FAITH AND ORDER

FAITH AND ORDER

Proceedings of the World Conference
Lausanne, August 3—21, 1927

Edited by
H. N. BATE
Canon of Carlisle

NEW YORK
GEORGE H. DORAN COMPANY
1927

ADDRESS OF THE SECRETARIAT:
P.O. BOX, 226
BOSTON, MASS., U.S.A.

Publications relating to the Faith and Order
Movement may be had on application to this
address.

First Published November, 1927

Printed by The Garden City Press Ltd.,
Letchworth, Herts, England

EDITOR'S NOTE

The Continuation Committee, meeting at Lausanne on August 20th, 1927, passed the following resolution :

Voted : to request Canon Bate to act as Editor-in-Chief of the official Report of the Lausanne Conference, and to refer the matter with power to the following representatives of the Business Committee : George Zabriskie, D.C.L., Rev. Bishop James Cannon, Jr., D.D., the General Secretary.

It was understood that an official Report should be prepared in English, French and German with the least possible delay. Arrangements were therefore made with the Publishing Department of the Student Christian Movement for the English edition : a French and a German edition, based on the English text, under the editorship respectively of M. le Pasteur Jules Jézéquel of Paris and Pfarrer Lic. Hermann Sasse, will soon be issued.

In preparing the present volume for the Press I have been greatly assisted by the kindness of Mr. Hugh Martin, of the Student Christian Movement, who has made special arrangements for passing the work through the Press with the least possible delay, and has provided us with accommodation in the office of the Movement for correspondence and editorial work. But above all my thanks are due to the Rev. Floyd W. Tomkins, Jr., who has prolonged his stay in England in order to help me, and whose assistance in preparing the material for this volume and for the French and German editions has been invaluable. Without the aid of his unremitting labour the production of this Report would have been impossible.

The longer speeches delivered at the Conference are printed here *in extenso*. Speeches delivered during discussion have been, for the most part, summarised or cut down. The Verbatim Reports have formed the basis of the

work, and I have not thought it necessary to indicate the
points at which I have substituted an English rendering
or summary for a French or German original. Some of these
translations are my own work, and for others I have to
thank Col. H. H. Wade, Mr. H. C. Kerr, and Miss M. Robertson, while acknowledging a general editorial responsibility
for the whole.

The volume is already longer than we could have wished :
and I hope this will excuse the editor in the eyes of any who
may feel that here and there it errs on the side of brevity.

H. N. BATE.

FAITH AND ORDER, 1910-1927

The origin of the Faith and Order Movement goes back
to the Edinburgh Missionary Conference of 1910. " It was
the sense of God's presence at that Conference, and the
wonderful and immediate results, that led some of us to
believe that a similar Conference on matters of Faith and
Order might be productive of good."[1] The actual initiation
of the Movement took place at the General Convention of
the Protestant Episcopal Church in the United States on
October 19th, 1910. A Joint Committee had been
appointed, on the motion of the Rev. Dr. Manning, now
Bishop of New York, " to take under advisement the
promotion by this Church of a Conference following the
general method of the World Missionary Conference, to be
participated in by representatives of all Christian bodies
throughout the world which accept our Lord Jesus Christ
as God and Saviour, for the consideration of questions pertaining to the Faith and Order of the Church of Christ."
This Committee reported its conviction " that such a
Conference for the purposes of study and discussion, without power to legislate or to adopt resolutions, is the next
step toward unity." On the basis of this report a Joint
Commission of Bishops, Presbyters and Laymen was
appointed to carry forward the project for a Conference.

The action thus taken by the General Convention co-
incided happily with other movements in the United
States. The National Council of Congregational Churches,
" in view of the possibility of fraternal discussion of
Church unity suggested by the Lambeth Conference of
Bishops in 1908," appointed a special commission to consider any overtures which might be made in that direction.
At the same time, and quite independently, similar action
was taken by the Disciples of Christ. The Joint Commission of the Episcopal Church, therefore, found that the

---

[1] Bishop Brent, in *Report of the Preliminary Meeting at Geneva*, p. 19.

ground was, at some points, prepared for its work. Its first task was the securing of the sympathy and co-operation of the Churches. Various Churches of the Anglican Communion gave prompt adhesion : and in 1912 a deputation was sent to Great Britain and Ireland. The Bishops of Chicago, Southern Ohio, and Vermont, with Dr. Manning, conveyed the invitation to participate in the Conference, and every assurance of readiness to co-operate was given them by the English Archbishops, as also by Bishops of the Scottish Episcopal Church and the Church of Ireland. Meanwhile the leading Protestant Communions in the United States had cordially responded to the call ; negotiations were set on foot with the Orthodox Church of Russia, conversations were held with leading Roman Catholic dignitaries, and preparations were made for the participation of the Old Catholic Churches.

By the summer of 1913 thirty Commissions or Committees representing various Churches throughout the world had been appointed, and the situation was reviewed at a meeting of the American Commissions. It is interesting to note that the task of preparation and the ultimate method of the Conference were anticipated, even then, with remarkable clearness. It was foreseen that it would be necessary to formulate in advance the problems which the Conference would have to consider, and that the business of the Conference would be, not the forcing of any particular scheme of unity, but the consideration "not only of points of difference and agreement between Christians, but also of the values of the various approximations of belief characteristic of the several Churches."

A deputation was now sent to confer with the non-Anglican Communions in the British Isles, and the Rev. Drs. Newman Smyth, J. H. Jowett,[1] W. H. Roberts, Peter Ainslie and Bishop J. W. Hamilton[1], were asked to undertake the journey, with the Rev. Tissington Tatlow to act with them in an advisory capacity. During their journey they conferred with thirty-one groups, and in this way, as

---

[1] Bishop Hamilton and Dr. Jowett were unable to join the deputation.

well as by private conference, they were able to secure promises from every Communion visited of a favourable consideration for the proposed Conference.

At a meeting of the Advisory Committee of the various Commissions in March, 1914, the progress hitherto made was reviewed, and a memorable speech outlining further opportunities for preparatory work in Europe and the Near East was made by Dr. John R. Mott.

Meanwhile, under the guidance of Robert Hallowell Gardiner, Secretary of the Commission, to whose memory the Conference of 1927 paid fitting tribute, a vast correspondence had been initiated, and some twenty-five pamphlets had been circulated in various languages throughout the world ; and it should not be forgotten that this great work of propaganda was made possible by liberal donors, among whom it is only right that the late J. Pierpont Morgan should have special recognition.

Then came the War, and for some four and a half years all the avenues of communication which had been so hopefully opened up, were hopelessly blocked. Yet, as soon as possible after the Armistice of November, 1918, the work was resumed. The first adventure on a large scale was a deputation to Europe and the East, in the spring and summer of 1919. The members of this embassy were the Bishops of Chicago, Southern Ohio and Fond du Lac, with the Rev. Drs. E. L. Parsons and B. Talbot Rogers : and they were joined in Athens by their secretary Mr. Ralph W. Brown, now General Secretary of the Conference. The report of this deputation (Pamphlet No. 32) is the record of a difficult, adventurous and astonishingly successful journey. The deputation as a whole visited Athens, Smyrna, Constantinople, Sofia, Bucarest, Belgrade and Rome. At Rome the deputation divided, the Bishop of Fond du Lac and Dr. Rogers going to Alexandria, Cairo, Jerusalem and Damascus, while the others went to Paris, London, Norway and Sweden. The results of this deputation have been manifest alike at Geneva and Lausanne, in the full and friendly co-operation which has been secured with the Orthodox Eastern Churches and with the Churches of Scandinavia. In Rome, through the great courtesy of Archbishop Cerretti, a formal invitation and statement about the Conference was presented to his Holiness the Pope through Cardinal Gasparri : and the official refusal of the invitation was balanced by the personal friendliness and benevolence of the Pope.

Sixty-nine Commissions had by this time been appointed, and it was felt that the time had come for a preliminary meeting of the Conference. A remarkable gathering therefore assembled at Geneva in the summer of 1920. That representatives of forty nations and some seventy autonomous Churches could be brought together, even in a neutral country, a year and a half after the War, was a notable achievement : and it was due, without doubt, to the vision and industry of Mr. Gardiner, who, at great cost of every kind to himself, had established personal contacts with men of many races and of all Churches, and had inspired in them that faith in the Conference which he held so firmly.

The value of the discussions held at Geneva under the presidency of Bishop Brent lay chiefly in the fact that they indicated, first, that fruitful Conference in a mixed body of Protestants and Catholics was not impossible, and second, that much organised study must now be undertaken, so that the work of the ultimate Conference might be focussed upon clear issues.

The Geneva Conference appointed a widely-representative Continuation Committee, and that Committee delegated its duties to two sub-committees : one, the Business Committee,[1] composed of Americans, to attend to the preliminary arrangements for the World Conference ; the other, the Subjects Committee, to prepare an Agenda and to promote preliminary discussion of the problems involved. That Committee consisted of the Bishop of Bombay as Chairman, with Dr. A. Lang of Halle, the Rev. Dr. Martin, Principal of New College, Edinburgh, the Rev. Dr. Selbie,

---

[1] Bishop Brent, Chairman, Rev. Drs. Ainslie, Boynton, Moore, Stevenson, Archbishop Germanos (or, Archbishop Alexander)., Bishop Cannon, Bishop McConnell, Mr. Zabriskie, and, by later addition, Rev. Drs. Barbour, Scherer and Cadman.

Principal of Mansfield College, Oxford, and Professor H. Alivisatos of the University of Athens. In the earlier stages, the Rev. D. C. Lusk acted as Secretary, and in 1923 he was succeeded by Canon H. N. Bate of Carlisle, who was given a seat on the Committee, which was subsequently completed by the appointment of the Rev. Dr. Lofthouse, of Handsworth College, Birmingham. An account of the work of the Subjects Committee will be found on pages 36-39 of this volume.

The Proceedings of the Conference (pages 12-13) also indicate how grievous was the loss sustained by the death of Robert Hallowell Gardiner on June 15th, 1924. It must suffice here to say that, whatever visible memorial is erected to his remembrance, his true memorial is in the World Conference itself. He seemed essential to the movement ; and yet it survived his loss simply because he had given it an inspiration which could not be allowed to fail.

For those who have followed the movement closely since 1924 its story is too multitudinous to be easily summarised. It consists in the maintenance of a worldwide correspondence and the output of much relevant literature ; in the gathering together of many local groups for discussion and prayer ; in the emergence and keen discussion of many problems connected with the Agenda ; in patient efforts to secure the adequate representation of great Churches, Catholic and Protestant alike ; in an energetic campaign in the United States for the raising of the necessary funds[1] ; and in the successive meetings of the Continuation Committee which brought the preparations for Lausanne up to their final stage. The focus of all this work was the Secretariat in Boston ; behind it, on the financial side, stood the Business Committee, with Mr. George Zabriskie, who has acted as Treasurer since the inception of the movement ; and the main driving power, under the inspiration and guidance of Bishop Brent, was

---

[1] Through the efforts of a Committee under the Hon. Charles Evans Hughes with the Hon. George W. Wickersham as executive chairman, the expenses of the Conference were provided by the generous gifts of some 700 churchpeople of many Communions.

supplied by the Head of the Secretariat, now Mr. Gardiner's successor as General Secretary of the Conference, Mr. Ralph W. Brown.

The meetings of the Continuation Committee were held, owing to favourable opportunities presented in connection with the Conference on Life and Work, at Stockholm and Berne in 1925 and 1926, and also at Lausanne both before and during the Conference itself. At Lausanne this Committee presented its final report (pages 404-406) and was succeeded by a new Committee whose names are printed at the end of this volume.

The Stockholm meeting was concerned with the place and Agenda of the Conference, the apportionment of representatives, and other preliminary business.

With regard to the apportionment of representatives, an approximate estimate made in 1924 was taken as the basis for further enquiry, and the following general guiding principles were laid down : that in most cases the co-operating Churches should be asked to send two representatives each (or one, in the case of some smaller bodies), and that more than two but not more than ten should be allotted to some larger bodies ; and that places not exceeding ten per cent. of the total number of delegates (about 500) should be reserved for persons whose presence would be for special reasons desirable and who might not be appointed by the Churches.

At Berne, the outline of a scheme for procedure was drawn up, and Committees (American, European and Eastern) for the nomination of speakers were chosen, the final decision being left to the following : Bishop Brent, Archbishop Söderblom, Dr. Garvie, Archbishop Germanos, and a second American to be chosen by Bishop Brent (Mr. Ralph W. Brown). This Programme Committee subsequently held two meetings in London, at which the list of speakers, chairmen, and leaders of devotions was completed. The action taken at Berne with regard to the Agenda is referred to on page 38. It was at this meeting that the subject " The Church's Message to the World—the Gospel " was added to the topics for discussion.

It was at Stockholm that the decision was reached which brought the Conference to Lausanne, a decision for which everyone connected with the movement has cause to be grateful. The negotiations for securing the required accommodation for the Conference and its delegates were greatly facilitated by the immediate and generous courtesy of the Swiss Federal Authorities and of the Association des Hôteliers Lausannois, under its President M. Haeberli. The University buildings in the Palais de Rumine, most generously lent by the authorities of the Canton of Vaud, proved to be even more admirably adapted to the purposes of the Conference than had at first been expected, or than the less robust delegates, faced by its vast staircases, were at first inclined to believe.

The main arrangements for travel and hotel accommodation were carried out through Messrs. Thos. Cook & Son, whose Agent in Lausanne, Mr. C. S. Alden, rendered invaluable assistance throughout; his unfailing courtesy and helpfulness will not be forgotten.

In the City of Lausanne a Comité de Réception was formed, and began its preparations long before the Conference ; its Chairman was Professor Alois Fornerod, with whom were Pastor Henri Laufer, M. Schnetzler, the Very Rev. Archimandrite Valiadis, Pastor Ulrich Gsell, Pastor Gustave Secretan, M. Gustave Fleury, Pastor Roger Bornand, Pastor R. Bergier, and M. Haeberli. To the assiduous kindness of this Committee was added that of the Syndic and Municipality of Lausanne ; with the result that from the moment of its assembling the Conference found itself in an atmosphere of gracious and friendly hospitality.

During July, 1927, and throughout the Conference, it was necessary to get a maximum of printing done with the greatest possible speed and accuracy. This work was entrusted to the Imprimeries Réunies, and to M. G.-A. Bridel, the Director, with his staff and workmen, the gratitude of the Conference is due.

In conjunction with the Comité de Réception and the postal authorities of Lausanne, elaborate arrangements were made for telephonic and telegraphic facilities, such as were required for the Press Bureau. That Bureau was under the able direction of Mr. Allan P. Ames, whose colleagues were Mr. Frank America, of the Associated Press, U.S.A., the Rev. Linley Gordon and Mr. Arthur Porritt, for the religious Press of the United States and of England, M. Hervier, for the European Press, and Prof. Dr. Hinderer, Director of the Evangelischer Pressverband for Germany. Every possible step was taken to secure publicity for the Conference, and the work of the Press Bureau was most effective throughout. An efficient staff of stenographers and manifolders under M. R. Kybourg, of Geneva, proved able to cope with the enormous task of providing Press and delegates alike with daily verbatim reports of the proceedings and with copies of necessary documents.

The many practical perplexities arising from day to day in such a gathering were ably disentangled by an Information Bureau conducted by Miss Stina Bredenberg and Mrs. Benedict.

The problem of securing efficient interpreters for the Conference occupied the Secretariat for many months. Eventually it was solved with complete success, and the gratitude expressed by the Conference to Colonel Wade, Pastor Rambaud, Pastor Sasse, Pastor André Monod and Mr. Kerr were abundantly merited.

It had been hoped that it would be possible to place at the beginning of this volume a preface by Bishop Brent. Greatly to the regret of the Editor and Editorial Committee, Bishop Brent's need for complete rest has proved to be so urgent that the book must go to press without any written commendation from his pen. In the preceding pages a very incomplete sketch has been attempted of an enterprise for which, and in which, he has lived for seventeen years. He has left upon this movement the impress of his devotion and faith.

We may be sure that his foreword, had he been able to write it, would have been an utterance of gratitude and a

summons to further endeavour. The Lausanne Conference
has been given what it sought ; it has been allowed to
reach, not an end, but a beginning. We trust that in the
next stage of the work we shall still have our friend and
leader with us, " speaking to the children of Israel that
they go forward."

H. N. B.

TABLE OF CONTENTS

xvii

CONTENTS

CONTENTS

Monday, August 15th

Subject VII—THE UNITY OF CHRISTENDOM AND THE RELATION THERETO OF EXISTING CHURCHES

Tuesday, August 16th

9.30 a.m.-12.45 p.m., and 4-6.30 p.m.

Wednesday, August 17th

CONTENTS

CONTENTS

PROCEEDINGS OF THE WORLD CONFERENCE ON FAITH AND ORDER

THE CALL TO UNITY

Wednesday Morning, August 3rd.

The Conference opened with a service in the Cathedral at 10 a.m. The service was preceded by the overture to the Messiah, played on the organ by Mr. SAINTSBURY, organist of the English Church. The Pastor of the Cathedral, M. le Pasteur Gustave SECRETAN, conducted the introductory devotions, which included hymn 36 from the quadrilingual hymn-book, *Communio,* and ended with the recitation of the Apostles' Creed by all present in their respective languages. The creed was followed by silent prayer ; after which the sermon was preached by the Right Rev. Charles H. BRENT, D.D., Bishop of Western New York. The sermon was followed by an organ interlude (How lovely are the messengers that preach us the gospel of peace —*Mendelssohn*) ; after hymn 6 had been sung the Lord's Prayer was said by all in their respective languages, and Bishop Brent gave the benediction. The following is the text of the sermon :

THE RIGHT REV. CHARLES H. BRENT, D.D.

Bishop of Western New York (Anglican)

Neither pray I for these alone ; but for them also which shall believe on me through their word ; that they all may be one ; as thou, Father, art in me, and I in thee, that they also may be one ; that the world may believe that thou hast sent me. And the glory which thou gavest me I have given them ; that they may be one, even as we are one : I in them and thou in me, that they may be made perfect in one ; and that the world may know that thou hast sent me, and hast loved them, as thou hast loved me.—*John xvii*, 20-23.

We are here at the urgent behest of Jesus Christ. We have come with willing feet. All the prayers and desires and labours of seventeen years meet in this hour.

The call to unity is primarily from God to man. It is for

our good that the appeal is made. Through unity alone can
the Kingdom of God be set up among men. Through unity
alone can the world believe and know that the Father has
sent Jesus Christ to reveal Him to the whole human race.
It stands as the unalterable condition on which He can
fulfil His mission to mankind. This no one doubts who
accepts Jesus Christ as Lord and Saviour.

Like all God's calls it is an invitation to co-operate with
Him. His will is part of His nature, and is set once for all
time. He lays no compulsion on us. He awaits our co-
operative response which will lay hold of His will and make
it our own. If unity has slipped away from our grasp it is
the common fault of the Christian world. If it is to be
regained it must be by the concerted action of all Christians.
Every section has shared in shattering unity. Every section
must share in the effort to restore it.

The call to unity is like the flow of a river ; it never ceases.
It has been sounding with varying accent through the
successive generations since the beginning. To us it has
of late come with new force through the voice of God's
Spirit speaking to the many divided communions of our
day, as the call of a shepherd to his scattered flock. We
have responded to His call. We are gathered here at His
bidding. He presides over us. In proportion to our obedience to His guidance we shall be able to promote His will
and embrace it as our own. He appeals to us to hush our
prejudices, to sit lightly to our opinions, to look on the
things of others as though they were our very own—all this
without slighting the convictions of our hearts or our
loyalty to God. It can be done. It must be done.

It is for conference, not controversy, that we are called.
As God appeals to us sinners to reason together with Him,
so we Christians mutually appeal to one another for a like
fellowship. Conference is a measure of peace ; controversy,
a weapon of war. Conference is self-abasing ; controversy
exalts self. Conference in all lowliness strives to understand
the view-point of others ; controversy, to impose its views
on all comers. Conference looks for unities ; controversy
exaggerates differences. Conference is a co-operative

method for conflict ; controversy, a divisive method. I do
not say there may not be occasions where controversy may
be necessary. This is not one of them. This is a Conference
on Faith and Order. We are pledged to it by our presence.
Let us play true to our tryst.

It is the call of Christ which arrests us. What He said
then with human voice He repeats now through His indwelling Spirit. The general need of unity is set down by
Him in a proverbial saying—" Every kingdom divided
against itself is brought to desolation ; every city or house
divided against itself shall not stand." This is as true to-
day as when it was first uttered. It has been accepted by
the world of men as applying to every department of life
in its separate groupings, political, intellectual, scientific,
social. In increasingly wide circles men are striving for
unity. Lying at the centre of all and providing the only
enduring cement is religious unity.

The Gospel provides for intimate relationship with
Christ. Our Lord speaks as He thinks. He thinks in terms
of reality. All life is a symbol. He declares that of which
it is symbolic. So He says not " I am like the vine, ye are
like the branches," but " Abide in me and I in you . . . I
am the vine, ye *are* the branches." Nature in its simplest
manifestations preaches its eternal sermon, points to Him
for whom it exists.

Again, have you not noted how to the very end of His
ministry Jesus Christ presents Himself and those whom He
commissions in pastoral terms ? It is not " I am like the
good shepherd." He is the reality of which the men who
watched their flocks were the shadow. It is " I *am* the
good shepherd " . . . " Other sheep I have, which are
not of this fold : them also I must bring, and they shall
hear my voice ; and there shall be one flock, one shepherd."
The Shepherd can fold His flock only if He lays down His
life in bringing them together. " Therefore," He says,
" doth the Father love me." He lays His life on His aim
and is unafraid.

All this was counted as axiomatic even before the
Gospels were written. St. Paul, writing when the Gospel

was oral, strikes sectarianism of all ages between the eyes
by calling divisions " carnal "—" for whereas there is among
you envying and strife and divisions, are ye not carnal and
walk as men ?   For while one saith, I am of Paul ; and
another, I am of Apollos ; are ye not carnal ? . . . For
other foundation can no man lay than that is laid, which is
Jesus Christ."   Division in the eyes of this intense man is
fatal to the life of the Church.

What I am about to quote is as familiar to you as anything in Scripture, but I repeat it as signifying at the
earliest beginning of Christianity the mind of Christ on the
indispensability of unity as read by His great apostle.   Now
it is the human body that is the symbol of which Christ
and His Church represent the reality.   " For as the body is
one, and hath many members, and all the members of that
one body, being many, are our body : so also is Christ.
For by one Spirit we are all baptised into one body, whether
we be Jews or Gentiles, whether we be bond or free ; and
have been all made to drink into one Spirit.   For the body
is not one member but many . . .   Now ye are the body
of Christ and members in particular."   In relation to the
Holy Communion " we, who are many, are one bread, one
body."   Again it is as of a household that the Church is
spoken—"built upon the foundation of the apostles and
prophets, Christ Jesus himself being the chief corner stone,"
or as a temple, or as the holy city, the heavenly Jerusalem.
In every instance the symbol has unity as essential to its
existence as light and heat are to the sun.   So inherent is
unity that it can admit of no racial, sex or social distinctions, but all are " one man in Christ Jesus."

But there are still greater heights towards which we must
rise.   Either in the words of our Lord Himself, or of the
Spirit of our Lord speaking through a disciple in the early
second century—it is all one—the kind of unity which the
Church must exhibit is that which unites the Father to the
Son.   Earthly imagery is inadequate and heaven is called
to bear its witness.   "Neither pray I for these alone, but for
them also which shall believe on me through their word ;
that they all may be one ; as thou Father art in me, and

I in thee, that they also may be one in us ; that the world may believe that thou hast sent me. And the glory which thou gavest me I have given them ; that they may be one, even as we are one : I in them and thou in me, that they may be made perfect in one ; and that the world may know that thou hast sent me, and hast loved them as thou hast loved me." If our Lord counts unity a necessity, how absolute must that necessity be ! Upon it depends our ability to know Jesus Christ in His full splendour, to do His works, to evangelise the nations. It is a tribute to the greatness of man that it needs the full weight of the whole Gospel for the miracle of a single conversion. The missionary quality of Christ's prayer is passionate—" that the world may believe that thou hast sent me . . . that the world may know that thou hast sent me." What a challenge to Christendom to set its own house in order before it further infect the Eastern world with sectarianism that robs the Gospel of its corporate power and gives people a stone instead of bread! The hundred missionary societies in China to-day are as suicidal for Christianity as the civil divisions are to her national peace and prosperity. The Christian orient to-day is in just revolt not against Christianity but against divided Christianity, not against foreigners either in politics or religion but against the domination of foreigners.

Jesus Christ revealed by His life on earth exactly what the unity was between Himself and His Father. It is not so mystical as to be unintelligible to the simple-hearted. We are not left as workmen without a pattern for their task. The kind of oneness exhibited by Christ with His Father on earth is clear beyond dispute—a paternal and filial relationship, and a liberty reached through absolute dependence consummated by supreme sacrifice. If individuals and groups were to practise these two principles, disunion would fade away like snow before a summer sun. When all Christians recognise God as Father and look on the things of others as of brothers in Christ, the family of God will be complete, a glorious Church without spot or wrinkle.

God calls man to unity—His ideal. Man calls to God for

unity—his need.   Unity is not only a thing of beauty but
a matter of practical necessity.   There are patches of unity
already, it is true, in an underlying loyalty to Christ.   But
not enough to make Christianity effective as a peace maker,
a liberator, a universal power, or to satisfy the mind of
God.

Some countries have a minimum of division at home,
especially where there is a State Church.   But purely national
Churches of whatever sort add to the rival denominations
which split Christ in the mission field, and make
Christianity contradict itself as a world religion.   In other
countries, as in America, Churches of every sort and every
name obtain.   The evil effect is most evident in rural
districts where the church-going population is divided into
impoverished rival groups without moral and spiritual
potency.   The Christian religion is often degraded into a
weak philosophy, incompetent and futile.   Some Churches
claim exclusive possesssion of the truth as found in Christ
and damn those who find other interpretations of His life
and teaching.   The result is that not fifty per cent.
of the population even profess to be followers of Jesus
Christ, many of them because they are sadly perplexed and
mystified by jangling claims and voices.   Churches which
have no real reason for holding apart still adhere to their
shibboleths.   Federative effort continues where organic
unity is the only logical step.   There is no one voice coming
with force from every pulpit in every country, as there
should be, on such great fundamental questions as peace
and war, what constitutes Christian marriage, the social
claims of Christ, the supra-national character of the Church.
The Catholic mind is rare.   In our hearts most of us are
devotees of the cult of the incomplete—sectarianism.   The
Christ in one Church often categorically denies the Christ
in a neighbouring Church.   It would be ludicrous were it
not tragic.   The situation is suicidal and we are here as a
solemn protest against it.   We try to get together in matters
of practical import, but as often as not we find ourselves
thrown back on our conception of Christ, the nature of the
Church, God's mode of governing His Church, the sub-

stance of the Gospel message. Christology may not be slighted. The value of theology must be admitted. The history of Christianity must be studied, if we are to get anywhere.

Were there no call to man from God to unity, our need would none the less make its high protest to God in heaven for unity. But we would be hopeless and helpless in the organised confusion to which we are party. It is God who takes the lead. His will that they may all be one must eventually be man's will if to do God's will becomes the passion of the human heart. When Christians accept Christ as supreme, they cannot but walk as companions and friends. His life as portrayed in the Gospels is His reliable teaching. His words as interpreted by His life are final and our duty to obey becomes our privilege, our joy. It is to encourage such faith in God made manifest in the flesh that we are in conference. That is the meaning of faith, rather than a form of sound words, however important they may be. To quote the words of Zinzendorf—" I have but one passion. It is He! even He! " Men like Sadhu Sundar Singh, Mahatma Gandhi, and Stanley Jones, are helping us to realise this more and more. In proportion as we rally around the living Christ during these days shall we banish our prejudices, enlighten our understanding, and correct our mistakes.

Again, as to the means of establishing intimate relationship with Jesus Christ—for that is our chief quest and goal, is it not?—we dare not be exclusive in sacramental, in mystical, or in intellectual modes of approach. Christ's agile feet journey to the human heart along many and diverse paths. That He comes by these and innumerable other routes who will deny?

After all, it is not these central principles that should give us great difficulty. Rather is it that which lies at the circumference—the government of the Church, or order. Personally, I should be well content were we to let this last vexed subject lie for the present rather than give it hasty consideration. We cannot pretend that it is unimportant. By means of it the Church is held together in

B

the fulness of organic life, world-wide and all-embracing.
But we cannot, in our brief Conference, cover the whole
vast field. Moreover, in that conciliar action did not break
unity, conciliar action cannot mend it. May it not be that
all other things being settled, we will grow into it as did the
early Church ?

But I must close. We are living in a world that has lost
its way. Religion as summed up in Jesus Christ and His
Kingdom can alone hope to rescue it. It must be, as God's
voice has warned us from the beginning, and our own experience has tragically confirmed, unified religion. God
has used, beyond anything we had a right to expect, our
divided Christendom. But now that we know the sin and
disaster of sectarianism, we cannot hope that He will use
it much longer. Though all time lies before us we may
not rest on our oars. We must move without haste and
without rest. Let us keep the purpose of unity firm in our
hearts and look on all Christians of whatever name as
brothers beloved. It is thus that, by practising unity, we
shall gain unity.

God's Spirit is presiding over us to make us will and do
His good pleasure. It is He that will change for us, in His
own way and in His own time, the impossible into the possible, and bring about that consummation of Christian hope
in a Church that will be one flock under one Shepherd. To
that end I make my own the impassioned appeal of St.
Paul, which is as applicable to this gathering of men of
many nations as to the Ephesians to whom it was originally
addressed : " I therefore, the prisoner in the Lord, beseech
you to walk worthily of the calling wherewith ye were
called "—note the moral qualities essential for unity—
" with all lowliness and meekness, with long suffering, forbearing one another in love ; giving diligence to keep the
unity of the Spirit in the bond of peace. There is one body,
and one Spirit, even as ye are called in one hope of your
calling ; one Lord, one faith, one baptism, one God and
Father of all, who is over all, and through all, and in all."

The opening service in the Cathedral being ended, the Conference assembled for its first session in the Aula of the University, the Palais de Rumine, at 11.30 a.m.

The Right Rev. Charles H. BRENT, D.D., Bishop of Western New York, was unanimously chosen as Chairman until such time as the President of the Conference should be appointed.

A message of welcome was then presented to the Conference by M. DUBOIS, Conseiller d'Etat. The ancient Cathedral of Lausanne, said M. Dubois, and the Aula of its University, though not presuming to match themselves with the splendours of the greater European cities, could still in some ways afford an appropriate scene for the inauguration of a great work of religious reconciliation. The Cathedral, once thronged with pilgrims to the shrine of Notre Dame de Lausanne, was linked with great names in the history of the Reformation ; the Aula, with its frescoes depicting the onward march of science and the great facts of the Christian revelation, represented the concordant movement of the spirit of man towards the Light. He trusted that the arduous labours of the Conference would be lightened in some degree by such hospitality as the Comité de Réception was proposing to offer to the Delegates, and that the discussions now to be inaugurated would tend to the promotion of Christian peace and goodwill.

The President of the Schweizerischer Evangelischer Kirchenbund, Dr. Otto HEROLD, then offered to the Conference the greetings of the Swiss Federation of Churches. That Federation, said Dr. Herold, owed its own origin to a movement towards the unification of cantonal Churches which had for centuries existed in isolation from each other ; it has watched with deep sympathy such movements as that of the Conference on Life and Work, and had gladly taken on itself the leadership of the work of relief for distressed Churches. It now welcomed with deep sympathy the Conference on Faith and Order as a truly Christian movement towards mutual understanding, inspired by deep charity and by a sense of the overwhelming importance of those things which all Christians possess in common ; and hoped that the blessing of God might rest upon the work to be done in Lausanne, and thereafter in the Churches to which the inspiration of this Conference would be handed on.

The Chairman gratefully acknowledged the greetings thus offered, adding a special word of thanks to the Rev. G. SECRETAN, Pastor of the Cathedral, for his generous help in preparing for and conducting the opening service.

Commemoration of Robert Hallowell Gardiner.

THE CHAIRMAN : I am sure that I voice the views of those who knew Robert Hallowell GARDINER in asking that our first business should be to pay a tribute to him, and I am going to ask Dr. Stevenson to present a memorial resolution.

DR. STEVENSON : I beg to present the following resolution :

Resolved.—That the World Conference on Faith and Order praise and magnify God for the life and work of Robert Hallowell Gardiner, whose single-minded devotion to our Lord and the unity of His Kingdom distinguishes him in his generation.

Like all great movements, reunion has been focussed from time to time in certain persons who, in their day and generation, became embodiments of its spirit. One such was Robert Hallowell Gardiner, whose work in connection with this Conference will never be forgotten, who was, indeed, while he lived, the organ of its energy.

The profound impression made upon the Christian world by what he was and did baffles description. It is not too much to say that there is not a Church in Christendom, great or little, ancient or new, that does not know his name and feel kinship with his lofty soul. Better than that, his name carries with it a vision, a responsibility and a purpose, for it was not himself but Christ whom he exalted. He counted himself but the cup-bearer of the King. He was one of those rare souls who are able to see that the unity of Christendom always outstrips its divisions. His catholicity was not a theory, but a character. His greatest weapon was his considerateness and his ability to understand others when they were busy misunderstanding him.

Now that we can take measure of him as never before we discover him to be one of the foremost leaders and inspirers of our day. Without his sort, hope would wither, faith decline and love grow cold. There is an ache in our hearts and a void in our fellowship which must abide. And yet all the while we rejoice that the Church raises up such men to enrich and inspire mankind. A bend in the road hides him, but he remains of our company, a little in advance of the rest, as he passes into the enjoyment of that unity for which he laboured diligently and well.

Resolved.—That the Conference send a copy of this resolution to his wife and family, rejoicing with them in their noble heritage and sympathising with them in their bereavement.

Resolved.—That in appreciation of all that we owe under God to Robert Hallowell Gardiner, this Conference erect in the church of his ancestral home, Gardiner, Maine, U.S.A., a tablet of appropriate character and design, the arrangements for which shall be entrusted to the care of a committee appointed by this Conference, each member of the Conference making such contribution to the fund necessary as he may desire.

The Resolutions were carried unanimously, all standing in silence.

The remainder of the session was occupied by the following three addresses on Subject I, The Call to Unity.

PROFESSOR DR. WERNER ELERT
University of Erlangen (Lutheran)

I

" He that is of the truth heareth my voice," saith the Lord. If we are of the truth we follow where He calls ; and He calls us to unity. So following, we are at one in Christ, and—which is the same thing—we are one in the Truth, for Christ called Himself the truth. Conversely, if we are not one in the truth, we are not at one in Christ. Therefore, all who seek for union in Christ must examine themselves whether they are in the truth. Truth indeed is not a thing which we can possess like a book which may be opened or closed at will. We can possess truth only in an act of recognition, which no wilfulness of our own can affect. To recognise truth is to feel its compulsion ; and this yielding to the compulsion of truth is faith. Faith is, indeed, more

than this : in faith we receive our individual deliverance,
the forgiveness of sins. Only in virtue of this faith are we
members of the one Holy Catholic Church. But what binds
Christians into a oneness that transcends individuality is
the objective force of that truth in which we, through faith,
come to have a share.

Since faith and truth are so closely linked, whenever
truth is obscured faith is imperilled, and with it our
membership of the Church of Christ is imperilled also. We
must, therefore, allow ourselves no communion with error :
truth and error can enter into no concordat. When truth
is involved there must be no compromise. The early
Councils were right in appending a rejection of error to
the positive clauses in which they expressed and acknowledged the truth. Not infrequently, perhaps, they failed to
distinguish rightly between the true and the false : still,
they did believe in truth, even though they discerned it only
in part. They knew that truth is no child of this world :
that truth betokens its presence, as Kierkegaard said, by a
challenge. There can be no recognition, no confession of
truth without a recognition and rejection of error. To say
this is not to demand a heresy hunt. We love those who
err, as our Lord and Master loved them. But unless we
would deny the truth, we must combat their errors.

The task laid upon the Church to discern between the
true and the false becomes more complicated as the centuries pass on. History evolves ever new forms of error which
seek to disguise themselves in the luminous garb of truth.
This is a process which we are unable to reverse, nor can
we silently evade the problems which it creates. As soon as
they are asked, the questions raised by the subjects of this
Conference demand to be answered. It is, therefore, our
desire that this Conference, seeking the unity of Christendom, may find it in the *truth*, and that it may express the
truth in plain terms, making no compromise with error.

II

The true cannot be discerned from the false until both
are expressed. Wherever the need has been felt to make a

common acknowledgment of truth as a basis of unity, it has always been found possible in the Church of Christ to discover terms which gave undisguised expression to that truth. This is the meaning and origin of the Creeds, Confessions and dogmas which are held to be valid, universally or locally, in Christendom. Our convictions, indeed, do not permit us to admit the existence of *laws* of belief. Councils cannot determine what must be believed : they can only establish what *is* believed.

I ask leave now to speak from the standpoint of the Church to which I myself belong : believing that the sense in which I declare my adhesion to the idea of this Conference is of cardinal importance.

It is true that the special Confessions of the particular Churches are in one sense divisive. But they did not create the divisions which they express : these already existed. Nor have they been merely divisive. They divide because error always dogs the steps of truth. Yet their primary purpose was not divisive but unitive. The Confessions have always expressed the common convictions of a multitude of individuals. And, further, they have served to hand on the convictions of one generation to its successors, and thus to form not only a link between contemporaries, but also a bond of unity between successive epochs and generations.

We Lutherans have, therefore, followed the activities of the World Conference on Faith and Order with close attention. The members of our Church present here to-day are in sympathy with the general aim and the work of this gathering. We thank God it has been possible to assemble a Council of the Christian Churches in which the problems of belief, doctrine, dogma, are to be taken quite seriously into consideration. We fear, indeed, that the discussions now about to begin will disclose differences of grave import. But we rejoice that the evil of disunion is here to be grasped by the roots. Our chief Confession teaches thus : *Ad veram unitatem ecclesiæ satis est consentire de doctrina evangelii et administratione sacramentorum. Nec necesse est ubique esse similes traditiones humanas seu ritus ab hominibus in-*

stitutos. We are glad, therefore, to note that the unity of Christians will be sought for in a *consensus de doctrina evangelii*. For history has shown us that there are spurious modes of unity which offer an illusory oneness in which true Christian unity, unity in the truth, is not found. We come, therefore, not as individuals, but as a great and world-wide community with centuries of history behind it. Indeed, we own our oneness with all those who in any age have confessed the Christian faith as we profess it. And thus our second desire for this Conference is, that the great unity towards which it strives may not destroy existing unities, but may rather, like a mother, gather within one home the mature and independent children of the house.

III

We believe that such a respect for existing unities does not imply the enduring perpetuation of confessional division. As far as our Church is concerned, this would only be a real danger if our Reformers in the sixteenth century had purposed to found a new Church and to cut themselves off from the Church Catholic. It was not so. Our chief Confession lays stress upon our agreement with the Church of antiquity, and it was thus that our theologians in the seventeenth century persisted in claiming membership of the true Catholic Church. The man who joins in the affirmations of the confession of our Church must have the will to be a Catholic Christian. Desiring, moreover, as we do, to find ourselves in agreement with the sound faith of the Church in all centuries, we give our assent to the development which history has brought. With all Christians we believe that Holy Scripture has Divine authority, as the document and evidence of the historical revelation of God. But we are convinced that it is impossible to reproduce the conditions and order of primitive Christianity as the Bible reflects them. It is for this reason that the leaders of the Lutheran Reformation would not consent to destroy the existing fabric of the Church, or to set in its place a structure framed on the pattern of the primitive Church. They knew that to do so would be Utopian. Therefore, while determined to do away with usages and teachings which seemed to them to stand in contradiction with the Gospels, they pursued a conservative policy wherever no such aberrations were concerned. And thus they were able to link themselves on to the dogma of the mediæval Church at all points where they observed no contradiction with the Gospels : they took over many liturgical forms ; they translated the hymns of the mediæval Church into their own language ; and they preserved much of the episcopal constitution of the Church.

It is upon this assent to the facts of historical development that the great tolerance of our Church in outward and temporal things is based. We tolerate much variety of constitution and rite ; and we yield to each other mutual recognition as equal members of the orthodox Christian Church, because we agree in one and the same confession of belief.

Our third desire for this Conference is, therefore, this : that varieties in constitution and rite may form no hindrance to that affirmation of unity in the truth, which it is our desire to achieve, and we feel in particular that all those forms which give external expression to our unbroken relationship with the ancient Church have a special claim upon our sympathy.

Patres reverendissimi! Fratres carissimi! The call of unity has been sounded. We have heard it and count ourselves bound in duty to obey. I have attempted to tell you what it is in this call that specially moves us, and have spoken from the standpoint of the Lutheran Church. I have done so because I believe that no one can abandon the standpoint of his own Church without losing his relationship to the Church of Christ in general. But we also believe that the best contribution we can bring to the deliberations of this Conference consists in the truths and the experiences which we have gathered in the Church which is our home. The great inheritance handed down to us by the fathers of our Church includes the will to Catholicity ; and I trust that this will to Catholicity has made itself plain to you all in the words that I have spoken.

There are two responsibilities of which we are gravely
conscious—our responsibility before God, and our responsibility before those whose faith we share. We, therefore, ask the help of the Holy Spirit that the great hour
of this Conference may find us not narrow-hearted, not
contentious, not self-assertive, not faithless or of little
faith, but broad-minded, peaceable, conscious of high
responsibility, filled with faith and with the wisdom of God.

THE MOST REV. ARCHBISHOP GERMANOS
Metropolitan of Thyateira (Orthodox)

It is exactly seven years ago since, in this beautiful
country and by the fair shores of Lake Leman, we made
the first step towards discussing a subject which should be
of interest to the whole of Christendom. After centuries
of separation and dire estrangement the first attempt was
once more made to mend the torn robe of Jesus in order
that the divided members of His mystic Body, the Church,
might again be bound together. To the call, sent forth from
beyond the ocean, the Orthodox Church of the East, the
most ancient of all, hastened with her younger sisters of
the West, to reply ; and though still " bearing in her body
the marks of the Lord Jesus " she regarded it as her duty
not to be absent from a Conference which set before it so
high and useful a purpose. And now after that first notable
contact, the Orthodox Church has been following with
ceaseless interest the untiring and inspired efforts of those
who conceived and initiated this work, and comes here a
sharer in the common endeavour. She who, for centuries,
has been a continuous witness to the apostolic Faith, comes
to contribute her share towards the building of reunion, the
erection of which is the object of this Conference.

Having been invited as representative of this Orthodox
Church to address you at this inaugural meeting, I thought
it would be of interest for you if I were, in a few words, to
explain to you the conception of reunion held by the

Orthodox Church ; this explanation, I think, will form a preamble, as it were, to the subjects to be discussed hereafter.

I

That those who believe in Christ and acknowledge Him as their Head must form one body, is self-evident according to the Orthodox Church. For the primary will and intention of the Saviour and Founder of the Church was that all who believed in Him " shall be one fold with one Shepherd." (John x, 16.) Our Lord, foreseeing the divisions that were to occur among those who were to believe in Him, asks during His last moments on earth of the Father who sent Him that He keep them in unity, " that they all may be one, as thou, Father, art in me and I in thee, that they also may be one in us." (John xvii, 21.) This unity of the faithful, a reflection as it were of the unity that is in God, was to be the most significant incentive for those who had not received the revelation to recognise the divine mission of Jesus and, being converted, to believe in Him—" that the world may believe that thou hast sent me." (John xvii, 21.) And even as our Lord, so the Apostles conceived of the Church as being, from the beginning, a unity ; to this the phraseology used by the Apostles when speaking of the Church bears witness, as for instance when they call it " the building of God," of which the corner-stone is Jesus Christ, and also " body," having as its head Jesus Christ. The wonderful picture especially which St. Paul draws of the Church leaves no doubt that the recreative force of the Holy Spirit in the body of the Church may then only be considered complete when each part keeps secure the bonds that tie one to the other, by means of its communion with the common Head, Christ ; that is, when they form a unity.

In this way, the Orthodox Church, regarding as it does the unity of the Church as being the will of its Founder, recognises at the same time that through absence of unity the work of the Church both external and internal throughout the world is greatly hampered.

Its external work is hampered because the principal mission of the Church, which is like leaven destined to leaven the whole lump and to draw into its fold all the nations, is frustrated. For is it not well known that the first question that comes to the lips of those who are called to enter the bosom of the Church is, " Which of the many churches am I to enter ? " And if they should happen to enter one or other of the Churches, the moment they come into contact with some Church other than the one they have entered they are so far confused as to be perpetually troubled by doubts as to whether they have " chosen the good part," or are drawn from the one to the other in turn. I do not even mention here the scornful comments of those outside the Church, which are heard by all those who have any relations with them.

Its internal work is hampered because, whereas modern conditions demand a united front against the subversive elements of the world which threaten the Christian edifice, the division of the Churches or, which is the same, of the striving forces of Christianity, seriously impairs the strength of their array. And even if we only take into account the recreative activity of the Church among its own members, it is obvious that it more fully achieves its purpose when it is undertaken by a united Church than by a Church divided and, at times, at variance.

Hence the Orthodox Church at all its gatherings prays for the reunion of all, and never ceases to hope that that which is considered humanly impossible, the reunion of the Churches, is not also impossible to God. But what does the Orthodox Church understand by the reunion of the Churches ?

Although the Orthodox Church considers unity in faith a primary condition of reunion of the Churches, yet it rejects that exclusive theory according to which one Church, regarding itself as the one true Church, insists that those who seek reunion with it shall enter its own realm. Such a conception of reunion, amounting to the absorption of the other Churches, is in every way opposed to the spirit existing in the Orthodox Church, which has always distinguished between unity on the one hand and uniformity on the other. The Patriarch of Constantinople, Photios, had already established the rule which in its practice the Orthodox Church has followed ever since. "In cases where the thing disregarded is not a matter of faith and does not involve disobedience to any general or catholic decree, a man capable of judging would be right in deciding that neither those who observe them nor those who have not received them act wrongly." (Encyclical Letter to Pope Nicholas I.)

As a consequence, only those things which have a direct reference to the Faith and which are by general consent accepted should be considered obligatory and as making for unity. Hence the Orthodox Church, following the advice of Augustine, *in dubiis libertas*, concedes to theologians freedom of thought as regards things which are not essential and which have no connection with the faith of the heart. But whilst it does not forbid such freedom, and willingly recognises that the nature of these questions is of such a kind that the solutions given to them are necessarily in the realms of doubt and probability, yet it stands by the principle that it is necessary to have agreement in essential things. *In necessariis unitas.*

But what are the elements of Christian teaching which are to be regarded as essential ? The Orthodox Church holds the view that it is not necessary that these should be discussed and determined at the present time, since they have been already determined in the old symbols and decisions of the seven Ecumenical Synods. Consequently, the teaching of the ancient undivided Church of the first eight centuries, free from every question which did not have a direct relation to these things which were to be believed, must to-day also constitute the basis of the reunion of the Churches. The soundness of this basis has been universally recognised in the discussions on reunion which in past years have taken place between Orthodox, Old Catholics and Anglicans. I may be permitted to say that no true Orthodox theologian would be found to deviate from this principle, and to enter upon a discussion of subjects which, according to his convictions, have already been decided,

except in cases where such discussion has for its sole purpose the justification of the faith held by his Church.

But while the Orthodox Church stands inevitably by
the basis laid down, it has at the same time no intention
of putting forward as a condition of reunion anything
that, after the first period mentioned, either is believed on
the authority of Holy Scripture and tradition or has been
defined in local councils and synods. And though we do not
deny that there have existed in the past, and still exist
among Orthodox theologians, those who insist on the
acceptance by others of these more recent decisions also,
yet those who judge aright confine themselves to those
decisions alone to which the common Christian conscience
of East and West had, of old, come. And when we take
into account how small is the number of decisions they
officially made, it becomes evident that there is a very wide
field of discussion remaining open to the Orthodox theologians and to those who are outside the Orthodox
Church but who are impelled by the same desire for
reunion of the Churches. And thus, subjects such as the
nature of the Church, its common creed, the significance
of Holy Scripture, the meaning of the sacraments, all of
which are due to be discussed by our Conference, are clearly
to be included among the number of these about which the
Orthodox theologian may formulate an opinion. In doing
so, he performs a duty towards his own Church, inasmuch
as he is thereby contributing to the removal of obstacles
which stand in the way of its unity.

My friends, at this moment when, having called down
upon us the guidance and inspiration of the Holy Spirit,
we are about to undertake our labours, let us call to mind
the deep signification of our mission, being at the same
time fully conscious that we all of us have a grave responsibility for the wasteful division of the Churches, and
feel repentance for the neglect we have hitherto permitted
of this duty, and devote ourselves to this work without
prejudice and with the requisite tranquillity. Above all,
let us cast aside all selfishness, and human calculations,
and rather be animated with respect for the convictions

of others, and beyond everything else, with love. Let us
not forget that, apart from all the points that divide us
one from the other, there exists a common bond which
binds all these gathered here, and that is faith in our
common Saviour and Redeemer, our Lord. I am not of
those who are so far confident as to imagine that the
question of the reunion of the Churches is one which requires only a short period of time and a short discussion
and exchange of views ; for that which long centuries have
divided cannot be reconciled in a single day. " Two
Churches," Döllinger said, " cannot at once throw themselves into each other's arms like two brothers meeting
after a long separation." We shall be happy if, before
departing from here, we are able to thank God that the
seed sown by the Conference on Faith and Order has not
fallen on barren ground. May God bless our labours.

THE MOST REV. THE ARCHBISHOP OF ARMAGH
Primate of Ireland (Anglican)

The call to Unity is the call of Christ. The great words
of our Lord which convey this call to all who profess
discipleship must sound in every heart here to-day. I need
not quote them : you have already heard them from the
pulpit of the Cathedral : they are the very charter of incorporation for this assembly. But let me quote an utterance of St. Paul's which forms an inspired and inspiring
comment upon them. It formed the preacher's concluding
exhortation. " Giving diligence to keep the unity of the
Spirit in the bond of peace. There is one body, and one
spirit, even as also ye were called in one hope of your
calling : one Lord, one faith, one baptism, one God and
Father of all, who is over all, and through all, and in all."
These words express the unity of the body in relation to
the unity of Christ, and under the supreme Unity which
dominates, pervades and penetrates the universal order—
the Unity of God. Traced thus to its source in God we must
gather that the unity of the body, in spite of all appearances

to the contrary, must be indestructible. And so surely it is. For what is the body ? It is the whole company of those who believe in Christ ; and if the outward side of the fellowship be taken account of, as it must be, the body is the whole company of those who believe and are baptized. Take the teaching of the New Testament in its simplicity, and as a whole, and no other definition is possible. So our great Anglican divine, Richard Hooker, most clearly declares : " Because the only object which separateth ours from other religions is Jesus Christ, in whom none but the Church doth believe, and whom none but the Church doth worship ; we find the Apostles do everywhere distinguish hereby the Church from Infidels and Jews, accounting them which call upon the name of our Lord Jesus Christ to be His Church. If we go lower," he continues, " we shall but add unto this certain casual and variable accidents which are not properly of the being, but make only for the happier or better being, of the Church of God." Here, Hooker points out, is the error of certain definitions. The persons who put them forward " define not the Church by that which the Church essentially is, but by that wherein they imagine their own more perfect than the rest."

Let us keep these great words in mind. The Church is one, and always has been, and must be, one ; because its essence is the relation of human souls to Jesus Christ.

Suppose, in illustration, that a visitor from some other world—Mars, let us imagine—were to come to this earth of ours and investigate our religions. Suppose him to try to form an estimate of the total effect of Christianity. Can you for a moment imagine that he would conclude that the influence of Jesus Christ upon human society is confined to the Orthodox Communion, or the Roman Communion, or the Anglican Communion, or the Lutheran Communion, or the great Communions of Presbyterians or Methodists ? It is surely clear that he must include them all—all indeed who profess faith in Jesus Christ. We can also see that he would be bound to take account of the fact that the other religions which claim universality, the Mohammedan and the Buddhist, are also divided into sects, and yet retain in all their divisions those peculiar qualities and produce those characteristic effects which are unmistakably theirs.

If this be true, we may well ask the question, why should we trouble about our divisions ? Why should we seek to heal them ? Why not adopt the view which was often adopted in the past, that the competition of the sects is a blessing in disguise, because it stirs us all to activity and so prevents stagnation ? It certainly does stir us to activity; it does prevent stagnation. But there is a better way. St. Paul's teaching points it out. Give " diligence to keep the unity of the Spirit in the bond of peace." The unity of the body depends upon the unity of the Spirit which animates it. And there are degrees of unity. Using the imagery of the living organism, we see that, in the realm of natural life, the degree of unity which any living thing possesses depends upon the degree of the control which the central principle of organisation exercises over all the vital processes of the whole. There are organisms which seem to be merely amorphous masses of living tissue ; yet they have a unifying agency of some sort or they could not hold together at all. Higher in the scale, we find organisms in which the various elements are so closely knit in living co-operation and mutual interdependence that there results a unity of function which produces a powerful effect upon the environment. In the control exerted by the conscious mind and will of man upon his own organism in relation to the material world outside it, in the mighty reactions which have given to man his dominant position, and which have in consequence changed the whole aspect of the globe, we find the supreme illustration from the natural world of a spiritual unification functioning through a material organism.

And so it would seem that, although the ultimate unity of the Christian Church cannot be utterly destroyed, the effect of our divisions is to lower the level of its life, to disorganise its proper functions, to weaken its power in the face of the tremendous forces which oppose its worldwide mission. Before the Church can become what our Lord intended it to be, it must attain to a higher degree of

organic unity. And this depends upon the attainment of a
new spirit.

May I then venture to say that if we are to find a way
to a solution of the great problem of Christian reunion, we
must follow the path pointed out by St. Paul ? The unity
of the spirit must come before the unity of the body. We
cannot, by devising any clever plans of adjustment between
the various organised Churches, overcome the difficulties
which stand in the way. No mere regulation of machinery
can bring about the end we have in view. We must begin
with the spirit, and the external adjustments will follow
as a matter of inevitable result. We have, I think, in the
past, counted too much upon settling our disputes by the
method of inventing a formula or framing a scheme. It
cannot be done. I know, indeed—and I speak as one who
had a share in the Lambeth proposals of 1920—that the
arrangement then proposed was the outcome of much
prayer and earnest attention to the things of the Spirit.
Behind the *Appeal to all Christian People* there was a deep
penitence for past failings, a sincere effort to look not only
to our own things but also on the things of others, and a
truly earnest desire to realise the great ideal of unity set
before us by our Lord. Yet it may be that, in spite of all
this, we did not discern as clearly as we should that the
unity of the spirit must come before any external arrangement.

Now here, it seems to me, is to be found the proper task
of the World Conference on Faith and Order. We are not
here to devise a scheme, an elaborate system of mechanically related parts, into which all the diverse elements of
organised Christianity will fall, as the various fragments of
a great puzzle, when duly disposed, combine to produce
a perfect picture. We are here, in the first instance at all
events, to unite in prayer, in thought, in expression, in
such a manner that the spirit of unity may find a home in
our hearts and in our counsels. In other words, we are
assembled in dependence on the Spirit of God, believing
that if we yield ourselves to Him, if we permit His directive
and creative power to guide our wills, we shall be drawn

together into a spiritual unity from which ultimately a great consolidation of the forces of Christianity must emerge.

What, I ask finally, are the principles which must guide our deliberations? St. Paul tells us to walk worthily of our calling, with all lowliness and meekness, with long-suffering, forbearing one another in love.

First, we should, each and every group of us, go into the Conference discarding any and every secretly treasured sense of our own superiority. We know how insufferable is the man who, failing in argument, puts on an air of superior wisdom. It is a poor sort of protective armour. It is indeed no real defence, and it must inevitably repel every thoughtful and sincere mind. Real conviction, fair and honest search for truth : these must attract the respect of all, and especially of those whose convictions are different. Therefore, as St. Paul says, let us walk worthily of our calling as followers of Christ, with all lowliness and meekness, with longsuffering, forbearing one another in love. No matter how different, or even opposing, our convictions may be, the spirit of humility, the spirit of forbearance, the spirit which, with patient and loving attention, hears the other side, will surely enable us to draw together with augmented esteem and better understanding.

Secondly, we must remember that the things which are impossible with men are possible with God. I know there has been in many minds the suspicion that the reunion of Christendom, however delightful as a beautiful dream, is incapable of realisation, things being as they are. And certainly, when we look back on the history of the Christian Church, and when we look round upon the world as it is to-day, we might well ask with incredulity, how it is possible to imagine that elements so diverse can be brought into an effective organic unity ? As a matter of worldly calculation, it does not, indeed, seem probable. But who dare set bounds to the forces of the Spirit if once the hindrances which spring from human pride and self-will are overcome ?

Finally, let us remember that the call to unity is the call of our Lord Himself. His will for His disciples is that they should form a world-wide Fellowship, under His leadership, inspired by His teaching, sharing that one life which is the very life of God imparted to man through Jesus Christ Himself.

The meeting rose at 1.15 p.m.

WEDNESDAY AFTERNOON, AUGUST 3RD.

The session was opened at 3.30 p.m. with devotions conducted by Bishop MCDOWELL. In continuation of the addresses given in the morning, Professor CHOISY spoke as follows :

PROFESSOR EUGENE CHOISY, D.D.
University of Geneva (Reformed)

The first and greatest call to unity is found in the high-priestly prayer of Christ, " That they all may be one as thou, Father, art in me and I in thee, that the world may believe that thou hast sent me." (John xvii, 20f.) So it is that the author of the fourth Gospel solemnly declares that Jesus the Christ was not to die for the people of Israel alone, but also that he might bring together in one body the children of God who were scattered abroad. (John xi, 52.) St. Paul utters the same thought in his epistle to the Romans, " We are one body in Christ, and members one of another." (Rom. xii, 5.) And in that to the Ephesians, "There is one body and one Spirit even as ye are called in one hope of your calling : one Lord, one faith, one baptism, one God and Father of all." (Eph. iv, 4f.) The call to unity is also heard in the writings of those disciples of the apostles whom we call the Apostolic Fathers ; first of all in the Eucharistic prayer of the *Didache* or *Teaching of the Twelve Apostles* : " As this broken bread which was scattered upon the mountains has been gathered together into one loaf, so may thy church be gathered from the ends of the earth into thy kingdom, for thine is the glory and the power by Jesus Christ for ever. . . . Gather together from the four winds this hallowed church into the kingdom which thou hast prepared for her, for thine is the power and the glory for ever. . . ." And later we have the significant declaration of Ignatius, Bishop of Antioch, who died as a martyr in A.D. 115 : "Wherever Christ is, there is the Catholic Church, so Christians each and all are one man in Jesus Christ, Son of Man and Son of God."

This unity of the faithful in Christ was openly manifested in those councils which could truly be called ecumenical, beginning with that at Nicæa in 325, councils which were general assemblies of the episcopate as representing the churches scattered throughout the world. Still, it must be admitted that this unity was never complete. Only too often serious differences in doctrine and practice divided the leaders of Christendom into hostile camps. A deep chasm came to separate the Greek from the Latin Church— a chasm which grew deeper and deeper as time went on, up to the definite breach which ensued in 1054. On the other hand, the Western Church, whose unity was so impressive, found itself confronted in the Middle Ages by a multiplication of hostile sects, and, what was worse, as a result of the scandals of the " Babylonian captivity," the removal of the papacy to Avignon, that Church was beset by a scandalous schism at the end of the fourteenth and the beginning of the fifteenth century ; it then showed itself deaf to the entreaties of those who demanded from it a reform in head and members, and so it suffered a complete disruption in the sixteenth century.

Believe me, it was not with a light or willing heart that Luther, Calvin and their allies broke with the hierarchy and severed themselves from the traditional Church. Compelled to choose between fidelity to Christ their Saviour —the only head of the Church—and submission to the demands of prelates claiming to be the sole authorised interpreters of Divine Truth, they could not sacrifice the rights of that Master who is the truth, of that Saviour in whom they trusted for their justification. Nor could they conscientiously sacrifice the conviction which had made them Christians. Far from desiring to wage war upon the

Church of Christ, they believed themselves to be called by God to restore it to its purity, and to reform it in conformity with the teaching of the apostles on the model of the Apostolic Church. You know how the development of the Churches of the Reformation gave rise to an excess of diversity and of division. After a long period of insistence upon the points which separate them they have now become aware of what they have in common, of the factors which unite them ; they have drawn nearer one to another, and have learnt to work together and to concentrate their energies for the work of mission preaching and social reform. This movement is at work also in the episcopal Churches, and in those of the East, so that to-day throughout the whole world a profound and notable tendency towards greater unity is making itself felt.

Tragic and painful experiences such as those of the Great War have been needed to open the eyes of Christendom to essential principles which have been too long ignored. In consequence of the sufferings through which it has passed, and thanks to the vast activity of theological thought and science in the nineteenth century, Christendom in our day has reached the conviction that Christianity is not primarily an ecclesiastical organisation : it is not the government of the Church by a hierarchy of prelates or representative bodies, nor is it essentially a collection of creeds or confessions formulating more or less faithfully the facts and truths of salvation, even though the organisation of the Church and the documents in which its faith is expressed can claim to be not only valuable but also necessary. Christendom to-day, I say, has come to recognise with all the great believers throughout the ages, that Christianity is the person of Christ Himself, who lived, and died, and rose again for us ; with Christianity is the gospel, the message which Jesus brought to mankind in its misery and sin ; it is His Spirit acting in the world to convert and regenerate it, so that he who has not the spirit of Christ is none of His. Moreover, Christendom yearns to see the Church becoming more and more truly the Body of Christ upon this earth.

Nowhere is this aspiration towards unity more keen than in the great non-Christian lands : in India, China and Japan —where native Christians for the most part are disinclined to attach themselves to a particular denomination, desiring to be members of the united church of Christ. Nearer home, great international organisations, such as the Y.M.C.A., the Y.W.C.A. and the Student Christian Movement, are overflowing the limits of all Churches and working eagerly for the manifestation of the oneness of the Body of Christ.

Further, one duty is evermore definitely and imperatively laid upon Christians and upon Churches, the duty of presenting a united front against those forces which are hostile to Christ and His kingdom ; how can the army of Christ fight when divided against itself, or move forward to victory over Mammon and Satan ? The royalty and sovereignty of Jesus Christ must be made manifest in the unity of His Church ; His servants and friends must rally round Him as their only leader to proclaim the gospel to the world, and to give effect to His law of righteousness, holiness and love ; the salvation of the world depends upon this. The admirable and effective efforts of the League of Nations will only attain their end if the Christian Church is able to utter a united protest against evil, and to stamp the character of the spirit of Christ upon that noble institution, which so sorely needs strengthening and completion.

The unity towards which we aspire must rest upon free consent ; it must be living and unfettered ; it will, therefore, be the fruit of discussion and the interchange of ideas and convictions ; it will be brought into being by a great and serious effort towards mutual understanding. Our great thinker, Alexandre Vinet, in his treatise on the manifestation of religious convictions, has a striking passage which expresses this truth :

" Without doubt, fellowship in religion and in worship requires an agreement and a consensus of many minds upon fundamental points of doctrine : even more certainly it requires a union of hearts ; but it is compatible with divergences upon any point which is less than fundamental. The existence of such points should neither be dissembled nor ignored, and the true interest of religious fellowship rather demands that they shall be frankly expressed."

" Such a candid expression of thought is, as a rule, a challenge—a battlecry of defiance. Living unity is a peace achieved upon a field of battle where the conquered becomes the conqueror's ally, and feels himself to be, as indeed he is, his fellow-victor."

Let us then be confident that our labours will be brought to a happy issue. We shall certainly find that there are among us serious differences of opinion upon the sacraments, upon church government, and upon the use to be made of the ancient rules of faith. I trust that these divergences will not hinder us from realising our deep inner unity. Let us affirm together our common faith in God who is Love, the Father of our Lord Jesus Christ, and our Father ; let us affirm our faith in Christ, the only and the perfect Saviour, the only head of the Church. Let us affirm our faith in the regenerating power of the Spirit of God. The unity of the Churches, the unity of the Church exists in Christ. May God help us to make manifest before the eyes of the world this spiritual oneness as a unity in divergence, a unity in love. Let us think the thoughts of Christ. May our work be the work which He would have done ; and under the guidance of His Spirit may we work towards the accomplishment of His purpose and towards the realisation of His prayer, " that they all may be one, as thou, Father, art in me, and I in thee."

Following the conclusion of Professor Choisy's address, the Conference took up the matters of business proposed by the Programme Committee for consideration at the afternoon session: The election of officers, the reception of the material prepared by the Subjects Committee, and the adoption of a programme and of rules of order.

BUSINESS SESSION

Election of Officers of the Conference.

On the motion of the Most Rev. Archbishop GERMANOS, seconded by Dr. DEISSMANN, the Right Rev. Charles H. BRENT, D.D., Bishop of Western New York, was elected President of the Conference.

THE PRESIDENT : My Brothers,—The honour you have conferred on me cannot fail to move me deeply. Of course, I knew that my name was to be presented, and at the Continuation Committee I expressed not only the willingness but the desire to draw aside and let another take my place, but now that you have given me this responsibility I pledge myself to you to do that which every man is bound to do—my best. I recognise that the real President of such a meeting as this is none other than the Lord Christ himself working through His Blessed Spirit, and it is with that conviction that I am prepared to place myself at His disposal and at your disposal.

There are just two things I should like to say. The first is that the most important work of this Conference can be achieved by united prayer. We are setting aside much more time that is ordinarily given at great assemblies for prayer; you will note in the last edition of the Programme that the full session begins with prayer, not *after* prayer, and we trust—and I earnestly urge it upon you—that every member, even at disadvantage to himself, will make it his duty as well as his high privilege to be present for the entire devotions which will begin at 9.30 every morning. At that time we can best put ourselves into relation with God in a corporate way, and I do trust that we shall gather together as a complete assembly every morning, and so begin our day aright as the family of God.

The second thing I have to say—and the last—is that in addition to prayer you and I must put ourselves in the right relation to God. I am in many respects as strongly convinced on many subjects as the rest of you, but I am anxious to get rid of prejudice and of ignorance, and it is for us, in a way that perhaps we have never

33

done before, to put ourselves at the disposal of God, to give our minds and our judgment and our hearts into His hands that He may sway us whither He will. I am not ashamed to change my opinions. I will not be ashamed to acknowledge that a conviction which I now have is wrong if God tells me it is wrong. It is in such a spirit that I believe all of us should approach God in this great Assembly, and if we do the results of our deliberations will be very far-reaching and the Church will stride forward with new hope and with new power toward that glorious day when there will be one flock under one Shepherd.

As you will recognise, the responsibility of a President is extremely heavy. My health is not what it might be, and therefore I need help, and I am going to ask your permission to nominate—although it is not usually the function of a Chairman to nominate—a Deputy-Chairman. I should like to present the name of the Rev. Dr. GARVIE, my friend, who has in the past year done much which in the same circumstances I would have been rather unwilling to do. He has taken my place at a moment's notice when I was kept by ill-health from attending the Continuation Committee, and he has constantly stood beside me at every moment when I have had any public office to perform since I came to Europe. Therefore I would hope that you would immediately respond in favour of the election of Dr. GARVIE as my Deputy-Chairman.

By unanimous vote, Dr. GARVIE was so elected.

In accepting the office of Deputy-Chairman, Dr. GARVIE said that nothing would have induced him to act in this capacity except the great respect and warm affection which he had for Bishop Brent, who had expressed the desire that he should be relieved in part of the chairmanship at the afternoon meetings when free discussions were to take place. The one advantage that he might possess as a deputy-chairman was that he understood the three languages in which the Conference was to conduct its deliberations.

The President then called for the nomination of a General Secretary of the Conference. Dr. Garvie put forward the name of Mr. Ralph W. BROWN, to whose industry, patience and diligence he paid a tribute which was warmly endorsed by the Conference. Mr. BROWN was unanimously elected.

The President nominated, and the Conference elected, Mr. George ZABRISKIE as Treasurer of the Conference. Mr. ZABRISKIE'S unique services to the cause of the Conference over a long period of years were cordially recognised by the whole Conference.

Arrangements Committee

Dr. GARVIE reported that the Continuation Committee had passed the following resolution :

Voted that the Continuation Committee appoint a sub-committee called the Arrangements Committee to assign the members of the Conference to Sections as provided, to consider reports if necessary, and to direct the Conference upon any questions which may arise regarding the conduct of the Conference. The members of the Arrangements Committee shall be the following :

Bishop Brent	Prof. Dr. Deissmann
Dr. Garvie	The Bishop of Bombay
Mr. R. W. Brown	Dr. F. L. Wiseman
Mr. Zabriskie	Bishop Iriney
Dr. Alivisatos	Pastor Thvedt
Dr. Atkinson	

This resolution was confirmed, and the Arrangements Committee named therein was appointed.

The Programme of the Conference

Dr. GARVIE : In submitting the Programme for your acceptance, there are some explanations which it seems desirable to make. At the meeting of the Continuation Committee last August in Berne, three committees were appointed—an American, a Continental and British, and an Eastern Orthodox—to nominate speakers. A central committee was also appointed consisting of the Archbishop of Upsala, Metropolitan Germanos, Mr. Brown and myself to deal with these nominations in preparing the Programme.

At a meeting last December, the Archbishop of Upsala was represented by Mr. Hellerström, the Swedish pastor in London. The other members were present and Canon Bate, Secretary of the Subjects Committee, was also invited. The first proposals for the Programme were then drafted, in which the effort was made (1) to use the nominations as far as possible, (2) to get the main ecclesiastical types represented each day, and (3) to secure also a representation of the different nations and the three languages. The Committee acted with a most conscientious effort to rise above both prejudice and partiality. The carrying out of these proposals was much hindered by the uncertainty of some of those invited regarding their presence at the Conference, the delay of others in answering the letters sent to them, and the unwillingness of a few to commit themselves. Some countries did not send in their suggestions until after the first proposals were drafted. Mr. Brown, the Secretary, has had incredible labour in getting the Programme into its present form, not because of any want of attention on his part but for the reasons given above.

The Committee met again this April, when the Bishop of Bombay, as Chairman of the Subjects Committee, was asked also to be present. In order to keep the Programme as representative as possible, some countries will find fewer of the names they recommended than they may desire or expect, but it may be pointed out that the afternoon discussions and, still more, the work in the sections and groups and committees proposed, will afford scope for the use of all the knowledge and ability which are at the command of the Conference in the representatives present. The procedure for the sections has been carefully thought out, as also have been the standing orders, and it is hoped that the Conference will accept these without spending time in debating the details so that it may give its time and strength to the main object.

The resolutions to be submitted, after Canon Bate has explained what the object is of the material and statements prepared by the Subjects Committee, are intended to make clear that the Conference is master of its own procedure and is not being led in any direction other than that in which its own judgment under the guidance of God's Spirit will freely lead it. Let that guidance be sought and used!

Bishop Brent: Before putting the Programme to the vote, I am going to ask Canon Bate to make a statement relative to the work done by the Subjects Committee.

Canon Bate : The task which I have been asked to undertake is a very simple one. I am to speak on the material prepared by the Subjects Committee, by the instructions of the Continuation Committee ; and what I have to say to you is relevant to a proposal which will be laid before you that the Conference shall receive the Material (Pamphlet No. 52) and the Statements of the Subjects Committee (Pamphlet No. 46) as summaries of the preparatory work done for the Conference under the instructions of the Continuation Committee.

I am concerned, therefore, with the two printed documents. The Conference will not be asked this afternoon to express its agreement or disagreement with anything which those documents contain : it will simply be asked to receive them both as embodying summaries of preparatory work done, and to accept one of them (No. 52) as suggestive of questions which must naturally arise in any thorough consideration of the general subjects which the Conference is invited in its Programme to consider.

Permit me then to remind you of one or two points relating to the history of these documents. Ever since the Preliminary Conference at Geneva, in 1920, a Subjects Committee appointed by the Continuation Committee has been at work under the Chairmanship of the Bishop of Bombay. That Committee was charged with the double task (1) of preparing for the discussions of this present Conference by promoting preliminary inquiry into the main topics of Faith and Order, and (2) of preparing an Agenda for this Conference. In pursuance of the first part of this task it prepared and sent out, in various languages, five series of questions for preliminary conference. The results of this process of inquiry, sent in from groups meeting all over the world, were considered and summarised at two prolonged sessions of the Subjects Committee, in 1923 and in 1925. At these sessions the Committee drew up statements in which an attempt was made to record the main agreements and differences revealed by the reports of the groups. These statements covered the subjects of the Church, the Creed, the Ministry and the Christian Moral Ideal. The fourth of these topics and statements, as belonging rather to the sphere of the Conference on Life in Work, was felt to be excluded from the purview of this Conference. There remained the subject of the Sacraments. By Midsummer, 1926, the work of those groups which devoted themselves to this subject was ready to be summarised, and although it was not found practicable to handle it in a full session of the Subjects Committee, a report was drawn up and submitted to the members of the Committee individually.

This, then, is the origin of the Pamphlet No. 46—" Statements by the Subjects Committee." It is available here for the use of any members who may desire to consult or use it, and it is simply what it professes to be—a summary, adequate I hope, though by no means complete, of that part of our preparatory work which has been done as a result of the activity of the Subjects Committee.

This pamphlet, I should add, is at the moment available only in English. Financial considerations have hitherto hindered its being circulated as a whole in French and German, although the greater part of it has been circulated for some years in German, French and Greek. If there is a demand or need for further translation no doubt this demand can be met.

I now pass to Pamphlet No. 52, which is available here in English, French and German. In 1925 at Stockholm, the Subjects Committee submitted to the Continuation Committee a Draft Agenda for this Conference. That Draft was there amended, approved and ordered to be circulated for wider criticism on the part of the constituents of the Conference. A year elapsed, and the voice of criticism was by no means silent. And when the Continuation Committee met at Berne last year it was decided to make a radical change, namely, to reduce the actual Agenda of the Conference to a list of subjects and speakers. The material contained in the Draft Agenda, together with all the criticisms sent in during 1925-6, and those made at Berne, was handed over to me, with the instruction that the material should be rewritten in the light—the fierce light—of the criticisms it had received.

The result of this process is Pamphlet No. 52, " Material prepared by the Subjects Committee." Part of that pamphlet—the subject No. II on the Church's Message to the World—was actually drafted at Berne by a sub-committee. The rest represents, like Pamphlet No. 46, a large mass of preparatory work, and chiefly the criticisms of groups and individuals on the Draft Agenda of 1925.

This document, like the other, is simply laid before the Conference for such use as the Conference or its sections may care to make of it. It is not directly the work of the Subjects Committee, as is plain from what I have said, but it is indirectly at least a fruit of their long preparatory work. It is intended only to supply starting-points for absolutely free discussion. Where it makes an assertion (if ever it does so) that assertion is intended to be treated as something that can be argued about ; where it asks a question—as it does very often—it does not intend to suggest that no more appropriate question could not have been asked ; rather it suggests a number of points which actually have been the subject of discussion among our constituents, and from which (it is reasonable to expect) many widely diverging paths will radiate out during the course of our explorations here. It is laid before you to be used, and used with entire freedom, and only to be used in so far as it may be found useful.

Finally, in regard to both Pamphlets No. 46 and No. 52, I feel sure that the Subjects Committee as a whole would allow me to say that they present them to you only as, on the one hand, records of what has actually been done, and, on the other, as instruments which they hope the Conference will put aside without hesitation should they not prove to be of service in furthering the work which we are called together to attempt.

DR. GARVIE : I have now to move the following resolutions :

1. That the members of the World Conference on Faith and Order proceed to the consideration of the subjects as listed in the Programme.

That means that you accept the Programme as it has been prepared for you by the Programme Committee. Some members may say that that deprives the Conference of the right of discussing other subjects, so in order to meet every possible objection we have drafted a second resolution which I will read, although I think it would be desirable to put the two resolutions to the vote separately :

2. That any subject not now listed in the Programme may be placed there at any stage at the written request of not fewer than three members of the Conference, if a two-thirds majority of the Conference so decide after consideration and report by the Arrangements Committee.

The Arrangements Committee can consider the subjects submitted and advise as to whether it is thought desirable that such subjects should be added. May I also add that the Programme is already pretty full, and I do not see how you can very well get much else into it.

Resolutions 1 and 2 were then carried, together with a further proposal moved by Dr. Garvie :

That the Conference receives the Material (Pamphlet No. 52) and the Statements of the Subjects Committee (Pamphlet No. 46) as summaries of the preparatory work done for the Conference under the instructions of the Continuation Committee.

Rules of Procedure

Dr. GARVIE then submitted to the Conference the following Rules of Procedure, pointing out that they had been prepared by a Special Committee and had been carefully discussed by the Continuation Committee :—

1. That during the Conference, matters of business and debated matters be considered at the afternoon sessions rather than at the morning sessions.

2. French, German and English shall be the official languages of the Conference, each interpreter translating into his own native language ; in the free discussions only a summary of each address shall be given in the other two languages.

3. During the free discussions in the sessions of the full Conference, the bell shall be rung after five minutes to indicate that the speaker must close, and again after seven minutes ; and only that part which remains of ten minutes shall be allowed for interpretations.

4. Those who desire to speak during the free discussions are expected to hand to the Secretary or place in a box to be provided for that purpose in the Aula, cards with their names, their church connection and the aspects of the subject on which they desire to speak, not later than 3 p.m. of the day devoted to that subject, so that the Chairman may in the exercise of his discretion be enabled to secure as varied and valuable a contribution to the discussion of each subject as possible. Groups who desire a particular conviction or point of view to find expression should select from among themselves a speaker, so that repetition may be avoided.

5. That besides the opening devotions provided for in the Programme, every session shall begin and close with devotion, and at the discretion of the Chairman there shall be other periods of devotion ; during the devotions the doors shall be closed.

6. No motion upon any Subject of the Conference shall be entertained until the appointed section shall have reported upon that Subject.

7.* When reports from the sections have been made to the full Conference, if alterations in them are proposed, the Conference may

* Revised August 6th. See p. 196-197.

refer them to a drafting committee for consideration and report. No statement shall be declared to be adopted by the Conference unless it be accepted either unanimously or *nemine contradicente*. In case a statement does not gain this measure of acceptance, the Conference shall determine what further steps, if any, shall be taken on that subject.

8. No motion under Subject I shall be entertained until Saturday August 20th. The officers of the Conference and the chairmen and secretaries of the sections should constitute a committee to prepare a resolution upon Subject I if the Conference determine upon such a course.

9. Arrangements for continuing the work of the Conference shall be determined on August 20th.

10. If the Conference desire that the discussion of a Subject should be continued, the Chairman may entertain a motion for adjournment to an evening session at 8.30.

11. That no literature shall be distributed to the delegates at the Palais de Rumine apart from the publications circulated by the Continuation Committee in connection with each day's discussions, and that such matter should be relevant to the subjects of the Conference.

Rules for the Sectional Sessions

12. That there be no section of the Conference upon Subject I.

13. That each member of the Conference be assigned to a section upon Subject II, III or IV, and also to a section upon Subject V, VI or VII.

14. In the assignment of members to sections, regard shall be given to their preferences. The section charged to deal with a given Subject shall include the persons who have opened the discussion of that Subject.

15. That, should it be desirable to charge more than 100 persons with the discussion of any Subject of the programme, the Arrangements Committee shall divide that section into two or more sub-sections meeting separately, except in such joint meetings of the sub-sections dealing with one subject as may be deemed necessary to secure that one report on each subject shall be submitted to the Conference. This course may be followed, if it seems desirable, even if the number for a section should be less than 100.

16. The procedure of the sections shall be as follows :

(*a*) A meeting of each section or sub-section shall be held for further division into groups and in order to determine the points of greatest importance for further discussion ;

C

(*b*) No group shall have more than twenty members. Each may be charged with the discussion either of the whole subject or of some part of it, and each group shall be made as widely representative of ecclesiastical types as possible ;

(*c*) The chairman and secretary of each section or sub-section shall nominate a reporter for each group, and these reporters shall constitute a Committee, who shall prepare the report for the section, to be submitted to the Conference ;

(*d*) A meeting of the whole section or sub-section shall be held to receive the report of this Committee, to determine the form in which it shall be submitted to the whole Conference. Where there are sub-sections, a joint meeting will also be held.

17. While each section and sub-section shall appoint its own chairman, the Arrangements Committee shall designate for each section and sub-section a secretary who shall act as its convener.

18. A member of one section who desires to speak upon another subject in the meeting of another section may do so at the beginning of a session upon the invitation of the chairman of that section.

A question was raised by Bishop GORE with regard to Section 7 of these Rules.

Dr. Gore recognised that the suggested Rule would preclude the adoption of any statement by the Conference upon which the Conference was not completely unanimous, but he desired to see some words inserted which would prevent statements approved merely by a large majority of the Conference from being regarded as receiving its approval. The question thus raised was discussed at length, and finally on the suggestion of Dr. Garvie, endorsed by Bishop Gore, the whole of Section 7 of the Rules was referred back to the Arrangements Committee for redrafting [see p. 196]. With this exception the Rules of Procedure were adopted by the Conference.

Death of a Delegate

THE PRESIDENT : It is with great regret that I have to announce the death of one of our members, the Rev. Norman NICHOLSON, who would have been sitting with us to-day had he not been taken from us yesterday. Mr. Nicholson, who was well known and beloved in Lausanne, was to have been here as a representative of the United Free Church of Scotland.

The Conference adjourned at 6.45 p.m.

THE CHURCH'S MESSAGE TO THE WORLD : THE GOSPEL

Thursday Morning, August 4th.

Full sessions of the Conference were held in the Aula of the University. The morning session was opened at 9.30 with devotions, led by the Rev. Dr. J. E. Roberts, and the Chair was taken by the Most Rev. Archbishop Germanos.

PROFESSOR DR. ADOLF DEISSMANN
University of Berlin (Evangelical-Lutheran)

The Church's Message to the World, the Gospel : this theme compresses into a single line four tremendous ideas packed with meaning. It speaks of the Church and of the world ; it asserts that the Church has a message for the world, and it calls this message " Gospel."

Church and world! On the eastern limit of the Roman Empire, on the distant boundary of the organised civilisation of the ancient Mediterranean world, in the troublous times of the early Cæsars, a prophet grew up. He came forth from the creative depths of those who labour and are heavy laden. A prophet indeed, but more than a prophet. From childhood onwards breathing the life-giving breath of prayer, early strengthened through a surrender of will to the living God, nourished and sanctified by the divine revelation working in the sacred history of His people, Jesus of Nazareth the youthful Galilean carpenter was first drawn along into the movement initiated by the Baptist under the influence of the resounding call of " Elias which was for to come," and then was Himself called out to work on the threshing-floor of the Messianic harvest, the harvest of the last day.

By His baptism in Jordan, the conviction of His own

43

mission which had long ago come to Him was concentrated, strengthened and raised for the first time to the level of Messianic consciousness. These two, Mission and Anointing, constituted the authority for His adoption of John's call to repentance as His own Messianic message, after the imprisonment of the Baptist. He spread this message abroad, both by His own mouth and by means of a multitude of followers, like a burning brand amid the people, while He humbly struggled with His ever-clearer consciousness of Messiahship, and obediently bowed to the necessity of a martyr's death. The glowing words " Repent, for the Kingdom of God is at hand! " (Matt. iv, 17, cf. Mk.1, 15) have this meaning : turn yourselves to the Living God, for His day is here, His kingdom is about to dawn, He Himself stands at the door, He Himself will come to you, to set up His rule over you as your Judge and your King. Watch and pray ! Perchance He comes even to-morrow, or this very day, while you listen to my voice!

This is the message which, viewed from the point of view of world-history, indicates the beginning of the greatest of all the spiritual movements of mankind—the beginning of Christianity. Once spoken quietly into trembling human hearts and proclaimed aloud throughout the land and to the ends of the earth, the waves of this message have now vibrated and expanded in circles with an eternal energy through two millenniums of human development. Undiscerned, or discerned but dimly by millions ; weakened, rendered trivial and no longer understood in its divine gravity by many, and that even by some who are themselves committed to spreading it, this message is yet indestructible in its primitive evangelical force, and from this primal source of strength it continually regains its ancient victorious Messianic passion.

Jesus entrusted this message to a little company of apostolic followers who, without knowing it, formed the primitive germ-cell of the Church. By them the message was rightly understood and, so understood, was passed on to others ; and thus it was that a cult-community of the glorified Master, exalted now as Lord, gathered together in the Mysteries of its Easter vision, awaiting His speedy coming with the prayer *Marana tha.*

That the Church which historically first appeared in the form of this cult-community felt herself to be the messenger of God to the world in the stead of Jesus Christ, is expressed with the utmost clarity by her greatest spokesman, the tent-maker of Tarsus : " We are ambassadors therefore on behalf of Christ " (2 Cor. v, 20). And that this apostolic message was directed not only to individual souls but also to the "world," that is to mankind in general, is also definitely known through the testimony of Paul. The apostolic message of the group of disciples, now become a Church, was nothing more than the true development of what was already present as ecumenical germ in the message of Jesus itself.

Thus the apostolic Church had already brought together in thought those great primitive words which we in Lausanne in 1927 compress into the theme " The Church's message to the world, the Gospel." The Church has a message, and this message, the Gospel, is directed to the world.

Now we must gain clarity about the meaning and essence of this message. In one of the greatest creations of the spirit of the Greek language, primitive Christianity itself brought to expression the meaning and essence of its message in the word εὐαγγέλιον, " evangelium." Not that the Apostles invented or coined this word. They found it already in use in the world about them, in a variety of senses. The glittering language of the Cæsar-cult shows the closest analogies : people were fond of using the word εὐαγγέλιον when some favourable news from the Emperor or the imperial house penetrated into the provinces.

This meaning " cheerful news," " joyful message " was also conveyed by the word εὐαγγέλιον in the usage of the primitive apostolic Church. But in this instance it became such an independent word, with a character and vividness so uniquely its own that it can with difficulty be translated into other languages. The Latin Bible therefore took it over untranslated in the form " evangelium," similarly the

Gothic Bible in the form " aiwaggeljo " ; both, by the way, by means of this transcription confirming the fact that the pronunciation of the original Greek word, even in very ancient times, was not " euangelion," but began with " ev," being pronounced " evangelion " in the popular Greek received by the Romance peoples, as also in late and in modern Greek.

Only one language has succeeded in finding an entirely true translation of this watchword and in creating for it a popular equivalent which was to experience a rich history of its own : the English language. The possession of the word " gospel " is one of the greatest spiritual treasures that are entrusted to English-speaking Christendom. The word " gospel " reflects indeed in its own history a considerable part of the history of missions in the West. For us it emerges for the first time in the Lindisfarne Gospels about the year 950 in the form " godspell," and there is no doubt that " godspell " is simply " good spell," that is " good tidings," " gute Zeitung," as Luther occasionally translates the word " evangelium." Popular etymology was fond indeed in early times of connecting " Godspell " with " God," and so understanding it to mean " God-tidings," " Gotteszeitung." In this misunderstood form " godspell " was carried over by British missionaries out of the Old English into the Germanic languages, in Old Saxon in the form " gotspell."

It is perhaps a pity that German Christendom of the early middle ages did not finally appropriate the Germanic word " gospel." But German Christians have always understood the true meaning of the word " evangelium." Luther in particular gives several excellent renderings : " gute Mär " (the good tale) and, as already mentioned, " gute Zeitung." And it has never been entirely forgotten that the subject of the Gospel is the good news of the Kingdom of God. The great American Congregationalist, Cotton Mather of Boston, wrote in 1715 an essay about August Hermann Francke, the bicentenary of whose death in 1727 has been celebrated by German Christendom this summer. When Cotton Mather gave this essay the title :

" Nuncia Bona e Terra Longinqua. A Brief Account of some Good and Great Things Adoing for the Kingdom of God in the Midst of Europe "—the expression " Nuncia Bona," applied by him to the account of religious facts of his own day, shows that he understood the Gospel to be inherently concerned with a joyful message of the Kingdom of God.

To this truth we, in our Conference, must attach supreme value ; the Christian watchword " Evangelium " in its original significance means the joyful message of Jesus of Nazareth that the Kingdom of God is at hand, that the kingly rule of the living God is about to come into this world. This includes both judgment and redemption. And this message is inseparably united with the inexorable demand for the inner transformation of each individual.

Thus the Gospel has a dual character. It is filled with the weighty moral seriousness that drives men to repentance in expectation of the judgment, and in spite of this it is finally the glad message of redemption.

A great misunderstanding in the sphere of spiritual history must here be averted. The Gospel of Jesus was not and is not the theological principle of a new school, not an idea in the philosophy of history, not the programme of a theoretical outlook upon the world. In the course of the spiritual history of Christianity, indeed, the Gospel of Jesus has exercised a profound influence on theology, on the philosophy of history, on law, and on men's outlook upon the world. In the spring of 1927 at a Conference held in Canterbury under the guidance of the Dean of Canterbury, twelve British and German theologians had for a week a wonderful and inspiring exchange of views on these matters. And truly, what a treasure of spiritual values would remain unexplored if we were debarred from following up as we did then the less immediate implications of the Gospel! But directly and in its original meaning the Gospel has nothing to do with these theoretical questionings. Rather the Gospel of Jesus is a religious message, a trumpet blast of the archangel, a moving call to repentance, a word of blessing and comfort, always a practical call, something whose aim is not to instruct people but to change them and turn them to the living God.

To anyone who looks for theoretical teaching the Gospel must needs appear as foolishness. And it is in fact foolishness (1 Cor. i, 18 and 21, cf. Matt. xi, 25), certainly a "foolishness of God" to which the understanding of the wise can never attain, a tale which, though a thousand times laughed to scorn, still simply means " *the* " truth.

Ultimately it is this foolishness of the Gospel which is emphasised when people insist on using the overworked, pedantic word " eschatology," and describe the Gospel of Jesus as an eschatological proclamation. For the last thirty years or so, the discernment of the eschatological character of the Gospel of Jesus has more and more come to the front in international Christian theology. I regard this as one of the greatest steps forward that theological enquiry has ever achieved. But to many, who before this had constructed for themselves a comfortable arm-chair Gospel for the study, whether it were an Aristotelian, a Neoplatonic, a Thomist or a Kantian Gospel, the discovery of the eschatological Gospel came as a terrible disappointment and as an occasion for indignant protests against "fanaticism" (" Schwärmerei ") ; we were confronted incessantly with the rival claims of a retrospective Gospel to be accepted as a new and ready-made system of soteriology.

Over against this we must insist not only that the Gospel, looked at historically, cannot be grasped by such doctrinaire methods, but also that we to-day in 1927 must lay the strongest possible stress upon the eschatological character of that Gospel which it is the practical business of the Church to proclaim ; namely that we must daily focus our minds upon the fact that the Kingdom of God is near, that God with His unconditioned sovereignty comes to us through judgment and redemption, and that we have to prepare ourselves inwardly for this coming of God by μετάνοια, by inner return. That is an eschatology which does not paralyse, but rather fortifies the *ethos* of the individual and of society in its contact with things temporal.

And as in the age of the Roman Emperors the watchword " Evangelium," " joyful news," revealed the inner form of contemporary human experience, in that it showed redemption as divine joy breaking in upon joyless, anxious mankind laden with guilt and wretchedness, so we too today, if the Church of Jesus Christ is to proclaim to the individual and the world the ancient message of the Master, must ever and again let the morning light of divine joy shine in upon a world which bleeds from a thousand wounds, a world stricken with individual and corporate guilt and unheard-of misery : " Lift up your heads, behold your redemption draweth nigh ! " (Luke xxi, 28).

The Gospel of the Master preserved for itself its fundamental tendency, combining severity and joy as it were in a parallelogram of forces, even when it became the message of the Apostles. The apostolic preaching remained eschatological, even when Paul and John succeeded in their profound attempt to combine the eschatology of the Kingdom with Christ-mysticism—when the ancient Biblical cry of exultation " the Lord is near " (Ps. xxxiv, 18 ; cxlv, 18 : Phil. iv, 5) came to mean alike " the *parousia*, the advent of the Saviour is at hand," and " the Saviour is near, because He dwells in us as the spiritual Lord who deigns to bestow His gracious presence upon us." The apostolic preaching of the Gospel was never reduced to a merely retrospective doctrine. It always contemplated the present marvellous world of the gracious God and His Anointed as an existing reality, and always directed its eyes forward to the still greater marvel (Cf. John i, 50 ; v, 20) of redemption yet to come.

Only in its whole content did the Gospel preaching of the Apostles possess a new fulness in comparison with the monumental simplicity and divine momentum of the message of Jesus. Without giving up the preaching of the Kingdom it concentrated increasingly on the preaching of Christ. The formulation given by the Subjects Committee and approved by the Continuation Committee of

our Lausanne Conference to Subject II, sentence 2, does
full justice to this fact :

" In the centre of the Gospel stands Jesus Christ Himself,
Son of God and Son of Man, who through His life, His
death and His resurrection, has redeemed mankind and
brought eternal life to light."

Only, perhaps, in order to reproduce the thought of
Paul and John with complete accuracy, we should add to
the words " has redeemed " the words " and redeems."
For with the Apostles redemption is thought of at least as
much in the present and future as in the past. By means
of the addition " and redeems " more justice is done to
the mystical and eschatological feeling of the apostolic
preaching.

Are we then compelled, we must now ask, to interpret
the two stages above mentioned, the Gospel of Jesus about
the Kingdom of God and the Gospel of the Apostles about
Jesus Christ, as a " twofold Gospel " ? The honoured senior
member of our Berlin Theological Faculty, Adolf von
Harnack, from whom we must all either directly or indirectly have learnt, sought to clarify the great problem
of the inner development of primitive Christianity with this
formula. Nevertheless, I cannot quite bring myself to
adopt the formula of the " twofold Gospel " for it does not
exclude at least two misunderstandings.

First, the misunderstanding lying in the idea that in
primitive times there were two different types of Gospel.
Now this is not the case : because in speaking of the Gospel
of Jesus and the Gospel of the Apostles we are dealing
not with two types, one following upon and taking the place
of the other, but with two expressions of the one Gospel
which grew up in inseparable combination.

Secondly, the formula " twofold Gospel " lies open to the
misunderstanding that the inner history of primitive
Christianity was the unfolding of a gradually developing
doctrinal idea : Chapter I, the teaching of Jesus concerning
the Kingdom of God ; Chapter II, The teaching of the
Apostles concerning Jesus Christ.

Over against that, it must be emphasised that what

actually happened, as a matter of historical sequence, was that in this successive appearance of the Gospel preaching of Jesus and the Gospel preaching of the Apostles there was a progress from the Gospel of Jesus to the Christ-cult of the Apostles, and that thus the later and enriched Gospel of the Apostles was actually a cult Gospel; it was that cult form of the primitive Gospel which worship and propaganda required.

Looked at in this way, the apostolic Gospel appears not only as a quantitative enrichment but also as the essential precondition for the future development of the Mother Church in Jerusalem into the ecumenical Church, the Church for all nations and all times.

Formulated in academic phrase, we may put this thought as follows : The ancient eschatology of the Kingdom as preached by Jesus acquired a personal concentration, and therewith a new capacity for gripping the popular mind, through the apostolic cult of the present and expected Lord (*Kyrios*), who was none other than the Crucified. Using New Testament language, we can express it thus : The petition of the Lord's Prayer " Thy kingdom come " (Matt. vi, 10 ; Luke xi, 2) uttered whenever two or three came together in His name, received a new enthusiastic intimacy and a new illumination by means of the prayer at the Lord's Supper, " *Marana tha*! " " Come, Lord Jesus! " (1 Cor. xvi, 22 ; Didaché x, 6 ; Rev. xxii, 20.)

Yet the moving seriousness of the original call to repentance, and along with it the original exultant joy which the Gospel of Jesus produced and still produces in the hearts of men, did not pass away when the Crucified, as the exalted Lord, had taken the central place in the proclamation of the Apostles ; it was still the heritage of the elect, who in Christ could confess alike that they were a new creation (2 Cor. v, 17 ; Gal. vi, 15), and that they were reconciled children of God (2 Cor. v, 18 ; Rom. v, 10).

In the providential ordering of history over a period of nearly two thousand years, the little Jerusalem community whose watchword was *Marana tha* has grown, as the cult-community of Jesus Christ, into a world-wide, an ecumeni-

cal Church, and behind every single expression of life
there lies its *character indelebilis* as the cult-community of
the Crucified and Living Lord Jesus Christ.

To-day, therefore, when in Lausanne in the year of
grace 1927 we discuss the Gospel as the Church's message to
the world, there still stands behind our thoughts and resolutions the living Christ, before whom we His followers bow
as fellow-worshippers, adoring Him as our crucified Redeemer and gloriously exalted Lord. From Him comes also
our personal mission, the mission of the Churches and the
mission of our Conference, " Go ye into all the world and
preach the gospel to every creature! " (Matt. xxviii, 19)—
that Gospel of the Kingdom of God soon to come, and yet
near us because the Lord is near us, the Kingdom for which
we ask in the prayer " Thy Kingdom come," and whose
bright dawn we behold when we pray " *Marana tha!*" For
when the believing Church of Jesus Christ prays her
Marana tha, her prayer is always heard : the Lord *is* near :
where two or three are gathered together in His name, there
He is in the midst of them (Matt. xviii, 20).

But it is for us, in the gracious presence of the Lord, to
transform the conviction of our own mission into active
work for a great new evangelisation. This new evangelisation must be a self-evangelisation of the individual and
self-evangelisation of the Churches, and through these
simultaneous processes must come the evangelisation of
national and social groups and associations, and finally
the evangelisation of mankind.

Both in content and expression this must not be so much
a retrospective and dogmatic teaching of the intellect as a
prophetic and authoritative shaking of the conscience and
will. It must not dictate paragraphs : it must sound the
trumpet. It must not set forth the Kingdom of God as an
institution long present in our midst ; rather, before the
eyes of those who have been awakened to be fellow-
labourers in God's harvest, it must present the Kingdom
with moving seriousness as the *unum necessarium*, the one
thing needful, as the great and unattained goal of all
things, as judgment to come, and as redemption to come.

And all this must be done with apostolic fervour and warmth, through concentration of the heart upon the living Master.

The Church must give up the attempt to demonstrate the rationality of the Kingdom of God to the healthy intelligence of mankind. It must have courage and joyfulness to proclaim paradox to the world and to expect paradox from the world : the paradox that by reason of the nearness of God and of His Anointed we must be new men, and that in following God's Anointed we must be the salt of the earth and the light of the world! It must preach the fearfulness of sin and the glory of grace. It must, however, because grace is greater than sin, ever have a *joyful* news, the Gospel, as its final message.

If the Christian Churches seriously accept the task of the new evangelisation, they will be compelled more urgently than ever to recognise the necessity of their unity. Not their uniformity. In their theology, in the details of their liturgy, in their methods of education and of practical work, in the productions of their art, of their poetry and music, the Churches may rightly continue to work out the manifold gifts entrusted to them in manifold ways. But in their message to the world they must be at one, they must form a united front. The unseen waves of the divine message of the Gospel which vibrate over the globe ought not to be destroyed and confused by contrary waves from those who are broadcasting a competition of ill-will. " If the trumpet give an uncertain sound, who shall prepare himself to the battle ? " (1 Cor. xiv, 8).

Therefore our special theme, the Church's Message to the World, is most closely connected with the fundamental idea of our World Conference : the necessity of the unity of the Churches. Our Conference, in so far as it concerns itself with the mission of the Church to the world, like the Zion of the second Isaiah (Isa. xl, 9) is called to preach— " O Zion, that bringest good tidings, get thee up into a high mountain "—to "lift up its voice with strength " and to proclaim to the world " Behold your God! "

So long as the Church preaches the Gospel from the

narrow valleys and deep abysses of mutual suspicion and isolation, her message does not penetrate to the world ; it dies away piteously on the hard rocky walls, it fades away in the shadow and cold mist of the valley bottoms. But if the united Churches together mount, as the Zion of to-day, to the topmost heights of the holy mountain, and call aloud from there to the world as ambassadors on behalf of Christ " Repent ye, for the Kingdom of God is at hand " (Matt. iv, 17), " Be ye reconciled to God " (2 Cor. v, 20), then indeed that Gospel which in the age of the Roman Cæsars gave a new direction to men's lives and even to the Mediterranean world as a whole, will do to-day, for a world grown vaster, that for which, in the misery of its pride and bestiality, of its hatred, its guilt and its perplexity, it is hungry and athirst.

THE REV. BISHOP FRANCIS J. McCONNELL, D.D.

Pittsburgh (Methodist Episcopal)

Probably there has not been a period in the history of the Church when we could say more positively that the Gospel in itself is good news than to-day. The Church has always maintained that the revelation in Christ is good news, but there has never been a day when the essentials of the message have been clearer than now. Differ as we may about some features of New Testament criticism, it is to-day manifest that even criticism has established anew at the centre of the Christian movement the personality of Jesus. Every attempt to explain away Jesus has ended in leaving Him more of a power than before. For example, the critic who would strip the life story of Jesus of every detail suggestive of the miraculous is faced at the end with the consideration that the followers of Jesus at least believed that He wrought miracles. How could they believe this ? The critic answers that Jesus was so forceful a character that the belief in miracles is a result of their belief in the sheer abundance of His power. Let this be granted. We have then a personality of such force that legends of miracle grew up easily and naturally. The sheer massiveness of this force, however, is not the chief problem for the critic, but rather the quality of the power. It is not incredible that stories of a mere wonder-making power should have got abroad concerning one who impressed his time as did Jesus, but when we see the stories elaborating kindly and benevolent purposes in the use of power our amazement increases. The marvel in the narratives of the miraculous in Christ is the use of such power for good will. A distinguished satirist has told us that if we wish to see what Christians would themselves do with extraordinary power, we have only to remind ourselves of what the New Testament tells us of the announcement of doom by Peter upon Ananias and Sapphira, and of the request of James and John that fire be called down upon the Samaritan village.

I refer thus to the stories of the miraculous in the life of Jesus purely for purpose of illustration ; not because I object to the explanations of these narratives by modern critical theory, but because the problem of the grace and power of Jesus remains with us even after the explanations. Again, it may be entirely possible to separate the New Testament narratives into separate strands or layers. It may be that back of Mark there were other documents, that the so-called Second Source was a composite of many sources, that Matthew and Luke each had access to facts and traditions whose origins we cannot now trace, that the needs of different congregations were determining forces in sifting out the important from the non-important in the story of Jesus. Nevertheless the conclusion is always urging itself upon us that the organising force back of this literary movement, the centre which marshalled the traditional material into order, was the conviction as to the enduring power and grace of the Lord Jesus—set forth in a many-sided portrait self-consistent enough to make Paul's word entirely intelligible to all the Churches, " Let this mind be in you which was also in Christ Jesus." We do not know much—speaking in quantitative terms—of the life of

Jesus. We know enough to generate the belief that if it had been possible for God to live on earth in human form, the life of Jesus, as set before us in the New Testament, would have satisfied our every expectation as to what such a divine life should be. More and more even those who do not believe in God admit that if there were a God, and if He could make a revelation of Himself to men, they could not suggest any qualitative improvement in the story of Jesus as given us in the Gospel. Modern criticism has made all this clear—or clearer than it once was. It is a part of the good news of the Gospel.

The fact of a mighty personality, so full of grace and truth that we can believe Him divine, is then an essential of the good news of the Gospel.

Carrying along the thought of a moment ago, let us imagine, if philosophy will be patient for a moment, that God could live on earth as a man. What should we desire most in God living under human conditions ? When we had brought ourselves to ask the question most worth while, what could we ask except as to a revelation of the spirit in which the universe is carried forward ? What does it all mean ? At what does it all aim ? Does the moral spirit count ? Is such spirit the chief fact about the universe ?

I have read many protests against the claims for the divinity of Christ. I have read very few based on the assumption that we do not have in Christ a revelation of spirit and temper which we should like to see established as holding good for God. Can we think of any spirit which we should rather see at the heart of the universe than that of Christ ? Can we think of any purpose which we should more readily believe to be the purpose of God than the righteous love revealed in Christ ?

The central spirit—the moral quality of the life of Christ—is evident, no matter whether we can find in the Gospels a detailed guide for moral conduct or not. We must not allow ourselves to be diverted here. I admit the uselessness of asking what Jesus would do as suggesting specific commands as to what we should do. It is not possible to make the Gospels a set of ethical regulations. All we can do is to catch the spirit of Jesus and strive to live in that spirit. The only answer there can be as to what Jesus would do on earth, is that Jesus would do whatever we ought to do, if He were put in our place.

In a word, the Church is concerned not merely to maintain the Godlikeness of Christ, but also the Christlikeness of God. This may seem to be a fine distinction; but fine as it may be, it is significant just now as marking a shift in emphasis in theological accent from that which we used to hear a quarter-century ago, a shift characteristic of a Christianity thinking in world terms. The former debate spoke in terms of the divinity, or deity, of Christ. The present emphasis is more on the Christlikeness of Deity. The movement at bottom is in line with all the great theology of the centuries. The aim in all important epochs of the history of the Church has been, and is, to interpret God in terms of Christ. The various theological formulas have been so many instruments of such interpretation. All the elaborately contrived doctrines of miracle, of incarnation, of trinity, of atonement, no matter how difficult to understand intellectually, are intelligent enough in their central intent, namely, to show God in Christ. Understand, I do not for a moment maintain that the soundness of the aim necessarily makes the methods intellectually sound. Back in the early ages of the Church there were some—probably only a few—thinkers who taught that Satan had a claim on the souls of men which only the death of the Son of God could satisfy, and that God met the obligation by sending the Son to the Cross. As an intellectual construction this theory arouses only amused pity to-day, but its aim is as self-evident as that of any theory of atonement ever built, namely, to declare that God Himself will do whatever is necessary for the salvation of men. All our formal theological creeds may be likewise inadequate as creeds, but all that are central aim at enforcing the belief that not only in Christ do we see God, but in God we see Christ.

It seems evident that if Christianity is to carry its Gospel to the whole world the stress must be kept on this

Godward reference in Christianity. For the question as to the fundamental powers at work in the universe is the one most insistently being asked to-day. How are we to conceive of the world and of life ? Do our natures supply any clue to the divine nature ? Is there a purpose back of the universe ? There may indeed be a turning from customary terms in the discussion of all such problems, but the problems nevertheless are being discussed. Probably there has not been in half-a-century such earnest questioning as to basic realities as to-day. When any such discussion as this begins in earnest and becomes widespread, much crudity forthwith appears, but it is the widespread character of the discussion to which I call attention. We do not have to arouse interest in religion. Taken the world over, the race is and always has been religious. To a greater extent even in non-Christian than in Christian lands does religion touch the daily life, as in the conceptions of ancestor worship in China, of the sacredness of animal life in India, as in dependence on medicine-men and in fear of witchcraft in Africa. It is this widespread interest about underlying world realities that Christianity must meet, especially since men are asking to-day with new insistence as to the validity and worth of any and all religion.

A query confronts us here. One asks us why we may not take the life of Jesus for what it is, the noblest realisation of the human ideal, and follow that. Why trouble ourselves as to the cosmic realities ? Is not Christ, considered as a human ideal, enough ? The answer is that if we begin really to follow Christ we must follow Him to God. If the revelation in Christ is merely the setting on high of a human ideal, without especial question as to whether such an ideal expresses anything essential for the universe itself, we sadly remind ourselves that we have in Christ just one more pathetic figure living a noble life, but in a universe unfriendly or indifferent. If we can believe that in the grace and truth and righteousness and love of Jesus we are on the path to the life of a God who is himself Christlike, we have an answer which we can at least claim the right to put before all men. If we are to have a Gospel for the world it must be a Gospel for all the world, that is to say, with a message about the total system of things which we call the universe.

The Gospel for the world must be for all men. We may have misgivings as to the use of the word " absolute " as applied to God, but a message for all men must maintain that there is a value in men which we must in the light of Christianity treat as absolute.

All Christian theories must base themselves on regard for the inalienable sacredness of every person. If we could once get social, national and international groups to a basis of mutual appreciative respect many of our Christian problems would solve themselves. It seems hopelessly trite and commonplace to say that in the light of Christianity men should always be approached as men, but events the world over are likely soon to make that trite and commonplace observation take on the force of a new discovery, significant enough fairly to stagger us into a realisation of the enormity of some social processes. Ought men to be asked to run the risk of disease and degradation in inhuman living conditions ? Ought men to be ordered into dug-outs or poisoned with deadly gas or blown to bits for the sake of the capture of sources of raw material ? Ought men of lower development in tropical lands to live under systems of compulsory labour imposed by men of professedly higher development ? Simple Christian questions like these, insistently put, may change or finally overthrow whole economic and social systems.

The Christian must start with a man's worth on his own account. Let me as illustration suggest that some things must not be done to men, no matter what the character of the men themselves. Suppose an offender against society has acted in a peculiarly animal fashion. Would it be tolerated if we were to advise that such an offender should be so punished as to suggest his animalism ? Should we not regard it as an outrage if such a man were so harnessed as to symbolise that he should be treated as a beast of draft or of burden ? In what would the outrage consist ? The man might not be hurt. No blows might be struck. Why,

then, speak of outrage ? Because a human ideal would be
sinned against. A man would be treated in a way in which
no man ever should be treated, no matter what he has done,
for even the punishments of men should conform to the
regards of essential humanity. Respect for humanity in
myself and in others is the first requisite for preaching a
Gospel of a Christlike God. A particular individual may
not be himself especially respectable—and it is admittedly
hard to give respect long to what is not inherently respectable. The question is not, however, wholly one of the
personal desert of the individual. The individual is made in
fashion as a man, and since he is a man he must be treated
as a man. He has an inalienable title to our Christian respect,
no matter who he is, or what he is, or whether he does or
does not care anything about such matters himself. While
we cannot in detail tell how to state the claim of humanity
on all occasions, in general Christianity must seek for a new
society on the basis that these claims are absolute. Fundamentally all men stand alike on the one plane of their
humanity. Even the punishments of wrong-doers, we
repeat, must not lose sight of that humanity.

Now, let us move to another point of view and speak in
phrases which may seem to contradict what we have just
been saying. If there is something which we hold as absolute in the claim of a man because he is a man, there is
something also relative in the same claim, which is for the
cynic excuse for bitter sport, and for the Christian the
ground for the largest charity. While men are all alike
men, it is also true that even the best men and the best
groups may be in process of continual improvement. It has
been said that the loftiest characteristic of man is his
capability for being endlessly improved. We are not dealing
with finished creations when we are dealing with men. We
have not to do with animals on the one hand, nor with
angels on the other, but with beings capable of passing
out of animalism into a state better than that of any angels
which have ever been described to us. All men are men,
with the differences between them slight and insignificant
as compared with the difference between man and anything

below him in the scale of being. Still, the differences between men, and the differences between social groups and
nations and races do count. It is a plain duty to recognise
that these differences between groups come out of the
differing rates of progress of the groups, and some differences may have a deep root pointing to something distinctive in the group. The absoluteness of man as man and
the relativity of men as men are alike real. This recognition of the aspect of relativity is a warrant for conceding
a measure of sacredness to the various types of group life
in which men live, racial, national, social. We have come
to see that no organisation has right of way over the welfare
of the individuals that compose the organisation, but the
group exists for the individuals and not the individuals
for the group. In so far as group distinctions further the
welfare of the individuals the Gospel must recognise their
worth, respect their instrumental sacredness, and work
through them.

In other words the Gospel must reach all phases of life,
all group activities, as well as individual activities. Religion
has long been regarded as the province of the individual
soul in its relation to God. This has been preached so
persistently and so long that the responsibility for making
all the group relations Christian has been thrust to one side.
Suppose that all men everywhere, in what we call the individual relation to God, could be converted to the service
of God. Would that solve all our problems ? It would not.
If the more social obligations, of the kind I now have in
mind, could be accepted by everybody as of sole importance, would all our problems be solved ? Certainly not.
As historic fact, however, the emphasis has been laid so
exclusively on the inner, subjective, individual phases of
religion that all civilisation is now in peril because of the
unchristian contacts between groups. So well have the
teachers of the limitation of religion to the personal wrought,
that one who tries to get any emphasis on the larger duties
between men is often charged with preaching a so-called
social gospel of doubtful standing, emphasising " environ-
mental " rather than spiritual factors.

If we are to have a God at all, we may as well have one of the widest interests. The idea that the Holy Spirit wells up in the individual consciousness, doing the essential work there, and then as by an after-thought tying individuals together, has incredibly slight basis. Society exists only in the persons that compose it ; but, for the sake of the persons themselves, the movement must be from a circumference toward the centre, as well as from within outward. The most is made of the individual when we think of him as essential in a system. Men arrive at their best as individuals through the social contacts. So that the time has come to preach the conversion of the wider relationships between men, or, if that sounds impersonal, the conversion of individuals in their group relationships of the wider order, all for the welfare of the individuals themselves.

It may be well for the ardent Protestant in particular to ask himself if the task of Christianity is now conceived in as wide terms as before the Reformation. Protestantism has not yet supplied effective substitutes for some agencies it cast aside. In those Middle Ages which we now see were not Dark Ages by any means, the Church brought all human group relations under its sway. The Church intervened between warring nations and quarrelling nobles, between feudal lords and serfs, between employers and employed, between wrangling individuals. That the Church was herself at times part and parcel of an oppressive rule, that she fell far, far short of her opportunities no one doubts ; but nevertheless the ideal of the Church was evident. It was to touch all phases of life with a redeeming impulse. Protestantism was a justified revolt against an ecclesiaticism which tried to redeem men by fiat, by arbitrary official authority, by force. When Protestantism, however, laid stress exclusively on justification by faith, it opened the door to an extreme individualism which slighted the group contacts. While the Protestant leaders have tried to correct this tendency in the name of infallibilities of one sort or another, quite as rigorous as the infallibility of the Church, the tendency still persists to the abandonment of vast spaces of group life to secularism, not to say paganism.

The field of international contacts, for example, has become secularised to such an extent that only by the accident of a Christian's now and again seeking on his own account as a statesman to guide a nation toward justice, have there been any notable attempts to make international dealings Christian. Only recently has there been any strenuous effort to create an international public opinion definitely and avowedly based on Christian principles.

Once more, the path to the knowledge of God must be one open to all men if the Gospel is to meet the needs of the world. That means that the path must be one not exclusively intellectual, if all men are to find it possible to walk in it. We rightly honour the scientific method of to-day as a path to God. In spite of all we say about the conflict of science and religion, there is a reconciliation in tasks undertaken by science and religion together for a Christly purpose. Still, we could not hold up science itself as the chief path to the knowledge of God, if we are to think in world-wide terms.

Mysticism, then, must be the path, says one who is impressed by the mystic seers who have appeared in all religions and by the large demand for a return to mysticism to-day. The mystic vision seems to such a one to be the common element in religious experience. What, however, does Christian mysticism imply? It implies the vision of practised insight, the insight coming out of the persistent doing of the will of God. This insight is at least to a degree possible to any who will do the will of God. One's will is enough under one's control to make it possible for one to set one's face toward righteousness, turning away from sin to seek the new life that goes with new light. The visions of the Old Testament prophets lent reinforcement to definite moral purposes and ideals. One of the noticeable features of Old Testament history is the stress laid upon the necessity of moral preparation for, and moral content in, any experience that claimed to bring a message from the Lord of Israel. Isaiah's vision of the glory of the Lord which like smoke filled the Temple, Amos' basket of summer fruit, even the stupendous dramas which rose before the gaze of Ezekiel, all had a moral meaning. They issued in messages of a righteousness to be worked into conduct in market-places and temple courts and council chambers.

Let now some student of non-Christian religion discourse to us of visions and trances of non-Christian saints, and we forthwith grant the validity of the experiences as testifying to deep and genuine religious instinct. We do not doubt or disparage. When, however, the student proceeds to inform us that such mysticism belongs in the same grade of religious importance and significance as the Christian mystic, we demur. I once heard an expert in Oriental religion dilating on the worth of some utterances of mystic ecstasy which were calculated to convey a fresh sense of the awful majesty of the physical universe, of the immensity of the void. If a sense of the awfulness of spacial distances were religiously important, a gaze at the stars, or a perusal of a treatise on astronomy, ought to be fully as effective. In this glad day of desire for better understanding among the followers of all varieties of religions, one voices a criticism of a non-Christian belief at one's peril. It is at considerable risk, then, that I ask as to the value of oriental mysticism. I urge the question with all proper hesitancy, because I think I am aware of the danger of judging Hindu mysticism, for example, by superficial appearances. Still, what does the mysticism amount to, in terms of the enlargement and betterment of human life? To stare at the sun, or at one's own navel, till all rational thought sinks toward unconsciousness—what does it amount to? What ideas, or ideals, come out of all this? To raise the question at all is to the Hindu, of course, a complete missing of the point. He replies to us that the absence of ideas and ideals, and of all specifically intellectual content, is itself the justification of the experience. Mysticism, in its very sinking toward the void, gives a hint of the process by which the soul which has let go of earth falls into the bosom of the infinite being characterised as plenitude, but practically treated as emptiness.

Again, what of it? He would, indeed, be hasty who would

deny that Western life would gain something from the reposefulness of the Hindu, for much Western life is forced and distorted. Any relaxation would to some souls be relief, but I doubt if Hindu or other non-Christian mysticism can be rated anywhere near Christian mysticism as tending to the welfare of human life. Let us not forget that Christianity judges everything by the outcome for larger and better humanity—that humanity being of distinctive worth on its own account and not for absorption into anything else—and finds its central strength in moral purpose.

Christian mysticism at its best appears to be that keen awareness of divine realities which comes out of persistent doing of the divine will. It is the awareness of the practised soul. Just as training of any faculty brings at last to that faculty a directness of perception and of execution which seems altogether mysterious to an uninstructed onlooker, so constant exercise of the whole life in righteousness brings an awareness of spiritual values, keener than eyesight, swifter than formal reasoning, and more instantaneous than deliberate resolution. Obedience leads to spiritual adjustment, and out of the adjustment arise those moral insights which are the best of Christianity—and obedience is possible to all men.

We are not quite through with mysticism, however. The mystics have, perhaps, too often and too readily assumed that what they call the direct gaze upon God, or direct communion with God, is the essential. If mysticism is communion in friendship, we may well ask whether communion is at its noblest in such direct gaze. Does not friendship, as we know it, come to its finest as each party to the friendship loses himself in a cause to which both are devoted? Which is better, to look directly at God, or at the objects to which God is devoted? If we could but learn the object of the divine thought, the sure road to friendship would necessarily be the contemplation of that object. Now, the Christ-revelation leaves us in no doubt as to the object of divine contemplation and effort, namely, a race of men, an organised humanity, redeemed into likeness to

Christ. If by some ineffable transport of emotion we could
be swept up into a vision of all things in God, the surest
testimony that we had actually been with God would be
that we had not only seen God more clearly, but had seen
the object of His thought and love more clearly. In the
friendships which mean most, each party to the friendship
finds the other most completely in losing himself in the
purposes to which that other is giving himself. So that
there is a world of significance for friendship with the
Divine in the organic bond which links together in Jesus'
word the second commandment with the first as "like
unto the first." In service for men we attain to the vision
of God. We see God by looking in the direction in which
God fixes His gaze. We meet Him at the far end of His
sweep of vision. The door of service is open to all men.

It remains to say a word about the dynamic of Christianity available for all men. The most depressing question
which is likely to arise in the thought of the ordinary man
the world over is : What is the use ? What better source
of power for such moods do we need than the conviction
that when all is said, God is like unto Christ ? What better
Gospel—good news—can there be than the Christlikeness
of God ?

Believing such a Gospel, the moral struggle is seen to be
worth while. We are helped, not by some strength that
seizes us and carries us along by compulsion, but by the
assurance itself that we are on the right track and that
we shall finally arrive. The reinforcement of the soul
comes through spiritual channels, through the admission
that the goal is, indeed, now far out of reach, but that our
paths lead toward it, that others are travelling thither,
that all is in the hands of a God like unto Christ, who takes
intentions for deeds, who helps not by miraculous wonders
but by opening up the best in human life through spiritual
contacts. The struggle is stern enough at the best, but the
sternness itself is joy, once the worthwhileness of the moral
attempt becomes clear. If God is like Christ, the attempt
is surely worth while.

PROFESSOR DR. NICHOLAS GLUBOKOWSKY

Sophia, Bulgaria (Orthodox)

Dear Brothers in Christ,—We are assembled here in the name of Jesus Christ and of the Gospel. That means that our " Message to the World " goes forth in the name of Jesus Christ and derives its whole strength from Him.

I

But our message will not create a deep impression and will not achieve a real success unless it is shown that this foundation of our belief is absolutely unassailable, and that a House of God, providing salvation for all mankind, can be built upon it.

This leads us to ask, is this foundation truly secure from this point of view? I am not thinking just now of atheists or rationalists—though these persons are often encouraged by our own tendency to free-thinking in regard to the Scriptures. What most concerns us is to be sure that we ourselves are united on this essential point, and that we regard it as a centre of peace and of unity, and as binding upon us all. St. Augustine wrote in the year A.D. 405 to St. Jerome, " The writings of the Apostles like all the sacred books are the fruit of divine inspiration. They are the words of God." And St. John Chrysostom says, in his Explanation of the Epistle to the Galatians, § 7, " Paul— and whenever I say Paul I understand Christ who was inspiring his thought—esteems the Holy Scripture above the angels who came down from heaven ; and very rightly so. For though the angels are mighty they are nevertheless the slaves and servants of God (cf. Heb. i, 14) and the whole Scriptures are given to us not as things written by servants, but by the Almighty Lord of All."

It was for this reason that the Lambeth Conference in 1920 proposed that the Scriptures should be taken as the primary basis of union, because " in the Holy Scriptures God reveals Himself to men, and they provide a complete rule and guide for our faith."

This principle was also unreservedly accepted in the

discussions between the Anglican Church and the Free Churches. It might have been supposed that all was now satisfactorily settled and that general unity was henceforth assured. But unfortunately the results have so far been very disappointing. The *Church Times* says in its issue No. 3339, p. 60, " It is now evident that the Nonconformists at any rate in England and Wales are, without exception, unwilling to enter upon any negotiations in the matter of Christian unity on the basis of the resolutions adopted at the Lambeth Conference."

And when we study the document itself[1] it is plain, beyond all doubt, that the Anglican Church is the only one which abides completely by that standard.[2] The other separated Churches, on the other hand, have refused to do so, with the same unanimity as if they had constituted a single body. They declare categorically, " We are Free Churches—claiming liberty in all spiritual affairs that we may be free to listen to and obey Him whom we all acknowledge as our only Head. And we are Evangelical Free Churches. We use the word in no party sense. But there is, we believe, a definite New Testament Gospel, and this— which carries with it the conception of the Church—we cannot and dare not compromise for the sake even of union itself. This, indeed, is our supreme and, in a sense, sole principle, for it contains the others : the Church is the outcome of the Gospel—hence the importance which has always been attached by Evangelical Churches to ' the preaching of the Word '—and the Church thus made by the Gospel must be free." . . . " In the Gospel, Christ is proclaimed as the Power and the Wisdom of God unto salvation. This salvation is essentially a personal relation of the soul to God—a relation which is immediate, and is constituted by grace on God's part and by faith on man's." . . .

---

[1] See *The Church of England and the Free Churches*. Proceedings of Joint Conference held at Lambeth Palace, 1921-25, edited by G. K. A. Bell, Dean of Canterbury, and W. L. Robertson, Secretary of the Federal Council of the Evangelical Churches of England, Oxford University Press, 1925.

[2] Thus, for example, the Church of Australia declared, at its General Synod in October, 1926, that it was in complete agreement with the Resolutions of the Lambeth Conference regarding the matter in question.

" The essentials of the Church are, therefore, in the Gospel, not in organisation." . . . "But we cannot allow any Church order or rite, or even the idea of the Church taken by itself, to displace the Gospel as the regulative and— under the Divine Spirit—the creative principle of all ecclesiastical doctrine and practice." . . . " We lay continual emphasis on the immediate and personal agency and sufficiency of Jesus Christ " (pp. 15-17). " The supreme standard of truth is the revelation of God contained in the Scriptures of the Old and New Testaments as summed up in Jesus Christ " (p. 38). But it is " the duty of the Church to keep its mind free and ready to receive from Him (the Living Spirit) in each day and generation ever-renewed guidance in the apprehension and expression of the truth " (p. 39). And for that reason they claim " a reasonable liberty of interpretation " (p. 38). And again, this " reasonable liberty " is referred to as being " the fullest freedom in the intellectual investigation of Truth and the most single-hearted discipleship to the Mind of Christ " (p. 41).

We have given these quotations not in any critical or polemical spirit, as that would involve a much more extended examination of the material. We are only seeking now to ascertain the facts. We merely ask you to consider the question as it has been stated, and to say in reply whether the unassailable and imperative authority of the Holy Scriptures can be regarded as assured ? I do not think anyone could confidently answer in the affirmative, having regard to the present relations between the Churches. At the outset they are all agreed in acknowledging the absolute and unconditional authority of the Word of God ; but a little later they demand freedom in its interpretation just as in any other " intellectual research." The governing factor is, consequently, human liberty. This liberty may, however, give " occasion to the flesh " (Gal. v, 13). And who is in a position or is entitled to set bounds to this liberty in the domain of Christianity ? Is it the Church ? But the Church is regarded as a secondary institution, relegated to a lower plane, in fact a superfluous institution, if every individual has the experience of direct access to God, and a personal and self-sufficing sense of the influence of Jesus Christ, and is endowed with "liberty in all spiritual matters." Does not such a liberty border on a licence which threatens the Holy Scriptures themselves and destroys the very foundation of our faith ?

On that path, in spite of our will and because of our weakness, we are exposing ourselves to dangers and catastrophes almost to the point of self-destruction! And the whole cause of our misfortunes is that we have accepted a single authority, the Holy Scriptures. But is not the integrity of the Holy Scriptures independent of any guarantee on our part ? For if it were otherwise, that integrity would be of a conditional character, and might even be transformed into its opposite if certain legalistic theories were pushed far enough. Absolute authority presupposes absolute submission to something which possesses antecedently an absolute and unchallengeable supremacy in no way depending upon ourselves. The Church, which stands forth as the judge in questions of knowledge and understanding of the Scriptures and of tradition,[1] has herself proclaimed this power of the Holy Scriptures. The Church is here seen as the " pillar and the ground of the Truth " (1 Tim. iii, 15), and she alone constrains us to do honour to the Word of God in spirit and in life.

This does not involve the suppression or absorption of personal by general authority, or the annihilation of free and rational activity. Within the Church, such a conflict is impossible : no sharp division between the individual and the universal exists ; on the contrary, within the Church we find an indivisible unity. It is true that redemption through grace is individual : but baptism brings

---

[1] As long ago as 1900 I had the honour to expound, publicly and officially, this basic dogma of the whole Christian faith, that the Church with Christ her Head, who is inseparable from her, and with the Holy Spirit as her constant guide, is herself the source of her own doctrine of faith. The Scriptures and tradition are seen to be an authoritative and binding expression of the doctrine which is fashioned from them both (i.e., from the Scriptures and from Tradition) for the benefit of the individual members of the Church. See the *Proceedings of the Russian Faculty of Theology*, 1900-1, page 371.

with it a mystical identification with Christ, who causes a man actually to become a son of God, and a brother of all God's justified children. Individual redemption without spiritual brotherhood is unthinkable : the latter, so far from superseding the former, gives it organic expression : it results in no suppression of reason or of freedom. Moreover, such a thing would be inconceivable in the Church, which is a community of true sons of God, in which we are all interpenetrated by the sense of complete independence, in unity with God, and of fraternal love with Christians of our own circle.

It is manifest that, in such circumstances, there is no restriction of reasonable rights or of research ; for to Christians, as the sons of God, the way lies open. All the specific claims of the rationalists are directed against tradition and are refuted by the evidence of the facts. To the religious consciousness the Church is in no sense an antirational institution, though in her realm she cannot employ mathematical methods such as appear to be advocated by some episcopal authorities.

II

As regards the means by which these principles are to be realised, it is claimed that everything should be done by the " Ministry of the Word." That is the governing practice and doctrine in many Churches and religious bodies who oppose ritualism and sacramentalism—institutions which we have lately heard stigmatised by a bishop as magic and paganism. Now as regards the reading of the Word at divine service, or the preaching of the Gospel in sermons, there is no well-ordered Christian organisation in the world where that practice is not regarded as of paramount importance and is not accorded the fullest prominence. But if it is sought to make use of this recognised attitude towards the Word as a means of despotically suppressing all other manifestations of piety, there is need for humble meditation lest we should bring the gravest dangers on ourselves without any justification in the Bible.

We know that the Apostles resolved to give themselves continually " to prayer and the ministry of the word," because " it is not reason that we should leave the word of God and serve tables." And for that reason they chose seven men for this service and appointed them to make daily ministration to the faithful (Acts vi, 1-4). Here, we are told, is a plain argument against our point of view ; but why ? We do not draw any such inference. This passage in the Acts certainly shows that great importance was attached to the work of providing for the material needs of the poorer and weaker Christians. The episode has in fact no direct bearing on the question we are discussing, and does not illustrate the nature of the " ministry of the word." Nobody would dispute that such a duty could not be made to give way to the daily cares of life. But how does that bear on the interpretation of the word " ministry ? " The answer is not so obvious. The eleemosynary activities of the synagogue were governed by established forms in the Jewish religion, and offered a useful model for the work of the early Christians. The latter did not feel it necessary to make a special solemnity of duties which had been carried on from ancient days and with great efficiency. Moreover, they appointed for this work " seven men of honest report full of the Holy Ghost and wisdom." In the case of Stephen we are specially told that he was a man " full of faith and of the Holy Ghost " (Acts vi, 5). Moreover, the first Church at Jerusalem is described as being composed of zealous disciples of Christ. Hence we may conclude that these seven men were in a special degree the élite of an élite body of men. Finally, we would observe that their appointment to their office was conferred on them by prayer and by laying on hands (Acts vi, 6). That is, by an act of undeniably mystical character similar to the laying on of hands on the priests (cf. 1 Tim. iv, 14).

Was a rite of so solemn and sacramental a character necessary for persons appointed to carry out charitable and administrative work, for which ordinary honesty and experience would seem to be the only requisites ? And if it was not so, must we not conclude that the act was of a different character, that it was a sacred act ? We know from Acts ii, 46 that all the faithful in Jerusalem used to resort daily and by one accord to the Temple, and that they broke bread from house to house, that they did eat meat together and praised God with gladness and singleness of heart. Therefore, there were daily " tables " at which they broke bread. But that was certainly not a usual procedure at meals—though indeed Christ made Himself known to the disciples at Emmaus in the breaking of bread (Luke xxiv, 30, 35). This was something exclusive, extraordinary, mysterious, although regularly occurring. Else why should we be specially told in the earliest Christian records that the faithful ate meat together every day ? And though this ceremony was conducted in an atmosphere of special piety and rapture, it was nevertheless related to the Jewish rites and usages.

We must admit that here we have something in the nature of a mystery, and realise that it is something entirely distinct from the " ministry of the word." This does not mean that the two things are in opposition, unless indeed anyone suggested abandoning the preaching of the Word, or binding the preaching of the Gospel in fetters of ritual and mysticism to the point of transforming sacred and mystical rites into magical exercises ; but that would be an extraordinary and anomalous situation, and it would be solely due to that course of action. But, normally, the two things were in close and organic relation with one another and were never disjoined in the evangelic work. Stephen was, for instance, a zealous disputant, a fervent apologist, and an enthusiastic preacher of the Gospel. The Apostles who had determined to give themselves entirely to prayer and the ministry of the word devoted the whole of their Christian efforts to ensuring that those whom they converted joined the Church through baptism, and held firmly to their mystic life in Christ.

From this standpoint the preaching of the Gospel is seen to be the compelling influence by which men are directed to the mystic life in Christ, which is an organic result of

D

Christian instruction. And here the words of the Apostle
Paul (1 Cor. i, 17) find their application, "Christ sent me not
to baptise but to preach the Gospel." Can anybody regard
these words as implying a condemnation or a neglect of
baptism ? If so, why did he baptise the whole household of
Stephanas (1 Cor. i, 16)? And is such an attitude conceivable
in an Apostle who has extolled the power and effect of holy
baptism with so much loftiness and rapture ? Is it conceivable in an evangelist who described his work as a preacher
of the Gospel of Christ as that of " a minister of Christ and
a steward of the mysteries of God " (1 Cor. iv, 1) ? Do not
the words " minister of Christ " also imply the mystic
acts ? Does this not show that his remark about baptism
is evidence of the caution which he had to observe, to
prevent it from being said that Paul had baptised in his own
name ? Was this caution not fully justified by the fact
that parties had been formed at Corinth (see 1 Cor. iii, 4)
and were probably using as party watchwords the fact that
certain of their members had been baptised by different
Apostles (1 Cor. i, 12)? And St. Paul thanks God that he had
shown this caution, but he does not say that it need necessarily have been so, or that it was a normal condition in the
work of an Apostle of Christ.

We know from St. Luke's Gospel (i, 2) that the first
Apostles were " eye-witnesses and ministers of the word."
This expression is not altogether clear, and from a gram-
matical standpoint it might appear that what is meant is
that they were the ministers of the word in its personal
sense, that is ministers of Him whose intimate companions
they had been and whom their eyes had seen. It would be
tendencious to object to this interpretation on the ground
that the Johannine " Logos " had a non-Christian origin.
I myself am rather inclined to consider the word αὐτόπται
as a particular technical term for the " eye-witnesses of
Christ." These direct witnesses of the events of the New
Testament proclaimed them to the world through the
" ministry of the word " (or through the Word). In this
connection they adhered closely to the instructions of
Christ, in which preaching and baptism are inseparable

(Matt. xxviii, 19, Mark xvi, 19, 16). This baptism guarantees the redemption of the members of the Church of Christ in brotherly community.

The preaching of the Gospel was not, therefore, an end in itself. It did not consist in " enticing words of man's wisdom," but it was " in demonstration of the Spirit and of power " (1 Cor. ii, 4), for it accomplished the regeneration of men and endowed them with the power of Christ. Thus it may happen that the " ministry of the word " may take the form of silence, as is indicated in many of the liturgical documents of the Orthodox Church. If we go by the Holy Scriptures we shall see that John Mark, whom Paul and Barnabas had taken as their " minister," was not an ordinary servant but an assistant in the work of proclaiming the Gospel. We note, further, that in the Christian narratives there is no record of Mark having received a call for preaching. The Gospel of Mark, in which he has given us the teaching of his " father " St. Peter, is the shortest and the least enriched with discourses of considerable length.

All these evidences convince me that the Christian " ministry of the word " cannot be confined to a theoretical exposition of a message, but that it must remain in perpetual and direct contact with the mystery of our life through grace in Jesus Christ. That is supremely important for the attainment of the loftiest expression of our Christian and brotherly communion in divine service. That is a sacrifice of praise and thanks to God for our mystic union in Christ, and, therefore, this communion should be a constant one—not less frequent than the daily breaking of bread among the first Christians. It is not meet that this " reasonable service " which is referred to in Romans xii, 1, should be held for all comers and that it should only include the Eucharist when one of the faithful is present to receive it or when the recipients are bound to be present under ecclesiastical ordinances. In all other cases one can content oneself with devotional exercises—though indeed these may be held elsewhere than in a church edifice, as I can testify from my own experience in 1910 in the blessed and godly household of Dr. Nathan Söderblom, the revered Archbishop of Upsala. Our sacrifice of devotion is presented through Christ in the Holy Spirit—with what benefit for us need hardly be said. But that sacrifice needs to be offered *by us*, and this implies a constant and unconditional surrender, a mystical surrender to God, when we receive by divine grace " the bread of heaven and the cup of life " for our spiritual growth.

It is only thus that the " ministry of the word " can find its fulfilment, and that the faithful can be enabled to participate in the grace and salvation of Christ. And if that end is assured by the Gospel it is clear that the " ministry of the word" cannot be carried on in the Church and by the Church as a mere question of preaching, but must consist in a living communion with the Gospel.

III

And now, what is the Gospel? Primarily and above all, it is not a theory, not a doctrine, not a sermon ; it is a redemptive act, fraught with great joy for all men who are freed from sin and from the curse and death. From this standpoint the Gospel is exclusively a " power of God unto salvation to everyone that believeth ; to the Jew first and also the Greek " (Rom. i, 16). This power places all men in a new and real situation of sonship with God, and enables them to live and grow in perfect peace and in perfect bliss. Just as the State has its political constitution, so the Gospel is the constitution of " the Kingdom " (see Matt. iv, 23, ix, 35 ; xxiv, 14), but being founded by Jesus Christ it is consequently the Gospel of the Kingdom of God (see Mark i, 14, rec. text), instituted by God and designed to bring its members to Him. And therefore we have a Gospel " of Salvation " (Ephes. i, 13) which is for us the " Gospel of Peace " (Ephes. vi, 15). We shall not attain to this goal by our own efforts or our own deserts, but solely " through the tender mercy of our God whereby the dayspring from on high hath visited us, to give light to them that sit in darkness and in the shadow of death and to guide our feet in the way of peace " (Luke i, 78, 79). In this sense the Gospel of

Christ was and must ever continue to be from its very nature a " Gospel of the grace of God " (Acts xx, 24), which has been poured out abundantly over mankind through His First-born ; and this Son of God is "full of grace and truth " (John i, 14). It is by virtue of these qualities that the Gospel opens to every man a straight and sure road to perfection and blessedness. Nevertheless it is necessary for each one of us to give reverent submission and observance to the Gospel if we wish to partake of its benefits. We must "obey" the Gospel (see Rom. x, 16 ; 2 Thess. i, 8), believe in it, with repentant acknowledgment of our sinfulness and our weakness (Mark i, 15) ; we must be ready to " strive for the faith of the Gospel " (Phil. i, 27), to " testify the Gospel of the grace of God " (Acts xx, 24), through self-immolation, through holy living, in order that we may become like the Apostle Paul " a partaker of the afflictions of the Gospel " (2 Tim. i, 8 and 1 Cor. ix, 23).

All these things are historically justified and confirmed by the words of Jesus Christ who was " the brightness of God's glory " (Heb. i, 3), and a reflection of that brightness is " the light of the Gospel of the glory of Christ " (2 Cor. iv, 4). For that reason the Gospel is "a glorious Gospel of the blessed God " (1 Tim. i, 11) and contains the " hope of the Gospel " (Col. i, 5), for it gives us the hope of that eternal Kingdom which is prepared for us. And for that reason it is manifestly an " eternal Gospel " for it is as eternal as Christ, the Lord of the Gospel.

It is in accordance with what has just been said that St. Ignatius wrote to the Church of Philadelphia (ix, 2) in the following terms : " The Gospel has something which is specially its own, namely the advent of the Redeemer, our Saviour Jesus Christ, his passion and his resurrection." That implies the whole of His redemptive work for humanity and for the regeneration of the world, but " great is the mystery of godliness " (1 Tim. iii, 16) " which has been hid from ages and generations " (Col. i, 26). And thus the Gospel is a complete mystery, which admits of no comparison with any other ; and the ministry of Jesus Christ cannot be limited to a preaching of the word, but is also a " priestly ministry of the Gospel of God " (Rom. xv, 16).

And now, bringing these observations to an end, we reach this conclusion : that the Gospel of Christ being essentially a mystery (*mysterium*), is always and wholly mystical, both in its appearance and in all its action. Therefore the preaching and the reception of the Gospel must always be accomplished by mystic (sacramental) processes, by constant, uninterrupted and complete submission to the " mystery of Christ " (Ephes. iii, 4) ; but this mystery only operates continuously within the Church of Christ.

Consequently the appeal to men on behalf of the Gospel must be made through the " ministry of the word " on the basis of the Church's authority, by participation in the mysteries of Christ, in order that we, living united in our Saviour, may " all come in the unity of the faith and of the knowledge of the Son of God unto a perfect man, unto the measure of the stature of the fulness of Christ " (Ephes. iv, 13, 15) and that we " may grow up into Him in all things which is the head, even Christ."

PROFESSOR WILLIAM ADAMS BROWN, D.D.

Union Theological Seminary, New York (Presbyterian)

Dr. Deissmann, in his opening address, has brought before us in a manner at once moving and restrained, four major points on which we may take agreement for granted. And Bishop McConnell has emphasised them in the address that followed. We are agreed that the Church has a message for the world. We are agreed that this message, in spite of all varieties of apprehension and presentation, is in its great essentials one. We are agreed that this message is a Gospel, good news for the individual and for society. We are agreed—though this point is often less vividly realised than the other three—that this good news concerns the future as well as the present and the past ; that our word to the world of our day must still be the Church's message

to the world of the first century. Lift up your hearts and
be of good cheer, for your salvation draweth nigh. The
Lord is at hand.

I desire to comment briefly on each of these four points
in their bearing upon the purpose which has brought us
together.

First of all, then, we are agreed that our Lord has entrusted His Church with a message for the world. We are
so familiar with this fact that we often fail to appreciate
it in its revolutionary significance. We have a message.
That means that our world has a meaning. It is not a
brute fact that we must take for granted without hope
of understanding whence it comes or whither it is tending.
It is a spiritual creation, the home of reason and value,
the scene in which our Father is working out His wise and
loving purpose for His children.

This message is a world-wide message. It is meant for
man as man. What it involves in all its details we may not
always clearly see. How it is to be appropriated and to
what extent it has already been received may still divide
us. But that God's message to us is not ours alone, but
is to be held in trust for all our brother-men, we are agreed.
Our message is a missionary message; to be preached
wherever there are ears to hear, hearts to feel, and wills to
respond.

This message is a divine message. It is not of man's
devising, or man's creation. It has been given to us by God.
Here again we may differ in our view of the method of
its impartation—some laying greater and some laying
less stress upon the human factor in the process; but that
God is its ultimate source we are all agreed; and that it
owes its authority and its convincing power to Him alone.

And this message He has committed to His Church.
This fact it is which brings us here. We are not a group of
individuals who have chosen to come together to discuss
some common plan of our own devising. We are members
of a society founded before we were born and to live on after
we have finished our earthly life—a society established by
our Lord and Saviour Jesus Christ for the very purpose

of proclaiming this message of good news to needy and sinful men, and to carry on the work to which He consecrated Himself. Here again we may differ in our understanding of the nature of the divine society. As to the fact, we all agree.

In the few moments that remain I wish to make certain suggestions as to ways in which we may make progress towards realising our divine mission. And I will attach what I have still to say to the other three points of Dr. Deissmann's opening address.

This world-wide message, he reminded us, in spite of all differences of outward expression and emphasis, is in its great essentials one. The conclusion I draw from this is that we shall make progress toward dealing intelligently and effectively with our differences by starting in every case from our admitted agreements.

I would not minimise, I repeat, the seriousness of our differences. They meet us in all three aspects of our Church life, doctrine, worship and organisation. It makes a difference, and a great difference, how we think of Jesus Christ ; whether we approach Him primarily from the side of His human nature, as a man who has been deemed worthy to be the vehicle of God's self revelation because of His ethical obedience, or whether we approach Him from the divine side as God entering humanity by a supreme act of divine self-abnegation that He may share with His suffering children His divine and immortal life. But important as this difference is, it is relatively less important than the fact on which we agree that in Jesus Christ God and man have met, that in Jesus Christ we have not only the disclosure of God's ideal for man, but the revelation of His own character and purpose. What would it mean for the individual ; what would it mean for society at large if this insight could be everywhere shared ?

Again it makes a difference how we think of the sacrament; whether we regard it as presenting us, in miraculous and extraordinary manner, with the very glorified body of our risen Lord Himself ; or whether we conceive it in less literal and more symbolic fashion as a spiritual feeding

upon the risen Christ ; a feeding in which the faith of the
recipient is the determining factor ; a feast of gratitude
and love in which the memory of Christ's past sacrifice
furnishes the inspiration to present consecration. But
significant and far-reaching as these differences are, they
are of minor importance compared to the one fact that
matters most, that in the sacrament, given to us of God
Himself for our spiritual food and growth in grace, we have
a means through which the work of Christ perpetuates
itself, and the consciousness of our common relation to Him
finds public and corporate expression.

It makes a difference finally what we think of the ministry ;
whether we regard it as a special order set apart by Christ
Himself to carry on His work and as such endowed with
spiritual grace which fits it to carry on that work effectively
—an order that finds its bonds of unity in the Bishop and in
the laying on of hands, the channel of the transmission
of its continuing spiritual life ; or whether we think of it
as but a part of a wider spiritual ministry, a ministry
embracing men and women of every calling and profession,
differing from this wider ministry only in this, that its members are concerned with a special form of activity, the
activity we call corporate worship. But however essential
it is that we should come to a clear understanding on these
points, our differences here are relatively unimportant compared with the fact on which we all agree, that there is a
body of men committed to the preaching of the Gospel of
Christ, and consecrated to His ministry—a body of men who
regard it as at once their supreme duty and their highest
privilege to hand down the Gospel as God has given them
to understand it, and to translate its principles into appropriate conduct.

If we are agreed so far, then I submit that agreement lays
on us a duty—the duty of making the fact known. Pending the solution of the larger and longer question which has
brought us together, the question of organic unity in its full
and complete sense, I believe that it is our duty, and that it
will prove to be entirely practicable, to devise some form of
intermediate organisation which while maintaining our

present ecclesiastical bodies for the time being unaltered, will express to the world the unity to which we have already attained. I hope before the Conference is over that it may be possible for us to consider the form that such an *ad interim* organisation might take—a consideration which could be followed up at the appropriate time and place. But my interest here is not with questions of organisation, but with the spiritual realities they symbolise and express. I wish, with all the power I can command, to voice what I am sure is our common desire, that God may burn into the heart and conscience of every one of us the intolerable scandal of the present situation, the spectacle of a Church professing a unity which it is impotent to express, and that He will give us grace each one to reconsecrate ourselves to doing whatever in us lies to bringing our existing unity to effective expression, as we have already found ways (and I believe rightly) of bringing our existing differences to effective expression.

This brings me to my next point, a point suggested by Dr. Deissmann's reference to the Gospel. This message of ours, in spite of its searching ethical challenge, is a message of good news. It is not addressed primarily to the mind, reasonable and intellectually consistent as it proves to be, but to the affections and the will. It is a message of judgment, as Dr. Deissmann has reminded us, but it is even more a message of salvation. Man of Sorrows though He was, Jesus was a bringer of good news, promising to those who accept the Gospel a peace that passeth understanding and a joy that the world can neither give nor take away.

There is a practical consequence which follows from this fact. As in our study of our intellectual differences we do well to begin with our points of agreement, so in our study of our emotional differences we shall do well to begin with our spiritual sympathies. Deeper than our intellectual differences, and more disastrous in their effect, are our suspicions and our fears. We do not really believe that those who differ from us can have experienced the grace of God as we know it ourselves ; and the only way to tell whether this is so or not is by an exchange of experiences. There is no remedy for a prejudice so efficacious as a common appreciation. Let each tell the other not only what the Gospel *means* to him, but what it has *done* for him. Let us approach each subject which now divides us—our view of the creed, of the sacrament, of the ministry, of the person of our Lord Jesus Christ Himself—with the question " What has my conviction done for me, and through me for others ? " " What change has it made, what change is it making in my life as an individual, and in the society in which I live ? " and we shall find a platform of agreement broader and firmer than many of us have regarded as possible.

One point more, and I have done. This Gospel which it is our privilege to preach to the world is a Gospel that faces toward the future. It is not only a Gospel of faith and of love but also of hope.

This is the most important point of all. We think of the Gospel as witnessing to a fact that is past, the sacrifice of our Lord on the Cross for the salvation of mankind ; and thank God it is such a witness! We think of it as good news for the present, the perennial source of power for all who put their trust in Christ ; and thank God it is such a source! But it is this and more. It is the Gospel of hope for the future ; the promise of better things in store for the individual and for society than anything we have as yet experienced—things that eye hath not seen nor ear heard, neither have entered into the heart of man, whatsoever things God hath prepared for those who love Him.

If this is true, then it ought to affect our attitude in this Conference. However much we may value the past, for us it can never be final. God has not yet spoken His last word or His best. Jesus Christ has not yet exhausted His power to redeem and to transform. There are still vast reaches of truth to be penetrated, new meanings in the old Gospel still to be disclosed. There are still great stretches of territory waiting to be subdued to Christ's obedience, millions of hungry hearts longing for the satisfaction He can bring. It is for His Church to win these conquests, to

appropriate this truth, and to render this ministry. But
we shall succeed in our mission only as we turn our eyes
from the past and even from the present to the greater
and better future that awaits us. Still the Master's promise
holds true for those who have faith to receive it. " The
works that I do shall ye do also, and greater works than
these shall ye do because I go to my Father."
May this promise be richly fulfilled in us.

Following this address THE CHAIRMAN summoned the Conference
to silent prayer. BISHOP OSTENFELD then continued the discussion,
speaking in English:

THE RIGHT REV. HARALD OSTENFELD, D.D.
Bishop of Seeland, Denmark (Lutheran)

When, as a young man, I stayed in England and attended
the May Meetings, which had an inter-denominational
character, one particular hymn was often sung. How it
began I do not remember, but two lines were especially
emphasised when sung :

> " One in hope and doctrine,
> One in charity."

It was the feeling of the Christian unity which here found
its expression, but a very unfortunate expression, I am
afraid, because it was just in the doctrine that we didn't
agree.

St. Paul speaks far more truly and more deeply when he
utters the following about his preaching : " By manifestation of the truth we commend ourselves to every man's
conscience " (2 Cor. iv, 2). In order to prevent the misunderstanding that it was his own religious experience and
feelings that he preached, he adds a little below : " For we
preach not ourselves but Christ Jesus, the Lord."

In these words he says two things about his message :
(1) that its essential element, the substance of it, is not a
teaching, not moral doctrines, not emotional sentiments,
but a person, Jesus Christ, and (2) that the purpose of his

preaching is to reach the conscience of man, not his logical sense, not his imagination, not his moods and not his will, but his conscience, i.e. the organ through which he is able to receive a message from God.

In this definition of his preaching there is also contained a definition of that soul-function in man to which the preaching appeals, but it is exclusively a positive fundamental definition which may be used at all times and under all circumstances.

This is confirmed by an experience which can be made nowadays too. When we hear a sermon which affects us so much that it will mean something in our own lives, then it is not the one which has a special doctrinal touch, either of the Anglican Church, of Methodism, Catholicism, the Lutheran Church or Presbyterianism ; nor is it the one which attacks the differences which arise from doctrinal peculiarities, but the one which takes its substance from a deeper-lying level in the soul than that to which these peculiarities belong. It is Christ Himself who meets us in a message like this, not a special doctrine about Him.

Perhaps there are not many people who have the opportunity of listening to speakers from the different denominations—to make this experience—but in spite of that they may meet it in their lives.

They meet it when they read the New Testament for their edification, and here they see the message of Christ and the message of the Apostles ; or when they read one of the classical books of edification : Thomas à Kempis' *The Imitation of Christ*, Bunyan's *Pilgrim's Progress*, Scriven's *The Treasure of the Soul*. We cannot confine these to any special denomination : they are the common property of Christ's whole Church. They do not give theories about the message and its contents, they give the message itself.

Still another example. We sing our hymns and express here what is living in the depths of our souls of praise, joy, worship, good-cheer, frankness and spiritual confidence. The differences in the theological doctrines of the hymn-writers do not come to the front, but on the other hand they are not covered. Possibly they have a theology and a theory which differ widely, but when they express their inmost experiences this does not appear.

But does this fact arise from the circumstance that these men are completely uniform and have the same theological way of thinking—these men who bring forward the strong message, these authors of books which never grow old, these hymn-writers whose hymns live in the hearts and on the lips of Christian people all over the world ? They did really belong to different denominations and in their theological systems they differed very much, but when their theology has been forgotten and their theoretical ideas have been destroyed, their message as it has been produced in their preaching and especially in their hymns still lives.

But whence does this uniformity in preaching come, when the difference on other points is so great ?

In the first place the message is not the message either of the Church or of its prominent members, but it is God's own message to sinful mankind, and after that it is the message of the Church and of the single followers of Christ who are to be the bearers of the message—which is not their own.

But how is the message to be delivered in the right way ? It may be said in many ways. Let me say it in my own way.

To be a Christian is to have a personal relationship with Christ, quite a simple, direct relationship. Through which function of the soul is a relationship like this attained ? Let us think of quite a human personal relationship which is nearer to us. We will think of the relation of a son to his father. It does not depend on the imagination, the intellect, the feeling or the will—it depends on a personal intimate trust. If a son has gone away from his father, the relations between them cannot be restored either through any intellectual reasoning or through any achievement on the part of the son by which he may develop his faculties in different directions. The only way homewards for him into the love of his father is to surrender himself to his father. This function of the soul which is to be used lies deeper than the point from which the different faculties of the soul separate and differentiate themselves. You might call it the personal ingenuousness.

Being a Christian is thus to be in a direct intimate personal connection with the living God. That is what Jesus expresses, saying, "This is life eternal, that they might know thee the only true God, and Jesus Christ whom thou hast sent" (John xvii, 3). "To know" is just to be in a direct intimate personal connection with.

With this is connected the understanding through contemplation, the apprehension of the feeling and the working of the will, but only as accessories which are of secondary importance ; the ingenuous surrendering is the kernel, and can never be replaced by any of those. This kernel is surrounded and enclosed in a different way by different people and persons, but the uniting thing is the direct ingenuous relationship.

So the preaching springs from our being apprehended in the depths of our soul by God, and the goal of the preaching is to lead man into the direct relationship with God, where he meets the living God face to face. The consequence of this is that preaching reaches its highest level, approaching nearest to its ideal, when it has Christ Himself as its substance, and is not satified either with our thoughts about Christ or with the doctrines concerning Christ or with the effects which come from Christ. Preaching Christ must be a representation of personal faith as fully as possible. Then the preaching will be a message. But it must be the whole Christ we preach, the Christ who gained the victory over the difficulties of life, the Christ who died and rose from the dead, the Christ who now lives and works in His Church, calls, unites and energises the whole of Christianity on earth, and is coming again to judge us. When I think of the preaching which grips me most, I cannot consider it sufficient to define it as the one that mostly refrains from disputed points in the doctrine, for that is a purely negative definition and gives as the result a thin, diluted preaching and message. There must be a positive definition, namely, the highest form of preaching is the one which most ingenuously and most directly renders what the teacher owns in his personal relationship with God.

That is the message which the Church is going to bring to the world, that world which we call the "heathen countries" and that world which surrounds us in the so-called "Christian countries." This message, which has Christ Himself as its living substance, has also as its dynamic force Him who has promised that He will be with His Church at all times until the world's end.

This may only be carried forward with full effect by a united Church which feels itself one in Christ. But it seems to me also to show the way towards unity, because this way cannot follow the course of compromise, whereby through agreement you try to reach a unity-formula. Neither will it be reached with a mechanical unity as goal, where all differences are obliterated. It must aim at an organic living unity, where the common spiritual property which embraces us has the whole emphasis, and upon which emphasis must always primarily be laid, whilst the differences come in a secondary place—never, so to say, operating by themselves and still less as greatest and most important, but only appearing in the light of that unity which arises from the common ownership of that which is most important and essential. Then the character of the Christian unity will be established in faith in Christ and not in doctrine about Christ; its goal will be laid down—to be one in Christ; and as a consequence it will distinguish itself from a lifeless, mechanical unity, which does not give room for those variations of life which do not damage but emphasise the true and living unity.

PROFESSOR WILFRED MONOD, D.D.

Protestant Faculty of Theology, Paris (Reformed)

I

Admitting that our dogmatics cannot be stated on a postcard, and that our message cannot be completely proclaimed in a paragraph, is then our Gospel a " good news " addressed to the whole world ?

One of the genuine prophets of to-day, Mahatma Gandhi, while travelling in India came to a station where the crowds, gathered to see him as he passed, demanded a speech. The non-Christian leader opened the New Testament, read the Beatitudes, and added " I have nothing more to say."

Jesus " preached," so our sacred text tells us. God speaks! The word He utters is the Church! A Church which affirms its inability to bless the soul apart from the soul's moral and intellectual co-operation—a Church which makes no claim to operate on humanity from without, as a surgeon might operate by injecting a serum. No, the Church, as it speaks and teaches, aims at effecting a change of heart, which is the only way in which man's destiny can be changed. It does not ask for subscription to a creed, but for the faith which can appropriate a Gospel.

When our Conference, then, declares that the Church has a message, it breathes the spiritual atmosphere of the prophets of Israel, the pioneers of the religion of utterance over against the religion of priesthood. Doubtless, it was not impossible for prophet and priest to work together in harmony, the prophet using the creative word and the priest the symbolic action ; the prophet addressing himself to the ear and the priest to the eye ; the prophet conveying the substance of truth, and the priest reinforcing the idea by an outward sign, and supplying the message thus with a tangible organism through which it could effect an entry into the practical sphere. In theory prophet and priest might co-operate thus as soul with body, as indeed the synagogue and the temple, lay and clerical religion, did work together. But when prophet and priest are forced into conflict, where does the Gospel take refuge ? It identifies itself with the spoken message.

Either the Church has no message, or it is the message which constitutes the Church. For the Christian conscience this is axiomatic. If Christ preached the good news, then evidently the task of Christianity in the world is to spread the good news. This brings us to the question—what is the message ?

II

The good news announced by Jesus took various forms. When He proclaimed the Kingdom of God, His own Kingship was implied, as in the words " Come unto me all ye that labour and are heavy laden, and I will refresh you." " He that followeth me shall not walk in the darkness but shall have the light of life." " No man knoweth the Father but the Son, and he to whomsoever the Son shall reveal him."

Rake out the dead ash of habit, and a shock of surprise awaits you! With a majestic monotony, faithfully reproduced in the fourth Gospel, Christ affirms " I am the way, the truth and the life." " Come unto me—unto *me*." The Gospel preached by Jesus is then a Gospel brought by Him, manifested in Him, incarnate in Him ; His revealing word was an act, a gift, a presence ; " the Word was made flesh."

An enigma is here, a paradox, a gift from heaven to earth ; the Gospel of Jesus was Jesus Himself preaching the Gospel. To that Gospel a new humanity makes its answer—" God hath visited and redeemed his people : Emmanuel, God with us." For two thousand years the Church has existed to point to the Revealer, the Son of God; to say, " We have found Him! " With the earliest witnesses the Church declares " We have found the Messiah : behold the Lamb of God which taketh away the sins of the world. . . . There is none other name by which we may be saved. . . . The eternal life has been manifested, and that which we have seen and heard, and our hands have handled, declare we unto you. . . The Word has tabernacled among us, full of grace and truth ; and we have beheld his glory as of an only begotten from the Father."

Such is the unchanging message of the Church. Its stress is not laid upon a theory of the episcopate or of sacraments, upon eternal predestination to heaven or to hell, not even upon a doctrine of the fall of man in Adam and its expiation

in the Second Adam. No, the constant message of the
Church has its centre in the person, or rather the spiritual
personality, of Jesus Christ.

It is this that the organisers of our Conference desired
to emphasize when they sent their invitation to the
Churches which confess the doctrine of the Trinity, a doctrine which as a matter of history was but a great and more
or less adequate attempt to find a metaphysical expression
for the inexpressible, but, on the side of religion, is the most
moving hymn of praise to the Risen Lord, the profoundest
homage to the Saviour. Moreover, in the New Testament
there are treasured for us various phrases of trinitarian
import freely and naively expressed, words coming spontaneously from the heart of the Church and giving abiding
utterance to the divine mystery of the Redeemer in simple,
poetic moving form : " He who hath seen me hath seen the
Father. . . . The Father is greater than I. . . . I and
the Father are one."

Briefly, the message of the Church may be summed up
in one Name—Jesus Christ.

III

But this luminous affirmation brings with it a question
of grave practical difficulty. No one can deny that Christ
existed in history before Christianity, which means that the
Gospel is in fact anterior to the Church. It follows that to
express the Gospel in its original purity the Church must
needs go back to its own pre-history, or, we might say,
must " go back into its mother's womb." The position
is unique. Using its own language, its dogmas, creeds and
rites, the Church must in every age proclaim the divine
message of the Gospel in a form different from that in which
the Redeemer gave it utterance. This does not mean that
the Church is bound to be unfaithful to the substance of
the message entrusted to it. But it does mean that even
if creed, sacrament and clergy can contribute to-day to the
maintenance, propagation and defence of the message, can
indeed enter into combination with it, still the means of

grace in their totality must not be confused with grace itself, any more than the Church with the Gospel or Christianity with Christ. No, the Catholic Church, august as it is, rich in spirituality, tenderly loved by all souls that are taught of God, the Church visible and invisible, the mystical Body of the Lord, and our Mother, is not itself the grace of God. She is right in affirming the perpetual presence of Christ whenever two or three are gathered together in His name ; but the Church is not to be confounded with her Head. She has a right to say that she is the bearer of the Gospel, but she is not herself the message—she is the messenger through whom it is made audible. She exists only to hand on the word of life ; she is but a providential instrument for the service of God's Kingdom, which the Messiah proclaimed. Yet again, all her message consists in this utterance—" Rejoice thou race of mankind ; *ave humanitas*, to whom God's grace has come. Rejoice that the feet of the Son of Man have trodden the ways of this world. Rejoice, for the Messiah has believed in mankind ; has believed that it is worthy of help and capable of being saved! "

If a man volunteers for the sake of a hospital patient to submit to the transfusion of his blood, it is a proof of his belief in the possibility of a cure. So the Son of God, on the Cross, gave His blood to renew the life of our dying race. He gave His blood, an invisible grace clad in a visible sign, His deepest self, with its resolve to love even unto death. He gave His spotless soul, His Spirit itself, inseparable from the Holy Spirit. He gave His blood, that is, the appeal to repentance and purification, the promise of new birth, the pledge of our immortality.

IV

One more question : why is a message so perfect in beauty so often rejected by the modern world ? Why do so many intellectuals, in the name of science, and so many working men, in the name of the common people, set themselves against the Gospel ? It is not merely a matter of the conflict between sin and holiness. Mankind was sinful in the days of Tiberius : it committed on Calvary a crime as indelible as the spot upon the hand of Lady Macbeth : yet that was the age when the gospel of St. Paul ran like a flame throughout the empire—a flame which lit up, in the black night of pagan darkness, the outlines of the palace of Nero. Why then is this message set aside to-day by the ridicule or the exasperation of the multitudes ?

Brethren, it is because we know the answer to that question that we are met together. It obsesses us ; we cannot evade it. " Whither shall I go from thy presence ? " cried the psalmist to the Almighty. Whither shall we go from the answer to this question ? For it is a voice from on high. When we ask, in our anxiety, why our Gospel is veiled, we are dismayed to receive from God this revelation— the Gospel is veiled by the Churches. The apostolic message was preached throughout the world by the Church of Jesus Christ, one and indivisible ; our message is set forth by rival Churches. *Kyrie eleison!*

Kyrie eleison! That moving invocation, borrowed from the mother-tongue of the New Testament, has found a place in all the liturgies of divided Christendom ; Churches which mistrust and compete with each other, which anathematise and persecute each other, have united in making their own the cry of the prodigal son—*Kyrie eleison!* May it unite us now in tears of humiliation and of brotherhood re-discovered!

Our message to the world is Jesus Christ ; it is, therefore, the one Gospel, and therefore it is also the united Church.

Traditional usage speaks of " the Gospel," though there are four evangelists each of whom gives a different version of the inscription on the Cross, and yet their diverse gospels form one Gospel. Well, Christendom to-day exhibits four main types of Christianity—Greek, Roman, Anglican, Protestant : and these four Churches ought to constitute the Church as the four Evangelists constitute the Gospel.

Here is another aspect of our message to the world. It is insufficient to speak of it, as does our Programme, as " the Gospel." This Conference ought to complete its motto, declaring that it stands for the One Gospel proclaimed by the One Church.

This means, of course, that no historic Church ought to claim a monopoly of absolute truth in the ecclesiastical sphere, none of them can claim as against the rest that it alone has built the flawless tabernacle " according to the pattern shown upon the mount."

You know that the Faith and Order movement owes its origin to the spiritual blessing which flowed from the Edinburgh Missionary Conference of 1910. Our presence at Lausanne, therefore, is a resultant of the obedience of Christians to their Leader's command—" convey the message to the ends of the pagan world." It is a good omen; in spite of appearances, we are not meeting upon a basis of doctrine, sacrament or hierarchy : we are met in the name of the true apostolic ideal, that is, of interests higher than the apostolate. I would recall to you, as I end, the prophetic words of a Chinese Christian uttered on June 21, 1910, at the Edinburgh Missionary Conference : " We look forward to the vision of a united Church ; all one in Jesus Christ. Let us climb the Mount of Olives with our divine Master, and from there we shall gain a far wider, fresher, larger view of the needs of the Church and the needs of the world."

Shall we understand that appeal ? Surely we have a message for mankind : but mankind also has a message for the Christian Church.

THURSDAY AFTERNOON, AUGUST 4TH.

The afternoon session, with Dr. GARVIE in the Chair, was opened at 4 p.m., with devotions led by Dr. Wilhelm PHILIPPS.

Messages of greeting to the Conference were read from the Ecumenical Patriarch, from His Holiness Damianos, Patriarch of Jerusalem, and from Bishop Christian Ludwigs of Denmark.

The President read a letter from Mr. CYRIL KERR, a member of the staff of interpreters, intimating his desire to serve the Conference without remuneration, and the Conference expressed its warm appreciation of Mr. KERR's generosity.

On the motion of the President the following were unanimously elected Vice-Presidents of the Conference : Archbishop SÖDERBLOM, Archbishop GERMANOS, Pastor CHARLES MERLE D'AUBIGNÉ, and Prof. ADOLF DEISSMANN.

The free discussion of Subject II—The Church's Message to the World : the Gospel—was opened by Prof. W. HADORN, who said :

PROFESSOR DR. WILHELM HADORN
Berne (Reformed)

The Committee of this Conference, which has so courteously invited me to address you on this memorable occasion, has asked me to state the attitude of the Swiss Churches towards the movement for a union of the Churches on the basis of faith and order. Our revered Chairman, Doctor Herold, has already referred in bidding you welcome yesterday to the special position of our Churches in regard to this matter, and I now venture to add the following observations.

Our Swiss Churches, which so joyfully accepted the invitation to Stockholm, are awaiting with eager expectation the result of these discussions at Lausanne. The Council of our Federation of Churches accordingly accepted the invitation to take part in your proceedings, not only out of courtesy, but in the firm conviction that the first step which had been taken at Stockholm in the direction of the union of the Church of Christ must of necessity be followed by a second step which would lead us still further from the circumference and nearer to the centre, and which would aim at a union in the matter of faith. May I also be permitted to remind you of those glorious and ever memorable meetings which were held a year ago in my own native city of Berne, and which crowned the work so well initiated at Stockholm.

A consideration which rendered it all the more easy for our Swiss Churches to take part in the discussions on faith and order was that the organisers of the Conference had made it clear in their programme that the message of the Church, the Gospel, was the centre from which the call to unity emanates, and in which unity must be sought. We regard this recognition of the Gospel as the message of the Church, as a step making for agreement and unity, and as such we welcome it with joy. If this Conference led to no other result than the acknowledgment of the Gospel as the message of the Church, that fact alone would justify us in speaking from this moment of a united Christianity, united in the Gospel.

The democratic organisation, which is the special characteristic of the Federation of Swiss Protestant Churches and of its several members (which regard the individual congregations as the vital and essential germ-cells of the Churches) must deter their representatives from making any declarations which might commit the Churches without first consulting them. I must therefore beg you, as you listen to me, to bear that reservation in mind. I can, however, without hesitation declare my cordial assent to the definition of the Gospel—a definition which is based upon the Bible—in the wording of the short title to the second Subject of discussion : " The Church's Message to the World—the Gospel." Our fathers the Reformers taught us, and bequeathed it to us as our heritage, that it is not the humanly subjective but the divinely objective action, not our faith or our trust-worthiness, not our perception or the terms in which we state it, but the Word of God, the revelation of God in Christ, God's appeal to us in the Scriptures, that is the foundation of our faith and at the same time the substance of the Church's message, that is, of the Gospel. Our acceptance of the Gospel does not mean that we give our assent to some human definition or statement of the Gospel, whether formulated by theologians or laymen, but that we know we are ranged under the Word of God, that we realise that it is God who speaks to us, who calls us, and who demands our obedience and our faith.

You know, honoured fathers and brethren, and it is fitting that we should recall it at this time, that our Swiss Churches have no longer any official definition of the Gospel possessing the canonical validity of a creed or confession; we have neither a Confession of Faith from the days of the Reformation nor any of the ancient Church Creeds. That is a result of the ecclesiastical conflicts of the last century. But in this tendency of our Churches and of our people towards freedom and democracy which dispenses with dogmatic formulation, we discern the guiding hand of God, in so far as it has put an end to an equivocal situation without obstructing the free course of the living Word of God, as it goes forth in the Holy Scriptures to the whole human race. It is this Gospel of the Scriptures which our pastors have the duty of proclaiming in all its purity and simplicity, to the best of their understanding and conscience. And, lastly, this Gospel has no need of a bridle in the form of an authoritative creed to make it effective. We acknowledge with joy and thankfulness that the liberating and redeeming power of the Gospel continues to be known and experienced among us, in our Churches and among our people.

I should not, however, be giving a complete picture of the situation in our country if I omitted to state quite clearly that this lack of any creed in our Churches is regarded by many of our Church people as a defect and grave obstacle, both among adherents of the Protestant Church Union, who are closely interested in the Faith and Order movement, and among the younger representatives of the theology of the Reformation, and, finally, also among the Free Churches of Switzerland. In these circles the present position is regarded as transitory, and they look forward, under God, to the day when our Churches shall once more be able—not by compulsion but in the fullness of the salvation given to them—to make their confession of what the Gospel means for them in experience and in life.

May I now touch very briefly on the other points which have been put down for discussion in these meetings regarding the ministry and the sacraments, and indicate the standpoint of the Swiss Churches, since our attitude in regard to these points is indissolubly connected with our attitude towards the Gospel.

As you are aware, the separation of our Churches—and subsequently of the other Reformed Churches—from the Roman hierarchy was a far more radical breach with the ancient and mediæval ecclesiastical system of Church government and ritual than was the case in other Churches. That was due, in part, to the hostility which the bishops of that time showed to the Gospel, and it led to this result, that not only were the powers of the bishops declared extinct, but that the government of the Church was transferred to the State authorities, who in turn delegated the management of the internal affairs of the Church to a Council acting under their superintendence. This Council is now appointed by the synods for a fixed term, and both clerics and laymen are eligible to sit on it. It is, however, important to note that the duty of preaching the Gospel and administering the sacraments is not regarded as an office that can be usurped by the first comer at his own will, but is recognised as a public, spiritual ministry of the Church, the exercise of which is only authorised after a thorough course of theological study through ordination by the Church and by the laying on of hands, matters in which an inward vocation is more important than the action of the Church. On the other hand, we find nothing which prevents us from freely and gladly recognising the ministry and constitution of those Churches which have been led by God in other paths, and we are always ready at any time to associate with them in brotherly and Christian fellowship. We do not, however, consider that uniformity of Church government is absolutely essential for the establishment of such a fellowship.

We should regard this fellowship—and here I touch upon the second point—as sufficiently vouched for and established if the Churches which know that they are already united through the Gospel would grant one another free access to the Lord's Table and participate in the celebration of the Lord's Supper, with which free access to the pulpit might also be combined. If this freedom were generally proclaimed and afforded, the unity of the Churches would be realised in all that is most essential.

And in this way we should have "*In necessariis unitas, in dubiis libertas, in omnibus caritas.*"

That is what we can declare now in advance. The future we must leave to the Lord, the Head of the Church. Let us state whatever we say to-day, so far as God enables us, *sub specie aeternitatis*; and let us remember that countless numbers of simple Christians in all lands are yearning for the day when the Churches shall hold out their hands to each other in the true unity of the spirit on the basis of the apostolic text (Eph. iv, 5), "One body and one Spirit, even as ye are called in one hope of your calling; one Lord, one faith, one baptism; one God and Father of all, who is over all, and through all, and in all."

THE REV. DR. ADOLPH KELLER

Secretary of the Swiss Church Federation (Reformed)

The task to which I wish to devote these few minutes is to sum up, as a basis for discussion, those points in to-day's speeches which are important to us members of the Reformed Churches. These speeches already appear to reveal a considerable body of agreement between the representatives of different Church groups.

The following remarks aim at discovering how far to-day's discussion may be held, from the standpoint of the Reformed Churches, to light the way towards a common understanding of the Gospel.

The Church's message to the world is the Gospel of Jesus Christ. On that point there is no difference of opinion between Christian Churches. The message of the Church is not the proclamation of a particular theory about the world, nor is it a moral doctrine, or any other merely pedagogic or social propaganda. It consists essentially and wholly in bringing the Gospel of Jesus Christ, which has been entrusted to the Church by the grace of God, in its purity and simplicity, to wretched and sinful men. This conception is so self-evident to the Swiss Reformed Churches that their delegates can proclaim it without need-

ing to obtain any special mandate from their Churches—a
mandate which would require many years of discussions
and carefully considered decisions by the numerous synods
of the Cantons.

For us the Gospel is the revelation of the living God.
Our evangelical faith teaches us that neither the human
intelligence nor the general religious experience of mankind
were capable, by themselves, of discovering the truth of
the Gospel. We regard this Gospel as something beyond the
range of all human endeavour, even of the highest order,
beyond the range of all mystical ecstasy, and as being
simply an act and a gift of God who, by grace and by judgment, has unfolded His love for mankind. Man is thus, both
as regards his creation and his redemption, wholly dependent upon God, and acknowledging this offers Him
thankfulness and reverence.

The gift of God's grace which we possess in the Gospel
consists, for our faith, in that which Jesus Christ brings
to us and does for us. It is indissolubly connected with
His words, His works, and His person. It cannot be considered apart from Him, as a purely spiritual message, but
is incarnate in His teaching and in the works in which He
manifested Himself and in the basic facts of His life. For
us, therefore, the life of Jesus Christ, His death and resurrection belong just as much to the Gospel as do His preaching and His call to us. We regard the whole manifestation
of Him, and not merely the words and teaching which He
bequeathed to us, as the Word of God to men. Thus our
faith is endowed not only with a personal conception of God,
but also with the assurance that the divine revelation is a
real and creative force breaking in upon a world of sin and
death. Jesus Christ is, therefore, not only the herald of a
new doctrine of life and a conception of God, but He is the
personal manifestation and operation of the redemptive
love and the forgiveness of God in a world of sin and death.

By the very fact that God, through the Gospel of Jesus
Christ, has given men the consciousness and the forgiveness
of sin, He has re-established communion with them, thereby placing them in communion with their fellow men ; and

this communion is the origin and the foundation of the Christian Church.

It is not the purpose of the salvation which God proclaims and offers to men in the Gospel, to liberate individuals only, but to redeem the whole human race. Hence the Gospel has both an individual and a social significance.

This message of the Gospel in its widest aspect is given to us, primarily, in Jesus' Gospel of the Kingdom of God, with its universal fulfilment of every expectation and promise, as the approaching and final victory of God over the powers of sin and death.

We have this heavenly treasure of the Gospel message in the earthen vessels of human tradition and ecclesiastical organisation. The necessity of apprehending the Word which God has given us in its pure and unadulterated truth impels us constantly to undertake fresh critical examination of tradition and of the human interpretation of the message of grace—a message which transcends all human intelligence.

The Gospel is, however, only to be apprehended through the faith which the Holy Spirit arouses in the hearts of men. Gospel and Faith are co-related ideas. And here we find a division of opinion as to the means by which this grace of God is obtained by men.

Though not disputing the value of other means of grace, such as the sacraments, Protestant belief lays the principal stress on the word of God as given to us in the Bible, heard in faith, and accepted in a spirit of obedience.

But the Gospel also includes the promise of the Holy Spirit, the present and living action of the grace of God. This Holy Spirit is One—whether He proceeds from the Father or from the Son or from both Father and Son. We believe that the Holy Spirit will, as promised by the Gospel, lead us to the unity of the Churches and also to fellowship and union with those who believe in Jesus Christ and His Gospel.

The Rev. Dr. FRANCIS J. HALL urged that the context of the Gospel must not be limited to the fact of the Incarnation, the proclamation of the Kingdom and the acts and deeds of the Lord here on earth. The Gospel is more inclusive than this, and the Church's message must have four main themes, namely (a) The Lord's recorded teaching; (b) His self-manifestation as God-man through His incarnation, life, works, death, resurrection, and the sending of the Spirit ; (c) the truths into which, as Christ had promised, the Holy Spirit led the Apostolic Church ; (d) the Church itself, as intended by Christ not only to be the abiding witness and proclaimer of the message but also, as the Body of Christ, to be the visible and corporate centre on earth of Christian grace, experience, and spiritual life. Further, to fulfil these tasks the Church must be visibly one : not merely one in spirit, for body and spirit are indissoluble. Thus the visible unity of the Church is a vital part of the Church's message. Unity and union are distinct ideas, but in realisation are inseparable.

Dr. FRIEDRICH GOGARTEN : The outline of the content of the Gospel which was given this morning is incomplete. The essence of the Gospel as the Reformers understood it is the forgiveness of sins : not merely a message about forgiveness, but forgiveness itself. To hear the Gospel with faith *is* to be forgiven, redeemed, holy. Everything else that can be said about the Gospel is only a corollary of this. For instance, the Gospel is a " message of judgment " only in the sense that it reveals a judgment of which we become conscious in the moment when we know ourselves to be delivered from it through faith. Or again, the Gospel reveals sin ; but it reveals sin only as that unfathomable depth from which the forgiveness of Christ has saved us. Even the right knowledge of Jesus Christ Himself, the bearer of this message, depends upon the centrality of *remissio peccatorum*. We cannot know Him as Lord and Son of God, unless we know Him as " made sin for us."

All this is not mere Lutheranism : it is the essence of the Biblical revelation, and of that Pauline exposition of the Gospel without which the " Jesus of the Synoptists " cannot be understood. The critical study of the New Testament has necessitated the liberation of the pure Gospel from the spirit of Hellenic philosophy ; but it also requires its liberation from the spirit of Hellenic mysticism. This is the pressing problem which our discussions ought not to evade.

The Right Rev. THE BISHOP OF DORNAKAL : I wish to urge the consideration of this subject in relation to the non-Christian world. The Church's message there, united in so far as it speaks of the Kingdom of God, realised in Jesus Christ, loses its distinctness when we pass on to ask the convert to separate himself from his past fellowship and enter the fellowship of Jesus Christ. We have no united answer to the questions—Should a man join the Church, and if so, what Church ? Should he be baptised, and if so, by what baptism ?

India has a great admiration for Christ, but we fail to carry it further because over against the anti-Christian divisions of caste we have no true Christian unity into which the convert can pass. Divided Christendom is a source of weakness in the West : in non-Christian lands it is a sin and a stumbling-block. If the non-Christian world is to be won for Christ our message must be one. If our message is to be one, we must be one.

After the singing of a hymn, and a few moments of prayer, the Rev. Dr. TIMOTHY TINGFANG LEW said :

We speak of a message to " the world," but do we realise what " the world " is ? Do we, for instance, include in our thought the teeming millions of China, one quarter of the human race ?

Again, our word Gospel is reproduced in Chinese by two words meaning " happiness from on high." China has a vivid notion of happiness as complete satisfaction. It asks what sort of man is a redeemed or reconciled man, one who is justified by faith : it asks how such a man differs from one who lives by the old religion, and what influence the corporate life of such men has upon social, industrial and international life.

It will not matter greatly if we fail here to attain agreement about sacraments or the ministry ; but it will be a failure indeed if we do not reach agreement on a better understanding of the Gospel. If we look out on the needs of the entire world, and then look up to God in the blazing sun of all His all-inclusive love, reaching out to His entire creation, our differences will dwindle into insignificance.

The Rev. Dr. SAMUEL ZWEMER desired to see, in the statement of the Church's Message and Gospel, a fuller emphasis upon the Cross of Christ. To speak of the Gospel as a message of repentance is inadequate : Mahommedanism and Buddhism know much about repentance. But the specific element in Christianity is its provision of a sufficient dynamic to produce knowledge of sin, sorrow for sin, and power to forsake sin. An experience of thirty-seven years as a missionary to Mohammedans makes it certain that wherever the Cross is given its rightful place the fruits of conversion follow : and therefore the centrality of the Cross should be emphasised in any statement which this Conference makes about the essence of the Gospel.

Professor Dr. NICOLAS ARSENIEW : Fuller emphasis should be laid upon the Resurrection of the Lord, which is the centre of the whole Christian preaching. Here, in a proclamation which is foolishness to the world, we have a cosmic event breaking through the law of death ; a message of victory, of the revelation of life eternal ; the incoming of a new reality. That reality will one day be fully revealed in the glory of the children of God, but in the presence of the Holy Spirit in the Church we already have a pledge and foretaste of that which is to be. Thus the Church is not an appendix to the Gospel but a part of it. To be in the Church is to be carried away by a stream of divine love, that took its rise in the Incarnation and Resurrection. The " love for one another " which Christ declared to be the sign of the disciples, the " love for our brother " which St. John required as a proof that we love God—this is the basis of the Church. To know " with all the saints, rooted in love, the length, breadth, depth and height," is to possess a new life, a victory over death : a life and a victory which began at the first Easter, and are at the very heart of the present life of the Church.

The Rev. D. N. FURNAJIEFF laid stress upon the centrality of Christ, and the importance of saying that the Gospel is nothing less than Christ Himself.

The Rev. BISHOP CANNON desired that the Gospel should not be summarised as a teaching or as the setting of a perfect example. It is the expression of the love of God for lost man, a message of sacrificial atoning love. Apart from this, the Gospels and Epistles are devoid of meaning. The Church of Christ can therefore have no Gospel but that of salvation through personal repentance and faith and the atoning sacrifice of a crucified and risen Lord ; it offers but one road of salvation, yet that road was built by the all-inclusive love of God for every creature. And although this message has the widest implications for industrial, social and international life, yet the need of the present time is an increased emphasis upon personal sin and personal separation from God. Further, the Churches, with their rites and institutions, have widely various ways of bringing the Gospel home to the individual. Each of these may have its value, but the essence of the whole is the simple underlying truth, transcending all organisation, that eternal life is given to us through the Cross of Jesus Christ. The acknowledgment of this fundamental truth is the only basis upon which the unity of the Christian brotherhood can be built up.

The Rev. Dr. LOFTHOUSE : Together with the impressive agreement which we have reached as to the substance of the Gospel we need also a synthesis between the message for the individual and the message for society. We need to say, when confronted with the demand for a spiritual principle applicable in the social sphere, that the peace of man must be peace with God, because when we learn to seek Christ in the least of His brothers we shall find Him. Side by side with St. John xvii, " that they all may be one," we need to put St. Matthew xxv, " Inasmuch as ye have done it unto the least of these, ye have done it unto me." The message of the redeeming love of Christ must bring us, not only to personal redemption, but to the discovery of the one family of which we are members, and of its claims upon us.

The session ended at 6.45 p.m.

E

THE NATURE OF THE CHURCH

FRIDAY MORNING, AUGUST 5TH.

The Conference met in full sessions both morning and afternoon in the Aula of the University, to consider Subject III—the Nature of the Church. The Rev. Dr. WILLIAM P. MERRILL being in the chair, the morning session opened at 9.30, with devotions led by the Rev. Pastor ANDRÉ N. BERTRAND.

Professor H. S. ALIVISATOS read the following address by

HIS BEATITUDE, CHRYSOSTOM

Archbishop of Athens and of all Greece (Orthodox)

The Church of Greece, gladly accepting the call to unity, extends to all the representatives of the several Churches and nations here present a hearty greeting; desiring, from the bottom of her heart, that the day may soon come when differences as to the faith will no longer bar the way to Christian fellowship and mutual goodwill.

The assignment of a first place in our discussions to the nature of the Church is, in my judgment, wise and right; for upon this the possibility of an understanding entirely depends : it is fundamental to unity. I have therefore gladly consented to give a brief explanation of the teaching of the Orthodox Church upon this subject, a doctrine which, as we believe, is in entire accordance—to use a current expression—with that of the ancient and undivided Church.

In speaking of the nature of the Church, we must first consider certain general characteristics of that holy fellowship called *Ekklesia*, and after this we must elucidate the particular marks which were attributed to the Church by the Fathers in the Nicene Creed, and which still represent the unchanging doctrine of the Greek Orthodox Church.

I

The Church as the divinely-instituted Body of the Faithful.

The founder of any society must of necessity be its original lawgiver. It is he who determines alike the aim for which the society is to exist and the means by which that aim is to be attained ; it is he who gathers its members into a unity for the accomplishment of that purpose. So we see in the New Testament that Jesus Christ, after choosing the twelve Apostles, delivers to them those laws and means and ordinances upon which the Church, having as its aim the salvation of the faithful, was to be built up. Receiving these instructions from Jesus Christ, the Apostles took the Christian religion out into the world by founding Churches in every place ; and they made it plain in doing this that they were acting in His Name and under the instructions received from Him. From the first century onwards the Church was regarded as a divinely instituted Society, and this was recognised by heretics, Jews and Gentiles, as well as by the Fathers of the Church. The early heretics, as is well known, claimed in self-defence that *their* Churches were founded by Christ ; and it is to Christ that non-Christian writers such as Celsus, Porphyry, and Pliny ascribed the foundation of the Church. Let us add that the prophecies of the Old Testament point forward to the establishment by the Messiah of a world-wide Kingdom, in which He Himself will teach the truth and bring about the salvation of mankind. There can be no doubt, as soon as we admit the Church to have taken its beginning from Jesus Christ, the Son of God, and Very God, that the Church is a divinely-instituted Society or foundation.

The Church founded by Jesus Christ is both visible and invisible.

The prophetic pictures of the Church in the Old Testament depict the Church as a visible society. The Church of the Old Testament, which prefigured the Church of Christ, was itself a visible society. It is clear, from the calling of the disciples and the sending of them forth to proclaim the

Kingdom of God, from the provision made for the preaching of the Gospel and from the institution of the sacraments, that it was the intention of Jesus Christ to constitute the Church as a visible communion or society. The fact that the Church is the instrument through which the faithful are to attain salvation implies directly the visibility of the Church. If the Church is to be a fellowship of human beings, it must of necessity be a visible fellowship ; it can have no existence as a community unless it has external marks by which it can be recognised. The primitive practice, dating from the first century, according to which heretics and schismatics were excluded from the Church, is in itself a proof of its visible character ; for exclusion from an invisible fellowship is impossible and meaningless, and in such a context the word " schism " has no significance. Further, the fact that the Church has among its members both bad men and good is a clear proof of its visibility. Thus before his excommunication the offender at Corinth was a member of the Church ; and before receiving Holy Communion we are bidden to examine ourselves because to partake unworthily of the Body and Blood of the Lord is to eat and drink judgment to ourselves : there are, therefore, in the Church, some who eat and drink unworthily. And the Sacrament of Confession also makes it plain that the Church includes sinful men among its members—a fact which is signified to us by the parables of the wheat and tares and of the fishing net.

The Church is, of course, invisible as well as visible. All its members are united in one body by grace, as St. Paul says (1 Cor. xii, 12 ; Eph. iv, 7 ; Rom. xii, 3-8) and this bond of grace is invisible. The faithful are also united by a common belief and by the sacraments, and these belong in part to the sphere of the unseen ; so that in this aspect, again, the Church has an invisible character. And this twofold nature of the Church, seen and unseen, can be inferred from the Bible and the Fathers, which teach us to regard the Church as symbolising the two natures, divine and human, in the one Person of the Lord, whose work the Church continues. Like Him, therefore, the Church must be at one and the same time outward and inward, human and divine, in virtue of its correspondence with the divine and human natures of its Founder : visible, therefore, and at the same time invisible.

The Church founded by Christ as a visible community is infallible.

The promise of Christ that He will be with the disciples till the end of all the ages (Matt. xxviii, 20) and that He will send His Holy Spirit to abide with them for ever (John xiv, 16) reveal to us that Christ and the Holy Spirit remain continuously in the Church and preserve it from every error. Christ, as the Head of the Church which is His Body, gives life to her continually and guides her : so that, inasmuch as Christ is the very Truth (John xiv, 6), it is impossible for her ever to fall into error. So it is that the Scripture calls the Church " the pillar and ground of the truth " (1 Tim. iii, 15) and declares plainly that " the gates of hell shall not prevail against her " (Matt. xvi, 18). It is evident that in that verse of the Epistle to Timothy Paul is not referring to the Church of Ephesus but to the Church Catholic ; also that he is not speaking of partial truth, or some special kind of truth, but of the truth as a whole ; so that the whole Christian Church is regarded as the pillar and ground of the whole Christian truth, and therefore as infallible. And in the quotation from St. Matthew, the invincibility of the Church involves her unerring infallibility.

Jesus Christ, the Founder of the Church, " gave to her apostles and prophets, evangelists, pastors and teachers . . . that we may be no more children, tossed to and fro, and carried about with every wind of doctrine " (Eph. iv, 11). Individually, of course, bishops or local Churches may err (Acts xx, 30 ; Rev. ii, 5ff.) but the Church as a whole is infallible. Tertullian (*de praescr.* 28), referring to the action of the Apostles under the inspiration of the Holy Spirit at the Apostolic Council (" it seemed good to the Holy Ghost and to us," Acts xv, 28), teaches with emphasis that the unity and unchangingness of the Church's faith is based upon the unique authority of the Church and the guidance given to it by the Holy Spirit.

The aim and purpose of the Church.

The aim of the Church is the sanctification of men and the building up of the Kingdom of God (Matt. vi, 33), that is to say, the uniting of man with God, who is the fountain of life and blessedness. Through the Church a share in the saving work of Christ is made possible for everyone who believes on Him (Eph. v, 26 ; Tit. ii, 14), through grace, unto life everlasting (John xvii, 3).

II

Thus understood, the Church is a divinely instituted fellowship of men united one with another by the same faith, sanctified by the same mysteries, and governed by those Pastors and Teachers whose office originated in the Apostles. This Church, according to the definitions attached to her by the ancient Creeds, possesses the following marks :

The Church of Christ is One.

Jesus Christ speaks of His Church as one (Matt. xvi, 15), and, therefore, there is only one Church, although its members are innumerable, dispersed throughout the whole world severed in time and in space, and although the local Churches are many. Our Lord teaches the unity of the Church in His parables, as clearly as He speaks of one fold and one Shepherd (John x, 16). The Apostles also spoke of one Church (Eph. v, 25), in which the unity of the faithful is derived from the oneness of the Body of the Church (Rom. xii, 5) : "For by one Spirit are we all baptised into one body " (1 Cor. xii, 13) ; "there is one body and one Spirit . . . one Lord, one faith, one baptism, one God and Father of all " (Eph. iv, 6 ; cf. 1 Cor. x, 17 ; xii, 14-27). The Church is one in her internal life, and this unity is based upon the one Christ, who, abiding with her, gives life to her through the Holy Spirit, uniting the faithful, the members of the one body, with Himself as its Head. This mysterious oneness of the members of the Church finds its special manifestation in the Sacrament of Holy Communion. Thus united, through the Holy Spirit, in Christ, the faithful are bidden to live one and the same life, the Christ-life. This unity is not affected by the use of varying languages in worship, nor by the external varieties of organisation in local Churches. But the Church, according to St. Cyprian, is "*una et sola a Domino constituta*"; religious communions divided from her whether by heresy or by schism cease to be members of the one Church (I John ii, 19), and their existence therefore does not destroy the unity of the Church. And the unity of the Church is not only to be thought of as a unity of the Church on earth, but as including also the Church in heaven, a unity transcending time and place since the Church, with Christ as its Head, lives with His life eternally. The maintenance of the Church's unity on the part of man depends upon fidelity to faith in Jesus Christ as the Church's head. By the power of a living faith the faithful have their share in the unity of the Church, and by the grace of God they form one spiritual community, the same in all ages.

As the Body of Christ, receiving its life by the agency of the Holy Spirit, the Church is Holy.

It is as a holy Church that the Saviour " presents " her (Eph. v, 25-27) having founded her through His blood. She is made holy by the Holy Spirit, sanctifying and enlightening her members, who therefore are called a " royal priesthood " (1 Pet. ii, 9-10), " fellow-citizens of the saints and of the household of God " (Eph. ii, 19), " children of light " (Eph. v, 8 ; 1 Thess. v, 5), " saints " (Rom. i, 7 ; 1 Cor. i, 2 ; Eph. iv, 12 ; 1 Tim. v, 10 ; Heb. iii, 1), " temples of God " and " temples of the Holy Spirit " (1 Cor. iii, 16-17 ; vi, 19 ; 2 Cor. vi, 16). Not that the members of the Church individually are all holy ; it is the Church that is holy, and this does not mean that it has none but holy members. Our Lord compared the Church to a field in which wheat and tares grow together (Matt. xiii, 24-30), to a net gathering of every kind (*ib.* 47), and to a supper at which there are worthy and unworthy guests (Matt. xxii, 2-13). He taught that in the Church there are good and wicked servants (Matt. xviii, 23 ff; xxv. 14 ff.), sheep and goats (xxv, 33 ff.). It was for this reason that He founded the Sacrament of Confession in the Church, for the forgiveness of sins (John xx, 22 ff.), and taught His disciples to pray for the forgiveness of their sins (Matt. vi, 12). Perfect holiness belongs to the condition of the life everlasting, but in this present life none is free from sin (I John i, 8). In the days of the Apostles, Ananias and Sapphira were members of the Church of Jerusalem, as the offender excommunicated by St. Paul was of the Church of Corinth. The holiness of her members is the aim which the Church aspires to reach through the means afforded to her. The inclusion of members who are not holy does not destroy the holiness of the Church, nor prevent it from making spiritual progress. A tree may have some withered branches, and yet go on growing, as long as its roots are strong and healthy. Deriving her sanctity from her Head, the Church ever seeks the betterment of her weak members, and only casts out from her fellowship those who cannot be made better— like the branches which, because they bear no fruit, are cast into the fire and burned (John xv, 1 ff.).

The Church, One and Holy, is also Catholic.

The Christian Church knows no local limitations. It is ecumenical and world-wide, as that Kingdom of God which Jesus proclaimed (Matt. viii, 11). It was not foreordained for one place or for one people. When our Lord was yet on earth, the Church needed but a little fold to contain it, but the Lord foretold that to this little flock His Father would give the Kingdom (Lk. xii, 32). Through the sending out of the Apostles to the whole world (Matt. xxviii, 19), and to the uttermost part of the world (Acts i, 8), the Lord foreshowed the Catholicity of the Church ; this Catholicity was made strikingly manifest at the moment of the Church's definite entry upon the world, on the day of Pentecost, when the Apostles were all filled with the Holy Spirit and began to speak with other tongues as the Spirit gave them utterance

(Acts ii, 4). Then came the founding of local Churches, particularly through the preaching of St. Paul : yet the local Churches in their totality constituted the one Catholic Church of Christ. In every Christian community in which there were believers in Christ, " brethren," a Church was constituted ; yet all the Churches of Achaia, Galatia, Macedonia and the rest formed together the Church of the Churches, the Catholic Church. This Church, as contrasted with the heretical communities severed from it, was the one and only true Church, and stood alone in the possession of the true faith. Though scattered over the world, it existed as one whole through the identity of its faith in our Lord Jesus Christ. Thus, Catholicity and the right and true faith of the Church were one and the same thing ; and so the term Catholic Church meant " the Church which possesses the true and right faith." And for the same reason the name Catholic was applied not only to the whole body but also to each local Church. The *Martyrdom of Polycarp*, which is addressed in the form of a letter from the Church of God in Smyrna to the Church of God in Philomelium and to all local communities of the holy Catholic Church, speaks of Polycarp as praying for the " whole Catholic Church in the world " ; and it also describes him as " an apostolic and prophetic teacher, and Bishop of the Catholic Church in Smyrna." In this sense of the word, at the time of the first and second ecumenical Councils the Bishops of the several cities and places were called Catholic Bishops of those cities (as, for instance, Meletios, Bishop of the Catholic Church in Antioch).

The Church is also Apostolic.

As God has sent His Son (Gal. iv, 4) the " Apostle and high-priest of our confession " (Heb. iii, 1), and the Son sent His disciples, whom he also named Apostles, so also the Church, founded in the world, sends out her own apostles to bring the world to Christ. But in order that the Church may be able to accomplish this aim, it must keep unspotted the apostolic doctrine and tradition, exactly as these existed in the time of the Apostles. Through them, whom the Lord chose and the Holy Spirit inspired, the Church was spread throughout the whole world ; through them their successors were appointed, by the grace of the Holy Spirit, to continue without interruption the work of the salvation of believers—" being built upon the foundation of the apostles and prophets, Jesus Christ himself being the chief cornerstone, in whom each several building, fitly framed together, groweth unto an holy temple in the Lord, in whom ye also are builded together for an habitation of God through the Spirit " (Eph. ii, 20 ff.). The apostolic doctrine and tradition, with the apostolic succession, are the elements in which the apostolicity of the Church consists. Only that Church can be apostolic which has and retains from the Apostles themselves the true doctrine and the gifts of the Holy Spirit. Through the divinely-constituted Hierarchy, and so alone, this Church is connected by unbroken succession with the Apostles and keeps the deposit committed unto it by them.

When in the second century the Gnostics attempted through their Bishops to corrupt the faith of Christ which the Catholic Church throughout the world was teaching, Irenaeus, Bishop of Lugdunum, wrote against them thus : " This teaching and this faith the Church has received : and, though scattered over the whole world, she preserves it as though it were dwelling in one house. And accordingly she preaches and hands on this faith as though with one mouth. For although in the world there are divers languages, yet the power and meaning of the tradition is everywhere one and the same : neither do the Churches founded in Germany, or in Iberia, or among the Celts, nor those of the East or of Egypt or in Libya or anywhere else in the world, teach or believe otherwise. But as the sun which God created is one and the same for the whole world, so also the preaching of the truth everywhere enlightens every man who desires to come to the knowledge of the truth. And neither will those among the Church's rulers who are mighty in speech teach otherwise than this (for the disciple is not above his Master), nor will those who are less powerful diminish the content of the tradition.

For in that the Faith is only one, he who is mighty in speech cannot add to its greatness, nor can he who is less powerful diminish it. For where the Church is, there is the Spirit of God also, and where the Spirit of God is, there is the Church and the grace of the Lord "—" *Ubi ecclesia, ibi et Spiritus Dei, et ubi Spiritus Dei, illic ecclesia et Domini gratia.*"

This, in a very brief compass, is our conception of the nature of the Church. Holding to this conception we are by no means far removed from that view of the Church's nature which was held in the ancient and undivided Church. And if, as we wish from the bottom of our hearts, all Christian bodies could find themselves united on this basis, which avoids both the extravagances of Romanism and the extremes of the theories most opposed to Romanism in the Western world, the Orthodox Church would be the first to rejoice over so great a blessing from God.

THE REV. S. PARKES CADMAN, D.D.

President, Federal Council of the Churches of Christ in America
(Congregational)

I

The gist of my contribution to the Conference is irenic. It is animated by the conviction that the Christian Church is the most characteristic creation of our common Faith, interpreting its realities to the world which too often judges them by the Church rather than the Church by them. The examination of the several theories of her nature and polity is best left to brethren of piety and learning who are qualified to judge them impartially. It is, therefore, not necessary for me to do more than trace in barest outline the genesis and development of the Church as God's living organism for the world's redemption. She has produced historic Councils and Synods ; powerful States and civilisations ; but her chief glory consists of regenerated souls who are the living stones built into her spiritual fabric.

I am cognisant of the definite differences of Christendom concerning the conception and constitution of the Church. These differences are not to be glossed over as useless impedimenta, but discussed in a fraternal spirit, and in the light of the totality of Christian experience and Christian history. Whether these relate us to Jerusalem, Alexandria, Constantinople, Rome, Wittenberg, Geneva or Canterbury, surely as believers in Christ we visualise the diversified wealth of our heritage, and as Churchmen we should feel at home in them all. Nor can the significance of our respective confessions and Communions be sufficiently appreciated by those who refuse to recognise them as indispensable parts of an organic whole in the Kingdom of the Holy Spirit. The fuller knowledge of their evolution should deliver Christians everywhere from the confusions of sectarian strife, and reveal to them the Catholicity which includes the historic Churches in the manifold wisdom and purpose of God. All are branches of the one Vine, and His life runs through every part.

The Reformed Communions, whether of Anglican, Lutheran, Zwinglian or Genevan roots, may learn that the Roman Catholic Communion has stood for nobler ideals than Protestantism is wont to concede. Roman Catholicism, on the other hand, might profit by recognising that Protestantism chartered a new freedom for Christian faith and progress. As I interpret the past of the Church Universal, few if any of her priesthoods or prophetic orders, her sacramental or evangelical theologies, her various concepts of holiness or oneness, have failed to confer lasting religious benefits on mankind. If that past has any lessons of unity or plans for its advancement to unfold to us, we shall do well to embrace them for the furtherance of the Gospel.

The saints who are Christianity's principal achievement, and also the ideals by which they have woven together the nations, sprang from our common Mother, the Church. Her life and doctrines were embodied in them, and they furnish satisfactory evidence of a divine design in her structure and development. Her numerous divisions did not drop out of space, but emerged in their succession from her pre-existent being. The Reformers, who either demanded a return to beaten paths, or struck out into others which seemed perilous to Traditionalists, did not imagine themselves alien from the Church, but defenders of her integrity and purifiers of her profession. Neither Greek, Roman nor Protestant were consciously lacking in loyalty and affection for the original *Ecclesia* to which they alike appealed for the teachings they championed. The Bible she had bestowed on them was their common possession. I dare to suggest that few if any real values have ceased to be, in the prolonged process of ecclesiastical evolution which confronts us to-day. Whatever transmutations time has imposed on the Body of Christ, its ideal has been preserved for our further realisation. The false perspectives of unlicensed power, the pursuit of minor or unreal ends, the disposition of huge impersonal organisations to annul the rights of individuals or minority groups of believers, could not obliterate that ideal. The conception of the Church as for ever one, holy and indivisible, God's new creation in Christ Jesus her Lord, has survived the perilous patronage of the great and noble. It still thrives in many hearts unwithered by the glare of sectional prejudice or national arrogance.

II

Her New Testament name *Ecclesia* signified (a) the whole number of the elect who have been, are being, or shall be gathered into one Commonwealth, (b) the entire body of those who throughout the world professed the Evangel of their Redeemer, as the Church Catholic and Visible, (c) the sum total of congregations in a given area, (d) the individual congregation, and (e) in at least one instance, the local Church as represented by its office-bearers. Her institutional forms first found shape in distinct isolated assemblies, attracted by their common life in Christ, and related one to another by the personal influence and authority of His Apostles and their messengers. They were not yet bound into a harmonious whole by any permanent organisation.

From these little groups of worshippers, with their local forms of government due to different circumstances, arose the conception of the all-inclusive federation of the Church Catholic and visible of the apostolic age. In a phrase reminiscent of her affiliation with the Jewish Ecclesia, St. Paul entitled her the "Israel of God" (Gal. vi, 16). St. Peter in his first Epistle referred to her members as "an elect race, a royal priesthood, an holy nation, a people of God's own possession" (ii, 9).

The terminology of the Hebrew Scriptures enlarged the Church consciousness of those early Christians of whom the New Testament speaks in realistic and idealistic senses as the Fellowship, the Family of God, the Body of Christ and His future Bride. The prestige imparted to the infant Society was nurtured by the noblest teachings of the Old Testament. Its sanctions explain in part why primitive Christianity was impregnable to the current legalism of Judaism, and also to the pessimistic vagaries of decadent paganism. The indwelling life of her Lord enabled her to overcome polemical criticisms within and beyond her borders, and to advance His conquests in every direction.

A comparison of St. Paul's epistles with the letters of St. Ignatius reveals the magnitude of the changes effected during the intervening period in the polity if not in the nature of the Church. For Apostle and Father alike she was the greatest of all societies, charged with the highest and most honourable of missions : to interpret God to man, and to reconcile man to God. But St. Ignatius also embodied those ecclesiatical developments whose actual origins are still a matter of debate. His determined spirit was intent on the three ruling ideas of contemporary Christian thought : the glory of martyrdom, the paramountcy of the territorial episcopacy, and the extermination of schism and heresy. "Do nothing," he peremptorily wrote to the Magnesians, "without the presbyters and bishops." The threefold order of the ministry was invoked by him, and later by St. Cyprian, not in behalf of subsequent theories of apostolic succession or sacerdotal prerogative, but for the unity of the Church and the defence of her doctrinal purity. St.

Cyprian's " high providential theory " that the Church is founded upon St. Peter, and her tangible bond one united episcopate, was set forth by the first martyred bishop of Africa to confute the Novatian heresy.

The original oneness of the Apostolic Church, both as regards its community in the Spirit and the later communion of all believers in a visible Society, was now attached to the episcopate to safeguard her against those centrifugal forces which became active after the death of the Apostles. Sectional tendencies were rife ; the heretical views of Docetists, Gnostics and Montanists sharply challenged current orthodoxy. The sole available remedy for these evils lay in the enlargement and vigorous assertion of episcopal control. Opposition to it was equally determined. Yet he ill understands Christian history's unveiling of the progressive nature of the Church who thinks that she was most honoured when least questioned. Dutiful and wise according to their lights, and encompassed by defences which a providential guidance supplied, these servants of God whom I have mentioned and their fellow-labourers heralded throughout the Greco-Roman Empire the Gospel of inwardness and power which our Lord had first announced in Galilee.

Moreover, from its beginnings, Christianity was deemed by its followers an independent, catholic, self-sufficient religion, universal in scope, and absolutely separated from the pagan systems which ministered to the ambition of Rome as an imperial World-State. Hence the persecution of the Church was but a matter of time, to be succeeded by an era of toleration, and finally by the edict which ended her humiliation and elevated her to the doubtful dignity of a State religion. It was at best a Pyrrhic victory. Nevertheless it meant that the Empire pledged itself to conduct its secular affairs in association with the officialism of the Church. If Constantine imagined she would reciprocate by becoming the willing instrument of imperial absolutism, he was doomed to disappointment. As a matter of fact she became its formidable and subtle foe.

Ever and anon she demonstrated that civilisation was the

heiress not only of Hellenism but of Hebraism, and still more of the Christian Evangel. The conviction that our Lord had founded and had intended to found a visible Church was fixed in the contemporary mind. She survived while imperial Rome perished, and at the dissolution of the old order she became the living centre around which the new order crystallised. The sequel justified the methods used for its success to a far larger extent than some who sit in judgment upon those troubled eras can conscientiously concede. We need not render their guides blind homage, but we may consistently reverence their love for the Church which as an institution, and acting under pressure, they transformed into a fortress.

Degeneration of methods did not blot out her sanctuaried life. However lamentably her leaders distrusted her divine origin in their efforts to constitute her a super-State, she continued to produce saints, theologians, pastors and missionaries whom it would be superfluous to eulogise here. Part of her past lives in all the present because she has been from the first a vital growth conditioned by environment. Every period of her history is the inalienable heritage of the Church as a whole, and is therefore organically related to what we consider in this Conference. The operations of God in her frequently used earthly agencies for ends far beyond themselves. But they confirmed the main contention that as His organic creation in Christ, the Church Universal may share every human fate, yet remain in essence divine. For the Spirit and the Truth which were before her have been within her from the beginning, and shall be within her to the end.

III

Time does not permit more than a passing reference to the mediæval Church, or the sixteenth century revolt which compelled the Holy See to set its house in order, and sharply defined the doctrinal system of modern Catholicism as against Protestantism. The European chaos that followed was a tribute to the notable service of the Papacy as a cohesive and federating institution. " For nearly eight hundred years," says Dr. Herbert B. Workman, " Rome had stood, not merely for righteousness, but solidarity. Her bishops were not only the vicars of God ; they were the symbols and source of a brotherhood that would otherwise have perished. Men remembered their services in the past ; how they had tamed the barbarians, enforced law upon the lawless, preached the subordination of the individual to society, curbed the lust and despotism of kings, held up ideals of purity and truth in the darkest ages, saved the Church from the triumph of the Cathari, maintained a unity of faith and hope in the days when all creed was in danger of disintegration."

Before 1564, the date of the canons of the Council of Trent, the conception of the Church as Catholic, not only in her faith but in her organisation, prevailed over the long-standing schism between East and West, and also against recurrent heresies. Nor did the continental Reformers anticipate the dissolution of this catholicity. On the contrary, they endeavoured to perpetuate it by their attempts to free the Church from mediæval accretions, and to restore her apostolic simplicity in the light of the New Learning. The present condition of rival and co-existent denominations, differing in certain fundamental doctrines and principles of organisation, would have been as obnoxious to the partisans of Luther and Calvin as to their most rigid opponents. But the conflict between them involved the State, and fostered its nationalistic tendencies in Catholic and Protestant countries. What was taken from priests was too freely given to princes. The divine right of the Civil Power was invoked against that of the Holy See, and in the outcome Protestant Christianity frequently submitted itself to the jurisdiction of the temporal sovereignty.

Rome, as we know, became one of the divisions of western Christendom. The splendid project of Hildebrand, for the moment successful and in part deserving success, to enforce in the monarchs and peoples of Europe a higher morality, respect for the spiritual mission of the Church,

and a sense of their common civilisation, was foredoomed
for lack of elasticity. It was ultimately defeated by the
expanding life of nations which the mediæval Church knew
better how to create than to control. Beneath the treach-
eries, grievances, complaints and conflicts of her Babylonian
captivity and its consequences lay the fundamental
error of her rulers, who could not or would not perceive
that feudalism was no longer possible as an organic system.
The outcome was far too complex and extensive to be
characterised in a phrase. But it may be said that northern
Europe's release from Roman supremacy was counter-
balanced by its loss of religious catholicity. The wounds
inflicted then and later have not been healed. The universality and unity originally shattered under Boniface VIII
and Clement V have not been repaired. Nor has the Papacy
resumed the spiritual lordship which it claims as the
sole inheritor of the tradition of the Pre-Reformation
Church.

In Protestantism the necessity of a logical basis for
conscientious dissidents from Established Churches, and
for large bodies of Christians living in lands that forbade
the union of Church and State, led to the formation of a
theory of the Church contrary to that of the early Reformers and deplored by the traditional Communions.
According to this sixteenth century idea[1] the Church
Universal is not a visible organisation, but the sum total
of all faithful souls who group themselves in fellowships
fashioned for their needs and convictions, and who obey
what they hold to be the precedents of Holy Scripture. An
historical survey of the Post-Reformation Church, considered as a definite and Catholic organisation, is beyond
our present scope. The stream of her continuity has been
diverted into many channels requiring specific exploration.
Yet I venture the assertion that all Christian Fellowships
have their synthesis in their mutual vitality, and that its
fuller realisation is responsible for this Conference.

---

[1] This date is accurate because, although the idea prevailed before this time,
the Elizabethan Congregationalists were the first to give it emphatic expression.
Their watchword was "Reformation without tarrying for any."

IV

Principal A. E. Garvie observes that " never before was the desire so keen and the endeavour so steadfast for the reunion of divided Christendom." He speaks authoritatively for the Congregational Church which I have the honour to represent. We accept without hesitation as our brethren all disciples of the Lord, and acknowledge the validity of the faith and order of all Christian bodies. It is our conviction that believers of every persuasion are one organism animated by a common religious life, knit together by the unity of one spiritual discipline, and held by the tie of a united hope. The recent reorganisation of the British Commonwealth of Nations upon the basis of absolutely free and equal self-governing States, between which there is no question of superior or inferior status, though all gladly recognise in the Motherland the *primus inter pares*, exemplifies the theory of Congregationalists that the Church is best united by flexible ties, unhampered by onerous restrictions, and having the pliability of life as against the rigidity of uniformity, combined with hearty acknowledgment of the historic past. The adaptation of her branches to their respective necessities is thus secured, and their contributions to the aggregate of human good facilitated.

We do not maintain that this form of organisation, or for that matter any other, can claim exclusive Scriptural or apostolic sanction. Yet it may be urged that the test of the true Church is not conformity to type, but effectiveness in fulfilling the will of her Lord, and therefore that organisation need not be of a single type. In the sequence, the Congregational position thus stated leaves us free to find, if possible, a *modus vivendi* which assumptions of finality in organisation would seem to exclude. If the principle of inclusion could predominate in our counsels, and some existing conditions of fellowship unknown to Christ or to His Apostles were submitted to the control of that principle, many of the barriers between us would fall like the walls of Jericho. The sense of unity that pre-

vailed in the earliest Churches is the lost secret which
may be rediscovered by this Conference of modern
Churchmen.

Christians cannot afford to hold lightly or neglect any
aids and expedients for the welfare of the Church Catholic
and of humanity. But aids and expedients should not be
elevated as part of the essence of God's message to man in
the Gospel, nor allowed to obscure the ideal of Christ for His
Ecclesia. The exaltation of means into ends and the ascrip-
tion of changeless merits to subordinate things are the
gravest obstacles to unity we encounter.

Nevertheless, one is aware that while as individuals all
Christians are alike priests, yet as members of a spiritual
corporation they have their several and distinct offices.
What the final organisation of the Church as a living, growing organism shall be is perhaps not within our power to
state. Neither our hopes nor fears, nor even the prophetic
soul within her decree her destiny. This is in the sole keeping of her living Head. Moreover her more heroic past has
so often proved too hard for the earth. Yet the nobler
eloquence of her message of peace and goodwill cannot be
hushed nor the formative powers she possesses abrogated.
In their operation they resemble those physical forces which
have raised man from the dust. They testify to the enduring tranquillity and strength at the heart of her ceaseless
agitation. But for God's life in her how could she face the
gigantic task of infusing order into chaos and discipline into
freedom, which is the acid test, not of the Divine Society
alone, but of every undertaking and economy of man?
Surely they should enable us to understand that the art
of Christian statesmanship is to know how to work with
things as they are in order to make them what they ought
to be.

Neither rampant individualism nor negative sectarianism
can for ever set aside the corrective witness of the Church
Universal. In her we may see the entire assembly of God's
faithful people held by a nexus stronger than that of race
or speech, and fused into spiritual homogeneity by her
living Lord. An informed consciousness of her catholicity

will not confine it to Sacramentalists, Legalists or Evangelicals. Are not her past, present and prospective align-
ments one story, one strife, one defeat, one victory, and one
undivided life expressed in diverse forms, pursuant to a
foreordained plan slowly emergent from the wear and tear
of human agencies ?

In behalf of her higher unity and loyalty, the wisdom
of this Conference, under the Holy Spirit's inspiration,
may bridge the gulf between freedom and authority. If
when clearly apprehended and defined these are complementary, why should not the very nature of the Church and
of her sacred ordinances imply an order which begins and
ends with freedom, passing from that freedom which obeys
lawful authority to the larger freedom to which such obedience leads ? At this juncture, however, her dogmas inter-
vene with their Roman Catholic assertion of infallibility
for an Office and their Protestant assertion of infallibility
for a Book. The strongest arguments against these out-
pacings of God's purpose in relation to Church or Bible
are derived from moral sources. If we are ready to admit
that both are essentially vital and progressive and subject
to the conditions imposed upon their revelation by human
elements, we have at our command those ethical weapons
that cut through the tangle of scholastic reasonings.

The Church as the extension of her Lord's Incarnation
has been and must always be the companion of earthly
circumstances. She has followed their lead, not always to
her spiritual advantage, but because in the main they
offered her the best available guidance for the shaping of
her course. If this is a correct statement of her historic
policy, I see no reason why we should have to appeal to
precedents, however venerable, for the solution of every
problem. We are not prepared to say that we do not in the
least care about what happened in the past except as it
enables us to see our way through that which is happening
now. Quite otherwise, the stress upon origins in creed or
organisation, whether conforming or non-conforming, is
illuminating. But I know no theory of the Church, her
doctrine, her ministry or her sacraments, which contains

their measureless significance for the transmission of God's
saving grace. In Gœthe's words :

" All theory, my friend, is gray,
But green is life's bright golden tree."

Our finest conceptions of the Church are therefore
tentative and predictive rather than absolute and final.
None has so wholly embodied the holy mysteries of redemption as to be immune to the ameliorating, expanding influence of time and the Lord. Hence institutions should be
studied, not in the abstract alone, but in the concrete ; in
their incessant contacts with those whose hearts their
ordinances have purified and ennobled. Their primal
energies were not hierarchical, nor born of organisation, nor
marshalled by officialism. They were begotten by the
Spirit of God in the spirit of man, and whatever draperies
they wear, they are by nature ethical and religious. Likewise, the nature of the Church is not regulated by her
history, but by the divine life within her as the maker of
that history. And her authority consists in her ability
to freely communicate that life for the regeneration of
human society.

V

I do not presume to discuss at length the contentions
crystallising around the affirmation or denial of Catholic
doctrine as the inevitable outcome of New Testament
teaching. Yet it seems clear that no historic or local communion has hitherto borne an exclusive witness to the
saving truths of God. This witness is to be found in the
joint consent and fidelity of all the Churches as guardians
of the universal tradition of the Gospel. The principle of
development, congenital to the living organism of the Church,
explains the evolution of her doctrinal and sacramental
systems. From the first, believing men made trial of new
theories for their faith, formulated the doctrine of the
Trinity, allowed some to maintain, without expulsion from
the Church, the " adoptionist " conception of our Lord's
Sonship for seven hundred years, and arrived at other

decisions of lasting significance. In brief, Christian theology was treated as a vital science in which no article was so perfect in its primary stages that it required nothing in addition. The Apostles and their successors received from our Lord the seed of faith, and the nucleus of a coherent system of belief; a vital seed, a vital nucleus, to be developed according to their potentialities under the Holy Spirit's illumination.

We reverently believe that He has brought us to this place for the furtherance of His will. We would not, therefore, needlessly restrict our conciliar activity. In truth, it is already narrow enough, and the avenues leading toward federation all too few, without being hampered by avoidable embarrassments. The reciprocal gifts of the Conference should confirm the truth that the Church has wrought successfully under diverse forms and policies. It should teach us that those who refuse to consider any other system than their own, labour under the mistaken impression that the Spirit abandoned His mission when their particular system was evolved. It should show us that Catholicity becomes sectarian when imprisoned within the frontiers of any single form of Church development. It should enforce afresh the lesson that God has been pleased to reveal Himself in sundry times and divers manners, ever old and ever new, the new being but an expansion of the old, and both a continuance of His redemptive purpose. It should lead us to those serener heights where hard and fast lines of system melt without change of creed, while spirituality and charity attain their native universality.

In firm reliance upon Him who has called us to do His work in the world, we may better understand whether the Church is an absolute or a relative institution; the episcopacy as an ancient and essential centre of Christian history, doctrine and work; and conceive of the Holy Sacraments in sympathetic and inclusive ways as against those which are separative. The connection of an absolute external authority over the Christian life with the individual believer's experience of that life requires elucidating. How the doctrine of an indispensable sacerdotal mediation through the ordained priesthood can be adapted to the religious needs of a democratic age, is a matter upon which I for one crave light. I appeal to historic Communions whose roots stretch back far and wide in the religious consciousness of the race to share with us any secrets of the Lord's Presence in Church and Sacrament which He has vouchsafed to them. Above all else, some of us would fain know if there is a possible agreement between those who seek God in man as the Reason within his reason, the Conscience within his conscience ; and others who, while assenting to man's creation in the divine image, confess the Deity's eternal and transcendent Being.

Indeed, the guidance of the Conference upon these and other momentous issues which are implicated in the subjective and objective ideas of the Faith is earnestly solicited by many of us who approach them with eager and open minds. The cherished elements of all the creeds must focus in our blessed Lord. Some of these are enriched by ageless memories of Apostles and Fathers ; others by the devotional enthusiasm of the Middle Ages ; still others by the Reformation and Counter-Reformation movements ; and not a few by the Puritanism and Evangelicalism which have played a signal part in modern Churchmanship, especially in Great Britain and America. All belong to the implicit or explicit Catholicism which shall yet regain undiluted its original significance, because the Church is God's living organism who shall fulfil Christ's own promise that against her the gates of Hades cannot prevail, for hers is the deathless life of the Deity Himself.

THE RIGHT REV. ALEXANDER RAFFAY, D.D.
Bishop of Budapest (Lutheran)

Like the individual, each human group is a living organisation, which reveals its character through its origin and the manifestations of its life. The Apostles' Creed calls the Church a " communion of the saints," that is, of believers. The first believers in Christ were those disciples who adhered to Him and from whose ranks He chose the Apostles ; and the Church at this day is still the fellowship of those who adhere to Christ and are ready to yield apostolic service.

The Church took its first steps along the road pointed to by the words " ye shall be my witnesses to the ends of the earth " (Acts i, 8). It is to a task of *witness* that the Church is called : to witness at home as well as abroad. But since " the Kingdom of God is not in word, but in power " (1 Cor. iv, 20), the work of witness includes the effectual exercise of those spiritual powers which give form and cohesion to human life ; for it is through the output of energy that Christianity is " a new creation " (2 Cor. v, 17). This spiritual energy of witness is active alike in preaching, in moral influence and in the sanctification of life (Eph. iv, 20 ff.).

The Church is essentially spiritual. Jesus said, " Ye shall receive power when the Holy Spirit is come upon you " (Acts i, 8). The Holy Spirit worked in the Apostles from faith to faith (Rom. i, 17), changing the unbelieving into believers. Force and compulsion are wholly alien to the being of the Church. The words " compel them to come in " (Luke xiv, 23) refer only to persuasion, to spiritual compulsion. It is of the essence of the Church to lead souls to the Redeemer ; the converted soul of its own accord brings its body for hallowing.

It is a corollary of the Church's spiritual nature and of its call to witness that its relation to externals and dogmas is that of a man to his clothing and speech. A man is fittingly clad if his clothes are well-made and attractive ; he gains dignity from the use of pure and winning speech ; yet neither clothes nor utterance can affect the value and obligation of his calling. The Church can change the external aids and the dogmas through which and in which it expresses truth, without changing its nature, its calling, or the truth with which it is entrusted ; of this, two millenniums of Church history are a sufficient proof. " The life is more than raiment," as Jesus said.

A mirror may be never so smooth and clean, yet the dust

will settle upon it. So it is with the Church. The dust of the world, as we can see from the changing story of externals and dogmas, settles on its mirror : it must be detected and removed. " Be not conformed to this world, but be ye transformed by the renewing of your minds, that ye may prove what is that good and acceptable and perfect will of God." The continuous purifying work of the Spirit of God is reformation ; to condemn the Reformation is short-sighted, for the Church essentially needs continuous reformation.

The law of development affects the Church as it does every living organism. Life is not mere existence : it is activity, and therefore it both can and ought to move forward and develop. The Church is also affected, like the physical world, by centrifugal and centripetal forces. Gravitation effects an equilibrium between physical forces of these two kinds : while in the life of the Church it is fidelity to the Word of God which balances the centrifugal force—that which diversifies confessions and makes for progress—against the centripetal, the orthodox tendency towards rigidity. Unchanging fidelity to the Word is essential to the Church, for the eternal changeless Word of God is the one sure ground, guide, hedge and plumbline of the Church's life. " Other foundation can no man lay than that is laid, which is Jesus Christ."

The Church, according to its nature, brings together into unity those who believe in Christ. It is thus not an end in itself but a means and a framework. It is the Body of Christ, in which His Spirit dwells. The body consists of members, none of which has equal value with the whole, and none of which can count the others to be superfluous or worthless, since each has its appointed calling and work. " There are diversities of gifts, but the same Spirit." The Church can, therefore, have no room for mutual condemna-tion : " Judge not, that ye be not judged " ; nor for affixing the stigma of heresy : " who art thou, that thou judgest another's servant ? To his own master he standeth or falleth." " He that judgeth me is the Lord."

In conformity with its nature, the Church owes to

believers, and believers owe one another, a duty of protection. " He that hath not the Spirit of Christ is none of His." " If we live in the Spirit, let us also walk in the Spirit." The keeping of this injunction excludes something more than sin : it precludes the danger of the intrusion of an alien spirit, and the perversion or extrusion of Christ's spirit from the Church. History shows clearly that whenever there has been a firm hold upon the life-giving Spirit of Christ, the Church has always been convincingly strong and victorious, whereas it has always fallen away when allied or identified with a spirit which is not His.

The Church is the executor of an ordinance of God, and thus it is its nature to serve. Within the Church all men are servants and none is master, far less lord. Her one Master, Lord and Ruler is Christ, who rules within her daily through His word. Believers are all equal in value and in vocation as branches in the one Vine, which is Jesus Christ. In God's sight there is no distinction of grade. The " clerical estate " has no basis or justification within the Church, since " one is your master, your father, your Rabbi : the greatest among you shall be your servant." Within the fellowship of believers the only distinctions which mark off brother from brother are those of task and service, since all are God's children. Yet the nature of the Church admits also of a need for overseers, " bishops," called to play the part of stronger branches, able to support the weaker and to nurture them with the life-force which flows from Christ. For the Spirit's sake, which we have received, we are responsible not for ourselves alone, but also for the brethren, whom the stronger are bidden to support.

It is of the nature of the Church to be a helper for those who seek and love God, leading them to God and keeping them in Him. The Church is a sign-post rather than an omnibus : it points faithfully along the road leading to the goal. Each man must traverse the road for himself, and to none is it guaranteed that he will reach the end. Of mediators the Church can know nothing, nor of ideas of propitiation. Jesus Himself said, " thy faith hath saved thee "; " he that shall endure to the end, the same shall be saved." " Be thou faithful unto death, and I will give thee the crown of life."

It is of the nature of the Church that the Spirit working within it reveals Himself in manifold ways. Historically the Church has taken various forms : yet ecclesiastical unity was not diminished by confessional division. Many flowers can grow on one stem. The human spirit can survive many processes of bodily change. The chief matter is unity of spirit. Confessional division serves to afford opportune expression for individual varieties which God allows and which have their warrant in psychology. " There must be sects among you, that they which are approved may be made manifest." Yet the Church as the fellowship of believers unites them all, to whatever historical organisation and fellowship they belong. This invisible Church is the only universal, Catholic Church indispensable to salvation, Orthodox, Roman, and Protestant Catholicism being three of its forms.

It follows from what has been said that " apostolic succession " does not depend on the imposition of hands, nor upon any outward act and solemnity, nor upon the creed. It depends solely upon the identity of the Holy Spirit, and of our vocation and calling. Therefore the effort of our Conference towards unity in faith and order is fully justified, practicable and doubtless well-pleasing to God. What the historic life of the Church has caused to err may, by the same life, be brought back to the right way. Nothing is needed for the task but firm faith and the Spirit of Christ. So may God ordain it to be!

THE RT. REV. THE BISHOP OF MANCHESTER
(Anglican)

Our purpose is to learn from one another, and to that end it seems to me that we can best help each other if, in these preliminary discussions before the Sections meet, we try to state our own opinions, especially on those points where there may be differences between some members of the Conference. We must first define our differences with precision if we are to be able to overcome them.

Dr. Parkes Cadman began his eloquent address by speaking of the Church as "God's living organism for the world's redemption" and closed it with the striking declaration, "The Church is God's living organism who shall fulfil Christ's own promise that against her the gates of Hades cannot prevail, for hers is the deathless life of the Deity Himself." I gather from the previous course of his remarks that the aspect of an organism which specially interests him in this connection is that which is expressed in the Hegelian definition : An organism is what it is, in that it is always becoming that which it is not. But of course Dr. Cadman, and also Hegel, would agree that in order to be any particular organism it must have a definite structure which sets limits to the kind of development that is possible for it. Moreover, the structure of an organism is determined largely by reference to its functions. So we go back to St. Paul's description of the Church as the Body of Christ, from which all thought of it as an organism takes its origin. As His Body it is the organism of His Spirit, through which normally and chiefly He accomplishes His work. That work is indeed the redemption of the world ; but that phrase too requires definition, for upon our conception of it will depend our conception of the Church which is to serve as the instrument for the accomplishment of this work. We may put it in two apparently different ways. We may say that it is a ministry of reconciliation whereby men are delivered one by one from the alienation of sin and are brought to that true sonship to God for which they were created ; or we may say that it is the fashioning of a society bound together in the bonds of a love which both answers to, and reproduces, the love of God, its Creator, Redeemer and Sanctifier. But these are only two ways of saying one thing. For the individual who becomes in the full sense a child of God finds himself by the same act a member of God's family ; and he who is brought into the fellowship of God, is brought into the fellowship of love (for God is love), so that salvation is always of its very nature social and not in any exclusive sense individual. For this reason St. Paul delights to speak of the Church as the society in which all natural divisions of men are overcome. Distinction of gift and function will remain, as he shows in his analogy of the many limbs in the one body. But division, either as separation or as antagonism, is abolished. " There is neither Jew nor Gentile "—the deepest of all divisions based on religious history overcome ; " there is neither Greek not barbarian " —the deepest of all cultural divisions overcome ; " there is neither bond nor free "—the deepest of all social and economic divisions overcome ; " there is neither male nor female "—the deepest of all human divisions overcome. (I have, of course, conflated the passages in Galatians and Colossians.) What then is the secret ? It is that " Christ is all in all " so completely that in place of all those divided groups there is " one man in Christ Jesus " : all men and women who are members of His Church so utterly possessed by His Spirit that, in a true sense, they constitute one Person, and that Person Christ. Here is a glorious corollary of the Lord's own promise that where two or three are gathered together in His name there should be found not merely a crowd or a group in the technical psychological sense, transcending the sum of its individual units as such a crowd or group always does, but there should be found the Lord in person.

St. Paul sees this " one man in Christ Jesus," who is also the " Body of Christ," growing towards a perfection as yet not revealed ; only when all races are converted and sanctified, only when Christ can live and work in all mankind with all its various capacities shall we see " the measure of the stature of the completeness of the Christ "— all that He is in Himself, all that He can be and do for us.

Such a vision kindles our hearts. But now come the difficulties. In the apostolic age no one called himself a Christian who was not in deadly earnest. There was little risk from a multitude of luke-warm adherents, and there was not a very prevalent danger of such disunion as would tear the Church into pieces, though the state of affairs at Corinth shows that this already existed. On the whole, unpopularity and persecution tend to purge a Church of indifferent members and to hold it together in unity, though it is worth noticing that they damage its spirit in other ways, tending to make it hard and unsympathetic. I suppose that what was unlovely in the Pharisees was largely due to Antiochus Epiphanes, and that certain clauses in the *Quicunque Vult* were indirectly the work of Gothic Unitarians. We cannot rely on persecution to keep the Church true to its central message or to preserve its unity. At the present time, all tendencies are towards unity. The individualism of the early and middle nineteenth century is dead. Collectivism in one form or another sweeps everything before it. On every side there is a disposition to slur over differences (except of class and of race) and to lay stress on agreement. Such a situation gives us our opportunity; but it is also full of peril, for it is as certain as anything human can well be that the pendulum will after a time swing back, and the divisive tendencies again come to the fore. The form of the unity towards which we work must be determined with reference to the strain to which that unity may be subjected. It is right that aspirations after Christian unity should be expressed when the general movement of thought and feeling is towards unity; but it is vital that the form of unity should be designed to curb and check the tendency to division when that once more is prevalent.

Of course this does not mean that the unity should be rigid or inelastic; still less that it should express itself in uniformity. Nothing could more effectively ensure its future disruption than that. It must be elastic, deliberately containing and welcoming a rich variety, so that all who do not lose the spirit of tolerance may find a place within it. If men go out not because there is no room for them inside but because there is room also for too many others, no scheme of unity can stop them. But our aim must be to comprehend all who hold the common faith and trust to the one Lord.

The obvious danger here is that the Church will become a society of men of good-will and lose all power through losing all individuality. What is necessary to avert this danger in the present and that of renewed disruption in the future is that all Christians should agree on certain principles as constitutive of, and essential to, the Church. First among these is the doctrine of God : of that we were thinking yesterday. But agreement upon that does not give us visible unity, unless we can agree to differ upon all other matters, including the ministry and sacraments. And I for one am convinced that such agreement to differ as regards the ministry and sacraments would be the way to ensure disruption almost as soon as reunion on such a basis were achieved.

For the unity we seek is a unity which effectively binds together in fellowship those who by nature tend to be at variance. It did not need incarnate God to tell men to love their friends ; we have not yet learnt how to obey His command to love our enemies. It is no miracle of grace when Evangelicals worship together in harmony, or when Catholics do the same. Differences of organisation based on differences of temperament, of taste or of tradition are real offences against the purpose for which the Church exists ; they stereotype the very divisions which the Church exists to overcome. A unity which was a mere federation of such elements would seem to me to have betrayed the cause for which alone that unity is truly desirable.

At this point most of us here should have a sense of guilt. Certainly the Church of England, for which alone I can speak with knowledge, does not at all perfectly succeed in welding into one living fellowship the persons of differing traditions and temperament whom it comprehends. But it is making some progress ; the tendencies towards synthesis are stronger than those of mutual exclusiveness.

Where in fact are we to find the principle of cohesion on which we may rely in times when men again tend to part asunder because of differing opinions ? There is the doctrine of God, based on Scripture and formulated in the historic creeds : of that we spoke yesterday. I would mention three others which in combination will, I believe, be effective, but any of which alone will, I believe, be insufficient. First there are the sacraments, of which we are to speak later. Secondly, there is the ministry, of which one aspect falls naturally into this place. The third is the living relation of the Church to Christ Himself. As the regards the ministry, some tell us that the Book of the Acts describes the Apostles as the nucleus of the Church, round whom the general body of believers was grouped ; some say that the general body was the primary fact and that this delegated authority to the Apostles. I believe that neither of these views is correct, and that each is possible because the truth in some sense includes them both. To me it seems, according to the record, that when the physical presence of the Lord was withdrawn there was found as fruit of His Ministry a society with the Apostolate, as the accepted focus of authority, within it. Neither is prior to the other ; each receives its significance from the other. But the actual fact is an Apostolic Church. And some steps at least were taken to provide for an Apostolic succession. Therefore, I am never much interested in claims to an Apostolic succession where there is no continuous body of believers ; but I am persuaded that a body of believers which has within it no ministry approved by Apostolic succession has let go something of real value. For our fellowship must be not only with contemporaries but with the saints of past generations and by hope also with saints that are yet unborn. It is a fellowship in the eternal things. The congregation in which we worship when we lift up our hearts to our Lord is not the few folk in the same building nor those alive on earth at the same time. It is angels and archangels and all the company of heaven. Therefore, a ministry more effective than the historic order for immediate purposes (if such could be devised) would still lack just that value which belongs to that order because it is the historic order. We cannot now cause any other order to be the historic order. As the outward symbol of fellowship both across the oceans and across the centuries the historic order of the

F

ministry is a potent, though manifestly not an omnipotent, instrument of unity. And as no other order can now have just this quality, the historic order is a necessary part of the expression of that unity which belongs inalienably to the Church as the whole number of those who confess in Jesus Christ their Saviour, Lord and God.

In any case, it is vital to recognise that the early Church shows no recollection of any moment when disciples of Christ met together to constitute the Church as an organised society. In germ its organisation was there from the outset. It is not a human contrivance. It is the continuation of that divine intrusion into human history which we call the Incarnation. And this has practical value. For in accepting the principle of a society, so given, as distinct from fashioning one to suit ourselves, we have some bulwark against Pelagianism, the most invidious, the most disastrous, and in our day the most pervasive of heresies.

So I come to the third and last principle of unity. It is the relation of the Church to Jesus Christ. The Church is His Body. The actual society of believers is only qualified to be called the Church in so far as it is organic to His Spirit, moving at once in immediate and perfect correspondence with His will. Here is the ground of the Church's unity, because here is the source of its life. It will never be sufficient, for while we are born as infants and reach maturity only by slow growth, there will always, even in a perfect Church, be those whose dedication is as yet imperfect and who need outward aids. For all of our very imperfect selves these are most necessary. Nevertheless, it is not in them that the unity of the Church is grounded ; not in creeds nor sacraments nor ministry. These are modes or expressions of its unity, and means of maintaining it in the experience of men. The unity is grounded in the one Lord. And it may be that the main upshot of this Conference will be to teach us all in a new way the need of deeper personal discipleship in ourselves and throughout the membership of our several denominations as the first condition to be fulfilled before the outward unity of the Church can be restored.

PROFESSOR FERNAND MÉNÉGOZ, D.D.

University of Strasbourg (Lutheran)

Certainly we are at one in rejecting two views of the nature of the Church : that which identifies a particular ecclesiastical organisation with the Kingdom of God, and that which makes a radical division between the visible and the invisible Church. Over against these two views, it would seem that theological reflection may well take the following as a starting-point for the consideration of our subject : the unity of the Church as a psycho-physical organism which, as a whole, unfolds itself spontaneously in a rich efflorescence of religious groups having each of them a marked individual character. In the reality of our earthly experience the Church is the totality of the various denominations claiming the name of Jesus Christ, being the sphere in which the divine " Pneuma " breathes, as the agent of human redemption : or briefly, the Church is the " Body of Christ," animated by the Holy Spirit.

From this solid basis we can move on one step to-day, I think, in a new direction. Let us apply to the Church the current distinction between *conscious* and *unconscious* spirit. Let us differentiate in the deep life of the Church between conscious and unconscious, or semi-conscious, levels. In so doing we can take for our guide the passage (1 Cor. ii, 6-16) in which St. Paul lays down the *charta* alike of the general theory of knowledge in religion and also of the special theory of the self-knowledge of the Church. We may then hope to make some progress in understanding the serious and anxious question with which we are confronted.

What is the specific property of *spirit* ? Self-knowledge, the passage from unconsciousness to self-consciousness. It is then the mark of the spirit of the Church—in which the Spirit of God and Christ is perpetually active—to rise, from the sub-conscious level, to an ever-clearer and more adequate consciousness of the purposes of God revealed by the purposes of Jesus Christ. What is the life, what is the tradition of the Church, but a ceaseless appeal of the " Pneuma " of Christ urging the soul of Christendom to rise from unconsciousness into consciousness, that is, to an increasingly complete knowledge of the divine plan, to a fuller sharing on man's part of that consciousness of Himself which the Spirit of God possesses ? In its normal structure the Church is so made as to *grow* into Jesus Christ, its head, in all things (Eph. iv, 15).

There are obviously members of the one true Church who remain, for the time at least, religiously unconscious or half-conscious. Such, for instance, are children ; then the indifferent or hardened, the dead-weight which the Church reluctantly carries, who are merely those members of Christ's fellowship who are not yet aware of, or have not aroused to action, the ideal of the Christian life ; then, too, those who formerly were called " heretics," who either allowed an alien philosophy to cut them off from the main life-stream of the " Pneuma " or, while still keeping contact with the " Pneuma," failed intellectually to discern the true spiritual realities on which their convictions were based ; lastly, those who, with a practical deification of their own individual religious group, and putting the authority of their Church in the place of divine authority, nurture themselves less upon the full rich consciousness of the authentic Christ-Spirit than on the relatively narrow and sectarian consciousness of a limited ecclesiastical body which takes its own unshared triumph to be the true end of human history.

Yet, are not all these types, for varying reasons, uninitiated as yet into a Christian consciousness which is ever growing in depth and width ? And are not all Church activities—teaching, edification (public and private), evangelisation, preventive or curative social work, theological enquiry—are not all these so many ways of trying to lead the spirit of the Church onward from unconsciousness to consciousness, and to provide for it a continuous extension of its field of vision ? To make us conscious of the grace given us in having been planted from our birth, through no merit of our own, within the family of God's children ; to make us more and more clearly conscious of those divine purposes which, while ever the same, require in every age fresh schemes of action for the solution of new problems incessantly opened up by the Christian consciousness—is not this the starting point of every work of God in and through the Church? And if we to-day, gathered here, have as our first problem the recognition of the true nature of the Church, is not this a remarkable confirmation of what I am saying? Does not the meeting of this Conference prove that in fact, through the activity of the living Spirit of Christ, the range of Christian consciousness has in these last days gained wonderfully in clearness and in breadth?

Obviously, we are becoming aware, over and above the diversity of complementary gifts, of a constitutional divergence between types of religious personality, a divergence of God's ordering and probably irreducible. One type tends to furnish the " divine presence " with *visibility* (in the letter of Scripture and of Creeds, in the Eucharistic elements and in the person of ministers duly ordained for teaching and for liturgy), while another holds strictly to a belief in an *invisible*, wholly spiritual presence of God and Christ, distinct in principle from any of its sensible manifestations. Still, if they take account of the contrast between these types, as the pivot on which most matters of dispute among Christians seem to turn, the members of the one true Church take account of it only in order to transcend it by accepting it humbly in a spirit of respect, helpfulness and brotherly love. For, at the same time, we have become aware at last of our profound oneness in Jesus Christ, our only Lord. We were one in Him, and yet we knew it not! But, by the grace of God, we know it now, and, knowing it, we must needs seek to give tangible expression to this oneness. To gain this end, to effect a concrete reconstruction of the " Body " of Christ, torn asunder hitherto, and to manifest in the world of sense that imperative desire for spiritual unification which belongs to the very nature of the Church of Jesus Christ, one means is requisite, primary, most sure in action : it is *prayer, common intercession*, in response to the light shed abroad in the Christian consciousness by the Holy Spirit. With intercession for them that were His, Jesus Christ built up the

Church; and the Church, by praying in every place in the consciousness of its incomparable mission, for its own restoration and the salvation of mankind, will take the first step, soon to be followed by others—that is, by action —towards accomplishing the work of its divine Founder.

THE REV. H. B. WORKMAN, D.D.
Principal, Westminster College, London (Methodist)

Let me explain the standpoint of this address. In any discussion we must never forget that a Church necessitates a confession of faith, a Christian fellowship and some form of ministry. These are not accidents; they are of its essence. They are all subjects that will be treated in other sessions; nevertheless, they must ever be present in our thought. A living confession of faith is the rock upon which the Church is built; a fellowship one with another is the inevitable outcome of the glad tidings; while a ministry or service for others is one of the privileges to which Christ Himself called His disciples. Of the sacraments also I will say nothing, though here again they cannot be far from our thoughts. The omission of these great notes of the Church somewhat reduces to an abstraction the whole discussion.

We are left to ask what is the one underlying necessity or function which lies at the root and constitutes the reality of this primary concept, remembering always that this fellowship only finds itself in conjunction with a confession of faith and a living fellowship.

I find this reality in life, a life that is divine in origin and end. The Church is not a loose envelope or a skin that in some vague way enwraps its members; nor is the Church the sum of its members—whether the *militia Christi* or the *universitas viatorum*, " the guild of travellers "—ideas that we find emerging at different times; much less is the Church the guild of its ministers; nor is it primarily the instrument for the profession of a faith.

The Church is a living organism with a life comparable

to that of any other organism in its laws of growth and retardation, only grander, richer, fuller, for it is an organism instinct with the divine life and with an oversoul in which we can find the workings of the Holy Spirit Himself. I would plead that we start here ; that our stress must be upon life ; that in all our thinking the uppermost thought should be that of a living organism giving value and vitality to all the several members, an organism in which we find a note possessed by no other organism, its deathless eternal character—the emphasis of its continuity—the gates of Hades powerless against it.

Let me put my plea in another way. There are two main ways in which we can view the Church—one static, the other dynamic. These, of course, are not exclusive. A dynamic view without static elements simply spells explosion; static without dynamic means fossilisation. Even the most static Churches must realise that something more is needed. Rome finds this in a theory of development. Purely static forms of Protestantism are being driven from their dug-outs by the shells of higher criticism. Every static, if it would live, must have in it something dynamic ; every dynamic that would deliver itself from the nebulosity and uselessness of a comet's tail must have due regard to a static balance. But with this caution I stand to plead here for the dynamic concept of the Church as the one in which we shall find best our lines of approach towards reunion.

What are the results of thus viewing the Church ? In the first place, creed as expressed in symbol or formula becomes no longer rigid and ceases to be the sole basis. Creeds will themselves have a growth, the growth of life. The old formula of Vincent, *quod ab omnibus, quod semper, quod ubique*, gives place to this concept of growth, though as in all other growth there will be the continuity of the divine sap, and as in all other growth change will lie in development of offshoots, not in change of structure, in new adaptations for a new environment, and not in new genus or species. The creed is a manifestation of life, the divine life immanent in the Church, a life expanding with the expanding ages which are another manifestation of the same immanence ; creed is not the basis, fixed, immutable of this life, but the outcome. Creed is thus the expression of living experience, slowly changing with the growth of that experience. All creeds are the attempts, poor at their best, to express in a sentence some great fact of spiritual experience. In themselves, apart from that experience, they give us no more insight into reality than the chemist's formula for water can give us a vision of the beauty of the lake at our feet (Geneva). We speak of Nicea. The struggle between Athanasius and Arius was not one of logic, a dispute about a Greek iota. The men who framed the creed had just passed through the persecutions of Diocletian, and in the midst of the fiery furnace they had seen at their side one like to the Son of Man. The Old Guard do not easily forget their emperor ; the martyrs could not surrender aught of the glory of the Christ through whom they had conquered. Logic may have been on the side of Arius ; life and experience won on the side of Athanasius. Other illustrations might be given of the dynamic basis of every creed, but time forbids. What I desire to point out is this : life, not creed, must lie at the root of our concept of the Church, inasmuch as creed so far as it grips the souls and intellects of men must be the expression of facts in the divine life and experience of the age. Do not let me be misunderstood. There is a continuity of life binding us with ancestors, two, three or four thousand years ago, possibly with lake dwellers in pre-historic Switzerland. But the main thing is not the continuity, valuable as that is, but the fact of life in the present with its vastly richer experiences and possibilities. So in the Church of God. It is the experience of to-day governed of course by a continuity with the past, an experience richer, fuller and with greater possibilities of bringing a larger world into touch with God and of seeing God at work in this larger world of life and thought, that must really govern us in all our efforts at reunion.

The Church is more than an institution. Institutions pass away ; the Church of God abideth. Her life is ever putting forth new forms in which she may find herself. As Bishop Brent preached to us his great sermon in the Cathedral, my thoughts went back to another scene in the same Cathedral seven hundred years ago, to the day when Rudolph of Hapsburg was present at its consecration. The Holy Roman Empire has passed away. The mediæval Church as then known has also passed away. But one thing has not passed away : the power of the pure in heart to catch a vision of the eternal and to enjoy the real presence of Christ. It is in life that we find the truest continuity ; life which is deeper, richer than any institution, giving to every institution its meaning and value.

Again, to view the Church from the standpoint of life is to recognise the proper place in the Church of the Holy Spirit. Only with difficulty can theology maintain a place for the Holy Spirit in a rigid, institutional or credal Church. The more sacramentalism emphasises the real presence of Christ to the exclusion of all else, or Protestantism treats Bible or Creed as the final word of God for all time, the more difficult it is to give full expression to the work of the Spirit, save indeed in His merely individualistic workings. But if we emphasise life, then the Spirit is this life, guiding a living Church to all truth. We get a unity, a plan underlying all the developments of Church activities, a goal to which we are being divinely led, a possible synthesis of all new knowledge in one ever-growing, richer faith.

To view the Church from the standpoint of life gives us also room for infinite variety in its manifestation. Life without variety is dead. This seems a truism, but how different history would have been if it had been recognised! The infinite variety of life in the Christian Church, the hermit, the monk, the friar, the mystic, the Covenanter, the Quaker, the Methodist, the Anglican, the Roman, the Orthodox, all alike are different manifestations of the one Divine Life. If the Church had conceived of itself as life, what anguish of soul, what schisms and splits, what wasted opportunities, would have been avoided! Only thus shall we discover our unity as we discern that our varieties, except in so far as they have been mere fashions of moments of time, have all contributed something to the totality of the one life. Institutions, forms, creeds—valuable and necessary as they are—will then all become secondary to the concept that where Christ is, there is His Church. " Is the Master with us ? " will become the acid test of our variety ; that He is with us, the bond of our unity.

The Conference adjourned at 12.30 p.m.

FRIDAY AFTERNOON, AUGUST 5TH.

The Session was opened with devotions at 4 p.m., with Dr. GARVIE in the chair, and the free discussion of Subject III—the Nature of the Church—was introduced by Dr. SIEGMUND-SCHULTZE.

PROFESSOR DR. FRIEDRICH SIEGMUND-SCHULTZE
University of Berlin (Evangelical-Lutheran)

The ten-minute speakers in the afternoon are expected to summarise the views that have been expressed. I feel it immensely difficult to make a summary of the views about the Church which have found expression to-day ; and I assume that I am only to summarise what may serve as a basis for bringing us together. In attempting to formulate propositions which could form such a basis, I would add by way of preface that in my judgment the truth about an organism like the Church, which is both spiritual and bodily, must take the form not of simple theses, each of which might have an antithesis to contradict it, but rather of " tensions." Thus in Christ Himself there is a " tension," an apparent incompatibility, between His human and His divine nature ; and so also there is a " tension " between the Church as a divine foundation and the Church as a human society. I will, therefore, set over against each other a series of twofold theses, balancing the divine origin of the Church on the one side against its human and social aspect on the other, and suggesting that the truth lies in a combination of both.

On the one hand, the Church is the highest thing with which our earthly knowledge brings us into contact. It is closely knit-up with Jesus Christ : it is the mystical Body of Christ.

On the other hand, the Church is not an institution apart from its human members, nor above or beyond those whom Jesus Christ has called ; it is identical with the fellowship of believers and thus embraces all who have come to believe in Christ.

There can be but one Body of Christ, as there is but one Spirit of Jesus which rules the Body.

Yet again, the word " Body of Christ " implies a plurality of members ruled by this Spirit ; it implies not only a difference between members but also a difference of functions. The uniformity of its members cannot be the goal of the Church ; rather, unity in diversity is a law of its being.

The Church, as being destined for all men, is universal.

On the other hand, the fact that the fellowship of Jesus is divided signifies the duty of working for union, as also the social responsibility of all members for each other, and that love of our neighbour which knows no limits.

The Church is holy, because the revelation of God is committed to it. Thus its continuity, from the Apostles whom Jesus sent out, to our own day, is an essential mark of the Church.

On the other hand the truth finds its sphere not in a transmitted official authority, but in the sanctification which lives in the Society. No Apostle and no Council is guaranteed against error ; it is only the Fellowship which follows the leading of the Spirit that is to be guided into all the truth. This is entirely true of the local church, but is also true of the Society as a whole, of ecumenical Councils.

The Body of Christ bears the " marks of the Lord Jesus." In this age the Church of Christ is a suffering and not a triumphant body. The resurrection must be preceded by the Cross. Yet the Church triumphant is closely related to the Church on earth.

The Society is more than the individual. As against that individualism which ascribes inspiration to the individual only, we must recognise that the loftier powers are at the disposal of the Society as a whole. Where two or three are gathered in Christ's name, there He is in the midst of them.

These antitheses between the divine mission and the human realisation of the Church are in fact so closely bound together that they might form a basis for the effort towards unity.

THE MOST REV. METROPOLITAN STEFAN
Archbishop of Sofia, Bulgaria (Orthodox).

The Church, the body of those who are *called*, is the Society of those who hold the true faith in the triune God, the faithful of all places, times and peoples ; the Society whose members have received baptism in Jesus Christ who called them, either directly or through the holy Apostles, who follow His saving doctrine, profess themselves to be His, and by Him are closely knit together, filled with life, and guided visibly towards life eternal by the active grace of the Holy Spirit. But the word " Church " has a wider meaning too. It means, above all, the aggregate of free and rational beings united in Jesus Christ as Head, summing up all things in the heavens and on the earth (Eph. i, 10, 20, 23). After the Fall there was a separation between the heavenly and the earthly, which disappears with the coming of Jesus Christ : all is made one in Him.

The first mark of the Christian Church is the unity of its members ; it is necessarily a closely-knit fellowship. As He left this world, the Saviour closed His converse with the Apostles by a prayer for His newly-founded Church (John xvii). He prayed that God the Father might give oneness in faith and in mutual love to the faithful in Christ, a unity rising into oneness with God Himself : " that they all may be one, as thou, Father, art in me and I in thee ; that they may be one in us, that the world may believe that thou hast sent me." "Father, that which thou hast given me, I will that, where I am, they also may be with me, that they may behold my glory which thou hast given me." So the Saviour prays for His whole Church, for its progress from strength to strength, from faith towards union with God, and from faith, through faith, towards the glory of the Son and of God : praying not only for the unity of the faithful, one with another, but also for that of the whole Church with its Head Jesus Christ, with God by Him, in glory everlasting and in the love of Father, Son and Holy Spirit.

To reach the glory of the Son and of God is to reach the lofty predestined end for which God created man. "And God said, Let us make man in our image and in our like-ness." "In the day that God created man, in the likeness of God made he him" (Gen. i, 26 ; v. 1). It is the high destiny of man to be made like God, to be made divine. "God became man," says St. Athanasius, "in order that we may be made divine." This is that "wisdom of God, hidden in a mystery, which was foreordained before the worlds for our glory" (1 Cor. ii, 7). But this end cannot be reached by pride, godlessness or separation from God, nor by that road of violence and usurpation into which our first fathers were led astray, but by the path which our Saviour followed and pointed out, by recollection, faith, and close union with God. And the close union of the faith-ful on earth in a spiritual organism is a thing so glorious that the world, be it never so unbelieving and antagonistic to the work of Jesus Christ, will draw nearer and nearer to the Saviour and, in the end, will believe in Him as the Messiah sent by God : "that they may be one is us, that the world may believe that thou hast sent me." The unbeliever, so says St. Paul, seeing this glorious thing, this unity, harmony, seemliness and good order of the Church, "will fall down on his face and worship God, declaring that God is among the Christians indeed" (1 Cor. xiv, 25).

Special emphasis must be laid on the fact that in His prayer for the Church the "Perfecter of our faith" is concerned not only that believers should be steadfast in the faith, but also that they should all be one. Here is a clear indication that if any man thinks himself to have the faith, and yet does not keep within the sublime unity of the faithful, he has reason to fear that he is outside the range of the saving prayer of Jesus Christ, and not within the sphere of salvation. For it is beyond doubt that only those are to be saved for whom the mediator between God and man uttered that prayer and in whom it is finding fulfilment. So it is that the Apostle, when bidding Christians to walk worthy of their vocation, urges them to " give diligence to keep the unity of the Spirit in the bond of peace," and adds, laying bare the foundation of Christian unity, " there is one body and one Spirit, even as ye are called in one hope of your calling ; one Lord, one faith, one baptism, one God and Father of all, who is over all, and through all, and in all " (Eph. iv, 3 ff.). From these last words not only does it follow that believers in Jesus Christ ought to form one single society, one spiritual union called the Church, but the basis of Church unity is made clear. The central and culminating point of Church unity, according to St. Paul, is God the Father : the Father who is " over all " by His supreme power, and " in us all " by the saving inward action of the Holy Spirit. In this same epistle St. Paul speaks of Jesus Christ as Head of the Church —His body. If the Church is the body of Jesus Christ, He is its heart, the principle of its life, and its head, its guiding wisdom. To be in union with Jesus Christ is to be one in Him with all believers : to be one with them in an indestructible alliance, far more closely knit than any merely human fellowship can be, an alliance which exists not merely for the supply of mutual need and for general advantage, but covers the whole of life.

But what is *belief in the Church* ? Orthodox belief in God's Church implies the conviction that all that the Church admits and teaches is true : and, more than this, it implies for the believer the duty of loving and honouring the Church as our common Mother, of yielding to her faithful and obedient sonship in all things, and extending as far as we can her spiritual blessings. The phrase " I believe in the Church " requires special attention. The Creed does not say " I believe the Church," but " I believe in the Church." The Church is a creature of God : why do we, whose belief is in God alone, profess belief in it ? And if faith is, as the Apostle says, the discovering of things unseen, why is belief required in the Church, which is primarily visible ? The expression " I believe in the Church " establishes the divine dignity of the Church : this belief is a habit of veneration for the Church. Although the Church is divinely created of human material, its Head is Christ Himself, very God, with the Holy Spirit who guides it perpetually by His divine teaching, a teaching which it is our duty to believe : as it is written, " believe the Gospel " (Mark i, 15). Belief in the Church is necessary, because the Church is not wholly visible : it carries with it belief in Jesus Christ its invisible Head, and in the holy sacraments, with their impartation of unseen grace to the faithful which is the proper object of faith.

According to apostolic teaching, the Church of Christ is a building, a spiritual house, a glorious temple, with a precious corner-stone as its foundation, the historic Christ, the God-man, the Redeemer. The Saviour Himself showed us this, in His promise to build the Church so firmly that the gates of hell would not prevail against it. On Christ then, as corner-stone, and on the foundation of the apostles and prophets, a spiritual building has been raised, a holy temple, made of living stones, of believers who have received the holy and life-giving Spirit and are not dead in sin. So St. Peter says, " unto whom coming, a living stone, ye also as living stones are built up a spiritual house " (1 Pet. ii, 4f.). " Ye are God's building," says St. Paul to the Corinthians. " According to the grace of God which was given me, as a wise master-builder, I laid a foundation ; and another buildeth thereon. But let each man take heed how he buildeth thereon. For other foundation can no man lay than that which is laid, which is Jesus Christ " (1 Cor. iii, 9-11). Faith and hope are the pillars which support the living stones on the sure foundation which is Jesus Christ, and love is the firm bond of union which unites them to the foundation and to each other.

Since the faithful of all ages are builders of the spiritual house, the Church is not finished once and for all : it is not a complete structure, but is still in course of building through the activity of the faithful, who labour " for the perfecting of the saints, unto the work of ministering, unto the building up of the body of Christ : till we all attain to the unity of the faith and of the Son of God, unto a full-grown man, unto the measure of the stature of the fulness of Christ " (Eph. iv, 12f.). In other words, the Church of God here on earth is a splendid but incomplete structure, which at the end of the world will reach up to heaven. The building of it, up to the measure of the fulness of Christ, is to go on for ages, and cannot be fully compassed by any one generation. Every believer, each age and generation doing its allotted part, achieves only a fragment of the great mission of the Church. It is thus that the Church is called Catholic and ecumenical.

When St. Paul says to the Corinthians that he laid the foundation and another is building on it, he does not mean that in his time there was no Christian Church at Corinth with its saving graces. St. Paul built a structure as well as laid a foundation, and each Corinthian who followed him became a " perfect " Christian, and all together formed a real Church. But he is speaking of the earlier stage of the building process, which was the basis of what followed, although the structure was in reality a complete building.

The body of Jesus Christ, the Church, the spiritual house, is to go on being built, St. Paul says, till all have one faith and one knowledge of the Son of God. One faith —there will be no more heathen. One knowledge of the Son of God—there will be no divergences between Christians, but all will have the same understanding of the Son of God, of the work of salvation which He has wrought on the earth, and of the right mode of apprehending it. To this end, Jesus Christ has given to His Church " some apostles, and some evangelists, and some pastors and teachers " (Eph. iv, 11) : that is, He has created in His Church a hierarchy of grace. At the head are the Apostles, who had every gift. These are the twelve, with St. Paul added to them ; they had seen and known the Lord, they were witnesses of His resurrection : they were sent directly by Him and filled with all the gifts of the Holy Spirit. They are also prophets, announcing the good news ; they are pastors, and possess the gift of healing. Every gift was in them and was by them set in its place in the Church. On them the Holy Spirit came in all His fulness, and by them He passed into the Church which He wholly fills. They are the channels of world-wide grace. The dignity of the apostolate, as held by the first Apostles, is unique. Nor does it need to be reproduced, for the Apostles put the Church in possession of their gifts ; they handed on the truths revealed to them by the Spirit of God, and the secrets of the hallowing of the faithful ; they ordained pastors to be their direct successors, whose mission and duty it was to keep that which the Apostles established in the Church and to maintain its effective influence upon the Christian Society and its members.

The Church lives on the apostolic treasure and on the grace proceeding from it, transmitted unbroken from one generation to another. And if anywhere this stream is interrupted, there is no true life in Jesus Christ the Lord.

Thus, if the holy apostolic Church is Catholic, universal, embracing the faithful of all nations, places and times ; if God is one, if the faith is one, if baptism is one, it is clear " what manner of persons we ought to be in all holy living and godliness, looking for and earnestly desiring the coming of the day of God " (2 Pet. iii, 11f.) ; it is clear that we all ought to press on towards that unity of the faith and of the knowledge of the Son of God which we have not yet reached : we must enter as living stones into the great spiritual structure, with full trust and hope that at its highest point, as it narrows towards heaven, we, though divided here below, may attain to the fulness of Christ and to full union one with another and with God our Saviour. Let us build! " But let each man take heed how he buildeth."

The Rev. Dr. Yoichiro Inagaki (Japan, Anglican)
expressed his general concurrence with the address of
Archbishop Chrysostom ; adding that the Nippon Sei
Kokwai stands for the two principles of continuity and
adaptation, as being a branch of the Holy Catholic and
apostolic Church which has found a way to adapt itself
in non-essentials to the environment and conditions of
Japanese life.

The Rev. Emile Vurpillot (France, Lutheran) : An
understanding upon the nature of the Church is vitally
necessary. We have before us many diverse and opposed
points of view : yet these all converge towards one centre,
and it is therefore possible to envisage a series of *syntheses*
retaining the essential truths which each represents.

Thus, if the Church is thought of on the one hand as
a society possessing absolute rights over the individual,
and on the other as a free association based on points of
agreement in faith or order, the conception of the Church
as an organism provides a possible synthesis here. As a
natural society in the order of grace, the Church is like a
family which has room both for the duties and for the
rights of the individual. Again, as between the thought of
the Church invisible (and yet real) and that of the visible
Church or Churches, the conception of a universal Church,
remaining one in the diversity of its members, is broad
enough to transcend these opposites. The sacerdotal and
the prophetic idea of the ministry can also both be sub-
sumed under the conception of responsible service in the
spiritual family, within which the ideas of succession and
ordination can easily find room. So also the two main
sacramental views, that of an *opus operatum*, and the
purely symbolic conception, can both be brought under
the notion of birth and growth within the spiritual organism which is Christ's Body.

The Rev. Dr. Theologos Paraskevaidis (Leipzig,
Greek Orthodox) : The work of our Saviour was not limited
to the proclamation and propagation of God's message, it
included the founding of a spiritual kingdom—the Church.
To that kingdom the prophets had looked forward, the

New Testament attests its presence. It was to be not merely a kingdom of the world to come, but a kingdom in this world, yet not of it, the ante-chamber of the perfect kingdom that is yet to be, in heaven. The parables, such as those of the net, or the wheat and tares, make all this plain. The Kingdom of Christ is not merely the reign of grace in the hearts of men : it is the organised and visible Church.

It is inconceivable that Christ should have left His kingdom without an adequate and permanent organisation : on the contrary, the structure left by the Apostles is the fulfilment of His intention. Christ handed on to the Apostles the teaching office, the priestly administration of the sacraments—Baptism, the Eucharist, the ministry of reconciliation—and gave them authority to demand and exact obedience—to bind and loose. The organisation of the Church rests, therefore, not upon the will of the Apostles, but on the supreme authority of the Incarnate. As Luther said, " He who would know aught of Christ must not trust himself, nor build a bridge of his own into heaven by his own reason, but must go to the Church and question her."

The Rev. Canon F. J. WESTERN, M.A. (India, Anglican) : One aspect of the authority of the Church over the Christian life of the individual is that of moral direction and discipline. The New Testament gives clear evidence of this fact. But the exercise of such authority is gravely hampered to-day in the mission field by disunion. Questions of the recognition of caste, particularly in the Holy Communion, of marriage, of semi-idolatrous or undesirable rites, and the like are answered differently in different Churches, and the result is gravely prejudicial to weak and confused souls. Nothing but a real unity of organisation can remove this practical difficulty : federation is quite inadequate. A living, growing Church needs an organisation by which in one country it can speak with one voice and act authoritatively as one body for the saving of souls.

Professor Dr. GOTTLOB HAUSSLEITER (University of Halle, Lutheran) reminded his hearers that they must look to Jesus as the good Shepherd, the seeker of the lost, the physician of the sick, the guide and teacher of the erring, and the house-father and friend. It was thus that He gathered His first flock around Him, and still gathers men to Himself. To learn of Him in humility is the way towards oneness. The Church and those who bear authority within it must think of themselves as still the erring sheep of the Shepherd, and of all Christ's sheep as having an equal claim upon His pity.

The Chairman called the meeting to silent prayer, and a hymn was sung.

The Right Rev. Bishop Gore (England, Anglican) urged the Conference, in view of the widely diverging statements that had been laid before it, to realise the vastness of its task—the seeking of complete reunion in the Christian Church universal. That would involve the admission that there is something deficient alike in Catholicism and in Protestantism as they now manifest themselves ; it would involve the attempt to envisage a conception of the Church on a basis tolerable to the Catholic mind, and capable of forming a substructure for building up all those elements of the life of the Spirit which have been identified with Protestantism. And all this must be attempted without forgetting the great Roman Church, with its vast and deep attraction for storm-wearied souls the world over. It would be well, at this stage, to recall the magnitude and difficulty of our ideal. It is this impracticable thing which we feel to be in the purpose of God.

Professor Dr. E. Gaugler (Switzerland, Old Catholic), while paying a tribute to the spiritual qualities of Dr. Cadman's address, ventured to question that view of the development of the Church which accepted the facts of division as a normal part of that development, endorsed by the will of God in history. We cannot regard the Church as a natural phenomenon, which is what it should be and must be as it is. And so our task is not merely to continue an existing development : we must rather search for the essence of the Church, we must face the difficulty of seeking the objective truth which will judge and give pain to us all, and is yet greater than anything we possess. The nature of the Church is spiritual, objective, divine : it cannot be gathered merely from the course which development has followed. If each special Church had, at its origin, some special word of value for the Church as a whole, yet the great Christian groups have also a record of lost opportunities behind them. We must find our way back to that essential Church which no existing body fully represents. It may be that in our disunion God has " shut us all up under unbelief, that He may have mercy upon all."

The Rev. Dr. H. J. Wotherspoon (Scotland, Presbyterian) : Is the Church, as has been said, to be identified with the Kingdom ? Was it not rather Christ's last resource, because the world would not receive Him nor the Kingdom of God ? This is the Church's sacred appeal to our faithfulness. The company of Christ's baptised servants is in stewardship for this last creation and gift of Christ. The Church has three primary gifts, the Gospel, the Sacraments and the Ministry, and we should regard them as gifts with which the Churches ought not to tamper.

But while we may think rightly of the Church as indefectible (rather than infallible) we should not pitch our claims for it too high. We are but administrators of Christ's substance ; and, in itself, what is the Church but a company of poor sinners gathered at the foot of the Cross and seeking to offer themselves to the will of the Lord ?

We are stewards, and this makes us anxious lest in the quest for unity we should misinterpret our trust. Yet it also simplifies our task, which is to examine the terms of our trusteeship.

Professor Lic. Benjamin Unruh (Germany, Mennonite) : Our minds go back from Lausanne to Jerusalem, to the first great conference of the Church, with its double aspect. Its leaders were, on the one hand, pardoned sinners and, on the other, sinners entrusted with a great task— *remissio peccatorum* led to a *missio peccatorum*. So the Church always moves on from Good Friday to Easter, and this is its calling to-day : the tragedy of the world is a day of God for the Church. We who come from Russia feel this truth most deeply; after judgment comes reconstruction and a new beginning.

This task calls for a Church full of vigour, clearness and charity, far-seeing and, in all its diversity of gifts and tasks, united. The closer we all come to the centre, to God in Christ, the nearer shall we be to each other. We have a conflict to wage in the sphere of the individual soul, of the intellect, of society, of international life. As we wage this war we shall discover that the oneness of the Church militant is not our achievement but God's gift, given to us through Cross and Resurrection, conflict and victory.

Professor Dr. OTTO SCHMITZ (Germany, Evangelical): The New Testament presents us with the vision of a Church which is more than an idea, invisible in itself but symbolically represented in the actual Churches; with a divine sphere of salvation, energising in this world with the powers of the world to come and yet essentially contrasted with this world. Faith requires us to discern this Church *in* the organised Churches; yet it is not identical with them, nor even in a reunited Church could it ever be so, since no mode of Church order can guarantee to the Church a complete freedom from contamination with the world. Faith must therefore distinguish the Church *from* the Churches; it must never relax its hold upon the reality of the Church invisible.

Yet the problem of Church order is of the utmost importance, since it is within the ordered Churches that the Church is, for us, to be found. It is, however, not the problem of discovering the one and only valid order: we have rather to judge of order only by its value for service, for the Kingdom.

The conception of the Church as Christ's body implies only the unity of many and diverse members, their dependence on Christ, and their organic relation to each other; it has nothing to do with the visibility of the Church. Faith discerns Christ's body in the Churches, without identifying it with them.

Two consequences follow: (1) We might here attempt a constitutional task of reunion by welding together existing types of order; this is a temptation from which we must pray to be preserved. (2) We might strive towards unity by the removal of barriers which wrongly divide Churches that belong to each other in Christ; this is our true task. Constitutional reunion, whether federal or centralised, is a perilous ideal; we must leave it to God to bring about such unity as He wills, and not confuse His will with our desires.

The session was closed at 6.30 p.m., with the singing of a hymn and with prayer by the Archbishop of Upsala.

THE CHURCH'S COMMON CONFESSION OF FAITH

SATURDAY MORNING, AUGUST 6TH.

The Conference met in full session in the Aula of the University. The Chair was taken by the Most Reverend NATHAN SÖDERBLOM, Archbishop of Upsala, and the session was opened at 9.30, with devotions led by the Rev. A. T. HOLDEN, C.B.E.

The PRESIDENT announced the appointment of the following Committee to have charge of the erection of the memorial tablet to Robert Hallowell Gardiner, in the church in Gardiner, Maine, U.S.A. :

> Mr. George Zabriskie, the Rev. Dr. Peter Ainslie, the Rev. Dr. J. Ross Stevenson, the Rev. Bishop Cannon, President Kenneth C. M. Sills.

The first addresses on the subject for the day were those of the Rt. Rev. Bishop GORE and General Superintendent Dr. ZOELLNER.

THE RIGHT REV. CHARLES GORE, D.D.

Bishop, Church of England

It is obvious that our conception of "The Church's Common Confession of Faith" is bound up with our conception of the meaning of the Gospel (Subject II) and of the Church (Subject III). I stand for the conception of the Gospel which we gain from the Synoptics and especially from St. Mark. It is the "good tidings of the Kingdom of God," and that means the present arrival of that which the prophets had foreseen—the sovereignty of the good God realised in Israel among men. The idea of the kingdom in the prophets is not simply that of the reign of God, but of His reign as realised in Israel and through Israel in the world. It is a concrete conception. When our Lord found Himself rejected by Israel in bulk, He behaved like the

160

prophets of old. He turned from Israel in the mass to
" the faithful remnant "—the disciples. So the Church was
by our Lord prepared, organised and sent out into the
world under the leadership of the Apostles, as the New or
True Israel, a visible institution or society. " Fear not,
little flock, (He said to His disciples) it is your Father's
good pleasure to give you the kingdom." And to the
Twelve He said, " Ye shall sit upon twelve seats judging
the twelve tribes of Israel." It was not indeed yet the
kingdom in its full power and glory. For that to be made
manifest, the Church must wait for the presence of Christ
or what we commonly call His Second Coming, with the
profound transformation which that is to bring ; but the
Church—as we see it in the Gospels, in process of being
refounded and re-equipped with a rudimentary organisation
by our Lord, or as we see it later at work in the Acts and
the Epistles, as the body and organ of the glorified Christ
inspired by His Spirit—is the authoritative representative
of the Kingdom of God in the present world. Thus "the
Gospel of the Kingdom " includes the Church. The Church
indeed is not identical with the kingdom, which is a wider
conception. But it is the first stage of the kingdom—a
visible organic society representative of the kingdom in the
world. Holding this high commission, its cohesion, as a
widely-dispersed society of all kinds of men, is found in
certain links which we are going to discuss—the apostolic
ministry and the sacraments ; but also and even more
fundamentally in the fact of agreement in receiving as the
Word of God a certain doctrine " to which " in St. Paul's
expressive phrase " ye were delivered " (Rom. vi, 17).
This body of doctrine was in part what Jesus taught, but
in part also a doctrine about Jesus, involved in the acts of
His earthly ministry, death, resurrection from the dead,
ascension to heaven, and the mission of the Spirit. First
it appears as the doctrine that " Jesus is the Christ " or
" the Christ is Jesus " ; then that " Jesus is the
Lord " ; then that He is the only Son of the Father, or
the Word of God, existing with the Father before all time,
His Agent in His whole creative work, who, in the fulness

of time, was born of a human mother and so " made flesh," and was therein crucified, raised and glorified, who again from the right hand of the Father has sent the Holy Spirit to constitute the Church His own body, to inspire it for its universal mission and to prepare it for its final perfection. This is the meaning of the Name of the Father and of the Son and of the Holy Spirit. This is what " the name of the Lord "—the One God of the Jews—had become through the manifestation of the Christ and the mission of the Spirit.

Now, speaking generally, our modern critics are not disposed to deny that the New Testament as it stands presents us with this idea of the Church as a visible and sacramental society, the home of the great salvation, grounded upon a positive Word of God, which it holds in common and which has the content which I have just described. It is very generally agreed that the doctrine of the Trinity and of the Incarnation is found implicit in the New Testament as it stands and that the doctrine of what we call the Nicene Creed is not more than the doctrine of St. Paul or St. John made explicit, with the one word *homoousios* added to exclude the Arian interpretation of the Son as a demigod—a word in which it is not likely that St. Paul or St. John would have found, under the circumstances of its selection, anything to object to. So through Church history the Creed maintained its ground as the summary of the scriptural and apostolic faith. And at the time of the Great Schism and the later schisms of the Reformation this doctrine of the Trinity and the Incarnation of the Eternal Son in the person of Jesus of Nazareth— the doctrine of the Nicene Creed—was the agreed point among all the divisions of Christendom, Catholic and Protestant.

But though modern rationalist criticism is not indisposed to concede the coherence and continuity between the doctrine of St. Paul or St. John and the Creed of Nicæa, it is disposed to deny the continuity between St. Paul and Jesus of Nazareth. Paul, we are constantly told, was the creator of the idea of the Catholic Church with its sacraments and its metaphysical creed. This is a quite unhistorical idea.

The institution of the Apostles by our Lord as stewards of His Household and rulers of the New Israel and the institution of the Eucharist—which St. Paul received as a fixed tradition at his conversion and handed on to the Churches which he founded—must be regarded as true history, if anything is true history. If the critics in considerable numbers deny this, it is probably only a passing fashion. However, we must reckon with it. Jesus, whether we are to represent Him as an ethical prophet of wonderful personal magnetism and authority, as Renan and Harnack have represented Him, or as an apocalyptic enthusiast with Schweitzer, never (it is suggested) aimed at founding any sacramental Church or other institution and never proclaimed Himself the Son of God except in a sense in which Israel was the Son of God. The " metaphysical " ideas of the Creed—the doctrine of the Trinity and the Incarnation —are the development (only in the minds of His disciples) of the belief that He was the Christ exalted to the right hand of God. Thus there is very widespread rebellion in the Protestant world against any " metaphysical " creed. More than that, though it cannot be denied that by St. Paul and St. John the Holy Spirit is thought of only as something or Someone indwelling the Church, imparted as a new gift from the ascended Christ to His members, and though this new gift of the Spirit of Truth is inextricably associated in their minds with the assurance of a divine revelation such as we have described which the Church receives as the Word of God, the modern world has developed a quite different idea of the Spirit of God as the inspiration of humanity, universal and progressive, which is man's birth-right ; and it quite repudiates the idea of an authoritative message once delivered. It puts the " religion of authority " which it rejects into contrast with " the religion of the Spirit," which knows no bound and no finality, and owns no allegiance to any once-spoken word, but only to the progressively realised truth. This is a really crucial question. Here is the ground on which we must join issue with the critics.

Now we are brought here together to seek the path of

reunion. Reunion in any large sense, in the sense in which this Conference is contemplating it, means the bringing together of Catholic and Protestant. Perhaps we are all agreed in feeling that the Catholic Church needs the contribution of the Protestant Churches and movements, and the Protestant Churches and movements need the strength and spirit of Catholicism. We must be very patient with one another after these long centuries of alienation. But if we are to make any progress at all, we must start from some fundamental agreement on central ideas. Are we agreed that the Church, which is Christ's organ in the world, is meant to be a coherent body, based on a belief in a positive and final revelation of God, made in and through Jesus Christ, which it is its constant business to carry into all the world as the message of God for man's salvation ? Again are we agreed that the doctrine of St. Paul and St. John, given under the inspiration of the Spirit of Christ, is the true expression of His mind for men ? If so, we belong to the religion of authority. If so, the Church stands before the world as professing a common creed which is accepted as the Word of God. It does not seem possible to believe that St. Paul or St. John would have taken exception to the idea of a binding creed. They seem to me to assert quite clearly the principle of such a creed, and to recognise as inevitable the conception of an orthodoxy (*orthe doxa*) which binds Christians into one. That is the answer which I desire to see given to the first question suggested by the Subjects Committee : " Is it requisite to Christian Unity that there should be general agreement in an explicit declaration of the Christian Faith ? "

I have already stated the answer which I desire to see given to the second : " Is it admitted that among the historic statements of that Faith the Creeds commonly called the Apostles' and the Nicene Creed have such weight that with regard to these forms, at least, it is desirable that the Churches should attempt to reach an agreement ? " I cannot perceive where the Apostles' and the Nicene Creeds fail to find their justification, clause by clause, in the New Testament. I cannot, moreover, see how there can be any hope of reaching agreement between Catholic and Protestant on any other basis.

As to (*b*) under the third question : " Could a united Church agree to leave the occasions for the use of these Creeds to the decisions of local Churches ? " supposing that the whole reunited Church is officially committed to these Creeds, I suppose that there is no obligation to use them in any particular way in the Church services. But that is a minor matter for future discussion, if we can agree to accept baptism in the Name of the Father and the Son and the Holy Ghost.

As to (*c*) : " Could a united Church agree to recognise, while firmly adhering to the substance of these Creeds, that the Holy Spirit, leading the Church into all truth, may enable the Church to express the truths of revelation in other forms according to the needs of future times ? " I should wish to leave this question until some substitute for the Creed, in whole or in part, has been suggested which is at all likely to find general agreement. If here and now we are agreed in accepting the Creeds as authoritative statements of the common faith, we can perhaps leave the abstract question of the necessary finality of the formulas for future discussion. We shall have accepted the principle that the thing to be expressed, in the future as in the present, must not be a different faith from the faith of the New Testament, but the same.

The question then for us to-day is whether we are prepared to accept the Creeds as adequately representing the apostolic faith and that apostolic message as really the message of Jesus and the Word of God. If so, we can go forward in our large enterprise. If not, we can go forward in certain large districts of the field. There could be reunion among large sections of the Protestant world, or again, perhaps, reunion between the Orthodox and the Old Catholics and the Anglican Churches. But any reunion between Catholic and Protestant in a large sense is inconceivable except on the basis of acceptance in common of the Creeds as authoritative statements of the Faith in Christ. If such acceptance is at present, in such a representative body as this, plainly impossible, I think we must abandon our present attempt (though only for a time) and devote ourselves to the more feasible task of consolidating all those who profess the Name of Christ, without regard to doctrinal and sacramental differences, in an earnest pursuit of the moral and social aims of Christianity. If we can learn to act as one body on the moral and social field, we may become better fitted in another generation to approach doctrinal and sacramental questions afresh.

GENERAL-SUPERINTENDENT DR. WILHELM ZOELLNER
Church of Prussia (Evangelical-Lutheran)

I must, at the outset, lay down a principle relating to my subject which is common ground for all Christian Churches, namely, that the final criterion for all that claims to be acknowledged, believed and preached as Christian is to be found in Holy Scripture. In spite of all varieties of interpretative method, and of the very different ways in which the relation of Scripture to tradition is conceived, in this we are all at one. But to the Lutheran, it is of special importance to emphasise this one supreme principle : for it is in this peculiar emphasis laid upon Holy Scripture, the Word of God, that the ecumenical character of Lutheranism consists.

I

The critera to be employed in the discussion of this subject and of the questions it involves must be deduced from Holy Scripture.

The evidence of the New Testament forbids us to treat the word " Church " as though it meant merely a Christian " social contract." The Church is not an institutional coalition of Christians, resting on a foundation of sociological law, and determined in the last resort, as an existing structure or as one in course of construction, by their ideas. That conception is the product of those currents of thought, originating in Humanism, Deism, the Enlightenment and similar movements, which during the last two centuries have first isolated the individual, cutting him loose from divinely-ordered modes of fellowship, and have then re-organised him in man-made social constructions of every sort. This movement culminated on the one side in the doctrine of the " Super-man," and on the other in a process of agglomeration in which we observe the Super-man, like a twentieth century Messiah, attempting to weld together the masses into one single will in order to embody that will in himself ; whether as its master or its servant, whether apart from God or in defiance of God, it is his aim to dominate the stream of circumstances and to create a kingdom of happiness in which redemption has no place, to the honour and glory of the Spirit of Man. Call it individual-ism or socialism as you will, we have here but two sides of one and the same tendency, which in both its forms, and in all that it asserts or denies, is set upon the destruction of all social order which rests upon the Divine will and ordin-ance.

It is no accident that in the Epistle to the Ephesians, the *magna charta* of the Church in the New Testament, St. Paul sets the mystery of the Church side by side that of marriage—marriage as God ordains and wills it to be. For marriage is the prototype of human social life as God wills it to be, and the source from which other groupings, the family, the tribe, the nation, derive their origin ; marriage, with the husband in his appointed sphere as the head, the wife as the soul, and children realising as developing per-sonalities their place within the order in which they find themselves. Here we have the joint action of past and future, talent and development, authority and freedom, with governance realised as service, and variety as the enrichment of unity ; and all this ennobled by the fidelity of the individual to his appointed task, and by dependence upon God, in whose service perfect freedom is realised by the operation of His love.

True social fellowship is a mystery ; it can only exist as between persons, and personality demands self-assertion while fellowship involves self-surrender. But apart from

God, self-surrender and self-assertion are mutually destructive ; and here is the reason why no social fellowship apart from God ever endures. But just as God, holy and loving, asserts Himself man-ward in self-giving, so we also find ourselves in complete surrender to Him, and that is why, in human social fellowship, it is possible for us to make surrender of ourselves without loss, self-surrender being rather the way through which we come to ourselves—" He who loveth his own life shall lose it : he who loseth . . . shall find."

The breach of fellowship between God and man is the real and ultimate cause of the break-up of any other fellowship. Any social edifice which lacks the foundation of fellowship with God is built in vain, and can but lead to further confusion and incoherence.

For this reason the Church, the power-centre of the kingdom of God, is the highest form of fellowship, and gives strength and coherence to all other human associations in the forms which God has ordained for them. From Him who is the Father all fatherhood on earth, as St. Paul tells us, takes its name (Eph. iii, 15).

It is in this sense that the Church is of God's founding, willed by Him in eternity, made manifest upon earth in time through Jesus Christ, and given substantial existence among men through the Holy Spirit, that it may come to its fulness in eternity (Eph. i, 3-12).

When the fulness of the time came and God sent His Son, when the Word was made flesh, then the Church came into being on earth ; for the incarnate Son of God is virtually and potentially the Church. But if Christ is potentially and virtually the Church, then His word and work is the Church's confession, alike in its inexhaustible fulness and in its wonderful unity and simplicity : it is *the* truth.

From the Lord of the Church, dwelling on earth, a Church upon earth comes into being. Through Him, and from His word and work, faith takes its beginning, and the dawning faith of His disciples is the dawn of the Church on earth.

But this germinal faith is the germinal confession of the

Church, the first outline of the way of truth and of that Life which is the Lord Himself.

The confession of Peter is the first point of climax in the movement thus begun : " Lord, to whom shall we go ? Thou hast the words of eternal life, and we have believed and known that thou art the Christ, the Son of the living God " ; a confession which the Lord takes up and ratifies— " Thou art Peter, and upon this rock will I build my Church, and the gates of hell shall not prevail against it."

It is to the Kingdom of God that our Lord applies the similitude of the grain of mustard-seed. The logic of the principles just stated justifies us in applying it also to the Church : and so far as the Lord is Himself virtually and potentially the Church, He is also the grain of mustard-seed.

What He says elsewhere of the corn of wheat has the same meaning : " Except a corn of wheat fall into the earth and die, it abideth alone, but if it die, it bringeth forth much fruit " ; words which He, crucified and risen for us, translated into action. St. John's Gospel (13-17) makes the significance of the picture clear, and St. Paul brings out its meaning in Eph. ii, 14, where he says, " Christ is our peace, who hath made of both one, and hath broken down the wall of partition . . . in his flesh . . . that he might reconcile both unto God in one body by the Cross."

The germinal Church and its confession : recall the disciples, seated at Emmaus, who say, " Did not our heart burn within us as he talked with us by the way " ; or Thomas standing and saying, " My Lord and my God " ; or how our Lord, after that strange questioning by the lake of Tiberias, judging and gracious, true and loving, restores Peter to his office and in so doing gives the Church its ministerial commission, " Feed my lambs, feed my sheep " ; recall the confession which followed, so utterly humble and so blessedly whole-hearted, " Thou knowest all things, thou knowest that I love thee."

Then comes the day of Pentecost, when the Father sends the Spirit through the Son, the moment of spring-time when the buds come into flower, when that which was hid comes to light and, through a miracle, the Church stands

G

out visibly in the world, the one Holy Church, alike the fulfilment of all the promises and the promise of ever new fulfilment ; the day when the discord of Babel is transformed into the one language of the children of God by the power of the Spirit.

But that day of the entry of the Church upon the world must needs be also the day of the Church's confession. Peter, the appointed mouth-piece of the Church, declares it. It is the great Amen of the New Testament to the Old— Jesus, the risen one, the Christ, Messiah, Anointed, the Lord (*Kyrios*). And Paul, to whom is committed the great mystery of the oneness of Jew and Greek in the Church, of the chosen people and the Gentiles, declares its fundamental import : " I delivered unto you first of all that which I also received, how that Christ died for our sins according to the Scriptures : and that he was buried, and that he rose again the third day according to the Scriptures " (1 Cor. xv, 3ff.).

And, in a wider sense, the three first Gospels come to us as the great confession of the primitive Church, owning Jesus as Christ and Lord. The apostolic letters take it up— " Great is the mystery of godliness : God was manifest in the flesh, justified in the Spirit, seen of angels, preached unto the Gentiles, believed on in the world, received up into glory " (1 Tim. iii, 16). The Apocalypse gives us a moment's vision of the worship of the Church triumphant, as it casts its crowns before the throne and gives voice to the great confession, " Worthy is the Lamb that was slain," and the Spirit and the Bride say, " Amen : even so, come Lord Jesus." And John the aged utters the final word— " We beheld his glory, the glory as of the only begotten of the Father, full of grace and truth . . . and of his fulness have we all received, and grace for grace."

II

There we have the Church's confession, in that first period which lays the foundation and establishes the standard ; there we have the " foundation which is laid," the corner-stone Jesus Christ, the initial courses on which the whole building is to be reared.

It is with this preparation that the Church goes out into the world.—As its extension increases, the resistance which it encounters demands a more intensive coherence. This is plainly seen in the Pastoral Epistles, with their increasing emphasis upon " sound doctrine " and upon that " good confession before many witnesses " which St. Paul's disciple is bidden to bear in mind. It becomes clear also in the necessity for a baptismal creed. The springs which rise in their purity from the rock of the primitive Church are merged into one stream : the Creed is unified. The *militia Christiana*, the mortal conflict against apparently over- whelming odds, required a password (*symbolum*) and a banner round which the army could rally. It was thus that the Apostles' Creed, *symbolum apostolorum*, came into being. Who was its author ? The same question is often asked with reference to our folk-songs, and the answer is— no one knows. It was a birth or a growth : a product of Christian " common-sense," the great inner unity of the brotherhood. Its content is that which God, the Three in One, has done and revealed. It speaks in monumental accents of the great acts of God in creation, redemption, completion : in birth and re-birth. It moves from eternity into time and from time into eternity ; past Christmas, Good Friday, Ascension and Pentecost, on to the fulfilling of the day of the Lord, the coming-again of Jesus Christ. Its last words lay stress upon the sphere of the Spirit's activity, the one Holy Church, wherein, out of the depths of forgiveness and redemption, the great purpose is wrought out towards its end.

Side by side with the Apostles' Creed comes the Nicene ; the one is the folk-song of the people of God, the other the product of the conscious art of its theologians. The latter took shape, as we know, through conciliar enactments, yet it was none the less significant, none the less truly a product of the Spirit. Let me note another difference as well—how that in the Apostles' Creed we have the Holy Spirit in a Latin guise, and in the Nicene the same Spirit uttering Himself in Greek : on the one side the language of the people of hard fact, a race which expresses itself in granite blocks and monumental phrases, and on the other the swift-moving stream, whose mighty waters catch and reflect the majestic beauty of the eternal sunlight.

Yet objective and subjective are here in close alliance. How massive are the initial words—Credo, I believe! It is the *fides quae creditur* and the *fides qua creditur* at the same time : alike the faith which is believed and the faith by which the act of belief is made. Objective and subjective are here at one : here we have the one holy Church, that fellowship which does no despite to personality and in no way obliterates its varieties, but perfects them and welds them together in the great polyphonic chorus of the πολυποίκιλος σοφία, the manifold wisdom of the One, of whom and through whom and to whom are all things : to whom be glory for ever and ever.

III

These creeds, the Apostles' and the Nicene, are the common heritage of the severed Churches. This is the weightiest general statement on which I must now lay stress. This is not the place for a descent from the heights which I have depicted, into the depths in which those severances came about. One point alone must be stressed. A German theologian, Prof. Dr. Elert, subsumes the entire development of the relation between Church and world under a law of *synthesis* and *diastasis*, to which the continuous process of inspiration and expiration in the human lungs affords a rough analogy. The first period is one of *diastasis*, a period in which the Church is concentrated upon its individual character and upon all that distinguishes it from its environment in the world : it is dominated and controlled by its sense of *difference*. Yet inasmuch as the Church is necessarily a missionary Church (just because it is aware of its own uniqueness), this first period leads of necessity— accurate dating is obviously out of the question—to a second, a period of *synthesis*, in which the Church presses forward into the world. But the further the Church presses on into the world, to overcome it, the greater is the peril of its becoming overburdened by the world. Then comes an inevitable reaction. The world-church has gone too far in the direction of *synthesis :* the turn of *diastasis* must come. The desire to set the seal of authority upon one's own achievements is an ever-present peril. And thus there emerges an unavoidable cleavage between those who remain attached to the results of *synthesis,* and those who, in order to preserve the authentic essence of the Church, are compelled to insist upon its *diastasis* from the world. For a historical reinforcement of this contention, I need only refer to the movements of the fifteenth and sixteenth centuries.

However this may be, one thing is indubitable, that all Christian Churches have in all essentials actually taken as their heritage the Apostles' and the Nicene creed. Developments beyond this point were exposed to a twofold peril. I have already called attention to the close interaction between the objective and the subjective in the creed. The peril lay in the dissociation of the two elements thus combined. Such a dissociation left the objective element lifeless, and exposed to petrifaction : a relic, in itself only a historical specimen, and yet anxiously guarded. What was left of faith was little more than an external assent devoid of life and power. Or if on the other side the subjective element was overpressed, the objective was exposed to the danger of losing so much of its coherence and solidity that the essential content of the Christian religion was mis-conceived as consisting in subjective emotions and conditions, opinions or views. It would be impossible to indicate more closely here all the forms, of the former or the latter type, with which history confronts us. Nor would I presume here to function as the critic of other Churches, or to express a judgment on the question how far, in those Churches, the danger of overpressing the objective has tended in the direction of excessive rigidity. All I will say is that in Protestantism over a large area the second of the two dangers has become acute. And even upon this point I must not enter into further detail, especially as it has received further attention in the first speech upon this subject. I therefore content myself with a particular reference to German critical and idealistic theology. Yet I must observe with emphasis that in spite of the considerable influence of that theology in our time, the Evangelical Churches in Germany have held fast, through the whole period, to the Apostles' Creed. It has maintained its place unshaken in their liturgies and ordinances, in Baptism and Ordination. And while, quite recently, an extreme religious subjectivism which is a law unto itself has been striving hard to free itself from all that is specifically Christian, there is a very manifest movement of reaction against it which perceives the abyss into which a one-sided subjectivity must fall and is putting out all its strength for the recovery of the objective, recognising, of course, that subjective and objective are one, and that the revealed grace of God must be accepted and grasped by the energy of a living faith.

IV

From this point we have now to draw the inferences which are relevant for the purposes of this Conference.

If our hearts are stirred by the question whether there is any road of return from the inward divisions of the Churches back towards unity, the first thing to be said is that no genuine road can evade the question of credal confession. Its creed is the inmost expression which any Church can give to its life ; and therefore nothing can truly help us forward unless it grows out of what is thus most inward, and grows out of it through that power of the Spirit from above which leads us ever onward into the fundamental depths of the word of revelation. It follows from this, again, that no inward union can be really promoted by the construction of artificial formulæ. Such formulæ are like a piece of paper stuck over a crack in a wall, which may hide the crack for a while, but cannot repair it. The French proverb says that everyone has the defects of his qualities ; and the saying, if taken with a grain of salt, is true of the Christian Church. That is a rather too delicate topic for detailed exposition. I must leave it to the representatives of other Churches to reveal what their merits and their demerits are. As far as

Lutheranism is concerned I think I have already spoken plainly enough. Let us draw the conclusion which the matter, as it is now before us, demands : namely, that each should keep a firm hold on the talent God has entrusted to him, and do his utmost to renounce all misuse of it ; he should develop what God has given him in consonance with its character, and yet develop it in such a way that each, as the process of growth demands, may learn from others what they have to teach. Our common heritage, the *Symbolum Apostolorum*, must be and must remain the basis upon which this work is done.

" What thou hast inherited from thy fathers, that shalt thou ever anew strive to make more and more profoundly thine own, that it may be thy possession." The mutual interaction of the two elements, the subjective and objective, is the goal we must keep in view ; and, as a Lutheran may rightly urge with particular stress, in seeking it we must give to the Holy Scripture, more and more, its rightful place as *norma normans*. However long and hard the road ahead may be, it is the road. And God's Spirit, the more we cease to limit His working, can lead us up even the steepest places more quickly than we can here and now imagine to be possible.

Is it our task to-day to attempt the formulation of new confessions of faith, in order to hasten the coming of unity ? The thoughts I have laid before you lead me to answer the question, so far as it concerns the present moment, in the negative. So far as I can see, we are not in a position to formulate any new creed. Artificial ingenuities of restatement, so far from helping us, can only increase confusion. Creeds must grow out of inward actualities : and only if a time is vouchsafed to us in which the music of belief finds spontaneous expression once more, will a new confession of faith become possible.

Let us fix our eyes, however, upon the goal : that each one of us should grow up in his measure into Him who is the Head, until we come to the measure of the fulness of Christ ; not to a flat uniformity, but to oneness in the Spirit through the bond of peace, to *una sancta ecclesia*, one Church with one confession, held fast with the grasp of life.

After short devotions and the singing of a hymn, the presentation of the subject was continued as follows :

PROFESSOR DR. GEORG WOBBERMIN
University of Göttingen (Evangelical-Lutheran)

For the sake of order and clearness, I will first express my opinion on certain points, which appear to me of particular importance, and then I will consider the conclusions which may be drawn from them in regard to the questions stated in the programme.

A point which is emphasised by the writers of both papers is that the Holy Scriptures, and more particularly the New Testament, are in the last resort the authoritative test by which any Christian confession of faith must be judged. For my own part I would most heartily endorse that statement, but to prevent any misunderstanding I would immediately add that the Holy Scriptures can only be understood aright through Christian experience and through Christian obedience, in faith. So Luther insisted that the Word of God was the only article of faith, but that no one could understand the Word of God unless he was touched by it, and worked with it, and made it his own by experience. It is in this experience, Luther added, that the Holy Spirit teaches us, so to speak, in His own school, and whatever we learn from any other source is merely pretence and vain babblings.

What strikes me as specially important in Bishop Gore's paper is the idea that every one of the Christian confessions of faith must necessarily have a metaphysical basis. As the word metaphysical is not quite unambiguous—for it might include philosophical speculation—I would prefer to say ontological. Every Christian confession of faith must, indeed, be understood in a metaphysical-ontological sense ; in other words, all its articles must relate to the supreme ultimate reality, to the absolute reality, indeed, to be exact, to the only absolute reality. I would, however, supplement that statement by pointing out that there are ideas and expressions in the creed which cannot be unreservedly accepted as perfectly corresponding with its basic metaphysical-ontological substance. These terms and ideas require, indeed, to be constantly re-examined with a view to determining whether they truly correspond, beyond all possibility of misunderstanding, with the all-important ontological basis.

A point which appears of the highest importance in Dr. Zoellner's paper is his affirmation that a Christian creed must always give equal expression to the subjective and the objective aspects—to the *fides quae creditur* and the *fides qua creditur*. This illuminating statement needs, however, to be still more deeply fathomed and more minutely elaborated. Its real justification lies in the fact that both the subjective and objective factors are most intimately related, in fact interdependent, so that each is conditioned by the other. For not only does the *fides quae creditur* (the objective factor) govern our apprehension of the *fides qua creditur*, but the latter also, in its turn, governs our apprehension of the former.

This leads us to take a further step. Protestant theologians of the last fifty years have, not infrequently, passed very one-sided judgments on the ancient creeds. The problem has been stated and examined exclusively in the following manner : how were the declarations and conceptions in these creeds understood, from a dogmatical point of view, at the time when they were first drawn up ? Such an investigation of their historical origin is undoubtedly justified. But it is far from exhausting the problem. Its effect has been to cause these creeds to be regarded chiefly as historical memorials, and to deprive them of any validity or authority for Christian belief in the world of to-day. If we desire to realise the extent of this validity and authority, we must supplement this historical investigation by another of a very different kind. We must enquire : what is the purely religious, the specifically Christian foundation which underlies these forms of expression and ideas ?

In order to see quite clearly in this question, it would be useful to consider not only the two first ecumenical Creeds, but also the third, the so-called Athanasian Creed. It is no doubt of less importance than the other two, but this difference is only relative, and does not involve any principle. The Reformers themselves took over all three of the ancient Creeds, not only into the Lutheran but also into the Reformed-Calvinistic Churches. If one examines the last-named of these three Creeds, one is immediately struck by the point to which I alluded just now. I refer to the famous introductory words of that Creed: *Quicunque vult salvus esse ante omnia opus habet ut teneat fidem catholicam ; fides autem catholica haec est.* (Whosoever will be saved, before all things it is necessary that he hold the Catholic faith ; and the Catholic faith is this.) Now if these words are read exactly in the sense which they were originally intended, both they and the whole Creed which follows are utterly and entirely incompatible with the evangelical conception of faith. Yet this Creed was taken over by the Reformers and is officially recognised in many Protestant Churches. That can only be accounted for on the ground that these famous words were not understood as applying to the actual dogmatic statements which follow, concerning the Trinity and Christology, but to the purely religious convictions on which these dogmatic statements were based and to the specific Christian faith by which they were inspired.

The same observation applies to the Nicene Creed. I would remind you of the well-known difference between the two texts of this Creed in the Eastern and Western Churches —I mean the question whether the Holy Spirit proceeds from the Father only, or from the Father and the Son. This distinction is all the more important as it expresses a trinitarian doctrine built up in quite a different way. If we regard this distinction in a purely historical sense, and if from that standpoint we examine the intellectual formula in which the doctrine was expressed, the difference appears even sharper, so that the Creed would conduce, not to a reconciliation, but rather to an accentuation of the distinction. The result is entirely different if, in addition to purely historical researches, we seek to ascertain the underlying religious foundation of these articles and to perceive their ultimate intention. Then we discern that both these texts, in spite of their differences, have in the last resort the same motive, and consequently bear the same construction. Both of them aim at establishing the strictly monotheistic character of the Christian Trinity. The Eastern doctrine sought to secure that end by considering the Father as the Principle and Source of Divinity, and, therefore, by describing the Holy Spirit as proceeding from the Father only. The Western doctrine sought to attain the same result by keeping the Three Powers of the Godhead in the closest possible relationship, and, therefore, by describing the Holy Ghost as proceeding from the Father and the Son.

Finally as regards the Apostles' Creed, Luther himself at various points in his great Catechism resorted to the method of disregarding the historical origin of the terms used and seeking to discover their ultimate religious significance or the convictions upon which they were founded.

I will now draw some conclusions for the questions which are put to us in the Programme.* To Question 1, it might be answered : It is not absolutely necessary, though it is extremely desirable, for the sake of unity, that there should be agreement on a particular statement of the Christian faith. It is not necessary, in the sense of a *conditio sine qua non*, since the intellectual formulæ in which a belief is stated cannot be unreservedly identified with the underlying Christian conviction. Nevertheless, it is extremely desirable, for it is only the intellectual formulation of a belief which can safeguard its genuinely Christian character and prevent it from drifting into legal religion or into magic and mythology.

In answer to Question 2 : The ancient Christian so-called Ecumenical Creeds, especially the Apostles' and the Nicene Creeds, are undoubtedly so important that the Churches should make an attempt to agree upon them. A

*i.e. in Pamphlet No. 52, "Material Prepared by the Subjects Committee," p. 9.

pre-requisite for such an agreement is that we should maintain the distinction between the actual Christian substance of the Creed, and the intellectual formulæ in which it is expressed. To speak plainly : it must be left an open question whether the formulæ used in those Creeds represent, in all points and in all respects, a satisfactory expression of the Christian faith, or whether in one respect or another a modification of the formula might not be desirable.

As regards Question 3 (*a*), the answer is already implicit in that given to Question 2. This question, like Question 2, must, therefore, be answered in the affirmative.

Question 3 (*b*) must also be answered in the affirmative. The occasions on which these Creeds should be employed must be left to the judgment of the Churches.

Finally, Question 3 (*c*) must be answered in the affirmative. The right to formulate the Creeds anew must be admitted in principle. But I would add to this reply that we must distinguish between two possible cases. I agree with the two speakers that, at any rate for the present, we should reject any idea of re-formulating these Creeds for use in Church services. But on the other hand, it is worth considering whether a re-statement of the Creed might not be attempted purely with a view to assisting discussion and agreement. I mean a re-statement which would bring out what we hold in common, and which would not seek to debate or ignore the issues on which we disagree, but would leave these differing beliefs to the Churches as their special possessions. I see no reason why such an attempt should be postponed. On the contrary, it is a task which should be undertaken by us, here and now, at this Conference. Indeed, in my own opinion, we should be neglecting our duty if we did not undertake this task.

If we wish to attain unity we must begin with it here. The foundation must be laid here, if the structure is to be sound. All the further questions, all discussions about church polity, the ministry and the sacraments, are governed by the question of the foundation of our faith with which we are now occupied.

If we feel assured that we are working here, according to the will of God and of Jesus Christ, in the power of the Holy Spirit, for a union of the Churches, we are justified in holding the same assurance that it is God's will that we should carry our task through to the end, to its utmost depths and its farthest boundaries. This reliance is grounded on that which is the ultimate and objective foundation of our common Christianity : one God, one Christ, one faith, one holy and universal Christian Church.

THE REV. JONAS LINDSKOG, D.D.
Rector of Braennkyrka, Stockholm (Lutheran)

There are in our evangelic Lutheran Churches many who in the main agree with Bishop Gore in his conception of the Apostles' and the Nicene Creeds as the authoritative, adequate and norm-giving summary of the Christian faith and as the indispensable basis for that union between the Churches which we are hoping for. But there are also many who, on the question of these creeds, their significance, aim and value, have a rather different view. I could, for instance, refer to several articles by well-known men in *Die Eiche* and other periodicals, and I will try in the following to put forward a similar conception.

Cardinal Bellarmin says : " *Non in verbis, sed in sensu est fides, non ergo habemus idem symbolum, si in explicatione dissidemus.*" The important thing is not in the words, but the meaning behind them. The same words do not guarantee even agreement in thought. It is well known that several clauses in the creeds, for instance, " descended into hell," " ascended into heaven," " the resurrection of the body," have been interpreted in quite different ways according to different minds.

But more important is realising that agreement in thought does not necessarily imply a real and deep unity between the souls. Unity in thought and unity in spirit are not the same thing. The former is not even a necessary pre-supposition of the latter. The spiritual unity lies on a deeper plane than the intellectual or historical though the latter by no means is unimportant.

To be sure, the New Testament speaks of the truth as the basis of unity between Christians. That men be of the truth and live in the truth—that matters more than anything else. But the word " truth " has a deep sense and is not the same as a sum of doctrines, conceptions, historical facts, etc. We see the truth, St. Paul says, only as through a glass darkly and partly. Our words and thoughts are never anything more than groping efforts to grasp it. The truth is a relation of life. According to the Gospel of St. John, Jesus calls Himself the truth and the life, two words which, although not synonymous, are intimately connected. To live in the truth is, therefore, to build one's life on the right basis, to gain the right relations of life and the right aim and mission in life.

St. Paul speaks of the true unity as a unity in Christ. To be in the Lord, as the branch in the vine, to imbibe life and nourishment from Him, His word and His person, to be inspired by His spirit and through Him get the right relation to God—that gives the right foundation for the real unity between Christians.

Such a unity of faith and life exists between the different Churches, in spite of all misunderstandings (otherwise this Conference could hardly have been called together). All of them call Jesus their Lord and testify that in Him we have the redeemer from sin and death and the mediator between God and men. All are looking up to Him as the truth, His path being the way of duty and of life. All believe—more or less clearly—in the remission of sins in His name and in the power of sanctification through His Spirit. For all of them, the Bible, the document of God's special revelation, is the matchless guide and source of life. There are Churches that are without the Apostles' Creed, or the Nicene or the Athanasian Creed, but none that is without " Our Father, which art in heaven," none that does not approach our heavenly Father with faithful prayer in the name of Jesus.

But this essential unity wants visible or audible expression. The common confession of the common faith is a spiritual need. At the Conference in Stockholm, 1925, it sometimes seemed as if all barriers had gone down, and the feeling of unity broke out spontaneously in common confession. We said jointly the Lord's Prayer, which prayer in a certain sense includes the whole Christian religion and reflects the Saviour's own soul, or we sang jointly from the bottom of our hearts hymns which became the expressions and confessions of our faith.

The feeling of unity expressed itself also, though more seldom, in common reading of the creeds. When the Patriarch from the altar in the Cathedral of Upsala read the Nicene Creed in the Greek language, the impression was strong and moving. The beloved Creed of the Orthodox Church became a symbol and an expression of the existing unity. As symbols—guiding symbols—of an essential unity the ancient creeds are of great importance, as they are also as a golden chain through history binding the generations together. But they are not adapted to be the proper foundation in the work towards a united Church, and this also on account of their content. It is true that they in a fine way enclose and confine the faith, which is the strongest bond of unity between the Churches, the faith in God our Father, declared in the only begotten Son through the Spirit. But this faith is partly clothed in words and terms which by many Christians in the present time are understood and must be understood in a different way than they originally were meant. It is combined with metaphysical thoughts which were influenced by the philosophy of the age, on account of which a distinction is to be made between their substance, the great religious truth they really stand for, and their temporary form. And there are important, indispensable elements in our religion which these formulas leave out of account. Bishop Gore has pointed out that the doctrine delivered by the Apostles was partly what Jesus taught, partly a doctrine about Jesus. During the development of the Church's doctrine the first part was, however, more and more passed over. It may be true that the central ideas in the creeds—the doctrines of the Trinity and the Incarnation—find their justification in the New Testament and correspond to the conceptions of St. Paul and St. John. But when these doctrines are made the principal thing in the creeds and what Christ taught is mostly passed by, there is a shifting of the emphasis, which has contributed to the intellectualism that more than anything else has separated the Churches and made them enemies instead of brethren. If we were now going to give the ancient creeds a position by which they practically would appear as binding and ruling laws for the doctrine, it is to be feared that hereby, just in the work for the reunion of the Churches, a seed would be sown which in the future would become a cause of new separations.

As the evangelic Churches' retaining of the ancient creeds at the time of the Reformation could not hinder the great schism, " a renewed acceptance in common of the creeds as authoritative statements of the faith in Christ," could hardly help us one step forward towards the real " reunion between Catholic and Protestant in a large sense." The fundamental differences between the Roman Catholic and the Protestant branches of the Church are so great that they nearly exclude the idea of a reunion in the present circumstances. But a deep organic unity between the sections of the Protestant world as well as between the Orthodox Church and the Evangelic Churches will, I hope, be found possible, even if we only should give the ancient creeds a position of being not binding laws but means, helping us not to lose certain important aspects of Christian truth and to attain a deeper understanding of the Gospel.

This is, in fact, the purpose of the creeds according to our latest Lutheran confession, the Formula Concordiæ of 1577, which says : The Holy Scripture alone is the normative, *norma normans* for the doctrine and the ethics of the Church, all other writings, the creeds included, are only witnesses how the Holy Scripture at different times has been understood by Christian people and testifying to the common faith.

The vital question for us is, then, if we in true faith in

God, and as true disciples of Christ, can gain and deepen that inner unity, which—as all true peace—is the fruit of the Spirit, the unity in Spirit. Then the more external unity will certainly, sooner or later, come, as the Primate of Ireland has pointed out, and we pray that this Conference may be a step towards the goal. The prayer " Our Father which art in heaven " will become a symbol and an expression of this unity. So also the Apostles' and the Nicene Creeds, even though the one thinks that they adequately represent the Christian faith, the other that they, just as all work of men (also our old fathers), are not infallible, the one that they must be interpreted according to the letter and the original meaning, the other allowing a freer and more spiritual interpretation. A certain agreement as to order will certainly also be forthcoming, if also a still greater liberty in this sphere should be allowed. But the strongest expression of the inner unity will be that confession which consists of life and deed, the confession on which our Saviour lays such a tremendous stress in His sermon on the Mount and His parable of the last judgment (Matt. vii and xxv).

THE HON. LORD SANDS, LL.D.
Procurator of the Church of Scotland, 1907-1917 (Presbyterian)

When the Apostles went forth to preach Christ to the world they went as the professed bearers of a message of new truth hitherto unfamiliar to men. They went forth not to create an atmosphere but to announce facts. The Apostles, a small united band with first-hand information as to the matters which they taught, probably felt no need for a definitely formulated creed. But conditions changed. The coming of the Lord who was to make all things plain, was delayed. Doubts and questionings arose. The need came to be felt for an authoritative formulation of the content of the message of which the Church was the repository. So we have creeds and confessions. The need for these, however, is not in our day universally acknowledged, and indeed in certain schools of thought there is even a fashion to decry them. But whilst there may be room for difference of opinion as to the measure of particularisation that is desirable, there is really no substance in the general objection. The Church must stand for something at once important and distinctive. Without community of faith in some truth which possesses these characteristics there can be no community of purpose. Life is more than doctrine, but life without doctrine is empty. Life gives value to the doctrine, but without the translation of life into intellectual form life cannot endure. Further, the communication of life must be through the body of this intellectual form, and this intellectual form must be capable of embodiment in human laguage. Otherwise there can be no assurance of community among the members of the Church and no communication of a message of truth to the world.

We are not concerned, however, here and now, so much with the general question of the need for creeds or confessions, as with the practical question of what common profession of faith is a necessary preliminary to any comprehensive Church reunion. If there is to be reunion there must be a measure of common faith. Otherwise, union can have no meaning or purpose. Assurance of such community of faith as reunion postulates seems to require agreement in a common formulation of faith. Language may not be adequate to express all the deep things that belong to God, but language is the instrument given us and that instrument we must employ.

I agree with Bishop Gore and General-Sup. Zoellner that we must find our doctrinal basis of union in the catholic symbols. Whilst not differing from these speakers in any way, as becomes a layman, I perhaps look at the matter in a somewhat more severely practical aspect.

I can hardly regard as practicable the formulation of a new common creed by the Churches represented in this Conference. By a new creed I do not mean a creed which is new in substance, which imports new doctrine or discards old doctrine, but merely a creed which restates cardinal doctrine under new forms of expression. Discussion would be interminable, suspicion would be acute. In the days of the undivided Church, councils framed authoritative definitions. But if such a conference as is gathered here were to frame definitions with a view to reunion, before any effect could be given to these definitions they would have to run the gauntlet of meticulous criticisms in a hundred different communions in all parts of the world. Authoritative restatement may some day be a task for the reunited Church; it can hardly be a preliminary to reunion.

There is, however, a perhaps more decisive objection to any new creed or confession as a basis of union. A large part of Christendom will take nothing else, or at all events nothing less, than one or both of the two great creeds. There might not perhaps be any insuperable objection to supplementary declarations upon matters not covered by these creeds. I apprehend, however, that the inclination of those who would seek some substitute for the catholic symbols would be not towards elaboration but towards simplification. In my view it is not profitable to consider that suggestion upon its merits. Large sections of the Church, without whom there can be no general reunion, are not prepared either to supersede or to curtail the catholic creeds.

There is one respect in which as a doctrinal basis for reunion the catholic symbols enjoy an immense advantage. Their language and their forms of expression are not those of our times. I am satisfied that if these creeds did not exist, if no such creeds had come down to us, and a body of modern divines—the most learned, orthodox and authoritative—with Dr. Gore and Archbishop Chrysostom as joint chairmen, were to formulate a creed, the forms of expression would be somewhat different from those which we find in the catholic creeds. But whatever forms of expression might now be chosen they would be keenly criticised as contemporary statements in contemporary language framed in the light of contemporary scientific and philosophical conceptions. The catholic symbols are upon a

different footing. We need not be too anxious about forms
of expression. These were chosen in an age which is not
our age, and were influenced by philosophical conceptions
prevalent in that age. The truth is unchangeable, but the
forms in which it clothes itself vary from age to age. There
are many verses in the Holy Scriptures in which we recognise deep spiritual truth, but which are expressed in
language which would not now be chosen. We accept the
truth, but we do not re-write the Scripture.

But the catholic symbols have another great advantage ;
the acceptance of these symbols as the doctrinal basis of a
reunited Church calls for no compromise, no concession
upon the part of any Church. However widely certain
Churches may have diverged from the norm of the mediæval
and the Eastern Church in certain matters, there has been
no repudiation of the catholic creeds. No Church need feel
that she is being asked to adopt something that belongs
to another Church. The creeds are the heritage of the whole
Church. The Church of Scotland, to which I belong, is not
a Lutheran or historically a Protestant Church, but it is a
reformed Church. In that Church the Apostles' Creed is
recognised as " a brief sum of the Christian faith agreeable
to the Word of God and anciently received in the Church
of Christ."

The confession prepared by Calvin in 1559 for the French
Reformed Church sets forth : " On all articles which have
been decided by ancient councils touching the infinite
essence of God and the distinction of three persons and the
union of two natures in our Lord Jesus Christ we agree and
receive all that was therein resolved as being drawn from
the Holy Scriptures." Similarly, the second Helvetic confession recognises the authority of the catholic symbols.
The confession of Augsburg, too, begins with a reaffirmation
of the Nicene Creed.

Whilst, as I have indicated, for practical reasons in relation to reunion the only path is the acceptance of the
catholic symbols, I venture—still keeping the practical
before me—to point out a certain difficulty. There are
some who, whilst prepared to accept these symbols, will

tell us that they deem them not wholly adequate as a profession of the living faith of the Church. They were framed, it will be said, under conditions and to meet difficulties different from those which confront us to-day. Church reunion needs a great spiritual dynamic and, in relation to the needs of our time, the creeds are static rather than dynamic. The love of God, the personal relation of the soul to the Saviour, the free offer of salvation to men, these may be implicit in the creeds but they do not find adequate expression. In the Apostles' Creed, for example, the only direct relation affirmed of the Master to mankind is that of a judge. I am not volunteering these criticisms, I am merely stating what I know will be put forward by orthodox and pious men, not against the creeds, but against their adequacy as a complete summary of the saving truth round which the Church must rally, the banner under which we who have so long been severed can gather triumphantly together and go forth to conquer the world.

Conditions have changed since supplementary definitions were made at Chalcedon, and the difficulty I have indicated is not, as I think, to be met by any formulation of supplementary doctrinal statements in the language of to-day. Rather I think it must be met by language more ancient than was that of the catholic creeds. It is perhaps premature to consider the form which any supplementary declaration might take. But when reunion comes further above the horizon may we not perhaps agree that the Churches in uniting shall not merely declare their adherence to the catholic creeds but shall with equal solemnity declare their acceptance of the evangelical message which the Church is to promulgate to the world.

" God so loved the world that he gave his only begotten Son that whosoever believeth in him should not perish but have everlasting life. For God sent not his Son into the world to condemn the world but that the world through him might be saved." " We have not an High Priest which cannot be touched with the feeling of our infirmities, but was in all points tempted like as we are . . ." " The Spirit and the Bride say come, and let him that heareth say come, and let him that is athirst come, and whosoever will let him take of the water of life freely."

One cannot, I am well aware, construct a creed or a substitute for a creed from Scripture passages, but here we have strikingly set forth in language at once authoritative and appealing, the love of God, the Saviour both as Redeemer and as friend and brother, and the free offer of salvation to man.

Some such form of declaration in the language of Scripture would, I believe, help to remove difficulties among some of those who, whilst loyal to the creeds as statements of doctrine, find that they do not wholly satisfy their evangelical and activist impulses.

Creedless reunion is a foolish and idle dream. Credal reunion might give us a Church of Sardis. We need not merely a common creed, we need a spiritual dynamic. Where shall we find it ? By the grace of God and under the guidance of His Spirit we shall find it in common devotion to our Master, in common recognition of His humanity as our elder Brother, in common recognition of His supreme claim to our obedience as the Son of God, in a common faith that " God hath highly exalted him and given him a name which is above every name, that at the name of Jesus every knee should bow, of things in heaven and things in earth and things under the earth, and that every tongue should confess that Jesus Christ is Lord to the glory of God the Father."

PROFESSOR DR. STEFAN ZANKOW
University of Sofia, Bulgaria (Orthodox)

I

For us of the Orthodox Church it is a self-evident axiom that where the one Church, or Christian unity, is found, there also is found the one Christian truth, and consequently one Christian faith, and hence one Christian Confession of Faith.

The well-known passage in which the Apostle speaks of

" one faith " (Eph. iv, 6) cannot be construed, whether from a natural or historical point of view, in any other sense than as a " doctrine," a creed.

A faith and a doctrine (or a creed) can only fail to correspond with one another in the sense that the substance and the idea may fail to correspond with the form and words in which they are expressed or rendered. Nevertheless, bearing in mind the dualism of human nature, we have no right to treat the idea and the words (or the faith and the doctrine) as opposite conceptions. Corresponding to every idea, there is a word ; corresponding to every faith there is a doctrine, or a creed.

Moreover, it follows from the very nature of the subject that when the Apostle spoke of one faith, he was also speaking of the one religious truth which is apprehended by that faith, and at the same time of one doctrine (or confession of faith) which is the expression of that truth.

Moreover, the whole tenour of the Holy Scriptures, indeed the very Scriptures themselves, and the whole history of the Christian Church from the time of the Apostles and their disciples convince us that, in the first place, there was always one faith, held and required, in the one Church of Christ ; and secondly, that the true faith was never and could never have been distinguished from the one religious truth and from the one religious doctrine (or confession of faith).

For even from an entirely empirical standpoint there never was, nor is there, nor can there ever be, any religious body, far less a Church, not possessing a fundamental faith and a doctrine (or confession of faith) as the expression of that faith. Christianity without its principle would be something utterly inconceivable, and a Christian Church without a principle would be even more inconceivable and absurd.

It is, indeed, the extraordinary importance, nay more, the indispensability of a correct confession of faith as an expression of the true Christian doctrine, which accounts first for the diversity and multiplicity of the creeds in use in the different Churches, and secondly for the steadfast attachment of every Christian Church to its own confession of faith.

To have one Church, and at the same time to allow the widest possible diversity of faith and creed within its bounds, would mean either that the essential nature of the Church as a unity was not understood, or that the Church in question was not in reality the Church of Christ; or else indeed that there was indifference towards the Church and towards ecclesiastical unity.

The chief argument which is used against the necessity of having a single faith or creed in a single or unified Church is that all faith is a matter of personal conviction, and that personal conviction can only be possible where there is personal freedom. We of the Orthodox Church consider that though these words may be correct in themselves, their use in this connection rests on a misconception, and that the argument is not relevant to the real point at issue. Undoubtedly, every person is free, according to his conviction, to believe in and acknowledge Christ or not to do so. But if he does not believe in Christ, he is not a Christian, and has no interest in the Christian Church; whereas, if he believes in Christ he must also confess Christ. And so long as he holds this belief it is illogical to speak of a freedom which would make it lawful for him to be a Christian, and yet not to believe in Christ! And this applies with the same force to the acceptance of all other fundamental truths of the Christian religion and the Christian Church. It is therefore idle, in discussing this problem, to seek to establish an antithesis, and to represent truth and faith (hence, doctrine and creed) as standing in opposition to freedom and conviction. The religious truth is objective (God, Christ, and so on); that is to say it exists, and will continue to exist, even independently of our personal conviction and freedom of judgment. Faith is the inward, personal, spiritual path through which the religious truth is apprehended, experienced and discerned, and it is also the inward vessel in which this truth is contained. The creed is the external expression, formulated in words, of this truth and this faith. These three elements are thus one in source and origin. They are in no way antithetical to freedom and conviction, which rather form a background for them.

For the same reasons we regard it as an error to suppose that the creed, because it is an external form, fetters or might fetter the living faith. If this view were to be generally applied, the Bible and the Church must themselves be regarded as external forms, so that the whole movement for the unity of the Church would be stultified.

Nor can we attach any value to the objection that the creed is related to and conditioned by historical events. All things are related to history : the Incarnation, the Bible, etc. But this relation does not imply any relativity in religious facts or truths, although their accomplishment and revelation have their place in history and have found verbal expression in the creeds.

Accordingly, we of the Orthodox Church hold steadfastly to the belief that where the Church is found, there must also *ipso facto* be found Faith, Doctrine, and Creed ; and that where the one Church of Christ is found, there are found, or ought to be found, one Faith, one Doctrine and one Creed.

II

What then is the confession of faith of a united Christendom ? Or what could or should such a confession consist of ? Should it be a new confession of faith, or one of the ancient symbols ?

The extraordinary difficulty of drawing up a new form of creed or securing its acceptance is plain to everybody, more particularly in the present situation of Christendom. Any new creed drawn up for a united Christendom would need to be so formulated as to express in its articles the essentials of Christian truth in a manner that would be acceptable to the individual Churches—since the object aimed at would be to have a single creed, which would form a single bond of faith. But at the first attempt to determine the articles of such a creed, every one of the issues which now keep Christendom disunited would immediately

arise. In short, it is evident that any new " midway "
creed, which aimed at reconciling the extreme right and the
extreme left, would be a futile undertaking, because, in
matters of religion, no reconciliation is possible between
truth and error, between affirmation and negation ; and
any such creed would, in effect, be a more or less un-
substantial and consequently valueless collection of phrases.
The same argument applies to any attempt to formulate a
new creed containing a minimum of Christian truth. For
there can be no minimum or maximum in Christian truth.

And again : What generally accepted standard could
we find for the numerous Christian Churches of to-day,
when we come to draw up the articles of the new creed ?
And what guarantee could we have that this standard
would be a correct one ? And what would be the prospects
of securing universal acceptance either for that standard or
for the new creed which would be founded upon it ? When
we begin to fathom the difficulties of drawing up a new confession of faith, we are compelled, in spite of ourselves,
to admit that there is grave danger lest these very difficulties might wreck our endeavours to re-unite Christendom,
and lest, after all our efforts to compile such a creed, the
Churches should be more widely separated than before
the attempt was made.

We find that the situation is exactly reversed if we take
the Nicene Creed as the Symbol of Christian unity.

First as regards the inward truth of the Creed. From
our Orthodox standpoint, the only guarantees of truth are
first the Church itself, and secondly and allied to the first,
the catholic character of the truth, as being the truth of the
Church. Outside the boundaries of the Ecumenical
Church and of Catholicism, there is nothing which is not
open to challenge. But the converse is not true—unless we
are advocates of ecclesiastical nihilism or of some Christian
atomic theory ! The Church is the "fulness " and the "pillar
and ground of truth," and the truths of the Christian
religion can only be apprehended in all their aspects if
they are given to us as " catholic " truths, that is to say,
if all the Christian Churches, going back to the times of the

former undivided Church, have endorsed them. Now that is the case in regard to the Nicene Creed. If it were otherwise, that Creed would be a document possessing only an historical or archæological interest for us. But, as it is, the Nicene Creed is the confession of faith of the whole undivided ancient Church, and we cannot perceive any reason why this Creed should not, or might not, become the Creed of a later united Christendom.

The acceptance of the Nicene Creed as the confession of faith of the united Church would be all the more intelligible and natural because it is already the Creed of two-thirds of Christendom and is held in great honour in the remaining third.

Moreover, the Nicene Creed has two advantages : first, that it is short, being a statement of the primary essentials of the Christian faith ; and secondly, that its acceptance would exclude all questions of equality or inferiority, such as might arise in the selection of a single confession of faith for a united Christendom.

Surely it must be admitted that, if Christendom of to-day is not ripe to accept the Nicene Creed as a common confession of faith, then this same Christendom is far less ripe for the attempt to draw up, and secure acceptance for, a new common creed.

For these reasons, we of the Orthodox Church hold that the only possible and the only necessary confession of faith for a united Christendom, to-day, is the Nicene Creed— that is to say, the Symbol of the ancient united Christian Church—and that the acceptance of this creed must precede any attempt to draw up a new common confession of faith.

III

At the same time, we must say frankly that in our veiw the acceptance of this Creed would only be of real significance if its validity, in the fullest sense of that word, were generally admitted.

IV

We do not think that the occasions on which this Creed would be used in Church services or the manner of its use are issues of primary importance, at any rate at the beginning.

And now, beloved Fathers and Brethren, we will conclude our observations with an appeal borrowed from the liturgy of our Orthodox Church :

" Let us love one another, so that we may confess God in unity of Spirit."

The Conference rose at 12.45 p.m.

SATURDAY AFTERNOON, AUGUST 6TH.

The afternoon session opened at 4 p.m. with devotions led by the Rev. H. SUMITRA, B.A.

On Thursday, August 4th, the Syndic and Municipality of Lausanne had graciously invited the delegates and their friends to an evening reception at the Hotel Beau Rivage. The fine weather made it possible for their guests to enjoy to the full the very hospitable entertainment provided for them in the grounds of the Hotel. The following resolution was unanimously adopted by the Conference on Saturday, August 6th :

That this Conference desires to convey to the Syndic and Municipality of the City of Lausanne its most cordial thanks for the gracious and generous hospitality offered to its members on the evening of August 4th. Acknowledging with gratitude the privileges which it enjoys as the guest of this beautiful and historic city, the Conference would also wish to express to the Syndic and Municipality its sincere good wishes, trusting that the blessing of God may rest upon them in the execution of those high and responsible duties which the citizens of Lausanne have entrusted to their care.

Rules of Procedure.—An announcement having been made as to sectional meetings for August 8th in the Aula, the *Eglise de Saint-Laurent*, and the *Eglise allemande de la Mercerie*, the Chairman submitted the following revised text of Rule 7, stating that it had received the approval of those who took exception to the Rule in its original form :

When reports from the sections have been made to the full Conference, if alterations in them are proposed, the Conference may refer them to a Drafting Committee for consideration and report. In any such report any differences remaining shall be clearly indicated, as well as the agreement reached. No statement shall be declared to be accepted by the Conference unless it be accepted either unanimously or *nemine contradicente*.

The amended text was adopted.

The Chairman then called upon Bishop LEON TOURIAN, of the Armenian Church, to address a few words to the Conference, introducing him as the representative of a nation still in peril, and of a Church which must claim the sincerest sympathy of all Christian people.

THE RIGHT REV. LEON TOURIAN
Bishop of Manchester (Armenian Church)

Dear Brethren,—I, as representative of the National Apostolic Church of Armenia and His Holiness the Catholicos, the Supreme Patriarch of all Armenia, cordially greet the members of this pan-Christian Conference, and declare that our ancient Church takes part with the greatest sympathy in its deliberations, seeing that this Conference tends to bring about closer relations and hearty co-operation among the Christian Churches, and aims at animating the Christian world by giving effect to Christ's express precept of love and union among His followers.

Deeming it essential that reciprocal and full knowledge of the Christian Churches should precede the closer relations and co-operation between them, and at the same time having in view the programme of the proceedings of the present Conference, I am instructed to lay before the Conference a short outline of the administrative and doctrinal principles of the Armenian Church.

The Catholicos or Supreme Patriarch of all the Armenians, at Etchmiadzin, as Head of the entire Armenian Church, is regarded as the successor of the Apostles Thaddeus and Bartholomew.

The organisation and the rule of the Armenian Church have emanated not from the activities of an ecclesiastical legislative body, but from the history of the Armenian nation. It is interesting to note that the Armenian nation is the custodian of not only the purely administrative prerogatives of the Church, but it also has a voice in doctrinal (non-dogmatic) questions as well.

The organ of the Armenian nation from the very beginning has been the Ecclesiastical Supreme Council, which met for the first time in the year 365, and at which both laymen and clergy were present. Through historical development the Supreme Ecclesiastical Council meets nowadays by the invitation of the Supreme Patriarch of all Armenia. The people in every diocese elect one layman and one clerical delegate, and all the delegates meet under the presidency of the Supreme Patriarch, and discuss questions and pass resolutions by a majority of votes, which resolutions are binding on all.

Thanks to the council system, the elective principle has taken root in the Armenian Church, and therefore every ecclesiastical functionary, from the highest to the lowest, is elected by the people.

The Creed adopted by the Armenian Church for its offices is the Athanasian formula, which had its beginning during the Council of Nicæa. It contains almost exclusively the dogma of the Incarnation, which our Church preserves with neither modification nor addition. The unity of the nature of Christ, or the *monophysitism*, which is accepted by the Armenian Church, is identical with the Ephesian formula, which is that of St. Cyril of Alexandria, namely, one nature of the Word Incarnate. The monophysitism of the Council of Ephesus, which the Armenian Church upholds, is altogether different from that of Eutyches.

With regard to the differences which divide the Armenian and Greek Orthodox Churches, these apply solely to the rejection by the Armenian Church of the Council of Chalcedon, and in the non-recognition of the succeeding Councils. In all other dogmatic questions the two Churches are in perfect accord.

It is with singleness of purpose and a minimum of elaboration that the Armenian Church has steered her course in the matter of dogmas. The lofty principle expressed by a learned divine of the Western Church, Saint Augustine, has been and ever remains the watchword of our Church. The expression " unity in essentials " has been carried by her to the furthest point of application ; that of " liberty in doubtful matters " she has applied in the broadest of senses ; and it is only on the basis indicated by common agreement that it will be possible, to our thinking, to ensure to the Universal Church " charity in all things."

Consequently, I declare from my heart, charity, more charity!

The Chairman then called the meeting to prayer for the persecuted Christians of Russia, China, Armenia, and other parts of the world ; after which the discussion of the subject of the day was resumed by Prof. Dr. OLAF MOE.

PROFESSOR DR. OLAF MOE
University of Oslo (Lutheran)

The question of the necessity of a Common Confession of Faith for a reunited Church is complicated for the Protestant Churches by the fact that Protestantism relies fundamentally on the Holy Scriptures as the sole authoritative guide in questions of faith. However, it cannot be disputed that the Reformed Churches have not only drawn up Confessions of Faith of their own, but have always expressly acknowledged their attachment to the ancient Creeds of the Church ; and only in exceptional cases do we find Protestant Churches which regard the Bible as their sole binding authority on questions of doctrine. As a matter of fact, recent historical research in the New Testament has shown with increasing clearness that the New Testament so far from excluding a special confession of faith actually implies its existence.

The two first and the two last speakers at this morning's session both gave affirmative replies to the first question which was formulated in the documents prepared in view of this discussion (Pamphlet No. 52). The Church is held together, above all, by the common recognition of a particular doctrine as the word of God, and neither St. Paul nor St. John would have had any objection to a binding confession of faith, in other words, to the idea of correct doctrine (Bishop Gore). The Church creeds are already implicit in the New Testament (Dr. Zoellner). A common confession of faith is not absolutely indispensable, but it is highly desirable (Dr. Wobbermin, Dr. Lindskog). The most important creed is that of life and action (Dr. Lindskog). Again, in regard to the second question, most of the speakers gave similar answers. The Apostles' and Nicene Creeds are simply co-ordinated statements of the confessions of faith which are to be found in various passages in the New Testament, and they were shaped by the opposition which they had to encounter (Dr. Zoellner). The essence of the apostolic teaching, particularly in the writings of St. Paul and St. John—the acknowledgment of Jesus as Messiah and Saviour, as the only Son of God, the Eternal Word, who became incarnate in the fulness of time, who in the flesh was crucified, slain and raised from the dead, and who after His ascension sent the Holy Spirit that His disciples should baptise in the name of the Father, Son and Holy Ghost—all these truths are merely stated with greater precision in the Nicene Creed. Indeed, theological critics are willing to admit this ; they only dispute that Paul understood his Master aright (Dr. Gore). On the other hand Dr. Lindskog objected that the Creeds have caused a shifting of the proper emphasis in the Gospel of Jesus.

It cannot therefore be denied that both the above-named Creeds possess special importance, owing to the fact that, as regards their substance, they are in accord with the New Testament.

There is, in addition, another consideration to which great weight must be attached for the purpose of this Conference, namely, that the Apostles' and Nicene Creeds constitute the common heritage of the Churches which were separated by the schism of the eleventh century and the Reformation of the sixteenth century. We can only secure a common basis, as Dr. Gore has pointed out, for the reunion of all the Churches—Catholic and Protestant—if this Conference will admit that the doctrines of the Trinity and the Incarnation are a natural corollary of the Gospel. Dr. Stefan Zankow has emphasised this point with even greater force.

For these reasons I entirely concur with the two first and last speakers of this morning's session in giving an affirmative reply to Question 3 (a) : " Could a united Church agree to accept the Faith of Christ as taught in Holy Scripture, and handed down in the Apostles' and Nicene Creeds ? " If the Churches will begin by agreeing that baptism shall be in the name of the Father, the Son and the Holy Ghost, it should be possible, as Dr. Gore has observed, to leave the local Churches to decide for themselves regarding the use of the above-mentioned Creeds at divine service.

As regards the last question, the same speaker has very shrewdly observed that he preferred to leave it unanswered until some substitute for the ancient Creeds has been suggested which is at all likely to find general agreement. The confession of faith, as Dr. Zoellner has said, must grow out of inward actualities, and no inward union can be promoted by the construction of artificial formulæ. Artificial ingenuities would only increase the confusion.

In conclusion, if I am asked my own opinion, I would say this : The Bible and the Lord's Prayer form an already existing bond which links all the Churches. Let us thank God that this is so. But that bond does not suffice, because the Bible itself is subject to such diverse interpretations. A Confession of Faith is an absolute necessity. And if we really desire a union of all the Churches which acknowledge Jesus as God and Saviour, we must take the ground which was common to the ancient united Church as our starting point—that is to say, the Apostles' and the Nicene

H

Creed. Evangelical catholicity is our motto ; and we ought not to fling aside all that is catholic or all that is ancient. The *Una Sancta* of the future can only be built upon the *Una Sancta* of the first days of Christianity, and the present divergence between the Churches can only be eliminated by converging towards the ancient Church and its Creed.

If all the divided Churches would lift up their eyes to our beloved Saviour and seek to be one in Him, and if the now disunited Churches would look back to the ancient united Church, then we might indeed expect a brighter future for Christianity.

The Bishop of GLOUCESTER (Dr. Headlam) : We have been told many times that we cannot unite the Churches on formulæ ; that is, of course, quite true. We cannot unite the Churches unless there is the spirit of unity. But I think it is equally true that we cannot unite the Churches unless we are able to have a concrete expression of faith. I think, after the speeches that we have had this morning, the time has come for someone to be so bold as to try to express what we have come to, in a way that may be agreed upon, and I would at once, therefore, read out a formulæ that I would propose :

We accept the faith of Christ as it has been taught us by the Holy Scriptures; and as it has been handed down to us in the Creed of the Catholic Church set forth at the Council of Chalcedon, and in the Apostles' Creed.

Those words have been very carefully chosen, and I will briefly expound them. First of all, we accept the *faith of Christ*, we do not accept the *Creed*. We accept the Creed as the expression of the faith of Christ, and it is very important that we should say that what we are united upon is the faith of Christ, because though it may be well expressed by the Creed it is far deeper, broader, and fuller than any Creed can express. Secondly, we put in the forefront the Holy Scriptures as the source of our knowledge of the faith of Christ. On that we are all agreed. Thirdly, we accept the great Ecumenical Creed, which is the almost universal authority of the ancient Church, which is agreed upon by East and West, which is accepted by almost all the modern Churches, and is the only possible basis of union. I would add to that, perhaps, the Apostles' Creed as being a simpler expression of the same thing.

The great value of putting the formula in that way is this : there are some who fear the ancient Creed because they think it commits them to a philosophy they do not hold. But we do not accept the Creed, we accept the faith which is taught in the Creed, of which it is the accepted expression.

I venture to think that on those words it may be possible for us to unite with the great majority (at any rate) of the Churches. May I say that I do not think, perhaps, that all the professors will unite ; I have been a professor myself and have been associated with them all my life, and I do not think that you would ever get all the professors to unite.

There is one thing more. The same Council of Chalcedon which promulgated the Creed which we accept, anathematised also those who put forward any other creed or who added to the Creed. My own belief is that almost all the divisions of Christendom have arisen because people have neglected that side of the wisdom of the ancient Church. It began with the *filioque* clause. It went on with the doctrine of transubstantiation. It ran riot at the Reformation when every Church tried to redefine the Creed so minutely as to exclude almost everyone from its walls.

Unless we are prepared to say that there will be no other necessary condition of union with the Christian Church than the Creed of Christendom, we shall fall into exactly the same difficulties in the future as in the past, and this must apply, I am afraid, to the suggestion made by Lord Sands. We cannot pick out any particular expressions of Scripture because they happen to be the ones we like ; we build ourselves on the faith of Christ, the Holy Scriptures, and the expression of the faith in the Ecumenical Creed.

The Chairman pointed out that the Bishop of Gloucester's suggestion would properly come up for discussion in the Section dealing with this subject.

Professor Dr. KARL PRÖHLE : This Conference is undertaking a gravely responsible task, which must not end in
a fiasco and still less in unreality. We are now dealing with
the very foundations of Christianity, and asking what confession of belief is essential to Christian unity. Surely we
need a purely religious confession of faith rather than a
theological one. We are met, on the terms of our invitation,
as confessing Jesus Christ as God and Saviour : this itself
is a confession. And it is only upon a common confession
that we can dream of building a common organisation. I
would plead for a new confession : not that we can dispense with the old creeds, but that they need supplementing. We need—and this is our difficulty—a creed broad
enough to be universal, and yet not so phrased as to be
devoid of definite content. We need to study the particulars
of Christian belief in the light of the whole, and the whole
in the light of the particulars ; and this would be a hopeless
task if we had not before us the person of Christ, in whom
the sum of revelation consists and who yet embodies it in
a living concrete historical person and character. Our task
is not hopeless, so long as we take Him as the basis and
content of the creed which is to bring us together.

The Right Rev. WILLIAM T. MANNING, D.D. : In connection with the subject of the day, the Common Faith of
the whole Church of Christ, I venture to add a few words
to what Bishop Gore has said in regard to that great Communion, the Roman Catholic Church, which is not represented here.

First, we all deeply regret that the Roman Catholic
Church did not feel able to accept the invitation which was
extended to her to send representatives to this World
Conference.

Secondly, although the Roman Catholic Church has not
felt that she could send representatives, we want her to
know that our feeling towards her is one of love and fellowship, and that it is our desire to take fully into account her
place and her great witness in this world for Christ.

Thirdly, while the Christian Communions, Catholic and

Protestant, which are represented here can, and we pray that they may, make true progress towards reunion, we recognise that Christian unity cannot be attained until it includes our brethren of the Roman Catholic Church. What we who are gathered here seek is not a unity of Protestants alone, or of Catholics alone. This might only accentuate differences, and perpetuate divisions. We seek a unity which shall include all Christian Communions throughout the world, both Catholic and Protestant, which confess our Lord Jesus Christ as Saviour, Lord and God. It is the united testimony of the whole Church of Christ that is needed in the battle against sin and unbelief, and especially at this time against the world-wide concerted attack, disguising itself often under new and high-sounding terms, upon Christ's standards of sexual morality and of marriage.

Fourthly, may I not venture to say that there goes out from this gathering the hope that our Roman Catholic brethren, clergy and people, will send up their prayers along with ours that in this Conference we may be guided by Him who prayed that we all may be one, and that by His Spirit we may all be led into that peace and unity which are agreeable to His will.

After a minute of silent prayer the discussion was continued by the Rev. Pastor ANDRÉ BERTRAND :

We are studying the relation between the Person of Jesus, Holy Scripture, and the ancient Creeds. We who hold to the Reformed tradition, in large agreement with Prof. Wobbermin, would urge the following considerations. The Person of Christ is at the centre of the Gospel, a living divine reality which cannot be compressed within the limits of any formula. For the knowledge of that Person the New Testament—the evangelic record and the apostolic confession—is the one primary source at our disposal.

Creeds, as has been said, must be metaphysical, ascribing to Jesus, as they do, a value which transcends history and belongs to the realm of the timeless and the universal. The "metaphysic" of St. Paul and St. John is not alien from the Synoptic tradition, but is its necessary complement. Similarly, the ancient Creeds were not arbitrary excrescences of Christian thought : they represent an evangelical conquest of Hellenism rather than a mere Hellenisation of the Gospel. Yet the work of creeds and councils, based though it was on Scripture, was not simply a transmission of the scriptural faith : it involved a re-statement of that faith in intellectual rather than in religious terms.

Christian unity requires an acknowledgment of the work thus achieved, and an endorsement of its guiding principles. It should not require the imposition of this or that creed upon Churches whose basis is purely scriptural. Calvinistic Churches, for instance, could not place any creed, however venerable, on the same level as Scripture. Union in Christ, who is the Truth, transcends the limits of all historic creeds.

The Rev. J. VERNON BARTLET, D.D. : Everything depends upon the principle, fully recognised in the Lambeth Appeal, of mutual consideration for each other's consciences. For Congregationalists, the type of creed which we desire to retain is one which expresses the attitude of personality to the personality of Jesus Christ, making this the fundamental bond between Christians. We endorse Alexandre Vinet's description of faith as a steadfast gaze (*le regard*) whereby the object, Jesus Christ, passes into the very substance of the soul of believers. Others may approach faith rather from the point of view of those inferential safeguards by which the early Church protected itself from certain misinterpretations of the faith. We accept those safeguards as indicating the lines within which the interpretation of the personality of Christ shall be developed : yet for us they are indirect and abstract as compared with that expression of belief which we consider primary.

It is much to be hoped that our closer consideration of this subject may bring us towards some common expression of that religious aspect of faith ; this would enable those who are primarily Evangelicals, but who are also deeply catholic in their outlook to draw nearer to brethren whose primary attachment is to the historic creeds.

The Archbishop of NUBIA : A general agreement as to the main principles and bases of the faith is essential for any stable union of Churches. The Greek Orthodox Church has for sixteen centuries adhered to the Nicene Creed alone, and this Creed, backed as it is by the consent of all ancient Churches, is the basis upon which the fabric of unity could most naturally rest. The faith of Christ as taught in the holy Scriptures and handed down in the tradition of the Church, of which tradition the Nicene Creed is a part—this is the standard which we, who use this Creed in Baptism and the Eucharist, have always accepted.

Freedom in the use of the Creed may be conceded : the possibility of the emergence of another creed, from a future Ecumenical Council, need not be excluded ; but as a stable foundation the Nicene Creed ought to be respected and retained.

The Bishop of TINNEVELLY (Dr. Tubbs) : The ground covered by the great Creeds is common to all of us Indian Christians. Divisions between us begin with matters, such as Orders and Holy Communion, to which the Creeds do not specifically refer.

In view of this fact, the movement towards reunion is more urgent among us than it is at home. Our Conference recalls to me that great Conference which we read of in Acts xv, when the ideals of a home Church and of a mission Church stood out in vivid contrast, the one adhering to ancient institutions, to tradition, and the other moved by a world-wide vision and opportunity. Unity was actually being achieved on the mission-field, yet the home Church could not see the wood for the trees, and had to be converted to the spirit of inclusive unity.

So it is to-day. In the mission-field we are actually solving the problems of unity. We in South India, for instance, are drawing nearer to the realisation of a great united Church ; but we are hampered by the doubts and difficulties of our leaders at home. Greatly as we respect the authoritative learning of those leaders, we find it hard to reconcile their reluctance to move with the actual facts as we know them at the front.

We therefore earnestly ask the home Churches not to strain the loyalty of the mission Churches and of native Christians. If to move forward is dangerous, it is more dangerous to sit still. We also ask that decisions shall not be postponed. Let us not disappoint the Church throughout the world. The Church of Jerusalem took a vast risk when it allied itself with Gentile Christianity ; cannot we, also, take risks ? God has not given us the spirit of fear, but of power and of love and of a sound mind.

Professor Dr. SERGIUS BULGAKOW : The universal acceptance of the Nicene Creed, hallowed by antiquity, is in itself desirable : yet it ought to be something more than a diplomatic concession. The Church is the fulness of the divine life : we are now speaking of something which, like the Gospel, falls within that fulness and is a part of it. The road to unity is the way along which we progress together from a minimum towards a maximum, towards an ever-increasing appropriation of the fulness of life in God.

The Church is the sphere of sanctification : it is a worshipping fellowship : it is charged with a prophetic mission ; on these three sides we are called to realise its ideal more fully.

Holiness is the goal and essence of the Church's life : the holiness of the manhood of Christ, actualised in the communion of saints. But we cannot separate the humanity of our Lord from that of His mother, the unspotted *Theotokos*. She is the head of mankind in the Church ; Mother and Bride of the Lamb, she is joined with all saints and angels in the worship and life of the Church. Others may not yet feel drawn, as I do, to name her name in prayer. Yet, as we draw together towards doctrinal reunion, it may be that we are coming potentially nearer even in this regard.

The Church, again, has a rich and growing treasure of liturgical worship, a treasure which the Orthodox Church has guarded faithfully as an inspired well-spring of faith.

She desires a great Christian unity in worship, but hopes for it not so much through the common acceptance of liturgical forms as through the energy of love, drawn out by the irresistible attraction of spiritual beauty.

Thirdly, the Church looks forward to new tasks and not only backward towards tradition ; its task is the consecration of all life, and the fulfilment of the " earnest expectation of the created world." The Spirit bloweth where it listeth : it is for us to be ready to follow His guidance. We are now only at our beginning ; we must be ready for new roads, for the opening-up of new horizons. Let us invoke our Guide : Come, O Paraclete, and dwell in us!

The Rev. Pastor FRANÇOIS MÉJAN : Great as are the obstacles which confront us, we should thank God for the general accord in which we find ourselves in regard to the confession of our faith. The Reformed Churches of France do not confuse faith with knowledge, nor do they, on the other hand, limit it to a " trust of the believing heart." The object of trust is knowable, and to know that in which we believe is a power and a bond. We recognise, therefore, the necessity of an explicit declaration of faith.

Our Church confesses " the sovereign authority of the Holy Scriptures as touching faith and salvation by faith in Jesus Christ, the only Son of God, who died for our sins and rose again for our justification. Therefore, at the foundation of its teaching, worship and discipline, it guards and maintains the great Christian facts represented in its sacraments, celebrated in its acts of worship, and expressed in its liturgies, notably in the confession of sin, the Apostles' Creed, and the Liturgy of the Lord's Supper."

The Apostles' Creed is read every Sunday in our churches : it is impressed upon parents at the baptism of their children : it is recited at the burial of the dead. Thus for us the acceptance of the ancient baptismal formula as a common confession of faith presents no obstacle.

After the singing of a hymn, and prayer offered by Bishop BRENT, the Conference rose at 6.30 p.m.

SECTIONAL SESSIONS

MONDAY, TUESDAY, AND WEDNESDAY,
AUGUST 8TH, 9TH, & 10TH.

On these days the Conference met in Sections for the discussion of Subjects II, III, and IV, and for the preparation of Reports to be submitted to the Conference.

Under the Rules of Procedure, it was voted that there should be no Section upon Subject I, The Call to Unity, but that the officers of the Conference and the chairman and secretaries of the Sections should form a committee to prepare a resolution upon that Subject.

The members were allocated to Sections, each having previously expressed his preference in the matter, as follows:

SECTION II

Subject II: THE CHURCH'S MESSAGE TO THE WORLD—
THE GOSPEL

Convener: PROFESSOR DR. ADOLF DEISSMANN

Armitage, Archdeacon	Day, Dr. W. H.
Arseniew, Prof. N.	Dibelius, Prof. M.
Baer, Dr. S. H.	Dionisy, Archbishop
Bagnall, Mrs. Mary A.	Enniss, R.
Barbour, Dr. G. F.	Fisher, Bishop
Barnes, Dr. C. W.	Frank, Dr. G.
Bertrand, Pastor A. N.	Gaugler, Dr. E.
Bieler, Prof. C.	Garrett, Dr. A. E.
Bleakney, Rev. C.	Gibson, Theron
Boyd, Mrs. W.	Glubokowsky, Prof. N.
Brewis, Principal J. T.	Gogarten, Dr. F.
Bristow, J.	Goodall, Rev. C.
Budd, Rev. W. R.	Hadorn, Prof. W.
Budd, Mrs. Elizabeth	Haenisch, Pastor G.
Cannon, Bishop	Hamilton, L. A.
Claudius, Salib Pasha	Harvey, Rev. F. G.
Constantinidis, Archimandrite	Henry, Dr. J. M.
Davis, Dr. D. A.	Herold, Dr. O.

Holden, Rev. A. T.
Horne, F. A.
Horstmann, Rev. P. F.
Howie, Rev. R. H.
Hoyois, Pastor E.
Hurst, Bishop
James, Prof. J. A.
Jézéquel, Pastor J.
Jones, Rev. T. J.
Klein, Dr. W. F.
Koren, Rev. L.
Laun, Lic. J. F.
Lew, Dr. T. T.
Lewins, W. A.
Limerick, Bishop of
Lofthouse, Principal W. F.
McConnell, Bishop
Machichan, Dr. D.
MacCracken, President J. H.
Maclagan, Dr. P. J.
Maclean, Rt. Rev. N.
Macnutt, Archdeacon
Malan, Pastor A.
Margetson, Provost W. J.
Master, Dr. H. B.
Méjan, Pastor F.
Mill, W. H.
Monod, Professor W.
Moore, Dr. T. A.
Nooe, Dr. R. T.
Nygren, Professor A.
Ochiai, Dr. J. K.
Ostenfeld, Bishop
Peake, Prof. A. S.

Philips, Dr. W.
Pyke, Rev. R.
Reichel, Sir Harry
Richards, Dr. G. W.
Richards, Dr. T. T.
Rose, Rev. I. M.
Rosenkjar, Rev. J.
Roy, Rev. T. S.
Rust, Dr. J. A.
Sanford, Mrs. W. E.
Schenck, Rev. H. W.
Schmitz, Professor O.
Schneider, Prof. F.
Schou, Aage
Siebel, J. G.
Sjöstedt, Major A.
Smiley, Dr. W. B.
Soper, Prof. E. S.
Stejskal, Bishop
Stevenson, Rev. J. S.
Sturgis, Dr. W. C.
Sumitra, Rev. H.
Tarafdar, Canon
Thvedt, Pastor N. B.
Titius, Prof. A.
Turkevich, Rev. B. J.
Verner, Pastor A.
Vickrey, C. V.
Wilson, D. M.
Wiseman, C. Luke
Wiseman, Dr. F. L.
Woods, Canon
Zwemer, Dr. S. M.

Section III

Subject III : THE NATURE OF THE CHURCH

Convener : Professor William Adams Brown, D.D.

Adelaide, Bishop of
Alivisatos, Prof. H. S.
Andersen, Prof. J. O.
Atkinson, Dr. H. A.

Aulén, Prof. G.
Bagnall, T. St. J.
Baker, Rev. H. N.
Banninga, Dr. J. J.

Bates, President M. L.
de Bildt, His Excellency H.
Bird, Dr. P. S.
Blair, Rev. J. C.
de Boér, Prof. Alexis
Bombay, Bishop of
Bulgakow, Prof. S.
Brilioth, Prof. Y. T.
Cadman, Dr. S. P.
Clark, Chancellor L. C.
Dibelius, Gen. Supt. O.
Dixon, Very Rev. W. G.
Donald, Dr. G. H.
Dornakal, Bishop of
Douglas, Canon J. A.
Elert, Professor W.
Eulogios, Archbishop
Fehl, Konsistorialrat A.
Fiero, R. H.
Fotheringham, Dr. J. T.
Fyffe, Dr. D.
Gardiner, Rev. J. B.
Gardner, Miss Lucy
Geller, Dr. S.
George, Bishop of
Gerrard, T. L.
Giesecke, Dr. F.
Handmann, Prof. R.
Hauge, Pastor S. M.
Haussleiter, Professor G.
Heath, Carl
Herron, Prof. C.
Hertzberg, Pastor M.
Hindes, Rev. W.
Holland, Rev. W. E. S.
Hume, Dr. R. A.
Humphries, Prof. A. L.
Iriney, Bishop
Joyce, Archdeacon
Kaas, Baron A. von
Keller, Dr. A.
Kelley, Rev. W. M.
Kennink, Archbishop

Kulp, Rev. E. J.
Küry, Bishop
Lang, Dr. A.
Lang, Dr. T.
Lehtonen, Dr. A.
Leo, Pastor P.
Leontopolis, Archbishop of
Livingstone, W. P.
Lunn, Sir Henry
MacArthur, Rev. K. C.
Macaulay, Rev. J. J.
Manchester, Bishop of
Marquis, Dr. J. A.
Martin, Prof. A. von
Ménégoz, Prof. F.
Merle d'Aubigné, Dr. C.
Merrill, Dr. W. P.
Milne, Rev. J.
Morehouse, F. C.
Mosel, Pastor H. G. W.
Mudge, Dr. L. S.
Naupactos, Metropolitan of
Neander, Dr. H.
Neiiendam, Dr. M. N.
Neuschäfer, Studiendirektor C.
Ohlemüller, Dr. G.
Papadopoulos, B. K.
Paraskevaidis, Dr. T.
Parker, Rev. G.
Parsons, Bishop
Peel, Dr. A.
Peradse, Dr. G.
Perry, Bishop
Philip, Dr. A.
Philputt, Dr. J. M.
Piper, Lic. O.
Pröhle, Dr. K.
Raffay, Bishop
Riley, Athelstan
Ritchie, Dr. D. L.
Roberts, Dr. J. E.
Rogers, Dr. B. T
Sasse, Lic. H.

Scheer, Pastor C.
Schempp, Direktor J.
Scherer, Dr. M. G. G.
Schian, Gen. Supt. M.
Schmidt, Prof. K. L.
Selecman, Dr. C. C.
Shatford, Canon
Siegmund-Schultze, Prof. F.
Slosser, Rev. G. J.
Sommer, Rev. T. W. E.
Souček, Dr. J.
Stange, Dr. E.
Stefan, Archbishop
Steimle, Dr. A.

Stewart, Dr. G. C.
Stewart, Rev. R. W.
Swartz, President H. F.
Sydney, Archbishop of
Taranger, Prof. A.
Thomas, Dr. J. S. L.
Thompson, Rev. L. M.
Tinnevelly, Bishop of
Unruh, Prof. B. H.
Upsala, Archbishop of
Valiadis, Archimandrite
Wallau, Lic. R. H.
Williams, Bishop
Workman, Principal H. B.

Section IV

Subject IV : THE CHURCH'S COMMON CONFESSION OF FAITH

Convener : Canon Tissington Tatlow, D.D.

Aalders, Prof. W. J.
Abbott-Smith, Canon
Ainslie, Dr. Peter
Ankar, Lic. G. A.
Appia, Pastor L.
Armagh, Bishop of
Ashworth, Dr. R. A.
Balanos, Prof. D. S.
Bartlet, Dr. J. V.
Barton, Dr. W. E.
Bate, Canon
Bensow, Dr. O.
Bond, Dr. A. J. C.
Brodersen, Pastor P.
Brent, Bishop
Brown, Dr. A. J.
Burn, Dean
Choisy, Prof. J. E.
Cochran, Dr. J. W.
Comba, Prof. E.
Cooper, Rev. A. O.
Davey, Prof. J. E.

Davies, Rev. E. O.
Diobouniotis, Prof. C.
Dublin, Archbishop of
Dysinger, Dr. H.
Emerson, Dr. C. B.
Fabricius, Prof. C.
Falconer, Prof. J. W.
Fisher, Canon
Forgan, Dr. R.
Fornerod, Prof. A. A.
Furnajieff, Rev. D. N.
Garvie, Principal A. E.
Germanos, Archbishop
Gilmore, Dr. C.
Gloucester, Bishop of
Gore, Bishop
Gounelle, Pastor E.
Greever, Prof. W. H.
Hagemeyer, Dr. F.
Hall, Prof. F. J.
Heiler, Prof. F.
Hermelink, Prof. H.

Hinderer, Prof. A.
Hognestad, Bishop
Honduras, Bishop of
Houghton, Dr. R. M.
Hughes, Principal H. M.
Ihlen, Prof. C.
Inagaki, Prof. Y.
Irbe, Bishop
Jesch, Pastor A.
Katz, Pastor P.
Kay, Prof. D. M.
Kendrick, Prof. Eliza H.
Kennedy, Dean
Klingman, Dr. G. A.
Kortheuer, Bishop
Lencz, Prof. G.
Lindskog, Dr. H. J.
Lyman, Mrs. A. J.
Manning, Bishop
Mauck, President J. W.
M'Clymont, Dr. J. A.
McDowell, Bishop
Moe, Prof. Olaf
Monahan, Rev. A. E.
Monnier, Prof. H.
Moore, Bishop
Nash, Bishop
Nollen, Dean J. S.
Norberg, Dr. O.
Noyes, Dr. E. M.
Nubia, Archbishop of
Parker, Pastor L. D.
Pfannenstill, Prof. M.
Pongràcz, Prof. J.
Prochazka, Bishop
Prys, Dr. Owen

Pustowka, Pastor O.
Quick, Canon
Ravasz, Bishop
Reed, Dr. L. T.
Richmond, Rev. M.
Robinson, Principal W.
Roper, Bishop
de Saint-André, Pastor L.
Sandegren, Rev. P.
Sands, Lord
Shaw, Prof. J. M.
Sigmond, Rev. S. O.
Sills, President K. C. M.
Simons, Dr. W.
Sjöstrand, Prof. B.
Smith, Rev. J. C.
Stevenson, President J. Ross
Stören, Bishop
Thompson, Prof. E. T.
Thompson, President W. O.
Tourian, Bishop
Turk, Dr. M. H.
Vance, Dr. J. A.
Van Vlijmen, Bishop
Washburn, Dean H. B.
Watt, Rev. T. M.
Western, Canon
Wigham, Dr. J. T.
Wobbermin, Prof. G.
Wotherspoon, Dr. H. J.
Wright, Rev. H. C.
Zabriskie, G.
Zankow, Prof. S.
Zarnovicky, Pastor. M.
Zoellner, Gen. Supt. W.

REPORTS OF SECTIONS II, III & IV

Thursday Morning, August 11th.

A full session of the Conference was opened at 9.30 with devotions led by the Rev. Dr. Zwemer. The Chair was taken by the President, the Rt. Rev. Bishop Brent.

The following messages of greeting were read :

From the Synod of the Reformed Church of Vilno :

To the pioneers of the idea of the Gospel, to our brethren in Jesus Christ, to all who take part in the Conference, brotherly greetings : may the philanthropic ideal which you disseminate win its way throughout the world!

From the International Peace Bureau :

The International Peace Bureau, the senior institution of those which have been organised to promote the pacific settlement of international disputes, recognising the inestimabl evalue of the co-operation of the Churches in its task, begs you, Mr. President, to express to the Faith and Order Conference its ardent desires for the success of its undertaking, and for the achievement through our common efforts of the noble purpose of international peace.

From the Roumanian Orthodox Patriarchate :

Nectarie, Archbishop and Metropolitan of Bukovina, offers to the World Conference the greetings of the Roumanian Patriarchate, wishing it every success in its striving towards the union of the Churches, which would be the best of all means for securing that peace between the nations for which the whole world longs. The Orthodox Patriarchate will do all that it can to further this cause.

It was announced that on Sunday morning, August 14th, at 8.30, a service of Penitence and Intercession would be held in the Cathedral for members of the Conference (see page 320).

A message was received from Dr. John R. Mott, who was to have presided at the public meeting on Sunday evening, August 14th, saying that owing to his continued indisposition he would be unable to fulfil that engagement. It was resolved to send a message of sympathy to Dr. Mott.

It was announced that the Syndic and Municipality of Lausanne had generously arranged to take all the members of the Conference round the Upper Lake, visiting the Castle of Chillon, on Wednesday, August 17th, at 2.30 p.m.; also that members would have an opportunity, later on, of making a contribution for the poor of the city.

It was also announced that on Sunday, August 14th, a Pontifical Service would be held in the Greek Church at 10.30 a.m., Archbishop Germanos officiating, and that it would be followed by a Requiem in memory of the Patriarch Photios of Alexandria and of the martyr Archbishop Chrysostom of Smyrna, this being the anniversary of their deaths.

ADDITIONAL PROVISION FOR SECTIONAL SESSIONS

The Chairman reported that owing to the lack of time for the deliberations of the Sections under the original schedule, the Arrangements Committee proposed that, instead of the full sessions on the afternoons of Friday, Saturday and Monday, August 12th, 13th and 15th, sectional meetings should be held on the three remaining subjects of the programme.

Doubts were expressed whether this procedure was necessary and whether it would not preclude, or unduly diminish, the public discussion of the last three subjects; but finally the recommendations of the Arrangements Committee were ratified.

Reception of Sectional Reports

The Chairman, after expressing his thanks and those of the Conference to Dr. Garvie for presiding at the afternoon meetings, and for his tact, impartiality and linguistic skill, said that the Conference was now approaching its hardest phase. He had visited the Sections while at their work, and had been impressed by the considerateness which the delegates, while remaining true to their own convictions, had shown to each other. In considering the sectional reports, he trusted that the Conference would conduct its discussion on the same high level.

Mere improvements in language should not be lightly suggested, and only where conscience was involved should changes be proposed. Without seeking to disguise disagreements, the Conference should seek to attain the highest and most inclusive agreement possible; and it should be remembered that no vote of the Conference could commit the Churches represented at it—the Churches alone, acting in their corporate capacity, could accept, reject or amend the agreements reached by the Conference.

Dr. GARVIE, after thanking the President for the kindness with which his services had been acknowledged, added : There are certain observations which may have the effect of easing some difficulties and shortening the discussion. I would point out that the Conference is not now asked to *adopt* these Reports, but only to *receive* them, in order to have an opportunity of making suggestions, of indicating objections, and of showing how far agreement has been reached. If differences emerge in the consideration of these Reports, no attempts will be made to amend them here. According to the rule that has been adopted, all such suggestions for amendment will be referred to a drafting committee which will consider them carefully ; also, if agreement cannot be reached upon any point, it will be made quite clear what differences remain, as well as what agreements have been reached. This is not said with a view to encouraging difficulties, but rather with a view to protecting consciences against any feeling that the Conference desires to carry conclusions which have not been thoroughly accepted. At the final stage, it will be impossible to carry proposals by a mere majority ; it will be necessary for the Conference to be united, and members should do all in their power to bring about such unanimity.

It has been said that it will be impossible to discuss these Reports ; but I would point out that this is only a first discussion, and it will be necessary to take time next week for further discussion, when the advice of the Drafting Committee will be before the Conference. There will be no undue haste, and the Reports will not be voted on finally at the present stage.

Archbishop GERMANOS explained that the Orthodox representatives would defer taking part in the discussion of the Reports to be presented until the texts were available in all the three languages.

The Chairman, announcing that the Reports of Sections II and IV were ready in all three languages, but that Section III had not yet sent in its Report, called upon Dr. DEISSMANN to present the Report of Section II, on The Church's Message to the World—The Gospel.

Report of Section II presented

Professor DEISSMANN : The Section was composed of 111 members of the Conference, namely, 14 Anglicans, 4 Baptists, 2 Brethren, 6 Congregationalists, 4 Disciples and Churches of Christ, 6 Orthodox, 1 Quaker, 10 Lutherans, 24 Methodists, 1 Old Catholic, 8 German Evangelicals, 31 Presbyterians and other Reformed Churches.

The Convener was Professor Dr. Deissmann, who opened the first session held in the Aula, on Monday, August 8th, 1927, at 9.30 a.m. The devotions were led by Professor Dr. Wilhelm Hadorn, of Berne. The Section then elected Professor Dr. Adolf Deissmann as Chairman and appointed him Reporter. It also elected Bishop McConnell as first Vice-Chairman and Professor Arseniew as second Vice-Chairman; Canon Woods as English Secretary, Professor Méjan as French Secretary, and Licentiat Laun as German Secretary.

It was decided not to divide the Section into sub-sections until the need for such a step made itself felt. As it turned out, no such need was experienced. It was agreed to begin with a general discussion to be followed by a special discussion, and finally to elect a Committee to draw up a statement to Christendom on " The Church's Message to the World—The Gospel."

The Section agreed that it was not called upon to re-open the whole discussion on the Gospel, but rather to continue the debate which had begun on Thursday, August 4th, 1927. It took as a basis of discussion the material which had been submitted by the Subjects Committee, and all the speeches delivered on August 4th.

With this object in view the Chairman had arranged, in skeleton form, all the ideas which had been expressed . In this work the printed speeches and verbatim reports were found to be of the greatest value. The Section unanimously agreed to convey their thanks to the Staff of the Conference for the promptitude with which these indispensable reports had been prepared, and this I now beg to do in their name.

The material was arranged under the following heads :

1. The preparation of the Gospel.
2. Jesus' Gospel of the Kingdom.
3. The Gospel of Christ's Apostles.
4. The Oneness and Absoluteness of the Gospel.
5. The Gospel of Hope (Eschatology).
6. The Gospel as a message to individual souls and the social Gospel (Stockholm and Lausanne).
7. The Gospel and the Unity of the Church.
8. The Appeal from the Mission field (Edinburgh and Lausanne)
9. How should we spread the Gospel to-day ?

The general discussion which took place on Monday morning and the special discussion which followed in the afternoon, in both of which a remarkably large proportion of the Churches represented in the Conference took part, revealed extensive agreement on all substantial points and produced many highly valuable suggestions from individuals. Altogether, including those who took part in the debates on August 4th and 10th, over seventy speakers were heard, so that the requirements of free discussion were fully satisfied. It was seen to have been a great advantage that we had not sub-divided the Section into groups.

The following were elected as members of the Committee which was to draft the Statement : Bishop McConnell, Canon Woods, Professor Arseniew, Dr. Lew, Professor Monod, Rev. Mr. Sumitra, Principal Lofthouse, Dr. Zwemer, Dr. Maclean, Rev. Mr. Rose, and Professor Deissmann (Chairman). This Committee sat during the whole of Tuesday, August 9th ; and on Wednesday, August 10th, it submitted the text which it had unanimously adopted to a full meeting of the Section, which discussed it closely till 1 p.m. The Section then gave its unanimous approval to the draft, subject to the understanding that a sub-committee should devote further consideration to certain proposals for verbal improvements and should word the text in a manner best adapted to the three languages of the Conference. This sub-committee, which was composed of the Chairman, Canon Woods, Professor Arseniew, Professor Monod, Archdeacon MacNutt, Dr. Soper and Pastor Bertrand, concluded their task yesterday afternoon, after sitting for nearly four hours, and now begs to submit the text of the declaration to Christendom with the hope that the World Conference will unanimously adopt the present Statement.

The following is the text of the Report as thus presented :

REPORT OF SECTION II, FIRST DRAFT

Preamble.—After long and careful preparation, the World Conference on Faith and Order met at Lausanne, August 3rd-21st, 1927.

Many representatives of the Churches throughout the world, including many from the Churches in the Mission Field, assembled in a spirit of penitence, confessing the failure of Christendom to meet the demands of the Gospel, and bowing in submission to the will of our Lord Jesus Christ, firmly resolved to lay aside the weakening spirit of dissension and with God's help to make a new beginning toward the union of divided Christendom.

With deep thankfulness, the Conference records that the delegates of the several Churches, while conscious of the manifold variety of their gifts and historic heritages, have experienced and recognised their spiritual unity in Him who is their Head, Jesus Christ.

This common experience has led the Conference to express unanimously its conception of the Gospel which the Church of Christ has for the world.

1. The message of the Church to the world is and must always remain the Gospel of Jesus Christ. The Gospel is the joyous message of eternal redemption, which is the gift of God to sinful man in Jesus Christ. The world was prepared for His coming through the activities of God's Spirit in all humanity, but especially in His revelation as given in the Old Testament; and the eternal Word became incarnate in the fulness of time in Jesus Christ, the Son of God and the Son of Man, full of grace and truth.

2. He, through His life, His call to repentance, His proclamation of judgment and the coming of the Kingdom of God, His obedience in suffering even unto death, and His resurrection and exaltation to the right hand of the Father, has brought to us forgiveness of sins, and has revealed the fulness of the living God and His boundless love toward us. By the appeal of that love, shown in its completeness on the Cross, He summons us to self-sacrifice and devotion to His service and the service of the world which He came to redeem.

3. Jesus Christ, as the crucified and living One, as Saviour and Lord, is also the centre of the world-wide Gospel of the Apostles and the Church. Because He is its foundation and essence, the Gospel is and must remain the message of the Church to the world. It is more than a philosophical theory; more than a theological doctrine; more than a programme for social and secular betterment. The Gospel is rather the gift of a new world from God to this old world of sin and death; still more, it is the victory over sin and death, the revelation of eternal life in Him, who has knit together the whole family in heaven and on earth in the communion of saints, united in the fellowship of service, of prayer, and of praise.

4. The Gospel is the prophetic call to sinful man to turn to God, the joyful tidings of justification to those who believe in Christ. It is the comfort of the weary and heavy-laden; to those who are bound it is the assurance of the glorious liberty of the sons of God in this life as well as in the life to come. The Gospel brings peace and joy to the heart, and produces in men self-denial, readiness for brotherly service, and compassionate love. It offers the highest goal for the aspirations of youth, the rest that brings divine comfort to the toiler, the crowning joy of the martyr.

5. The Gospel is the sure source of power for social regeneration.

It proclaims the only way by which humanity can escape from those class and race hatreds which now devastate society, into the enjoyment of national well-being and international good-will. It is also a gracious invitation to the whole non-Christian world, athirst for redemption, to enter into the joy of the living Lord.

6. Sympathising with the anguish of our generation, with its longing for intellectual sincerity, social justice and spiritual inspiration, the Church offers in the eternal Gospel the answer to all the legitimate needs and providential aspirations of the modern world. Consequently, alike in the past and in the present, the Gospel is the only and the absolute way of salvation. Thus, through the Church, the voice of the Saviour is heard, " Come unto Me! . . . He that followeth me shall not walk in darkness but shall have the light of life."

Discussion

The Report was read in German, French and English, and the Chairman moved its formal reception, in order that it might be considered paragraph by paragraph.

After a moment of silent prayer, in thanksgiving for the unanimity of the Report, attention was drawn to certain discrepancies between its three versions. The Report was then formally received for discussion.

Some questions were raised with regard to the wording of the *Preamble*. The words " representatives of the Churches throughout the world," criticised by Bishop GORE as unduly wide, were found to be an incorrect rendering of the German " beschickt von zahlreichen kirchlichen Vertretern aus der alten und der neuen Welt " ; Dr. SCHERER desired to modify the expression of penitence in lines 4 and 5 ; but it was pointed out that the Preamble as a whole was relevant to all the Subjects rather than to Subject II, and on the motion of the Chairman it was decided not to consider it further.

Paragraph 1. The Rev. Canon DOUGLAS desired the insertion of a reference to the Church itself and its functions as included in the Gospel.

At this point the discussion was adjourned till 3 o'clock, and the Conference rose, after prayer offered by the Chairman, at 12.30 p.m.

Thursday Afternoon, August 11th.

The afternoon session was opened at 3 p.m., Dr. Garvie in the chair, with devotions conducted by the Rev. Dr. Peter Ainslie.

The Chairman announced that the original text of each Report would be understood to be that submitted by the Convener of the Section, and that care would be taken to secure complete conformity between the three versions.

Report of Section II (*Adjourned Discussion*)

On *paragraph* 2, the Rev. Dr. Wotherspoon suggested the addition of the statement that the primitive Gospel is the proclamation of the great redemption accomplished in Christ, from which all the other Gospels proclaimed to the world take their rise. The Archbishop of Dublin desired the remodelling of the paragraph in Christological terms free from all ambiguity : as it stood, the paragraph was open even to an adoptionist interpretation. The Archbishop of Armagh suggested the transposition of the terms " of judgment and of the coming of the Kingdom of God," and the deletion of the words " obedience in suffering even unto," as suggestive of a too definite doctrine of Atonement. Bishop Gore asked for the insertion of " and by the mission of the Holy Spirit " after " to the right hand of the Father." Herr Jacob Siebel suggested that for "suffering and death " should be substituted " His vicarious (or, atoning) suffering and death " ; and the addition of " and His holy Spirit " at the end of the paragraph.

Paragraph 4 : Dr. Atkinson suggested that the final sentence should read, in closer conformity with the German, " the rest that brings divine comfort to all those who labour and are heavy-laden."

Paragraph 5 : Dr. Aalders proposed that the following should be inserted : " The Gospel is also the inspiring power in intellectual and social life."

These suggestions, and a written suggestion by Dr. F. J. Hall on paragraph 1, were referred to the Drafting Committee for consideration.

Report of Section III *presented*

After an interval for prayer, the Report of Section III on the Nature of the Church was thus presented by the Rev. Dr. William Adams Brown, Chairman of the Section :

The problem which confronted Section III was different and in some respects more difficult than that which faced the other Sections. There are important and far-reaching differences both in our understanding of the Gospel and in our attitude toward the Creed, but these differences are not to the same extent confessionally determined as is the case with our view of the Church. They divide the members of each Communion even more than the Communions themselves. In the case of the Church, however, it was not possible to ignore our ecclesiastical differences in our method of procedure.

There were at least three main groups represented in our Section (numbering 122 members) whose convictions and traditions needed to be considered : one, including the Orthodox (11), the Anglicans (21) and the Old Catholics (2) ; another, congregational in polity, including the Congregationalists (6), the Baptists (2), the Disciples (2) and the Friends (2) ; and an intermediate group consisting of the Lutherans (18), the Presbyterian and Reformed (28), the Methodists (15) and the Evangelical Churches of Germany (21). We were fortunate in having all these bodies represented in our Section.

The Section organised by the election as Chairman and Vice-Chairman of the present speaker and the Bishop of Manchester. Five groups were constituted, interdenominational in character, each with its own Chairman : Dr. Cadman, Dr. Workman, General Superintendent Schian, Dr. Alivisatos and Dr. Merle d'Aubigné. In addition, a larger committee was appointed representing the different ecclesiastical groups, who, together with the Chairmen of the five groups, constituted the drafting committee which prepared the report which we now submit. This committee consisted, in addition to those already named, of Bishop Iriney of Novi Sad, the Archbishop of Upsala, the Bishop of Bombay, Dr. Roberts, whose place was afterwards taken by the Rev. Mr. MacArthur, Dr. August Lang, Präsident des Reichsgerichts Simons, and the Bishop of Dornakal representing the Church in the mission field. Three secretaries were chosen, one for each language : Dr. Peel, Professor Piper, and Professor Ménégoz, who were *ex officio* members of the drafting committee.

Monday was spent in general discussion of the subject and in perfecting the organisation already described. Tuesday morning was spent in free discussion in the several groups, the report of the Subjects Committee (Pamphlet 52) being used as a general basis and, in the case of two of the groups, the report of the Conference between Anglicans and representatives of the Free Churches of Great Britain, held at Lambeth in May, 1922, recorded in Bell's

" Documents on Christian Unity " pages 146, 147 and 148. The Drafting Committee then unified these reports in a single report which was presented to the full Section on Wednesday and discussed by them through the day. The discussion concluded at half-past six, when, to our deep gratitude, it was possible to adopt a unanimous report, namely, the report which is now presented to you.

A word of explanation as to the nature of the report is in order. For reasons which the Conference will easily understand, it has not been possible for us to present a finished document as has been the case with the other Sections. What we have here is rather a series of notes on points of agreement to which we have thus far been led, which can be used as a basis of any fuller statement which the Conference may desire to make. Had it been possible to remain in session another day, I believe we could have presented to the Conference a report which would in many respects have satisfied us better. In particular, many of us would have been glad to introduce a paragraph expressing our gratitude to God for the progress already made in removing the obstacles which stand in the way of our unity, especially those which are due to misunderstanding. Reference was made particularly to certain misconceptions which have hitherto blocked the way to reunion, such as (a) that in entering the fellowship of the reunited Church, the members of the so-called Free Churches would be obliged to renounce their spiritual ancestry and accept obligations inconsistent with the fundamental principle of freedom of conscience ; (b) that in objecting to the imposition of definite creeds, or the acceptance of a particular form of the ministry or sacraments as of divine order, the members of these Churches are indifferent to the great benefits of a common organisation or would be unwilling to co-operate in it if freedom of conscience could be preserved ; (c) that all, or even the most important obstacles to unity, are due to differences of organisation; (d) that in accepting the principle of common organisation, the different bodies which unite would be committed to uniformity as well as unity. On all these points we believe that great progress has been made toward better understanding, for which we would gratefully record our thanks to Almighty God ; but we have not found it possible to include them in our report.

Two principles dominated our procedure : first, the determination not to ignore, but frankly, honestly and generously to face any fundamental differences which we found existing. Such differences fell into three groups, all of which our report recognises, and with reference to all of which we were able to secure unanimous expression.

First, the differences of conviction concerning the nature of the Church represented by the different Communions ; secondly, the differences of spiritual significance attaching to membership in the organised Church ; thirdly, differences in the interpretation of our historic divisions in the past. Strong efforts were made at various times to induce us to ignore all three of these differences, and merely to affirm the points on which we agreed. We felt that to yield to this pressure would be to go contrary to our instructions and to rob the pronouncements of the Conference of the note of reality which is essential. We were able to overcome our difficulties by frankly recognising the existence of these differences, allowing each group to choose the form of statement which was satisfactory to its own conscience, recognising that the rest of us were not bound by that which was thus said.

A second principle which governed our procedure was the effort as far as possible to state what we meant clearly and unambiguously, and to defer to later commissions such vexed questions as the sacraments and ministry which it was not possible adequately to discuss for lack of time.

Among the differences of conviction to which it was not possible to give complete and adequate expression in the report was that of our Orthodox friends as to the apostolic foundation of the Church and the importance of associating tradition with Scripture, and that of other groups as to the interpretation which ought to be given to the spiritual significance of our historic divisions ; but we believe that no statement has been made which contradicts any conscientious conviction.

I am sure all the Section will wish me to voice on their behalf our deep gratitude to God for the spirit of fraternity and unselfishness which has marked our deliberations from the first to last. Deep differences of conviction were repeatedly given frank expression, and at times it seemed that it would be impossible to find any form of words to which we could all honestly assent, but the spirit of humility, of brotherly love, and of earnest desire to do the will of God so prevailed that it was possible for us at last to present a unanimous report. If we had to choose between rhetoric and love, we felt it our duty every time to let rhetoric go. I trust that the purists in the Conference will bear this in mind when they study the construction of some of our sentences. To the eye of the rhetorician they may seem clumsy and ineffective, but for us they have proved bridges by which we have walked across the rivers of our division to the fertile valleys of spiritual unity.

Two incidents in our discussion will be recalled by us with special satisfaction : the willingness of a large section of the Conference who would have preferred the simple word " believers " to " true believers " in paragraph 2, to insert the adjective in order to meet the conscience of some Anglo-Catholics in our midst ; and the willingness of the Friends, for whose presence with us we were continually thanking God, to add the words " and by public profession of faith " in paragraph 4 to the broader statement many preferred, in order not to embarrass our brothers of the missionary Church who feared lest the omission of this clause might embarrass them in their work.

I wish particularly to express the gratitude of the Section to the many who helped us to overcome the physical difficulties under which we laboured owing to the shortness of the time ; to the translators both German and French, namely Pastor Sasse and Pastor Merle d'Aubigné ; to the Rev. and Mrs. Caius J. Slosser, the Rev. Mr. Lytle, Miss Cox and Miss Gunning, who helped us in the transcription of our material; to the Underwood Typewriter Company for working before opening hours ; to Madame Chaban, the caretaker of the Church of St. Laurent, for her personal interest in our comfort ; and to Dr. Philip Bird for constant and indispensable help in matters of organisation.

Following the precedent set by the Second Section, I will now call upon the Bishop of Manchester, Vice-Chairman of the Section, to read the report in English. He will be followed by Dr. Simons, who will read it in German and Dr. Merle d'Aubigné, who will read it in French.

I would simply reiterate the hope expressed by our Chairman, Bishop Brent, that in such discussion merely verbal questions so far as possible be passed over and that we concentrate on the great central themes with which the report deals.

The following is the text of the Report as thus presented :

REPORT OF SECTION III, FIRST DRAFT

The Section thankfully reports that we have been able to arrive at substantial agreement on the following points :

1. The Church of the Living God is constituted by His own will, not by the will or consent or beliefs of men, whether as individuals

or as societies. Of this Church God is the Creator, Jesus Christ its Head, the Holy Spirit the source of its continuous life.

2. The Church as the communion of true believers in Christ Jesus is, according to the New Testament, the people of the New Covenant, the Body of Christ, the Temple of God, built upon the foundation of the Apostles and Prophets, Jesus Christ Himself being the chief corner stone.

3. The Church, in the Divine Providence, is the agency by which Christ, through the Holy Spirit, reconciles men to God through faith, bringing their wills into subjection to His sovereignty, sanctifying them through the means of grace, and uniting them in love and service to be His witnesses and fellow-workers in the extension of His rule on earth until His Kingdom be fully come.

4. As there is but one Christ, and one Life in Him, and one Holy Spirit who guides into all truth, so there is and can be but one Church, holy, catholic and apostolic, visible and invisible. There are different views as to the relation of the invisible and visible character of the one Church. For instance, some believe that the visible expression of this Church was determined by Christ Himself and is unchangeable ; others that the one Church under the guidance of the Holy Spirit may express itself in varied forms. Some, again, hold that the number of the faithful in the world to-day is not completely included in any existing branch of the visible Church, but that it is known to God, and the existence of such disciples is made known to men by public confession and through the fruits of the Spirit in their lives. But we are agreed that it is the will of Christ that the one Life of the one Body should be manifest to the world by the visible unity of its members.

5. Different views are taken of the divisions which have arisen in the course of history. A typical view in one direction is that no division of Christendom has ever come to pass without sin. A typical view in the other direction is that the divisions were the inevitable outcome of different gifts of the Spirit and different understandings of the truth. Between these views there is a large body of opinion which looks back on the divisions of the past with penitence and sorrow, coupled with a lively sense of God's mercy which, in spite of and even through these divisions, has advanced His cause in the world. But whatever may be our view of these divisions in the past, we are now agreed that they present obstacles to the accomplishment of the Church's task which it is our duty by God's help to remove. We therefore urge most earnestly that Christians, in fulfilment of the Saviour's prayer that they all may be one, must become

united if the Church is ever to accomplish His will for the salvation of the world.

6. As visible, the Church possesses certain marks whereby it can be known of men. These have been, since the days of the Apostles, at least the following :

(*a*) The possession and acknowledgment of the Word of God as given in Holy Scripture and set forth in the world.

(*b*) The profession and proclamation of faith in God as revealed and incarnate in Christ.

(*c*) The observance of the Sacraments.

(*d*) A ministry for the pastoral office, the preaching of the Word and the administration of the sacraments.

(*e*) A fellowship in prayer, in worship, in all the means of grace, in holiness of life and in the service of man.

7. All these are means, not ends, given us for the building up of the Body of Christ, the uniting of all believers in faith and love, until that day when every tongue shall confess that Jesus Christ is Lord to the glory of God the Father.

Discussion

In *paragraph* 1, the alteration of " by His own will " to " in His revealed will " was suggested by Prof. von MARTIN ; the omission of " or consent or beliefs of men " by the Rev. Dr. M'CLYMONT ; the substitution of " agent " or " medium " for " source " by the Rev. J. CROMARTY SMITH ; and the modification or suppression of the negative element in the paragraph by the Rev. Dr. BARTON.

In *paragraph* 3 the Rev. R. PYKE desired an acknowledgment of the truth that God works in reconciliation outside as well as within the Church, and the insertion of a reference to regeneration.

Note was taken of an apparent divergence between the English " until His Kingdom be fully come " and the German " bis dass sein Reich kommt in Herrlichkeit."

In *paragraph* 4, the emendation of the last sentence to run thus : " All probably hold that the number of the faithful in the world is not completely included in any existing Church, or in all together, but that it is known to God, and the existence of such disciples, whom the Church has not known how to win, is made known to men through the fruit of the Spirit in their lives," moved by Bishop GORE and supported by Dr. BARTON, was referred to the Drafting Committee.

In *paragraph* 6 two additions were proposed : that of a reference to the exercise of godly discipline, after (*d*) (Dr. ZWEMER), and that of a statement that " One of the marks of the Church is the zeal for the expansion of the Kingdom of God throughout the world " (LORD SANDS).

In *paragraph* 7, it was understood that the words " all these " would be expanded and made clear.

The Report as a whole was referred to the Drafting Committee for consideration and the incorporation of suggestions.

Report of Section IV presented

The Report of Section IV, on The Church's Common Confession of Faith, was then presented by the Rev. Canon TISSINGTON TATLOW, as follows:—

I will begin by saying that the official text of this Report is the English one ; in the case of the German translation, the translators were anxious that I should say that it was a literal translation to be put later into more graceful German.

The Section consisted of about 120 members and was fully as representative as the Sections described by Dr. Deissmann and Dr. Brown. We began with a full session of all the members, and it was at once plain what the main line of our work would be—that we were concerned as to what we should say about Holy Scripture ; secondly, that we were concerned as to what we should say about Creeds. It was at once apparent that there were two widely differing traditions amongst us—the tradition represented by those who are accustomed to the use of the Creeds, and that represented by those who are quite unaccustomed to the use of credal statements of any kind. The third main interest which very quickly emerged was the desire of many amongst us that we should make it clear in dealing with any of the questions indicated, or statements of the Faith, that the object of our Faith is our Lord Himself and not statements about Him.

In view of the discovery that that was the nature of our business, we at once divided into five different groups ; and after two sessions by those groups—each group taking the series of subjects I have indicated—each of the five groups presented to us statements, and

I may say that there was an agreeable similarity between these statements. These statements were then discussed by the whole Section, and were referred by the Section to a representative committee, perhaps the one piece of organisation that I may describe best by giving the names of those who composed it ; for although the document before you was finally submitted to and discussed by the entire Section, the main business of the editing of the five reports and of producing a single document was undertaken by this committee, consisting of seventeen members, namely, Archbishop Germanos, Prof. Zankow, the Bishop of Gloucester, Bishop Gore, Canon Quick, Prof. Choisy, Prof. Monnier, Dr. Hermelink, Dr. Nygren, Prof. Ihlen, Rev. Paul Sandegren, Dr. Ross Stevenson, Dr. Ashworth, Dr. Turk, Dr. Wigham, Dr. Garvie, and Dr. Tatlow. This Editorial Committee was presided over by the Bishop of Gloucester.

You will see that our Report consists of a first paragraph, which is really a preamble, and then a series of short paragraphs ; I should like to say a word of explanation in regard to the preamble.

Some of our members said they had come to this Conference uncertain as to what to expect, and perhaps not even expecting very much, and that they had found themselves sharing in a notable spiritual experience. We found that this was true of the entire membership of the Section, and all desired that we should give it expression in making our report. The first paragraph is, therefore, an attempt to state quite simply and sincerely that we were conscious of God with us.

As to the Report I feel that it will ultimately, in its final form, go out into the world without comment, and therefore I do not propose to make comment upon it, preferring to leave the rest of the time for members of the Conference to make comments which may go with the Report to the final Drafting Committee.

The following is the text of the Report as then presented :

REPORT OF SECTION IV, FIRST DRAFT

1. We members of the Conference on Faith and Order, coming from all parts of the world in order to bring the different Churches together, have with deep gratitude to God found ourselves united in common worship, adoration and prayer, in God our heavenly Father and His Son Jesus Christ, our Saviour, in the fellowship of the Holy Spirit.

2. We are united in the Christian Faith which is contained in the Holy Scriptures and is witnessed to and safeguarded in the Ecumeni-

cal Creed[1] called the Nicene and in the Apostles' Creed, which Faith has been continuously confirmed in the spiritual experience of the followers of the Lord Jesus Christ.

3. It is understood that the ways in which these Creeds may be used shall be determined by the competent authority in each Church. It is understood also that the several Churches will continue to make free use of such special Confessions as they possess.

4. We recognise that the Holy Spirit in leading the Church into all the truth, may enable it, while firmly adhering to the witness of these Creeds (our common heritage from the ancient Church) to express the truths of revelation in additional forms according to the needs of future ages.

5. Finally, inasmuch as in dealing with this subject of creeds, we have been occupied in considering the place and importance of a common Confession of the Faith, we desire at the same time to leave on record our solemn and unanimous testimony that no external and written standards can take the place of that inward and personal experience of union with the living Christ, which is the only evidence of spiritual vitality, and that the object of our faith is not any statement about Christ but the Lord Jesus Christ Himself.

[1]NOTE.—The Ecumenical Creed is that put forth at the Council of Chalcedon, formerly known as the Constantinopolitan and now as the Nicene Creed. The Apostles' Creed is the traditional baptismal creed of the ancient Western Church. It must be noted that the Orthodox Eastern Church can accept the Nicene Creed only in its uninterpolated form without the *filioque* clause, and that although it accepts the Apostles' Creed, that Creed has no place in its formularies.

Professor Dr. ARTHUR TITIUS spoke of the obstacles to agreement in the matter of Creeds, of the importance of assigning sufficient weight to the particular Confessions of the various Churches, and of the relative claims of the Apostles' and the Nicene Creed as expressions of the common faith.

It was agreed to adjourn the discussion of the Report to a special session at 3 p.m. on August 12th, preceding the afternoon sectional meetings.

The Conference rose, after prayer offered by the Chairman, at 6.30 p.m.

THE CHURCH'S MINISTRY

FRIDAY MORNING, AUGUST 12TH.

The Chair at the full session Friday morning was taken by General Superintendent Dr. OTTO DIBELIUS, and the session was opened at 9.30 with devotions led by the Rev. YOICHIRO INAGAKI.

Death of a Member of the Conference.

The President announced that Pastor MIKAEL HERTZBERG, of Oslo, a delegate from the Church of Norway, had died on August 11th. The Conference gave expression to its sympathy and deep regret.

Pastor HERTZBERG had prepared, in English, the following notes for an address to the Conference, which were read, as a tribute to his memory:

What is the way to Church Unity?

The different church bodies existing to-day point this out. May we take it for granted that the ancient Church, the original common Church, from which we all have come, is marked by the sign of St. James; that the Roman Church bears the sign of St. Peter; that the whole evangelical ecumenic Church, the sign of St. Paul?

And may we acknowledge that they have realised their types, symbolised to-day, as far as the two last are concerned, by the Cathedrals of St. Peter in Rome and St. Paul in London—the two largest temples of the said types of Christianity?

But is not, however, something lacking here? The last of the Apostles and surely the one who soared highest and fathomed deepest—St. John?

Which part of the Church bears his sign? It has not yet come—at least, none has realised his type of Christianity, his ideals. We are waiting. But we have already the prophecy, the finger points towards it. We have a dim prototype of the coming Church, the Christianity, the epoch of St. John, symbolised by the veiled Sophia Cathedral: that is to say, the Church of the Logos. That is the venerable Church of the East, when it rises again, inspired by the Christianity of St. Peter and St. Paul. *Lux ex Oriente!* as from the grave of St. John, where he is still resting and waits.

Through the Apostle John the way leads to Church unity. His scriptures and theology, his conception of Christianity, of his Church, the Church of St. John, the last Apostle, the great Apostle, the Apostle of love, who was nearest to the Lord.

May this be manifested at this Conference.

The consideration of Subject V, The Church's Ministry, was opened by the following addresses :

THE RIGHT REV. E. J. PALMER, D.D.
Bishop of Bombay (Anglican)

In this address I make several assumptions. It will be unintelligible unless I state them. They are these :

1. This is a Conference about truth, not about reunion. We engage in it because we desire the visible unity of Christ's Church on earth. Our disagreements about truth are considered by many to justify our disunion. Whether they do so or not, agreement about truth would be one of the firmest foundations for unity.

2. As we differ very greatly about cardinal matters, some of us must be wrong, and all may be to some extent wrong. We come here expecting to learn, and that must mean hoping to be corrected if we are wrong.

3. We seek God's truth about the whole of Christendom. We must necessarily begin by stating what we have learned in our part of it. We have no idea of imposing our conception of truth on others unless it really fits the whole of Christendom, and if it does there will be no question of imposition, for they will accept it gladly. But what I expect, even when I speak most confidently, is that others will have something complementary to add, not that I already know the whole that God means about anything.

I

4. We speak as representatives of the Churches to which we belong, but we must try to " look not only on our own things, but also on the things of others," and this should compel us to accept, or even to suggest, things which we know that our own Churches do not at present hold, if those things seem to correspond better to the whole of the facts than the traditional views entertained by our own Churches.

I propose to take up two main divisions of the subject of the ministry of the Church : one, the commission and authority of the ministry, the other, the functions of the ministry. I propose to preface these two main sections by a consideration of the question whether there is only one ministry in Christ's Church or several, and between the two main sections to say a few words about the question whether Christian ministers constitute an order or orders or are only office-bearers. I hope to conclude by pointing out the connection between some of the views held on these subjects and some ultimate conceptions of Christianity itself. My address will thus consist of five sections, of which the second and fourth are those of cardinal importance.

The whole will be treated in very general terms, leaving details to the second stage of our discussions.

I

Is there only one Ministry in Christ's Church, or several ? It seems strange that it should be necessary to discuss this question. The New Testament seems to answer it beyond a doubt. " God hath set some in the Church, first apostles, secondly prophets, thirdly teachers, then miracles, then gifts of healings, helps, governments, divers kinds of tongues. Are all apostles ? Are all prophets ? Are all teachers ? Are all workers of miracles ? Have all gifts of healings ? Do all speak with tongues ? Do all interpret ? " (1 Cor. xii, 28, 29).

" When he ascended on high, he led captivity captive, and gave gifts to men. . . . And he gave some to be apostles ; and, some, prophets ; and some, evangelists ;

and some, pastors and teachers ; for the perfecting of the saints, unto the work of ministering, unto the building up of the body of Christ" (Eph. iv, 8, 11, 12).

Though these lists were not intended to be lists of ministries, they certainly testify to more ministries than one.

The ministers actually mentioned in the Acts and Epistles undoubtedly had different functions. Certainly the Apostles stood above all—St. Paul gives orders to the prophets in Corinth—and there is no reason to suppose that all the others were on a level. Indeed obedience, according to him, was an essential element in the Christian society : " subjecting yourselves one to another in the fear of God" (Eph. v, 21). The peculiarity of the Christian Church was to be that distinction in it was to be measured by the reality and depth of service (Matt. xx, 26-28), and one of the words for minister (*diakonos*) and its cognates can consequently be applied to all those who hold any authority in the Church, from our Lord downwards.

This principle of the diversity of ministries in Christ's Church was challenged for the first time in the sixteenth century. The notion that there is only one ministry and all ministers are equal received classical expression in the *Confessio Belgica* Article XXXI : " But wherever the ministers of the word of God may be, they all have the same and equal power as well as authority, inasmuch as they are all equally ministers of Christ, that one and only universal Bishop and Head of the Church."[1] The ministers here referred to are those who, in the preceding article, were said to be " pastors and ministers whose duty is purely to preach and purely to administer the sacraments."[2] They are distinguished from the elders and deacons, who are not designated " ministers." How far modern Protestants hold to these definitions of the *Confessio Belgica*, I do not rightly know. But it is one of the greatest difficulties

---

[1] " Caeterum ubi sint locorum verbi Dei ministri, eamdem illi atque aequalem omnes habent tum potestatem, tum auctoritatem, ut qui sint aeque omnes Christi unici illius episcopi universalis et capitis ecclesiae ministri."

[2] " Pastores ac ministri, qui pure et concionentur, et sacramenta administrent."

in the way of mutual understanding, that there is a firmly-rooted presupposition among them, that there is only one ministry in the Church of Christ, and that a ministry of preaching which is also entitled to administer the two sacraments ordained by Christ Himself.

I hope that we may be able to move away from this presupposition. It is contrary to the New Testament, to common sense, to the order of human nature and to the pattern of the divine nature. Human nature is founded on the family, and in the family there must be obedience, as the fifth commandment teaches us. One truth about the divine nature our Lord taught us in the words, " The Father is greater than I." We should be prepared to find (as historically we do find) not one but several ministries in the Church, and not equality but subordination among them.

II

The commission and authority of Ministers : This is a matter on which there are extreme divergencies of view among Christians. We have preconceived opinions held with great warmth and involving condemnations of each other which make any project of reunion exceedingly difficult. Many Protestants regard the notions both of the apostolical succession and of the conferment of divine grace through ordination as superstitious. Many Catholics consider ministers who have not been ordained in the apostolical succession as laymen, gifted, it may be, and preachers of righteousness, but laymen, and therefore having no right to administer the Lord's Supper. Thus the Protestant and the Catholic ministries are respectively regarded with suspicion or even indignation by many Christians who are of the other persuasion. While this continues, unity is impossible. Where shall we turn ? Let us turn to Jesus Christ. He is on the throne, judging both the ministries—and using both. What is it that He sees in both ? Will this Conference come to see it too ?

The differences of our conceptions appear most plainly when we try to answer the question, *what happens in ordination* ? To that question the Churches which have preserved the traditional form of the ministry of Holy Orders answer : " It is Christ who consecrates or ordains, and in consecration or ordination He, using the bishop as His mouthpiece, makes a man a bishop, or a priest, or a deacon," or a member of any other order to which admission is believed to be given by ordination. The Protestant Churches, according to my friend Dr. Garvie, answer, generally, that " ordination is a corporate recognition of the grace-gift investing with the authority of the Church the exercise of that gift within the Christian community."[1] In other words, some of us say, " In ordination Christ ordains," others say " In ordination the Church recognises and authorises."

Let us try to put away preconceptions and prejudices, and reconsider both these theories. Is it possible that they are both true but that they apply to different types of ministers ?

I ask to be allowed to bear my witness about the traditional view of the Catholic Church. I hope to hear an equally convinced statement about the other view.

The traditional view contains two elements :

1. The bishop has inherited the authority of the Apostles, and he, like them, speaks for Christ in ordination.

2. The person ordained is made God's man, the representative of Christ to the Church.

1. The first of these points involves the apostolical succession. Some of you, I know, have long since completely closed your ears against this theory, because you say that the transition from the Apostles to the bishops cannot be proved. If it did happen, it happened in a time when our evidence is confessedly fragmentary. But, even so, there is real evidence. St. Paul writes to Timothy to provide for a succession in teaching (2 Tim. ii, 2). Clement of Rome (ad Cor. 44) says that SS. Peter and Paul provided for a succession in the episcopate (by which word he still means the same as the New Testament writers do). The whole Christian world used the laying on of hands from the

[1] Dr. A. E. Garvie in *Towards Reunion*, p. 158.

Apostles' times, and to a Jew that implied some kind of transmission (cf. Num. xxvii, 18-20), and it was Jews who started this custom. The whole Christian world at the end of the second century believed the bishops of certain sees to be the successors of Apostles in those places. It is true that these and other items which might be cited are only fragmentary pieces in favour of what tradition says. But no one can live on a mission-field, so long as I have, without seeing that tradition is right. The order of proceedings is universal. First the missionary itinerates, secondly he or his successor settles in a suitable headquarters, and from there superintends the Church in the surrounding district, thirdly, that duty of supervision passes into the hands of a local minister. That is the normal, natural, almost necessary development. That is exactly how the authority of the Apostles passed into that of the bishops. Calvin made the most amazing mistake for an able man when he tried to reform the Church by reconstructing it after the pattern of the apostolic age *minus* the Apostles. The Spirit that had directed the history of the primitive Church was wiser than Calvin. Consequently, I feel no reason to doubt, but every reason to accept, the tradition that the bishops succeeded the Apostles in everything that they could succeed to.

The part of the authority of the Apostles which concerns us here, is *the authority to send*. Its motto is our Lord's saying, " As my Father hath sent me, even so send I you." The Apostles acted continuously on that example. Though they bade the Church to select the Seven, *they* laid their hands on them, *they* " set them over this business " (Acts vi, 3, 6). Paul and Barnabas appointed presbyters in their infant Churches. " The Apostles," says Clement, " made their first fruits *episkopoi* and deacons." Every missionary repeats the process, and that tradition is quite secure as against any rival hypothesis of an appointment by infant Churches, though they would be consulted and considered. Paul ordained Timothy, after he was pointed out as a suitable person by certain " prophesyings." Later, he sent him to ordain in Ephesus, and Titus in Crete. That is the mainstream of the New Testament evidence, and it rolls on, unchecked and unaltered, down the history. The principle of the Church's ministry is *sending*, as from Christ, or rather sending by Christ through His Apostles and those that they sent.

This sending is not recognising a ready-made minister. It is commissioning a man who by the Holy Spirit's power may become a " sufficient minister." It does not exclude preparation. Our Lord Himself prepared the Apostles. It does not exclude the future minister's own conviction of his call, but it should be observed that in the Scriptural examples no stress is laid on that. It does not exclude selection by the Church, which the Apostles ordered in the case of the Seven. All these things are good, but all in the second rank.

2. The one primary matter is that the minister is to be *God's man*, one whom Christ has sent. This is evidenced by the prayers which from the first form an invariable element in every ordination. It should also be made clear by the method of making the minister. Here again I have learned from my eastern experience. In the East, men value institutions for what they mean—in the West for what they effect. There is a vital truth in the eastern view. To a great extent an institution is what it symbolises. The ordination by the bishop (to any simple mind) represents ordination by Christ, the Chief Shepherd, much more naturally than any other method. The bishop's irreviewable discretion with all its awful responsibility is the counterpart of Christ's single will as the action of no committee or assembly can be. Thus, in a picture, episcopal ordination proclaims that the priest or deacon ordained is Christ's man, not the choice of a handful of fellow townsman or fellow countrymen or sharers of the same religious views, nor the representative, nor the servant of any of those, nor responsible to them, but the representative and the servant of Christ and responsible to Him. Further, it is a symbol of the universality of the ministry. No local church, nor any body of adherents of a particular doctrine, could ever bestow upon a Minister universal authority in the Church of God. Only

either the whole Church (which very soon became impossible to assemble together) or Christ Himself could bestow this. And it was God's plan to give the Church a ministry with a universal commission.

It is principally because of the immense symbolical value of the traditional method of ordination that I believe that it is divine, and that Christendom, if it wishes to be united, will return to it for the general ministries of the Church.

Passing now to Protestant conceptions of ordination and of the authority of the minister, I think it will be convenient to consider three typical views, (1) the view of the earlier Presbyterianism, (2) the view of Independency, and (3) the view expressed in Dr. Garvie's definition which I have already quoted, which, I venture to think, represents the modern *rapprochement* of the children of Presbyterianism and the children of Independency in English-speaking lands.

1. In the older Presbyterianism, though the word " clergy " was rejected, there survived a strong sense of the distinction between the ordained and the unordained. Only the ordained had authority to ordain. Consequently a great deal of what I have said about the traditional method of the Church in ordination, could be said, and has been said, about presbyterian ordination. *A priori*, indeed, the authority of the Apostles might have passed to the presbyters—but the historical evidence, so far as I can judge, shows that it did not. But if it had so passed, then a presbyterian ordination, in which the final decision to ordain or not to ordain rests with the ordaining presbyters, would symbolise a commission to a universal ministry founded by Christ and responsible to Him. It is not surprising that we sometimes find Presbyterians setting value on ministerial succession.

2. The theory of the source of ministerial authority which is characteristic of Independency is, I understand, that any gathering of Christians may constitute themselves a Church and make a ministry for it. Such action relies on the promise " where two or three are gathered together in my name, there am I in the midst of them" (Matt. xviii,

20). In our own generation it draws support from the theory that every little local Church is a microcosm of the universal Church and possesses all the powers of the latter. Thus, if the universal Church can make ministers, so can the smallest Church. Now I am afraid that these arguments leave me unconvinced. Our Lord's promise is to those who gather in His name. Can it be claimed by those who gather to separate themselves from their brethren ? *They* are not gathering in His name, whose gathering breaks up His Body. Neither are *they* gathering in His name, who meet to make a minister who will be a centre and symbol of disunion when he is made, and for whose making they have received no authority. They say, that the Holy Spirit chooses this minister through the independent Church in its meetings. But where in Scripture is there any colour to be found for such an assertion ? Is there any real sign that local Churches had all the powers of the universal Church ? Did the Corinthian Church of St. Paul's day contain any Apostles ? If this is not true of a purely local Church, surely it is still less true of a sectional Church, formed of adherents of a particular man or a particular doctrine.

I recognise to the full the devotion and spiritual power of some Congregational Ministers. But God blesses faithful attempts to serve Him in spite of our mistakes, and I cannot but think that the Independent theory of ministry is a mistake. I am supported in so thinking by certain movements among modern Congregationalists. They tend in many countries to form themselves into unions, and ordinations are more and more connected with representatives of the unions. In several countries Congregationalists have formed a united Church with Presbyterians, and in those united Churches the theory and practice of ordination is largely Presbyterian. This leads me to hope that even the successors of the Independents are moving away from the typical Independent theory of the ministry.

3. Let us now consider Dr. Garvie's statement of the Protestant conception of ordination : " Ordination is a corporate recognition of the grace-gift, investing with the

authority of the Church the exercise of that gift within the Christian community." This statement might be called the formula of union between Presbyterian and Congregationalist ministries. But it is at the same time a correction or even a denial of the traditional theory of ordination, which held the field in the Catholic Church for many centuries.

Believing, as I do, that traditional theory to be true, I ask myself whether the Protestant theory can be also true? It appears to me that this recognition is the proper procedure with a Prophet. Only it ought not to be called ordination, for a prophet does not need to be ordained. And I am quite prepared to recognise that any kind of teaching into which the fervour and incisiveness of the Spirit enter is truly prophetic. But I encounter here two difficulties. On my own side the trouble is that I have no reason to suppose that the call to be a prophet is by itself a sufficient title to the general ministry of the Church. On the side of my Protestant friends, I find almost always a refusal to admit that theirs is only a prophetic ministry. They claim that it embodies everything that God intended the general ministry of the Church to be.

Thus I find myself unable to give an account of most of the Protestant ministries at once acceptable to themselves and consistent with what I have learned of the nature and history of the Church. Yet I cannot help feeling that the strength of the Reformation ministries has always lain in their prophetic character. The office of inspired teaching was being ill-performed in the Church of the early sixteenth century, and the Reformers, in concentrating attention on that office, re-emphasised one of the provisions that God means His Church to have. The Church in Israel had the service both of priests and of prophets, in different proportions at different times. All along the priest was a teacher. Sometimes a man of God was both prophet and priest. The Son of God was both. In the Christian Church men with the gift of the prophet have often been made priests or bishops. It may be that there are some prophets who are not called to the general or pastoral ministry. They would need to be formally recognised by the Church. If the Protestant description of " ordination " means such a recognition, I can see how it could find a place in the universal Church.

But if that description be intended to mean that in ordination the Church is making a minister, as a municipality instals its mayor, or Freemasons make a Worshipful Master, then I submit that there is either an error or a confusion.

There is an error if it means that the Church conceives itself as the source of the authority that the minister is to exercise, or holds the minister to be primarily the representative of the Church. The minister is the representative of Christ, and Christ is the representative man as well as the Son of God. Therefore the minister is secondarily the representative of the Church as well as primarily the representative of Christ. But the source of his whole authority and being is Christ alone.

It may be a confusion of thought which makes some say that the Church in ordination gives authority to a man to exercise his ministry. To secure its own orderly existence the Church must assign to every minister his sphere, and without a sphere a minister, however truly ordained, has no right to work. The methods of assigning this sphere of work are various and variously named, license, presentation, institution, induction, etc. Such proceedings are the Church's duty ; they give the minister what Dr. Forsyth called " social opportunity." Ordination does something quite different. It puts a man into an order, or company of persons who have a divine commission to share a particular part of Christ's work in the Church.

III

Do Christian ministers constitute an order, or orders, or are they only office-bearers? I find it difficult to appreciate the objection which some raise to the conception of an order. I submit that it is a true conception, which most of us in practice hold about the Christian ministry, and that it conduces much to clearness of thought to distinguish it from office. As the word is used in the expression " Holy Order," an order means a company of men who have received God's commission to perform certain duties or services for the Church, and that commission is lifelong. They require the Church's further authority to perform them in certain places or with regard to certain persons or in some peculiar relation. In short, the minister receives from God membership in an order which qualifies him to perform the duties of certain offices in the Church, but these offices he receives from the Church.

Offices are for instance the care of a particular congregation, the charge of a particular diocese, an archdeaconry or deanery, or provostship or principalship, an archbishopric or the papacy itself. All these are offices. A man is an office-bearer while he is in that office and no longer. He is instituted or in some other way put in possession of it, but he is not ordained to office.

A man once ordained to an order of ministry continues to be a member of it throughout his life, though the Church has a right, if he commits some great sin or fault, to forbid him either temporarily or permanently to perform the duties belonging to the order. The principle underlying this is that " the gifts and calling of God are without repentance."

Thus this distinction again witnesses to the principle that the minister is essentially God's man, the representative of Christ to the Church. Any theory that we have either of ministry or ordination, must rest upon this truth.

IV

The functions of the ministers : I fear there is no subject about which the sense of mutual alienation is greater than this subject of the functions of Christian ministers. Yet I believe that a real reconsideration of the subject in the light of Christ and of what He wants the Church to be and what He sends ministers to help it to be, might lead us to unexpected agreement.

Let us begin, if you will, with *the function of teaching.* " I am the light of the world." " Ye are the light of the world."

It is the duty of the Church to teach the world. It is possible for the Church because its Head is the light of the world. He gives the Church teachers for two purposes, that it may both learn itself and teach the world. How often has history shown that the great movements come when the rank and file are so much alive that they cannot but teach. Teaching is a perpetual necessity. It must be given afresh to every soul. But it is only a means. It is not the end. If it were, Christianity would be a system of philosophy and the Church a school of thought. The end is not the Gospel but the life; the life of Christ, and the Church is His Body which has the life.

The function of sacrifice. The life of Christ is the dying life, dying to self that we may live to God. Christ as priest gave and gives Himself wholly to the Father. In Him His body gives itself—thus we are a holy priesthood as a body. Those who represent Him by His commission and sending are leaders in this life of sacrifice. They are so, first of all, in that act of worship, the Lord's Supper, in which we proclaim the Lord's death till He come, in the only way that is sufficiently sincere, by uniting ourselves through His Spirit with Him in His death, and by offering ourselves in Him and with Him to the Father—acceptable only in the Beloved. The priest is the leader in this act of sacrifice in which he speaks and acts for the whole priestly congregation which with him is offering the sacrifice. And secondly, when we issue from that holy house where we have pledged ourselves to that share in the Lord's self-sacrifice, the priest is our leader in all the practical acts of self-sacrifice which by God's grace redeem our life from selfishness and sin, and make us all a holy priesthood.

The function of shepherding. " I am the Good Shepherd." Here the minister is very clearly distinguished from the people. Shepherds are not sheep. Here he derives a commission from Jesus and shares one of His functions. " I came that they might have life and have it abundantly." " I lay down my life for the sheep." The minister as shepherd is to feed the sheep with life, and to give his life in the feeding. This does not mean preaching only; it means passing on to the sheep the Lord's life in sacrament, in every seasonable word, and in the wholesome infection of personal holiness. It also means seeking and recovering lost sheep.

The function of reconciliation. " The Son of Man hath power on earth to forgive sins." Did He not mean to exercise that power through the ages? "Whose soever sins ye remit, they are remitted unto them, and whose soever sins ye retain, they are retained." At any rate, the Church as a whole has this ministry of reconciliation committed to it. One of the protests of the Reformation was for a purer discipline. But excommunication is only in order to bring about penitence and to lead to reconciliation. The Church forgives by readmitting to its fellowship those who have been, or ought to have been, cast out. All live Churches have done this in some way or other. It is surely inconceivable that this most solemn and touching ministry should *not* be put in charge of special persons. Think of Paul the Apostle. He took pains to associate the Church of Corinth with himself in excommunication and in reconciliation. But in the end of all he says : " What I have forgiven . . . for your sakes I have forgiven it *in the person of Christ* " (2 Cor. ii, 10).

It is much to be desired that according to the custom that prevailed for centuries the absolution by the bishop or priest should take the form of a prayer, and not of a declaration. But about the central facts of the ministry of reconciliation and their reasonableness, I venture to say there is no doubt, and to hope that we could agree.

The function of mercy. The whole Church ought to serve the weak and helpless of the world, and the deacons were meant to be the leaders and instruments in this exhibition of the divine mercy. We ought to ordain the persons who are in permanent charge of our charitable works to be deacons—then there would probably be more love in those works. Again, such works ought always to occupy a large part of any deacon's time.

The function of superintendence or oversight. Our Lord Himself is called the *Episkopos* of our souls. Some of those who are His commissioned representatives must have superintendence—and this is the more necessary, the larger the Church grows. The ultimate responsibility for the doctrine of the Church, for the exclusion of persons from the Church and readmission of them into its fellowship, for the principles of the conduct of public worship, and for the granting or refusal of the commission to the ministry, must rest somewhere. In the Catholic tradition these responsibilities, with some others, are placed in the hands of the bishops. The Protestant Churches, having ceased to have bishops, have raised the question, whether these functions of superintendence can be adequately or better discharged by other ministers or bodies, not whether they ought to be discharged at all.

I have taken six outstanding functions which have been and are being discharged by the ministry of the Church. I put it to the Conference that it is God's will that all these functions should be discharged by the different orders of the Christian ministry. I believe that if some Christians have denied this about some of these functions, it is only because the sins and frailties of men have led to abuses with regard to them. But I would submit that, while condemning and discontinuing the abuses, the Church must accept from God these functions of the ministries which His Son has given to His Church and endeavour to keep their exercise pure and uncorrupted.

V

Thus far my conclusion is that though we have, or might have, considerable agreement about the totality of functions which should be performed by the totality of the Church's ministry, we are as yet divided on three questions, the different orders or kinds of ministers which there should be in the Church, the proper distribution of functions among the different orders or kinds of ministers, and the right method of admission of persons to those orders.

In considering these questions let us keep ever before our mind two thoughts which must guide us in their solution, the nature of the Church and the generosity of God.

The Church is not a democracy but a monarchy, and Christ is its King. All its institutions must be consonant with, and expressive of, His sovereignty.

The Church is not a school of thought but a living Body. Christ gave to the Church, not a written word but Himself the living Word ; not ideas only, but men filled with the ideas. As He Himself is the Truth and the Life, so He gave to the Church *men* to bind it as a living body to Him in living truth and true life. That is the ideal of the ministry.

The generosity of God provided many kinds of ministers to do this great unitive work. Let us not deny the largeness of His provision. Again, even when men try to work for and with Him in wrong ways or not the best ways, He may bless them. Let us not be misled by His generosity. Let us seek to find His " first thoughts," the best ways of doing His work. Some of our institutions may be mistakes, though He generously blesses us in them : just as our sins are still sins, though He uses sinful men to great purposes. Lastly, let us never minimise God's intentions. Let us fear to rationalise or naturalise our conception of Christ's Body. It is a supernatural society. It is meant to contain and to dispense divine grace. We cannot exaggerate the generosity of God. Let it rule all our thoughts about the Church, the Body of Christ, His Son and our Lord.

THE REV. M. G. G. SCHERER, D.D.
Secretary of the United Lutheran Church in America

It may be worth while at the outset to call to mind two very different uses of the word ministry. According to the one use it means a service—something which one does in compliance with the will and command of another, or for the pleasure or the weal of another. In this sense the Church has a ministry to perform in the name of its Lord for the world. This ministry is carried on by the whole Church, all who are Christ's, great and small, having part in it. According to the other use of the word we understand by it certain members of the Church who have been solemnly set apart

to render service in special activities and with recognised
authority for and on behalf of the whole Church. These
are ministers, and taken collectively are called the ministry
of the Church. We take it that in using the word in this
latter sense we will be following the lead of those who proposed the subject and will be speaking about that which
now occupies the mind of this Conference.

I

The Church has always had its ministry ; but that
ministry, as seen at different times, in different parts of
the world and in different groups, has, in its constitution
and specialisation in regard to function, presented diverse
conceptions of what the ministry is and of the kind of
authority with which it acts. In the first period, covering
the lifetime of the Apostles and some years thereafter, in
addition to the Apostles we read of deacons, elders and
bishops—the last two names, however, designating in this
early period not different orders of the ministry, but being
used alike of the same officials. We may remark here, perhaps more conveniently than elsewhere, that the word
" elder " is English for πρεσβύτερος, and that from the
Latin form, *presbyter*, comes our word priest. In the New
Testament, however, the presbyters are never called
priests. The point to be particularly noted is that the New
Testament presbyter is quite distinct from the later priest.

There were facts and conditions, in the religious and
political *milieu*, and in the necessities of a church expanding and growing in experience, which would cause this
earlier form of the ministry to develop naturally, if not
legitimately, into that more specialised form which presents
itself to view in the early part of the second century.
Whatever the explanation, the fact is that at that time
there were ministers who were called deacons, others who
were designated as presbyters, and still others who were
distinguished by the name of bishop. Just what the
difference was between the presbyters and the bishops may
for the present be passed by. Whatever the difference of
function may have been, and however the development

may have been opposed and resisted here and there, the three orders mentioned became finally established and prevailed universally down to the Reformation of the sixteenth century.

Before that century had ended, practically the whole of northern Europe, including England and Scotland, had passed through the throes of the Reformation. The Church had been shaken to its foundations. Its institutions, its doctrines and traditions, its rites and ceremonies —everything—had been sorely put to the test ; and in the general break-up the ministry, too, was involved.

Notwithstanding the expressed readiness of the Lutheran confessors at Augsburg in 1530 to submit to the authority of the bishops, on condition that they would allow them to preach the Gospel, the canonical orders were by and by lost to the Lutherans everywhere throughout Germany. The office of bishop was continued in the Churches of Denmark and Norway. In Sweden, where the archbishop accepted the Reformation, the episcopacy was retained, and has been perpetuated to this day. Thence it was extended also to Finland. Likewise it has been retained in the Anglican communion. In some European countries the canonical orders were discarded or given up without regret.

In America there are many " denominations " and we have there every kind of polity pure and mixed ; Greek Catholic, Roman Catholic, Episcopal, Presbyteral, Congregational and Lutheran. The Lutheran attitude in regard to polity may be described as libero-eclectic—neither episcopal, presbyteral nor congregational as of divine ordainment, but freely appropriating elements from all sides and having something in common with each.

II

We are now discussing the subject of the Church's ministry as related to the larger question of the unity of the Church, and we are to inquire first whether any one form of ministry everywhere and throughout time be necessary to a united church.

If it be maintained that the ministry, as well as church

government, is by divine appointment purely *congrega-tional*, then it follows that every congregation is and must be strictly autonomous, a church unto itself, having no organic relation to other churches. This would be true whatever the form of the ministry in the local churches. In one or in all of them there might be only presbyters; or there might be in each of them a bishop, a presbyter and a deacon. None of these, however, would have standing as a minister outside of his own local church. Thus there might be myriads of churches, but if there were no other bond of unity than their ministry, there could be no such thing as one holy, catholic or universal Church ; and the only unity due to and marked by the form of ministry would be that which might be predicated of any one of the local churches which may have had an unbroken succession of ministers with no change of form—a unity of continuity in the congregation only. It should be remarked here that the congregational principle is perhaps nowhere consistently carried out in our time.

If the unity of the Church depends upon and is conditioned by the form of its ministry, and if the *presbyter-ministry* has been given divine right to the exclusion of other forms, what then becomes of unity and catholicity ? It might be argued with some plausibility that, in the years immediately following the death of the last of the Apostles, there was one Church, and that its unity was reflected in the presbyterate of the time. But if such a claim be granted, then the Church which appeared upon the establishment of the episcopate was something else ; and thus with this change even the unity of continuity was broken.

Once more, if the unity of the Church be posited in the episcopate, then there can be no unity without *episcopacy*. Then also it must be shown either that there was no unity in the period immediately following the departure of the Apostles, or that bishops, as distinct from presbyters and having what might be regarded as canonical orders, arrived in time to take the place of the Apostles as their successors in office.

Among all the ministers of the Church the Apostles, without question, constituted a very distinct group.

The Apostles died without leaving, so far as is recorded in the New Testament, any intimation of a succession in the apostolate, or providing therefor. Neither did they leave on record any distinction, as regards function, between the presbyters and the bishops. There is no account of the ordination or consecration of a bishop.

When the Apostles passed off the stage there were left, so far as our information goes, only deacons and presbyters, the latter of whom, on account of the special function of *oversight,* were also called bishops. They were appointed (χειροτεῖν) as presbyters ; if the bishop was in any sense distinguished from the presbyter, it was only as *primus inter pares.* This state of affairs continued for some years after the Apostles were all dead, and yet during this period every function of the ministry was duly performed. Later the " bishops " obtained a higher rank, and were recognised as the ones having authority to ordain and confirm ; they also acquired certain powers of jurisdiction.

In order that we may have everything clearly before us, it is necessary to inject at this point reference to certain doctrines which have from very early times been associated with the episcopate.

One of these, and the chief, is the sacerdotal character of the ministry. From the Apostles on down, the ministry, so it is maintained, is a priesthood. The Eucharist is an offering (in the Church of Rome regarded as propitiatory) : now an offering requires a priest.

The priesthood belongs to the bishop, and by him it is passed on through ordination to the priest (presbyter) with the gift of the Holy Spirit. Hence the insistence that episcopal ordination is necessary to the valid celebration of the Holy Communion and the granting of absolution.

Then comes the doctrine of apostolic succession, carrying with it authority first given by Christ to His Apostles and by them handed on down to the bishops as their successors.[1]

[1] The Primacy of the Pope is not mentioned here because the Church of Rome is not participating in this Conference.

This is not the time nor the place to discuss these doctrines. It need only be said that, if this sacerdotal theory be accepted and consistently carried out, not only is there an end to all discussion about the kind of ministry that is necessary for a united Church ; but what is more important to note is that Christ is no longer the sole Mediator between God and man, the universal priesthood of believers is degraded to an inferior position, and the doctrine of justification alone by faith in Christ, which Luther called " the article of a standing or a falling Church," is thereby endangered, if not surrendered.

Returning now to the main topic, it is important to observe that this question of the necessity of episcopal ordination to the unity of the Church is not a new one. It has been exhaustively studied before this, in the times when men were ready to give their lives for the principles which they avowed. This question had to be faced by the Reformers at Wittenberg very early in the Reformation.

The question with them at Augsburg was not whether they would have the bishops or not, but whether they could have the Gospel or not with the bishops. Long before the Diet of Augsburg the Reformers had found they could not submit to the bishops and still continue to preach the Gospel. Therefore falling back upon the principle of the parity of the ministry and the right of the Church to call and ordain its own ministers, they exercised this right themselves ; taking care, however, to ordain only such as had been regularly called. Melanchthon in his masterly Apology[1] prepared during the Diet for the eyes of the Emperor, said in justification of this course : " the bishops either compel our priests to reject and condemn the kinds of doctrine which we have confessed, or, by a new and unheard-of cruelty, they put to death the poor innocent men. These causes hinder our priests from acknowledging such bishops. Thus the cruelty of the bishops is the reason why that canonical government which we greatly desired to maintain is in some places

[1] *The Apology of the Augsburg Confession*, written in answer to the Confutation by Catholic theologians by order of the Emperor Charles V.

dissolved." It is to be observed furthermore that the
bishops refused to ordain to the priesthood men who
accepted the principles of the Reformation, and persecuted
the priests who espoused those principles.

The Reformers gathered at Augsburg were not unaware
that a deplorable schism was taking place ; but to them
there was something to be dreaded far more than schism,
that was, that they should lose the light of the Gospel and
be plunged back into the darkness and tyranny from which
God had graciously delivered them. Schism could at most
affect only the outward organisation of the Church. It
could not cut down into the true Church, the Body of
Christ, which to them was not to be identified with the
external organisation but which was the " congregation of
saints (the assembly of all believers) in which the Gospel
is rightly taught and the Sacraments rightly administered."[1] They declared it as their faith that this " one
holy Church is to continue for ever " ; and they said :
" We know that the Church is with those who teach the
Word of God aright, and administer the sacraments aright,
and not with those who not only by their edicts endeavour
to efface God's Word but also put to death those who teach
what is right and true."

Where they put the blame for the schism is expressed
in the following words : " Those who in the beginning
condemned manifest truth, and are now persecuting it with
the greatest cruelty, will give an account for the schism
that has been occasioned." " Furthermore, we wish here
again to testify that we will gladly maintain ecclesiastical
and canonical order, provided the bishops only cease to
rage against our churches. This our desire will clear us
both before God and among all nations to all posterity
from the imputation against us that the authority of the
bishops is being undermined, when men read and hear
that, although protesting against the unrighteous cruelty
of the bishops, we could not obtain justice."

Thus also the unity of the Church was placed by them
not in any outward organisation, nor in any form of

[1] *Augsburg Confession*, Art. VII.

ministry. This is what they wrote in their Confession :
" To the true unity of the Church, it is enough to agree concerning the doctrine of the Gospel and the administration
of the sacraments. Nor is it necessary that human
traditions, rites or ceremonies instituted by men should
be everywhere alike. As Paul says : ' One faith, one
baptism, one God and Father of all,'" etc. (Eph. iv, 5, 6).
They were speaking of " spiritual unity," and held that,
" those are one harmonious church, who believe in one
Christ ; who have one Gospel, one Spirit, one faith, the
same sacraments."

Nevertheless, their warfare was not waged against the
episcopate as such. Indeed, they said : " Now it is not
our desire to wrest the government from the bishops, but
this one thing is asked, namely, that they allow the Gospel
to be purely taught, and that they relax some few obser-
vances which cannot be kept without sin." They further
said : " We have frequently testified in this assembly that
it is our greatest wish to maintain church polity and the
grades in the Church, *even though they have been made by
human authority* [1], provided the bishops allow our doctrine and receive our priests." And seven years later at
Smalcald they adopted the following statement of Luther :
" If the bishops were true bishops, and would devote
themselves to the Church and the Gospel, they might be
allowed, for the sake of love and unity, *and not from
necessity* [1], to ordain and confirm us and our preachers."

So the Lutheran confessions really leave open the
question as to what polity, or what form of ministry, the
Church shall have. The Church has never rejected the
episcopate as such, nor has it pronounced in favour of any
other particular form. This is why I have called its polity
libero-eclectic ; not that it must, according to its genius
and principles, exhibit an eclecticism in the matter of
polity, but that it is free to choose between the episcopal,
presbyteral and congregational forms, or indeed to choose
elements from each of these, and if possible, to combine

---

[1] Italicised by the writer.

them in a harmonious polity in which each of them will have due recognition and constitutional standing.

One other plea that may be made in favour of the episcopate is that whether necessary or not, it was under the guidance of the Holy Spirit that the Church was led to the adoption of this form of ministry, and that this ministry has been blessed with the presence and power of the Spirit. This we would freely grant, and we rejoice that it is so. Doubtless at certain times, in particular countries, and under special conditions this form of Church government was best. But we cannot judge otherwise than that the Spirit of God was also moving in the Reformation, and that His guidance was with those who resolved to persevere, at all cost, in the preaching of the Gospel. We know also that He has abundantly blessed the ministry of those Churches to which, through no fault of their own, the episcopate was lost.

III

We come now to the inquiry whether, in view of the present divided state of Christendom, and notwithstanding all that can be brought up from the past, there remains the possibility of one Church with episcopal orders. For reasons easily understood, our inquiry is confined now to the Communions participating in this Conference; and the question is limited to the possibility of union under an episcopal polity, not because other possibilities are ignored, but because it is evident that, in the consideration of this matter, the discussion will turn upon the question whether, all things considered, episcopacy does not offer greater hope of solution than any other well defined polity.

In so far as Lutherans are concerned, it may be gathered from what has already been said that there is no confessional principle that rejects episcopacy *per se*, or that sets up any other form of ministry as necessary. The Lutheran position is that since there is no express command of God in this matter the Church is free, under the guidance of the Holy Spirit, to determine its polity according to the circumstances and requirements of time and place.

If, however, they should be called upon to consider the possibility and the desirability of turning to episcopacy, where their form is of another kind, they would desire conference on the following questions : first, Will the change involve the acceptance of the sacerdotal theory of the ministry ? Secondly, Will subscription to the necessity of episcopal ordination be requisite ? Thirdly, Must the theory of apostolic succession be received ? Fourthly, Will not the step lead logically to the acknowledgment of the primacy of the Pope ? And finally, In view of recorded history and of present conditions, is there a reasonable assurance that, without unity in the faith, the episcopate will be able to prevent schism ?

These questions settled, they would desire further to confer upon that which to them constitutes the true unity of the Church, viz., " agreement concerning the doctrine of the Gospel and the administration of the sacraments." With them the thing of chief importance is that the Word and sacraments, which are the divinely appointed means of grace, shall continue with the Church in their purity.

Let me say in conclusion that I have simply touched upon the main issues which are involved in this subject. These questions ought to be fully and carefully considered in love ; but, at the same time, with all seriousness. They are serious problems which this Conference lays before us.

The Chairman, as a preface to an interval for devotions, said :

We thank the two speakers who have thus set out their points of view upon this grave and weighty matter, without vagueness or concessions, and yet taking pains to indicate the points at which the contrasted lines of thought converge. In view of the divergences, the Bishop of Bombay asked, " Where shall we turn ? Let us turn to Jesus Christ." Let us do so, at this moment, and in view of our great differences and difficulties let us lift up our hearts to Him who binds us all in one.

THE VERY REV. DR. SERGIUS BULGAKOW
Professor at the Orthodox Theological Institute, Paris

The Church is Christ's body, in which there are many members, differing from each other and yet indispensable to the body, and in that sense each has the same value. They are many : the body is one. This we learn from St. Paul (1 Cor. xii), who reveals to us the fundamentals of the Church's hierarchy; for the Church has a hierarchy and its constitution is hierarchical, and yet it is an organism rather than an organisation, a mystical unity rather than a juridical institution. This does not run contrary to the fact that some sides of the Church's life are clothed in legal form, and express themselves alike in canon law and also in common, public and private law. This notwithstanding, the Church belongs in essence to an order above the legal plane, and this should not be forgotten when we speak of the hierarchical character of the Church.

Russian theology expresses the fundamental essence of Church unity in a word for which no other language has an equivalent. *Sobornost* connotes alike the catholicity of the Church—the integral totality of its being—and its spiritual character as the oneness of its members in faith and love; its outer aspect, as at all points resting on the freely-chosen unanimity of its members, and lastly its ecumenical character, which links it to all nations and subordinates to it all local churches. It is the conception of *sobornost*, summing up as it does the organic nature of the Church, which underlies the doctrine of the hierarchy in the Orthodox system. Every member of the spiritual organism has his part in the life of the whole ; receives his hallowing in baptism and his ordination in the sacrament of anointing, conveying to him the seal of the gifts of the Holy Spirit. In some measure every member of the Church has his *charisma :* "Ye are an elect people, priests and kings, a holy nation " (1 Pet. ii, 9).

The laity, no less than the clergy, has its place and value in the Church as a whole. The status of the layman is not negative, it is not merely a non-clerical status, but is rather a special order, imparted in confirmation. That is why the holy oil requisite for this sacrament has to be blessed by more than one bishop ; in the Roman use the sacrament cannot be administered except by a bishop.

Baptism, even without confirmation, imparts some charismatic gifts ; and because of this, baptism in the name of the Holy Trinity is valid even when performed by a layman, so that baptism is valid even among those Christian confessions which do not recognise Holy Orders and have lost the apostolic succession.

Societies of laymen, devoid of clergy—such as are those Protestant Confessions which have lost the Episcopate—possess only one ecclesiastical degree, the order of laymen. This order has its character and place in the Church, and though subordinate to the priesthood is in some sense independent of it. It is the mark of Protestantism to understand and to emphasise this independence of the laity within the Church : though they carry this to an excess, by way of reaction against the opposite excess of Romanism, in which the laity are bound to yield passive obedience to the clergy, and thus lose the value which belongs to them.

Priesthood within the Church is related inseparably to the laity, and the relationship is not merely that of ruler to subject : it is also a relation of mutual help and of unity within the *sobornost*. The priest requires the co-operation of the laity in the administration of the sacraments, and the laity take their share in service and sacrament through singing, responses and prayers. Laymen, in concert with the clergy, take their part in Church teaching, in the ministry of the word : they may even be entrusted with a mission, and permitted to preach under the oversight of the bishop. Laymen have an incontestable right to take part in the election of the clergy, in all its degrees, from that of deacon and reader to that of patriarch. Lay and clerical representatives of the diocese of Moscow shared in the election of the Patriarch Tikhon, first as Metropolitan of Moscow and then as Patriarch of all the Russias. The laity present at the ordination of a priest signify their approval by acclaiming him as *axios* (worthy) immediately after the imposition of hands, and ordination cannot take place without this approval. Church administration in like manner is always conducted by the bishop in concert with representatives of clergy and laity organised in episcopal, diocesan or presbyteral councils, or in special gatherings such as local or ecumenical councils. Even where bishops alone are present, as at an ecumenical council, or in many local councils, the bishop's position is that of the " angel " of his church, voicing the harmony of its opinions and doctrine. He does not impose his personal opinion upon his church but gives authoritative expression to the voice of the whole Church : and an episcopal council expresses not the sum of the personal views of the bishops assembled (which, in that case, would have binding force) but the harmony of the views of the local churches.

It would, however, be incorrect to describe these relationships in terms of public law as " representative and constitutional "—so judicial a conception would be out of keeping with the Church's nature. The relation between priesthood and laity is, on the contrary, that of the *sobornost*, a spiritual reciprocity, a union in love, a oneness in thought, and, as I said, an organic rather than an organised principle. The clergy is not above the people but in them and with them : it is not a judicial absolutism but a divinely-given authority. Yet, for the faithful, this authority is a spiritual power, based upon the mystical energy imparted in ordination to the priesthood for the fulfilment of its sacramental task. The sacrament which this energy of the priesthood brings into operation is a divine, not a human activity : not an idea, a doctrine, an institution, but an immediate divine Fact. The priesthood has the power to link the divine with the human, to bring heaven down to earth, and it is in this sacramental ministration that the efficacy and basis of Holy Orders consists.

The priest is above all an offerer of sacrifice : this is the quality in virtue of which he can become the shepherd of the faithful and minister of the Word. The episcopal prayer at the imposition of hands for the priesthood reads thus : " that he may be worthy to present himself at Thy

altar, to preach the Gospel of Thy Kingdom, to set forth
in holiness the word of Thy truth, to offer to Thee gifts and
spiritual sacrifices and to renew Thy people by the baptism
of regeneration." Among all these gifts, the ministry of the
altar and the giving of gifts and spiritual sacrifices—the
purely sacrificial offices—belong to the priesthood alone :
for the ministry of the Word, the authority to preach the
Gospel and even the power to baptise are compatible with
the status of the laymen. The priesthood has the privilege
of the ministry of the Word, not as a prerogative of its
status, as though it were an *ecclesia docens* in contrast to
the *ecclesia discens,* but in virtue of the fulness of its
charismatic gifts and sacerdotal authority. There is no
special *charisma* of the ministry of the Word and of infallible teaching, such as the Vatican decree attributes to
the Pope, and to all the Roman clergy in his name (*veritatis
et fidei nunquam deficientis charisma*). The truth of the
Church is committed to the whole body, to clergy and
laity as an integral whole. No part of the Church can claim
infallibility over against the others : even bishops and
patriarchs, as Church history sufficiently shows, can fall
into error. And thus, if even the collective episcopate
claims the *charisma* of infallibility, it infringes the *sobornost,*
and leans towards the Vatican dogma by admitting an
episcopal, collective *charisma infallibilitatis.*

Still, the episcopate has the right to use its power and
authority in the defence and proclamation of the truths
acknowledged by the Church, and this is what the bishops,
in local and ecumenical councils, have done, when speaking
in the name of the Church and expressing not their individual views but the faith of the whole Christian people,
with their expressed or implied assent. The presence of
representatives of the whole Church, clergy and laity, at
local councils, gives visible expression to this assent.

The ministry of the Word and the authority to preach
form a duty and privilege of those who serve the temple :
yet they are not restricted to the temple. Only one ministry
is withheld entirely from the laity, that of the mysteries—
the celebration of the holy Eucharist and the other sacra-

ments. No human consent or election can confer this power upon men, even though an act of election is a preliminary condition of ordination. The divine power of Christ alone, given to the Apostles and transmitted by apostolic succession, can confer it. The hands laid by the bishop upon the head of an ordinand are the hands of the Apostles. It is Christ Himself, our supreme Bishop, who ordains His ministers. And as the Church cannot live nor have salvation without a mystical union with Him by the communion of His body and blood, so the charismatic priesthood is a vitally necessary organ of the body of the Church : its suspension, or a break in the continuity of the sacerdotal status in any ecclesiatical group is the gravest of evils, and cuts it off from the fulness of life in the Church.

If then the charismatic source of the priesthood is the apostolic succession, episcopal authority is the continuous and primitive well-spring from which its fulness flows (*sine episcopo nulla ecclesia*), although the bishop is in and with, and not above, the Church. The charismatic authority of the episcopate is not an idea but a fact, before which we must bow in gratitude to God, humbling ourselves beneath His holy will. This authority alone conserves and fortifies the fulness of charismatic life in the Church, and restores to the right path such groups as have strayed outside Church unity into isolation.

The task of reunion remains merely abstract unless it is approached by way of intellectual interchange and the discussion of principles. As an idea, it requires an incarnation : as a problem, it demands to be realised. The union of Christians cannot be brought about otherwise than by a sharing of the same Cup at the Holy Table and by the ministry of a priesthood which is an integral unity and indubitably charismatic.

At the present time we find that the apostolic succession is broken and set aside in |some quarters, while in others it has lost its evidential clearness through the historical complications of the Reformation and the Western schism; while in all these quarters there is a historical reaction against the Roman clerical system, although the Papacy has not violated the apostolic succession.

The orthodox priesthood of the Eastern Church has preserved all its vigour and charismatic purity, and that Church embraces in love all who seek it, expecting from them no juridical submission but rather brotherly love. When it is God's pleasure to accomplish that work of re-union to which our prayers look forward, may all be kindled with the longing for one undoubted charismatic priesthood which will rebuild what has perished and complete what is doubtful, in such modes as the love of the Church and the grace of the Holy Spirit shall reveal. In that day the eyes of all will turn towards our Mother, the Orthodox Eastern Church, and towards its charismatic episcopate, for that healing of infirmities and renewal of exhausted energies of which a prayer in our Ordinal speaks.

This is the road which the reunion of the Church must needs follow : the whole past history of the Church, no less than its present condition, makes this clear. And from this point of view our present gathering is symbolic ; Christians from all over the world are here, and the only absentees are the representatives of the Roman hierarchy, which conceives of union as involving submission to the absolute power of the Pope. But here you behold, present among you, bishops and ministers of the Orthodox Church, and by their voice that Church summons all men towards oneness in faith, in love, and in sacramental grace, in the words which come before the creed in the liturgy of the holy Eucharist : "Let us love one another, unto the Confession, with one heart and soul, of the same faith."

THE REV. JOHN J. BANNINGA, D.D.
South Indian United Church

Fathers and Brethren : It is as a witness of an experience that I come to speak before you and not as an exponent of any theory, old or new, concerning the Christian ministry. The subject as assigned me reads, " The Church's Ministry." I would have preferred it if it read " The Christian Ministry," for it seems to me the holy ministry of the Word and sacraments is far more that of our Lord and Saviour Jesus Christ than it is that of the Church, though the Church is His Body, the Temple of the Living God.

The Bishop of Bombay has called attention to a quotation from Dr. Garvie's book *Towards Reunion*, and in commenting upon that quotation has laid emphasis on the second and by far the less important part of that quotation. The quotation reads, " Ordination is a corporate recognition of the grace-gift, investing with the authority of the Church the exercise of that gift within the Christian community." The first and most important part of this matter of ordination is the " grace-gift " mentioned by Dr. Garvie. The second part is the recognition by the Church of the gift.

What is meant by the " grace-gift"? It seems to me it is something like this. Jesus Christ wishes to use a certain person as His minister in the Church. Early or later in life, He begins to make known His desire to the person. The person responds in obedience to the divine will, and allows himself to be guided toward the goal. From time to time Christ bestows grace on him for the work that lies before him. Through prayer and Bible study and other means of grace the young man grows into a fuller maturity. He consults the leaders of his Church and guides himself in accordance with its rules and customs. Finally a day comes when his training is complete and he presents himself for ordination. In the meantime the Church has not been ignorant of his existence nor of his purposes, but now, through duly appointed officers, it examines the young man to see whether he has fulfilled the requirements. They also inquire into his spiritual experience and into his Christian life. If they find all in due order they vote to ordain him to the Christian ministry and the time and place for that ceremony are determined. At that time with impressive ceremonies he is publicly received into the Christian ministry by the laying on of hands and prayer.

No one who has not gone through this experience can realise what it means to one who has truly given himself in glad surrender to his Master for this high purpose. It is not so much the solemn assembly, nor the serious responsibilities that he is taking upon himself, nor even the part that men of high esteem and great respect are taking in the service. What he feels, above all else, is that he is then and there in the very presence of the Master Himself, and from Him receiving a special blessing which makes him in very reality " God's man." No Church, no Church officer, can make him such. It is a personal matter between him and his Master, and to the young man it is the Master Himself who lays hands on him and bids him go forth in His name to proclaim salvation to all men through faith. It is indeed a solemn hour, never to be forgotten. All about the ceremony itself may be forgotten. Even the names and faces of the men who took part in it may be forgotten. But the fact that, in that solemn hour, he and his Master stood face to face and that they there entered into a new covenant of service and of enduement with power will be something that can never pass from his mind but will abide with him as a constant inspiration though he live far beyond the allotted four-score years. And it is in the consciousness of that hour that he ministers in Christ's name to those who have been committed to his care.

And who will say that his ministry is not blessed by the Master Himself? Should we not apply the Master's own rule in trying to judge this ministry? The Master said, " By their fruits ye shall know them." And, for four hundred years since the days of Luther and Calvin, men thus ordained have in His name ministered both the Word and sacraments to multitudes of people in all parts of the world, and everywhere we find those who have been led to the foot of the Cross in glad self-surrender, who can testify to life and joy and peace found through such ministries. We dare not apply any external tests to the spiritual life but must apply only those tests that are spiritual. And when we do apply them we find that in the branches of God's Kingdom, in which such ministers have served, the fruits

K

of the Spirit have been and are found in abundance. St. Paul says, " The fruit of the Spirit is love, joy, peace, long-suffering, kindness, goodness, faithfulness, meekness, self-control ; against such there is no law." It seems to me that an unprejudiced examination of the facts will show that these fruits are found in all Churches and that, therefore, we must admit that the Spirit of Christ is in them all.

A stream of Living Water has flowed from the Throne of Grace in all ages. When the channel becomes blocked through the refusal of men to yield to the influences of the Spirit, the Waters burst forth into new channels. And the evidence of the continuity of the stream is not in the banks of the old channels, but in the fact that there is Living Water and that along the shores there is evidence of the fruit that is produced by that Living Water.

Christ chose twelve Apostles, and one of them betrayed Him. The eleven tried to fill the vacancy but we never again hear his name mentioned. But Jesus, the Risen Lord, Himself appeared to Paul and sent him forth as His special messenger to the Gentiles. At one time Paul had to " withstand Peter to the face " because the latter seemed inclined to limit God's grace and want it to flow only through Jewish channels. But Paul was able to show that the fruits of the Spirit were manifest among the Gentiles, and so the Council at Jerusalem bade him go forwards ; and their decision, they said, was in accordance with what " seemed good to the Holy Spirit and to them." What Christ did in those days He can do again at any time, for He is the Living Christ.

The writers of the New Testament used the Greek language and so they spoke of " Apostles " when referring to those whom Christ first " sent forth." Had Latin been the New Testament language they would probably have been called " missionaries," for such they were. And as the Bishop of Bombay rightly observes, missionaries during this past century have done just what they did. They have proclaimed the Word, they have gathered in the believers, they have trained and ordained ministers, and, just as in the first century, the blessings of the Spirit have been manifested in their work. It seems to me that, if we could have another Council like that held in Jerusalem, we too might say with them, " It seems good to the Holy Spirit and to us to recognise what God has wrought, and to acknowledge as Christ's ministers those through whom these mighty works have been manifested."

But some would say, " But are not these men prophets rather than priests in the Church of Christ ? " Yes, perhaps they are. But when the people came to John they asked, " Art thou Elijah ? Art thou the prophet ? " And when Jesus asked His disciples what men said of Him, they replied, " John the Baptist ; but others say Elijah ; and others, that one of the prophets is risen again." I cannot help but feel that it is significant that Jesus was not likened to one of the Old Testament priests. No one seems to have thought of Him as such. When years later, He is referred to in that way, He is called in the Epistle to the Hebrews, " a priest after the order of Melchizedek, without genealogy," that is, I take it, without predecessor or successor. But both John and Jesus seemed to have been included in the minds of the people as in the line of the great prophets of old. But this does mean that those whom Christ sent forth under the New Covenant were what some call merely " a prophetic ministry," for they are in very truth all that Christ intended that they should be—witnesses of what they had heard and seen of the life eternal given to them through the Son of God, ministers of the Word and sacraments given by Christ as means of grace for those who accepted Him as their Lord and Master.

It is not necessary to say more concerning this matter. What we need to do is to recognise what Christ Himself has ordained and to acknowledge that the fruits that they have borne are the fruits of His Spirit. The disciples at one time tried to get Christ to exclude one " who did not walk with them," but Christ said, " Forbid him not, for he that is not against me is for me." The Church of the future, if it is to be a united Church, must be an inclusive Church. It must be rich in all that pertains to the Kingdom of God. Within it must be found all that is manifestly of the Spirit, and therefore it is not for any to say, "this must be excluded or that must be excluded." Let us include all, so that God's Spirit may have free course through the hearts of men and draw all men unto Himself.

The highest and greatest realm of all God's creation is personality and we can never separate God's Kingdom from personality. God revealed Himself in a Person and Jesus Christ chose persons to be His witnesses. And so with high respect for personality we must conserve all that the Master has taught us. It is persons filled with His Spirit that will convey His grace to men. It is persons with His Spirit that will be the messengers of life unto men. It is personal fellowship with the Risen Lord Himself that will make us partakers of His life.

Let me close with a single verse from Edwin Markman :

"He drew a circle which shut me out ;
Heretic! Rebel! A thing to flout :
But Love and I had the wit to win,
We drew a circle and took him in."

THE REV. JOSEF SOUČEK, D.D.

Senior and President of the Evangelical Church of Bohemian (Czech) Brethren

I have been asked to speak on the Christian Ministry on behalf of the Evangelical Church of Bohemian Brethren, perhaps because she is the descendant of Hussite Churches and because through them for the first time a whole nation broke the unity of the Western Church. I want to say, therefore, a few words of our experience of the past and of the present standpoint on this subject of the ministry in connection with the reunion of the Churches.

The Hussites never thought of a separation from the Church. They wanted reform. Their intense yearning, awaked by Huss, aimed at a Holy Church, purified from all blemish according to the Scriptures, the very Kingdom of God. This ideal they defended for fifteen years with many sacrifices and great suffering. Then the Church sought reconciliation and subsequent negotiations about it resulted in certain compacts, *compacta*, agreed upon between them and the Council of Basel. Some points of the desired reforms of the Church were guaranteed to them, with which they were not satisfied but which they accepted for the sake of the unity of the Church. But what the Council had approved, the Pope did not sanction and refused also—though it was promised—to acknowledge the elected Hussite archbishop, who for that reason could not be consecrated. Now as they held, with the Church, the doctrine of apostolic succession, there was no authorised person who would ordain the Hussite priests, and they would not set apart and ordain their priests by some other way—unless they broke the unity of the Church and separated from her. Some of them advised it, but they would not do it. And so the consequence was that they had for a hundred years a great shortage of priests, and that in that need they accepted from the neighbouring countries any priests, even those who, for their iniquitous life, were put out of their charges, and that young Hussite clerics of doubtful character used to purchase ordination from Roman bishops abroad. The result of this state of things can be imagined. Demoralisation and corruption—and terrible disappointment. Where were now the ideals for which they suffered and that Holy Church which they so ardently desired and which they hoped to establish in Bohemia? They sacrificed the ideal of the pure Church of Christ for the idea of the unity of the Church. And they did not save that unity either, for they were always considered and fought by the Pope as heretics and schismatics—which, according to the Roman standpoint, they actually were. Later, the Utraquists—as they were commonly called—cast off, under the influence of the German and Swiss Reformation, these fetters of visible unity, and giving up the doctrine of apostolic succession freely called and ordained their ministers after the example and teaching of the German Evangelical Church.

The minority of Hussites, distressed by growing demoralisation of Utraquists, went a different way. For them the Kingdom of God, a Holy Church, was a greater good than Church unity. And in the year 1467 they parted from the others, broke with Rome utterly, became an independent Church and raised priests out of their own members. They were ordained through the mediation of a Waldensian Elder in Austria, and one of them was appointed and ordained to be their bishop. By this act the Church, which is known in history as the Unitas Fratrum, whose last bishop was John A. Comenius, got the necessary freedom for the full obedience of the Word of God and was thus enabled to grow in faith and knowledge and righteousness and to become a great and continuous blessing for the Bohemian people until this day.

The Brethren, as they were shortly called, had a sort of episcopal Church government with growing presbyterian elements. It might be called, indeed, a constitutional episcopacy. For the bishops were elected by the Synod of Priests, and the Synod alone had the power to decide in all weighty matters. Even in the administration of the Church the bishops had to take the Church's counsel. They never held the doctrine of apostolic succession, of which we read in their confession of faith, from the year 1535, thus : " This is the true apostolic succession which is founded not on certain places or persons but on the pure faith and teaching of the Apostles." They say also, " The priest, or presbyter, and the bishop are according to the apostolic canons one and the same thing, and the minister who preaches the Word of God in purity and walks in the steps of the Apostles can piously boast of the apostolic succession without which the other one is of no worth."

Such is our experience, showing that even the good and great idea of unity may sometimes quench the Spirit, and separation for the sake of conscience may open the way for the Spirit and be blessed by God.

Our present Evangelical Church of Bohemian Brethren is not an unbroken continuation of the old Churches which were destroyed by persecution —again for the sake of unity. Still we are their descendants by our traditions, by race, and through those dispersed secret adherents of the old Church who remained faithful during all those 160 years until better times came. We are of their faith and hold essentially the same view and theory of the church ministry, but we have not accepted their bishops. Our Church follows the presbyterian system, which we believe to be most in conformity with the Christian religion and with the example of the Apostolic Church. With our fathers we consider our ministers to be elders, or bishops, who have been called by God and by the Church to dedicate themselves wholly with all their abilities and time to the service of the Church of Christ, so as to make it their life's vocation. The responsibility of their ordination rests in our Church, partly with the local congregation which calls a minister, but chiefly with the General Church whose central Administrative Board decides whether they are qualified to be ordained or not. The Board consists of ministers and elders, and its chairman is a minister who is at the same time the president of the Synod, and is entrusted with the ordination of candidates who are found to be qualified. He is called, after the example of the Brethren, the Senior of the Church, and is elected for six years, though he may once more be re-elected. Ordination is lifelong and for the whole Church.

What do we mean by ordination ? What happens by it ? We cannot accept the teaching that in ordination, and through the act of ordination—be it conferred by whomsoever—God in answer to the prayer of His Church makes a man to be a minister and imparts to him or grants him such gifts as are needed for his ministry. We believe that God, if He calls a man to the ministry, has granted him and, if he continues to be obedient to Him, will continue to grant him such gifts as will enable him to perform his duty faithfully and successfully. Ordination means setting him apart before the congregation of Christian people to this sacred office, and the Church through the ordaining minister, by the laying on of hands and invoking of God, invests him with her authority, and lays on him before God the duty of being a minister of Christ and His ambassador to His people. It means that he is to preach the Gospel and administer the ordinances of Christ, not in his name but in the name of the Church of Christ, and therefore in the name of Christ Himself.

What shall we think of the ministry of the united Church, and of the difficulty of the universal recognition of ministers ? I think that the best solution would be to acknowledge that the question of the form of church government, and how its ministers should be ordained, is not an essential question of the Christian religion and of the true Church, and that for this reason it might be left to the different Churches or the branches of the united Church, to decide what shall be the form of their organisation and of the calling and ordaining of their ministers.

But it seems that it is impossible for some Churches to recognise the ministers of other Churches, and that perhaps the solution of the difficulty might be a constitutional episcopate. I believe—and here I speak personally—that this suggestion need not be *a priori* rejected by non-episcopal Churches, and that for two reasons : there are Churches which we cannot consider episcopal in the full sense of that term, but they have bishops. There are Methodist bishops, Lutheran bishops and also Presbyterian bishops, and we have with us at this Conference two such Presbyterian bishops. I know that they and their Church are decidedly Presbyterian ; they have changed the name " superintendent " to " bishop," and many other Reformed Churches with the presbyterian system have or have had superintendents. Comenius in one of his writings defends the title of bishop as a Biblical name. And if that is possible now in some non-episcopal Churches, why not in others, if by such a concession Church unity could be achieved ?

With reference to the second reason, I said that the presbyterian system answers best to the spirit of Christian religion, but we must admit that there are no strict and clear instructions of Christ or of the Apostles in the matter of church government, and that therefore the form of church organisation is not of fundamental importance, and that for the sake of the unity of the Church it might be advisable to accept this solution, or at least not to reject it *a limine*. For unity cannot be realised without self-denial on all sides.

But such a solution is possible only on the following condition—that it shall be purely a question of Church government and not a question of faith and doctrine. But there are some doubts. We are told that some Churches find it impossible to recognise the ministers of other Churches. I believe, though I may be wrong, that these Churches number among them some episcopal Churches, and why is it impossible for them ? Is it because ministers of non-episcopal Churches have not been ordained by bishops ? But there are Protestant Churches with bishops which have no difficulty in recognising ministers ordained without a bishop—as for instance, I am sure, the Danish or the Swedish Lutheran Church with bishops recognises the Lutheran ministers in Germany though they have not been ordained by a bishop. The reason is the doctrine of apostolic succession, which some of the episcopal Churches hold. If a non-episcopal Church should elect and appoint bishops and give them authority to ordain, would the Churches who now find it impossible to recognise the ministers of other Churches recognise those bishops who have not been ordained or consecrated in the way of apostolic succession, or would they demand their submission to a special consecration by a bishop already consecrated in that way ? If that should be the case then the difficulty about the universally acknowledged ministry would not be solved by the constitutional episcopate. For it can scarcely be expected that non-episcopal Churches would consent for the sake of unity, or for the universal recognition of ministers, to accept the doctrine of apostolic succession or, without accepting it, to let their ministers be ordained bishops by those who are believed to have been consecrated through the apostolic succession. It would be a matter of conscience, and agreement would not be easy. In this connection I take the liberty to mention one instance in the past of how such a difficulty was solved on a small scale. The Hussite Churches—the Utraquists and Brethren—united, in the seventeenth century, into one Church of two distinct branches. Each branch retained its own form of worship and church government. They had only a common Consistory whose president or administrator was one of the Utraquist ministers, and the vice-president one of the bishops of the Unity. The ordination of Utraquist ministers was performed by the Administrator with the assistance of the bishop and the ordination of ministers of the Unity by the bishop with the assistance of the Administrator, but both of them laid hands on the ordained. And so, seeing the wonderful spirit of mutual goodwill and considerateness which the delegates of all Churches show towards one another in this Conference, we may hope that in this question also some way will be found toward reaching an agreement.

THE REV. DAVID FYFFE, D.C.L.

Moderator of the Presbyterian Church of England

I propose, with the time at my disposal, to present the perspective in which Presbyterians generally envisage the ministry of the Church of Christ.

From the comparative silence of our Lord about the corporate form the Kingdom of God on earth should take, the most reasonable conclusion to draw is that it would find for itself a body, fashioned in conformity with the divine family life of which it would be an expression, a building fitly framed together to house its own inner spirit which is the Holy Spirit of Jesus, a temple adorned for the indwelling of God.

If such were our Lord's mind, it was amply justified by subsequent events and by nothing so conspicuously as by the appearance of Paul, acting in the full, joyous and triumphant discharge of the duties of an Apostle, impelled thereto by the Spirit of Christ which dwelt within him, though he had neither sojourned with Christ while He lived on earth nor been commissioned by any of the existing Apostles. Already the power of Christ had begun to find for itself a home and an active body. And as a matter of history it is to Paul, made a minister of the Gospel " not by man, nor by the will of man, but by the will of God," that the foundations were laid for this temple, this divine building which was to be. He preached the Gospel, he lived the life of the holy brotherhood, debtor to everyone whom he could lead to Jesus, and he urged his converts to the use of those means of grace which Christ had either instituted or approved, the usage of public and private prayer and the due observance of the sacraments of Baptism and the Lord's Supper.

It is characteristic of St. Paul that in all his labours to build up the corporate Society of Christ, he kept close to the word and mind of his Master. Every society requires some form of organisation, some allocation of its different functions to different persons, some provision for government and rule : but the Body of Christ must be so formulated as to be a fitting expression of the Spirit of Christ's Kingdom.

Four considerations, native to the temper of the Kingdom demand recognition.

1. The Christian community, consisting of brethren in the family of God, enjoys equality in spiritual rights. All have immediate access to the Father and to the infinite resources of widom and love stored up in Him. In such a community it would be impertinent, if not ludicrous, to introduce differences of rank or order. The only recognisable ranks in a genuine family are degrees of usefulness. To this principle the founders of the first Christian Church were loyal. If some brother seemed worthy to be entrusted with rule he was warned " not to lord it over the household of God " ; to whatever office any member was called he was to regulate his conduct on the principle " that we are members one of another."

2. In the second place the possession of gifts was to be considered as a stewardship. Our Lord had taken pains to

bring this somewhat unpalatable fact home to the hearts of the disciples. In various parables to the people at large, in private instructions to the Twelve and by His own example Jesus taught the law of stewardship as an obligation each owed to God. In a noble passage Paul also derives the varied gifts which men possess from the sovereign grace of God who liberally endows His children for the service of His Church.

3. If it was necessary, as always amid the fluctuations of imperfect and self-willed Christian folk it will be necessary, to find some trustworthy vehicle for the Spirit of God, that will have to be sought in the body of believers, in the household of God. If any question of authority arise it can only be settled by reference to God, the Fount of truth and love ; but should there be further question about God's will in any given circumstance, or for any specific duty, that is to be found where the Spirit of God resides, among the members of God's household. When all have equal access to truth and to right judgment, and are presumably exercising that privilege, the one seat of authority under God is the common mind of the brethren. This fact is not to be established by subtlety of argument —it belongs to the thing which a divine family is.

Should the question arise of a brother's fitness for some office, that of preaching, for example, it is taken for granted that the company of believers has the necessary knowledge to discover the presence of these gifts. Thus when brethren were needed to relieve the Apostles from the strain of their duties, they appeal to the Christian community. " Look ye out among you seven men of honest report, full of the Holy Ghost and wisdom " (Acts vi, 3). Again, it was to the Christians in Antioch that the Holy Spirit said, " Separate me Barnabas and Saul for the work whereunto I have called them " (Acts xiii, 2). And again it is the Christian brethren who are urged to deal with any member found in a fault.

From the people of God rises the authority of the Church and the functions of the Church are by them delegated to those thus chosen.

4. The fourth consideration is unity. As all faithful members of the body of Christ are brethren together of the same family, the objective of the Kingdom of God must be a corporate Society in which all are included and in which the spiritual bond transcends all other differences. This life in the divine household can only enjoy its full measure of enlightenment and love in a Church as universal as the brotherhood itself. It is not only the passionate appeal of our Lord for unity among believers which urges us forward under the spell of one united Church—the impulse is native to the Kingdom. The motive which prompted this World Conference is organic to the Gospel.

So in the New Testament, while there may be many Churches, there is in fact but one Church. This one Church, gathering into itself all scattered Churches, is the conception which fires the heart of St. Paul as it regulates all his exhortations, instructions and entreaties to different communities of the faithful.

Roughly, but quite in the order of nature, the duties for which provision had to be made were, first, supervision of things temporal—the distribution of charity and the like ; and, second, the preaching of the Gospel and supervision of the flock. The principle of selection was manifestly fitness for the specific duty. As every office was to be exercised within the brotherhood and for the prosperity of the Kingdom, the men chosen must possess the spirit of the community in marked degree: they should be men " filled with the Holy Ghost." Alike on grounds of common sense and apostolic injunction, this is a *sine qua non* for the Church for all times. How to raise such men and how to recognise them is one of the primary tasks of Church organisation.

If there were two quite definite functions, one temporal and one spiritual, the officials of the Church would be of two kinds. Whether any particular brother were suited for spiritual or for temporal office depended upon the gifts he possessed. For the oversight of temporalities " wisdom and discretion" were required (Acts vi, 3) ; for leadership in spiritualities—teaching and preaching—in addition to the possession of the Holy Ghost, a man " should be of blameless life, discreet in the conduct of home and business, charitable, sound in the faith and apt to teach."

There seems to have been at first no clearly marked line of division between these two offices, the deacon and the presbyter or bishop—Philip, for example, was ordained to the service of tables, but he is found preaching the Gospel and administering Baptism.

The early Church adopted the initiatory practice of the " laying on of hands." This initiatory act was employed when converts received the gift of the Holy Spirit, when Paul received his sight, when the leaders of the Church at Antioch appointed Barnabas and Saul to their missionary work, and when Timothy was sent forth to the duties of the pastorate. Nowhere is specific instruction given respecting the person who might ordain.

So far as the New Testament records give information, the gifts come first and the ordination afterwards ; there seems to be no evidence of particular gifts being bestowed upon brethren at ordination. It is agreeable to the nature of the Gospel and the dictates of sound judgment that so imperious and consecrated a person as Paul should be accepted as leader and worthy of the honour conferred upon an Apostle ; that Barnabas be appointed to accompany Paul, because of his gift of consolation ; that Timothy was selected because of his knowledge of Scripture, and John Mark because of his general serviceableness for the Gospel.

Such was the first organisation of the Church, such its two classes of officials and such its method of initiating into office. Various functions were distributed between the two offices, those of the evangelist, the prophet, the teacher and the ruler ; but manifestly the chief functions of the elders or bishops were teaching, preaching and government, while the deacons were specially charged with the material concerns of the sacred community. It was a simple organisation, whose officers were chosen because of the gifts Christ had bestowed upon them, deriving their authority from the Holy Spirit resident in the body of believers. And we are compelled to insist that, so organised, Christ had found for Himself a body or a Church. Other forms of government might be added in the future, other officials might be appointed, but such an organisation and ministry as the Kingdom of God required was there present in the days of St. Paul. It was of this community that Paul could declare: "God hath put all things under his feet, and gave him to be head over all things to the Church, which is his body, the fulness of him that filleth all in all."

Among those sections of Christendom which have adopted this primal and apostolic type of Church organisation it has been found necessary, as life became more complicated and the general standard of education had risen, to give more attention to the qualifications of the teaching elder. The first consideration in the making of a minister is that he be a man God has called and chosen ; he must possess the *ethos* of the Kingdom which is always the gift of the Holy Spirit. Who is to decide on any man's claim to possess this qualification ? The candidate may himself be mistaken. There is then a reference to the brotherhood, to the members of a particular congregation. If after prayer, this company of believers is satisfied that he is fitted to lead them in the things of God, the Presbytery, representing the whole Church, confirms his calling, ordains him a minister of the Gospel and inducts him into a particular charge or function. Following apostolic practice the Presbytery solemnly lays its hands upon the ordained. This practice of ordination, accompanied by the laying on of hands, the Presbyterian Church retains, accepting it as an ancient practice and also in the interests of Church unity.

Though ordination follows the recognition of gifts, and does not bestow them, there can be no doubt that a sincere Christian man, believing himself called of God to the holy office and confirmed in that belief by the choice of his brethren, feels himself further committed and more deeply engaged to the winning of souls at the solemn act of ordination. It may be, surely it cannot but be, that he realises more richly then than ever in his life the presence and blessing of God who is always present in love with His family on earth, but present most fully when together they are praying and planning for the extension of His rule in the world.

For God's heritage is His people, and His glory their prosperity.

PROFESSOR DR. MARTIN DIBELIUS
University of Heidelberg (Evangelical-Lutheran)

The first part of this discussion has made us all realise how different are the views which exist in regard to the ministry of the Church. We have heard the extent to which the representatives of the different Churches are bound by tradition and conscience, and I do not feel called upon to put an end to this multiplicity of opinions regarding the ministry by suggesting some formula of compromise, which would necessarily be colourless or would satisfy nobody ; nor would it be right for me to add yet another opinion to the number. My own standpoint, which is closer to that of Dr. Scherer than to that of any other speaker at this morning's session, would probably not interest you so much as my reflections on the cause of this variety of views and an appeal which I would make to your sense of responsibility.

It is indeed a matter in which we have great responsibilities : to the past, the present and the future.

First, we have a responsibility to the past : there seem to be two schools of opinion among us : one which holds to the tradition of the centuries, and regards the validity of the ministry as dependent upon adherence to this tradition ; and another school which regards this tradition as containing later accretions that it cannot accept, and which, therefore, feels bound to defend the position of the primitive Church against the claims of tradition. We cannot debate the historical evidence here. I will merely say, briefly, that it depends very largely whether we rely on the Epistle to the Romans and the First Epistle to the Corinthians, or whether we turn for guidance to the Pastoral letters and the first letter of St. Clement. The difference in our opinions as to what was the primitive position arises out of the difference between these documents. Nor can we debate our different attitudes towards the historical question; the difference is due to the fact that some of us see in history chiefly the working of human factors—the effects of national and geographical conditions, and also of human weakness and wickedness—whereas others see in it rather the action of divine providence, and regard history as being confirmed by the indisputable divine blessing bestowed upon all the Churches. No individual Church can renounce its allegiance to tradition or to what it believes that it knows about the primitive Church. That constitutes our responsibility to the past, a responsibility which none of us can disown.

We have also a responsibility for the present. In that connection I wish to remind you of what a representative of an Indian Missionary Church told us at the first afternoon meeting of the Conference. And I would further remind you that our western Churches are living in the midst of a non-Christian world, and are, therefore, also missionary Churches from this point of view. The world is watching us; heathen and Christians, laymen and Church people—all expect something. What is it they are expecting? So far as concerns the present subject the answer is that they expect, at the very least, that the question of the ministry should not set us at variance. For they, more especially the Christian laity, will certainly feel that men who are united in the service of the Lord Jesus Christ may indeed be divided in opinion, but ought not to be disunited by the question of how this service is to be performed through the ministry. It is precisely because I myself feel so strongly about the different historic conceptions of the ministry in its historic aspect that I feel bound to remind you that these questions are not the last or the deepest in the group of problems with which we are confronted. And do not let it be said, as a result of our present discussion, that we have incurred the reproof which

Paul addressed to the Jews who were over-proud of their customs : " The name of God is blasphemed among the Gentiles because of you."

And, lastly, we have a responsibility towards the future. What is it we can do, seeing that on the one hand there are these deep historical divisions among us, and that on the other hand we have to be mindful of our responsibility to the present ?

I think we should first recognise that this Subject cannot be dealt with in the same way as Subject II, or even as Subjects III and IV. There can be no question of finding a formula on which we might all agree. If we were to return to our Churches with such a formula we should discredit the work of Lausanne from the standpoint of the future.

What can be attained now and in the immediate future is that respect should be accorded to the ministry of other Churches even by those who do not regard such ministries as ecclesiastically valid. It would mean substantial progress if we could depart from the old standpoint of denominational particularism which regards the sacred things of others as unworthy of respect. Let us remember that Paul warns us to respect the conscience of our weaker brethren, because Christ died for our weaker brother also. How much more is it incumbent upon us to respect the ministry of another, which he regards as sacred! Perhaps in this direction we might arrive at some sort of neighbourly recognition of each other's ministries ; that might be a useful subject to discuss in the proper Section. But in any case, when we are examining the conceptions of the ministry which are held by others let us say to ourselves : " Take thy shoes from off thy feet, for the place whereon thou standest is, to another, holy ground."

The Conference rose at 12.30 p.m

FRIDAY AFTERNOON, AUGUST 12TH.

A short full session, for the further discussion of the Report of Section IV, was held from 3 to 4 p.m., and was opened with devotions led by Bishop JOHN HURST.

On the motion of the Rt. Rev. Bishop GWYNNE the following message of sympathy was sent to the Coptic Orthodox Church, in view of the loss sustained by it in the death of its Patriarch :

"Delegates from seventy Churches assembled at World Conference on Faith and Order desire to express deep sympathy with Coptic Orthodox Church in sustaining the death of his Beatitude the late revered Patriarch. We thank God for lives of Egyptian Christians which have enriched the Universal Church and pray that you may experience God's especial guidance and power in the time of your bereavement."

It was announced that the Pastor of the Cathedral and the council of the Cathedral parish would welcome any members of the Conference at a service of Holy Communion to be held on Sunday, August 14th, at 9.45 a.m.

Report of Section IV—Adjourned Discussion
[The text of this Report as presented will be found on p. 230.]

The Bishop of GLOUCESTER said that in spite of many difficulties a substantial measure of religious agreement had emerged with regard to the Creeds. Unanimity, indeed, appeared to have been reached, but it seemed that the Lutheran position had not been sufficiently well understood. There was a difference of intellectual attitude, rather than of religious thought or theology. The Drafting Committee would meet that evening, and full attention would be paid to the points that had been raised.

He hoped that the short introduction to the Report would be retained. As for the pre-eminence assigned to the Nicene Creed, it was placed before the Apostles' Creed as being accepted by East and West, and as having a place in the western Confessions and in the doctrine of the Huguenot Church ; and in fact it could not be said that the Apostles' Creed was the older. To put the Nicene Creed first would be a natural and rightful deference to the strong wishes of the Orthodox. The footnote, elementary as it might seem, was inserted for the sake of clearness. And not much had been said about particular Confessions because the Conference was rather concerned with a creed for the whole Church.

The Rev. PAUL SANDEGREN, speaking in English, said that he had been asked to make the following statement on behalf of a considerable number of members of the Section :

The Report was not unanimously accepted. Some decisions were carried by a majority in the face of a strong minority, handicapped as it was with regard to language. But I am personally of the opinion that if we had had only one day more we should have been able to present a unanimous report. I have every hope that we shall be able to do that even now after some additional committee work.

We were charged with the task of preparing a statement on Unity and Confession of Faith. In accordance with the assurance that we were quite free to make or not to make use of Pamphlet 52, we have, in order not to offend the legitimate susceptibilities of some groups of members, struck out a new line which seems to us to be of greater importance. We have, therefore, looked at the actual facts, and have found something which was not entirely expected. We had come here to bring the Churches together, though some of us no doubt had a much higher aim. But we found a deep and real unity already established on a common religious basis.

We emphasise that this is not a unity of doctrine or of intellectual terms ; many would, I imagine, consider such intellectual unity would neither be possible nor desirable.

But here we found a stronger unity, which in a vital union binds together men of perhaps widely different conceptions, even of important aspects of the Christian religion. We have endeavoured to describe this fact with regard to the Confession of Faith. It is here related to the Holy Scriptures, the old Symbols and the Christian experience.

We now propose a small addition before the second paragraph in order to make our meaning quite clear and to avoid the fatal misunderstanding which has been alluded to. This is for many a matter of conscience. Paragraph 2 should now read : " Fully respecting the differences in doctrinal conception, we are," etc.

It is further to be emphasised that the three points in this paragraph have here no relation to historical considerations. Such things belong to footnotes ; what we wish to express in this paragraph is that the Scriptures, the old creeds, and the always living personal experience, connected as it is with the tradition of experience of all times, have a common present-day religious value for us. We reiterate that we have found this to be a fact. Some verbal changes may be urged upon the editors who would probably be able to adopt them.

As the chief contents of the report are the emphasising of certain facts I strongly believe that we shall be able to arrive at unanimous agreement.

The following suggestions were made for submission to the Drafting Committee :

In *paragraph* 4, the Rev. J. MILNE desired the addition of some re-statement of the relations between Church and State.

In *paragraph* 5, the Rev. J. C. BLAIR suggested the substitution of some such word as " supreme " for " only," in the phrase " the only evidence of spiritual vitality."

The Convener stated that any further suggestions which reached the Drafting Committee in time would be fully considered.

The Report as a whole was then referred to the Drafting Committee ; and, after prayer by Bishop BRENT, the Conference separated at 4 p.m. to continue its sectional discussions.

THE SACRAMENTS

SATURDAY MORNING, AUGUST 13TH.

The Conference met in full session on Saturday morning to consider Subject VI, The Sacraments. The chair was taken by Sir HENRY LUNN, and the session was opened at 9.30 with devotions led by General-Superintendent Dr. SCHIAN.

The following paper, prepared by the Rt. Rev. NICHOLAI, Bishop of Ochrida, was read, in his absence, by Archbishop GERMANOS.

THE RIGHT REV. NICHOLAI
Bishop of Ochrida (Orthodox)

There are seven Sacraments in the Church militant on earth : Baptism, Confirmation, Eucharist, Penance, Ordination (*Cheirotonia*), Marriage and Extreme Unction. In the East the Sacraments are still called the Mysteries. Why ? Because each one of them hides in itself a mysterious and miraculous action of God the Holy Spirit. The very kernel of each one of them consists of this mysterious and miraculous divine action. In the Christian Mysteries we do not know *How* but we know *That*, i.e. we do not know how the Holy Spirit works in a Mystery but we know that He works in and through it.

In the Mystery of Baptism God the Holy Spirit cleanses the soul from sin, so that the soul receives God's sonship by grace and is recruited into the army of Christ the Saviour. Baptism effectuates such a tremendous change in a man, that is called the new birth (John iii, 5). Baptism was ordered by the Lord (Matt. xxviii, 19). " Whosoever be unbaptised cannot be saved, except the martyrs, who even without the water (but by the blood) receive the Kingdom of God " (Cyril of Alexandria).

In the Mystery of Confirmation, God the Holy Spirit fills the soul previously cleansed and emptied from sin by Baptism, with positive powers or gifts. And the gifts are different. Confirmation was ordained and instituted through the practice of the Apostles (Acts viii, 15-17; xix, 1-6; 2 Cor. i, 20-22).

In the Mystery of the Eucharist and at the moment of the priest's invocation, God the Holy Spirit descends on the bread and wine which have been set forth and sanctified, and transubstantiates them into Christ's body and blood (not transforms them but transubstantiates them; for the substance is changed while the form of bread and wine remain to our eyes unchanged).

This Mystery of the perpetual love of God through sacrifice was ordered and instituted by the Lord (Matt. xxvi, 26-28; John vi, 53-57; 1 Cor. x, 16-17; xi, 23-26). So Christ Himself is our real food; He communicates Himself to us, that He may make us true men, citizens of the Kingdom of Heaven, the very members of His immortal Body. So great is the love of God that in this Mystery the Lord gives us not only His gifts, as in other Mysteries, but Himself. Greater love than this does not exist either in heaven or on earth.

In the Mystery of Penance, or rather of Absolution, God the Holy Spirit forgives the man his new sins done after Baptism. Thereby the man becomes again clean before his God. A sinner travels away from his God into a foreign land and becomes a companion of swine, throwing his pearl—his soul—to the swine. Sin being repented of, confessed and forgiven, man gets the liberty to enter again the house of his Father. The parable of the Prodigal Son explains clearly the origin and the nature of sin, of true repentance, of confession and absolution (Luke xv, 11ff.). The Lord Jesus ordered and instituted this Mystery through His words and actions (Luke vii, 47; Matt. xviii, 18). The Apostles understood their Master and followed faithfully His example and His commandment (1 John i, 8-10; Acts iii, 19; xix, 18).

In the Mystery of the Ordination of priests, God the Holy Spirit gives the special grace of Orders to the priest, the minister of the mysteries in the Kingdom of God on earth, i.e. in the Church militant. This grace He gives through the act of the laying-on of the hands of the

Apostles and their successors upon the head of those who have been found worthy. In the priestly performance of a Mystery man counts almost for nothing, but the grace of God the Holy Spirit is all-important. The priest, therefore, is not allowed to say, " I baptise thee," or " I forgive thee," or " I unite you " in marriage, etc.; but " the servant of God, James or John, has been baptised, or forgiven, or united " in marriage, etc.; for the real performer of a Mystery is the Lord the Holy Spirit. This Mystery was commanded and instituted by the Lord and His Apostles (John xv, 16; Acts vi, 2-6; xiv, 23; xx, 28; 2 Timothy i, 6).

In the Mystery of Marriage, God the Holy Spirit by His grace unites two human beings, man and woman, for the special purpose of the growth of the Church of God according to God's commandment (Gen. ix, 1) and for the mutual help of husband and wife in the work of their salvation. This Mystery was ratified by the Lord Jesus (Matt. xix, 5-6). He Himself sanctified the bond of marriage through His presence at the marriage in Cana of Galilee (John ii, 1). The Apostle Paul, seer of the highest Mysteries, declares to us that marriage is a great mystery (Eph. v, 22 ff.).

In the Mystery of Extreme Unction, God the Holy Spirit comes to man's life in its last emergency and heals the sick. The purpose of the Mystery thus performed is described by St. James (v, 14-15) as the restoration of health and the remission of sins. This Mystery was practised and ordered by the Apostles from the very beginning (Mark vi, 13).

And thus we have seven divine Mysteries as the seven different workings of God the Holy Spirit, who is the true Dispenser, the Lifegiver, the Mover and the Treasurer of all divine gifts in the Church of Christ on earth. Five of these Mysteries are related rather to the personal life and personal salvation of each member of the Church, namely, Baptism, Confirmation, Eucharist, Penance, and Unction; and two of them are related to the good of the whole Church, namely, Orders and Marriage. The first five mean : emptying (Baptism), filling (Confirmation), feeding (Eucharist), freeing (Penance) and healing in the last emergency (Unction). The last two mean: the increase of the Church (Marriage) and the ministration of the Mysteries in the Church under the all-powerful God the Holy Spirit (Orders).

Now when the question is raised as to which of these seven Mysteries is more and which less important, the question inflicts a wound upon the conscience of a believer. It seems almost an offence to the Holy Spirit. Throughout its whole past, down to our own times, the Church has gathered a rich experience of the effective workings of God the Holy Spirit in all these seven Mysteries. One chariot might look more sumptuous and another less sumptuous, but it is not the chariot that matters but the charioteer. Whenever the Holy Spirit descends upon men through His grace, is it not indifferent how He arrives, sumptuously or simply ? It is He that matters. And since we know even from the present experience of the Church as well as from Holy Scripture that His grace descends and works in the Mystery of Extreme Unction, why then ask whether Confirmation, or Penance, or Marriage is something greater than Extreme Unction ? The greatness of all the Mysteries, their brilliancy, their beauty and their miraculous character come from Him—God the Holy Spirit. Ask a doctor which is more important for a person in bodily sickness, that he should be cleansed from impurities, or that he should be filled with fresh vitality ; that he should be fed or healed or helped in his last agony ; what would he say ? He would be bewildered. Or ask a householder which is more necessary for a house, that it should be cleaned or filled with fresh air and light ; that it should be maintained or kept in repair, or saved when in danger of falling ; he, too, would be bewildered. We empty our soul from the impurity of sin through Baptism ; we fill it with fresh powers in the form of God's gifts through Confirmation ; we feed it by Christ the living Lord through the Eucharist ; we free it from new impurities of sin through Penance ; we heal it and save it in a great emergency through Unction ; and since we are many and not one, we need the growth of our sacred society, i.e. of the Church, and we get this growth through Marriage; and again, since we are many and not one, we need a divinely ordered dispensation to prepare the soul for immortal life in the eternal Kingdom of God. Thus the seven Mysteries represent the sevenfold drama of the Christian soul's ascent from the dark pit of sin to the height and glory of the Kingdom of God.

And if anyone should think that perhaps Baptism and the Eucharist (or other two or three of the seven Mysteries) are the only Mysteries, the only Sacraments, well—let him ask God about it ; by fasting and praying tears let him ask God, and He will reveal to him the truth as He has always revealed it to the saints. As to us of the East, we are afraid to depreciate any of the seven marvellous Mysteries, we are afraid of God the Holy Spirit. For He whispered to the Apostles and to the saints the truth about everything necessary to man's salvation. Therefore all that we have said about the great Christian Mysteries is not an opinion of our own (if it were an opinion of our own, it would be worth nothing), but it is the repeated experience of the Apostles in the ancient days and of the saints up to our own days. For the Church of God lives not on opinion, but on the experience of the saints, as in the beginning so in our days. The opinions of intellectual persons may be wonderfully clever and yet be false, whereas the experience of the saints is always true. It is God the Lord who is true to Himself in His saints.

May the Lord God the Holy Spirit, with the Father and with the Son, give to all those who tearfully pray to Him the grace of wisdom and the power to see and recognise the whole truth, necessary for the salvation of all of us, the baptised and the never sufficiently penitent children of God.

PROFESSOR J. VERNON BARTLET, D.D.
Mansfield College, Oxford (Congregationalist)

We have now come, in due sequence of thought, to the last of those aspects of the Church's divine-human life as to which we are exploring our differences and the possibilities of fuller unity, viz., the sacraments, or rather on this occasion the two Sacraments having clear New Testament authority. These present also our most crucial problem, as being the point at which the diversities of conception under which we hold certain common Christian ideas come to a head in practice. This is the case particularly with the Sacrament of the Lord's Supper, that Holy Communion in which inner unity ought to find its most typically Christian expression, but which has in fact become the great dividing line and barrier to fuller fellowship. It is concern about this, and all it implies, which has chiefly brought us together in conference.

But what is there to give us any hope that our dealing with this topic, which has proved so divisive in the past, will yield a fresh result, and prepare the way for reunion even at this crucial point ? I answer, the new spirit and method of our present approach. For as compared with our predecessors in this task, not only in the sixteenth century and later but also since the schism between Eastern and Western Churchmen at the end of the Patristic period, we have a twofold advantage. We are meeting, firstly, with a new sense of our common Christian *experience*, as sincerely and conscientiously disciples of the One Lord Jesus Christ, in spite of differences in the way we understand that experience ; and, secondly, with an unparalleled sense of the part played by past *history*—in addition to varying temperament and personal environment—in making our divergent conceptions what they are in the Church-groups which we represent. The combined effect of all this is a fresh sense of the limited or relative importance and value of those forms of thought which divide us, and a humbler estimate of that part of the total truth of Christ's Gospel, as realised in His Church Universal, which our branch of it has been able to assimilate and witness to. In a fuller sense than when Lord Bacon coined the phrase, " we are the Ancients," in length of historical experience : and we must not shrink from the present duty of asking where and how *bona fide* misunderstandings have arisen, including our own.

To help us, we have to-day, as part of the general culture of our age, what our forefathers had not, namely the historical method and historical sense, the habit and instinct of seeing old words in the light of their context and past usage, rather than unwittingly reading back into them later meanings and our own native or acquired fixed notions. To make full use of this help should be the effort alike of Catholics and Evangelicals. By Catholics I mean those who view " the mind of Christ " primarily through the meaning put on His teaching and that of the apostolic writers by the Ancient Church of the Greek and Latin Fathers ; by Evangelicals, those who rely more on direct study of the New Testament read in its own light and usage —made the more clear by a comparative study of the Old Testament writings, as illustrative of the forms of thought in which Biblical revelation is couched. These contrasted methods of approach deeply affect both the experimental and the theoretic apprehensions distinctive of the two main Christian types among us, particularly in their respective emphasis—which means so much in religion. All Biblical religion, as conditioned by its Hebraic psychology, emphasises *will* as the root of the matter, and personal relations between man and God—whether grace in God, or faith, both receptive and active, in man—as the sphere of human salvation or well-being. As Biblical religion develops, this emphasis grows with the deepening conception of personality. It becomes more inner and self-conscious in quality, so that external forms and rites are seen less as sacred in themselves and more as relative to their meaning for human experience, in its moral and personal relations with God ; they are made for man, not man for them. Finally the whole form of revelation became more intensely personal when Divine Law, as medium of revelation, was replaced by a Divine-human Personality.

Christian Sacraments, then, as Evangelicals see them, are relative to prophetic Hebraism as determining the distinctive spirit of Christian religion. But no less are they relative to it as giving the key to the manner in which the language in which they are described in Holy Writ is to be understood. Hebrew speech is characteristically poetic, metaphorical, symbolic, as distinct from literal or scientific; and the context is relied on to settle where words are to be taken in a literal or in a symbolic sense. Further, the prophets were specially given to the symbolic manner of speech; and Jesus Himself conformed closely to the prophetic type in this respect. All this must be given due weight in a truly historical reading of the Gospels and the Epistles—one, that is, which takes them as the original hearers, for whose understanding they were intended, would naturally have taken them. These facts were certainly not before the minds of the Ancient Church of the Fathers, when Scriptures couched in terms of Hebraic mentality came to be read by men of a very different mentality and culture, to-day known as Hellenistic, which was then prevalent in the Roman Empire outside Palestine. The probability, then, of unconscious misunderstanding of Biblical Christian Sacraments, alike in their psychological and linguistic meaning, was obviously very great; and we have to be prepared for more or less change of conceptions appearing as time goes on. Such misunderstanding, going back to the Ancient Church, Evangelicals believe to be the main source of the differences between Catholics and themselves in this matter of sacramental doctrine and practice. In what follows, then, I attempt to set forth these differences, first in their historical aspect, and then in more positive form : after which a few words will be said on the limits of such diversity and on the unity of idea underlying differences of conception.

We begin with Baptism. John the Baptist affords our surest line of historical approach. He called for moral repentance on prophetic lines and as the condition of readiness for the " Kingdom of God," the perfected state of His holy or devoted People. Radical repentance, as the prophets taught, meant a moral renewal of personality which was likened to a cleansing bath, fitting for a new devotion to the divine will. " Wash you, make you clean," was the human aspect of the matter : the divine side was equally needful, " Then will I sprinkle clean water upon you, and ye shall be clean." Such a message fitly took symbolic form in a baptism or bath of repentance, objectifying to its recipients the reality and meaning of their inward attitude of obedience and self-dedication. But John realised the merely provisional nature of his own work : the positive inspiration needful to achieve the great change to a new level of life, one really divine in quality, would come as a baptism with something of more transforming power than water, what he called " fire." The author of *Ecce Homo* caught the contrast exactly when he said that the moral purity of true goodness must be impassioned, possessed by the enthusiasm of a vision and motive able to lift and sustain human nature above its own normal level of sense-ruled and self-centred life. To impart such a baptism, John taught, was the vocation of a personality mightier than his own, that of Messiah Himself. And this *rôle* of baptiser with " holy Spirit," or divine inspiration, Jesus fulfilled in virtue of the inspiring quality of His personality as medium of the Divine Spirit's action on persons.

As seen originally, on the Day of Pentecost and during the Apostolic Age, Christian Baptism was essentially baptism or drenching with " holy Spirit " as a fact of human experience, both for the recipient and for onlookers, but a fact in which God as Holy Spirit was manifest as immediate agent. The water was simply a symbol, sometimes being added, as in the case of Cornelius and his friends, after the Spirit-baptism had already occurred : it was not his channel or necessary concomitant, as later came to be conceived, when the Spirit's action ceased to be a fact of experience and became matter for imaginative theory. A striking confirmation of such a view is the early Syrian usage, in the second century and long after, by which anointing with holy oil, symbolising " participation in the Holy Spirit," preceded descent into the water, the " symbol of death " to sin (*Apost. Const.* vii, 22, 2). No doubt, too, the symbolic act of Baptism itself, as a dramatic objectification of the inner act by which faith made its open confession (hence the use of the middle voice in Acts xxii, 16, cf. 1 Cor. vi, 11), did enhance by suggestion the rapt spiritual experience which usually accompanied the rite in the Apostolic Age. Yet the fundamental baptism, " the purification of the heart by faith " (Acts xv, 9), in virtue of which the convert took the momentous step of associating himself with Jesus as Christ and with His visible Body the Church, and thereby received the Divine " seal " of acceptance (confirmation, in the original sense) in such manifest " holy inspiration " (Eph. i, 13)—this inner and prior change was itself traced to the Spirit, applying " the word " of the Gospel to the soul as the living seed of new life.

Primitive Baptism, then, moved wholly in the sphere of religious experience and moral personality in the case of those capable of personal faith. With children not yet capable of this the case was different. They were by their Christian birth-right " holy," within the sphere of the Covenant and not of " the world " : for according to the thought of Hebraism, and indeed of all ancient religion, the offspring shared its parents' religious status in a sub-personal manner. According to this deep sense of family solidarity, and of the wider solidarity of " the family of faith " as the psychological atmosphere of the child's awakening consciousness, it was also the natural thing that the symbol of the parents' religious relation should be administered even to the infant children of believers, as being by right potential believers. The absence of any sign of ancient controversy about this usage, as if other than apostolic, virtually precludes its being of later origin. On the other hand, it is most unlikely that as long as Hebraic modes of thought prevailed in the Church—i.e. until the original Apostles had died out—any notion of baptismal regeneration, in the actual sense proper to faith, was associated with the practice. Once, however, the prevailing mentality of the Church changed decidedly to one non-Hebraic and Hellenistic in sacramental conception, confusion between the two species of Christian Baptism would readily come about, and in fact did so. Here lies the justification of the historic protest of those who at the Reformation rejected anything but "believers' baptism," even if largely in ignorance of the difference between the corporate mode of apostolic thought and their own more individualistic one. Most Evangelicals, however, have adhered to what they believe to be both apostolic usage and thought in the matter. Here surely is a case for that " mutual deference to one another's consciences " for which the Lambeth Appeal of 1920 pleaded. The fact that most branches of the Church regard Church membership as incomplete until Confirmation or some other form of personal confession has marked the baptised child's appropriation of its birth-right of faith, should help Baptists to regard infant baptism as the first stage of the full rite, and so allowable.

The Sacrament of the Lord's Supper should also be approached historically through the known forms of Hebraic thought and usage, and nothing foreign to these be read back into Christ's own intention. Nor again should any associations which cannot be verified as part of what the historical context implies that He meant those actually present in the Upper Chamber to gather from His acts and words be treated as having His direct authority. Even where Biblical in idea, these are not to be made integral to the Sacrament as instituted by Christ Himself, but treated as secondary enrichments for devout meditation.

Read in its historical context in Jesus' ministry, the one idea of this Sacrament which He (especially in the text of Mark, the earliest Gospel) desires to bring home to His disciples is the same that He had again and again tried to convey, but had ever found them so unreceptive of, viz., the redemptive significance of His coming death, in keeping with Isaiah liii. Once more, and for the last time, He repeats in a fresh and more impressive way the central truth of His later ministry, that " the Son of Man " is about " to give His life as a ransom for many " (Mark x, 45). Taking advantage of the Paschal season which was filling their minds (whatever the exact day of the Supper) with the idea of redemption through the life-blood of an innocent lamb, Jesus in prophetic manner makes use of it to suggest, by this most acceptable approach, that Israel's final salvation will come through the breaking of His own body and the shedding of His own blood "for many." That this is the one thought here present, the one with which He desires in yearning sympathy to fortify His disciples against future despair, is borne out by St. Paul's declaration in 1 Cor. xi, 26, that in this Sacrament it is "the Lord's death" that is proclaimed. This, then, underlies Jesus' words in distributing the broken loaf, over which He had given thanks to God, doubtless (in the absence of any indication to the contrary) in the usual form for the familiar rite before the meal of a group of male Israelites. As to those crucial words, "Take this—my body," there is in the Aramaic original no verb expressive of the relation between "this" and "my body," but the sense is defined by the circumstances as "represents." (Compare Gal. iv. 24, "these women are two covenants.") Thus the words simply attach to the familiar ritual a new and special symbolism, a prophetic object lesson of what was so soon to be, but was not yet, objective fact. When these conditions are realised, in the Hebraic atmosphere of the occasion, they simply preclude[1] the literal and realistic sense which once seemed to men who had little or no sense of the full historical context more natural than the prophetico-symbolic. The one really valid meaning of this Sacrament, then, is that implied in the "words of Administration" in the Anglican Prayer Book of 1552, "Take and eat this in remembrance that Christ died for thee, and feed on Him in thy heart by faith with thanksgiving."

Other associations came more or less naturally to attach themselves to the suggestive symbolism of this acted parable. Those of a Biblical type are, the unity of the Church as sharing in the *one* loaf (1 Cor. x, 17, cf. *Didache*, ix, 4); Christ as the Bread of Life to the soul (the idea of John vi, though not one really suggested in the Last Supper, where the Bread and Cup together set forth the single *redemptive* idea under two aspects); and, though it is not actually

[1] See Prof. R. H. Kennett, *The Last Supper, its significance in the Upper Room*, Cambridge, 1921, and Bishop Temple, *Christus Veritas*, pp. 246-249.

L

in the New Testament, the association of the Church's self-oblation with the supreme example of the principle in the person of her Head. On the basis of His self-giving, the Church came in time to offer her " gifts " in kind as homage of thanksgiving or " Eucharist." This, the Church's one recurring " Sacrifice," was a specialised symbolic form of the general Christian " living sacrifice " of oneself, body and soul, in " spiritual service " (divine *latreia*), in virtue of the priesthood of all believers (Hebrews xiii, 15, 1 Pet. ii, 5). In the Eucharistic Sacrifice of the ante-Nicene Church —though this fact is often overlooked—there was no thought of propitiation for sins, but only of " the sacrifice of praise." This has a vital bearing on the idea then held of the ministry as a specialised priesthood. As to the idea of " the Real Presence " of Christ's *body* and *blood* in the elements, rather than of His spiritual humanity under bodily forms—available as that is at all times to believers for communion through the Spirit—it is a pure accretion of a non-Hebraic and sub-personal order. It came in originally to satisfy the Hellenistic mentality, in its craving after a quasi-physical " food of immortality " for the corruptible human body. It is expressed with different degrees of realism in different circles of the Ancient Church ; and it strongly influenced both the language and sacramental thought of the Patristic and Mediaeval Church long after its original bodily rather than devotional interest was forgotten. Evangelical grounds of objection to any realistic theory of Christ's bodily presence, however attenuated its corporeal nature may be, are not only its exegetical impossibility (as above argued), and the physical impossibility of bodily ubiquity; they include also its irrelevance to the communion of persons, and the fact that, in claiming a superiority *in kind* for the sacramental species of grace, it lowers in idea the level of normal or abiding spiritual communion of Christians with Christ, and so creates a dualism in the life of grace as a whole. In neither of these two latter regards can the doctrine be brought into harmony with the genius of the Gospel of Christ and of His Apostles, and of the nature of grace and faith in the New Testament sense.

Yet such harmony is the final test of all properly Christian sacramental theory.

In the above historical survey I have tried to state frankly the essential Evangelical doctrine of the Sacraments as rooted in Scripture, with some passing allusion to the points at which the Catholic doctrine has come to diverge from what Evangelicals regard as the lines of true development, into serious changes in conception. I have distinguished, moreover, even what I regard as true developments in the Church sacramental doctrine, from the essential idea of the Sacraments, as these have the full sanction of Christ Himself. Such true ecclesiastical developments have a relative value for the Church, both in its different specific groups and as a whole : and it is the ultimate aim of our Conference to appraise and use them aright. As to those conceptions and usages which Catholics or Evangelicals cannot but continue to view as mistaken or defective, and so cannot adopt from each other for the enrichment of their Christian life, they need not in the last resort hinder intercommunion : for they do not cancel the unity of underlying idea as apprehended in personal experience. Thus in the Holy Communion of the Lord's Supper there is experienced by both a special spiritual union between Christ and His own, in death to sin and new life unto God. And while deeply convinced that the Evangelical understanding of them best preserves generally and at the most vital points the original New Testament emphasis and perspective, and that this is the abiding test of true developments, I yet acknowledge that at certain points Catholic piety has better safe-guarded in its own way true Christian values, those most closely connected with its strong sense of the corporate nature of the Church. These will doubtless be duly brought out by those who represent the Catholic standpoint.

I would add a few words on what may be called the philosophy of sacraments. First, then, Evangelicals hold the true order to be " word and sacraments," not *vice versa* : for the former psychologically conditions the latter, as means by which the Holy Spirit works graciously on the soul. Next, by Sacraments they mean the rites as a whole, not the material elements characteristic of each. So regarded, namely as symbolic acts of the Church, Sacraments are, in Augustine's phrase, " visible words." Thus the difference between them and the " word of the Gospel " fades away ; and they are seen as special forms of the same spiritual appeal to personality which words convey in a less concrete and sensibly vivid manner. Hence they are valuable complements to the spoken word, their suggestiveness often speaking with silent eloquence, as the Holy Spirit interprets them to the heart, when the more abstract appeal of the audible word has for the time lost its full power. Being unargumentative, they penetrate the more by suggestion to the semi-conscious and intuitive levels where lie deep springs of emotion and volition. On lines such as these, rather than on those of Catholic theory as to objective change in the elements, should we conceive the true " spiritualisation of the material " which we all aim at.

I will close on two notes of a synthetic tendency. While I have stressed the nature of Christianity and of its Sacraments in terms of personality, and personal rather than sub-personal conceptions of sacramental means of grace, I rejoice to recognise that personality is far from one and the same as individualism, or even individuality in any restricted sense : it is the soul of corporate and even institutional life also, so far as these attain their highest human forms. It may be common, then, to the Catholic and Evangelical emphasis on the corporate and the individual aspects of religion respectively. As regards the feeling among Catholics that the Evangelical conception of the Sacraments is too subjective, I would beg them constantly to remember that Evangelicals regard all grace as due to the action of the Holy Spirit, and that to them this makes sacramental grace as objective as it need or can be for persons as such. All sacramental grace, so far as verifiable and actually enjoyed in mystical experience, is and must be subjective in form, whatever our theories of its causes.

Finally, and most emphatically, I plead for the largest tolerance of diversity in the various constituent groups of any future closer unity of organised Church communion, in the spirit of the golden words of the Lambeth appeal: " We believe that for all the truly equitable approach to union is by the way of mutual deference to one another's consciences."

PROFESSOR DR. AUGUST LANG
University of Halle (Evangelical-Reformed)

It is impossible to reach any agreement on the subject before us to-day! That is what many people think, and we are all tempted at first to repeat it. For indeed when we look back into history we see nothing but bitter conflicts in regard to the Sacraments, and these conflicts contributed not a little to the dismemberment of the Church. What was the reason for all this? It would be an error to ascribe it simply to opinionatedness or culpable obstinacy. The memory of the Reformers of this hospitable country, of Zwingli, Calvin and Vinet, to mention only a few— memories which we are so glad to revive during this Conference—should suffice to banish any such suggestion. Those men searched the Scriptures, amid bitter sufferings, in order to secure a firm basis for their convictions, no matter what might be the consequences. And that applies not only to them but undoubtedly to their opponents as well. The conflicting doctrines with regard to the Sacraments have been sealed with the blood of martyrs, and have been maintained in hard fought wars. Let us pay homage to such heroic courage! How can it be imagined that we could shake the reputation of such men by the speeches or observations which we may offer here? We must leave every Church free to hold such opinions regarding the Sacraments as it desires to maintain, according to its understanding and to the enlightenment granted to it by the Holy Spirit in the past and in the present. So far as I myself am concerned, I may say that, as a member of the German Reformed Church, I adhere to the view stated by Dr. Vernon Bartlet, a conception which comes down to us

through the line of Augustine, Luther, Zwingli and Calvin.
But though we all remain firmly rooted in the beliefs of
our different Churches, does that mean that we must
renounce all hopes of union? Would it not be possible,
in spite of the bloodstained controversies which have been
provoked by the Sacraments, to find something which is
common ground to all parties, something which was overlooked in the heat of strife, but which may be revealed to
us to-day if we approach the question in a pure spirit of
peace and of the frankest sincerity? To find what we hold
in common—however small it may be—and to exalt it as a
symbol of unity, that is, as I conceive it, our task at this
Conference.

I think I may assume, to begin with, that we all regard
the Sacraments with the deepest reverence. No one considers to-day's subject as inferior to the others in importance. If, however, this reverence may have waned somewhat among the masses of the people in any Church, it
might be strengthened and fortified by a joint declaration
issued by this great Conference. For it is *reverence*, in the
first place, that we all feel in common for the Sacraments.

Now why is it that we all feel this reverence for these
sacred rites which were entrusted to the Church by its
Head? That is the second point. The first speaker to-day,
who was unfortunately unable to read his speech in person,
the Bishop of Ochrida, laid great stress on the *divine
mystery* which is enacted at every Sacrament, and which is
its inmost essence. Christ instituted the Sacraments, but
Protestants of all denominations only apply this term to
Baptism and the Lord's Supper. But we also regard the
five other Sacraments—Confirmation, Marriage, Penance,
Extreme Unction, and Ordination—at least in part as
ecclesiastical rites, in which the Holy Spirit exercises His
secret and most beneficent influence. Even that revered
and illustrious reformer, Zwingli, whom many regard as
having gone furthest in detracting from the value of
Sacraments, never refused to admit the element of mystery,
of sacred mystery, in every Sacrament, although he preferred to seek this mystery through the awakening of faith

by that chief means of grace, the Word of God. We of the Reformed Churches gladly admit that there is in the Sacraments an element of mystery which eludes the intelligence, something which makes its appeal to the heart, which stirs our spirits as a call to us from God and from His Church. What it is would not be easy to define in words ; for I think that all doctrines regarding Sacraments are like the stammerings of an infant. But all of us in this Conference are willing to bow together before this holy mystery and in so doing to find a bond of union.

But there is a third factor, a thing which I believe is felt, recognised and acknowledged in all quarters, namely, the relation of the Sacraments to the *Church*. No doubt there are considerable divergences on this point also ; yet every Christian knows that where there is a Church there he will find the Sacraments, and where there are Sacraments there he will find the Church. The only exception, so far as I am aware, is that of the Society of Friends, the Quakers, which is so highly respected, and not least in Germany ; and perhaps that is only an apparent exception. The different ideas on the subject of the Church and the Sacraments have their origin not only in the questions which we discussed in connection with the Church, but in our different conceptions of the nature of divine grace. Doctor Vernon Bartlet has just drawn our attention to that point, and I would like to do so again. In the belief of one group the divine grace is instilled, so to speak, drop by drop, from the beginning of a man's life and on through all its culminating experiences. Another group holds that it is the personal element, the Christian personality, which derives its strength from the means of grace ; that it is the personal love of God for us, the personal salvation of the sinner, the personal laying hold on salvation, which are the essential factors. These are truly very profound and serious differences ; but is there any reason why the Churches should not, in spite of their different views, dwell under one roof, acknowledging that the Sacraments are gifts of the Holy Spirit and the expressions of the Church's life ? It is the Church which by means of the Sacraments goes forth into the world, which works through them in the name of God and of the Lord Christ, which saves and educates men, and finally, as we hope, leads them into eternal salvation. It is the Church which builds itself up with the Sacraments, creates community between Christians, and sets a boundary between itself and the world. Owing to the shortness of the time at my disposal I will content myself with having indicated these common factors, which other speakers will elaborate further.

Before concluding I would like to refer to an idea expressed by the Subjects Committee, or rather by the Bishop of Bombay, distinguishing between " God's part " and " man's part " in the Sacrament. That is a very important point. The gift of God which He offers in the Sacrament presents to us that sacred mystery by which God elevates common objects such as water, bread and wine to the level of signs and witnesses, nay more, to channels of His marvellous grace. " It is true that grace "—I am quoting verbatim—" is also given through the Word. . . . But those who have experience of the difficulties of translating words from one language into another are specially able to recognise the wisdom of God in providing means of expressing His gracious purposes which need no translation." In the case of the Sacraments it is not one of our senses only—as in the case of the Word—which is called into service, but every one of our senses ; not only our ears but our sight, hearing, taste and sense of smell. It is true that the Word still holds the foremost place as the interpreter of the mysteries ; but is it not marvellous that God has employed every avenue of man's nature in order to present to him the working of His grace ? And these ideas again are common ground to all the Churches.

As regards man's part in the Sacraments we must above all avoid the danger of imagining that man can do anything by himself. For whatever man is able to do in order to experience the effects of divine grace is merely owing to the action of the Holy Spirit which draws us towards God. However, there is one point on which all the Churches can agree, and that is that in the Sacrament there is something which has to be experienced ; that the divine gift in the Sacrament can never be without its effect.

The abuse, which consists in administering the Sacrament as a purely external rite and then dismissing the communicants as though everything necessary has been done, is not approved—at any rate in theory—by anyone at all. The human factor in the Sacrament needs to be stimulated, aroused and made worthy to receive the grace. That is why most Protestants are so assiduous in maintaining that the Sacrament is valueless without faith. If that statement is understood in its true sense it should be possible, from that starting point, to build a bridge and so to draw nearer together.

I speak of drawing nearer because it would suffice, in my opinion, if the individual Churches were to recognise that in this question of Sacraments they have a common basis, which is witnessed to by the Bible and by history. We shall find this common ground if we can come to see, not only by charity but by faith, that Christ has many ways of entrance into the soul. There are diversities of gifts, but one Spirit.

THE REV. O. C. QUICK, M.A.
Canon of Carlisle (Anglican)

I propose to confine what I have to say almost entirely to the first of the questions in Pamphlet No. 52, that concerned with the parts of God and man in the Sacraments. I have it in mind to state briefly four cardinal principles which might conceivably receive a general assent, or at any rate help to clarify discussion. Two are concerned with God's part, and two with man's. And each pair forms to some extent an antithesis.

(1) *In every Sacrament the principal inward reality* (*res sacramenti*) *is a divine act.* In Baptism, in the Eucharist and in every other rite to which the name of sacrament may be properly applied, our chief and dominant aim should be, not so much to declare our own faith before God,

not so much to express our own unity with one another, as
to receive into our own souls some actual blessing or gift
from God. As we perform the appointed signs in obedience
to what we believe to be God's will, we look to God to come
among us in the living and present power of His Spirit.
We declare our faith, our penitence, our fellowship, in
order that by these means our souls may be more open
towards the divine beneficence. The chief end is not in a
reminder of the past, nor in men's mutual encouragement
of one another to lead a Christian life, but rather it is to
receive the full efficacy of the present act of God.

(2) *On the other hand, the Sacraments in no way limit
God's gracious activity, so as to restrict its range. Deus non
alligatur sacramentis.* We dare not affirm that apart from
some particular sacramental sign, or from all sacramental
sign whatever, any divine grace or gift is unobtainable.
Rather, we rejoice to believe that our Saviour is also the
light that lighteth every man, and leads in the way of
salvation all men who do not wilfully and of their own fault
reject His guidance. Moreover, God alone knows the hearts
of men ; many that are last shall be first, and the first
last. May it not be true to say that nothing will more surely
condemn us before the Father of all, than that we should
refuse to recognise the presence and work of the Spirit,
on the ground that these show themselves outside an
appointed system of ordinances, or because God the Holy
Spirit, no less than God the Son, may sometimes "come
out of Nazareth."

The acceptance of the principle just stated evidently
necessitates some kind of distinction between validity and
efficacy in sacraments. A valid sacrament is one in which
all the appointed signs are duly performed ; but it is not
necessarily efficacious for salvation in the individual, since
it may be unworthily received. On the other hand, a rite
or service in which appointed sacramental signs are imperfectly performed, or not performed at all, may certainly
be used by God to bestow His spiritual gifts ; and undoubtedly is so used where true penitence and faith are
present. It follows then that services which are not valid

sacraments at all may nevertheless be efficacious in bestowing grace ; just as valid sacraments themselves fail to bestow grace where the soul is not open to receive it. Nothing, perhaps, confuses discussion on the Sacraments so easily or so fatally as a failure to distinguish validity from efficacy. It does not of course follow that, because God may and does bestow gifts apart from the appointed signs of Sacraments, therefore it does not matter whether a sacrament is valid or not.

(3) *True faith and penitence are necessary conditions for the effectual receiving of God's gifts in the Sacraments.* In other words, God gives to the soul only that grace which it is spiritually capable of receiving ; according to their capacity some will receive more and others less. It is characteristic of our Lord's whole method of work and teaching as recorded in the Gospels, that He constantly requires some measure of co-operation or at least receptiveness from those whom He seeks to help. " To him that hath, it shall be given." " Those who seek, find." " According to your faith be it done unto you." We cannot believe that divine action in the Sacraments follows a different law. The Sacraments, therefore, do not work for man's salvation mechanically or in any magical way. The Western Church indeed has long taught the doctrine of sacramental grace *ex opere operato*, which has been severely criticised for its magical tendencies. But that doctrine has never been authoritatively held or taught so as to remove the need for due preparation on the part of those who are to receive sacraments to their soul's health. Indeed, it has been more usual in the past to surround the Eucharist with an almost excessive dread of unworthy reception and its awful penalties, than to allow men to suppose that the mere outward act of partaking was enough to profit them. *Hagia tois hagiois* has always been, and must remain, a recognised principle of sacramental doctrine. And yet, in saying this, we need not forget that it is the sick, not the whole, who most need the great Physician. Solomon, we are told, received the gift of wisdom because he was already wise enough to know his need of it and to ask God for its

supply. Socrates claimed to be the wisest of men on the ground that he alone knew himself ignorant. So it is that they who are most aware of their own spiritual poverty, have already most of that real wealth which God delights to increase and multiply. It is only to him that hath, that the gift is given. Yet he who has most, is the beggar in spirit.

(4) Nevertheless *the soul can receive infinitely more in the Sacraments that it is itself aware of.* To say that we must prepare ourselves to receive in faith and penitence is not to say that our consciousness can grasp all that is bestowed upon us. The Sacraments, as the Bishop of Ochrida's paper has reminded us, are God's mysteries. In them God acts upon us. Who shall say that he is aware of all that God so does ? This is a point, I fear, on which some divergence of opinion is likely. The reason why many of us find something more, or at least something other, in a sacrament than in a sermon is precisely this. Spoken words are only meant to affect us in so far as their meaning is made clear to our understanding. At least that is the only use of words which is legitimate, if we follow the teaching of St. Paul. Music, again, acts not on the understanding, but more directly on the feelings. Both words and music may truly be inspired. But in a sacrament there is something more or something different. It consists also of something *done* to us, an act of God upon our souls, which does not depend wholly either upon conscious understanding or on conscious feeling for its effectiveness. True, the effectiveness, the efficacy, of a sacrament does and must depend in some degree upon the human *will.* We must be endeavouring in some way to hold communion with Christ, before Christ can communicate Himself to us. But if we are sincerely making that tremendous effort of faith, we must not be told that, if our conscious success is small, we have therefore in reality received as little. The understanding may be darkened and the feelings hard to stir, but Christ is greater than our minds or hearts and we believe that in the breaking of the bread He has come to us again.

PRÄLAT DR. SCHOELL
Evangelical Church of Wurtemberg (Evangelical-Lutheran)

It seems very difficult to discuss at the same time both the concordance and the divergences in sacramental doctrines and usages. Sacraments are something so sacred that the smallest criticism expressed by one group may be felt as an offence against the sentiments and intimate convictions of the other. May it be granted to us to discuss this most delicate aspect of our faith without, on the one hand, being false to our own consciences and convictions, or on the other hand, offending the consciences and convictions of our brothers!

Following the lines indicated by the Subjects Committee, I will first discuss our conceptions of the Sacrament. Here we are agreed on three fundamental points : first on the necessity of both Word and Sacrament for the foundation and maintenance of the Christian life. No doubt some will attach more value to the preaching of the Word, others to the use of the Sacraments ; but it is certain that none of us would desire to have only one without the other. Secondly, we are agreed that in the Sacraments we are concerned with a divine means of grace. The Sacrament is certainly not a purely human institution deriving its sole value from the action of men. It is a divine institution, and we believe and know by experience that what is presented to us in it is derived, not from men, but from God. Lastly, we should be able to agree that the benefit of the Sacraments is only obtained by those who desire to receive it. The Sacrament is not some magic charm which produces its effect by the mere fact of being employed, irrespective of the attitude of the recipient. God's grace is offered to us in the Sacrament, but it is not imposed on us.

After thus predicating the points on which we are agreed we can talk with greater freedom of the points on which we disagree. The chief divergence arises in regard to our understanding of the nature of divine grace. On this question we have two radically different conceptions. According to the first the grace of the Sacrament is bestowed by the penetration of the divine essence into the human nature, by a combined physical and super-physical process. From this standpoint it is naturally of the greatest importance to insist that the elements in the Sacrament are not merely symbolical signs, but are really of a super-natural character, a *materia coelestis*. And it is also evident that, from this point of view, the grace which is bestowed by the Sacrament is something new, something different from the grace conveyed by preaching the Word. The means of grace by the Word and the means of grace by the Sacrament are regarded as two separate channels of grace running parallel to one another.

According to the other conception, the grace of God is always the same, at all times and in all circumstances; and it does not consist in a supernatural gift, but it is the will of divine love manifested in Christ which judges and saves the sinner. The Sacrament is also a preaching of the Word; it is the Word preached through a visible sign: *verbum visibile*. Its importance is, therefore, in principle, the same as that of the Word; it calls us to repent and to accept sonship with God. In this conception the question of the transubstantiation of the sacramental elements becomes of secondary importance.

If we follow this divergence between the doctrines of grace a stage further, we finally discover a divergence of views in our conceptions about God Himself. I say a divergence, not a conflict of views. Some persons lay the chief stress on the metaphysical aspect of God; others on the ethical aspect, on the thoughts of God. The first group of thinkers emphasises the supernatural essence of God, the second lays stress on His loving purpose, and the will and person of God. From the standpoint of the first group the Sacrament is the penetration of the divine essence into the human nature, enabling the Christian to participate in the divine nature. From the standpoint of the other group the Sacrament is the proof of divine love, witnessed to by signs and ritual, which gives the Christian the assurance of forgiveness and of sonship with God. Either of these conceptions is perfectly clear and justifiable in itself;

but for that very reason any combination of them results in obscurity and inconsistency.

The correctness of the above considerations may be tested by applying them to the questions of Baptism and the Lord's Supper, about which I have a few words to say. I will not refer to divergences regarding the manner of Baptism—whether by immersion or by sprinkling with water—for these appear to me of secondary importance. Nor can I discuss the far more important question of infant baptism or adult baptism, as that would involve a discussion on the whole question of a national Church. I would like first to point out that we are really in agreement on the essentials. That is to say, we all agree in acknowledging that Baptism is necessary and must be performed in the name of the Father, the Son and the Holy Spirit; in regarding Baptism as an act of admission into the community of Christ and of Christians; and in the mutual recognition by the Churches of the validity of Baptism in the name of Trinity. The essential difference lies in our attitude to the question whether, and in what sense, we regard Baptism as related to a re-birth. Those who hold the first conception of the Sacrament which we referred to above will regard Baptism as the penetration into the soul of the germ of divine life, and for them Baptism is the beginning of a genuine re-birth, of a transformation of the human nature into the divine nature. Those who hold the second conception of the Sacrament will regard Baptism as a token of God's will that a child of man is to be transformed into a child of God, and he will only acknowledge it as the beginning of a re-birth to the extent that the divine will for salvation is accepted by the baptised person through faith, either at the moment of Baptism, or subsequently during his life.

The Lord's Supper needs to be discussed with the greatest reverence. We can all regard three points as established. First, that the Lord's Supper is a feast of remembrance for the sacrificial death of Christ, not in the sense of a mere memorial of the fact and circumstances of His death, but as a Eucharist, as a thanksgiving for all that our Lord won for us by the sacrifice of His body and the shedding of His blood. Secondly, that the Lord's Supper is a real, and not merely imaginary union with our ascended Lord, the Head of the Church. And thirdly, that the Lord's Supper is a feast *in common* which binds the disciples of the Lord together in a communion of love. Since we are agreed on such important points of belief and experience, our differences— which, I grant, are far from insignificant—should no longer give occasion to such passionate conflicts and accusations of heresy as marred the history of Christianity in the past. These divergences arise out of our different conceptions of the Sacrament. For those holding the first of the two conceptions referred to above it is of vital moment to declare that the elements are the actual vehicles of a physical and super-physical salvation ; and for them it becomes an essential condition for true communion that the elements should be consecrated in the prescribed form by a priest who has been validly ordained in that capacity. The idea of the sacramental sacrifice is intimately allied with reverence for the consecrated elements. The effect of the Sacrament is a union of spirit and body with Christ. To those who hold the other conception, it is the spiritual action which is of importance. For them the symbolic betokening of the gift which Christ offers us of His body and His blood is a means whereby faith may be fortified, the stricken conscience may be consoled, and the assurance of sin forgiven and of life made holier may be obtained.

These divergences are fundamental and very great. It appears scarcely possible to attain unity in regard to the doctrine and use of the Sacraments. It would not greatly help us if we evolved some formula of compromise here ; our Churches would not accept it, for they will continue for reasons grounded in history and practice to hold sted- fastly to their own conceptions of the Sacrament. What we can do is to banish all unchristian or polemical sentiments when we discuss these divergences—as it is necessary to discuss them. We can rejoice and be thankful that we have so much that is essential and precious in common, and we can learn to understand and support each other in brotherly love, until the day when we shall attain to a common faith and a common knowledge of the Son of God.

THE REV. ROBERT A. ASHWORTH, D.D.
Yonkers, New York (Baptist)

It will perhaps best serve the purposes of this interchange of views if I present, in the interest of unity and in bare outline, without any attempt at justification, the general conception of the sacraments—or ordinances, to employ the term in use among us—held by members of my own Communion. The fact that Baptists acknowledge no credal formula as authoritative, and that, receiving the New Testament as the only rule of faith and practice, they accord, in theory at least, full liberty of individual interpretation, provides abundant opportunity for divergences of view within their fellowship. That there should prevail under such conditions so large a measure of agreement in doctrine as actually exists is deeply significant.

Holding firmly to the spiritual competence of the soul, Baptists assert the privilege and the ability of every individual to seek and to find God in Christ directly, without the mediation of any man or any institution whatsoever.

While recognising fully that Christian fellowship is essential for the enrichment of Christian character and the fulfilment of our Lord's will for His disciples, no church is deemed necessary to bring God and man together or to make available to man the benefits of the divine grace.

According to this view, moreover, no special order of the ministry with priestly functions is essential to introduce man to God or God to man. Affirming the priesthood of all believers, all members are equal in spiritual privilege and station within the Church. Those who believe themselves to be called of God to preach the Gospel and to devote their time and strength wholly to the service of the Kingdom of God, if that call is recognised by the local church, are, in the interest of orderly administration, set apart or ordained, by the laying on of hands and by prayer, for the work of the ministry, and, if sanctioned by a council composed of messengers from other churches, such ordination is generally recognised throughout the entire Communion. This endows its subject, however, with no spiritual graces, gifts or authority which he did not possess before. All endowment for the ministry must come direct from the God who calls men into it.

From this point of view must be interpreted the significance of the ordinances of Baptism and the Lord's Supper instituted by Christ. Their efficacy does not depend upon the official position of him who administers them, but only upon the presence of the Lord and the faith of him who receives them. We are saved by faith alone. The ordinances are related to faith as aids and reminders. Nothing is conveyed or effected by the ordinances in and of themselves. Each is a symbol, nourishing in the believer and keeping before his mind essential elements in a Christian experience which, being wholly spiritual and inward in nature, cannot be produced by nor be dependent upon any outward physical act or rite whatsoever. The ordinances can serve to fortify the life of the spirit only as by the stimulation of faith they may quicken man's spiritual-rational nature. In this sense they are means of grace, and highly valued among us.

To say that the ordinances are symbols only is not to depreciate their worth nor to imply that they are negligible. The schoolboy's salute to the flag, the soldier's oath of allegiance (the Roman *sacramentum*), putting on the marriage ring—these do not create loyalty where it does not already exist, but they may powerfully stimulate loyalty and constantly remind us of its object. That God is truly present in the ordinances to the soul that devoutly receives them, and that they may be the occasion of the deepening of that mystical union with God, revealed in Jesus Christ, which is the highest privilege of the Christian life, the experience of the generations makes it impossible to doubt.

The spiritual experiences which the ordinances serve to keep before us and to intensify are conversion, or regeneration, and the abiding presence of Christ upon which the maintenance of the Christian life, thus begun, depends. In Baptism the believer openly identifies himself with his Lord, dramatically setting forth in symbol that initial act of consecration by which he has died in penitence with Christ to the old life of sin, and by the power of God has been raised from death to walk in the new life with the Christ who is the source of it. At the Lord's Supper the believer draws more closely to his Saviour in mystical fellowship, and as he receives the bread and wine it is his privilege truly to experience through communion with his Lord the replenishment of those vital spiritual energies upon which the vigour of the Christian life depends. There, too, the Christian meets his brother Christian upon the highest plane upon which human fellowship is possible—a common devotion to all that is most holy and sacred in life, sanctified by the memory of Him who is their incarnation and who, in His death, supremely set them forth. Thus the disciples of the Lord keep green the memory of His sacrifice and steep themselves in the spirit of it.

It is because of this conception of the meaning of the ordinances that Baptists practise the baptism of believers only, and employ the New Testament mode of immersion, and maintain the simplicity of the Lord's Supper as it was first instituted. Obviously participation in either of these must be a man's own act ; no one can do either for him. The form of the symbol also must be congruous with the experience symbolised or it is meaningless.

From such views flow certain inferences that bear directly upon the propositions set forth in Pamphlet No. 52 for this Conference, as a possible basis for further discussion. That " in each Sacrament there is an act of God ministered by His Church," or that " the grace of God is offered to man through the Sacrament," would be allowed by Baptists only in a sense which would apply as fully to any exercise of faith apart from the use of physical symbols, or directly to the influence of the Word of God. It is the " Gospel of Christ " that is supremely " the power of God unto salvation," and not the Sacraments.

With that understanding of the meaning of the terms involved, Baptists could accept the second proposition, that " the only necessary intentions in the Church, the ministers or the recipients, are to do what Christ commanded to be done and to receive what God wills to give through each Sacrament."

The third proposition, which asserts that " the administration of the Sacraments of Baptism and the Lord's Supper as instituted by our Lord is of perpetual obligation on the Church," would also be generally accepted. Whether there is a corresponding obligation on the part of all believers to observe the Sacraments, would, however, be called in question by many. Attendance at the Lord's Supper is nowhere obligatory among us. It is a privilege to which believers are urgently invited in the interest of their spiritual well-being and growth. So in many churches it is also with the observance of Baptism. It is offered to all converts as a sign and seal of their discipleship, which all are urged to observe in obedience to the Gospel ; but in the so-called " open membership " churches, in which are included a considerable fraction of English Baptists and a growing number of Churches in the United States, it is not demanded as a pre-requisite of Church membership. Conceived, from their reading of the New Testament, as an obligation arising from the relation of the believer to his Lord, and not from his relation to the Church, its observance, like that of the Lord's Supper and that of other Christian privileges or duties, is left to the individual conscience. To such Churches it appears that the ordinances, being made, like the Sabbath, for man and not man for the ordinances, they are of value only to those whose spiritual life they stimulate and feed ; and since in their view they convey no grace of themselves, the Church should not insist upon their observance on the part of those to whom they afford no spiritual ministry.

We must conclude that the attainment of agreement in doctrine upon the subject of the Sacraments is not a very hopeful objective, so far as Baptists are concerned, as a basis for organic unity. Agreement at this point, indeed, would not be sufficient to effect such unity. The Communions which now agree most closely in this regard are not correspondingly united. On the other hand, there are divergences of conception as to the Sacraments now existing within single Communions sufficient to assure us that differences here do not make impossible union in worship, service and Christian fellowship. In a united Church the widest liberty would be necessary in views as to the mode, subjects, number and function of the Sacraments.

Desirable as agreement upon these and other matters may be, the abiding basis of unity will be discovered below any and every form of ceremony in a common loyalty and a common purpose. The lasting bond for the unity of the Church is to be sought not solely in the field of doctrine, government, or sacraments, but also in the spiritual experiences which the Sacraments portray, a living faith in Jesus Christ, together with the dedication of the will to Him in service which such faith involves, the essential elements everywhere recognised throughout Christendom to-day as the marks of discipleship, the same to-day as in the first days of the Church, capable of being perpetually reproduced in the lives of men of every age, and so of continual renewal and verification for each generation as it appears. We can build hopefully only upon Jesus Christ, the chief corner-stone, " in whom all the building, fitly framed together, groweth unto an holy temple in the Lord."

THE REV. H. MALDWYN HUGHES, D.D.
Principal of Wesley College, Cambridge (Methodist)

I believe that the Conference will wish me to emphasise agreements rather than differences. There were agreements deeper than all the differences in the papers of the Bishop of Ochrida and of Dr. Bartlet. Both speakers emphasised the importance of Christian experience, and, as it seems to me, hinted that the true basis of unity is to be found in the realm of Christian experience.

The Bishop dealt with the Seven Sacraments recognised by some branches of the Church, Dr. Bartlet spoke only of the two Sacraments which are universally recognised, and in order to keep common ground, I shall follow his example. Indeed, I propose to confine my remarks to the Sacrament of the Lord's Supper, and further, to limit them to the practical aspects of the question.

We have already reached agreement on some carefully-worded formulæ, but thousands of our fellow Christians and the great world outside look for some act which will give a practical demonstration of the reality of the unity which we all believe already exists amongst us. What act could be so effective and convincing as some step or declaration which should prepare the way for intercommunion between all those who are members of the Body of Christ?

Doubtless at this point some may be thinking that it is unwise to raise so thorny an issue at this stage, but I am not unaware of the difficulties of the situation, nor do I regard lightly or with indifference sincere conscientious convictions. I do not think that we can hope to solve the problem along the ordinary lines of approach, dogmatic and historical. The discussions in England on the basis of the Lambeth Appeal have shown that that road ends in a cul-de-sac.

But I want to ask whether there is not another method of approach. Is it not possible for us, under the inspiration of the Spirit of God, to rise to a higher spiritual plane on which our differences will be transcended? I would suggest that whatever our doctrinal explanations, fundamentally and experimentally the Sacrament of the Holy Communion means very much the same thing to all of us. We all believe in the Real Presence of our Living Lord, if not in the elements, yet in the whole sacramental service, and our purpose is " to feed on Him in our hearts by faith with thanksgiving." I believe that all here would agree with an honoured teacher of my own Church in likening the Sacrament of the Holy Communion to the trysting-place of the lover and the beloved. Cannot we be content with that great reality of experience and agree to differ as to doctrinal interpretations? Cannot we be content to go together to meet our Lord at the appointed trysting-place, willing to leave it an open question as to exactly *how* He meets with us?

As the Bishop of Ochrida said: " Whenever the Holy Spirit descends upon men through His grace, is it not indifferent how He arrives? . . . It is He that matters." The same is true of the Living Christ. Confronted by the secularising and paganising tendencies of the age, are we not bound in loyalty to our Lord to achieve a visible expression of the unity which none of us denies? After all, we are not considering a Table or Feast of our own, but the Table and Feast of our Living Lord. He is the Host who invites us to be His guests, and have we any right to refuse fellowship with any whom we have every reason to believe He would not repel? As our Lord said when speaking of the Bread of Life: " All that the Father giveth me shall come to me " (John vi, 37).

I know that there are many who are deeply distressed that they are unable to communicate with their fellow-Christians, but who feel conscientiously that the course which I am advocating would hinder rather than hasten the real unity which is desired.

But I would ask, is it conceivable that the fellowship of love can prove a barrier to vital unity? To quote St. James: " Doth a fountain send forth at the same place sweet water and bitter? " (James iii, 11).

Even if we can rise to this higher plane on which we can agree to forget our doctrinal differences and to concentrate on the pursuit of brotherly love, we shall certainly be confronted by great practical difficulties which will have to be overcome if inter-communion is to be practised on any worthy scale. The situation will call for sacrifices from us all. But we shall surely be ready to make any and every sacrifice which does no violence to conscience. Only let us all ask for grace to distinguish between conscience and prejudice, and between dead tradition and living truth.

The fact is that the Sacrament of the Holy Communion, which ought to be the trysting-place of all the redeemed, has unhappily become the centre of our disunity. There we have an open wound in the Body of Christ. May God give us light and love that we may initiate at this Conference the process that shall heal the wound.

The Conference rose at 12.45 p.m.

SERVICE OF PENITENCE AND INTERCESSION
SUNDAY, AUGUST 14TH

The members of the Conference united in a Service of Penitence and Intercession in the Cathedral on Sunday, August 14th, at 8.30 a.m. The service, which was drawn up by Canon E. S. Woods, was conducted jointly by Bishop Brent, Pastor Merle d'Aubigné and Pastor Sandegren. It began with the hymn " Holy, holy, holy," and with an act of worship and praise, ending with the Lord's Prayer. There followed a call to reliance upon Christ, who wills unity for us, and to penitence for our thwarting of His purpose ; and the whole congregation kneeling together acknowledged their own shortcomings and those of the Churches—their lack of mutual understanding, humility, faith and love.

After the hymn " Now thank we all our God," and a reading from Scripture, a common act of thanksgiving was made for God's past and present mercies to His Church, and particularly for the new hopes arising out of this Conference. Intercession was then made for the Church, in English, German and French, and the hymn " When I survey the wondrous Cross " was sung.

The Apostles' Creed and the Beatitudes were then recited by all, each in his own language ; then, after an act of self-consecration to the service of God's kingdom and a moment of silent waiting upon God, the Blessing was given and the service thus brought to an end.

THE UNITY OF CHRISTENDOM AND THE RELATION THERETO OF EXISTING CHURCHES

Monday Morning, August 15th.

The full session opened at 9.30 a.m. with devotions led by the Chairman, the Rev. Pastor Henri Monnier. Archbishop Söderblom, who had prepared a speech which was printed and circulated before this session, delivered a supplementary address, speaking in English, as follows:—

THE MOST REV. NATHAN SÖDERBLOM, D.D.
Archbishop of Upsala (Lutheran)

Christian unity expresses itself in love, in faith and in the organisation of the Church.

How shall Christians show their unity? Perhaps it is reasonable to ask rather, how do Christians most clearly show their Christianity? Hereupon our Lord answers unequivocally in the Sermon on the Mount (Matt. vii, 16), "Ye shall know them by their fruits." Our fellowship in the Universal Christian Conference two years ago was a *communio in serviendo ecumenica.* In asking God how we should best fulfil His service in our time, we had a wonderful experience of coming nearer to our Saviour and therefore nearer to one another and of feeling ourselves to be one. We were brought together in Life and Work. The Church's unity round the Saviour's Cross was revealed.

In the preface to the report of one of the English Archbishops' Commissions, we read : " We do not underestimate the theological and constitutional questions involved. But we say deliberately that *in the region of moral or social questions we desire all Christians to begin at once to act together as if they were one body, in one visible fellowship.* This could be done by all alike without any injury to theological principles. And to bring all Christians together to act in this one department of life as one visible body would involve no loss and manifold gain. We should get to know and trust one another : we should learn to act together : we should thus prepare the way for fuller unity."

Life, work, love, has its foundation in faith, trust. And that unity of faith which we experience deeply also here, must find its expression in clear, thoroughly thought-out words and forms. It must also be realised in worship and Church order. There is little use to speculate about the forms of a United Church before we have attained the *conditio sine qua non* for such unity, I mean fellowship at the Lord's Table.

How do the existing Communions feel and teach and act in relation to such a unity of the Church ?

In order to describe the different attitudes towards such a unity, it will be necessary to distinguish between the soul and the body of the Church. The soul is the divine inspiration conveyed to the Church by the Holy Spirit through Word and Sacrament, the soul is God's revelation received through faith. The body is the system of creed, doctrines, rites and institutions of all kinds, which serve as channels or means or vehicles of God's grace.

Here we find three general answers to the questions about unity in Creed and Order. I venture to call those three positions (1) Institutionalism, (2) Spiritualism, and (3) Incarnationalism.

1. Institutionalism arises from time to time in different Communions often as a reaction against a one-sided and extreme spiritualism.

Outside Rome, institutionalism has in Western Christendom, as far as I know, never been taught and expounded in a more consistent and explicit way than in the Evangelic Lutheran Communion in the early nineteenth century. The primary thing is, according to that conception, the sacramental institution created at Pentecost. It must be remembered that great and lasting religious values were and are connected with that theology. But the controversy about the origin of the Church reminds one sometimes of the discussion whether the hen made the egg or the egg made the hen. A saying from Upsala tried to characterise that institutionalism : " The ministry is the primary, the divinity the secondary thing."

Institutionalism is a hindrance to unity. One single example : a real and important step towards Church unity was taken when, after long and mature deliberations, intercommunion was opened between the Church of England and the Church of Sweden by the Lambeth Conference of 1920 and the Swedish Bishops' Council of 1922. We praise God for such a boon. In our epoch the Lambeth Conference is the greatest and most representative official spokesman for Christian unity. But criticism and grievances were heard and are still made from that High Church or Stiff Church Lutheran institutionalism. It criticises faith, order and discipline in the Anglican Communion. It says, for instance, there is no guarantee in Anglican ritual and creed for the Real Presence in the sacrament, safeguarded in our Church by the doctrine of the ubiquity of the glorified Lord and of the *consubstantio* in the Lord's Supper. Further, there is no consistent and defined body of doctrine, nor any sufficient claim for theological university training of clergy, not sufficient doctrinal preparation for Confirmation. One finds in Anglicanism sometimes an archprotestant, anti-catholic individualism which thinks that the individual priest can arrange worship and his ecclesiastical duties as he likes and not according to the discipline and fixed rules of the section of the Church in which he serves.

We have had to meet such objections, and we have met them. I quote such criticism as an *advocatus diaboli* only, in order to show you how institutionalism is a hindrance to unity. I am happy that such Lutheran institutionalism has in no wise prevailed in the Church of Sweden, although it exhibits its exclusiveness in other important sections of our Communion. Such an institutionalism is not in harmony with the doctrine of the prophets and of the Apostles, nor with the essence and spirit of our creeds and of the Church renewal in the sixteenth century.

The religious institution is as old as history. It has had

the form of a tribe, or a family, or a nation or a fellowship for celebration of mysteries. Sometimes an ascetic or a teacher or a prophet gathered round him a new religious society. According to the Gospel story Jesus in calling His disciples had no idea of founding a new institution. He stayed inside the Jewish national religious institution until He was put on the Cross. His disciples stayed in that same community until they were expelled from it. Hence the difficult problem : did the creation of a new religious institution as separate from the Jewish one belong to our Saviour's intention and vocation ?

2. If I am bound to choose between Institutionalism and Spiritualism I prefer the latter. We " must worship God in spirit and truth." " It is the spirit that giveth life, the flesh profiteth nothing." If a priest is ordained by all bishops and archbishops of the Church, if he behaves in a perfect sacerdotal manner and knows the doctrine, but lacks the spirit, he is good for little. But the waiter whom I happened to meet here in Lausanne, and who has but one reality and passion in life, to follow His Lord and Master, exercises without any ecclesiastical consecration a priestly task.

The danger of Spiritualism is that in neglecting the doctrine and order of the Church it becomes too much dependent on men's capacity or incapacity. As Professor W. A. Brown shows in his beautiful recent book on Prayer, a formless worship easily becomes monotonous and poor. The mystery of revelation and salvation and the Church's own life is easily transformed unto a more or less idealistic society, which sometimes becomes somewhat aristocratic, reserved for a few. The continuity with the first Christian community and with the Church as a whole is broken. Without a body of creed and tradition the religious society loses its coherence and duration.

3. I try to call the relation to Church unity taught by the Communion to which I belong, *Incarnationalism*. Will you say, " Wenn der Gedanke fehlt, stellt sich ein Wort herein ? " This third group emphasises, as against the first, that religion is not essentially a body, a fixed form,

a doctrine, a hierarchy, but primarily a soul, a spirit. It emphasises as against the second group that for us, in this earthly existence, every spirit must receive bodily form, be incarnated in words, in deeds, men, institutions, doctrines and forms of service in order to become active and lasting.

Let me try to state first what I for my part regard as the relation of the Evangelic Lutheran Communion towards unity, and secondly a few words about the special situation of the Church of Sweden. It will be more useful than to try to tell the relation of all existing Churches to the unity of the Church. If the section of the Church known as Lutheran —although Martin Luther himself vehemently protested against his name being used for a group of Christians—has proved and proves to be difficult in these strivings for unity, there are several obvious reasons :

We are, in Western Christendom, next after the Roman Institution, the most numerous Communion, with something between seventy and eighty millions of baptised people.

Secondly, much more difficult is the fact that Lutheranism has not, as e.g. Anglicanism, the natural unity of expressing the sacred story of one great nation. The Evangelic Lutheran faith has, after the Roman Church, the largest number of national Communions, representing in a more or less authentic way the religious life of the larger part of a nation. We here of Evangelic Lutheran faith at this Conference speak some dozen mother tongues and very few of us speak the English-American language as our mother tongue, which fact handicaps us in this Conference. Our Communion all over Christendom speaks many more languages. More than one third of the Evangelic Lutheran Communion in the world has not sent representatives to this gathering. Many stand aloof as yet. We do not all agree on unity.

Thirdly, what the Bishop of Gloucester said the other day about the difficulty of making professors agree is applicable to our Communion, which has always been very much concerned with professors. It regards university studies as necessary for Holy Orders, akin in this respect to the Presbyterian or Calvinistic Communion.

Further, when Martin Luther, the passionately devoted son of the Church, was expelled from the papal Institution, then it became a hard necessity to him and his friends to organise, *contrary* to their will and intention, a Communion of their own. But they could never see or recognise that the action of the Pope excluded them from the One Holy Catholic and Apostolic Church. On the contrary, they felt themselves in a more authentic continuity with the revelation told in the Holy Scriptures, concentrated in Jesus Christ and preserved and developed under the guidance of the Holy Spirit in the ancient Church and in the Middle Ages, than those who separated them violently from temporal communion with Rome. It became also a necessity to formulate new expressions or symbols of faith, not in order to replace the old creeds, but in order to express more clearly and explicitly in the language and the thought of the epoch what the great theologians of our Evangelic Lutheran Communion later called the Catholicity of the evangelic faith, or " the Catholic Evangelic confession," in full acceptance of the ancient creeds of the Church. Those symbols or creeds of the Evangelic Lutheran faith constitute a *corpus* which, in comprehensive theological learning and explicit treatment of doctrine and life has, as far as I understand, *mutatis mutandis*, its analogy in one section of the divided Church in the sixteenth century, namely in the Roman Communion, in the *Tridentium*.

You will not find any official document that calls the Church in my country Evangelic Lutheran ; it is simply called " the Church in Sweden " or " the Swedish Church." But the Church in our country has, in 1593, against the Roman Catholic King and under a regent with some tendency toward a mitigated Calvinistic doctrine, emphasised the genuine Evangelic Lutheran conception as expressed in the whole treasury of creeds and symbols from the so-called Apostles' Creed until the Formula Concordiæ. They form a very bulky book. We possess thus a great and developed dogmatic tradition which makes it necessary for us to seek consistency when with whole-hearted earnestness we try to realise the unity of all Christians.

I agree that such a tradition makes this undertaking more difficult to us than to most of our sister communions.

Now four statements on our relation to unity :

1. I need not insist upon what we all recognise, namely the foundation of our faith in Holy Scriptures, not as an oracle or a collection of oracles, but as a divine revelation concentrated in the Word, *Logos*, who became flesh, and in what our creeds call " the prophetic and apostolic doctrine."

2. It is to us self-evident that the unity of faith and order cannot be found in another direction than that indicated and defined by the ancient creeds. It is said that the Holy Spirit who teaches us all things shall guide us unto all the truth ; but He shall not invent any new things. He shall not speak from Himself. He shall take from Christ's.

The drawback of the ancient Creeds, as Lord Sands and Professor Wobbermin and others have told us, is of course that they are expressed in a way of thinking and in a language very different from our way of thinking and our language, so that historic and theological learning is needed ; otherwise the creeds are easily interpreted in a heretical, not in an orthodox way. Therefore, the question arises of the creation of new creeds, new expressions, new symbols. I quite agree with General Superintendent Zoellner that we cannot sit down here to write a creed. Let us clearly see our limitations and the superhuman greatness of the task, because the divine truth will never be fully expressed in human words. The Bishop of Gloucester writes about the Eucharist : " It is easy for us to unite in worship, it is impossible for us to unite in definition, for no human language can be equal to so great a mystery."

It will interest our brothers in other Communions that we have in our creed a very clear definition of what a creed means. In the introduction of the Formula of Concord the prophetic and apostolic Scriptures of the Old and the New Testaments are proclaimed as rule and standards according to which all dogmas and teachers shall be esteemed and judged. Then it is said : " Other writings of ancient or modern teachers, whatever reputation they may have, should not be regarded as of equal authority with the Holy Scriptures, but should altogether be subordinated to them, and should not be received other or further than as witnesses in what manner and in what places the doctrine of the Apostles and Prophets was preserved."

It is most necessary to keep in mind and to acknowledge that character of the creed. As Professor Titius stated the other day, we find that we have since the ancient Church gone further under the guidance of the Spirit.

3. To our Communion, Church unity is a necessary, self-evident corollary of the Gospel. But " to the true unity of the Church it is enough to agree concerning the doctrine of the Gospel and the administration of the sacraments. Nor is it necessary that human traditions, rites or ceremonies, instituted by men, should be everywhere alike. As Paul says : 'One faith, one baptism, one God and Father of all.' "

4. I may also add, I think, in the name of our whole Communion, that we feel it most necessary to give time to ourselves and to our brethren to think and talk and write these things over very thoroughly, before we venture to issue any kind of proclamation about doctrine and order.

Now a few words about our peculiar Swedish position.

We have the so-called constitutional episcopacy, and the episcopal and presbyteral continuity without break is proved beyond any doubt— which, of course, in no wise makes our priestly office perfect. Even some Roman Catholic writers find in the Church of Sweden a stronger and more faithful continuity with the institutions of the Church of the Middle Ages than in any other non-Roman section of Western Christendom. Thus the Church historian J. Martin of St. Sulpice writes : " Encore aujourd'hui le Missel Suédois, basé sur celui d'Olaus, est le moins éloigné peut-être du Missel catholique " (*Gustaf Vasa et la Réforme en Suède*, Paris, 1906). The learned North American Roman prelate, J. M. Spalding, in his *History of the Protestant*

Reformation, New York, 1875, II, page 424, note 2, wrote about the first Bishop of Upsala, elected and consecrated September 22nd, 1531, after the Church renewal in Sweden, " the consecration having been duly performed by bishops having undoubtedly the episcopal character themselves, though uncanonical and unlawful, was certainly valid, and thus the present Swedish Lutheran bishops, unless the rite of consecration has since been materially altered, are invested with the episcopal character ; though being severed from the communion of the Church, they have not canonical jurisdiction or any lawful authority whatever." According to that view the bishops in Sweden are schismatics, but bishops in the Roman Catholic sense as in no other part of non-Roman Western Christendom. Of course, we have never asked Rome about the validity of our orders, because we regard the Church in our country and the section of the Church to which we belong, as at least as authentic a continuation of the Historic Church of previous ages as the Roman Communion.

The value of episcopacy was accentuated by Laurentius Petri, Archbishop of Upsala, in his Church Ordinance of 1571, which has authority in our Church as a kind of particular symbolic book : " Wherefore as this law was most useful, and without doubt proceeded from God the Holy Spirit, the Giver of all goodness, it was also universally accepted and approved over the whole of Christendom, and has ever since been and ever must be so long as the world endureth ; albeit abuses which have been exceeding great herein, as in all other of those beneficial and needful things, must be doffed." The Swedish Church Commission of 1911 says that the doctrine of freedom " in nowise makes our Church indifferent to the organisation and the forms of ministry which the cravings and experiences of the Christian community have produced under the guidance of the Spirit in the course of history. We not only regard the peculiar forms and traditions of our Church with the reverence due to a venerable legacy from the past, we realise in them a blessing from the God of history accorded to us."

The only way for us to decide what part of formulated

M

doctrine and Church organisation is necessary for unity, is to consider its ability to bring the supernatural divine content to man, society and mankind (Phil. iii, 4-8).

The Commission continues : " No particular organisation of the Church and of its ministry is instituted *jure divino*, not even the order and discipline and state of things recorded in the New Testament, because the Holy Scriptures, the *norma normans* of the faith of the Church, are no law, but vindicate for the New Covenant the great principle of Christian freedom, unweariedly asserted by St. Paul against every form of legal religion, and instituted already by our Saviour Himself, as for instance when, in taking farewell of His disciples, He did not regulate their future work by *a priori* rules and institutions but directed them by the guidance of the Paraclete, the Holy Ghost."

So far about our peculiar situation and doctrine in the Church of Sweden.

Such a principle makes the task more complicated and difficult. But we must not shrink from difficulties. Difficulties are there in order to be overcome. The bliss of Church unity is great enough to demand the price of our patient and prayerful consideration together in order to distinguish what is necessary and what is, in different situations, useful and important in creed and order.

A lady at table quoted the other day in this connection the words that Pascal heard in the silence when, in the emptiness of the infinite space, he was asking for God : " Tu ne me chercherais pas si tu ne m'avais pas trouvé "— " You would not seek me if you had not already found me." We experience this wonderful fact, an earnest and free and frank and brotherly conversation on our faith and our different traditions. I feel that such a seeking after a fuller joint expression of our unity indicates that *we have* already at the bottom of our Christian trust and experience such a unity. Is it excluded that, to quote once more the Formula of Concord, the Church in this epoch also might create a witness " in what manner the doctrine of the prophets and the Apostles has been received and preserved " and left to future generations by our time ?

We who have experienced the miracle of unity in the Stockholm Conference and here will not deny the possibility of a new expression of faith in the living God through Christ under the guidance of His Spirit in the language and fabric of the thought of these times, whether it may be made in the future united Church or before that time in a brotherly fellowship of Christian communions, not as yet organically united, but on the way to such a unity in multiplicity. My generation shall not see that wonder.

But we have come together here to experience our spiritual unity and to witness to it and at the same time to consecrate before God our thought upon what is essential in what unites us and in what separates us. We have to learn from one another. We must all of us make a real effort to come out from the self-complacent confessional laziness of thought into a seeking for fuller truth. We must pray and work whole-heartedly for unity and with patience await God's hour.

THE RIGHT REV. THE BISHOP OF GLOUCESTER
(Anglican)

The subject on which I am asked to address you to-day is The Unity of Christendom and the relation thereto of existing Churches. It is, of course, somewhat difficult to decide what the relation of existing Churches shall be to our future united Church until we have made up our minds on what lines the unity of Christendom is to be attained. I believe that the ideal that we have put before us is a unity which should have in it great possibilities of diversity, but that unity is not to be a mere federation, it is not to be a combination of different bodies merely for the sake of efficiency : the unity of the Church, as St. Paul teaches us, is a spiritual unity, a unity in Christ, a sacramental unity, a unity built up on a divinely appointed and divinely inspired ministry. Within this unity diversity might be possible. I propose, therefore, first of all to sketch shortly the principles of unity, and secondly the principles of diversity.

The unity of the Church must be a unity of faith, a unity in the sacraments, and a unity in the ministry.

First as to the unity of faith. This should be in words which have already been suggested, " The faith of Christ as taught in Holy Scripture and handed down in the Apostles' and the Nicene Creeds." It is not the Creeds or the Scripture that we believe in, but the faith that they teach, and this is of extreme importance, for it means that we are not committed to any particular theory of inspiration, and we accept the Creeds not as infallible or inerrant or necessarily unchangeable documents, but as the traditional expression of the faith in Christ. That faith means the belief in God as revealed in Christ ; it means fundamentally the doctrines of the Incarnation and the Trinity ; it means that reality is expressed to us in the words God, Son, Spirit, in the Life and Death, the Incarnation and the Atonement of Jesus Christ.

Just one thing more would I say, and I think it is fundamental. The same Council of Chalcedon to which we owe the document we now describe as the Nicene Creed condemns, not only those who reject that Creed, but also those who add to it in any way. I cannot think but that many of the evils of Christian disunion have arisen from the attempts that have been made from time to time to add to that Creed. We should unite on the fundamental revelation of reality which comes to us in Jesus Christ, and not impose as in any way necessary for salvation any further interpretations or elucidations.

Secondly, the union is to be a sacramental union. " In one spirit are we all baptised into one body." " We being many are one bread, one body, for we are all partakers of the one bread." Now this unity in sacrament means the acceptance of the sacraments and not of any particular teaching about them. For twelve hundred years the Christian Church was satisfied with that. There was much theology on the sacraments, some good and some bad. The traditional belief was enshrined in liturgies which might still form a common basis of union. But no particular acceptance of any theory was required or enjoined or forbidden by the Church. I believe that that must be our basis of union in the future ; we can unite in worship, we cannot unite in definition. The future Church will look upon Baptism as the one means of entry into it ; it will look upon the Holy Communion as the great corporate act of worship ; it will endeavour to express its belief about these in the best way that the revelation of Scripture and theological thought has taught it, but it will not impose as a condition of entrance into the Christian society or of membership of it any particular belief about the sacraments, nor will it prohibit any particular belief. Each worshipper will receive the sacrament with the meaning that he himself attaches to it.

Then thirdly, the union must be a union in ministry. The Christian minister is not merely an official appointed for the convenience of society. His appointment comes from God ; " God has appointed in the Church apostles, prophets, teachers." " The apostles, the evangelists, the prophets, the pastors and teachers " have received in a marked way the gifts of the Spirit and that " for the perfecting of the saints, for the work of the ministry, for the building up of the body of Christ." Nor have I any doubt that this union in the ministry must mean the acceptance of the traditional form of the Christian ministry, the acceptance of episcopacy and of episcopal ordination. It is not my purpose at this time to discuss how that may be brought about ; I would only say this, that I do not think that it is possible for any one Church to go to any other and say, " Our Orders are valid, yours are not." It is not possible for them to say, " We have the succession, you have not." The only full and complete Orders would be those given in a united Church, and because the Church is divided therefore all Orders are irregular and no succession is perfect. The unity of two branches of the Christian Church must come by each giving what it can to the other in the ordination of its clergy.

This, then, is our Christian unity, and I believe on this

basis a strong, elastic society would be built up allowing within it for the manifold divergences which have come through the different types of human nature. The Gospel of Christ is far deeper and fuller than anything which any one man or any one nation can grasp. All the different nations and churches of the world bring their honour and glory to the building up of the heavenly city, and if we attempt to impose upon the different Christian societies an ordered uniformity, we will destroy much life and the expression of new aspects of the Christian faith.

Let us now pass to the problem of variety.

There are, I think, two separate problems. There is first of all the relation to one another of the different National Churches. In most European countries there is an established National Church with definite relations to the Government of the country, often supported in some way or other by public money. In some countries the National Church includes the vast majority of the population. What is to be the relation of these Churches to one another, and how far, if there were to be full Christian unity between them, could they retain their distinctive customs, manner of worship, and religious teaching ? It is this problem that meets us most prominently in Europe.

Then, secondly, there is the problem which presents itself most prominently in America, where there is no National Church, but there are a vast number of separated Religious Societies or Churches, often differing from one another in points which seem to the outsider to be matters of slight importance, but yet having their own independent traditions and life. How far can these co-exist with one another, and in countries where there is a National Church, how far can they co-exist with that Church ?

I will speak first of the problems raised by the relations of the different National Churches one to another. How far can their individual usages and customs be retained ?

First, variety in worship. There are many different types of Christian worship existing in the world. There is the worship of the Roman Church, of the Greek Church, of the Anglican Church, of the Lutheran Church, of the

Presbyterian. In all these I have at different times taken part. In all of them I have received edification. They have gradually been developed corresponding to the aspirations of different sections of the Christian society ; in their turn they have helped to mould the character and temperament of nations. I do not think that we can say that any one of them represents the perfect form of service. We may have our own particular desires depending largely upon habit and custom, but what may appeal most to us will not appeal in the same way to others, and therefore I see no reason why in the united Church these different forms of service may not remain ; although no doubt when the Churches are united together, each will learn from the other and there will be more tendency to assimilation.

In fact, already in the Church of England we have begun to find that complete uniformity in worship is not attainable. Particularly in the mingled life of our great cities the various needs of mankind to be satisfied are far greater than any one form of service can content. There are many who wish to worship in different ways, and I do not know that the worship of one is a deeper or more real expression of Christian piety than the worship of another. The same diversity that exists within the Church of England might be extended and exist in greater variety in the united Christian Church.

The second point will arise as to the particular confessions of particular Churches. What are we to say to the Westminster Confession or the Augsburg Confession or the Formula Concordiæ ? It will clearly be necessary to have in any Christian Society other statements of the Christian faith than the Creeds. They alone are not sufficient to teach what Christianity is. They concentrate the mind on the essential truths, they do not explain those truths. Every Church will need its catechism for the instruction of the young, it will need some manual or book of directions for its clergy to tell them the lines on which they should teach. The aspect of Christian truth presented to us in England is somewhat different to that presented in Germany. It is not that the one is true and the other false ; it is that they are different interpretations of the one truth, and that clearly must remain. If suddenly Christianity as taught in England were to be taught in Spain, or the Christianity of Spain be taught in England, it would mean something difficult for those who heard it to understand. So I believe that for a time at any rate the different confessions of faith will continue, but they will continue not as documents excluding from the Christian society, but as manuals of instruction putting before the clergy traditional lines of Christian thought and teaching. No doubt each Church will learn from the other, no doubt these formulæ may gradually be modified, no doubt in time they may give place to some new manual of instruction or some new catechism putting the traditional truths in a way more suited to the change of thought of modern times, and to a united Church. But that should be a slow process gradually going on. We do not wish to say at once that these traditional types of theological expression should be banished.

Then, thirdly, within the Christian ministry there may be different methods of expressing the relationship of the different parts. It is not so much the administrative unity of the ministry or its aspect with regard to organisation, but its spiritual unity that is essential. Episcopacy may be autocratic, constitutional or democratic. The authority given to the Christian congregation may vary. Different forms are suited to different stages of civilisation or to different national temperaments. I do not see that it is necessary for us to impose one particular form on everybody. The tendency at the present day is to what is called a constitutional episcopate, to emphasise the congregational or the democratic elements. It has not always been so ; it might not always be so again. At any rate, what I am desirous to suggest is that the adoption of episcopacy does not mean the adoption necessarily of one particular type.

Then, fourthly, the relation of the Christian Church to the national life may vary very greatly, and I see no reason why we should necessarily impose one particular type ; and

I think that it is particularly necessary to emphasise this, for there is great variety existing at the present time, and that variety should not necessarily be changed. We have, for example, in Scandinavian countries strong national Churches in a close connection with the State ; we have in America a loose form of establishment of all religious ideals ; the attitude of the Church of Rome towards the Government has varied much in different countries. I am not prepared necessarily to say that one particular type of national Church is necessarily the right one. I have sometimes seen it suggested that the ideal put before us by the English Free Churches should be considered the one possible relation of Church and nation. Personally, I dislike that ideal intensely. For me the building up of one national Church in any nation in close union with the State seems the ideal to be attained. I have far greater sympathy with English Nonconformity as a religious movement than as a political movement. But it is not by my business to discuss what should be the relation of Church and State. What I wish to point out is that each nation and each national Church should be left free to make its own arrangements for the relation between the two great societies in accordance with its own traditions and the characteristics of its people.

So far I have been discussing the question as it concerns the relation of national Churches to Christian unity; but we have to pass now to the consideration of those societies which have organised themselves apart from national Churches. I should look forward to the unity of the Church finding its natural expression in a local unity of administration or organisation. That is to say, I believe that in some form or other the diocesan and parochial systems which prevail in almost every country of Europe should be the basis of Church life. But in no times of religious earnestness has that ever been quite sufficient. In the Middle Ages we find the local organisation supplemented by the great monastic system, and always there have been religious societies within or without the fold of the local Church expressing different and sometimes intenser forms of the religious life. It would be a grave misfortune to Christianity if such variety should cease. The only thing that we should demand is that these societies, whether Anglican, Roman, Methodist, or whatever they may be, should not call themselves Churches. And as I see it, the relation of these societies towards the Church might take one of two forms. The one form would be that represented at the present time by the position of the Uniate Churches in the Roman Catholic Communion. These bodies have their own hierarchy, their own liturgies, their own canon law, and they exist in the same locality side by side with the churches of the Latin rite. I do not see why such a variety should not. exist in our united Church. Quite clearly, even if there were to be unity between the Church of England and the Church of Rome, those in England who have been in the habit of using the Latin rite would not want to give it up. I can well believe that other Christian Churches existing at the present time might like to organise themselves on the same basis. They would have their own episcopate, their own properly ordained ministers, in communion with the localised ministry, but adding to the intensity and variety of religious life.

But there is another relationship which is possible. I can well believe that these separate bodies might exist without a separate religious organisation of their own, as societies for promoting religious life : that I believe in some of the Scandinavian countries is the relation of their free Churches. They have their separate religious life, but they have not their separate Communion service. They would communicate in their parish church. The relationship of the Salvation Army might be the same as the relationship of the Church Army. Methodist societies might be religious societies in quite close union with the National Church.

Let us take some concrete instances.

First of all let us picture to ourselves a country where there is a Lutheran Episcopal Church, as the National Church, with a considerable minority belonging to the Orthodox Eastern Church. Each of these has its traditional form of service, each its traditional Church life. It would not be very easy for either of them to change suddenly their ways of thought, nor can I see any reason why they should change. We want them to be one Church and not two, and that we should secure if their ministries were unified ; if bishops from both Churches should take part in all consecrations, and perhaps also if, in the ordination of presbyters, presbyters from both Churches should take part. They would unite in Synodical meetings to discuss all those matters which formed the common interest of both Churches, especially the regulations as regards religious education. They would unite in solemn service from time to time, and where necessity and occasion demanded the members of each would be admitted to Communion at the altars of the other, but they would each live their own religious life and continue to observe their own religious customs and methods of worship. No doubt if thus united there would be considerable influence from one and the other. Each would learn from the other, and probably the unity between the two would become greater, but I see no reason at all why the two forms of worship should not go on side by side.

Or again, let us picture the way in which religion might organise itself in England. We have a National Church, which ministers directly to about half the population and has attached to it by nominal ties a considerably larger number. We have a body of Roman Catholics, about half a dozen considerable Nonconformist bodies, and a very large number of smaller sects. As regards the latter, it is not quite possible to say whether, if there was a general move towards unity, they would desire to retain a separate existence. Some would, some would not. Some would probably be quite implacable, like the Plymouth Brethren. Others would tend to be absorbed in larger bodies. But there will always be separated bodies so long as men think for themselves and think incorrectly. The Churches we should be concerned with would be the Roman Catholic, the Methodists (who will probably become a united body), the Congregationalists, the Presbyterians, and the Baptists.

I do not know whether the Baptist Churches will ever desire or accept unity. As regards the others, the Roman Catholics might well continue as a separate body of Christians observing the Latin rite, living side by side with those following the English rite. The bishops of the two societies would mutually assist in consecrations. I do not know whether the Methodists, the Congregationalists and Presbyterians would care to have bishops of their own. They would I think tend to become, what they really are to a large extent at present, religious societies organised on a somewhat democratic basis, supplementing the religious life of the National Church and correcting its deficiencies. Only in the future they would do this in union with the National Church and not in opposition to it. That would mean that the ministries of these Churches would be episcopally ordained, that they would assist in ordinations as presbyters of the Church, that they would meet in Synods and Councils, and that they would communicate with one another. But they would preserve each their own religious life and customs and manner of worship. No doubt when once united together they would tend to learn more from each other than they do at present. In some cases they might gradually approximate to one another, but I doubt if that approximation would proceed very far. The form of worship and religious life which is presented in Nonconformist Chapels in England makes a definite appeal to many persons and would remain as a permanent type of religious worship.

As regards America, it is difficult for any one outside to speak, but sometimes the observations of an observer looking on are of value, and from such a point of view it would appear that the one thing that is needed for that country is to construct out of its vigorous but disorderly religious life an organised territorial ministry, to build up a proper parochial system, as the only method to prevent the overlapping of rival religious bodies, and to secure that every person throughout the country shall, if he claims it, have the ministrations of religion available. I believe that if the principles of unity I have laid down were accepted, such a system would come very quickly. No doubt, especially in towns, it would need, as in England, to be supplemented by greater religious variety. I imagine that America would never have an Act of Uniformity. That a certain unity having been secured, it would be left to each separate congregation to continue to develop its own life, only there would be a decided tendency for different forms of worship to approximate to one another. The problem really in America is to create a unity out of the great number of very varying religious bodies which are yet not separated from one another by any fundamental point of doctrine. Once grant unity and a sufficient uniformity would be quickly developed.

I have endeavoured to sketch out as well as I can what I conceive to be the proper relationship of the Christian societies. Of course, anything put forward must be very much in the air. We do not know whether we are going to unite or how we are going to unite, but it is important, I think, to have clearly before us an ideal which leaves great room for diversity and variety. One thing only I would like to say, in conclusion, and that is that a fundamental postulate of our united Christianity must be freedom and toleration. It seems strange that this is a lesson very slowly learnt. It must mean freedom for those who do not care to join the United Church; it must mean freedom within the Church for those types which do not have any desire to conform to the organised life of the National Church; it must mean, above all, educational freedom. It is strange how difficult people find it to learn these lessons. I am shocked when I hear that only in recent years in one country the Roman Church has joined with the socialists to despoil a Protestant Church of its building. I am equally shocked when I hear that in another country a Protestant Church has joined with the anti-clerical State to prohibit Roman Catholic schools. I am shocked at the way in which modern liberalism has failed to realise that educational freedom means freedom to teach your children your faith as well as freedom from a State or Church imposing its creed upon your children. It will be useless and dangerous for us to build up any form of United Church unless all alike, Romanist, Anglican, Protestant, Non-Conformist, have learnt the fundamental doctrines of Christian liberty.

THE REV. PETER AINSLIE, D.D.
Baltimore, Maryland (Disciples of Christ)

We have all listened with profit to the noble utterances of the Archbishop of Upsala and the Bishop of Gloucester. To the former we are indebted for his brilliant leadership in making possible the Stockholm Conference of 1925, and to both we are indebted for their fine contributions through their books and magazine articles on the subject of a united Christendom, so that to speak where they have spoken is to come into a field that has been somewhat cleared by reverent and careful thinking.

The unity of Christendom is the greatest issue of modern times, not a mechanical unity born of compulsion or compromise, but a unity that is pulsating with the warm affection of a brotherhood that shall include all who have accepted Jesus Christ as Lord and Saviour. To this ideal every Church is directly or indirectly related. To the Protestant Episcopal Church of America belongs the leadership in making this Conference a reality and all of its steps have been marked by statesman-like advance. Seventy-odd Churches from all parts of the world are represented here. The Roman Catholic Church, although not responding by the appointment of a delegation, has had more to say on Christian unity in its periodicals in consequence of this Conference than ever before in its history.

Over against a powerfully entrenched denominationalism, with its stubborn facts and almost insurmountable obstacles, is the law of action and reaction first announced by Newton and practically demonstrated in the field of physics, and more recently in the field of finance by that genius in statistics Roger Babson, and now most interestingly observed in the field of religion, before which the divisions of Christendom are as sure to go slowly down as the ebb and flow of the tides. The Church, in all parts of the world, is beginning to see that these divisions, however sacredly guarded now, are artificial, abnormal, and unspiritual, and diversity within unity is the spiritual and normal possibility towards which we must work. That which gives life and vitality to every Christian Communion is that which is common to all, and everything that bristles in antagonism toward another Communion is not of vital consequence. Unity is the first and the highest law of the universe, written in the constitution of mankind and released by Jesus Christ for the brotherhood of the world.

Our greatest difficulty lies in getting our eyes off of the Communion of which we are parts and seeing only Jesus Christ, the crucified and glorified Son of God. Our denominationalism has obscured Him (and I am using the word denomination as applied to all the divisions of Christendom). Denominational loyalty is a foreign phrase in these days of an agonising world, Christ is supreme and to Him our loyalties belong. My denomination must grow less in my eyes if I am to grow more towards Christ. I am willing that my denomination shall be forgotten if thereby may be hastened the unity of the Church of our Lord. That denomination is most prophetic that is willing to disappear for Christ's sake—to go to its disappearance as deliberately as Christ went to His crucifixion.

Mr. Robert H. Gardiner, to whose memory a beautiful and deserved tribute was expressed by this Conference at its opening session, has left us a striking and appropriate paragraph. I wish he were living to say these words, and since he has passed from us, I wish I could put into them the humility and gentleness of his voice. He says, " Our divisions arose, and are being perpetuated, by the pride and diversity and instability of the human will. Finite man has undertaken to delimit the relationship of God to the world, and, in the pride of his self-opinion, has dared to act as if to him had been trusted the whole counsel of the Almighty, and as if God were shut into this or that particular means for the salvation of the world. Hence we have sought our own will, not God's, and our prayers for unity are too often in substance only that God will bring the world to agree with us. Prayer is not to bend God's will to ours, but to bring our will in harmony with His, and we can pray only that God will manifest to us the unity He wills and give us grace to follow it."

We are here as parts of the divided Church of Christ, seeking to courageously face the scandal of our divisions and to try, by the grace of God, to loosen up to some extent in our outlook and attitude as a contribution to the healing of this running sore. History records no greater scandal than the broken brotherhood of the Church of Christ. We cannot shift this guilt upon the shoulders of our forbears, but we ourselves are the sharers of the guilt. St. Paul, writing to the Church at Corinth (I am using Moffatt's translation) says, " Brothers, for the sake of our Lord Jesus Christ, I beg of you to drop these party-cries. There must be no cliques among you ; you must regain your common tempers and attitude. By quarrelling I mean that each of you has his party-cry, ' I belong to Paul,' ' and I to Apollos,' ' and I to Cephas,' ' and I to Christ ' . . . I could not discuss things with you, my brothers, as spiritual persons. . . . I had to address you as worldlings, as mere babes in Christ. For with jealousy and quarrels in your midst are you not worldly, are you not behaving like ordinary men ? "

What were but mere saplings in the Corinthian Church have become a forest of giant trees, some of them centuries old, whose roots and trunks and branches are sacredly guarded in the affections of the party to which each of us belongs to the exclusion of all others. In the Corinthian Church St. Paul appears to have made no reference to their doctrinal differences. In the fact of their party-cries they had assaulted the law of love. This both in the mind of Christ and of St. Paul was primary ; because the Church is a brotherhood, division is sin. To claim that this or that is *the* Church and others are schismatics or " the sects " or " the denominations " is but playing with words in order to dodge repentance. Humility is the path of God

—let us be careful that we do not get out of God's path. In the Corinthian Church those who formed the "Christ party" doubtless assumed superiority over those of the Paul and Apollos and Cephas parties, but St. Paul puts them all on an equality of guilt, and until every party in the modern Church feels the sting of guilt, until every one of us is embarrassed when he is compelled to line up with his party, there can be no substantial growth toward a united Christendom. I wish I could escape my party name, although it is the first name worn by the followers of Christ. My denomination has sectarianised some of the holiest names in the Scriptures. I know that it is as wrong to wear any Scriptural name in a party sense as to wear non-Scriptural names for Christian parties. I am embarrassed in being so classified. But joining another party does not afford an escape. I have only two alternatives. I must either follow the example of my great countryman, Abraham Lincoln, and refuse to identify myself with any of the Churches in consequence of our divisions, as he did, or remain in my party and work and pray constantly for the union of the divided Church. I have chosen the latter course, conscious, however, of multitudes, among whom are some of the finest souls on earth, having chosen the former. If we who are members of the Church are not really in heart and will genuine advocates of unity, it is a question whether we are Christians at all.

In consequence of these things and also the many prophetic utterances that have marked this Conference, I lay before you these three possible steps of action.

First, whatever may be our theories or practices, the very fact of this Conference is a call for all the Christian parties to get together in our various countries and work side by side in such causes as circumstances will permit. The method must be suited to the local conditions, but the need is so great that where the circumstances do not justify this co-operation the Church should be adventurous enough to create the circumstances.

Second, the time is here and now when there should be the recognition of the equality of all Christians before God.

The barriers that have been set up to keep other Christians out or to keep our Christians in, or both, must be loosened up by a spirit of tolerance, like that of St. Paul in his interpretation of Christianity when he exhorted his fellow Christians to practise forbearance in the spirit of love. No finer expression of this equality of all Christians before God could come than to close this Conference next Sunday with the celebration of the Lord's Supper with its whole conduct in your hands, Bishop Brent. I know, Sir, that some would dissent from that suggestion on the ground that many at home in various Communions would be offended. For these I have great respect, be they great or small in the affairs of their Communion, but I remember that also at home is a great multitude who are slowly turning away from the Church because of our unbrotherly traditions. I assume to be spokesman for that multitude for whom so few will dare to speak but for whom Christ died. I hope, Sir, that this suggestion may be favourably considered. If we cannot now observe the Lord's Supper together after these centuries of separation, I ask when can it be done ?

Third, in the political affairs of the world the nations have formed a League whose merits are daily rising in public esteem. Is it not high time that the Churches of the world should form a league or fellowship, already hinted at by others, each Church holding to all that it has and seeking to contribute something to that divine life that has been released for the growth of mankind toward God ? The Covenant need be no more binding than this Conference, but it would afford an opportunity for larger understanding by future conferences and co-operative efforts, making possible the way for growth into unity, which can never come so long as we remain isolated from and indifferent to the causes of others. We have been entrusted with such a spirit in this Conference that, if we did not go forward, it would be disloyal to one of the greatest experiences in the history of modern Christianity. If the adoption of these three steps is going too fast, wherein lies our moral right to go so slow ?

The day of penitence is here. Let us, brethren, not be

afraid to express it in such a manner as will prove its practicability and permanency, neither let us be afraid to trust others with that with which Christ has trusted all.

PROFESSOR J. M. SHAW, D.D.
Halifax, N.S. (United Church of Canada)

That a divided Christendom, especially a divided Protestant Christendom, is one of the main obstacles to the spread of Christianity in the world and to the realisation of Christ's purpose through His Church, weakening the Church's witness and in large measure confusing and discrediting her message—this is the conviction back of this momentous World Conference on Faith and Order in which we have the privilege and responsibility of taking part. To the question how this obstacle is to be removed and a closer union of Christendom to be attained, different answers may be and have been given. Some hold that the best hope is along the line of federation, rather than of union—federation in which the different denominations, while still maintaining their separate identity and separate organisations and governments, yet come into closer co-operation and alliance for the sake of the realisation of their common ends. As to this, I can only express my personal belief, without waiting now to support or defend it, that federation can only be regarded as a half-measure, and but a first step towards a more complete and organic union.

For the attainment of this closer organic union different methods have been proposed. Two in particular : *First,* some hold that such a union when attained must be a doctrinal and sacramental union, a union, that is to say, on the basis of a common creed and a common order. Such is the answer in particular of the Greek Orthodox Church in the East and of the Church of England in the West. The former takes the position that the Nicene Creed and the doctrinal decrees of the Seven great Ecumenical Synods, in which it is claimed the substance of the faith of the still undivided Church was finally and infallibly interpreted, should form the basis of union. The latter, the Church of England, as its mind was expressed in the Lambeth Appeal of 1920, suggests as the basis of union "the whole-hearted acceptance" not only "of the Holy Scriptures as the record of God's revelation to men and as the rule and ultimate standard of faith," but further of the Creed commonly called Nicene as the sufficient statement of this faith, and either it or the Apostles' Creed as the baptismal confession of belief; together with the acknowledgment of the "divinely instituted sacraments of Baptism and the Holy Communion as expressing for all the corporate life of the whole fellowship in and with Christ."

As to this method—apart from the fact that some Churches, for example the Congregational and the Baptist, object to the adoption of any creed or formula as obligatory or authoritatively binding, as being a hindrance to the free expression of the Christian faith—if we are to accept the Apostles' and Nicene Creeds, it can only be the faith expressed in these Creeds, not the particular formulation of this faith in thought-forms which are in large measure meaningless for us to-day. What is of truth and value in this position in our judgment is that there can be no real union apart from agreement on the fundamentals of the Christian faith, in particular without agreement in our thinking about, or rather, attitude to, Jesus Christ.

This is the answer we would give to the *second* proposed method of bringing about closer organic union, often spoken of as the method of ethical or moral union, a union namely of all Christian bodies in the law of the love of Christ, regardless of diversities of faith, worship and order, a union in practical brotherhood and fellowship.

As against these two ways of attaining closer organic union among the Protestant Churches, we would suggest and support a *third* and, as we believe, more hopeful way, namely, that the several Churches or denominations, repudiating a dogmatic attitude and endeavouring to rise above their own particular preconceived ecclesiastical theories or traditional predilections, should agree to reconsider these theories or predilections in the light of the New Testament and of New Testament scholarship, and ask themselves what, according to the New Testament standard and perspective, is fundamental and essential to the very existence and purpose of the Church as the Body of Christ, the organ and instrument of the manifestation and realisation of His mind and will in the world ; what is that fundamental essential Christianity on which all the Churches as members of the Body of Christ should unite, and how should the Church to-day in the light of history and experience be constituted or organised so as to express and realise this fundamental and essential Christian faith and life, and thus fulfil Christ's intention through her.

What is thus fundamental, first, as regards the Church's *faith* ? I believe the net result of modern critical scholarship has been to enable us to recover the proper New Testament emphasis and perspective with regard to what is primary and what is secondary, what is central and what is circumferential ; and to realise that the essentials of faith are not certain doctrinal or credal formulations which change with the changing forms of the age—these are the variables of Christianity—but properly religious convictions based upon Christian experience, convictions verifiable afresh by every generation because the experience is permanent and abiding from age to age, the true Christian *continuum* or constant, constituting the faith once for all delivered to the saints, convictions centering in Jesus Christ and His relations to God and to man.

As regards *order* or *polity*, modern scholarship has shown that so far from any specific order or form of Church government and organisation being able to be pointed to as ordained by Christ or His Apostles, the particular form of organisation adopted by the Church in each age has been determined by the particular historical circumstances of the age and situation. In the New Testament itself no plan or theory of Church order and organisation was thought out in advance and applied in all circumstances, but the plan or form of organisation adopted in each case was determined by the compulsion of events or, in more Christian phraseology, by historical circumstances under the leading of the Spirit of God. Not uniformity of organisation, that is to say, but continuous adaptation to the needs of the historical situation under the guidance of the Spirit —in Sanday's words, not " code law," but " case law "— was the law of the Church's action in the apostolic age and should be the law of the Church's action in every age, just because the Church is not a static corporation or institution, but a living, vital, developing organism. As in the natural sphere vital function precedes and creates its specific organ, so here in the spiritual sphere life or function determines organisation, and the best form of Church organisation in each age, and I will add in each country, is that which best expresses in that age and in that country the life of the Body which is Christ's and realises His purposes in the world. Unity in the essentials of the Christian faith, together with liberty to follow the guidance of the Spirit in each age and place both as regards doctrinal and institutional expression of this faith—such would seem to be the New Testament indication as to the proper method of attaining closer union between the Churches.

Not that the differences between the Churches, the distinctive characteristics of the several denominations as regards doctrinal and institutional expression, are thus to be thought of as light and unimportant, and to be simply disregarded or sacrificed in order to obtain a Least Common Denominator among the Churches. Such a method would be one of spurious simplification. So far from this, it may rather be argued that " every great Church of Christendom bears witness to some aspect of Christian truth and experience which either in form or in content was insufficiently emphasised by other Churches and should be preserved and lived by." Any real reunited Catholic Church must conserve and include the true spiritual or religious values for which each Church has historically stood. In a reunited Christendom there must not be one lost good, but each Church must bring its distinctive contribution to the thought and life and order of the Church as a whole, that through this manifold or many-sided contribution we may in the reunited Church not only provide for varying forms of faith and worship, but may also the more fully apprehend the manifold wisdom and grace of God and attain the nearer to the measure of the stature of the fulness of Christ. From the episcopal Churches, for example, a reunited Church might well adopt the episcopal form of government, not indeed as of the very *esse* or being of the Church, but only as of its *bene esse* or well-being, as the form of government most likely in present circumstances to promote and preserve the unity and historic continuity of the Church—an episcopacy, however, not of a monarchial but of a constitutional or representative type in which the rights and privileges of the whole Christian community, the body of believers, in the Church's government shall be adequately recognised and preserved; while from non-episcopal bodies might be adopted that evangelical liberty of prophetic ministry and worship and service which has its roots in immediate personal relationship with God in Christ. Thus would centralised authority and solidarity be combined with local freedom or spontaneity. In any case, not uniformity but unity in diversity or unity in multiformity—a unity within which diversity of thought and of religious and institutional expression are recognised and made use of—is, it would seem, the New Testament ideal of Church unity.

Such a United Church, allow me to say in closing—such a method of bringing about closer organic union between the Churches, is no mere dream or abstract speculation. It has been realised. An outstanding concrete example of it, the first large-scale achievement indeed of organic union between separate denominational bodies since the Protestant Reformation, we have in the Church which I have the honour to represent and to speak on behalf of at this Conference, namely, the United Church of Canada, brought into existence two years ago through the union of three independent Protestant denominations, each rich in spiritual history and in traditions of doctrine and government, the Presbyterian, the Methodist and the Congregational

Churches. It is a Union inspired and brought into existence
—this is its great distinction—by purely religious considerations and motive, *i.e.*, for the fulfilment of the task for
which the Church as such exists, the task which the
Churches in Canada came to feel beyond their separate
resources and their separate strength, the building up of
Christ's Kingdom in every corner of our great Dominion.
The Churches that have been set up in different countries
at different times since the one Church of the earlier days
began to disintegrate have been variously motived and
based. Some were founded in vindication of doctrines
which had been obscured and some in assertion of liberties
which had been curtailed either by national or ecclesiastical
authorities. But this Church, our Church—while true to
and carrying on the essential traditions and spiritual heritage of the several uniting Churches—was conceived and
brought to birth for the one great purpose of creating a
fitter and more effective instrument or organ for the meeting of the religious needs of Canada, specially of the new
communities which are filling up the great empty spaces
in the West ; and thus making our land a land where Jesus
Christ shall have dominion " from ocean unto ocean " and
" from lakes to northern lights."

It is a union brought about by the subordination of
denominational loyalties to loyalty to Christ and the
advancement of His Kingdom in Canada and beyond.
While there is a doctrinal basis of union, a statement and
interpretation of the living faith of the three uniting
Communions, the faith by which the Church lives and in
which is the very life of the Spirit, yet the union itself
is more religious or practical than theological or doctrinal,
based not on theological uniformity but upon common
devotion to a living Saviour and Lord and to the demands of
His service. It is a Church one in a common heart-beat, yet
including variety within this vital unity, a Church in which
the religious and Christian values of the separate uniting
Churches have been conserved, each denomination finding
in the others gifts and qualities complementary to its own,
gifts and qualities needed for a full appreciation and

appropriation of the whole round of Christian faith and life.

With such an exemplification and concrete illustration in our land in present-day history of a great new adventure of faith for the worthier fulfilment of Christ's purposes through His Church, what hinders that there should not be in every land a United Church suited to the conditions of each land, a United Church of India, a United Church of China, a United Church of Africa, as well as a United Church of England and a United Church of Scotland? With penitence for our weakening divisions and with full purpose of and endeavour after new obedience to the Spirit's leading, let us in every land press forward steadily and patiently towards the fuller realisation of Christ's prayer for the visible unity of His Church, bearing in mind the truth which that catholic-minded episcopal divine of the seventeenth century, Bishop Stillingfleet, enunciated when he said that "without all controversy the main inlet of all the distractions, confusions and divisions of the Christian Church has been the adding of other conditions of Church connection than Christ Himself hath done "; and convinced that the true way of peace and fuller union among the Churches is that indicated long ago by one Rupertus Meldenius in that saying of his quoted by Richard Baxter in his work entitled *The True and only Way of Concord of all the Christian Churches*, the saying namely, " *In necessariis unitas, in non necessariis libertas, in utrisque caritas* "—" In essentials unity, in non-essentials liberty, in both essentials and non-essentials charity."

THE RT. REV. DR. ADOLF KÜRY
Bishop of the Old Catholic Church of Switzerland

It is obvious that union in the Church cannot involve uniformity in religious and ecclesiastical life. The conception of the Church as the Body of Christ implies that it is a living organism. St. Paul's picture of its manifold character (1 Cor. xii, 4 ff., Rom. xii, 4 ff.) is as applicable to the whole

Church as to a local community. The several members, with their particular functions and tasks, are servants of the whole; each retains his distinct place and character. Nor could any one branch of the Church be asked to make concessions which would involve the compromising or surrender of the special gift which it knows itself to have received.

Such diversity in unity was the mark of the primitive Church. In the apostolic age Jewish and Gentile communities existed side by side. How striking were the contrasts, and how impressively was the unity of the whole expressed in the Pauline collection for the saints at Jerusalem! St. Ignatius of Antioch, an oriental, felt himself to be at one with the western brethren in Rome, although the episcopate was not yet as fully developed in Rome as in Asia Minor. St. Cyprian, the inspired champion of Church unity, claimed for each bishop the right of administrative freedom, on the ground that a bishop was responsible for his official acts to God alone. The great Ecumenical Councils guaranteed the individual rights of provincial churches : and down to A.D.1054 the East and the West were united, although the centre of religious and theological interest lay, for the Easterns in Christology, for the Westerns in soteriology : although the East continued to recognise the collective authority of the episcopate, while the West developed in the direction of a primacy: although Eastern liturgical forms adhered to tradition, while Western liturgies struck out lines of their own.

The reunited Church of the future will be even richer in the manifold variety of the particular Churches within it. They must have assurance that each will be free to place its own gifts at the disposal of the entire body, not as occasions of division, but as energies which will stimulate and enrich other communities in the deepening of their own religious fellowship and life. It must needs be so : for the various ecclesiastical types have their roots in the diversities of national temperament, culture and religious outlook, and these have a claim to be respected. If the Churches of the East, for example, appear to a Western eye to be a unity admitting of no difference, yet closer knowledge reveals how variously the life of religion expresses itself in each Church and people.

It is not for us here and now to lay down a minimum of principles for a united Church. God will give His guidance to men of good will. One thing, however, we can say : Christendom will be near its goal on the day when members of all Churches can approach the same altar, to kneel there with one heart as brothers in the Lord, brought thither not merely by individual sentiment, but by the inward moving of the spirit of their own Church, to celebrate there the sacrificial feast of communion with Christ and the brotherhood, to the glory of God. With our eyes upon this goal, we cannot but see how distant it is, and what obstacles beset the road to it. Yet we know that not all the Churches of the East—still less those of the West—are now in communion with each other. We might well here express the wish that this Conference might bring Churches which are already close to each other to consider the problem of inter-communion more closely. Inter-communion presupposes a mutual recognition of ministries and a common basis of doctrine. These matters, which in the course of controversial history have given rise to apparently irreducible antagonisms, will surely become less acute when they are regarded from the standpoint of inter-communion, of full fellowship in sacred things.

Step by step with this, an important task among the masses of our people in the Churches must be pursued. Even if our Conference does not fulfil all expectations, it certainly has been a first step towards mutual understanding. Different as our views and positions are, we are able to respect, value and understand each other in love, untouched by the virus of controversy. We all feel that in spite of all differences in teaching, worship and order, there are strong links of positive belief which unite us : the difficulty is to find the right expression for them. Let us carry this experience of ours into the Christian fellowships of the whole wide world, to fight down the prejudice, mistrust and ill-feeling which still exist in communities

whose representatives have here met in brotherly intercourse ; let us emphasise what unites us rather than what
divides.

We Catholics are exposed to special prejudices : the
word " catholic " itself awakes much mistrust—perhaps
because it is used as the attribute of one particular Church.
Let us restore the old significance of the word to its due
place of honour, not as merely synonymous with " universal," for Catholics do not simply hold fast to the universal Church, but also regard as essential in faith and
order that which is common to all : it is this that is catholic.
So also with the priesthood. Priests are not mediators
between God and man : we know only one Mediator, Jesus
Christ (1 Tim. ii, 5). Priests are His servants, called to
serve as " examples to the flock " (1 Pet. v, 3) within the
Church : " not that we are lords over your faith, but are
helpers of your joy : for by faith ye stand " (2 Cor. i, 24).
The Holy Mass is no idolatry ; the often-repeated assertion that it is linked with magic and superstition is baseless.
It is to us, with the Gospel, the highest and holiest thing
in the life and religion of the Church. Those who do not
share our faith may criticise as they will what we value,
but we can ask our brethren to respect what to us is holy.

I venture to say these things to you, because our bishops
at Utrecht in 1889 made this declaration : " We trust that
theologians will find a way, while holding fast to the faith
of the undivided Church, towards a real understanding
upon those differences which have arisen since the great
divisions took place. We would urge the clergy who serve
under us to lay primary stress in preaching and teaching
upon those essential Christian verities which the divided
Confessions unite in acknowledging, and, in dealing with
outstanding differences, to avoid inflicting wounds upon
truth and love ; and by word and example to lead the
members of our Churches to treat those who do not share
their faith in the spirit of Jesus Christ who is the Saviour of
us all."

Here is the first task, in preparation for reunion, which
the several Churches must undertake. Not only our leaders,

but the whole Christian people must be filled with the desire for mutual comprehension and reconciliation. There is a word of St. Paul which applies as much to particular Churches as to individual Christians : they should not " think more highly of themselves than they ought to think " (Rom. xii, 3). High and holy as the gifts of any Church may be,it possesses them "in earthen vessels" (2 Cor. iv, 7). To recognise this enables us to treat our separated brethren " with all lowliness and meekness, with long-suffering, forbearing one another in love" (Eph. iv, 2). I would commend, as the first preparation of the Christian people, the people of God's grace and power, the spirit of comprehension, mutual recognition, deep respect and love. It would be well if we could express this spirit in prayer, in a prayer which all the Communions gathered here for common council and supplication could use at Pentecost in all their churches and chapels. The whole Christian people would then experience, in a hallowed hour, what has been so clearly brought home to us, that the spirit of love and understanding unites us all. Thus will it become possible to " give diligence to keep the unity of the Spirit in the bond of peace" (Eph. iv, 3). And may fellowship in prayer prove the first step towards fellowship in kneeling at one and the same altar.

G. F. BARBOUR, D.Phil.
United Free Church of Scotland (Presbyterian)

Mr. President, Fathers and Brethren, it is a great honour for a layman to be called upon to address this historic Conference, representing so large a proportion of the Churches of Christendom, but I could wish it had fallen to some other member—to some one with fuller theological equipment than mine—to speak almost at the close of the varied and memorable series of addresses to which we have listened at our plenary morning sessions.

First, as to the differences which confront us. Those which are significant and which have a real measure of value, may, I think, be traced to two main influences. The first is the passage of time, which alters the thoughts of men far more rapidly than it transforms the face of nature. In our day changes of outlook and custom, which might formerly have occupied a generation or a century, take place in a decade or less ; and to these changes the Church cannot be indifferent. She must adapt the form of her message to the thought of her own age. She must answer *its* questions, not those of an earlier age. Hence it is said that Apologetics is the most rapidly changing branch of theology ; and different Churches necessarily adapt themselves to the circumstances and problems of their times in various ways.

Mingled with these differences due to a changing world, are those due to the other great fact that we live in a varied world. There have always been differences in the Church due to the various temperaments and aptitudes of the races to which the Gospel has successively come. Some have been subtle in intellect, others rich in emotional response, others again predominantly active and energetic. Hence in the early centuries the Greek, Roman and Celtic Churches all showed distinctive and notable marks.

But at this stage of the Conference it is needless to analyse such " varieties of religious experience " and ecclesiastical type. We ourselves form a living museum of such differences as have survived into, or developed in, the twentieth century. The point which I wish rather to make is that these differences are not fortuitous or casual. We should all admit that differences due to the character and endowment of different peoples have a providential origin and that without them " the glory and honour of the nations " cannot be brought into the Holy City (Rev. xxi, 26). But this is no less true of differences brought about by changes in the social and intellectual life of men. As we look upon a wide landscape on a day of sunshine, wind and cloud, our attention is drawn now to one feature— mountain or valley, lake or woodland—and now to another, as the sunlight and shadows pass across the landscape ; but its grand outlines remain the same. So in Christian experience. Certain doctrines—that of the Atonement, for example, or of Immortality—on which Christians of one epoch have dwelt with especial gladness, may take a minor place in the preaching of another land or time. But they have not vanished ; the light has only ceased for the time to fall on them. This may be in part due to failure and forgetfulness on the Church's part. But that is not the only cause. As in the illustration just used, the changes in the aspect of the landscape are due to the action of the free wind upon the clouds of heaven ; so we may believe that the wind of the Spirit controls the attention of the Church and focusses it upon those aspects of truth which have a primary importance for the men and women of a special generation.

If, then, the differences which we see in the universal Church have a providential origin and use, can the same be said of her divisions ? That is one form of the great question which we have been gathered here to answer ; and I do not know of any shorter or better answer than that given by Mr. J. H. Oldham to the great Conference at Birmingham three years ago : " Differences were meant by God, not to divide, but to enrich." Difference ought not to mean division, hostility or even separation. That is surely a great principle to which we have been steadily guided during these last years, and which has resounded through many speeches here at Lausanne.

It does, indeed, represent a radical change from the idea which long prevailed in certain countries, and not least in that from which I come—that only those who think alike and worship according to the same forms can be fellow members in the same Church. That conception of utter uniformity was impossible, and I believe, unchristian. It was a narrow ideal, and it resulted in the multiplication of Churches divided only by narrow boundaries ; whereas the conception that differences are meant for the enrichment of the Christian community has an enlarging effect. Professor Shaw has told us how that influence has been felt in Canada ; and I may also refer to the way in which the Churches of England and of Denmark have been able to contain within their borders widely differing types of piety and schools of theological thought. It may, perhaps, be said that this has been done at the price of occasional strain and tension, but even if this were true it would not give cause for regret, for strain and tension bear witness to life and growth ; complete uniformity, if we could ever attain it, would spell death.

The duty thus laid upon the Church in all her branches to welcome forms of Christian experiences as yet unfamiliar, was clearly stated thirty-six years ago by a voice to which it is our privilege still to listen. In his *Bampton Lectures* Bishop Gore said : " Lest we should be arrogant we need to remember that other ages and other races have caught more readily in our Lord what we ignore—His antagonism to pride or to the selfish assertion of property—and that the whole is not yet told." Dr. Gore went on to foretell the time—now very near, or perhaps already come—when " the existence of really national Churches in India and China and Japan . . . will bring out new and unsuspected aspects of the Christian life."

A word as to practical methods of drawing together in a Christian fellowship, wide enough to include great diversity. Much has necessarily been said in this Conference about unity of belief and doctrine ; but it is good that other avenues to unity have not been forgotten. Especially have the representatives of the Swedish Church, Dr. Lindskog at an earlier session and Archbishop Söderblom to-day, reminded us of the unity that comes through service and through worship ; and to their testimony to the *communio in serviendo ecumenica*, and to the unity in worship experienced at Stockholm, I should like to add mine to the very memorable sense of unity which developed in one short week last August at Helsingfors among 1400 Young Men's Christian Association members gathered from 47 countries. In our present Conference more than one of the Sections has already expressed its sense of the unity of the Church in service, prayer and praise.

As to unity through service—" the cup of cold water,' said Oliver Wendell Holmes, " does not need to be translated for a foreigner to understand it." And regarding unity in worship, we have two auxiliaries at hand which also are independent of translation, and ought to form part of the language of the united Church—Music, and its complement, Silence.

There must, indeed, be wide varieties in the form of worship. We are all loyal to those forms of prayer, those psalms and hymns whose words and music are inseparably linked with our earliest and most sacred memories, and we inevitably wish to pass them on to our children. But we can learn, and are in some measure learning, to value other forms also ; nor can I see why I, as a Presbyterian, should need to go to another Communion to prove the value of silence with the Society of Friends or to take part in the great historic canticles and prayers with the Anglican Church. And in proportion as we add to our own treasured forms of worship, forms borrowed from other branches of the Church, we are insensibly led nearer to a further and fuller unity.

But all this spells liberty—an end hardly less great than unity itself. Those of us who come from the Reformed Churches in particular can never forget the great summons, " Stand fast therefore in the liberty wherewith Christ hath made us free " (Gal. v, 1). This includes the liberty of the whole Christian community to contribute to the common life. The Bishop of Gloucester has rightly emphasised certain special applications of this ideal—educational freedom and the liberty of the local or national Church to determine its relation to the society in which it lives. But within the Church, and especially in the wider borders of a reunited Church, liberty can only exist on the basis of forbearance and charity. Surely the first application of the Golden Rule should be within the Church itself ; and we should allow to others the freedom which we ourselves claim to worship God and to express our loyalty to the Master in the ways most satisfying to our hearts and consciences.

In the sphere of belief this involves that those who find rest in the authority of the Church and in time-honoured expressions of the faith should be very slow to condemn

N

others who feel impelled to find new modes of expression and who may even seem to venture at times into dangerous paths ; while these in their turn should respect those ancient symbols which they may not be able fully to make their own.

So a united Church, strong in love, which "is the bond of perfectness" (Col. iii, 14), might go forward to bring peace to the nations and unity to a distracted world ; might go forward also to that task of intellectual interpretation whose greatness was thus described by a thinker and leader of the Scottish Church, Dr. Robert Rainy : "To take a sufficiently comprehensive view of all the elements ; to gauge and test their relations to one another . . . and to those modes of human thought by which we strive to explain them to ourselves or to one another : this is a great work. And it is a gradual work, in which no man, and no Church, and not the whole Church, is perfect all at once." Yes, a great work ; for tributes of many kinds and from every age are His due of whom it is written : *Ipse enim est pax nostra.*

May I add one final word ? As we gathered this morning we must all have remembered that the first word in the discussion of this theme had been already spoken by a voice from the other side, and in Pastor Hertzberg's message, which came to us so solemnly on Friday, surely we heard not only a summons to unity, but also a note of urgency. The time is short ; be ye also ready!

THE RIGHT REV. PETER HOGNESTAD, D.D.
Bishop of Bergen, Norway (Lutheran)

In Article 7 of the Lutheran *Confessio Augustana* it is said : *Ad veram unitatem ecclesiae satis est consentire de doctrina evangelii et administratione Sacramentorum. Non necesse est ubique esse similes traditiones humanas, seu ritus aut ceremonias ab hominibus institutas. Sicut inquit Paulus : Una fides, unum baptisma, unus Deus et Pater omnium.*" (" For the true unity of the Church it is sufficient to be agreed about the doctrine of the Gospel, and about the administration of the Sacraments. It is not necessary that human traditions should be everywhere the same, or that rites and ceremonies instituted by men should be identical. Thus Paul has said : One faith, one baptism, one God and Father of all.")

It is evident that we Lutherans could not conceive of a single ecclesiastical unit which would do away with all individual Churches and create one uniform Church. On the contrary we think that it is a richer unity which manifests itself in a variety of forms. If it is permissible to use such a parallel, I would ask, " If God is Three in One, why should not His Church be three in one or many in one?"

Where then does unity reside ? In faith. Faith unites, life multiplies. One may use various similes to denote the many Churches which are linked together in a single unity. One may describe them as branches of the same tree. But the most appropriate term is " sister Churches " ; and that name we apply to the Churches which love and respect one another because they belong to one home. How is the love of sisters to be kept alive and caused to grow ? We have to know each other, to visit each other's homes. In Scandinavia we speak of different Churches—the Danish, the Swedish, the Norwegian Church, and so on. But they are all Lutheran sister Churches, and we have a rule that the clergy of other Churches may preach in our pulpits and may even celebrate at the altar. English Churches have often held services for tourists in Norwegian churches. Would it not be possible to extend this exchange ?

The Conference of Lausanne ought to found a common organ, a Church periodical which might be called the *Ecclesia*. It should be brought out in German, English and French, and perhaps also in Greek. Its columns would contain reports from all parts of the whole united Church : things which make for union and also things which bring out the special characteristics of individual Churches. It might publish sermons delivered in different Churches, and also extracts from liturgies, church anthems and hymns.

The effect of these personal visits and the possession of a common organ might be to develop a spirit of emulation in which each Church would seek to give its utmost, not in a spirit of strife, but in the desire to impart its richest spiritual treasures. In the Scandinavian Churches we have learned a great deal from each other through sermons. We have also gained experience of new liturgical forms. If only such a mutual exchange could be carried further! Then we should have a silent reform movement beginning first in one Church and then in another, and perhaps extending to the whole of the united Church. The Church needs reformation just as the individual Christian needs daily penitence.

The deepest form of union in the Church is that effected by the *communio mensae Domini*. This communion should above all be practised here at this Conference. I am aware that certain Churches have met in their church edifices for the Lord's Supper. But I have enquired in vain for a communion service which would be held in common for all of us. I would like to ask my brothers of the Anglican Church, who initiated this movement for a Conference on Faith and Order: Will you not hold a common service for the Lord's Supper here at this Conference? I should feel deeply disappointed if we should have to separate without any such service. I feel indeed that it would be a discredit for this Conference. I am a Lutheran, and I hold the same belief as Luther about the Lord's Supper. For that reason I prefer to communicate in my own Church, and I did so on the last day before leaving Norway. But our Norwegian Church does not see any objection to receiving guests at the Lord's Supper from other denominations. Nor do I feel any objection to being a guest at the Lord's Table in another Church, just as in everyday life I may be a guest in other people's houses, where other customs prevail than in my own home. If a joint Communion service were to be held here according to the Anglican rite I would gladly attend it. I would also attend it if it were held under the Swiss rite. And I believe that in either case Christ would give me what I am glad to believe that He does give us at the Lord's Supper : His own body and His sacred blood. I ask, in the name of Jesus, that we may be one in the *communio mensae Domini*.

We seem to be agreed in desiring a form of unity which will not exclude diversities. We may conceive of this unity as existing in the essence, in the soul of the Church, and the diversities as finding their place in its outward expression. But the soul has its individuality as well as the body ; and therefore we must look deeper and seek the unity in the Spirit, in the Holy Spirit. I believe in the Holy Spirit, in the Holy Catholic Church. That which one believes in is invisible. God who sees the invisible and who knows His own, sees the one Church. But we desire that men and the unbelieving world should also see it ; and therefore we desire a visible unity in faith and in life. It has been said that the way to unity leads through the following stages : federation, union, unity. It is evident that we cannot attain unity at one stride, so we must begin with federation. If it is objected that federation is too loose a bond, I would point to the Swiss Confederation, in whose territory we are now assembled. I have seen here in Lausanne memorials to heroes who fought against the Bernese for the liberty of their Canton. And yet Vaud and Berne are now members of the same Confederation, and as I trust, united by a stedfast and enduring bond.

In a federation we might learn to know one another. Such an end might be promoted by (1) a common organ, a periodical, which we might call the *Ecclesia*; (2) by personal visits and exchanges of divine service ; and (3) by conferences, including special meetings of Churches of the same denomination and general inter-church conferences.

It has been found that it is not always fundamental differences which separate Churches. External usages are more often causes of division than are questions of faith. If the Holy Spirit has now given us a desire for unity we must ask for His guidance that we may learn anew to discern between essentials and non-essentials. And thus a federation will lead us first to a union and finally to unity.

But, at present, we have not reached that point. With deep regret I learned yesterday that we cannot have a common Communion service. The Church of this Canton had given us a fraternal invitation to meet at the Lord's Table Many of us accepted the invitation, but not all of us. I consider that, though I availed myself of it, I have remained a good Lutheran. If there are so many of us who cannot join in such a Communion service, why has the Conference itself not taken steps to organise a service of such a kind that all the members of the Conference could take part in it? The Apostle has exhorted us to show hospitality, but the Churches do not yet manifest enough of this virtue. Can we not learn it anew? If we were to practise full inter-communion I am absolutely convinced that we should gain an increasingly real conception of the Lord's Supper.

If we truly desire to be one in Christian faith do not let us be separated by differences of usage.

The Rev. Dr. GREGOR PERADSE, of the Georgian Church, then spoke briefly as a member, though not an appointed representative, of that Church. He referred to the freedom with which he had been able to study in Germany, Belgium and England without encountering anywhere a proselytising spirit, and asked that the Georgian Church should not be regarded as a field for missionary enterprise from without. It was itself a Church with a real missionary tradition and opportunity in relation to Mohammedans, and would welcome help in the fulfilment of that responsibility. On the other hand it was intensely independent and national, and through its many sufferings had identified itself profoundly with the life of the Georgian people. It would welcome friendship and sympathy from all sides, and assistance in building up an educated priesthood, a task which the destruction of its seminaries had interrupted.

The Conference adjourned at 1 p.m., and the afternoon was devoted to sectional meetings

SECTIONAL SESSIONS

TUESDAY, AUGUST 16TH.

On this day the morning and afternoon were devoted to meetings of Sections V, VI and VII, into which the whole membership of the Conference was divided. These Sections had already held sessions on the afternoons of August 12th, 13th, and 15th. The lists of members are given below:

SECTION V
Subject V : THE CHURCH'S MINISTRY
Convener : THE BISHOP OF GLOUCESTER

Abbott-Smith, Canon
Adelaide, Bishop of
Alivisatos, Prof. H. S.
Andersen, Prof. J. O.
Ankar, Lic. G. A.
Appia, Pastor L.
Bagnell, Dr. R.
Barber, Principal W. T. A.
Barton, Dr. W. E.
Bate, Canon
Bell, Dr. W. C.
Bensow, Dr. O.
Blair, Rev. J. C.
Blake, H.
de Boér, Judge Alexis
Bombay, Bishop of
Brewis, Principal J. T.
Brown, Dr. W. A.
Davey, Prof. J. E.
Deissmann, Prof. A.
Dickey, Prof. S.
Dornakal, Bishop of
Dublin, Archbishop of
Elderdice, President H. L.
Furnajieff, Rev. D. N.
Fyffe, Dr. D.
Garvie, Principal A. E.

Geller, Dr. S.
George, Bishop of
Germanos, Archbishop
Gilmore, Dr. C.
Gogarten, Dr. F.
Gore, Bishop
Greever, Prof. W. H.
Hadorn, Prof. W.
Haenisch, Pastor G.
Hall, Prof. F. J.
Hauge, Pastor S. M.
Heath, Carl
Held, Dr. G.
Herron, Prof. C.
Hinderer, Prof. A.
Holland, Rev. W. E. S.
Honduras, Bishop of
Horne, F. A.
Houghton, Dr. R. M.
Hoyois, Pastor E.
Hume, Dr. R. A.
Inagaki, Prof. Y.
Jenkins, Rev. T.
Jesch, Pastor A.
Kaas, Baron A. von
Kay, Prof. D. M.
Kennink, Archbishop

367

Koren, Rev. L.
Laun, Lic. J. F.
Lehtonen, Dr. Aleksi
Leontopolis, Archbishop of
Lewins, W. A.
Limerick, Bishop of
Lofthouse, Principal W. F.
Marquis, Dr. J. A.
McDowell, Bishop
M'Clymont, Dr. J. A.
Merrill, Dr. W. P.
Milne, Rev. J.
Moore, Dr. T. A.
Mosel, Pastor H. G. W.
Mudge, Dr. L. S.
Naupactos, Metropolitan of
Neiiendam, Dr. M. N.
Nooe, Dr. R. T.
Noyes, Dr. E. M.
Nubia, Archbishop of
Ochiai, Dr. J. K.
Papadopoulos, B. K.
Parker, Rev. G.
Parker, Pastor L-D.
Parsons, Bishop
Peake, Prof. A. S.
Peel, Dr. A.
Pfannenstill, Prof. M.
Piper, Lic. O.
Pröhle, Dr. K.
Pustowka, Rev. O.
Pyke, Rev. R.
Reichel, Sir Harry

Richards, Dr. G. W.
Ritchie, Dr. D. L.
Roper, Bishop
Rose, Rev. I. M.
Roy, Rev. T. S.
Sandegren, Rev. P.
Sands, Lord
Scherer, Dr. M. G. G.
Schian, Gen.-Supt. M.
Scoumperdis, Archimandrite
Selecman, Dr. C. C.
Smith, Rev. F. E.
Smith, Rev. J. C.
Stange, Dr. E.
Steimle, Dr. A.
Stevenson, President J. Ross
Stören, Bishop
Sumitra, Rev. H.
Swartz, President H. F.
Taekema, Rev. P.
Tarafdar, Canon
Thomas, Dr. J. S. L.
Thompson, Prof. E. T.
Thompson, Rev. L. M.
Tinnevelly, Bishop of
Titius, Prof. A.
Walker, Dr. G.
Washburn, Dean H. B.
Williams, Bishop
Wotherspoon, Dr. H. J.
Zarnovicky, Pastor M.
Zoellner, Gen.-Supt. W.

Section VI
Subject *VI* : THE SACRAMENTS
Convener : Bishop Cannon

Armitage, Archdeacon
Ashworth, Dr. R. A.
Bartlet, Prof. J. V.
Bird, Dr. P. S

Bulgakow, Prof. S.
Brilioth, Prof. Y. T.
Brodersen, Pastor P.
Burn, Dean

Burntvedt, Rev. T. O.
Choisy, Prof. J. E.
Clark, Chancellor L. C.
Cochran, Dr. J. W.
Cooper, Rev. A. O.
Davies, Rev. E. O.
Diobouniotis, Prof. C.
Dionisy, Archbishop
Donald, Dr. G. H.
Dysinger, Dr. H.
Elert, Prof. W.
Fisher, Canon
Gardiner, Rev. J. B.
Garrett, Dr. A. E.
Gaugler, Dr. E.
Gerrard, T. L.
Glubokowsky, Prof. N.
Goodall, Rev. C.
Handmann, Prof. R.
Heiler, Prof. F.
Hermelink, Prof. H.
Hindes, Rev. W.
Holden, Rev. A. T.
Hornyanszky, Prof. A.
Hughes, Principal H. M.
Humphries, Prof. A. L.
Jensen, Bishop
Jones, Rev. T. J.
Joyce, Archdeacon
Kelley, Rev. W. M.
Kendrick, Prof. Eliza H.
Klingman, Dr. G. A.
Kortheuer, Bishop
Lang, Prof. August
Lang, Dr. Theodore
Lindskog, Dr. H. J.
Livingstone, W. P.
Lunn, Sir Henry
Lyman, Mrs. A. J.
Macaulay, Rev. J. J.
Maclagan, Dr. P. J.
Manchester, Bishop of

Manning, Bishop
Margetson, Provost W. J.
Martin, Prof. A. von
Master, Dr. H. B.
McConnell, Bishop
Méjan, Pastor F.
Ménégoz, Prof. F.
Mill, W. H.
Moe, Prof. Olaf
Monahan, Rev. A. E.
Monod, Prof. W.
Moore, Bishop
Morehouse, Dr. F. C.
Nash, Bishop
Nectarie, Archbishop
Neuschäfer, Studiendiretkor C.
Norberg, Dr. O.
Nygren, Prof. A.
Paraskevaidis, Dr. T.
Perry, Bishop
Prochazka, Bishop
Prys, Dr. Owen
Quick, Canon
Riley, Athelstan
Robinson, Principal W.
Rogers, Dr. B. T.
Rust, Dr. J. A.
de Saint-André, Pastor L.
Sasse, Lic. H.
Schempp, Direktor J.
Schmitz, Prof. O.
Schoell, Prälat Dr.
Siebel, J. G.
Sigmond, Rev. S. O.
Sills, President K. C. M.
Smiley, Dr. W. B.
Soper, Prof. E. S.
Soucek, Dr. J.
Stefan, Archbishop
Stewart, Dr. G. C.
Stewart, Rev. R. W.
Sturgis, Dr. W. C.

Sydney, Archbishop of
Thompson, President W. O.
Thvedt, Pastor N. B.
Turkevich, Rev. B. J.
Valiadis, Archimandrite

Vance, Dr. J. A.
Vlijmen, Bishop van
Vickrey, C. V.
Watt, Rev. T. M.
Wiseman, Dr. F. L.

Section VII

Subject VII : THE UNITY OF CHRISTENDOM AND THE RELATION THERETO OF EXISTING CHURCHES

Convener : Archbishop Söderblom

Aalders, Prof. W. J.
Ainslie, Dr. Peter
Armagh, Archbishop of
Arseniew, Prof. N.
Atkinson, Dr. H. A.
Aulén, Prof. G.
Baer, Dr. S. H.
Bagnall, T. St. J.
Bagnall, Mrs. Mary A.
Baker, Rev. H. N.
Balakian, Bishop
Balanos, Prof. D. S.
Banninga, Dr. J. J.
Barbour, Dr. G. F.
Barnes, Dr. C. W.
Bates, President M. L.
Bieler, Prof. C.
de Bildt, His Excellency H.
Bond, Dr. A. J. C.
Boyd, Mrs. W.
Brent, Bishop
Bristow, J.
Brown, Dr. A. J.
Budd, Mrs. Elizabeth
Budd, Rev. W. R.
Cole, Dr. E. W.
Comba, Prof. E.
Constantinidis, Archimandrite
Cowden, Rev. J. B.
Davis, Dr. D. A.
Day, Dr. W. H.

Dibelius, Gen.-Supt. O.
Douglas, Canon
Enders, Dean G. C.
Eulogios, Metropolitan
Fabricius, Prof. C.
Fehl, Konsistorialrat A.
Fiero, R. H.
Fisher, Bishop
Forgan, Dr. R.
Fornerod, Prof. A. A.
Fotheringham, Dr. J. T.
Frank, Dr. G.
Gardner, Miss Lucy
Gibson, Theron
Giesecke, Dr. F.
Gounelle, Pastor E.
Gwynne, Bishop
Hagemeyer, Dr. F.
Hamilton, L. A.
Harvey, Rev. F. G.
Haussleiter, Prof. G.
Heard, Bishop
Hognestad, Bishop
Horstmann, Rev. P. F.
Howie, Rev. R. H.
Irbe, Bishop
James, Prof. J. A.
Katz, Pastor P.
Keller, Dr. Adolf
Kennedy, Dean
Klein, Dr. W. F.

Kulp, Rev. E. J.
Küry, Bishop
Lencz, Prof. G.
Leo, Pastor P.
Lew, Dr. T. T.
MacArthur, Rev. K. C.
MacCracken, President J. H.
Machichan, Dr. D.
Macnutt, Archdeacon
Malan, Pastor A.
Mauck, President J. W.
Merle d'Aubigné, Pastor C.
Neander, Dr. H.
Nollen, Dean J. S.
Ohlemüller, Dr. G.
Peradse, Dr. G.
Philputt, Dr. J. M.
Pongràcz, Prof. J.
Reed, Dr. L. T.
Richards, Dr. T. T.
Richmond, Rev. M.
Rosenkjar, Rev. J.
Sanford, Mrs. W. E.
Schenck, Rev. H. W.
Schneider, Prof. F.
Shatford, Canon

Shaw, Prof. J. M.
Siegmund-Schultze, Prof. F.
Simons, Dr. W.
Sjöstedt, Major A.
Sjöstrand, Prof. B.
Slosser, Rev. G. J.
Sommer, Rev. T. W. E.
Stejskal, Bishop
Stevenson, Rev. J. S.
Taranger, Prof. A.
Tatlow, Canon
Turk, Dr. M. H.
Unruh, Prof. B. H.
Verner, Pastor A.
Victoria, Bishop of
Wallau, Lic. R. H.
Western, Canon
Wigham, Dr. J. T.
Wilson, D. M.
Wobbermin, Prof. G.
Woods, Canon
Wright, Rev. H. C.
Zabriskie, G.
Zoch, Bishop
Zwemer, Dr. S. M.

REPORT OF SECTION V

Wednesday Morning, August 17th.

Under the chairmanship of the Rev. W. O. Thompson, D.D., the Conference met in full session in the Aula, opened at 9.30 a.m. with devotions led by the Rev. Pastor Gustave Secretan.

Business of the Conference

It was announced that there would be no afternoon session, the afternoon being reserved for the tour of the lake, to which the Conference had been invited by the Syndic and Municipality of Lausanne ; but that on the following day there would be three sessions, in the morning and afternoon for the consideration of the Reports of Sections VI and VII, and in the evening to discuss the continuance of the Conference's work and to receive the Report of the Continuation Committee.

The President said that the Continuation Committee appointed at Geneva in 1920 had now finished its work, in bringing about the present Conference. It was therefore necessary to form another Continuation Committee. He therefore appointed the following to draw up a list of thirty names which would form a nucleus of the new Committee, which, on appointment, should be given power to add to its number : Lord Sands (Convener), Prof. Alivisatos, Dr. Bagnell, Prof. Brilioth, Canon Woods, Dr. Martin Dibelius, Dr. Keller.

Memorial by the Women Delegates to the Conference

The following Memorial was then presented by Miss Lucy Gardner :

In this great Conference assembled to try to discover the will of God for His Church, it has been laid upon the hearts of the women delegates to ask the Conference to realise the significance of the fact that out of nearly 400 delegates only seven are women. We do not wish to raise any discussion on the subject, but we believe that the right place of women in the Church and in the councils of the Church is one of grave moment, and should be in the hearts and minds of all.

In the great fight to bring light unto the dark places of the world, as well as for the upbuilding of the Church, it is essential that all

available power at her command be used, and to every member of
the Church must be allotted his or her right work and right position
of responsibility.

The signatories of this document make no claim to state what is
the right place of women in the Church, and in fact not all of them
are agreed on all points. But on one they are agreed—that this is a
matter that cannot be decided either by men or by women alone.
It is not for women to claim and for men to give, but as the Church
unitedly sets out on a quest for deeper spiritual unity, we believe
that in this matter also we shall unitedly see fresh light and a fresh
revelation of God's will.

Some outcome of this Conference there must be, some mission of
evangelisation undertaken as we realise afresh the precious healing
of the Gospel of Jesus Christ for the sin and sorrows of the world—
of the great multitude, as Dr. Ainslie reminded us, "slowly turning
away from the Church."

We believe that the call must go out from this Conference to all
men and women alike, for faithfulness in giving the message, lest
the differing gifts and opportunities be unused.

At this hour in the Conference we do not ask that this, one of the
problems of "Order," be discussed. We do ask the prayers of all,
that the gifts of women as of men may be offered and used to the
full in the great task that lies before us—that of the evangelisation
of world through a Church united.

Signed :

Eliza H. Kendrick	Lucy Gardner
Elizabeth Hill Lyman	Mary A. Bagnall
H. S. Sanford	Elizabeth Budd

Declaration by Members of the Lutheran Communion

The following declaration by members of the Conference belonging
to the Lutheran Communion was read in German by General
Superintendent Dr. Zoellner, in English by the Rev. Dr. Steimle,
and in French by the Rev. Pastor Louis Appia :

Members of this Conference, who belong to the Evangelical
Lutheran Communion, desire to lay before the Conference the
following declaration :

Our participation in this Conference proves more than any statement could do how deeply we deplore the divisions in the Church
and how profoundly we feel the need of unity among Christians. As
Evangelical Lutherans we feel it to be our sacred duty to labour for

the unity of the Church in faith and hope, and especially in this day of dire need, in serving love to mankind. Of course, according to our Confessions, it is not necessary to the unity of the Church that human traditions, rites or ceremonies, should be everywhere alike, but this unity consists in agreement concerning the doctrine of the Gospel and the administration of the sacraments.

To give accurate expression to the existing spiritual unity is, of course, possible only in the direction pointed out by the Ecumenical Creeds. It is a large task, whose difficulty must not deter us, but which we dare not take lightly. The current discussions are, in large part, important and illuminating, and we desire that they may continue to the end of the Conference. But we question whether it is possible, and whether it comports with the dignity of this Conference and is worthy of Christendom, to announce at once as finalities the formulations here made on fundamental principles of faith and order.

It is therefore our judgment that the Conference should in its public proclamation strongly express the great significance of this gathering, that deep spiritual unity which we recognise with gratitude to God, the serious will to unity which prevails, and the value and necessity of thorough and fraternal discussion in continuance of the labours here begun.

Accordingly no final vote should be taken on the propositions formulated here. They should be added to the proclamation as material for further consideration.

In order to secure a thorough and adequate consideration and to give the desired effect to the labours of this Conference, the whole material should also be referred to a small commission composed of trusted representatives of the various groups, namely the Orthodox, the Evangelical Lutherans, the Reformed and the Presbyterians (Calvinist), the Anglicans, the Methodists, the Baptists, the Congregationalists, etc. This commission should be charged with the duty carefully to examine these propositions in the light of the discussions during this Conference and to set forth the points of agreement and difference in doctrine and practice.

Commissions should also be appointed in the various Communions in order to give thorough study to the propositions and report to the joint commission, which should submit the results of its labours to a future conference.

In behalf of a Meeting of Evangelical Lutheran members of the Conference:

LOUIS APPIA, Inspecteur Ecclésiastique, Paris.

PETER HOGNESTAD, Bishop of Bergen[1]

KARL IRBE, Bishop of the Lutheran Church in Latvia.

M. G. G. SCHERER, Secretary of the United Lutheran Church in America.

D. DR. SCHOELL, Prälat in Stuttgart.

NATHAN SÖDERBLOM, Archbishop of Upsala.

A. STEIMLE, Pastor, New York, United Lutheran Church in America.

W. ZOELLNER, D. General Superintendent, Münster i.Westf.

Preamble to the Reports

The PRESIDENT recalled that it had been proposed that the President of the Conference should attempt to provide a Preamble preceding all the Reports. With the invaluable aid of Dr. FRANCIS HALL, the Bishop of BOMBAY, and the Lutheran members who had presented their statement, he had drawn up, somewhat roughly, such a preamble. If the proposals contained therein met the Conference's approval, he would proceed to draft it in final form.

The following is the text of the preliminary draft :

We, the representatives of many Christian communions throughout the world, assembled to consider, under the guidance of the Holy Spirit, the things wherein we agree and the things wherein we differ, receive the following series of Reports as containing subject-matter for the consideration of our respective Churches in their common search for unity. Each subject was first discussed in plenary session. It was then committed to one of the three sections into which the whole Conference was divided for the purpose. The report was finally drawn up and adopted by the section to which it had been committed. It was twice presented for further discussion to a plenary session of the Conference when it was referred to the Churches in its present form.

Though we recognise the Reports to be neither exhaustive, adequate, nor in all details satisfactory to every member of the Conference, we submit them to the Churches for that deliberate consideration which could not be given in the brief period of the Conference. We further recommend that the whole material should be referred to a small Commission of qualified men representative of the various groups—Orthodox, Evangelical Lutheran, Presbyterian, Methodist, Anglican, etc.—and charged with the duty care-

---

[1] The other Norwegian delegates desire a vote of the Conference on the other Subjects, but not on the Church (Subject III), the Ministry (Subject V) or Sacraments (Subject VI).

fully to examine these propositions in the light of the discussions and to report thereon to the Churches.

Where the Reports record differences, we call the Christian world to an earnest reconsideration of the conflicting opinions now held, and a strenuous endeavour to find the truth as it is in God's mind, which should be the foundation of the Church's union.

The President was invited to complete this draft and to submit it again to the Conference. [The final form of the Preamble will be found on p. 460.]

Report of Section V presented

The Bishop of GLOUCESTER, in presenting the Report of Section V, on The Church's Ministry, said:

Before reading this Report there are a few remarks I want to make. In the first place, I should like to say that in my opinion you have entrusted us with an extraordinarily difficult task to accomplish in a very short time. We have produced the best we could under the circumstances, but we could not have produced anything at all if it had not been for the happy and friendly way in which the whole Section worked, everyone contributing all that he could to make our work as good as was possible.

Secondly, it is an agreed Report, but I must explain in what way it is an agreed Report. At the beginning of the Conference some people thought they were defining terms for the reunion of Christendom; others, that they were engaged upon making a statement of the Christian faith as they accepted it. Neither of these purposes, as we understood it, were before us. Our purpose was to explore lines of unity and to submit suggestions for the consideration of the Churches, so that this Report does not give exactly what each person thinks, but gives what we all think ought to be put before the Churches as lines of investigation.

In accordance with that idea, the Report divides itself into sections. It begins with a section on the nature of the ministry, which is, I think, agreed to; it passes on to consider the difficulties of the situation, giving a short summary of the various opinions held, and puts forward suggestions for the consideration of the Churches, concluding with the statement that far more study than we have been able to give it is necessary for settling these very difficult questions.

The Bishop of Gloucester then moved that the Report be received by the Conference. The following is the text of the Report as thus presented:

REPORT OF SECTION V, FIRST DRAFT

I

The representatives of the Churches here assembled are happy to report that they find themselves in substantial accord in the following five propositions :

1. The ministry is a gift of God through Christ to His Church, and is essential to the being and well-being of the Church.

2. The ministry is perpetually authorised and made effective through Christ and His Spirit.

3. The purpose of the ministry is to impart to men the saving and sanctifying benefits of Christ through pastoral service, the preaching of the Gospel, and the administration of the sacraments, to be made effective by faith.

4. The ministry is entrusted with a government and a discipline of the Church, in whole or in part.

5. Men gifted for the work of the ministry, called by the Spirit, and accepted by the Church, are commissioned through an act of ordination by prayer and the laying on of hands to exercise the functions of this ministry.

II

Within the many Christian Communions into which in the course of history Christendom has been divided, various forms of ministry have grown up according to the circumstances of these several Communions and their beliefs as to the mind of Christ and the guidance of the New Testament. These Communions have been, in God's providence, manifestly and abundantly used by the Holy Spirit in His work of " enlightening the world, converting sinners, and perfecting saints." But the differences which have arisen in regard to the authority and functions of these various forms of ministry have been and are the occasion of manifold doubts, questions and minsunderstandings.

In this way the difficulties of inter-communion have been accentuated, to the distress and wounding of faithful souls ; while in the mission field, where the Church is fulfilling its primary object to preach the Gospel to every creature, the young Churches find the lack of unity a very serious obstacle to the furtherance of the Gospel. Consequently, the provision of a ministry acknowledged in every part of the Church as possessing the sanction of the whole Church is an urgent need.

III

We now pass to the differences above alluded to :

A.—The following is the view of the Orthodox Church:

The Orthodox Church, regarding the ministry as instituted in the Church by Christ Himself and as the body which, by a special *charisma*, is the organ through which the Church spreads its means of grace such as the sacraments, and believing that the ministry in its threefold form of bishops, presbyters, and deacons cannot be based except only on the unbroken apostolic succession, regrets that it is unable to come, in regard to the ministry, into some measure of agreement with many of the Churches represented at this Conference ; but prays God that He through His Holy Spirit will guide to union, even in regard to this difficult point of disagreement.

B.—In Western Christendom also there are conspicuous differences. One representative view includes the following points :

(*a*) That there have always been various grades of the ministry, each with its own function.

(*b*) That ordination is a sacramental act of divine institution, and therefore indispensable, conveying the special *charisma* for the particular ministry.

(*c*) That bishops who have received their office by succession from the Apostles are the necessary ministers of ordination.

(*d*) That the apostolic succession so understood is necessary for the authority of the ministry, the visible unity of the Church, and the validity of the sacraments.

C.—On the other hand it is held in many Churches represented in the Conference :

(*a*) That essentially there is only one ministry, that of the Word and Sacraments.

(*b*) That the existing ministries in these Churches are agreeable to the New Testament, are proved by their fruits and have due authority in the Church, and the sacraments ministered by them are valid.

(*c*) That no particular form of ministry is necessary to be received as a matter of faith.

D.—Further we record that there are views concerning the ministry which are intermediate between the types just mentioned. For instance, some who adhere to an episcopal system of church government do not consider that the apostolic succession as described above is a vital element of episcopacy, or reject it altogether ; and some who adhere to presbyteral and congregational systems of church government believe that the apostolic ministry is transmissible and has been transmitted through presbyters.

IV

Certain suggestions as to possible church organisation have been made, which we transmit for the consideration of the Churches :

1. In view of the place which the episcopate, the councils of presbyters, and the congregation of the faithful, respectively, had in the constitution of the early Church ;

2. And in view of the fact that episcopal, presbyteral and congregational order are each to-day, and have been for centuries, accepted by great communions in Christendom ;

3. And in view of the fact that episcopal, presbyteral and congregational order are each believed by many to be essential in the order of the Church, therefore, we recognise that these several elements must all, under conditions which require further study, have an appropriate place in the order of life of a reunited Church, and that each separate Communion, recalling the abundant blessing of God vouchsafed to its ministry in the past, should gladly bring to the common life of the united Church its own spiritual treasures.

If the foregoing suggestion be accepted and acted upon, it is essential that the acceptance of any special form of ordination as the regular and orderly method of introduction into the ministry of the Church for the future should not be interpreted to imply the acceptance of any one particular theory of the origin, character or function of any office in the Church, or to involve the acceptance of any adverse judgment on the validity of ordination in those branches of the Church universal that believe themselves to have retained valid and apostolic orders under other forms of ordination, or as disowning or discrediting a past or present ministry of the Word and Sacrament which has been used and blessed by the Spirit of God.

It is further recognised that inasmuch as the Holy Spirit is bestowed upon every believer, and each believer has direct and immediate access to God through Jesus Christ, and since special gifts of the Holy Spirit, such as teaching, preaching, and spiritual counsel, are the treasures of the Church as well as of the individual, it is necessary and proper that the Church should make full use of such gifts for the development of its corporate spiritual life, and for the extension of the Kingdom of Jesus Christ our Lord.

There has been no time in this Conference to consider all the points of difference between us in the matter of the ministry with that care and patience which could alone lead to complete agreement. The same observation applies equally to proposals for the constitution of the united Church. But we are not content to leave these statements of differences and proposals without expressing the hope that common study of these questions will be pursued by members of the various Churches represented in this Conference, and will produce results most advantageous to the cause of union.

VI

In conclusion, we should express our thankfulness to Almighty God for the great progress which has been made in recent years for the mutual approach of the Churches to one another, and our conviction that we must go forward with faith and courage, confident that with the blessing of God we shall be able to solve the problems that lie before us.

In particular we share in the conviction—repeatedly expressed in this Conference—that pending the solution of the questions of faith and order in which present agreements have not yet been reached, it is possible for us, not simply as individuals but as Churches, to unite in the activities of brotherly service which Christ has committed to His disciples. We therefore commend to our Churches the consideration of the steps which may be immediately practicable to bring an existing unity in service to more effective expression.

Discussion

The Rev. Dr. W. E. BARTON, speaking in favour of the reception of the Report, said that he wished to say a word for his own Communion—so far as he had any right to represent it—and he believed his view represented that of a very large body of Christians and Christian Churches in the United States.

Leaving on one side the powerful Roman Catholic Church, there were about 27 million communicants in the Churches in the United States, of whom roughly one million were Episcopalians. The remainder (about 26 millions) went freely into each other's pulpits, received members from them and sent members to them, and there existed among them a certain bond of fellowship which they wished their brothers of the Episcopal Church might more fully share.

It was not because their Churches felt themselves unworthy or possessed of an inadequate ministry that they were represented at the Conference, nor could the Report be presented to them on any such basis. It must be presented to them—and he begged the Conference's forgiveness in putting the matter bluntly—as a needless and almost unreasonable concession made to satisfy what, from the point of view of their people, was a prejudice founded upon nothing that could be found in the Scriptures, but to which they were willing to lend themselves, without negation, in order to further the cause of unity.

The Rev. Pastor APPIA said that while this Report represented on the whole the convictions of the greater Churches, he would wish to speak on behalf of other bodies. He would ask what would be the Lutheran or Reformed opinion of such a Report. There would be some resistance to the introduction of the idea of the episcopate : to many, the possibility of a non-Roman episcopate had never presented itself. The Report would throw a new light upon this situation. Secondly, it would serve the purpose of showing that some important non-episcopal Churches had been led to envisage the possibility and the utility, in the cause of reunion, of an episcopate such as would not involve any renunciation of their basal principles. Thirdly, it would show that for the Orthodox and Anglican Churches this was not a question of expediency but of principle, and of the removal of a serious barrier to unity ; that those Churches had made very remarkable advances from their side ; and that the vision, now dawning, of the integral and visible unity of Christ's Church, was a great contribution to the spiritual treasure of Christendom, a contribution through which the Anglican communion had earned the gratitude of other Churches.

The following suggestions upon the Report were brought forward : By the Rev. J. C. BLAIR, that the explicit reference to differences in paragraph III should be deleted; by the Rev. L. S. MUDGE, that the following should be inserted in paragraph III D: " Those who adhere to the presbyterian system of church government believe that the apostolic ministry is transmissible and has been transmitted through presbyters orderly associated for the purpose;" by the Rev. W. E. BARTON, that the following be attached to the words suggested by Dr. Mudge : " Those who adhere to the congregational system of government are careful to define their ministry as having been and being transmitted, according to the precedent and example of the New Testament, through presbyters perpetuating a valid episcopate, and to be possessed of full validity and apostolic authority;" by Bishop FISHER, that in paragraph III D, after the words " described above," the words " or the historic episcopate are vital elements," should be inserted; by Dr. BARTON (with general assent), that in the first line of paragraph VI the word " should " should be deleted.

These suggestions were referred to the Drafting Committee, and the Report as a whole was received. The session closed, with devotions and the singing of a hymn, at 12.30 p.m.

REPORTS OF SECTIONS VI AND VII

Thursday Morning, August 18th.

The Conference met in full session, morning, afternoon and evening. The morning session opened at 9.30 with devotions led by the Rev. Canon Woods, the chairman being the Rev. Dr. Garvie.

The President expressed the gratitude of the Conference to the Syndic and Municipality of the city for their hospitality in arranging a tour of the lake on the previous day, and undertook to send them a written message of thanks.

Presentations to Bishop Brent, Archbishop Söderblom and Professor Monod

On behalf of the syndical Commission of the National Church of Vaud, Professor Fornerod, of the University of Lausanne, Chairman of the Comité de Réception, presented to Bishop Brent, Archbishop Söderblom and Professor Wilfred Monod, copies of the Liturgy in use in the pulpit of Lausanne Cathedral, in remembrance of the discourses delivered by them in the Cathedral on August 3rd and 14th, and of the choice of the city of Lausanne for the meeting-place of the World Conference. Professor Fornerod spoke in cordial terms of the stirring messages delivered by Bishop Brent and Archbishop Söderblom, as also of the close kinship between French and Swiss Protestants of which Professor Monod's discourse was a symbol. The gifts presented by him were warmly acknowledged by the recipients.

The Archbishop of Syria offered to the Conference the greetings of the ancient Orthodox Patriarchate of Antioch, a Church whose history, he said, went back to the very beginnings of Christianity ; it was in the province of Syria that our Lord Himself was born. He commended the Conference to the peace and grace of God.

Declaration on behalf of the Eastern Orthodox Church

The Rt. Rev. Archbishop Germanos, Metropolitan of Thyateira, then presented to the Conference the following declaration, in English, on behalf of the delegates from the Orthodox Church :

Brethren, on receiving the invitation of the Organising Committee of the World Conference on Faith and Order seven years ago, the

Orthodox Church answered readily by sending representatives from her particular Orthodox Churches to the preliminary Conference in 1920 at Geneva. That delegation of the Orthodox Church put before the Conference a united declaration in general terms of the teaching of their Church in the matter of faith and order and at its conclusion recommended that before any discussion of the reunion of the Churches in faith and order, a League of Churches should be established for their mutual co-operation in regard to the social and moral principles of Christendom. Further, when the Orthodox Church was invited a short time ago to take part through her representatives in the present Conference, although many of her particular Churches are in distress so grave as to threaten their very existence, she hastened to send her delegations to it.

Accordingly, we, the undersigned, delegates of the Orthodox Church, being inspired by a sincere feeling of love and by a desire to achieve an understanding, have taken part in every meeting held here for the purpose of promoting closer brotherhood and fellowship between the representatives of the different Churches and for the general good and welfare of the whole body of Christians. But while sharing the general labours of the Conference both in delivering addresses as arranged in the programme and in taking part in the open debates, as also in the work of the Sections, we have concluded with regret that the bases assumed for the foundation of the Reports which are to be submitted to the vote of the Conference, are inconsistent with the principles of the Orthodox Church which we represent.

Therefore, we judge it to be a matter of conscience that with the exception of the first we must abstain from voting in favour of the two Reports which are now ready. Although both in the papers read, in speeches, in debate and in statements made in the three Sections, we Orthodox have already made plain and clear what are the points of view and the conceptions of the Orthodox Church in regard to the subjects under discussion, we hold it to be of importance that we should specify here certain points in order to make manifest the differences which separate us from other members of the Conference. For example, while the Report on the Message of the Church, since it is drafted on the basis of the teaching of the Holy Scripture, is in accordance with the Orthodox conception and can be accepted by us, it is otherwise with the two other Reports, on the Nature of the Church and upon the Common Confession of the Faith of the Church. The drafting of these two latter was carried out on a basis of compromise between what in our understanding are conflicting ideas and meanings, in order to arrive at an external agreement in the letter alone : whereas, as has often at other times been emphasised in statement by representatives of the Orthodox Church, in matters of faith and conscience there is room for no compromise. For us, two different meanings cannot be covered by, and two different concepts cannot be deduced from, the same words of a generally agreed statement. Nor can we Orthodox hope that an agreement reached upon such statements would remain lasting.

That the drafting committees have realised the existence of this disagreement is apparent from many of the notes which they have placed in the Reports and which leave full liberty upon matters which at least we Orthodox hold to be fundamental. Thus for example, we Orthodox cannot conceive a united Church in which some of its members would hold that there is only one source of divine revelation, namely, Holy Scripture alone, but others would affirm that apostolic tradition is the necessary completion of Holy Scripture. While the full freedom so accorded in the Report to each Church to use its own confession of faith would make those confessions of indifferent value in themselves, on the other hand, nothing but confusion as to the one common conception of *the* Faith of the so united single Church could arise.

The Orthodox Church adheres fixedly to the principle that the limits of individual liberty of belief are determined by the definitions made by the whole Church, which definitions we maintain to be obligatory on each individual. This principle holds good for us not only as to the present members of the Orthodox Church, but also as to those who, in future, may become united with it in faith and order. Moreover, the symbols which would be accepted by the united Church acquire their importance (in our conception as Orthodox) not only from the fact of their being historical witnesses of the faith of the primitive Church, but above all because the Church has affirmed their validity in her Ecumenical Councils. It should be unnecessary for us to add that the Orthodox Church recognises and accepts as an Ecumenical Symbol only the Creed of Nicea-Constantinople.

That which holds good for us in regard to the Ecumenical Symbol, holds good also in regard to the dogmatic definitions of the Seven Ecumenical Councils, the authority of which no Orthodox would be justified in shaking.

Therefore the mind of the Orthodox Church is that reunion can take place only on the basis of the common faith and confession of the ancient, undivided Church of the seven Ecumenical Councils and of the first eight centuries.

Although the Reports of the other three Sections are not yet to hand, the process of debate upon them makes it evident that agreement on them can be reached only by vague phrases, or by a compromise of antithetical opinions. Thus, for example, we cannot conceive how agreement can be made possible between two conceptions which agree that the existence of the ministry of the Church is by the will of Christ, but differ as to whether that ministry was instituted by Christ Himself in its three degrees of bishop, priest and deacon. In the same way we judge there to be no practical value in an agreed formula as to the necessity of sacraments in the Church when there is a fundamental difference between the Churches not only in regard to their number but also as to their general significance, as to their particular essential nature and as to their particular effects.

This being so, we cannot entertain the idea of a reunion which is confined to a few common points of verbal statement ; for according to the Orthodox Church, where the totality of the faith is absent there can be no *communio in sacris*.

Nor can we here apply that principle of economy which in the past the Orthodox Church has applied under quite other circumstances in the case of those who came to her with a view to union with her.

In consequence, while we, the undersigned Orthodox representatives, must refrain from agreeing to any Reports other than that upon the Message of the Church, which we accept and are ready to vote upon, we desire to declare that in our judgment the most which we can now do is to enter into co-operation with other Churches in the social and moral sphere on a basis of Christian love. Further, we desire to add that as Orthodox Delegates we should view a partial reunion of those Churches which share the same principles with satisfaction as a precedent to general reunion, inasmuch as it would thus be easier for our Orthodox Church to discuss reunion with the Churches which had so united into a single Church and had a single faith, than with many Churches with different faiths.

In making it plain that we have arrived at our decision only in obedience to the dictates of our conscience, we beg to assure the Conference that we have derived much comfort here from the experience that, although divided by dogmatic differences, we are one with our brethren here in faith in our Lord and Saviour Jesus Christ. Declaring that in the future we shall not cease to devote ourselves to labour for the closer approach of the Churches, we add that we shall pray to God without ceasing that by the operation of His Holy

Spirit He will take away all existing hindrances and will guide us to that unity for which the Founder and Ruler of the Church prayed to His heavenly Father : " that they all may be one as we are one."

We close with the intercession that our Lord will richly give His blessing to one and all who labour in sincerity and in His fear for the establishment of His kingdom among men.

Delegates from the Ecumenical Patriarchate : Archbishop of Thyateira, GERMANOS ; Archimandrite MICHAEL CONSTANINIDIS ; Dr. PARASKEVAIDIS, Archimandrite ; C. VALIADIS, Archimandrite.

The Patriarchate of Alexandria : CHRISTOPHOROS, Archbishop of Leontopolis ; NICOLAS, Archbishop of Nubia.

The Patriarchate of Jerusalem : KALLINICOS, Archimandrite ; BENEDICTOS, Deacon.

Archbishopric of Cyprus and the Church of Greece : AMBROSIOS, Metropolitan of Naupactos ; CONSTANTINE DIOBOUNIOTIS ; H. ALIVISATOS ; D. S. BALANOS.

The Patriarchate of Serbia : IRINEY, Bishop of Novi Sad.

The Patriarchate of Roumania : NECTARIE, Archbishop of Cernauti and Metropolitan of Bukovina.

The Church of Bulgaria : Proto-presbyter Prof. Dr. STEFAN ZANKOW ; Professor NICHOLAS GLUBOKOWSKY, D.D.

The Church of Poland : DIONISY, Metropolitan of Warsaw and all Poland ; Archpriest BENEDICT J. TURKEVICH ; Dr. NICOLAS ARSENIEW.

Russian Delegates : EULOGIOS, Metropolitan of the Russian Church in Western Europe ; Archpriest Prof. Dr. SERGIUS BULGAKOW.

Georgian Delegate : Dr. GREGORY PERADSE.

THE CHAIRMAN : We sympathise with our Orthodox brethren in their difficulty and appreciate most sincerely the tone in which this declaration has been offered to us, and we welcome with great thankfulness the indication of their desire as far as possible to continue in spiritual unity with us. It is too great an issue for me to venture to say anything about it, and I will call upon the President of the Conference, Bishop Brent, to indicate what seems to him the proper course of action.

BISHOP BRENT : A Conference such as ours, which pays mutual deference to the consciences of all present, cannot take any exception to the statement made on behalf of the Eastern Orthodox brethren by Archbishop Germanos.

We appreciate his frankness, but I would point out the fact that the paper is but a declaration of the manner in which the Orthodox Church will act with regard to the Reports when finally presented, and being such—and in this Archbishop Germanos agrees with me—there should be no discussion of it. I should, however, like to point out one or two things :

In the first place, this Conference was not called to provide a sufficient basis for unity in its first inception ; it was stated clearly that it was to be a Conference in which both agreements and disagreements were to be carefully noted, and we thank our Orthodox brethren for making so distinct the differences which prevent them from taking a more positive position in relation to the Reports. We thank them because we are now in a position to consider the stand they take with more clearness than we could otherwise have done.

I would further say that in our Reports we have tried to be frank, and have tried to avoid compromise. We have given the Eastern Orthodox every opportunity to express their differences. They have expressed them to a certain extent, and we are glad to have their statements incorporated in the Reports in the final form in which I believe this assembly will receive them. But their further statement gives us a large responsibility, and we only hope that they will study the positions which are contrary to their own position with the same earnestness and lack of prejudice that the balance of the Conference will study their position.

I do not think it is necessary for me to say anything more. This is not a Conference that aims at a complete agreement, and there can only be a complete agreement reached when everyone faces the convictions of others with honesty, and we congratulate our Orthodox brethren on the frankness with which they have made their statement, because I recognise that it is an extremely difficult thing to take the position which they have taken and which I will say they have taken with great grace.

THE CHAIRMAN : The matter now before the Conference was not on the agenda for to-day, but Bishop Brent and myself felt it to be a matter of such importance that it was due to our Orthodox brethren that they should have an opportunity of bringing the matter forward now. It does seem to me, however, that it would be a departure from the proper order of business if we were to engage in any discussion of it at the present stage. The proper occasion for such a discussion would be at the time of the discussion on Report VII or when we are debating the question of the reception of the various Reports.

Continuation Committee

The following list of names, drawn up by the Nominating Committee as a nucleus for the new Continuation Committee, was then presented by Lord SANDS, who said that the list was intended as a basis for enlargement, and that the question of substitutes would be left to the new Committee :

Rt. Rev. CHARLES H. BRENT, D.D.
GEORGE ZABRISKIE, D.C.L.
Rev. PETER AINSLIE, D.D.
Dr. HAMILCAR ALIVISATOS.
Rev. ROBERT A. ASHWORTH, D.D.
Rev. HENRY A. ATKINSON, D.D.
Rev. Canon H. N. BATE, M.A.
Rt. Rev. the BISHOP OF BOMBAY.
Rev. Bishop JAMES CANNON, Jr., D.D.
Judge ALEXIS DE BOER, LL.D.
Prof. Dr. ADOLF DEISSMANN.
Prof. Dr. WERNER ELERT.
Miss LUCY GARDNER.
Rev. ALFRED E. GARVIE, D.D.
Most Rev. ARCHBISHOP GERMANOS.
Rt. Rev. PETER HOGNESTAD, D.D.
Rt. Rev. IRINEY, Bishop of Novi Sad.
Rev. ADOLF KELLER, D.D.
Rt. Rev. Dr. ADOLF KURY.
Sir HENRY LUNN, M.D.
Rt. Rev. WILLIAM T. MANNING, D.D.
Rev. Bishop FRANCIS J. McCONNELL, D.D.
Rev. WILFRED MONOD, D.D.
Rev. T. ALBERT MOORE, D.D.
Rt. Rev. HARALD OSTENFELD, D.D.
Rev. J. E. ROBERTS, D.D.
Hon. LORD SANDS, LL.D.
Rev. M. G. G. SCHERER, D.D.
Prof. FRIEDRICH SIEGMUND-SCHULTZE, D.D.
Rev. P. CARNEGIE SIMPSON, D.D.
Most Rev. NATHAN SÖDERBLOM, D.D.
Most Rev. METROPOLITAN STEFAN.
Rev. J. ROSS STEVENSON, D.D.
Rev. F. LUKE WISEMAN, M.A.
Rev. Canon EDWARD S. WOODS, M.A.

Report of Section VI presented

The Conference then passed to the consideration of the Report of Section VI, which was presented by Bishop CANNON in the following terms :

The Section of the Conference appointed to prepare the draft of the statement on the Sacraments met on Friday afternoon, August 12th, and organised by the election of Bishop James Cannon, Jr., Chairman ; Vice-Chairman, Dr. F. L. Wiseman ; Joint Secretaries, Canon O. C. Quick, Dr. Eugène Choisy and Lic. H. Sasse.

The Section had helpful illuminating general discussions on Friday and Saturday afternoons. Afterwards four groups were formed of approximately twenty each, under the respective chairmanships of Bishop Manning, Dr. Vernon Bartlet, Dr. Hermelink and Dr. E. S. Soper. These four groups held meetings on Monday and again on Tuesday, and each group appointed a drafting committee of three. The four drafting committees prepared separate reports and then the four committees met together with the officers and prepared a report which was submitted to the full Section on Tuesday afternoon, which discussed the report for about three hours, after which the whole question was then committed to a drafting committee of nineteen which was fairly representative of all the varying views. This Committee held two lengthy meetings at which the difficult questions involved were fully discussed with great frankness. But while there were statements made setting forth the most widely divergent views on some points (for it must be remembered that the Section contained bishops of the Greek Church and members of the Society of Friends) there was the most delightful spirit manifested in all the discussions, and while neither the Chairman not any member of the Committee delivered any exhortation on brotherly love, it was evident from the beginning to the end that the members of the Committee in the statement of their honest convictions were governed by the apostolic exhortations, " let love be without dissimulation " and " speaking the truth in love ; " which exhortations to frank, positive, loving speech having been followed with interest and profit, the further exhortation " let brotherly love continue " was followed to the end. While emphasising the limitations put upon its work by the shortness of time and the widely divergent views mentioned above, your Committee presents this report as a result of earnest discussion, meditation and prayer, hoping that it may prove to be a real contribution to the cause of Christian unity, the spirit of which unity dominated all its labours.

Moreover, the fact that there is this divergence of conception and interpretation on some points pertaining to the Sacraments surely must not be permitted to retard or to hinder in any way the continued growth of co-operative activity by the various denominations or Churches in applying the teachings of Jesus Christ to the redemption of both the individual and the entire social order throughout the world.

The Committee respectfully requests that following the reading of the Report, Dr. Wilfred Monod be given an opportunity of presenting a brief statement of his views, which were heard with interest and profit by the Committee.

The following is the text of the Report as thus presented :

REPORT OF SECTION VI, FIRST DRAFT

1. We are convinced that for the purpose in view in this Conference, we should not go into detail in considering Sacraments—by some called "Mysteries." The purpose therefore of this statement is to show that there may be a common approach to and appreciation of Sacraments on the part of those who may otherwise differ in conception and interpretation.

2. We testify to the fact that the Christian world gives evidence of an increasing sense of the significance and value of Sacraments, and would express our belief that this movement should be fostered and guided as a means of deepening the life and experience of the Churches. In this connection we recognise that the Sacraments have special reference to the corporate life and fellowship of the Church and that the grace is conveyed by the Holy Spirit, taking of the things of Christ and applying them to the soul.

3. We agree that Sacraments are of divine appointment and that the Church ought thankfully to observe them as divine gifts.

4. We hold that in the Sacraments there is an outward sign and an inward grace, and that the Sacraments are means of grace through which God works invisibly in us. We recognise also that in the gifts of His grace God is not limited by His own Sacraments.

5. The Orthodox Church and others hold that there are seven Sacraments and that for their valid administration there must be a proper form, a proper matter and a proper minister. Others can regard only Baptism and the Lord's Supper as Sacraments. In this Conference we lay stress on these two Sacraments because they are Sacraments which are generally acknowledged by the members of this Conference.

6. We believe that in Baptism administered with water in the

name of the Father, the Son and the Holy Spirit, for the remission of sins, we are baptised by one Spirit into one body. By this statement it is not meant to ignore the differences in conception, interpretation, and mode which exist among us.

7. We believe that in the Holy Communion our Lord is present and that we have fellowship with God our Father in Jesus Christ His Son, our Living Lord who is our own Bread, given for the life of the world, sustaining the life of all His people, and that we are in fellowship with all others who are united to Him. We agree that the Sacrament of the Lord's Supper is the Church's most sacred act of worship, in which the Lord's atoning death is commemorated and proclaimed, and that it is a sacrifice of praise and thanksgiving and an act of solemn self-oblation.

8. There are among us divergent views, especially as to (1) the mode or manner of " the Real Presence " ; (2) the conception of the commemoration and the sacrifice ; (3) the relation of the elements to the grace conveyed ; and (4) the relation between the minister of this Sacrament and the validity and efficacy of the rite.

9. We are aware that the reality of the divine presence and gift in this Sacrament cannot be adequately expressed in human thought and language.

10. We close this statement with the prayer that the differences which prevent full communion at the present time may be removed.

Discussion

It appeared from Bishop CANNON's statement that although a preliminary Report had been submitted to the whole Section, the Report as presented came to the Conference directly from the Drafting Committee of the Section. But it was ruled that it must be taken to be the Report of the whole Section, and that members speaking upon it should speak as members of the Conference rather than of the particular Section.

Professor WILFRED MONOD then presented the statement referred to by Bishop Cannon.

The point now reached, he said, is most critical : either we must face the acute metaphysical difficulties which for ages have divided the Churches, or, if we refuse to do so, we incur the risks spoken of by our Orthodox brethren, of contenting ourselves with merely verbal agreement. Deeply conscious of this difficulty, I drew up certain propositions treating of the sacramental problem on a purely spiritual plane. I submitted them to Professor Heiler, who endorsed and signed them at once. Heiler was born a Roman Catholic, is a ritualist, and communicates with the old Catholics ; I am a Huguenot, a Calvinist and perhaps a Quaker too. Surely our concord is deeply significant ? It may indicate the lines along which spiritual unity in Jesus Christ is still possible for this Conference. This is our statement :

All Christians are bound by the same spiritual experience common to the universal, that is, the Catholic Church.

This experience expresses itself in two ways :

1. In terms of *psychology*, the perpetual presence of the Lord is a personal and experimental reality : " Not I, but Christ in me."

2. In terms of *solidarity*, the presence of the Lord is joined to a social reality, that of the Communion of Saints: " Where two are gathered in my name, I am there."

THESES

I. The Gospel shows us Jesus Christ, visible, in Palestine.

The Church is a second " Holy Land " where Jesus Christ, invisible in the soul, manifests His spiritual presence through the Christian institutions.

II. In the sacramental life of the Church, we find, enlarged and glorified, the two commandments of which our Lord said that they sum up the perfect law : " Love God, love your neighbour."

III. The love of God gives an infinite expansion to the individual soul, and introduces it, even here, into eternal life.

The love of one's neighbour replaces the struggle for life by fraternal collaboration in the service of God's Kingdom.

Now, in the mystical realm of the Church, Body of Jesus Christ, the Sacraments of Baptism and of the Lord's Supper widen and transfigure, through grace, the first and second commandments.

IV. Baptism is the divine seal, imposed in the name of Jesus Christ on each individual, a vocation addressed to the soul, a prophecy of unfoldings, offered or promised.

The Lord's Supper is the mystical pledge and the food of human unity in the name of the blood shed by the Saviour for all mankind ; it remains a never-ceasing call to service and consecration.

V. Morally speaking, Baptism—the sacrament of personality— signifies : " Thou art the child of God. Become it ! "

Morally speaking, the Holy Supper signifies : " Thou art the brother of Jesus Christ and of the Brothers. Behave accordingly ! "

So the Sacrament of Regeneration and the Sacrament of Communion fundamentally unite all the disciples of our Saviour and establish the catholic basis of a true Christendom.

VI. Consequently, the Christians of the whole world, giving due respect to the dogmas, rites, symbolic interpretations and sacraments of every Church, do humbly and fraternally turn their hearts towards practical inter-communion.

" By this shall everyone know that you are my disciples, if you have love one for another."

F. Heiler.   Wilfred Monod.

The Report of Section VI, of which it was made clear that Professor Monod's statement did not form a part, was then considered in detail.

The following suggestions were made and referred to the Drafting Committee : By the Rev. Dr. Atkinson, that the position of the various paragraphs should be considered, and that, for the sake of logical sequence, the last two paragraphs should be incorporated after the word " mysteries " in paragraph 1 ; by Dr. J. A. Rust, that the words " through faith " should be inserted in paragraph 2.

Dr. William Adams Brown asked permission to submit, for the consideration of the Drafting Committee, the addition of the following clauses in the appropriate place in the Report. He thought that the members would be very grateful that the Report had been so unanimously received, a Report which so fully expressed the degree of unity attained, but there were some among them who would like— if it could be done with perfect accord—to have attention called a little more specifically to certain particular practical difficulties under which the Conference was labouring, and without any commitment whatever to urge that the consideration of the Churches be concentrated upon those difficulties in the immediate future. The following clauses had been carefully drafted in order to avoid as far as possible any doctrinal difficulty :

In particular we commend to the Churches for their earnest consideration the following points of immediate practical importance :

1. The possibility, pending the solution of the larger and more important difficulties above referred to, of some provision at future Conferences for united or simultaneous celebration of the Sacrament, in a form consistent with the present law of the several Churches, which could express to the world the spiritual unity to which we have already attained.

2. The possibility, without prejudice to the doctrinal position of

o

each Church, of providing in communities where no other possibility of partaking of the Sacrament exists for the admission to communion, under proper safeguard, of members of other Christian bodies resident in or visiting those communities.

3. The possibility, under similar safeguards, of making early provision for some form of inter-communion or, if that be not immediately possible, joint or simultaneous celebration in the new Churches in non-Christian lands.

The suggestion that these proposals be referred to the Drafting Committee was felt to involve considerable difficulty. The Archbishop of DUBLIN thought that they ought not to come before the Conference until the members had seen them in writing; the Rev. Dr. GEORGE CRAIG STEWART, that they were not relevant to the Report; Bishop GORE, that they raised controversial questions which went beyond anything that the Conference could adequately consider. The Rev. I. M. ROSE hoped that they would not be withdrawn, as they represented an ideal, and would not be out of place in a Report which took account of disagreements and difficulties.

Dr. BROWN said that he had been aware that this was a matter which would raise difficulties, and it had been for that reason that he had simply asked the privilege of reference to the Committee where it might be quietly considered and where, if it appeared advisable, it could be decided not to bring it before the Conference. He added that Bishop Gore was well aware that many of the members of the Conference had contended that they should not go one step further than the consciences of their brothers permitted, but he felt that the matters referred to in his proposal lay so closely on their hearts that they might at least be referred for consideration to the Committee before being dismissed, in order that they might all feel that they had done everything possible in moving forward to the end in view. In conclusion he said that he would immediately withdraw his motion if it were deemed advisable.

BISHOP CANNON pointed out that the Committee had not shirked any work which it had thought it should properly undertake, but it had recognised limitations of time and diverging views and had not discussed questions upon which it had not thought any helpful conclusion would be arrived at.

Dr. GARVIE said that after the expression of feeling on the part of the Conference he was quite sure that there would have been no inclination on the part of the responsible committee to raise, at this late stage in their discussions, a subject which was evidently open to so much difference of opinion. In view of this, and the fact that the proposer had expressed his willingness to withdraw it, if the Conference deemed it wise, he thought they might regard the matter as ended.

The Conference adjourned, with prayer offered by Bishop GORE, at 12.30 p.m.

THURSDAY AFTERNOON, AUGUST 18TH.

The afternoon session was opened at 3 p.m. with devotions led by the Rev. Prof. FORNEROD.

The Chairman, Dr. GARVIE, introduced the Rt. Rev. Bishop BALAKIAN of the Armenian Church, who desired to make a statement of which the following is a summary :

We are assembled from all parts of the world in this hospitable city to perform a sacred task, that the Christian Churches may be united and new power may thus be given to the Gospel.

The growth of materialism in our day has been accompanied by a decrease in the spiritual power of Christianity, especially since the War, which has gravely affected every nation which took part in it. We find men speaking of the Church as out of date and needing to be replaced, or turning their eyes to the East in search of a new religion. The facts of division have enhanced the apparent inadequacy of the Church.

But in fact mankind needs no new religion : it needs a renewal of the fire of Christian love, a work to which we can contribute here. We need first of all to believe in our task, whoever else may doubt its value. There are those who regard our task as impossible, or attribute our activities to motives of policy. I am an optimist, and believe that the impossible goal of unity can be reached through fellowship in work. We need no new Creed to unite us. The words of Jesus, " By this shall all men know that ye are my disciples," suffice. To secure the true peace of the Church and the world, instead of the vain shadow of peace which now exists, we of the clergy must make a beginning by manifesting Christian love in all its simplicity and sincerity.

It is not true that we are powerless, and that politicians must rule the world : ideals are the true governing forces. The ideal of Stockholm, a noble germ, must be brought to maturity.

This country of Switzerland, maintaining unity and peace in spite of, or by means of, the freedom and independence of each Canton, is the type of that union in which the divided Churches should come together. Our meeting is the pledge and foretaste of such a unity. We have but to follow out our task in the spirit in which we have begun, and its successful accomplishment is certain.

The order of the ancient Armenian Church is simple and democratic : its countless martyrdoms give it a right to a place of honour among the other Churches, ancient and modern. It has always felt itself at one in Christian love with other Churches : has never anathematised any, or failed to recognise its ordinances ; it greets you now, and is prepared to throw itself whole-heartedly into a fellowship in work.

It was upon Ararat, the holy mountain of Armenia, that the ark of Noah came to rest after the flood, and the dove brought the olive-branch as an assurance that the time of God's wrath had passed away. A flood of slaughter drowned the world again in the years of the War; let us send out from this Conference to the world a message and assurance of peace, co-operation and mutual love.

Report of Section VII presented

The Report of Section VII on the Unity of Christendom and the relation thereto of existing Churches was introduced by Archbishop SÖDERBLOM, the Archbishop of ARMAGH, and General-Superintendent DIBELIUS.

Archbishop SÖDERBLOM said that the Section had worked together in brotherly concord, and had before it two distinct conceptions, that of alliance and collaboration, and that of a reunited Church. With regard to the first paragraph of their Report, Professor Balanos had written that by " union " the Orthodox understand a dogmatic union, and, since this under present conditions seemed unattainable, it would be well for us to concentrate upon a fellowship between the Churches, while continuing to study that which unites us and that which divides.

In the second paragraph, the Archbishop would prefer to read, instead of the phrase, " the idea of one Church," " the idea of a united Church."

The Archbishop of ARMAGH said that the section had worked in happy fellowship and had reached its conclusions without acute differences of opinion. They considered that Section VII was in effect the summing up of the work of the whole Conference, with the practical aim directly in view, and in order to keep that aim well in view they had felt it better to begin a little further back, approaching the whole question from the point of view of fellowship in life and work.

The first section dealt with what had already been done in relation to Christian unity in Life and Work ; Section 2 with Fellowship in Faith and Order, sub-section 5 of which had given rise to a difference of opinion. Then followed section 3, " Ways of Approach," and 4, " Complete Fellowship," which was presented as the great aim of the Conference, for until complete inter-communion was possible the purpose in view could not be attained.

General-Superintendent Dr. DIBELIUS said that Section VII had performed its task, which was a summary of the whole work of the Conference, with a sense of its responsibility and without discord. Starting with the common practical Christian work of all Churches, they had passed on to the ideal of a unified Church, based on one Faith, one Baptism, one Eucharist, and one Ministry, while leaving room for constitutional liberty. The approach to unity must be made step by step through fuller mutual knowledge and co-opera-tion, such as had already become manifest in the mission field. The will to unity would persist in spite of all differences : premature steps, such as projects of inter-communion, were likely to do more harm than good.

The following is the text of the Report as thus presented :

REPORT OF SECTION VII, FIRST DRAFT

Christian unity expresses itself in love, in faith and in the order of the Church.

1. *Fellowship in Life and Work*

As the individual is tested (" ye shall know them by their fruits ") so also the unity of the disciples is proved by their fellowship in the service of the Master.

In fulfilling the Master's law of love, all Christians should act together as if they were one body in one visible fellowship without any injury to theological principles. In 1920 the Ecumenical Patriarchate issued to Christendom an encyclical letter proposing a *koinonia ton ekklesion*, a league of Churches for practical purposes, without authority to commit the Churches. It was followed up by the Universal Christian Conference on Life and Work (Stockholm, 1925). This work must be continued and strengthened and will surely prepare the way for fuller spiritual unity through faith in God and our Lord Jesus Christ, the faith underlying and inspiring all Christian life and work. A council of the Churches for practical purposes might well be evolved from already existing organisations such as the Continuation Committee on Life and Work, consisting of representatives officially appointed by almost all Christian Communions, and the International Committee of the World Alliance for Promoting International Friendship through the Churches.

2. *Fellowship in Faith and Order*

The present movement towards unity in Faith and Order which has found expression at Lausanne, yields the idea of one Church including diverse types of doctrinal statement and of the administration of church ordinances.

Every existing Church has its own *charisma* and its own historic tradition. It has, therefore, a contribution to make to the whole. The common historic tradition of Christianity has also to be considered. In the primitive Church there was variety in the expression of doctrine and also diversity of practice. Yet the Body was one.

We envisage the characteristics of the united Church as follows :

1. A common Faith, a common Message to the world.

2. Baptism as the rite of incorporation into the one Church.

3. Holy Communion as expressing the corporate life of the Church and as its signal act of corporate worship.

4. A ministry in all parts of the Church recognised by the whole Body.

5. For all the uniting Communions, liberty in regard to interpretations about sacramental grace and ministerial order and authority.[1]

6. Due provisions for the exercise of the prophetic gift.

3. *Ways of Approach*

In preparation for closer fellowship each section of the Church should seek more intimate knowledge of faith and life, worship and order in other Communions. Differences founded in complicated historic developments may sometimes prove to be less important than they are supposed to be. As our several Communions come to understand each other better, they will refrain from competitive propaganda to exalt one by depreciating another.

When different Christian denominations are represented in the same community, differences in creed, worship and practice should not prevent individuals and Communions from working together

---

[1] Professor Balanos made the following statement :
The Greek Church, which regards the holy tradition of the Church besides the Holy Scriptures as *norma fidei*, cannot recognize liberty in regard to interpretation about sacramental grace and ministerial order and authority.

in recognition of the principle of comity, mutual consideration and Christian courtesy.

We note with gratitude to God the effective co-operation and union prevailing in the mission fields. The purpose of all Christian missionaries is to carry the eternal Gospel in manifold ways to the ends of the earth. The greatness and urgency of this task is leading to the speeding up of unification which has already set an example to the older Communions and should not be retarded by their long-standing divisions.

4. Completed Fellowship

Complete fellowship in the Church will not be realised until the way is opened for all God's children to join in communion at the Lord's Table. Only through prayer and thoughtful deliberation can steps be taken towards inter-communion between the different sections of Christendom. Ambiguous statements and hasty measures may hinder the work of unification. Only when full mutual recognition has been attained, can the visible unity of the Church be effectively realised.

Nor should we forget that, greatest of all, God's mercy and our sonship in His family are granted to every faithful soul. God give us wisdom and courage to do His will!

Discussion

The Rev. ROBERT A. HUME, D.D. : It is my joy to report that in India two large denominational communions have been really united to form one large, congenial, active and hopeful Church which has no denominational titles which formerly characterised the ecclesiastical fruits in India of foreign missions from the United States, Canada, Great Britain and the Continent of Europe. All the Congregational Churches and most of the Presbyterian Churches in Northern and Western India have been united to form a single Church called the " United Church of North India." So, casting off every denominational title, there is not now a single Congregational Church and there are few Presbyterian Churches in those sections of India.

This happy result is under God due to the determination in the hearts of the Indian and foreign leaders of the two Communions to do what the Christian movement requires. On the foreign field Church union is more urgent and is more easily accomplished than in old communities, and the desire for union is growing stronger and stronger.

The union of all Congregational and most Presbyterian Churches in Northern and Western India was accomplished without requiring either of the uniting Communions to change their theological views or their modes of worship or government. The uniting Communions continue locally to administer their worship and order much as before.

Such happy union would have been impracticable if either Communion had required some of the churches of the other Communion to disown their hallowed past, or to discredit the validity of the apostolic and fruitful ministries of the regularly consecrated ministers of either body.

In all the churches of the United Church of North India all Christians in good standing in any Communion who love the Lord Jesus Christ and strive to obey His commands are welcomed to participate in the Holy Sacrament of the Eucharist, and neither in thought, word or act is any regular minister stigmatised as schismatic because he is ordained in any supposedly inadequate manner.

This united Church of North India lives in the hope that eventually nowhere shall the disciples of our one Lord be excluded from joining Christian brothers at the uniting Sacrament of Holy Communion.

The Rev. Harold Schenck : I have but one suggestion to bring to this Conference. In deference to the scholarly and exactly worded addresses that have edified us and stimulated our minds day after day, I have been quite reluctant to ask even for these few moments and have kept hoping that someone, more eloquent than I, would feel constrained to speak in the interest of the group—nay, the thronging multitude—whose plea to the ecclesiastical statesmen of the day and whose earnest prayer to the Almighty I am venturing to lay before you in these inadequate words. I have listened in vain for the sounding of that note in positive, ringing tones. There has been a faint echo here and there in some of the Sections, but certainly no emphasis that would do justice to the importance of the issue. I refer to the passionate plea of the youth of to-day—the youth of all Churches and countries and continents—for greater unity among Christian forces, and unity that will be expressed in a practical form that the world will understand, " that the world may know that thou has sent me," the Christ, the Son of the Living God, not in vague terms that require the service of a highly developed theological mind to interpret and explain.

Whatever satisfaction we find in the deliberations of this Conference, in its findings, in its statement of agreements and disagreements, we might just as well ask ourselves this question now, for we must face it later—each delegate for himself—and I care not what creed or Church he represents, " What will the youth of my country, my Communion, have to say to the pronouncements of this Conference and to the measure of hope it offers to the world ? " Will youth feel that we have grasped the opportunity that has been lingering in our midst ? Will youth feel that we have been courageous ? Will youth feel that we have been open-minded ? Will youth feel that we have been self-effacing ? Will youth feel that we have been absolutely Christ-like ? Can we say that it has been the spirit of the law rather than the letter of the law that we have sought after humbly, penitently and with open minds ? It would be blind and foolish of us to discount the importance of such searching questions and of this searching challenge. Unless this Conference can feel the pulse of Christian youth, sound its aspirations, and know its yearnings, it is only reviewing the failures of yesterday and confessing the shortcomings of to-day ; it is not sounding the trumpet-call of hope and advance for to-morrow.

The position we face together is this—and it is a critical position, for there is not a single delegate here but who is aware of the fact that millions upon millions of young people are refusing to give allegiance to the Church because of our timidity in this matter : the youth of to-day are eager, passionately eager, to see real unity practised, unity revealing itself in the humble heart, the tractable mind, the broad outlook, the tolerant attitude, co-operative effort. It does not expect all of this to be done in a few years—it realises that this is a transition, an evolution that requires time—but it does urge, and it will continue to urge in more emphatic terms in our respective Church Councils that we move on beyond the talking stage to the acting stage, that we wrench ourselves loose from the bonds of the past and resolve to practise unity instead of merely eulogising it. I would not speak so boldly if I were not confident that I am speaking for the youth of many countries. It has been my privilege to feel the pulse of youth and study the attitude of youth towards ecclesiasticism in some fifteen countries of the world, and it is stating it mildly to say that youth is plainly apathetic, indifferent toward much of the credal emphasis of the Church, and is chafing under the restrictions that these inherited forms impose. It is saying to priests and clergymen, " Why are you so zealous and insistent on perpetuating differences that mean little or nothing to us, when we desire simply to walk in the footsteps of Jesus, to follow the Christ of the Galilean Road and the Indian Road and apply His teachings ? Your discussions are largely academic ; they are as the grass of the field—green to-day and parched to-morrow. They are for the passing day, certainly not for eternity." Youth is praying, pleading, reaching out for a brotherhood of understanding throughout the world, and it urges, and urges rightly, that we provide a practical demonstration of this in our Christian communities.

Bishop GORE took general exception to the Report, as having been drawn up in such a way as to make it very difficult for those whose standpoint was Catholic to continue their participation in the movement. Section 2 laid all its stress upon diversity, while saying nothing about the duty of unity; its third paragraph, which attempted to enumerate the characteristics of the Church—a matter which had better have been left to the previous Reports—said nothing about a common moral discipline. Moreover, it would be unwise to give unqualified approval to the speeding-up of unification in mission churches : too rapid a movement might merely lead to new divisions.

The Archbishop of ARMAGH maintained that, in spite of Dr. Gore's criticisms, unity was the keynote of the Report.

Professor GLUBOKOWSKY, as an Orthodox member of the Section, supported the Report as neither an end in itself nor a means, but as a good beginning.

The Rev. TIMOTHY TINGFANG LEW begged that the Report might be received without modification ; section 3 was especially valuable in view of the needs of the mission field, especially in China ; any weakening of it would cause suspicion and disappointment. The Rev. Dr. MACHICHAN endorsed this plea. Prof. ARSENIEW asked that, as a means towards unity, Churches should be asked to pray for each other, and especially for Churches in distress.

The Rt. Rev. Bishop MANNING moved that the Report be referred back to the Section without further debate : the motion, opposed by Archbishop SÖDERBLOM and Bishop FISHER, was not carried.

Detailed suggestions of amendment were then offered as follows :

In section 1, second paragraph, by the Rev. Dr. GILMORE, to delete the reference to the World Alliance, the paragraph to end with " appointed by almost all Christian Communions."

In section 2, first paragraph, by Bishop GORE, to insert after the words " unity in " the words " fundamental faith, order, and administration of sacraments " ; and in the second paragraph, to add after the words " in the primitive Church," " there was not only a marked unity of faith and practice, but also a considerable variety " ; this last suggestion was accepted by Archbishop Söderblom and the

Archbishop of Armagh. In the same section, third paragraph, several amendments were suggested. The Rev. Dr. F. J. HALL hoped that sub-paragraph 5 would be omitted, as peculiarly difficult for those of a Catholic mind. The Bishop of BOMBAY asked for a reconsideration of the whole paragraph, which, he thought, lay outside the reference of the Section. On the other hand he desired at this point a consideration of two matters: (1) the relation of local or national Churches to the reunited Church, and (2) the future position, in the reunited Church, of Churches which exist to represent certain doctrines or practices. Bishop GORE proposed to redraft the paragraph thus:

" We envisage the characteristics of the united Church as follows:

1. A common moral standard and discipline.

2. A common confession of faith (see Report IV).

3. A common administration of the Sacraments according to certain conditions recognised as necessary (see Report VI).

4. A ministry recognised throughout the whole universal Church.

5. Liberty of interpretation with regard to all matters not accepted as essential.

6. Due provision for the exercise of the prophetic gift."

Licentiat J. F. LAUN laid stress upon the liberties indicated in the Report, which, he said, were vital to those who belonged to the tradition of the Reformers.

In section 3, second paragraph, Bishop GORE moved that after the word " community," there be added " they should first of all strive to make the most of their agreements, and, after that, exhibit a larger spirit of toleration." In the third paragraph, the Bishop of BOMBAY intimated that, with the aid of the Bishop of DORNAKAL, he had prepared a new draft for this paragraph, which would be submitted in writing.

In Section 4, the Rev. A. E. MONAHAN proposed to substitute "full communion" for "inter-communion," as being less ambiguous.

Canon TARAFDAR pleaded, in the name of Indian Churches for which the problems of union were less difficult than those which Westerns discover, for the approval of the Report with the suggestions which had been made.

The Report was then referred to the Drafting Committee for the consideration of the proposed amendments.

After prayer by the Archbishop of ARMAGH, the Conference adjourned at 6.30 p.m.

Thursday Evening, August 18th.

At the evening session, at 8.30 p.m., the President was in the Chair, and the opening devotions were led by the Rt. Rev. Bishop Nuelsen.

Report of the Continuation Committee

The President read and presented the following Report :

The Continuation Committee of the World Conference on Faith and Order was organised by appointment of the preliminary Conference at Geneva on August 18th, 1920. Under the following resolutions of the Preliminary Conference, it was decided :

" That a committee be appointed to be known as the Continuation Committee ; that it consist of approximately forty members chosen by this Conference ; that the Business Committee be instructed to present nominations for this Committee, as broadly representative as practicable of the various groups of Communions ; that this Committee shall elect its own officers, an executive committee and such sub-committees as it may deem expedient ; that it shall have power to fill vacancies, to add to its membership, and to provide or accept a substitute under due limitations in case of the inability of a member to attend a given meeting ; that it shall meet at least once a year, and oftener if necessary, provided not less than six months' notice shall be given ; that it shall be charged with the duty of carrying on the work of preparation for the World Conference or Conferences on Faith and Order, correspondence and co-operation with the Commissions of the various Communions, fixing the time and place of a Conference, and performing all such other duties as may be necessary to arrange for the Conference ; that it shall call a meeting of representatives of the various Commissions if and when it is requested to do so by a majority of the Commissions, on six months' notice, and that such a meeting, if held, shall have power to resume any or all of the powers now granted to the Committee."

Its officers were : the Right Reverend Charles H. Brent, D.D., Chairman ; George Zabriskie, D.C.L., Treasurer ; Robert H. Gardiner, Secretary. On August 19th, 1920, the Continuation Committee was divided into two sections : a Business Committee of which Bishop Brent was the Chairman, and a Subjects Committee of which the Bishop of Bombay was the Chairman. Both these Committees have functioned up to the present moment.

It has been the function of the Business Committee to attend to all matters that pertained to the business of the World Conference, and the Subjects Committee has prepared material for the Conference now in session. The two sub-committees have had frequent meetings. The whole of the Continuation Committee has met three times : at Stockholm on August 15th-18th, 1925, at Berne in Switzerland, August 23rd-25th, 1926, and at Lausanne on July 30th and August 1st, 1927. We have also met twice during the Conference. We now submit this report as accounting for our stewardship. Our Secretary, Robert H. Gardiner, died June 15th, 1924. A graver loss could not have been sustained than that which came to us through Mr. Gardiner's death. The tribute paid him at the beginning of the sessions of the Conference in Lausanne was fully merited. No man could have been more devoted, more intelligent or more single-minded in the prosecution of his task. Many of us have thought of him constantly during the present sessions, thanking God for the firm foundations which he, more than anyone, laid for us to build upon. Ralph W. Brown was appointed Corresponding Secretary upon the death of Mr. Gardiner.

In accordance with the injunction laid upon it by the Continuation Committee, the Business Committee planned for the Conference in Lausanne and attended to all the details in connection with it. Too much praise cannot be bestowed upon Mr. Ralph W. Brown for the manner in which he consummated the preparations made by an Arrangements Committee appointed at Berne. It is due to him that our comforts have been so carefully attended to and all the details for our meeting have been arranged.

To my regret, I was unable to preside at the meeting of the Continuation Committee at Berne in 1926, but Dr. Garvie stepped into the breach and more than filled my place. His ability as a Chairman is far beyond mine and his knowledge of language gives him power which I could not hope myself to possess. As the report of the Arrangements Committee was presented to this Conference, there is no need of further reference to its work The Subjects Committee, under the Bishop of Bombay, drew up a programme which was adopted at Stockholm. Later on, however, at Berne, it was felt advisable to swing from the consideration of resolutions to that of topics. We are deeply indebted to the Bishop of Bombay and to Canon Bate, who was associated with him, for the extremely valuable material which the Subjects Committee prepared and which has been at our disposal. In addition to all other services rendered by Canon Bate, I desire publicly to recognise the selfless way in which he has thrown himself into some of the more tedious preparations for this Conference. He has worked incessantly on details and has overseen the translations of, and in some instances translated himself, between forty and fifty of the longer speeches delivered at the Conference. I doubt if there are many men who could have done such a herculean task with the effectiveness and quietude of Canon Bate. This whole Conference owes him an unpayable debt of gratitude.

In addition to what I have said in relation to the work of the Continuation Committee, there is that which has been carried on by Robert H. Gardiner during his lifetime in the Secretariat in Boston, and since his death by Mr. Ralph W. Brown. An enormous correspondence has been kept up with Christians of various Churches all over the world. There have been times, especially shortly after Mr. Gardiner's death, when Mr. Brown has for considerable stretches of time given himself no sort of respite or recreation, even sleeping at the office in order to be at his work from 7 o'clock in the morning until late hours at night. This correspondence, which has all been carefully filed, is extremely valuable for historical purposes and also for purposes related to the study of the various Churches of Christendom.

Our Treasurer, Mr. George Zabriskie, who has filled this office for seventeen years, has done us incalculable service. There have been many moments in which he shared with Mr. Gardiner the grave anxiety of having insufficient funds, but he has always carried his burden with serenity, and we were able to present a financial situation on the 1st of August, 1927, which will enable us to conclude our task with funds sufficient to meet all our responsibilities up to the end of December of the calendar year.

I have not gone into details, inasmuch as the minutes of the Continuation Committee have been published. With this Conference we complete our labours and pass on our responsibilities to such other committee as the Conference may be pleased to appoint. In closing, I would say that as I look back on the long stretch of years in which the Continuation Committee has been working in behalf of this Conference, I thank God for the many manifestations of His presence and blessing. The knowledge that our labour has been manifestly in accord with God's will has brought its own and its sufficient reward.

The adoption of this Report was proposed by Dr. GARVIE, and seconded by the Archbishop of ARMAGH. It was felt on all sides, however, that the Report should include some reference to the invaluable labours of Bishop BRENT himself, and on the suggestion of the Archbishop of ARMAGH and Dr. GARVIE the following insertion was adopted :

" The Conference on Faith and Order takes this opportunity of expressing its warm appreciation of the great work which its President, Bishop BRENT, has done in the cause of Christian unity, and its deep sense of the sincere spirit of Christian devotion to the service of Christ and His Church which has animated all his labours."

The Report was then adopted unanimously.

The Rev. Dr. PETER AINSLIE informed the Conference that many suggestions of names had been sent in to the nucleus of the new Continuation Committee, and that in considering these the following principles would be borne in mind :

(1) To retain a nucleus of members from the former Committee ;

(2) To choose members who had taken an active part in the work of the present Conference ;

(3) To secure the appointment of men of the younger generation

Continuation of the Work of the Conference

Dr. AINSLIE then presented a Report of the Committee charged to present suggestions with regard to the continuation of the work of the Lausanne Conference.

Of this Report, after discussion, the following paragraphs were retained and adopted by the Conference :

That the Continuation Committee, which shall meet at the call of the Chairman, may distribute its work sectionally, if, in its judgment, such distribution is needed.

That to all of those Churches which have sent delegates the findings of this Conference shall be sent through their official channels at as early a date as possible, asking those Churches to consider the findings and report back to the Continuation Committee the results of their deliberations, in view of which the Continuation Committee shall consider what steps need to be taken for another Conference.

That the participating Churches be asked to continue their commissions or committees dealing with the subject of this Conference, both for educational purposes at home and in order to keep in touch with the Continuation Committee.

That the annual budget be $20,000, which shall be raised from the participating Churches and such individuals as may be interested.

That all the subject-matter of this Conference be referred to a Committee which shall be appointed by the Continuation Committee.

That the Continuation Committee be authorised to take whatever steps it may think wise and necessary, within the purpose of the Conference on Faith and Order, to advance the cause of Christian unity.

After prayer, offered by Archbishop GERMANOS, the session closed at 10.45 p.m.

REPORTS OF SECTIONS II, III & IV

Friday Morning, August 19th.

Full sessions were held morning and afternoon in the Aula. At the morning session Dr. Garvie was in the Chair, and the opening devotions at 9.30 a.m. were led by Bishop Jensen.

The following announcements were made during the session : a telegram had been received, which Bishop Manning was asked to acknowledge in the name of the Conference, from Bishop Gailor, "Sewance prays God's blessing Unity Conference—Gailor."

A collection was taken for the poor of Lausanne, amounting to 916.25 Swiss francs, 78 French francs, 0.28 Belgian francs, 2.00 German marks.

Preamble to the Reports

The President read a second draft of the Preamble, enlarged from the draft submitted on the morning of August 17th, and also a draft of a Report on Subject I, "The Call to Unity." As no copies were available for distribution to the members at this session, it was decided to postpone detailed discussion of the documents until Saturday morning, August 20th. The texts will be found in the record of that session.

After a brief interval for silent prayer, the Chairman announced the sessions of the day would be devoted to considering the final drafts of the Reports of Sections II, III and IV; those of Saturday morning and afternoon to the Preamble and Subject I, and to Reports V, VI, and VII.

Statement by a Group of Reformed Protestants on the Historic Significance of the Lausanne Conference

Prof. Choisy read the following statement :

In harmony with the declaration of our Lutheran brothers, a group of delegates belonging to the Protestant Churches of Switzerland, the Union of Reformed Churches of France, the Reformed Church of Alsace and Lorraine, the National Reformed Church of the Netherlands, the Waldensian Church of Italy and the Belgian Missionary Church, recognises as gifts from God the brotherly spirit which has been maintained throughout this Conference and the will to unity which has been manifested in communion and prayer ; these delegates are deeply grateful for the spiritual unanimity which has become manifest, beyond all that could have been hoped for, during the course of the Conference's labours.

However important may be the efforts made to translate this unanimity into definite terms, they hold that the historic significance of the Conference is to be found above all in the fact that the Churches have shown themselves resolved to seek the basis of their unity henceforward in the Person of their Master and Saviour, exalted as the supreme object of their faith above all particular creeds

Those of our contemporaries who live without hope and without God cannot comprehend the interest of our discussions of the successive forms in which Christian faith and life have clothed themselves in history ; but they are eager to learn whether the Churches which claim to be Christian can show themselves capable of setting the example of spiritual unity realised through love to a world which is torn asunder by hatred. They will not dream of giving themselves to Christ unless they see the Churches living by the life of Christ.

May the grace of God, which has allowed us to take the first steps towards the visible unity of Christ's Church, grant that the Lausanne Conference may mark the end of dissensions and anathemas between Christian Churches!

Statement by Mr. Carl Heath

Mr. CARL HEATH, a member of the Society of Friends, made the following statement :

We, who follow a freer way of Christian practice than would probably be acceptable to most of those present, feel that there are certain things to be said by us before this Conference closes.

We are glad that the organising committee of this Conference should have decided that the Reports of the Sections are to be submitted to the Churches for consideration and are not to be accepted as definitive statements of agreement, for, like our friends of the Orthodox Church, we cannot adopt them, though we warmly receive them for study. We do not in any way belittle the importance of the problems we have been working upon, but we believe that " the unity of Christians never did, nor ever will or can, stand in uniformity of thought or opinion, but in Christian love." And we believe that a corporate practice of the presence of God, a corporate knowledge of Christ in our midst, a common experience of the work of the living Spirit, constitute the supremely real sacrament of a Holy Communion.

In this Lausanne Conference no question of church order has

arisen in our daily inter-communion one with another in God. We *know* that we have been bound together in the bonds of the love of the living Christ. For we have met in the life, and we feel and we know that the sacrament of communion in God is a thing to be experienced, and not one to be known only or primarily in symbol or in rite, useful as these may be to many in concentrating thought upon supreme things in the Church. We, who practise a very free way, are wholly sacramentalist in our effort to reach unto God. Jesus Christ is the centre of a Gospel that is not primarily a creed or a doctrine but a life. The Spirit of God in its working in the world, prompting men to service and to sacrifice, cannot be confined to any institution that can be conceived, for the Spirit is Life, and Life cannot be so limited. When we have settled church order we shall have made no great progress with that vast " multitude of men that is slowly moving out of the Church "—indifferent to church order, but greatly interested in the reality of spiritual life. And by spiritual life we do not mean a world-wide social activity, but an increasing liberation of God's Spirit in men, finding its expression in *all* human relationships.

Communities of free religious life, such as is the Society of Friends, want to be at one with the whole Church of Jesus Christ. But we feel in the depths of our spirits, and with a certain poignancy, as we have struggled to find unity in definitions of faith and order in this Conference, how supremely important it is that we should not lose sight of the freedom in which God guides men, by His Spirit, from truth to truth. There is a freedom of God to which we lay claim. And we do so, not because we desire to escape a right order or dis-cipline in spiritual life. Rather it springs from an intense feeling that the realisation of this freedom is essential to the dynamic power and the vital attractiveness of the Church, if it is to meet the need and reach the heart of the young and strong life of men in the world of to-day.

Bishop GORE said he received with all respect the statement made on behalf of the Society of Friends, but pointed out that the prin-ciples asserted therein would prevent almost any of the Reports being passed unanimously. He asked whether they were prepared to let them pass *sub silentio* or whether they intended to vote against them ? If none of the Reports—or hardly any of them—could be passed *nemine contradicente*, it was better to know immediately.

Dr. GARVIE replied that there was no intention on the part of the representatives of the Society of Friends to vote against any

Report; they simply desired that their position should be clearly understood.

Mr. ATHELSTAN RILEY : You have just heard the speech of Mr. Heath, who has placed before you his general opinion as a member of the Society of Friends, and I would ask your permission to speak for a few moments as an Anglican layman.

Speaking as an Anglican, I wish to make it clear that my attitude is very largely that of our Orthodox friends. I believe that the Church of England, in which I was baptised, sets forth the Catholic faith and order. To these I am pledged, and these I have endeavoured to maintain in all these friendly discussions in which I have been privileged to take part in Lausanne. I believe all baptised people to have received thereby the character of membership of the Catholic Church, and I confess that many have used this grace which flows from baptism in good works which put me to the deepest shame. But I believe in One Holy Catholic and Apostolic Church, and I do not believe it can be, or is, divided into " Churches," holding widely different and even opposite opinions on what I am bound to consider fundamental questions. I believe this Conference, under God's good guidance, will be productive of much that will lead to Christian unity if we can have met together for mutual explanations without compromising anything really fundamental which we hold.

Dear brethren in Christ, believe me, when I say that my heart goes out to you, the heart of a great sinner to godly men, the heart of one whose highest ambition it is to be the least in heaven and bring up the rear. Believe me when I say that I have a passionate desire to see you united with me in faith, in order and in worship. But I cannot allow you to be deceived as to my attitude. The reunion of Christendom will never be accomplished by ambiguity of language or concealment of thought.

Pastor MERLE D'AUBIGNÉ said that the members of the Reformed Evangelical Church of France had not signed the Statement read by Professor Choisy, not because they disagreed with it—on the contrary they were entirely in accord with it—but because they thought something was missing from it; they considered that there was something beyond the fraternity shown in the meetings of the Conference. They wished to continue furthering the aim of the Conference—unity!

The Bishop of BOMBAY, on behalf of the Anglicans as a whole, said that they had decided to make no declaration as a Church. They all honoured Mr. Riley, and those who desired the free expression of personal opinion would honour the expression of his, but there were many who did not know about the Anglican Church, and he desired it to be clearly understood that they did not wish to make a Church statement before the Conference. They hoped to work for many years towards a better apprehension of the truth of God as it is offered to the universal Church, and to put behind them every kind of sectional opinion.

The Chairman pointed out that it would be unfortunate if the impression were given that the wording of the Reports was " ambiguous." This suggestion had been made by some members : but it should be remembered that while the Conference allowed full liberty of expression, it did not necessarily endorse the terms used by any speaker.

Report of Section II, second draft, presented

The Rev. Dr. LOFTHOUSE presented the Report of Section II, on the Church's Message to the World—the Gospel, in the form finally approved by the Drafting Committee of the Section.

The following is the text of the Report as thus presented :

REPORT OF SECTION II, SECOND DRAFT

The World Conference on Faith and Order, met at Lausanne, August 3rd-21st, 1927, expresses the Message of the Church to the World as follows :

1. The message of the Church to the world is, and must always remain, the Gospel of Jesus Christ.

2. The Gospel is the joyful message of redemption, both here and hereafter, the gift of God to sinful man in Jesus Christ.

3. The world was prepared for the coming of Christ through the activities of God's Spirit in all humanity, but especially in His revelation as given in the Old Testament ; and in the fulness of time the eternal Word of God became incarnate, and was made man, Jesus Christ, the Son of God and the Son of Man, full of grace and truth.

4. Through His life and teaching, His call to repentance, His proclamation of the coming of the Kingdom of God and of judgment, His suffering and death, His resurrection and exaltation to the right hand of the Father, and by the mission of the Holy Spirit, He has brought to us forgiveness of sins, and has revealed the fulness of the living God and His boundless love toward us. By the appeal of that love, shown in its completeness on the Cross, He summons us to the new life of faith, self-sacrifice, and devotion to His service and the service of men.

5. Jesus Christ, as the crucified and the living One, as Saviour and Lord, is also the centre of the world-wide Gospel of the Apostles and the Church. Because He Himself is the Gospel, the Gospel is the message of the Church to the world. It is more than a philosophical theory; more than a theological system; more than a programme for material betterment. The Gospel is rather the gift of a new world from God to this old world of sin and death; still more, it is the victory over sin and death, the revelation of eternal life in Him who has knit together the whole family in heaven and on earth in the communion of saints, united in the fellowship of service, of prayer and of praise.

6. The Gospel is the prophetic call to sinful man to turn to God, the joyful tidings of justification and of sanctification to those who believe in Christ. It is the comfort of those who suffer; to those who are bound, it is the assurance of the glorious liberty of the sons of God. The Gospel brings peace and joy to the heart, and produces in men self-denial, readiness for brotherly service, and compassionate love. It offers the supreme goal for the aspirations of youth, strength to the toiler, rest to the weary, and the crown of life to the martyr.

7. The Gospel is the sure source of power for social regeneration. It proclaims the only way by which humanity can escape from those class and race hatreds which devastate society at present, into the enjoyment of national well-being and international friendship and peace. It is also a gracious invitation to the non-Christian world, East and West, to enter into the joy of the living Lord.

8. Sympathising with the anguish of our generation, with its longing for intellectual sincerity, social justice and spiritual inspiration, the Church in the eternal Gospel meets the needs and fulfils the God-given aspirations of the modern world. Consequently, as in the past, so also in the present, the Gospel is the only way of salvation. Thus, through His Church, the living Christ still says to men, "Come unto me! . . . He that followeth me shall not walk in darkness, but shall have the light of life."

Discussion

Professor Dr. MARTIN DIBELIUS said that while the importance of this Report was incontestable, it was impossible to define the Gospel in such terms as every member of the Conference would approve; this applied especially to paragraphs 6, 7 and 8, in which the Section had attempted to define what the message of the Church should be in view of modern conditions. Still, it would be almost impossible to amend the Report at this stage and on these points by discussion ; he hoped that it would be left unchanged, particularly as it had received a large measure of acceptance from the brethren of the Orthodox Church.

Canon DOUGLAS said that he could be content to vote for the document, if allowed to make clear his objection that the word " Church " in it appeared to cover two opposed conceptions.

Pastor ELIE GOUNELLE urged that the Report had not given sufficient prominence to the conception of the kingdom of God, which ought to have had the first place in it.

Only two substantial changes were suggested in the Report. Prof. Dr. HAUSSLEITER asked, in the interest of simple readers of the Bible, that the following should stand in place of paragraph 4 : Jesus Christ, in the days of His flesh, fully revealed the grace and judgment of the Kingdom of Heaven through His compassion, His teaching, His example, and His witness to Himself. His death upon the Cross is, according to Scripture, the propitiatory sacrifice of the God-Man for the sins of the whole world, and His Resurrection is the power of justification unto newness of life in the Spirit for all believers.

Dr. Wilhelm PHILIPPS desired to substitute the following for paragraph 5 : The Gospel is rather a power of God which saves all who believe thereon, a gift of God our Heavenly Father, in Christ Jesus, to this world of sin and death. Dr. PHILIPPS was content, however, that his suggestion should merely be recorded in the Minutes.

The Rev. J. C. BLAIR suggested that the Report should not only be received, but also adopted, as being the only Report on which the Conference was unanimous. The Chairman pointed out that this would be contrary to the rules of procedure and unfair to absent members. The Report was unanimously received and the Conference adjourned, after prayer, at 12.30 p.m.

FRIDAY AFTERNOON, AUGUST 19TH.

The afternoon session opened at 3 p.m., with devotions led by the Very Rev. Dr. M'CLYMONT.

Report of Section III, second draft, presented

After observations by the Rev. Dr. WILLIAM ADAMS BROWN, and Reichsgerichtspräsident SIMONS, the revised Report of Section III, on the Nature of the Church, was read in English by the Bishop of MANCHESTER, who said :

The changes which appear in the present form of the Report, apart from verbal changes which will explain themselves and to which it is not necessary for me to make further reference, are the following :

1. A change in the order of the treatment of subjects. As the Report is at present presented, our definition of the nature and functions of the Church is succeeded at once by the description of the characteristics by which it is known on earth ; the account of our historic divisions is relegated to a footnote ; and the Report concludes with a brief enumeration of our differences and the expression of our hope and prayer for eventual reunion.

2. The relegation of the full statement of our differences to footnotes. This has made it possible to define them more accurately without interrupting the progress of the main thought.

3. The introduction of certain clauses emphasising aspects in our thought of the Church which had not received adequate recognition in the previous draft, notably one on the missionary responsibility of the Church.

4. The change of certain words which were open to misunderstanding.

Taking up the paragraphs of the Report in order, we begin the first paragraph with an introductory clause which relates our Report to the preceding Report on the Message of the Church—" God has given us the Gospel for the salvation of the world and has appointed His Church to witness by life and word to its redeeming power." We have omitted the phrase " God is the Creator," partly because it has been rendered unnecessary by the insertion of the new clause, partly because of the ambiguity of the word " Creator." We have inserted after the word " societies " the phrase " though He uses the will of men as His instrument " in order to meet the desire of those who wished a clearer recognition of the fact that God works His will through the will of men, a thought more fully expressed in paragraph 3. In paragraph 2, the word " true," which appears before " believers " in the original draft, is omitted with the consent of those who had requested its insertion.

In Paragraph 4, the introductory sentence which describes the nature of the Church is separated from the rest of the paragraph in order to complete the statement of points of agreement. The remainder, so far as retained, is transferred to paragraph 6.

Paragraph 5 in the original draft, so far as retained, is treated in part as a note, in part as embodied in paragraph 6.

In the present paragraph 5, the word " marks " has been omitted as having a particular dogmatic meaning in American Lutheran circles, and the word " characteristics " has been substituted. Under 5 (1) we have substituted for the clause " and proclaimed in the world " the words " interpreted by the Holy Spirit to the Church and to the individual," which are further explained in note A, where the different ways of understanding this interpretation are given— the understanding of the Orthodox being that this interpretation is given through the tradition of the Church ; that of the Evangeli- cals, through the immediate witness of the Spirit to the heart and conscience of the believer. Other Christians combine both. In order to do full justice to the missionary responsibility of the Church, clause (3) has been added : " The acceptance of Christ's commission to preach the Gospel to every creature."

Paragraph 6, which describes our differences, has been much shortened, the fuller statement of these differences being relegated to notes B and C. The added space thus gained has enabled us to deal in a manner more satisfactory to the different groups repre- sented with two difficulties in our first draft ; namely, the mis- understanding as to the meaning of the terms " visible Church " and " invisible Church," and the misunderstanding caused by the different way in which different groups relate their recognition of the existence of devout souls outside of any form of organised Christianity to their theory of the Church. The fact itself is recog- nised in note B,1 : "All true believers on earth whether contained in any organisation or not."

We commend to the thoughtful and prayerful consideration of the Churches the statement of differences contained in paragraph 6 to which much time and care have been given. The previous statement of our differences was inadequate because it did not make perfectly clear some of the more important reasons for misunder- standing (e.g., the fact that the Orthodox have no term which corresponds to the Evangelical idea " the Church invisible on earth "). We believe that our present form of statement will more accurately represent our real points of difference. There is no way to remove an unreal difficulty so effectively as to state the real difficulty clearly.

The German version was presented thus by Reichsgerichtspräsident SIMONS :

May I be permitted to add a few brief words of my own? Although

I cannot claim to be their accredited spokesman, I feel sure that I am speaking in accordance with the views of my German brethren and friends when I say that we participate who͵e-heartedly in the feeling of deep thankfulness to God which has been expressed by Dr. Brown, the revered Chairman of our Section. We are thankful that the preamble to our Report recognises the preliminary and incomplete character of our work, and that, as it has been framed without too narrow restrictions, no conscience can be offended. Nor are we less thankful that it has been granted to this Conference to take so important a step forward in the direction of the unity of the Churches, of the different branches of the Church of Christ, and we trust that we may continue to move onwards in a gradual approach to our distant and exalted goal. Few of us, when we set out for Lausanne, imagined it to be possible that we should achieve so much. And, in truth, when we think back upon the past, upon thousands of years of religious strife, the course of this Conference on Faith and Order must seem little short of a miracle of God.

Here at Lausanne we have been united in prayer, united in song, united in mutual Christian love and human sympathy, just as we were previously united at Stockholm. But over and above all this, we have begun to understand and respect one another's faith, even though we may not have been able to agree upon the exact formulation of our articles of faith. It is much indeed to have accomplished, and let us therefore render thanks and praise unto God. May His help continue with us.

The Rev. Pastor MERLE D'AUBIGNÉ, presenting the French version, said that the revised form of the Report was better, clearer and more logical than the first draft. Its three main divisions dealt first, with the nature and functions of the Church visible and invisible, as established by God and proceeding from His will, and having for its end the reconciliation of the world with God ; next, with the marks by which the visible Church is known—the Word of God, the sacraments, the ministry, the fellowship of the brotherhood—an important paragraph relating to the missionary task of the Church being added ; thirdly, a brief summary of the different conceptions of the Church held by Christians, this being repeated, so as not to break the sequence of thought, in the appended notes. Lastly, there was an expression of the conviction that Christians should never lose sight of the unity of the Church as thus conceived—a unity primarily of spirit, but leading, it may be, to an organic unity—but should labour unremittingly towards its realisation.

The speaker desired to pay a tribute to the brotherly cordiality which had marked the discussions ; there had been an encouraging sense of a sacred unity transcending all divergences. He expressed the gratitude of the Section to the Chairman, Dr. William Adams Brown, and the Vice-Chairman, the Bishop of Manchester, whose tact and consideration had built up in the section, with all the contrasting traditions it represented, a genuine Christian unity.

The English text of the Report as thus presented is as follows :

REPORT OF SECTION III, SECOND DRAFT

The Conference further reports that it has been able to arrive at substantial accord on the following points :

1. God, who has given us the Gospel for the salvation of the world, has appointed His Church to witness by life and word to its redeeming power. The Church of the Living God is constituted by His own will, not by the will or consent or beliefs of men whether as individuals or as societies, though He uses the will of men as His instrument. Of this Church Jesus Christ is the Head, the Holy Spirit its continuing life.

2. The Church as the communion of believers in Christ Jesus is, according to the New Testament, the people of the New Covenant; the Body of Christ ; and the Temple of God, built upon the foundation of the Apostles and Prophets, Jesus Christ Himself being the chief corner stone.

3. The Church is God's chosen instrument by which Christ, through the Holy Spirit, reconciles men to God through faith, bringing their wills into subjection to His sovereignty, sanctifying them through the means of grace, and uniting them in love and service to be His witnesses and fellow-workers in the extension of His rule on earth until His Kingdom come in glory.

4. As there is but one Christ, and one Life in Him, and one Holy Spirit who guides into all truth, so there is and can be but one Church, holy, catholic, and apostolic.

5. The Church on earth possesses certain characteristics whereby it can be known of men. These have been, since the days of the Apostles, at least the following :

(1) The possession and the acknowledgment of the Word of God as given in Holy Scripture and interpreted by the Holy Spirit to the Church and to the individual. (Note A.)

(2) The profession of faith in God as He is incarnate and revealed in Christ.

(3) The acceptance of Christ's commission to preach the Gospel to every creature.

(4) The observance of the Sacraments.

(5) A ministry for the pastoral office, the preaching of the Word, and the administration of the Sacraments.

(6) A fellowship in prayer, in worship, in all the means of grace, in the pursuit of holiness, and in the service of man.

6. As to the extent and manner in which the Church thus described finds expression in the existing Churches, we differ. Our differences chiefly concern :

(1) The nature of the Church visible and the Church invisible, their relation to each other, and the number of those who are included in each. (Note B.)

(2) The significance of our divisions past and present. (Note C.)

Whatever our views on these points, we are convinced that it is the will of Christ that the one life of the one body should be manifest to the world. To commend the Gospel to doubting, sinful and bewildered men, a united witness is necessary. We therefore urge most earnestly that all Christians in fulfilment of our Saviour's prayer that His disciples may be one reconsecrate themselves to God, that by the help of His spirit the body of Christ may be built up, its members united in faith and love, and existing obstacles to the manifestation of their unity in Christ may be removed ; that the world may believe that the Father has sent Him.

We join in the prayer that the time may be hastened when in the name of Jesus every knee shall bow and every tongue confess that Jesus Christ is Lord to the glory of God the Father.

NOTES

A. Some hold that this interpretation is given through the tradition of the Church ; others through the immediate witness of the Spirit to the heart and conscience of the believer ; others through both combined.

B. For instance:

1. Some hold that the invisible Church is wholly in heaven ; others include in it all true believers on earth, whether contained in any organisation or not.

2. Some hold that the visible expression of the Church was determined by Christ Himself and is, therefore, unchangeable ; others that the one Church under the guidance of the Holy Spirit may express itself in varying forms.

3. Some hold that one or other of the existing Churches is the only true Church ; others that the Church as we have described it is to be found in some or all of the existing communions taken together.

4. Some, while recognising other Christian bodies as Churches, are persuaded that in the providence of God and by the teaching of history a particular form of ministry has been shown to be necessary to the best welfare of the Church ; others hold that no one form of organisation is inherently preferable ; still others, that no organisation is necessary.

C. One view is that no division of Christendom has ever come to pass without sin. Another view is that the divisions were the inevitable outcome of different gifts of the Spirit and different understandings of the truth. Between these, there is the view of those who look back on the divisions of the past with penitence and sorrow coupled with a lively sense of God's mercy which, in spite of and even through these divisions, has advanced His cause in the world.

Discussion

The Chairman pointed out that the introduction to the Report would need re-casting so as to indicate closely the nature of the Report and its relation to the Conference.

The Rev. H. SUMITRA urged that the attention of the Conference should be centred, not so much on the Church of the past, as on the Church in its entirety, past, present and future ; and that it should take account of that " supplement to the Acts of the Apostles " which was now being enacted in the infant Churches of the East. He added :

For we believe that in the Church in the mission field the Spirit is revealing to us truths that are perhaps obscure in Christian lands. For example, " faith " in the mission field means belief in the Lord Jesus Christ and not a statement of this belief. The emphasis on creed and doctrine is conspicuous in the Far East by its absence. All the emphasis is placed on life in Christ, and so far no attempt has been made to define this life in doctrine. As regards the organisation and order of the Church, the Indian Christians have no preferences and no prejudices. We feel that keeping true to the Spirit of Christ we are at liberty to develop that form of organisation which is most helpful to our corporate life in Christ. We are also bound to consider seriously the religious organisations of India in preference to the religious organisations of the West. Similarly, the supreme task of the Church in mission lands is obviously the preaching of the Gospel to those who are outside the Church. Before this urgent and all-important task, questions of faith and order take a secondary place.

Many of us feel that these changes in emphasis are not only necessary and proper but also that they are in harmony with the Spirit of Christ. We are of opinion that through His Church in the mission field our Lord is calling us to a freer and fuller life. The Church is the living Body of the living Lord, and as such there should be room for growth and adaptation. The more we look to the past, the more hopeless do some of us become of the union of all Churches. But we believe in the living Church. Let us believe in the Spirit of Christ, who lives in His Church and is able to recreate the Body to serve His purpose in the world. The world is eagerly looking for the living Christ and the living Church. As we think and study and plan for the formation of one united Church, I humbly plead that we should study the history of the Church in mission lands as well as the past history of the Church, with an open mind, determined to be led by the Spirit of God into all the truth.

In the discussion of the Report, Bishop JENSEN asked that in paragraph 5 (2) it should suffice to say, " the public confession of faith in God as revealed in Christ " ; and it was suggested by the Bishop of ADELAIDE that in paragraph 6, first sentence, " existing Communions " should be substituted for " existing Churches." Some discussion took place upon a suggestion of Bishop GORE, which in the following form was supported by Dr. BARTLET, that this paragraph should be incorporated in the notes to the Report: " Most of us probably hold that the number of those who are being saved in the world to-day is not completely included in any branch of the Church, or in all together, but that they are known to God, and the existence of such disciples whom the Church has not known how to win is made known to men through the fruits of the Spirit in their lives." This suggestion was opposed by the Rev. W. B. SMILEY, the Bishop of DORNAKAL (who held that it would have an unfavourable effect upon missionary enterprise), and by Dr. WILLIAM ADAMS BROWN, who, however, thought that an appended note might fittingly record the substance of the suggestion. The Conference not being unanimous, the Chairman and President decided that the suggestion could not be further considered.

The Report and Notes were then unanimously received.

Report of Section IV, second draft, presented

After an interval for silent prayer, Canon TATLOW presented the Report of Section IV, on the Church's Common Confession of Faith, in the form in which it is printed on page 467.

The Report and Notes were unanimously received without discussion: and after silent prayer the Conference adjourned at 5.30 p.m.

REPORTS OF SECTIONS V, VI, VII

The Conference met in full session morning and afternoon. The morning session opened at 9.30 a.m., with devotions led by Bishop MANNING.

Continuation Committee

The President referred to the gift of a silver clock, which had been made to him by the members of the old and new Continuation Committees. "Next to being allowed to love," he said, "the greatest privilege in life is being loved ; and as this is an expression of the affection and loyalty of the Continuation Committee to whom I owe unspeakable things, I wish to let everybody who had any part in this gift know how very deeply I appreciate it."

A preliminary list of members of the new Continuation Committee was then read. (The full list will be found on page 531.)

Report of Section V, second draft, presented

The Bishop of GLOUCESTER, with thanks to Lord Sands, Dr. Titius, and Pastor Appia for valuable help in drafting and translation, presented the following revised Report of Section V, on the Church's Ministry, and moved that it be received :

REPORT OF SECTION V, SECOND DRAFT

I. The representatives of the Churches here assembled are happy to report that they find themselves in substantial accord in the following five propositions :

1. The ministry is a gift of God through Christ to His Church and is essential to the being and well-being of the Church.

2. The ministry is perpetually authorised and made effective through Christ and His Spirit.

3. The purpose of the ministry is to impart to men the saving and sanctifying benefits of Christ through pastoral service, the preaching of the Gospel, and the administration of the sacraments, to be made effective by faith.

4. The ministry is entrusted with the government and discipline of the Church, in whole or in part.

5. Men gifted for the work of the ministry, called by the Spirit and accepted by the Church, are commissioned through an act of ordination by prayer and the laying on of hands to exercise the function of this ministry.

II. Within the many Christian Communions into which in the course of history Christendom has been divided, various forms of ministry have grown up according to the circumstances of the several Communions and their beliefs as to the mind of Christ and the guidance of the New Testament. These Communions have been, in God's providence, manifestly and abundantly used by the Holy Spirit in His work of enlightening the world, converting sinners, and perfecting saints. But the differences which have arisen in regard to the authority and functions of these various forms of ministry have been and are the occasion of manifold doubts, questions and misunderstandings.

III. These differences concern the nature of the ministry (whether consisting of one or several orders), the nature of ordination and of the grace conferred thereby, the function and authority of bishops, and the nature of apostolic succession. We believe that the first step toward the overcoming of these difficulties is the frank recognition that they exist, and the clear definition of their nature. We therefore add as an appendix to our Report such a statement, commending it to the thoughtful consideration of the Churches we represent.

IV. By these differences the difficulties of inter-communion have been accentuated to the distress and wounding of faithful souls, while in the mission field where the Church is fulfilling its primary object to preach the Gospel to every creature the young Churches find the lack of unity a very serious obstacle to the furtherance of the Gospel. Consequently, the provision of a ministry acknowledged in every part of the Church as possessing the sanction of the whole Church is an urgent need.

V. There has not been time in this Conference to consider all the points of difference between us in the matter of the ministry with that care and patience which could alone lead to complete agreement. The same observation applies equally to proposals for the constitution of the united Church. Certain suggestions as to possible church organisation have been made, which we transmit to the Churches with the earnest hope that common study of these questions will be continued by the members of the various Churches represented in this Conference.

P

In view of (1) the place which the episcopate, the councils of presbyters, and the congregation of the faithful, respectively, had in the constitution of the early Church, and (2) the fact that episcopal, presbyteral and congregational systems of government are each to-day, and have been for centuries, accepted by great Communions in Christendom, and (3) the fact that episcopal, presbyteral and congregational systems are each believed by many to be essential to the good order of the Church, we therefore recognise that these several elements must all, under conditions which require further study, have an appropriate place in the order of life of a reunited Church, and that each separate Communion, recalling the abundant blessing of God vouchsafed to its ministry in the past, should gladly bring to the common life of the united Church its own spiritual treasures.

If the foregoing suggestion be accepted and acted upon, it is essential that the acceptance of any special form of ordination as the regular and orderly method of introduction into the ministry of the Church for the future should not be interpreted to imply the acceptance of any one particular theory of the origin, character or function of any office in the Church, or to involve the acceptance of any adverse judgment on the validity of ordination in those branches of the Church universal that believe themselves to have retained valid and apostolic orders under other forms of ordination ; or as disowning or discrediting a past or present ministry of the Word and Sacrament which has been used and blessed by the Spirit of God.

It is further recognised that inasmuch as the Holy Spirit is bestowed upon every believer, and each believer has direct and immediate access to God through Jesus Christ, and since special gifts of the Holy Spirit, such as teaching, preaching, and spiritual counsel, are the treasures of the Church as well as of the individual, it is necessary and proper that the Church should make fuller use of such gifts for the development of its corporate spiritual life and for the extension of the Kingdom of Jesus Christ our Lord.

VI. In particular, we share in the conviction, repeatedly expressed in this Conference, that pending the solution of the questions of faith and order in which agreements have not yet been reached, it is possible for us, not simply as individuals but as Churches, to unite in the activities of brotherly service which Christ has committed to His disciples. We therefore commend to our Churches the consideration of the steps which may be immediately practicable to bring an existing unity in service to more effective expression.

VII. In conclusion, we express our thankfulness to Almighty God for the great progress which has been made in recent years in the mutual approach of the Churches to one another, and our conviction that we must go forward with faith and courage, confident that with the blessing of God we shall be able to solve the problems that lie before us.

NOTES.

A. The following is the view of the Orthodox Church, as formulated for us by its representatives :

" The Orthodox Church, regarding the ministry as instituted in the Church by Christ Himself, and as the body which by a special *charisma* is the organ through which the Church spreads its means of grace such as the sacraments, and believing that the ministry in its threefold form of bishops, presbyters and deacons can only be based on the unbroken apostolic succession, regrets that it is unable to come, in regard to the ministry, into some measure of agreement with many of the Churches represented at this Conference ; but prays God that He, through His Holy Spirit, will guide to union even in regard to this difficult point of disagreement."

B. In Western Christendom also there are conspicuous differences.

One representative view includes the following points : (a) that there have always been various grades of the ministry, each with its own function ; (b) that ordination is a sacramental act of divine institution, and therefore indispensable, conveying the special *charisma* for the particular ministry ; (c) that bishops who have received their office by succession from the Apostles are the necessary ministers of ordination ; (d) that the apostolic succession so understood is necessary for the authority of the ministry, the visible unity of the Church, and the validity of the sacraments.

On the other hand, it is held by many Churches represented in the Conference, (a) that essentially there is only one ministry, that of the Word and Sacraments ; (b) that the existing ministries in these Churches are agreeable to the New Testament, are proved by their fruits and have due authority in the Church, and the sacraments ministered by them are valid ; (c) that no particular form of ministry is necessary to be received as a matter of faith ; (d) that the grace which fits men for the ministry is immediately given by God, and is recognised, not conferred, in ordination.

Further we record that there are views concerning the ministry which are intermediate between the types just mentioned. For instance, some who adhere to an episcopal system of Church government do not consider that the apostolic succession as described above is a vital element of episcopacy, or they reject it altogether. Others do not regard as essential the historic episcopate. Those who adhere to presbyteral systems of church government believe that the apostolic ministry is transmissible and has been transmitted through Presbyters orderly associated for the purpose. Those who adhere to the congregational system of government define their ministry as having been and being transmitted according to the precedent and example of the New Testament.

A suggestion by the Archbishop of DUBLIN, that in Section V, paragraph 3, the term " apostolic orders " should be made clear, was referred to the Drafting Committee.

The whole Report and appended Notes were then unanimously received by the Conference.

The amended form of the Report of Section VI, on the Sacraments, was then presented by Bishop CANNON, with explanations, as follows :

REPORT OF SECTION VI, SECOND DRAFT

1. We are convinced that for the purpose in view in this Conference we should not go into detail in considering Sacraments—by some called " Mysteries." The purpose, therefore, of this statement is to show that there may be a common approach to and appreciation of Sacraments on the part of those who may otherwise differ in conception and interpretation.

2. We testify to the fact that the Christian world gives evidence of an increasing sense of the significance and value of Sacraments, and would express our belief that this movement should be fostered and guided as a means of deepening the life and experience of the Churches. In this connection we recognise that the Sacraments have special reference to the corporate life and fellowship of the Church and that the grace is conveyed by the Holy Spirit, taking of the things of Christ and applying them to the soul through faith.

3. We agree that Sacraments are of divine appointment and that the Church ought thankfully to observe them as divine gifts.

4. We hold that in the Sacraments there is an outward sign and an inward grace, and that the Sacraments are means of grace through which God works invisibly in us. We recognise also that in the gifts of His grace God is not limited by His own Sacraments.

5. The Orthodox Church and others hold that there are seven

Sacraments and that for their valid administration there must be a proper form, a proper matter and a proper ministry. Others can regard only Baptism and the Lord's Supper as Sacraments. In this Conference we lay stress on these two Sacraments because they are the Sacraments which are generally acknowledged by the members of this Conference.

6. We believe that in Baptism administered with water in the name of the Father, the Son and the Holy Spirit, for the remission of sins, we are baptised by one Spirit into one body. By this statement it is not meant to ignore the differences in conception, interpretation and mode which exist among us.

7. We believe that in the Holy Communion our Lord is present, that we have fellowship with God our Father in Jesus Christ His Son, our Living Lord, who is our one Bread, given for the life of the world, sustaining the life of all His people, and that we are in fellowship with all others who are united to Him. We agree that the Sacrament of the Lord's Supper is the Church's most sacred act of worship in which the Lord's atoning death is commemorated and proclaimed, and that it is a sacrifice of praise and thanksgiving and an act of solemn self-oblation.

8. There are among us divergent views, especially as to (1) the mode or manner of the presence of our Lord ; (2) the conception of the commemoration and the sacrifice ; (3) the relation of the elements to the grace conveyed ; and (4) the relation between the minister of this Sacrament and the validity and efficacy of the rite. We are aware that the reality of the divine presence and gift in this Sacrament cannot be adequately apprehended by human thought or expressed in human language.

9. We recognise that under certain conditions the spiritual values of the Sacraments may be realised by divine grace where the outward signs are absent.

10. We close this statement with the prayer that the differences which prevent full communion at the present time may be removed.

Discussion

On paragraph 7 a suggestion by Dr. BARTLET that the word " specially " should be inserted before " present " failed to gain the acceptance of the Conference.

A prolonged discussion arose upon paragraph 9. Dr. BIELER suggested altering this paragraph to read, " We recognise that under certain conditions the spiritual values of the Sacraments may by divine grace be realised where the outwards signs are absent."

Bishop CANNON said that the Committee was prepared to accept this suggestion. Dr. SCHERER asked whether the words "where the outward signs are absent" meant where the Sacraments were not available. Bishop CANNON replied in the affirmative. He pointed out that this paragraph had been considered very carefully by the Committee, and had been drawn up in its present form in order to meet the views of the Society of Friends.

Archdeacon JOYCE explained that the clause, with the emphasis on the words "under certain conditions," meant that where the Sacraments were not available God could give the special grace of the Sacraments independently of the outward signs. He thought they would all agree that the impossibility of receiving the Sacraments was not always a physical impossibility, but might be a moral impossibility. The Section had considered that the clause covered the needs of those who at present practised Christianity without the Sacraments. It was, however, possible that the words were open to misconstruction, and he suggested, for the consideration of the Drafting Committee, that a note might be added to the Report intimating that the expression "under certain conditions" was differently interpreted by different Communions in the Christian Church.

Bishop CANNON suggested the following redrafting : "We recognise that there are those among us who hold that under certain conditions the spiritual values of the Sacraments may by divine grace be realised where the outward signs are absent." This suggestion was approved by Dr. Scherer.

Bishop GORE hoped that the Conference would agree to the paragraph as originally drafted, as it merely represented what had been said in the final words of the fourth paragraph : ". . . in the gifts of His grace God is not limited by His own Sacraments." He could not imagine anyone refusing to recognise that under certain conditions—of which God alone was the Judge—He could give what He pleased to any human soul. In conclusion, he said that he had observed with regret on several occasions a tendency on the part of the Conference to refuse to say what was true because they thought it dangerous.

Dr. SCHERER did not question the right of the Society of Friends to say for themselves whether they believed the outward signs of the Sacraments to be necessary or not. There was no criticism of that ; his only contention was that if he did not recognise the Sacraments, and did not use them, he could not claim the benefits which they conveyed.

Prof. MONOD supported the view expressed by Bishop GORE. After further discussion of this clause, during which suggestions were made by Pastor Thvedt, Dr. Wotherspoon and Archdeacon Joyce, it was decided, on a motion by the Bishop of Bombay, to ask the Drafting Committee to draw up another form of words in writing, to be submitted to the Conference at an early hour in the afternoon session for approval. It was agreed to hold over the report until such time as the new draft of paragraph 9 was received.

Dr. GARVIE drew attention to the very arduous duties that were being carried out by the multigraphing staff, which had been obliged to work through the entire night in order that the documents might be ready for to-day's session. He was sure that it would be the desire of the Conference to convey its thanks to them for the manner in which they had so faithfully worked.

Preamble and Subject I, second draft, presented

The President presented the Preamble in its revised form and the draft of the report on Subject I, the Call to Unity. Introducing these documents he made the following observations :

In presenting this Preamble which I have been charged to write, I present the judgment of many minds of varying views, all of which coincide in what I have written. There is an avoidance of compromise, to which I am opposed, and as strong a recognition of differences as of agreements. The differences which our Reports present are the material for that careful study which must be the new starting-point in our quest. These differences are, many of them, not vertical, dividing Communion from Communion, but rather are horizontal, running through many Communions. They exist as schools of thought within a given Church, not as divisive agencies, but as bearing testimony to that diversity in unity which I believe will be characteristic of the whole united Church. It would be in many instances difficult to pronounce a given position as representing the mind of a given Church. The most that could be honestly done would be to denominate it as representing a school within the Church. In our Reports this has, I am convinced, been given adequate recognition.

You will note that the Preamble as I present it looks only for the reception of the Reports and passing them on to the Churches we represent for such action as God's Spirit may guide them to take. They do not hamper the Churches in any way. They but draw attention to the unities manifested and the differences registered.

Had there been no Conference on Faith and Order the duty of the Churches to give these matters consideration would have been unabated and binding. The Conference itself would be powerless to attempt more than to formulate these things to aid the Churches in their obvious duty. It could not do less.

Our effort is a synthetic effort. It is following the lines of all movements of the day—unitive movements in every department of life. Best of all, it is following the method of God's Holy Spirit who creates a Body having many members with many gifts and functions.

There is one thing that has been brought to my attention, and to which I should like to give expression in this connection, namely, the thankfulness to God for the lead which mission Churches abroad have given to the home Churches in the matter of Church union. Could we not, for their encouragement, express in some way the hope and prayer that the union toward which they are looking may be consummated according to God's will, and that a still wider union throughout the whole Church may, under the blessing of God, come to pass ?

PREAMBLE, SECOND DRAFT

We, the representatives of many Christian Communions throughout the world, assembled to consider, under the guidance of the Holy Spirit, the things wherein we agree and the things wherein we differ, receive the following series of Reports as containing subject matter for the consideration of our respective Churches in their common search for unity.

This is a Conference summoned to consider matters of Faith and Order. It is emphatically *not* attempting to define the conditions of future reunion. Its object is to register the apparent level of fundamental agreements within the Conference and the grave points of disagreements remaining ; also to suggest certain lines of thought which may in the future tend to a fuller measure of agreement.

Each subject on the agenda was first discussed in plenary session. It was then committed to one of the sections, of more than one hundred members each, into which the whole Conference was divided. The report, after full discussion in sub-sections, was finally drawn up and adopted unanimously or by a large majority vote by the section to which it had been committed. It was twice presented for further discussion to a plenary session of the Conference when it was referred to the Churches in its present form.

Though we recognise the reports to be neither exhaustive nor in all details satisfactory to every member of the Conference, we submit them to the Churches for that deliberate consideration which could not be given in the brief period of our sessions. We further recommend that the whole material should be referred to a small commission of qualified men representative of the various groups—Orthodox, Evangelical, Lutheran, Presbyterian, Methodist, Anglican, etc.—and charged with the duty carefully to examine these propositions in the light of the discussions and to report thereon to the Churches. We thank God and rejoice over agreements reached; upon our agreements we build. Where the reports record differences, we call upon the Christian world to an earnest reconsideration of the conflicting opinions now held, and a strenuous endeavour to reach the truth as it is in God's mind, which should be the foundation of the Church's unity.

SUBJECT I, THE CALL TO UNITY

God wills unity. Our presence in this Conference bears testimony to our desire to bend our wills to His. However we may justify the beginnings of disunion, we lament its continuance and henceforth must labour, in penitence and faith, to build up our broken walls.

God's Spirit has been in our midst. It was He who called us hither. His presence has been manifest in our worship, our deliberations and our whole fellowship. He has discovered us to one another. He has enlarged our horizons, quickened our understanding, and enlivened our hope. We have dared and God has justified our daring. We can never be the same again. Our deep thankfulness must find expression in sustained endeavour to share the visions vouchsafed us here with those smaller home groups where out lot is cast.

More than half the world is waiting for the Gospel. At home and abroad sad multitudes are turning away in bewilderment from the Church because of its corporate feebleness. Our missions count that as a necessity which we are inclined to look on as a luxury. Already the mission field is impatiently revolting from the divisions of the Western Church to make bold adventure for unity in its own right. We of the Churches represented in this Conference cannot allow our spiritual children to outpace us. We must gird ourselves to the task, the early beginnings of which God has so richly blessed, and labour side by side with the Christians who are working for indigenous Churches until our common goal is reached.

Some of us, pioneers in this undertaking, have grown old in our search for unity. It is to youth that we look to take the torch of unity from our failing hands. We men have carried it too much alone through many years. The women henceforth should be accorded their share of responsibility. And so the whole Church will be enabled to do that which no section can hope to perform.

It was God's clear call that gathered us. With faith stimulated by His guidance to us here, we move forward.

Discussion

Three suggestions were made as to further changes. That of Dr. von Martin, to enlarge the opening sentence of the Preamble thus : "We, representatives of many Christian Communions throughout the world, united in the common confession of faith in Jesus Christ, the Son of God, our Lord and Saviour," was accepted by the President ; on paragraph 3 of the Call to Unity, a proposal of Dr. Forgan, to read in the final sentence " We and they must gird ourselves to the task, the early beginnings of which God has so richly blessed, and labour side by side until our common goal is reached," and various verbal emendations of the phrase, " Christians who are working for indigenous Churches," were left to the President's discretion. Note was taken of the Bishop of Ottawa's desire to omit in paragraph 4 the words, " from our failing hands."

The Bishop of Bombay desired that the Preamble should be not only received, but also adopted : but the Chairman pointed out that this could not be done, as some members had abstained from voting. (See, however, the afternoon session, page 439.)

The Preamble was then received by the Conference, and the session closed, after devotions, at 12.30 p.m.

Saturday Afternoon, August 20th.

The afternoon session opened at 4 p.m. with devotions led by the President.

Report of Section VI (continued)

It was reported by Dr. Garvie, the Chairman, that the question which had arisen in the morning with regard to paragraph 9 had been considered by the Drafting Committee. The Committee submitted the following clause to be inserted in paragraph 5, after the sentence " others can regard only Baptism and the Lord's Supper as sacraments " :

Others, again, while attaching high value to the sacramental principle, do not make use of the outward signs of sacraments, but hold that all spiritual benefits are given through immediate contact with God through His Spirit.

The insertion of these words, which was understood to involve the deletion of paragraph 9, was carried, on the motion of Dr. SCHERER, seconded by Miss LUCY GARDNER.

The Report was then unanimously received by the Conference.

Report of Section VII, second draft, presented

In the absence of the Archbishop of Upsala, the revised form of the Report of Section VII, on the Unity of Christendom and the Relation thereto of Existing Churches, was presented by the Archbishop of ARMAGH, who spoke of the almost insuperable difficulties of the task entrusted to the Section. It had been quite clear to the Section that they were nowhere near the practical working out of the relation of existing Churches to a united Christendom, and that they could not do more than present certain principles of approach, with a summary of what had been done towards the solution of the tremendous problem before them. It was notable that the conclusions reached in the Report ran parallel, in many points, to the Lambeth Appeal of 1920.

The following is the text of the Report as thus submitted :

REPORT OF SECTION VII, SECOND DRAFT

Christian Unity expresses itself in love, in faith and in the order of the Church.

1. Fellowship in Life and Work

As the individual is tested by the divine rule (" ye shall know them by their fruits ") so also the unity of the disciples is proved by their fellowship in the service of the Master.

All Christians in fulfilling the Master's law of love should act together as if they were one body in one visible fellowship without any injury to theological principles. In 1920, the Ecumenical Patriarchate issued to Christendom an Encyclical letter proposing a *koinonia ton ekklesion*, a league of Churches for practical purposes, without authority to commit the Churches. It was followed up by the Universal Christian Conference on Life and Work (Stockholm, 1925). The task of that Conference should be continued and strengthened, and will surely prepare the way for fuller spiritual unity through faith in God and our Lord Jesus Christ, the faith underlying and inspiring all Christian life and work. A council of the Churches for practical purposes might be well evolved from the Continuation Committee on Life and Work, consisting of representatives officially appointed by almost all Christian communions, and from other organisations of a similar nature.

2. *Fellowship in Faith and Order*

The present movement towards unity in faith and order which has found expression at Lausanne, yields the idea of one Church united in the essentials of faith and order, and including diverse types of doctrinal statement and of the administration of Church ordinances.

Every existing Church has its own *charisma* and its own historic tradition. It has, therefore, a contribution to make to the whole. The common historic tradition of Christianity has also to be considered. In the primitive Church the Body was one, yet there was variety in the expression of doctrine and also diversity of practice.

In the united Church there must be :

1. A common Faith, a common Message to the World. (Reports II and IV.)

2. Baptism as the rite of incorporation into the one Church.

3. Holy Communion as expressing the corporate life of the Church and as its signal act of corporate worship. (Report VI.)

4. A ministry accepted throughout the universal Church. (Report V.)

5. Freedom of interpretation about sacramental grace and ministerial order and authority.

There is a difference of view as to the extent of this freedom. Professor Balanos made the following statement :

The Greek Church, which regards the holy tradition of the Church besides the Holy Scriptures as *norma fidei*, cannot recognise liberty in regard to interpretation about sacramental grace and ministerial order and authority.

6. Due provision for the exercise of the prophetic gift.

3. *Ways of Approach*

In preparation for closer fellowship, each section of the Church should seek more intimate knowledge of faith and life, worship and order in other Communions. Differences founded in complicated historic developments may sometimes prove to be less important than they are supposed to be. As our several Communions come to understand each other better they will refrain from competitive propaganda to exalt the one by depreciating another.

The unity of the Church is most effectively promoted by constant prayer for one another on the part of the various Communions : and such prayer is especially needed for all those who are passing through suffering.

We would also stress the value of different Communions engaging in joint evangelistic work. There is abundant evidence that when Communions undertake together the divine task of bringing the love of Christ to those who do not know Him, they find themselves in the closest spiritual unity.

When different Christian denominations are represented in the same community, differences in creed, worship and practice should not prevent individuals and Communions from working together in recognition of the principle of comity, mutual consideration and Christian courtesy.

We note with gratitude to God the recent increase of effective co-operation on the mission field. The purpose of all missionary work is to carry the eternal Gospel to the ends of the earth, so that it may meet the spiritual needs of every nation and bring all men to their Saviour. The urgency and greatness of that task has led to the accomplishment of some unions, and to the proposal of plans which are attracting the attention of the older Communions and may prove to provide examples for them. We trust that the old, long-standing divisions will not be permitted to frustrate such plans.

4. Completed Fellowship

Complete fellowship in the Church will not be realised until the way is opened for all God's children to join in communion at the Lord's Table. Only through prayer and thoughtful deliberation can steps be taken towards full communion between the different sections of Christendom. Ambiguous statements and hasty measures may hinder the work of unification. Only when full mutual recognition has been obtained, can the visible unity of the Church be effectively realised.

Nor should we forget that, greatest of all, God's mercy and sonship in His family are granted to every faithful soul. God give us wisdom and courage to do His will!

Discussion

Dr. F. C. MOREHOUSE made detailed criticisms of the form and substance of the Report, and moved the following resolutions :

1. That the Report be referred, without recommendation, to the Continuation Committee.

2. That Bishop Brent be asked to write a concluding section.

After some discussion, the President said that in view of the absence of unanimity the reference of the Report to the Continuation Committee would be the best way to keep the subject open. The skill, experience and learning which had been given to the compilation of the Report, under the guidance of the Archbishop of Upsala, was recognised by all the delegates.

The Chairman said that probably the Conference was not ready at this stage for the discussion of so difficult a problem : nevertheless, the Report would prove valuable for its future study. He added, in reply to a question from Dr. FORGAN, that the Report, as having been duly presented, would necessarily appear in the records of the Conference.

The reference of the Report to the Continuation Committee was strongly opposed by the Rev. T. TINGFANG LEW, and Bishop CANNON held that it would be better to hold an evening session, for detailed discussion of the Report, than to refer the Report without comment.

After further argument, the President suggested, as a proposal likely to meet all difficulties, that the Report should be received by the Conference in the same way as the other Reports, but on the understanding that it should be referred to the Continuation Committee for further consideration. This proposal was seconded by Canon WOODS. Rev. J. S. STEVENSON intimated his readiness to acquiesce in the motion, it having been explained by the Chairman that the document would only go to the Continuation Committee for further consideration, whereas the other Reports had been received for transmission to the Churches.

The Chairman also explained, in answer to the Bishop of BOMBAY, that the Continuation Committee would take such action as it considered advisable in view of the knowledge it had of the situation.

The motion was carried ; and note was taken of the following suggestion of Dr. FORGAN, who desired that the records should state plainly, in this form, that the document was not to be transmitted to the Churches :

In view of the extreme difficulty of the task assigned to this Section and the raising in the Report of questions which have not been discussed, the Conference, while recognising the high value of the Report, resolves to receive it and refer it to the Continuation Committee for such consideration as the Committee is competent to give it, without sending it to the Churches for their consideration.

Dr. F. C. MOREHOUSE then moved his second resolution in these terms : That the President of the Conference be requested to draft a concluding section to be added to the documents which this Conference has received.

This motion, seconded by the Rev. Dr. Lofthouse, was carried.

The Conference accepted for consideration a proposal by the Rev. Prof. D. M. KAY : That a standard text for the various versions in French, German and English of the fundamental conclusions of this Conference should be prepared, and also in the Greek language of the Apostles and Evangelists.

Dr. MERLE D'AUBIGNÉ moved the following resolutions, which had been endorsed by Dr. Dibelius, Dr. Hermelink, Pastor Gounelle and Dr. A. Lang :

Considering that it is of the utmost importance that there should be no ambiguity in the documents originating from the Conference ; that most of these documents were first written in the English language ; and that the translations into French and German had sometimes to be made rather hastily ; it is decided that the English should be regarded as the authoritative text in cases of doubt, and that a committee of revision be added to the general drafting committee entrusted with the care of revising the German and French translations and of making such changes as may be found necessary.

The Chairman undertook that these resolutions should be considered by the Continuation Committee.

Adoption of Preamble

The Chairman reported that at the morning session he had acted upon a belief that there were members who were not prepared to support the adoption of the Preamble : that belief, he now discovered, was unfounded, and he therefore asked the Conference whether it was now prepared unanimously to adopt the Preamble.

The Conference assenting, the Preamble was unanimously adopted on the understanding that Bishop Brent would perfect the wording in the light of suggestions made in the morning's discussion.

A Personal Statement

Dr. F. C. MOREHOUSE desired to make it clear that he had not moved his motion at the instance of the delegation of the American Episcopal Church : he had discussed the matter with many delegates, but had acted, as it had been understood throughout that delegates should act and vote, on his own initiative.

Letter from the Syndic of the Municipality of Lausanne

The President read the following letter from the Syndic of the Municipality :

SIRS,

You are coming to the end of the three weeks of assiduous discussion which you have undertaken. Coming from distant countries, and representing as you do a variety of Churches, diverse groups, and many peoples, you have laboured for the union and consolidation of the Churches in order to further the development of Christianity in the world.

It was a moving moment, and one which will abide as a historical memory, when churchmen, scholars and laymen, gathered together in Lausanne Cathedral, in fellowship with our pastors and with a crowded congregation of our people, recited the Lord's Prayer together.

In the spirit of knowledge, charity, and mutual good-will you have sought to find every possible point of agreement: and these agreements have enabled you to appoint an influential Committee of your members for the continuation of your work.

At this moment of your separation, when you are about to return to your distant homes and spheres of work, permit us to express to you our hope that the days spent in Lausanne will be remembered by you as a period of useful work. If, through the large-minded application of the spirit of Christian comprehensiveness, and the exercise of theological skill, you have found it possible to establish basal principles and to form new ties of friendship, you may be sure that the city which you have honoured by making it the home of your Conference will recall that result with deep satisfaction.

We would assure you once more of our respect and esteem, and of our best wishes for your safe return to your homes.

ROSSET.

Syndic.

Close of the Conference

The Chairman (Dr. GARVIE) : I wish to thank the Conference for the way in which it has helped me to conduct the meetings. I thank God that through many difficulties we have been guided and helped, and although we have had these difficulties we have, after some storms, reached haven. I hope that haven will only be the starting-point of some further voyage. What has added greatly to my appreciation of the task entrusted to me is the fact that I have been able, in this way, to relieve the very heavy burden of responsibility that has fallen upon Bishop Brent.

The PRESIDENT of the Conference (Bishop BRENT) : Brethren, Captain Garvie has brought the ship safely into port. He was very free in the way in which he conferred high titles on others, and so I venture to call him the Captain of this Conference.

I am extremely grateful to him, and have already expressed what I feel. I do not think I can add anything except to assure him that I hope in the future we may still work side by side.

Every member of the Conference owes great gratitude, in the first place, to our very efficient staff, and while it is invidious to mention any names, there are two names that I should like specially to bring forward as having done prominent service : the Rev. Floyd W. Tomkins, Jr., and Mr. T. H. Ringrose. It is a very trying thing to undertake to do all sorts of petty jobs and to be called at any moment to do something that seems to be necessary. Mr. Ringrose and Mr. Tomkins have both fulfilled that rôle from the beginning of this Conference, and they are in large measure among those hidden servants to which society owes a very great debt.

I should also like to mention the great service rendered to the Conference by the interpreters, and also to thank the Conseiller d'Etat for the use of this building and this fine hall in which we have held our meetings. In due course a formal letter will be presented to him.

Then there is the Reception Committee of which Prof. Fornerod was the Chairman. We owe them a great deal for the many conveniences they have afforded us, and to them also a formal letter will be addressed.

I would also mention Pastor Secretan and the authorities of the Cathedral, who are among our benefactors, as well as the authorities of the Church of St. Laurent, and the authorities of the German Church where we have held our meetings.

Dr. Garvie spoke this morning about the girls who have been doing our multigraphing, and I should like to add another word. I have had a great deal of experience of secretariats, including the secretariat of the League of Nations which, up to the present, I had supposed to be the most efficient secretariat in the world. I now place the secretariat of the League of Nations second to that which we have had here. This is very largely due to the efficiency, faithfulness and hard work of the girls whom none of us have seen, but who have felt that they have been doing a service for the Church of God in the work they have undertaken.

Now may I speak of things that are personal to you and to me. I wish to thank every member of the Conference for the faithful way in which he has fulfilled his duties ; I do not think there has been a slacker in the Conference. Day by day in rain or shine you have been in your places attending to your work. More than that, you have been prompter than I have ever known any large assembly to be. Every morning at devotions we have had a large number, on many occasions a majority of the members of the Conference, here for those prayers which we offered, and I venture to think that in large measure it was due to the emphasis that we gave to prayer that this Conference has gone as happily as it has. I am indeed glad that we put the devotions as part of our work under the heading of " Full Session." I wish to thank you for your co-operation in what I conceive to be the most important part of our gathering.

We have formed new friendships, we have enlarged our horizons ; we have had new hope, new faith kindled in us, and now we are looking forward to the day that is to be when all these struggles for unity will have been consummated—we cannot say when or how— but we look forward to the day when there will be a great world gathering representing all the Churches to consider how they can best in their unified form fulfil their responsibility to God and to man. I should like to have the gift of an orator in order to place in word pictures before you just what such a gathering should be, and yet I venture to say that we have had glimpses during this Conference of such a gathering.

I said that Dr. Garvie had guided the ship into port, but it is not the final port ; we are already making preparations for a new voyage, and we trust that everyone will be in his place, that everyone will fulfil his peculiar and special responsibility in relation to the great task, and that when we next gather (and I trust it will not be a great many years hence) we shall feel that the accomplishments of this Conference have far exceeded anything that we at present are able to conceive.

There is one further word I should like to say. In the Report which we have just referred to the Continuation Committee there is a clause in which prayers for our suffering brothers are asked. To-day, in Russia, there are conditions among the clergy which we cannot afford to overlook. There is suffering to which we must give our attention. A petition is being passed round for our signatures, but we must not rest with that, and I am going to take the privilege, inasmuch as you have kindly asked me to write the closing words of our series of Reports, to make reference to this matter in that last section and to ask the prayers of the whole Church.

There is nothing further that I ought to say, except again to thank you for the co-operative spirit and friendliness which you have manifested throughout the Conference.

Bishop Brent then called upon the Bishop of MANCHESTER to address the Conference, who was followed by Mrs. WILLIAM E. SANFORD, Archbishop GERMANOS and Professor BENJAMIN UNRUH.

The sessions of the Conference were closed, at 7 p.m., with the Benediction, pronounced, after prayer and the singing of a hymn, by the PRESIDENT.

THE CLOSING SERVICE

Sunday, August 21st.

The closing Service of the Conference was held in the Cathedral on Sunday, August 21st, at 3 p.m. The order followed was similar in the main to that of the opening Service on August 3rd; but it had been arranged that there should be one leading subject on which, after an introductory word from the Pastor of the Cathedral, three addresses should be given, one in each of the languages of the Conference. The subject chosen was " Jesus Christ, the same yesterday and to-day and for ever." Pastor G. Secretan took for his theme, " To whom shall we go ? "; the address on Jesus Christ *yesterday* was given by Bishop Jensen; that on *to-day* by Bishop Parsons; and that on *for ever* by Pastor Elie Gounelle. The Service ended with the saying of the Lord's Prayer, the singing of the hymn " Abide with me," and the blessing pronounced by the President of the Conference.

The following is the text of the addresses:

THE RIGHT REV. PAUL TH. JENSEN, D.D.
Bishop of the Moravian Church

I. Jesus Christ—Yesterday

On the occasion of this closing service of the World Conference on Faith and Order, we are called upon to give an answer to the question, Whither shall we go ? Whither shall we go with all the unrest of our hearts, with all the troubles which oppress us ? The answer of the Church, the answer of the Christian community, can be but one: Jesus Christ, yesterday, to-day, and for ever.

" Come unto me, all ye that labour and are heavy laden, and I will give you rest." So He Himself calls to us again and again. In no other is there salvation ; no other name under heaven has been given unto men in which we may find salvation—so says the apostolic witness.

444

He who is eternal, for whom there is no yesterday, to-day, or to-morrow, entered by the grace of God into the *yesterday* of our history. " The Word was made flesh and dwelt among us, and we beheld his glory, the glory as of the only begotten son of the Father." " Behold the Lamb of God, which taketh away the sin of the world." " God made him to be sin for us who knew no sin, that we might be made the righteousness of God in him." " He was delivered up for our sins and rose again for our justification." " By his own blood he entered in once into the holy place, having obtained eternal redemption for us."

We have spoken much during these days of the distress of the Churches, of the distress of their disunion. Yet their diversity does not signify only distress, it signifies also the abundance of grace. In so far, however, as it does signify distress, true distress, it is but a part of a far wider distress, the distress of this world. Let us reflect for a moment upon this distress.

A world given over to sensuality, self-seeking and lies. A world of men, created by God in His own image, yet it hearkened to the voice of temptation, " If ye eat of the tree of the knowledge of good and evil ye shall be as God." And the world took its own way and placed itself beside God, and thus in opposition to God. And now its ways are evil, evil even when it would be righteous. For even in its religion the world serves but its own ends.

God has not forsaken this world. His Spirit is at work in it. But again and again the world has turned against the prophets, the chosen ones of God. And what is God's answer ? It is the answer of love. " God so loved the world that he gave his only begotten Son, that whosoever believeth on him should not perish, but have everlasting life." " For herein is love, not that we loved God, but that he loved us and sent his Son to be the propitiation for our sins." And thus the Son of God, our Lord Jesus Christ, came to confront His world, the small Jewish world of His day. That world is our world. He gave it His love. In Him dwelt only love. And the world's answer to this love ? It was, as we all know, the Cross. He was despised and re-

jected of men, and those of His disciples who were closest
to Him betrayed Him, denied Him, understood Him not.
Lonely He went His way. He, the One, stood over against
all others. He turned not away from them, but cast Himself into the depths that divided them from Him. He died
for their sins, for the sins of all of us. And He overcame
sin and death. The grave had no hold over Him. He rose
again—the only one who had ever returned from the
kingdom of death to the kingdom of our life, who lives and
reigns among us as our invisible, ever-present and living
Lord and Saviour.

We cannot fathom all this with our intelligence, but we
have the testimony of the Scripture, confirmed by the
experience of faith, and we know that in our crucified and
risen Saviour, and in Him alone, we have access unto the
house of God our Father.

He was crucified and rose again, and it is He who says,
" Come unto me all ye that labour and are heavy laden, and
I will give you rest." He it is who brings back the prodigal
son to his father. But it is given to us, the members and
representatives of His Church, His community, to be
ambassadors for Him and to pray in His stead, " Be ye
reconciled to God."

And now one final word. He found the way into our
distress, and it is just *in* our distress that He finds us.
When we become conscious of the chains which hold us
prisoners, when we begin to tremble in God's holy presence,
then His work in us has begun, then the Saviour is bending
over us and the glory of the Cross shines upon us. Then
are we born, for now and for all eternity. He, our crucified
and risen Saviour, has accomplished His work, has accomplished it once and for all. Nothing is lacking. God made
Him to be to us wisdom, righteousness, redemption.

" Who shall lay anything to the charge of God's elect ?
It is God that justifieth ; who is he that condemneth ? It
is Christ that died, yea rather, that is risen again, who is
even at the right hand of God, who also maketh intercession for us. . . . I am persuaded, that neither death
nor life, nor angels nor principalities nor powers, nor things

present nor things to come, nor height nor depth, nor any other creature shall be able to separate us from the love of God, which is in Christ Jesus our Lord." Amen.

THE RIGHT REV. EDWARD L. PARSONS, D.D.
Bishop of California (Anglican)

II. Jesus Christ—To-Day

I have been asked to speak to you of " Jesus Christ To-day," of Him who is to-day the same as yesterday and forever, the centre of our faith, our love and our hope—and asked to speak of Him as to-day He has been known and revealed in the great Conference which has now closed.

The Christ whom we adore to-day is the Christ of yesterday : He who died, who sent the early Church out upon its conquering mission, who guided its growth and bound its followers into one. But He is likewise the same Christ who, when the sad days of division came, was still the Incarnation of that Eternal Truth, in loyalty to which men found themselves compelled for conscience' sake to separate. Like a great mountain peak some saw Him in cloud, some in sunshine. They looked from north or south, from east or west, and failing to see what others saw, they fell apart. But the same great peak rose above the land. It was the same Christ whom all adored.

To-day it is still the same Christ ; but a change has come. Men rejoice in their own visions of Him, but they are no longer content to see those visions in loneliness, to know only one aspect of the Christ. They will to share what they have with their brethren and to see what their brethren see. They will not live on one side of the mountain and know no other.

From a hundred Churches and fifty lands, with diversity of language, of tradition and of view, we have been together that we may explore the riches of our Master's love and manifest to the world that we have the same Lord.

It is not for us who speak to-day to tell of the work of the Conference nor of those of its achievements which are to be set forth in print. But let me try to interpret to you something of its spiritual achievement as it manifests the glory and significance of the great Figure in whose name we gathered and at whose feet we bowed—the Christ of yesterday, to-day and for ever.

Christ is the Incarnation of Eternal Love. It is through Him that there comes to men that supreme message of hope, that all are God's children, that all belong to God's great family. Love is therefore—I speak truths familiar to us all—Love is therefore the fundamental principle of Christianity as it translates itself into motive and conduct. God is love and men must love. If we have not love, as St. Paul reminds us, there is something hollow, sham-like in our faith. As I think over the events of these three weeks I wonder whether ever in the history of Christianity there has been a nobler revelation of the Eternal Christ who is Love than in this Conference. It has not been the revelation in martyrdom or in the dangers of the battle-front in the mission field. It has not been heroic in its appeal. But how superb in its call to charity and considerateness and reasonableness! No gathering like this Conference has, I think, ever been held. In smaller groups men have met. But a Conference of world-wide scope to discuss frankly the most extreme differences, to touch the most sensitive nerves in the great body of Christian teaching, is unprecedented. There were not lacking souls who prophesied that it must fail, must break up in dissension. But it did not. In love and thoughtfulness and consideration for one another, through long days of wearying discussion, men of different views sat side by side and learned of one another ; men whose forefathers had separated in bitterness, whose traditions were filled with memories of persecution or insolence or neglect, prayed and sang together and adored the same great Christ. The youngest and smallest of the Churches of the Reformation received the same attention and the same privileges as the ancient Mother of Churches from the East. It was a marvel—yes, a miracle wrought by the Holy Spirit of Love. But the miracle was that which our Lord can always work for the humble in heart.

We could hear with confidence what we had before dreaded, we could trust where before we had suspected, because we knew in the very depths of our souls that we had the same Lord, the Eternal Christ—and having kneeled and prayed and worshipped at His feet, the miracle was wrought. And as we realised this miracle of love, we must have found ourselves wondering whether among all the heresies there is any which in the sight of the dear Christ can be compared with the spirit which would break the fellowship of love. We are finding our way to that fellowship again, and under the sway of love the claims of truth must be adjusted and the broken Body healed.

For next to the manifestation of Christ as Love was the manifestation of Christ as Truth. I am the Truth, He said. In Him the meaning of this universe is brought to light, the secret of God revealed. He is all Truth, for in Him all truth unfolds itself to men—that message is everywhere in the New Testament ; and for those who gather round Him to-day in adoration it is the present-day message as well. Who would be true to Christ must be true to Truth. Who would manifest Christ must manifest unswerving devotion to the Spirit of Truth. And every day in the Conference that has been done. It was because Christians desired to be true to truth that they fell apart. It is because they would be true to truth to-day that they have been able to come together to explore those ranges of truth which they have not known before. The frankness of men towards one another has been a Christlike thing. No man has been asked to hide his faith nor minimise his convictions. Each has spoken as the Lord has given him utterance ; and to those who have listened in the teachable spirit of the child new visions of the one truth have been revealed. New light has fallen upon the one Christ or shone from Him.

And there are still ranges unexplored. No one who has that heart of a child can have left this great gathering without a sense of the immeasurable depths of Christ. We have only begun to know Him. We are but children in His school. These nineteen hundred years have but started us to chart the depths of the Divine revealed in Him. Those ancient symbols which express the heart of our faith—even of them in some sense we may cry in awe, " Lo, these are but the outskirts of His ways."

Christ the Eternal Love, Christ the Truth, Christ the Power of God ; Let me remind you, finally, how the sense of the Power of Christ penetrated all the work of the Conference and rang out with the joy of victory to the world.

There have been many Christians in these latter days who, seeing the weakness of the Church and its oft-repeated failures, seeing a divided Christian world plunged in fratricidal strife or torn by industrial and social dissension, have cried out, " How long, O Lord ? " Where is the power of Pentecost ? Is the Christ no longer a conquering Master ? Is there no longer a Christ with power to save ? Dear discouraged hearts! Loyal fainting souls! But think back over these weeks. What a note of triumph and of power has gone forth! How the Christ whose Spirit of Power fell at Pentecost has been among us!

" The Gospel is the victory over sin and death. . . . The Gospel is the sure source of power for social regeneration." So reads the Message of the Church to the world. The Holy Spirit is the spirit of Power. Look back if you will over the long days of our discussions. Many men have spoken and of many minds. Some have pressed for unity with an impatience of detail. Others have cautiously scrutinised every step. Doubts and questions have been uttered. But never has there been one doubt or one question about the Power of Christ to save the world. Men have deplored the irreligion and the anti-religion of to-day, but they have never questioned the mastery of the Lord Christ and the certainty of His Kingdom. Tired we have been and perhaps sometimes disheartened, but when we feel our way back into the solemn and deep experiences of these days we know that we have met the Spirit of Pentecost and received new power.

One word more : if I have rightly interpreted the spiritual achievements of these days, if in truth, for all our disappointments and shortcomings and the little way to

unity we seem to have come, we have nevertheless manifested the Christ of Love and Truth and Power, if we have
seen Him in new lights and He has grown more glorious
before our eyes, does not it mean that to every member
of the Conference, and through them to the world, there
must come the vision of a Church greater, wider, richer,
more splendid than any has dreamed before—a Church
which, being His Body, is rich with all His richness, filled
with the fulness of the divine, vaster than you or I may
dream ? The Body of Christ must reveal to the world all
the wealth of the knowledge of Christ, it must show forth
the fulness of Him who is all in all.

To the Christian world, then, we who have been here
may say : Brethren, in the special task entrusted to us
we have made some progress—more than some expected,
less than others hoped. It has been a hard and technical
task. We go home to our several Churches not as an army
with banners calling them to a triumph. We go calling
them to further study and further self-sacrifice.

But back of our technical achievement, great or small,
lifting us in real triumph to God, is our consciousness that,
imperfectly as yet but truly, we return with a new knowledge of our Lord and Master. We have found His power
in the miracle of love, in the unswerving devotion to truth,
in the joyous certainty of victory. The Lord has come to
us in new glory.

THE REV. ELIE GOUNELLE, Légion d'honneur

Pastor of St. Etienne, France (Reformed)

III. Jesus Christ—For Ever

At the close of this world-wide Conference, in which for
the first time in history divided Christendom has humbled
itself and been uplifted to search for unity, in study and in
prayer, on the ground of Faith and Order, it has seemed
necessary in this last service to proclaim aloud Him who
alone can bring us together ; that transcendent Master of
whose acts past and present, as Saviour and as Chief

Shepherd, we have just been reminded. It remains for me, with the help of that Holy Spirit whose aid in my weakness I implore, to tell you that this same Jesus who prayed, suffered and laboured to save us and to make us one "yesterday and to-day" is for ever active, and that His victory is at hand.

The Saviour of souls will be the Head of mankind ; the chief Pastor of the Church will make it one ; the Prophet of the Kingdom of God will establish that Kingdom and rule in it, by right alike of birth and of conquest, "for he must reign, till he has put all enemies under his feet, and then shall the Son also be subject unto him who put all things under him, that God may be all in all."

Let me group under three heads the dominant impressions left by this Conference, and the visions of hope which it justifies. I am no prophet ; yet it is permissible for a believer in God's grace and the victory of Christ to lift a corner of the veil which hides the future from us, and from the experiences through which we have passed in these days to focus his vision upon an assured prospect of the near future—on the threefold vision of a Church united through faith, liberty and love, the three secrets of the eternal Christ.

I. Unity Through Faith

This World Conference offers a tangible proof that in spite of all diversity, and even of contradiction, Christendom as a whole can unite, if it wills and when it wills, on the ground of faith, by the grace of Jesus Christ, round the Person of Jesus Christ, or rather *in* Christ and for His glory.

The problems unsolved are formidable : how to bring about a visible union, a reunion of Christendom, an organic unity, the character and form of which—whether federal, co-operative or constitutional—we have not yet succeeded in determining, though its absolute necessity and its spiritual presuppositions are plain to us all.

For the first time in history, a hundred denominations have been able to spend three weeks in discussing dogma, discipline, sacraments and ministry without contioversy, without exclusions or anathemas or excommunications. This is a new thing and a marvel : it is a proof that the Spirit of Christ is doing and preparing great things, for which we are bound to make ourselves ready.

Lord, we believe : increase our faith!

We have with us, to bring this movement to fruition, the great Unifier. Pastor Charles Wagner, at a memorable Conference which led, after the separation of Church and State, to a re-grouping of the Reformed Churches of France, spoke of Him as " the Eternal Contemporary," " who alone can reduce all ecclesiastical fractions to the same denominator." We have experienced, have we not, this unifying power of Christ throughout our Conference : in our discussions, with their intervals for fervent prayer and impressive silence ; in our worship, public and private ; in the efforts which we made to set aside prejudice, custom, rooted antipathies, and to find and understand each other ; in those memorable services in the Cathedral, where we knelt together to confess with one heart and voice the guilty cause of our divisions—our selfishness and pride ; where hundreds of us, looking towards the day when believers of every confession will be able in full liberty of conscience to meet at the table of the Lord, received the one Bread which is the body of Christ and the one Cup which is His blood.

There have been novel *rapprochements* here, and spiritual happenings as wonderful as they were unexpected. Quakers, for instance, who admit neither formulated dogmas nor definite sacraments—doubtless because all nature is to them the sacrament of grace—have abstained from voting in order that it might be possible to adopt certain documents *nemine contradicente* ; their conciliatory spirit was admirable. And we have found high-minded men of a sacramentalist and sacerdotal type caught up by a generous and liberal impulse above the level of their individual thoughts, attitudes and rites, and meeting thus on the spiritual heights with presbyterian or congregationalist minds such as ours. In the words of Bishop Brent, our revered President, " God's Spirit has been in the midst of us. It was He who called us hither. His presence has been manifest in our worship, our deliberations and our whole fellowship. He has discovered us to one another. He has enlarged our horizons, quickened our understanding, and enlivened our hope. We have dared, and God has justified our daring. We can never be the same again."

Let us give thanks for all this to the Father of Jesus Christ, in the Holy Spirit. It is but a beginning, a first stage towards unity, which, like salvation, comes only from grace and from faith in Jesus Christ. That faith in a Christ who is ever the same in manifold activities, demands and confirms faith in one Church ever the same in its manifold manifestations. The cause of unity, of the one holy Catholic Church, is going forward, and nothing henceforth can arrest it.

II. Unity Through Freedom

Secondly, this world-wide Conference of non-Roman Christendom attests the growing triumphs of freedom, of that moral liberty which in a scientific and critical age like this is the very condition of sincerity, dignity and robustness in thought as in faith ; and of a Christian freedom, which in daily life is tolerance, breadth, generosity, tenderness, considerateness and co-operation. " Where the Spirit of the Lord is, there is liberty." At our Conference we have breathed this wholesome air. The labour of critics and interpreters, of philosophers and theologians throughout the nineteenth century, has not been in vain. In this pulpit from which the liberating message of reform was preached in 1536 by Viret, Farel and Calvin, when the utterances of those young Reformers was followed by the whole noble country of Vaud, how could we forget the wonders wrought by Christ the Liberator, the rights and blessings won and kept through a holy war for freedom and for faith ?

Above every separate creed and beyond our diversities of doctrine we have sought and found the basis of our unity in our adored Master, who frees us from sin but not from duty and conscience, who is a prophet and no scribe, who is more and better than the Law because He is grace, and who wields supreme authority just because He is the incarnation of sacrifice and perfect freedom.

We need, then, the sacerdotal Church which has done so much and so worthily for mankind and stands for order and spiritual authority, and yet too often has dominated, divided and alienated human souls. But also and above all we need the prophetic Church, the Church of a new age, the Church of that Kingdom of God which is to be set up on earth as in heaven, the Church which, whilst it awaits the eternal reign of God, shall be the unwearied builder of the social kingdom of Jesus Christ. This prophetic Church will represent, first, the equal right of every soul in God's sight, in other words, the " laymanship " of every Christian; secondly, the glorious liberty of the children of God, and as its corollary " the right and duty of every believer and every Church to reconcile modern thought with the Gospel,"[1] " Civilisation with belief,"[2] democracy with the Church ; and thirdly, that brotherly solidarity of which Jesus, Son of God and Son of Man, is the eternal principle. " A prophetic Church is humanity's greatest need."[3]

In all our international religious gatherings, we observe something like a new controversy between the ancients and the moderns. A prophetic Church could synthesise both points of view : the ancient is good, the modern is excellent, but the eternal is better. Jesus is identically the same for ever : the same Saviour, the same Priest, the same Messiah, herald of the City of God, the same Peacemaker of a world divided and at war, the same Restorer of a fallen world whose problems He is ready to solve, whose misery and evil He is ready to cure. For that same Christ who saves souls, wills also, in an age of social and international questions, to be the Head of humanity.

---

[1] Déclaration de Foi des Eglises réformées de France (Jarnac).

[2] Title of a notable work by Charles Secrétan.

[3] Carl Heath.

III. Unity Through Love

Lastly, it is Love alone, the eternal prophet, which can unite us. The great Vaudois Christian, Alexandre Vinet, finely said, " To name Jesus and to speak of charity are one and the same thing." How can love, the love which Jesus incarnates, unite us ? In two ways : by abolishing the guilty causes of our divisions—our sins ; and by increasing and hallowing the special gifts of the Spirit, which impel us to create and develop a diverse function and a novel ministry to meet every legitimate need of the soul and of society.

Let me borrow from St. Paul, the first theologian and the great poet of Love, the wings of his inspiration : and, at the close of our memorable gatherings, let me utter not a declaration of faith but a confession of love, the hymn of charity, which I would fain hear from the lips of the Church of to-day : Though, to confess my faith in God and in Christ, to sing my hymns and offer my sacramental worship, I speak with the noblest of human tongues and the music of angels, if I have not love, I shall only set up altar against altar, symbol against symbol, cross against cross, and my song will only be sounding brass or a tinkling cymbal. And though I, the Christian Church, for the defence and propagation of the Gospel have an army of prophets, apostles, doctors and pastors, furnished with every gift for their task, with the understanding of mysteries, with knowledge, with eloquence that electrifies and dominates the multitude ; though I should have all faith, yes, faith as belief, faith as trust, faith as the light of my whole being, faith as the power which comes from God and makes us sharers of His omnipotence ; though I should have that faith of which Jesus said that, were it as small as a grain of mustard seed, it would remove mountains into the sea ; yet, if I am not the Church of Love, if my pastors and the faithful do not love each other, if the many Christian denominations are strangers to each other, if they do not share with each other in the bread which is Christ's body and the cup which is His life-blood, I am nothing, and I effect nothing, nay, more, all the priceless treasures which have been entrusted to me to be utilised, the Bible, tradition, the creeds, ministry, worship, sacraments, all this wealth becomes an obstacle, and I, instead of being Christ's witness and the servant of humanity, the joy of the whole earth, am a scourge and a stumbling block.

And if I give my goods and those of my people to feed the poor, in splendid social institutions for the abolition of poverty and for the solving of economic and international problems, if I have not the true inspiration of charity, all this is nothing.

And if I am a Church of martyrs as were the Waldensian, Hungarian, Hussite, Puritan, Hugenot Churches of old and as the Orthodox and Armenian Churches are to-day, I must remember that without the love that inspires Christian heroism, this is devoid of worth.

Ubi Christus, ibi ecclesia. The Church of Christ, the Church of love, is patient, good, athirst for righteousness ; it weeps like Jesus over the multitudes ; it goes to the people to save it in all possible ways. It hates compromise, strife for precedence, and all the lesser and greater vanities, presbyterian or episcopal, which seek for display and believe themselves exalted when the foundations are giving way ; it hates pride, and spiritual pride above all. The Church of love seeks not its own, knowing that the Church is made for man and not man for the Church, and that like its Divine Pattern it ought not to be ministered unto but to minister, and to give its life a ransom for the souls of men and nations.

The Church of love co-operates with every spiritual family, and banishes divisions, excommunications and anathemas for ever. It rejoices not in others' failures, but only in the triumphs of truth—wherever truth is found, wherever it leads and whatever it says. It pardons all things, believes all things, hopes all things, even for the ending of vice, poverty, and war, for the renewal of country and town, for comfort in the worst sufferings, for the ending of evil, for victory over death and for the coming of the glory of God.

Q

That is the Church that I fain would see : the *Una Sancta Catholica*, the pure and spotless Bride of Christ, which in the fulness of love will partake of the banquet of eternity.

Love never faileth. Creeds, theologies, denominations, will have an end ; sacred eloquence will be silent, prophecy will vanish as the Dayspring approaches. Now we think, believe and speak in part. By the light of the Pentecostal fire, I, the Church, have seen something of the absolute and the eternal. Then, for ages, I thought and reasoned as a child, borrowing now the tongue of the simple, now that of Greek wisdom, now that of Councils and Popes. But when I became a man, I put away some of the imperfections of infancy and youth. Now we see our Christ and His kingdom confusedly, in the darkened mirror of creeds : but then I shall see face to face.

And now abide these three things : faith in the living Christ, the hope of the kingdom of God, and the eternally creative and re-creative power of Love : and the greatest of these is Love, because Love is Christ, Love is God.

Have you noted the last thought and petition of Jesus in His high-priestly prayer ? " That the love wherewith thou hast loved me may be in them, and I in them." Jesus dares to ask that we may love Him as God has loved Him, that our love may be like the love divine. And as Christ's love utters no empty phrases, He adds " and I in them." His prayer culminates in a total gift : He incarnates Himself, offers His life, His blood, His soul, His entire self.

As is Christ, so is the Church. The Church cannot desire oneness otherwise than in the hope of giving herself more completely ; and, like Jesus, she will only give herself for a cause infinitely beyond herself : the service of the kingdom, the complete conversion of mankind, the honour of God.

To the Church as we know it, imperfect and divided, let us proclaim at Lausanne that deep utterance of the genius of Goethe—*Stirb und werde* : renounce thyself to make Christ King : die to rise again : go up upon the Cross as thy Master went, and thou shalt rise again for time and for eternity. Amen.

DOCUMENTS RECEIVED BY THE CONFERENCE FOR TRANSMISSION TO THE CHURCHES

The following are the final texts of the Reports as received by the Conference for transmission to the Churches represented, and of the Preamble and Concluding Statement.[1]

PREAMBLE

Unanimously adopted by the full Conference, August 20th, 1927.

We, representatives of many Christian Communions throughout the world, united in the common confession of faith in Jesus Christ the Son of God, our Lord and Saviour, believing that the Spirit of God is with us, are assembled to consider the things wherein we agree and the things wherein we differ. We now receive the following series of reports as containing subject matter for the consideration of our respective Churches in their common search for unity.

This is a Conference summoned to consider matters of Faith and Order. It is emphatically *not* attempting to define the conditions of future reunion. Its object is to register the apparent level of fundamental agreements within the Conference and the grave points of disagreements remaining; also to suggest certain lines of thought which may in the future tend to a fuller measure of agreement.

Each subject on the agenda was first discussed in plenary session. It was then committed to one of the sections, of

[1] At the evening Session, August 18th, the Conference voted, " that to all of those Churches which have sent delegates the findings of this Conference shall be sent through their official channels at as early a date as possible, asking those Churches to consider the findings and report back to the Continuation Committee the result of their deliberations, in view of which the Continuation Committee shall consider what steps need to be taken for another Conference."

more than one hundred members each, into which the whole Conference was divided. The report, after full discussion in subsections, was finally drawn up and adopted unanimously or by a large majority vote by the section to which it had been committed. It was twice presented for further discussion to a plenary session of the Conference when it was referred to the Churches in its present form.

Though we recognise the reports to be neither exhaustive nor in all details satisfactory to every member of the Conference, we submit them to the Churches for that deliberate consideration which could not be given in the brief period of our sessions. We thank God and rejoice over agreements reached ; upon our agreements we build. Where the reports record differences, we call upon the Christian world to an earnest reconsideration of the conflicting opinions now held, and a strenuous endeavour to reach the truth as it is in God's mind, which should be the foundation of the Church's unity.

I. THE CALL TO UNITY

Unanimously adopted by the full Conference, August 20th, 1927.

God wills unity. Our presence in this Conference bears testimony to our desire to bend our wills to His. However we may justify the beginnings of disunion, we lament its continuance and henceforth must labour, in penitence and faith, to build up our broken walls.

God's Spirit has been in the midst of us. It was He who called us hither. His presence has been manifest in our worship, our deliberations and our whole fellowship. He has discovered us to one another. He has enlarged our horizons, quickened our understanding, and enlivened our hope. We have dared and God has justified our daring. We can never be the same again. Our deep thankfulness must find expression in sustained endeavour to share the visions vouchsafed us here with those smaller home groups where our lot is cast.

More than half the world is waiting for the Gospel. At home and abroad sad multitudes are turning away in bewilderment from the Church because of its corporate feebleness. Our missions count that as a necessity which we are inclined to look on as a luxury. Already the mission field is impatiently revolting from the divisions of the Western Church to make bold adventure for unity in its own right. We of the Churches represented in this Conference cannot allow our spiritual children to outpace us. We with them must gird ourselves to the task, the early beginnings of which God has so richly blessed, and labour side by side until our common goal is reached.

Some of us, pioneers in this undertaking, have grown old in our search for unity. It is to youth that we look to lift the torch on high. We men have carried it too much alone through many years. The women henceforth should be accorded their share of responsibility. And so the whole Church will be enabled to do that which no section can hope to perform.

It was God's clear call that gathered us. With faith stimulated by His guidance to us here, we move forward.

REPORT OF SECTION II

Received by the full Conference, nem. con., August 19*th,* 1927

THE CHURCH'S MESSAGE TO THE WORLD— THE GOSPEL

The message of the Church to the world is and must always remain the Gospel of Jesus Christ.

The Gospel is the joyful message of redemption, both here and hereafter, the gift of God to sinful man in Jesus Christ.

The world was prepared for the coming of Christ through

the activities of God's Spirit in all humanity, but especially in His revelation as given in the Old Testament ; and in the fulness of time the eternal Word of God became incarnate, and was made man, Jesus Christ, the Son of God and the Son of Man, full of grace and truth.

Through His life and teaching, His call to repentance, His proclamation of the coming of the Kingdom of God and of judgment, His suffering and death, His resurrection and exaltation to the right hand of the Father, and by the mission of the Holy Spirit, He has brought to us forgiveness of sins, and has revealed the fulness of the living God, and His boundless love toward us. By the appeal of that love, shown in its completeness on the Cross, He summons us to the new life of faith, self-sacrifice, and devotion to His service and the service of men.

Jesus Christ, as the crucified and the living One, as Saviour and Lord, is also the centre of the world-wide Gospel of the Apostles and the Church. Because He Himself is the Gospel, the Gospel is the message of the Church to the world. It is more than a philosophical theory ; more than a theological system ; more than a programme for material betterment. The Gospel is rather the gift of a new world from God to this old world of sin and death ; still more, it is the victory over sin and death, the revelation of eternal life in Him who has knit together the whole family in heaven and on earth in the communion of saints, united in the fellowship of service, of prayer, and of praise.

The Gospel is the prophetic call to sinful man to turn to God, the joyful tidings of justification and of sanctification to those who believe in Christ. It is the comfort of those who suffer ; to those who are bound, it is the assurance of the glorious liberty of the sons of God. The Gospel brings peace and joy to the heart, and produces in men self-denial, readiness for brotherly service, and compassionate love. It offers the supreme goal for the aspirations of youth, strength to the toiler, rest to the weary, and the crown of life to the martyr.

The Gospel is the sure source of power for social regeneration. It proclaims the only way by which humanity can escape from those class and race hatreds which devastate society at present into the enjoyment of national well-being and international friendship and peace. It is also a gracious invitation to the non-Christian world, East and West, to enter into the joy of the living Lord.

Sympathising with the anguish of our generation, with its longing for intellectual sincerity, social justice and spiritual inspiration, the Church in the eternal Gospel meets the needs and fulfils the God-given aspirations of the modern world. Consequently, as in the past so also in the present, the Gospel is the only way of salvation. Thus, through His Church, the living Christ still says to men " Come unto me! . . . He that followeth me shall not walk in darkness, but shall have the light of life."

REPORT OF SECTION III

Received by the full Conference, nem. con., August 19th, 1927

THE NATURE OF THE CHURCH

God who has given us the Gospel for the salvation of the world has appointed His Church to witness by life and word to its redeeming power. The Church of the Living God is constituted by His own will, not by the will or consent or beliefs of men whether as individuals or as societies, though He uses the will of men as His instrument. Of this Church Jesus Christ is the Head, the Holy Spirit its continuing life.

The Church as the communion of believers in Christ Jesus is, according to the New Testament, the people of the New Covenant ; the Body of Christ ; and the Temple of God, built upon the foundation of the Apostles and Prophets, Jesus Christ Himself being the chief corner stone.

The Church is God's chosen instrument by which Christ, through the Holy Spirit, reconciles men to God through faith, bringing their wills into subjection to His sovereignty, sanctifying them through the means of grace, and uniting them in love and service to be His witnesses and fellow-workers in the extension of His rule on earth until His Kingdom come in glory.

As there is but one Christ, and one life in Him, and one Holy Spirit who guides into all truth, so there is and can be but one Church, holy, catholic, and apostolic.

The Church on earth possesses certain characteristics whereby it can be known of men. These have been, since the days of the Apostles, at least the following :

1. The possession and acknowledgment of the Word of God as given in Holy Scripture and interpreted by the Holy Spirit to the Church and to the individual. (Note A.)

2. The profession of faith in God as He is incarnate and revealed in Christ.

3. The acceptance of Christ's commission to preach the Gospel to every creature.

4. The observance of the Sacraments.

5. A ministry for the pastoral office, the preaching of the Word, and the administration of the Sacraments.

6. A fellowship in prayer, in worship, in all the means of grace, in the pursuit of holiness, and in the service of man.

As to the extent and manner in which the Church thus described finds expression in the existing Churches, we differ. Our differences chiefly concern :

1. The nature of the Church visible and the Church invisible, their relation to each other, and the number of those who are included in each. (Note B.)

2. The significance of our divisions past and present. (Note C.)

Whatever our views on these points, we are convinced that it is the will of Christ that the one life of the one body should be manifest to the world. To commend the Gospel to doubting, sinful and bewildered men, a united witness is necessary. We therefore urge most earnestly that all

Christians, in fulfilment of our Saviour's prayer that His disciples may be one, reconsecrate themselves to God, that by the help of His Spirit the body of Christ may be built up, its members united in faith and love, and existing obstacles to the manifestation of their unity in Christ may be removed ; that the world may believe that the Father has sent Him.

We join in the prayer that the time may be hastened when in the name of Jesus every knee shall bow and every tongue confess that Jesus Christ is Lord to the glory of God the Father.

NOTES

(A.) Some hold that this interpretation is given through the tradition of the Church ; others through the immediate witness of the Spirit to the heart and conscience of believers; others through both combined.

(B.) For instance

1. Some hold that the invisible Church is wholly in heaven ; others include in it all true believers on earth, whether contained in any organisation or not.

2. Some hold that the visible expression of the Church was determined by Christ Himself and is therefore unchangeable ; others that the one Church under the guidance of the Holy Spirit may express itself in varying forms.

3. Some hold that one or other of the existing Churches is the only true Church ; others that the Church as we have described it is to be found in some or all of the existing Communions taken together.

4. Some, while recognising other Christian bodies as Churches, are persuaded that in the providence of God and by the teaching of history a particular form of ministry has been shown to be necessary to the best welfare of the Church ; others hold that no one form of organisation is inherently preferable ; still others, that no organisation is necessary.

(c) One view is that no division of Christendom has ever come to pass without sin. Another view is that the divisions were the inevitable outcome of different gifts of the Spirit and different understandings of the truth. Between these, there is the view of those who look back on the divisions of the past with penitence and sorrow coupled with a lively sense of God's mercy, which in spite of and even through these divisions has advanced His cause in the world.

REPORT OF SECTION IV

Received by the full Conference, nem con., August 19th, 1927

THE CHURCH'S COMMON CONFESSION OF FAITH

We members of the Conference on Faith and Order, coming from all parts of the world in the interest of Christian unity, have with deep gratitude to God found ourselves united in common prayer, in God our heavenly Father and His Son Jesus Christ, our Saviour, in the fellowship of the Holy Spirit.

Notwithstanding the differences in doctrine among us, we are united in a common Christian Faith which is proclaimed in the Holy Scriptures and is witnessed to and safeguarded in the Ecumenical Creed, commonly called the Nicene, and in the Apostles' Creed, which Faith is continuously confirmed in the spiritual experience of the Church of Christ.

We believe that the Holy Spirit in leading the Church into all truth may enable it, while firmly adhering to the witness of these Creeds (our common heritage from the ancient Church), to express the truths of revelation in such other forms as new problems may from time to time demand.

Finally, we desire to leave on record our solemn and unanimous testimony that no external and written standards can suffice without an inward and personal experience of union with God in Christ.

NOTES

1. It must be noted that the Orthodox Eastern Church can accept the Nicene Creed only in its uninterpolated form without the *filioque* clause ; and that although the Apostles' Creed has no place in the formularies of this Church, it is in accordance with its teaching.

2. It must be noted also that some of the Churches represented in this Conference conjoin tradition with the Scriptures, some are explicit in subordinating Creeds to the Scriptures, some attach a primary importance to their particular Confessions, and some make no use of Creeds.

3. It is understood that the use of these Creeds will be determined by the competent authority in each Church, and that the several Churches will continue to make use of such special Confessions as they possess.

REPORT OF SECTION V

Received by the full Conference, nem con., August 20th, 1927

THE MINISTRY OF THE CHURCH

We members of the Conference on Faith and Order are happy to report that we find ourselves in substantial accord in the following five propositions :

1. The ministry is a gift of God through Christ to His Church and is essential to the being and well-being of the Church.

2. The ministry is perpetually authorised and made effective through Christ and His Spirit.

3. The purpose of the ministry is to impart to men the saving and sanctifying benefits of Christ through pastoral service, the preaching of the Gospel, and the administration of the sacraments, to be made effective by faith.

4. The ministry is entrusted with the government and discipline of the Church, in whole or in part.

5. Men gifted for the work of the ministry, called by the Spirit and accepted by the Church, are commissioned through an act of ordination by prayer and the laying on of hands to exercise the function of this ministry.

Within the many Christian communions into which in the course of history Christendom has been divided, various forms of ministry have grown up according to the circumstances of the several communions and their beliefs as to the mind of Christ and the guidance of the New Testament. These communions have been, in God's providence, manifestly and abundantly used by the Holy Spirit in His work of enlightening the world, converting sinners, and perfecting saints. But the differences which have arisen in regard to the authority and functions of these various forms of ministry have been and are the occasion of manifold doubts, questions and misunderstandings.

These differences concern the nature of the ministry (whether consisting of one or several orders), the nature of ordination and of the grace conferred thereby, the function and authority of bishops, and the nature of apostolic succession. We believe that the first step toward the overcoming of these difficulties is the frank recognition that they exist, and the clear definition of their nature. We therefore add as an appendix to our Report such a statement, commending it to the thoughtful consideration of the Churches we represent.

By these differences the difficulties of inter-communion have been accentuated to the distress and wounding of faithful souls, while in the mission field, where the Church is fulfilling its primary object to preach the Gospel to every creature, the young Churches find the lack of unity a very serious obstacle to the furtherance of the Gospel. Consequently the provision of a ministry acknowledged in every part of the Church as possessing the sanction of the whole Church is an urgent need.

There has not been time in this Conference to consider all the points of difference between us in the matter of the ministry with that care and patience which could alone lead to complete agreement. The same observation applies equally to proposals for the constitution of the united Church. Certain suggestions as to possible church organisation have been made, which we transmit to the Churches with the earnest hope that common study of these questions will be continued by the members of the various Churches represented in this Conference.

In view of (1) the place which the episcopate, the councils of presbyters, and the congregation of the faithful, respectively, had in the constitution of the early Church, and (2) the fact that episcopal, presbyteral and congregational systems of government are each to-day, and have been for centuries, accepted by great communions in Christendom, and (3) the fact that episcopal, presbyteral and congregational systems are each believed by many to be essential to the good order of the Church, we therefore recognise that these several elements must all, under conditions which require further study, have an appropriate place in the order of life of a reunited Church, and that each separate communion, recalling the abundant blessing of God vouchsafed to its ministry in the past, should gladly bring to the common life of the united Church its own spiritual treasures.

If the foregoing suggestion be accepted and acted upon, it is essential that the acceptance of any special form of ordination as the regular and orderly method of introduction into the ministry of the Church for the future should not be interpreted to imply the acceptance of any one particular theory of the origin, character or function of any office in the Church, or to involve the acceptance of any adverse judgment on the validity of ordination in those branches of the Church universal that believe themselves to have retained valid and apostolic Orders under other forms of ordination ; or as disowning or discrediting a past or present ministry of the Word and Sacrament which has been used and blessed by the Spirit of God.

It is further recognised that inasmuch as the Holy Spirit is bestowed upon every believer, and each believer has an immediate access to God through Jesus Christ, and since special gifts of the Holy Spirit, such as teaching, preaching, and spiritual counsel, are the treasures of the Church as well as of the individual, it is necessary and proper that the Church should make fuller use of such gifts for the development of its corporate spiritual life and for the extension of the Kingdom of Jesus Christ, our Lord.

In particular, we share in the conviction, repeatedly expressed in this Conference, that pending the solution of the questions of faith and order in which agreements have not yet been reached, it is possible for us, not simply as individuals but as Churches, to unite in the activities of brotherly service which Christ has committed to His disciples. We therefore commend to our Churches the consideration of the steps which may be immediately practicable to bring our existing unity in service to more effective expression.

In conclusion, we express our thankfulness to Almighty God for the great progress which has been made in recent years in the mutual approach of the Churches to one another, and our conviction that we must go forward with faith and courage, confident that with the blessing of God we shall be able to solve the problems that lie before us.

Notes

1. The following is the view of the Orthodox Church, as formulated for us by its representatives.

" The Orthodox Church, regarding the ministry as instituted in the Church by Christ Himself, and as the body which by a special *charisma* is the organ through which the Church spreads its means of grace such as the sacraments, and believing that the ministry in its threefold form of bishops, presbyters and deacons can only be based on the unbroken apostolic succession, regrets that it is unable to come in regard to the ministry into some measure of agreement with many of the Churches represented at this Conference ; but prays God that He, through His Holy Spirit, will guide to union even in regard to this difficult point of disagreement."

2. In Western Christendom also there are conspicuous differences.

One representative view includes the following points : (a) that there have always been various grades of the ministry, each with its own function ; (b) that ordination is a sacramental act of divine institution, and therefore indispensable, conveying the special *charisma* for the particular ministry ; (c) that bishops who have received their office by succession from the Apostles are the necessary ministers of ordination ; (d) that the apostolic succession so understood is necessary for the authority of the ministry, the visible unity of the Church, and the validity of the sacraments.

On the other hand it is held by many Churches represented in the Conference (a) that essentially there is only one ministry, that of the Word and Sacraments ; (b) that the existing ministries in these Churches are agreeable to the New Testament, are proved by their fruits and have due authority in the Church, and the sacraments ministered by them are valid ; (c) that no particular form of ministry is necessary to be received as a matter of faith ; (d) that the grace which fits men for the ministry is immediately given by God, and is recognised, not conferred, in ordination.

Further we record that there are views concerning the ministry which are intermediate between the types just mentioned. For instance, some who adhere to an episcopal system of church government do not consider that the apostolic succession as described above is a vital element of episcopacy, or they reject it altogether. Others do not regard as essential the historic episcopate. Those who adhere to presbyteral systems of church government believe that the apostolic ministry is transmissible and has been transmitted through presbyters orderly associated for the purpose. Those who adhere to the congregational system of government define their ministry as having been and being transmitted according to the precedent and example of the New Testament.

REPORT OF SECTION VI

Received by the full Conference, nem. con., August 20th, 1927

THE SACRAMENTS

We are convinced that for the purpose in view in this Conference we should not go into detail in considering Sacraments—by some called " Mysteries." The purpose therefore of this statement is to show that there may be a common approach to and appreciation of Sacraments on the part of those who may otherwise differ in conception and interpretation.

We testify to the fact that the Christian world gives evidence of an increasing sense of the significance and value of Sacraments, and would express our belief that this movement should be fostered and guided as a means of deepening the life and experience of the Churches. In this connection we recognise that the Sacraments have special reference to the corporate life and fellowship of the Church and that the grace is conveyed by the Holy Spirit, taking of the things of Christ and applying them to the soul through faith.

We agree that Sacraments are of divine appointment and that the Church ought thankfully to observe them as divine gifts.

We hold that in the Sacraments there is an outward sign and an inward grace, and that the Sacraments are means of grace through which God works invisibly in us. We recognise also that in the gifts of His grace God is not limited by His own Sacraments.

The Orthodox Church and others hold that there are

seven Sacraments and that for their valid administration there must be a proper form, a proper matter and a proper ministry. Others can regard only Baptism and the Lord's Supper as Sacraments. Others again, while attaching high value to the sacramental principle, do not make use of the outward signs of Sacraments, but hold that all spiritual benefits are given through immediate contact with God through His Spirit. In this Conference we lay stress on the two Sacraments of Baptism and the Lord's Supper, because they are the Sacraments which are generally acknowledged by the members of this Conference.

We believe that in Baptism administered with water in the name of the Father, the Son and the Holy Spirit, for the remission of sins, we are baptised by one Spirit into one body. By this statement it is not meant to ignore the differences in conception, interpretation and mode which exist among us.

We believe that in the Holy Communion our Lord is present, that we have fellowship with God our Father in Jesus Christ His Son, our Living Lord, who is our one Bread, given for the life of the world, sustaining the life of all His people, and that we are in fellowship with all others who are united to Him. We agree that the Sacrament of the Lord's Supper is the Church's most sacred act of worship, in which the Lord's atoning death is commemorated and proclaimed, and that it is a sacrifice of praise and thanksgiving and an act of solemn self-oblation.

There are among us divergent views, especially as to (1) the mode and manner of the presence of our Lord ; (2) the conception of the commemoration and the sacrifice ; (3) the relation of the elements to the grace conveyed ; and (4) the relation between the minister of this Sacrament and the validity and efficacy of the rite. We are aware that the reality of the divine presence and gift in this Sacrament cannot be adequately apprehended by human thought or expressed in human language.

We close this statement with the prayer that the differences which prevent full communion at the present time may be removed.

REPORT OF SECTION VII

THE UNITY OF CHRISTENDOM IN RELATION TO EXISTING CHURCHES

This report was received by the full Conference on August 20th, 1927, for transmission to the Continuation Committee, which then appointed a committee with the duty of considering the whole situation with regard to Subject VII and reporting to the Business Committee.

Those directions are being carried out.

CONCLUDING STATEMENT

Drafted by the Chairman of the Conference at its Request

We have finished our immediate task. From first to last we are able to express it in constructive terms written and received, whether they be statements of agreement or statements of difference, in brotherly love and mutual consideration. They are the product of the minds of men who earnestly desired and strove to place and keep themselves under the guidance of God's Holy Spirit. Human imperfections which mingle with them we pray God to pardon. In offering to Him our handiwork, we are but returning to Him that which He has given to us. We pray His acceptance of and blessing upon our offering.

However, we have not finished our whole task. We have but taken a step on a long journey. The Conference was only a new starting point. What we did there will crumble into dust unless the representatives at Lausanne bring home to their several Churches the duty and responsibility of studying the Reports which they themselves received for this very purpose. The Conference should be repeated in every main ecclesiastical assembly, as well as in each separate congregation, throughout our entire Christian constituency if we are to take full advantage of the progress registered. By our presence and activity at Lausanne we are solemnly pledged to reproduce, each in his own local circle, the spirit and method which made the World Conference on Faith and Order what it was. " I pray you to give me the utter joy of knowing you are living in harmony, with the same feelings of love, with one heart and soul, never acting for private ends or from vanity, but humbly considering each other the better man, and each with an eye to the interests of others as well as to his own. Treat one another with the same spirit as you experience in Christ Jesus."[1]

We who have been privileged to labour together have done so in the joyousness of unhampered freedom. We must not forget, in the liberty which is to us a commonplace, the sufferings which some of our Christian brethren are at this very moment undergoing. Deprived of liberty, in hostile surroundings, their cry goes up to God from the house of their martyrdom. Our prayers enfold them and our sympathy stretches out affectionate arms toward them.

Finally, we commend the Christian Churches, whether represented in the Conference or not, to our Heavenly Father's guidance and safe keeping, looking earnestly toward the day when the full mind of God will control all the affairs of mankind.

[1] Phil. ii, 2-5, Moffatt's translation.

THE NECESSITY OF CHRISTIAN UNITY

PUBLIC MEETINGS IN THE CATHEDRAL

AUGUST 7TH, 10TH, 14TH, AND 17TH.

During the sessions of the Conference a series of four meetings, dealing with various aspects of the necessity for Christian unity, was held in the Cathedral.

The following is a record of the substance of the addresses delivered at these meetings.

I. THE NECESSITY OF CHRISTIAN UNITY FOR CHRISTIAN FELLOWSHIP AND CO-OPERATION

SUNDAY, AUGUST 7TH, 8.30 P.M.

Chairman : PASTOR CHARLES MERLE D'AUBIGNE, D.D.

PROFESSOR DR. FRIEDRICH SIEGMUND-SCHULTZE
University of Berlin (Evangelical-Lutheran)

What is it that we are striving after in this World Conference on Faith and Order ? Uniformity ? In these days of general levelling, men are already becoming too prone to similarity. So, too, nations are tending more and more to resemble one another. Yes, even in the Churches, there are movements which aim at copying the characteristics of others. If this development is pursuing a natural course, then let it be. But deliberately to compress the various types of Christianity into a homogeneous mass, to reduce all individuality and personality to one pattern, this is a purely human ideal—the desire to form others in my own likeness, a race of men that shall resemble me—and it is an ideal that the Church should not set before herself. Uniforms are needed by the State for its officials, for its army ; they are not needed by the Church.

But *unity* can be of more importance to the Church than uniformity. Unity may, of course, be interpreted so as to apply merely to some external form, to union under a Pope, or any outward union in a hierarchical system under a visible head. How low are the summits in systems of this kind! But if we seek higher for the Head of the Church, then of itself comes unity : the Body of Christ. If Christ is the Head, then the Body must be one. It is well that there are divers members, with diversity of gifts and functions, for how else could they be members of the body of Christ ? But that which makes them one, which unifies them, must be the single will which directs them, that is, the Spirit of Christ.

Thus concord, at the very least, is necessary. The various members of the body must not strive among themselves. There must be a living and brotherly understanding among them. We need a *Unitas Fratrum.*

How far distant we still are from such a unison! Is there not sharp antagonism between Roman and Protestant Christendom ? Are not the Free Churches the hostile brethren of the State Churches ? In the face of such strife, long indeed is the way to true unity. For such unity is without meaning, unless it proceed from an inward union.

Shall we, then, set before ourselves a lower goal ? Shall we content ourselves with such fellowship as arises now and again between certain denominations ? To speak only of one great Church which is absent from this Conference, are we to be content because in the Roman Catholic camp a few of the devout are praying with us for unity ? Is it sufficient that one true Catholic priest of that Church sings a new melody to the Stockholm song, and that we can unite with our Catholic friends in our common admiration for St. Francis and St. Clare ?

Or, again, shall we content ourselves with the fact that now and again co-operation is possible between the Confessions, that the various Churches meet together, for instance, for the campaign against alcohol or for juvenile welfare ? For the last few years in Germany we have held social-ethical meetings at which men of all denominations and ways of thought, including men of all political parties have gathered together. Is that sufficient? Just at these very meetings we became aware that something more is needed than mere outward co-operation. If we wish to make clear to one another the deepest of those foundations on which our convictions are based, then neither the discussion of objective questions nor the adoption of common resolutions will suffice. Both in order to find the truth, and in order to make old things new, we needed to press on further towards unity. We needed to allow one another to participate in what we all hold most holy. We needed to become one in God. And thus we were led to hold services in which our Roman Catholic brothers and we Protestants could join.

In the working-class quarter of East Berlin we had the same experience. When the members of so-called educated classes and working-men had joined together for the service of their neighbours —work we had come to look upon as the true way towards a new national fellowship, inspired from within—the " workers " became as intent as we were on determining the source of this will to serve. And more and more deeply we came to realise that the man who does not allow himself to be served, but who serves, stands in some direct relation to man's prototype, the Son of Man, who came not to be ministered to but to minister, and to give His life as a ransom for all. Fellowship in work had to pass into fellowship of the spirit, which seeks its unity in the depths. Should not the Churches also feel this urge towards unification, towards oneness ?

If the representatives of the Churches have worked together for peace since 1914, if, since 1925, they have founded a great social fellowship of work, then in their joint work and in the resulting fellowship they should endeavour to press forward towards a deeper unity. So long as I know that a friend who is a member of another Christian Church must, according to the tenets of his Church, hold me to be damned and lost ; so long as the Lord's Table, which should represent the deepest fellowship of the disciples of Christ, remains the symbol of their disunion ; so long as the representatives of Churches must make reservations before they can join in Christian fellowship; just so long must fellowship still be incomplete, must love remain imperfect, and the results which should proceed from the unity of the Head be unattained.

And, therefore, we yearn for a fuller unity, for the fulfilment of the wish of Christ Himself that we should be one. Therefore we earnestly pray, together with all those who have united with us, that we may be able to remove all obstacles that hinder the will to unity. Therefore, we ask every man to set aside and sacrifice his personal pride, if, in this ecumenical work, it stands in the way of the attainment of true unity. Therefore we expect of all Churches that they also will be prepared to sacrifice their pride for the sake of that unity to which Christ calls us. Therefore we pray each of you to honour his neighbour more highly than himself. Therefore we expect each to care not solely for the interests of his own Church, but also for that which concerns another. Therefore we rely upon our

Churches to understand the difficulties and needs of the other Churches, and to bear the Cross of Christ together. Therefore we fully accept that saying which promises, to everyone who lays upon his own heart the load of another, that he shall know himself to be at one with Christ's purpose: "Bear ye one another's burdens, and so fulfil the law of Christ." The appeal of the apostle is made to all of us : " If there is, therefore, any comfort in Christ, if any consolation of love, if any fellowship of the Spirit, if any tender mercies and compassions, fulfil ye my joy, that ye be of the same mind, having the same love, being of one accord, of one mind."

THE REV. T. ALBERT MOORE, D.D.
Secretary, The United Church of Canada

The United Church of Canada has been realising the increasing value of Christian unity for Christian fellowship and co-operation, through the developments which culminated in Church union a little more than two years ago. Needless to say, the movement for Christian unity antedates by years the negotiations which began in 1902 when committees were appointed by the General Conference of the Methodist Church, the General Assembly of the Presbyterian Church, and the Congregational Union of Canada to consider the possibility of the organic union of these denominations. From 1867, when the various Canadian Provinces were federated into the political entity known as the Dominion of Canada, there has been a continual and persistent demand for the elimination of denominational divisions. In 1872 the different Presbyterian communions united, and became the Presbyterian Church in Canada ; in 1884 the several Methodist communions united, and became the Methodist Church. In 1906 the Provincial Unions of the Congregational Church united and became the Congregational Union of Canada. At the times of these unions each denomination envisaged a church union that would include all Christian Communions. Early attempts at church union revealed that denominational differences are grounded in temperamental proclivities, national prejudices, different conceptions of life and of ethical standards, as well as in specific theological dogmas and ecclesiastical convictions.

The twenty years of negotiations were a period of ever-enlarging fellowship and ever-increasing co-operation. The association of the three Communions both through their committees on church union, in their congregations, their courts, and their many Christian activities, developed a better acquaintance with each other, an increased confidence in each other's motives, methods and missions, and a firmer bond of Christian unity. As they worked together for the common purpose of improving the facilities for worship, bettering the moral conditions in communities and establishing the Kingdom of Christ throughout the Dominion, they entered more fully into real living fellowship and experienced a more vital realisation of beneficent and successful co-operation. These actual contacts in fellowship and co-operation were invaluable to the whole movement, bringing the Communions to a better understanding and establishing a well-grounded confidence which helped to overcome the apparent obstacles to church union and to discover the very satisfactory basis of doctrine, order and polity which became mutually acceptable to the uniting Communions.

There were many in 1902 who honestly questioned the possibility of uniting the Congregational, Methodist, and Presbyterian denominations into one Communion. Their histories, traditions, doctrines, attitudes to life, and associations of thought were far separated from each other. These persons still doubted when the joint committees on church union unanimously declared " that organic union is both desirable and practical," and " that no insuperable obstacles have been discovered which should prevent such a consummation."

The negotiations continued from year to year, the three denominations endeavouring to meet the religious needs by various forms of co-operation and different methods of federation. All these activities of Christian unity, however, produced a never-ceasing and ever-increasing demand for a closer relationship. The colleges of the three denominations federated or co-operated in various ways ; the mission boards planned multifarious methods for federation or co-operation of local congregations, and many plans were evolved to aid the local congregations and the denominations in their responsibilities to minister adequately to the people's spiritual needs. As people poured into our Provinces to advantage themselves by the development of our natural resources, constantly establishing new communities, demands were made that the *isms* of older communities should not be fastened upon them, but that as they were compelled to co-operate in plans for the education of their children, the founding of their social life and the carrying on of their business, so they should co-operate in their worship and all forms of religious activity.

In June, 1925, the union " was consummated by the free and independent action of the negotiating Churches, with the sanction of the supreme court of each denomination, in accordance with their respective constitutions," after the ministers and membership and the lower courts, by very large majorities, had given their hearty approval. The official documents declare that " believing the promotion of Christian unity to be in accordance with the divine will, and recognising the obligation to seek and promote union with other Churches adhering to the same fundamental principles of the Christian faith, and having the right to unite with one another without loss of their identity upon terms which they find consistent with such principles," they have adopted a Basis of Union. All congregations of the Methodist Church, all but eight congregations of the Congregational Church, and more than four-fifths of the congregations of the Presbyterian Church entered the Union. With approximately 4,000 ministers and 700,000 members, the United Church ministers to upwards of 2,120,000 persons, organised into more than 8,700 congregations. Our Sunday Schools are attended by more than 1,000,000 scholars, and our Young People's Societies have a membership of half a million. Our thirty-two colleges enrol more than 7,000 students, our eight missions in Asia, Africa and South America enrol more than 600 missionaries, and our Home Missions send more than 1,000 missionaries to our sparsely settled communities. Our numerous institutions for social betterment minister in most practical ways to needy children and adults of Indian, Anglo-Saxon and other races, while we heartily co-operate with many others in the practical applications of the principles of the Gospel of Jesus in the social, industrial, economic and political relations of life.

Our two years' experience of Church Union has abundantly justified the most sanguine expectations. The personal relations between ministers and members who were accustomed to different methods and different forms of church government have been most cordial. The harmony which has existed in the various Church Courts and throughout our congregations since the union of these three denominations has been effected, has proved that union has been an enriching experience in Christian fellowship and co-operation, and has increased the degree of Christian unity.

The new conceptions of the widening claims of social life; our responsibilities to men, women and children; the vital and unceasing needs of the poor, the toilers, and the under-privileged, together with the perpetual duty to preach the Gospel to every dweller in our far-flung provinces, constituted a persistent challenge to a heroic task. The experiences of the World War forced upon us with immeasurable influence the conviction that religion must become not merely the service of humanity, but its high priest and liberator.

Nothing must interfere within our own country, or between our country and other lands, to prevent Christian fellowship and co-operation with the children of God in every land. Shall not organised Christianity in this day gather round its Lord and Redeemer and pledge itself, not merely to fidelity to the memory of a great creed and a glorious past, but also to a new crusade to lead the world to practice the imperishable ideals of Jesus Christ at whatever cost, in order that all the people of all the nations may realise that supreme reconciling message of our Lord, " Look unto me, all ye ends of the earth, and be ye saved," " Come unto me all ye that labour and are heavy laden, and I will give you rest." In that highest experience of Christian co-operation may we all come into that unity of faith and knowledge of the Son of God, which will produce that Christian fellowship which ever maketh increase of His body unto the edifying of itself in love.

II. THE NECESSITY OF CHRISTIAN UNITY FOR THE PRESENTATION OF THE CHRISTIAN TRUTH

WEDNESDAY, AUGUST 10TH, 8.30 p.m.

Chairman : His Excellency HARALD DE BILDT

PROFESSOR DR. KARL LUDWIG SCHMIDT
University of Jena (Evangelical-Lutheran)

Concerning Christian truth, which proceeds from God, the assurance has been given that it shall overcome the world, which lies in wickedness. The Church of Christ, having received from her Lord the mission of expounding Christian truth, encounters from time to time as she carries out her mission the antagonism of the world, which points with doubt, despair and scorn to the differences that divide the Christian Churches. It should be observed that all efforts made by the Church against this severance of Christian truth tend to give her fresh impetus, seeing that the world's opposition diminishes or ceases if *one* Church becomes visible behind the multitude of individual Churches.

The modern world, in particular the modern Western world, having lost its unity in the material and intellectual spheres and pining for the social and mental unity of former days, has put forth the " Internationals " of education and economics. Both are upheld by the force of strong moral principles. The ideal of enlightened citizenship and the ideal of a socialist state of the future have laid hold on many minds, and wrestle with each other in one and the same human breast and within society in general. Into this contest of truths laying claim to universal validity the Church of Christ, preaching her truth which is to overcome the world, is drawn. The Christian International fights among the other Internationals for her existence and development. The outcome of the resulting debates is very various ; for the most part they issue either in mutual antagonism or in agreeing to differ. Visible success, as expressed in the numerical increase of adherents of this or that International, brings enhanced prestige in its train. There can be no doubt whatever that a World Church Conference constrains the world to listen and procures esteem for the Churches and the Church, even though there may be opposition to the Churches and the Church. And must not the world, with its desire to attain some outlook on life which shall be intelligible to all, pay heed when an association of persons meeting together as a so-called religious society, by its appeal and the successful overcoming of differences, further and further increases the circles of its adherents ? It is easily comprehensible that such discussions should lead to reciprocal relations between the Christian International and the Internationals based on intellectual or economic principles. This fact is familiar to us all ; we need do no more than call to mind the synthetic expressions, Christian Idealism and Christian Socialism.

An expounder of the Bible and a member of the Lutheran Church may be allowed to dwell in the first place and mainly on this fact, that neither the Scripture nor the Lutheran Confession has, wishes to have, or can have, any concern whatever with the prestige of a Christian International before the world, or of any synthesis with worldly wisdom or society. But the Old and the New Testament as well as the Reformed Confessions, derived as they are from the early ecumenical Confessions, do expressly speak of Christian unity, of the unity of the Church of Christ, because they lay stress on the uniqueness and individual character of Christian truth. For not unless its unity is manifest does Christian truth emerge. To speak of Christian truth is but to speak of Christian unity.

What have Christian truth and Christian unity to do with one another ? The differences between men, exemplified most clearly in their diversity of tongues, are represented in the story of the tower of Babel as being a consequence of the sin of man, a divine punishment. It is only through the Church of Christ, in the Christian Pentecost, that this sinfulness and punishment were removed. For then the obedience of Christ became manifest, the one perfect obedience because of which we, the disobedient, the sinners, have received forgiveness. The Apostle Paul never wearies of speaking of this unity of the Christian Church, which has its foundation in the crucified and risen Christ, nor of alluding to Christian truth as a stumbling-block to the Jews and to the Greeks foolishness. No law or philosophy, no social system or school of thought, form the basis of the unity of the Church which expresses, and must ever express, the Word of Christ alone, that is the Word of the Cross, the Word of perfect obedience.

The call has gone forth to us to enrol ourselves in this united front which God promised to His people and which He constituted in the Messiah whom He sent to His people, and not to imagine that we can strengthen His front by any action of our own. It is a natural instinct to desire, by means of our personal resources, to identify ourselves with God's work or at least to supplement it. That, and that only, constitutes the error of justification by works, that is, of co-operationism, which was pilloried by the Reformers and in which nevertheless hourly and daily we become entangled. Stern and severe is the saying of Jesus, that the Kingdom of Heaven shall be for the poor : for those, that is, who do not take but accept their places, thereby showing obedience and nothing but obedience. Paradoxical is the knowledge, vouchsafed to Paul in prayer, that the power of God is mighty only in the weak. We must not speak of the *Una Sancta* unless in dwelling on the *Una* we also bear in mind the *Sancta*, the fact that God called, justified and sanctified His people. The prophets of the Old Testament were zealous for the recognition of God's call and God's promise, which was applicable to the people as being the host called by God and therefore not to the People of Israel as such, that is, as possessing a natural individuality. It was precisely because of Israel's own misunderstanding that God hardened its heart. To lay stress on one's own individuality is to force one's own speech arrogantly and frowardly into God's Word. And it was the disobedient People of the Jews which constantly insisted on its own special character and spoke foolishly of itself as destined by God to be the *Una Sancta*. When the last of the prophets before Jesus, His precursor, John the Baptist, ventured to proclaim that the coming of the Kingdom of Heaven and of Jesus was at hand, he ventured to do so with the proviso, made by God, that out of the stones God could raise up children unto Abraham.

On the threshold of a new age the Baptist uttered his denunciation of human self-sufficiency in words which we have no right to evade. Yet religious history, Church history, has obliterated them ; and with their disappearance the *Una Sancta*, the Church of early Christendom, the Church of the New Testament, has also passed away. Even the New Testament itself has already much to say on the subject of divisions in the Church, rooted in human egotism. Sectarianism threatened to overwhelm the first community of Jerusalem, which instituted God's People, the remnant of Israel, that is, in fact, the Church. It was in Jerusalem, as a result of what happened at Easter, that the Church had first emerged ; and it was in Jerusalem, the City of God, that the coming of the Kingdom of God was expected. Then, however, it came to pass that the first Apostles claimed as a consequence of this prerogative, of this mark of preference, that certain powers of command were vested in themselves as the authorities and in Jerusalem as the Holy Place. The conduct of Peter in Antioch is a typical specimen of this early history of Christian theocracy, of self-seeking ; Christian truth, and hence Christian unity, was injured, nay sacrificed, for the Church of Antioch was torn into factions, Christian Jews and Christian Gentiles. Paul passed a severe judgment on these degenerate growths of theocracy. Where he speaks of the Body of Christ, he means the Body of Christ visible in all Christian Communities, in which Christ Himself is the master, and not man, self-appointed and thrusting himself to the front. But further, the decisive fact in this fight for truth and unity is that Paul, notwithstanding all his wealth of experience, his spiritual gifts, his mysticism, his enthusiasm, his visions, his raptures, laid no stress whatever on his own personality but based his apostolate solely on the special vision of Damascus, because as an episode of the Resurrection it connected him directly with the first disciples.

The collection for the poor in Jerusalem which was taken among the Christian Gentiles of the world was a visible and notable expression of the truth that the one Body of Christ is the one and only Church of God. If it were otherwise, the Body of Christ would have no connection with Christ as the Son of Man made flesh but would be a mere human organisation. So also any Church which neglects this truth, which assigns to itself its own place and calls attention to its own wealth, beauty and exclusive character, is no more than a human organisation.

From this rich diversity we are called back to a stern unity. Our poverty is God's riches. God, who ordained His Church, will not suffer us men to glorify what we add to His ordinance. The marks of the Church are but few, only God's Word and Sacrament. In the discussion with the Roman Catholic hierarchy on the question of justification by works, in which the first and last word was not left to God, the Augsburg Confession takes up the message of the Apostle Paul : " It is also laid down that for all time there is and shall remain but one Holy Christian Church, which is the Assembly of all the Faithful, in which the pure Gospel is preached and the Holy Sacrament administered according to the Gospel."

From the Holy Scriptures and from this Confession of the Reformers it is evident that we may not think to bring about the unity which is of God's making by sweeping away secondary diversities which have their roots in the world and in human sin. That unity has its inspiration in the Gospels and not in human traditions.

Thus in the Apology for the Augsburg Confession we read : " Those men are the true Church who here and there in the world, from the rising of the sun to the going down thereof, truly believe in Christ, who have one Gospel, one Christ, one Baptism and Sacrament, and are ruled by one Holy Ghost, albeit their ceremonies may differ." To forget this is to repeat the history of the Tower of Babel. God having spoken in Christ, this would be a sin against the Holy Ghost.

Proceeding from Christian unity rightly understood—in which connection we must note both the need for and the dangers of unitive work—the contrast between Christian truths and secular truths stands out clearly. If then we cannot set forth with one meaning and one mind the one straight Christian truth, it is because we constantly become entangled in the worldly truths with their self-ordained values, and sacrifice the *Una Sancta*. Unfortunately, theology, whose task and responsibility it is to speak of the truth of the one Church, has in the course of history become relatively blind to the spirit of self-appraisal. It must, moreover, be conceded that affairs in the modern world are so inexpressibly complicated that the "discernment of spirits" becomes well-nigh impossible. Antichrist at all times appears clad in shining raiment. And the most seductive of all garments is to be found in metaphysics, a product of the self-appraising mind of man, which fails altogether when the spirit of man is called the Spirit of God. It is intelligible, indeed necessary, that Socialism should pass judgment on a Church of this kind, which is nothing but a civil, cultured, aesthetic, religious union. And there are Christians in the Socialist movement who look anxiously for a protest of the Church against this self-appraisal of man. Yet it must, at the same time, be pointed out that the socialist International, in so far as it is inspired by socialist metaphysics, itself falls under the bann.

The promise of the Kingdom of God applies solely to the Church. And we must only think and speak of the *Una Sancta* as *ecclesia militans*. There is no such thing as an *ecclesia triumphans* which unites all men under her sceptre. Our unity lies in the hope of the Kingdom of God which is to come, in which God will be All in All. It is only the obedience of Christ which has rent the veil woven about us by the hardness of heart, the disobedience, the self-appraisal of man. And the Kingdom of God, visible behind the veil, can only be discerned by him who, despite all wealth, bears in mind the commandment which is nearest, the simplest and yet the most difficult law : Thou shalt love thy neighbour as thyself. To speak of the unity of the Church of Christ ordained by God, and to work for it, is therefore judgment and grace in one, as the saying of Jesus implies : " Where two or three are gathered together in my name, there am I in the midst of them.".

THE RIGHT REV. THE BISHOP OF MANCHESTER
(Anglican)

These public meetings in the Cathedral serve the great purpose of recalling to our minds the wider issues which depend on all our detailed work. Our present concern is the bearing of our divisions on the presentation of Christian truth. There can be no doubt that our divisions do seriously weaken the effectiveness of that presentation. But I wish to call attention to something deeper. We can only present what we can apprehend ; and our divisions fatally hinder the presentation of Christian truth because they first hinder our apprehension of it.

The evil is as old as the Church. There was a people prepared by national experience, as interpreted to it by saints and prophets, to receive the Lord and His Gospel ; with the exception of a very few they failed to respond. The repudiation of the Gospel by Israel was the first mutilation of the Church, and its consequences are past all calculation. Some would tell us that in the patristic age Christianity was completely transformed under Hellenic influences. That seems to me a gross exaggeration ; but it is not a mere falsification of the facts. How vast a difference it might have made if during the formative age of Christian theology the strongly intellectual influences of the Greek tradition had been balanced by the prophetic note which is most of all characteristic of the Hebraic tradition ! But Israel was not within the Church to supply its own contribution. So Christianity became definitely a European religion. It is worth while to reflect on the significance of the fact that when we speak of the East as distinct from the West in church history we do not refer to the Christianity of India or China, but to the Christianity of Eastern Europe—of a region west of the birthplace of Christianity. If Israel had not failed at the outset, the Indian or the Chinese would not feel to-day that Christianity is European. The injury of that first failure to the Church's missionary work is deep and terrible, and only now is its meaning becoming apparent.

Thus the Church has been mutilated from the first. And other divisions have had the like effect. Our civilisation has three historic roots—Palestine, Greece and Rome. Palestine dropped out from the beginning. The next great division separated the other two. Can anyone doubt that the intellectual passion, which is the glory of Greek culture and which expressed itself in philosophy and sculpture that are unsurpassed to this day, and the instinct for political order and for law, which is Rome's great gift to the world, could have accomplished more for the human race in combination even than all that Constantinople and Rome have brought to it in their separation ?

That was a division of East and West ; the Reformation brought a division of North and South. We are not now considering whether or not in the circumstances of that time the separation was necessary or desirable. In an evil situation the best course possible may only be the least bad. The Reformation in fact involved a division between Rome, with its strong sense of the value of order, and the Teutonic races with their long tradition of local self-government and liberty. Rome, left without their balancing influence, moved towards a regimentation of the spiritual life which seems to many of us mechanical and ultra-legalistic ; while the Teutonic tradition moved towards chaos, especially in the Anglo-Saxon countries, and again especially (if I may venture to say so) in Anglo-Saxon America where it could follow its own genius untrammelled by the historic traditions of the Old World.

From such a summary it seems to be beyond all reasonable question that every division injures both parties that are concerned in it. Each of them tends to become weak in its hold upon that aspect of the truth which is specially stressed by the other, and each tends to lay a disproportionate emphasis on the points for which it had stood at the moment of separation. Thus, for both, the apprehension of truth is warped and distorted.

It is not possible that any sectional group, above all any group of like-minded persons, should exhaust the " unsearchable riches of Christ." The measure of the stature of His fulness can only be revealed by the completed Church, when all races have brought their special contribution to the common apprehension. Only the truly Catholic, the truly Universal, Church can have a living grasp of the whole Christian faith. From this point of view it would be true to say that there is not in the world to-day a Catholic Church with many schisms around it ; from this point of view it would be true to say that there exist only schisms, and that this must always be true so soon as any schism has taken place at all. There are other points of view leading to another verdict : but this is the truth of the matter as regards one vital aspect of it.

If all this is true, how deep our penitence for our share in the sin of

R

disunion ought to be! It is not any question of our own satisfaction or peace which is at stake ; it is not only a question of efficiency in organisation. The great question is whether the Lord Christ shall be truly and fully presented to His people. We read in the Gospels of people among whom He could do no mighty work because of their unbelief. If we are not seeking with all our hearts the way of unity which may be followed with full loyalty to truth as we see it, then upon us in our day must lie the heavy load of responsibility that because of our failure to live together as members in the one Body, the Saviour cannot do the mighty works He would, cannot speak to our distracted world the healing words He would.

III. THE NECESSITY OF CHRISTIAN UNITY FOR THE MISSIONARY ENTERPRISE OF THE CHURCH

SUNDAY, AUGUST 14TH, 8.30 P.M.

Chairman: The Rev. Bishop JOHN HURST, D.D.

THE RIGHT REV. THE BISHOP OF DORNAKAL
(Anglican)

Our Lord's prayer for unity was based on the one plea " that the world may believe that thou didst send me." The revelation of God in Christ, says our Lord, would only be recognised and acknowledged by the world when it sees visibly before it an exhibition of unity which will be after the pattern of the divine unity. In this world of strife and conflict, unity is so rare and so uncommon that when it is seen in the Church the world will recognise it as supernatural and coming from God Himself. We shall now consider some reasons why unity is necessary for the missionary enterprise of the world.

1. *Unity is necessary in view of the World Opportunities open before the Church to-day*

After nineteen centuries of Christianity, two-thirds of the world's population still remain outside the Church. In India alone we reckon that at least one hundred millions of the people, or a third of the entire population, are beyond the reach of existing missionary organisations. China with its four hundred millions has even a sadder story to tell. Africa with two hundred millions is not Christian yet. Moreover, the world is open to-day to the Gospel as it was in no previous generation. Africa is emerging out of its heathenism of ages. India is throbbing with new life from end to end. Educated India is, more and more, coming under the spell of the teaching and person of our Lord. Rural India is even more ready to accept Christ and His Gospel of regeneration and uplift. The outcastes are entering the Church at the rate of about 3,000 a week. In my own diocese we have admitted during the last seven years 70,000 people. It has been said repeatedly that if only the Church had the vision and the devotion, the fifty-million outcastes could be swept into the Church in our generation!

491

And yet, with these world opportunities before it, the Church is feeble, its missionary work everywhere is under-manned, and its resources pitifully inadequate for this world-task. The Church is feeble because it is divided. It has been confidently asserted that if only the Church were one, at home and abroad, we have now at our disposal all the resources in men and money required to evangelise the whole world in our generation.

You know better than myself the wastage of Christian forces in the home lands. An Indian visitor is often saddened by seeing in some places churches built and ministers appointed, not to meet the needs of enlarged membership, but to have different denominations represented in the same locality. This—often unnecessary—multiplication goes on all the time that continents are asking for Gospel messengers, and backward and primitive races are clamouring for light and for the Gospel. Similar wastage is reproduced in the mission field. Four places of worship stand within a hundred yards of each other in one of the cities of India, each barely half full at any ordinary Sunday service, all ministered to by underpaid ministers, each too often engaged in unceasing warfare, not against the sin and suffering all round, but each against the supposed defects in the beliefs and practices of the others. Seven missionary societies are at work in my area among a population of a million people, five of which claim the exclusive possession of the Gospel truth and, therefore, the right to enter and plant churches anywhere. Such a multiplication of churches in the same area renders church discipline exceedingly difficult and ineffective. By our divisions, we not only waste our resources, but also diminish the Church's effectiveness for righteousness and purity in non-Christian lands. Unity, organic unity, is the only remedy.

2. *Unity is necessary for a common witness before the non-Christian World.*

Where the Gospel has entered in, the divisions in the Church cause the non-Christian to stumble. Thinking men ask why, while claiming loyalty to the one Christ, we still worship separately, we still show exclusiveness in the most sacred acts of our religion. The divisions confuse the thoughtful enquirer. " Which church shall I join ? " is often asked by such a convert. There have been many such " little ones of Christ " who have been caused to stumble by our divisions. Then again, hundreds of men in India to-day are hesitating to acknowledge Jesus as Lord and God because of the demands He is making upon them to break caste by entering into the fellowship of all believers for service in India. And the Church cannot speak with a united voice; its witness is confused by contrary voices; men are not certain of their duty, and their consciences are not touched by the united authority of the One Church. We are unable in our divided state to give an authoritative call to repentance, faith and baptism. This confirms men in their doubt and hesitation, and weakens their will for the sacrifice which Christ demands. To present a common front and preach a common faith to the non-Christian world *we must be one.*

3. *Unity is necessary for the life of the Church in the Mission Field.*

The divisions of Christendom do not appeal to the Christians in these lands. Christians in India, for instance, did not have a share in creating them. They entered into this ready-made system, and it has not really taken hold of them. Men become attached to this or that form of church organisation or polity only because their spiritual fathers belonged to that particular section. " I am a Baptist," said an Indian friend to me, " not because of theology, but because of geography." Having accidentally become attached to a Church, Indian Christians do not find it difficult, when necessary, to change their ecclesiastical allegiance to a Church other than their own. Restriction of such intercourse hurts them. It drives them either to be disloyal to their own Church, or to find fellowship with non-Christians and thus often to become indifferent to all religion.

The feeling of very many Indian Christians is that they were not responsible for the divisions of Christendom, neither would they perpetuate them. Force of habit, financial dependence, denominational training and, above all, loyalty to their spiritual fathers, now keep them in denominational connections. But these circumstances cannot keep them apart for ever.

Another factor must be mentioned. The rising tide of nationalism cannot be ignored. This new national spirit calls for national unity. The young Indian Christian cannot help being influenced by this new spirit. His patriotism moves him to do what he can to advance the interests of his own country, while his loyalty to Christ makes him long for his country to come into the full inheritance of eternal life in Jesus Christ. This national and Christian consciousness in consequence unites him with his fellow Christians of all Churches in the common task of the material and spiritual regeneration of his country in and through Christ. The Church, alas, divides; with the result that spiritual fellowship with his countrymen is coming to be valued more than participation in common sacraments, and belief in institutional Christianity is in danger of disappearing in the younger generation. The young Indian Christian wants Christ, he throws himself heartily into every institution that unites him with his brethren in fellowship and service, but he has no use for a Church that divides.

There is still another, even more serious, danger in India. Through our divisions we unconsciously become parties to the creation of caste churches. Caste is the bulwark of Hinduism. This religion, as was told me by one of its great exponents, does not stand for doctrine or belief, it stands for a life. It is very accommodating in religious practices ; it is relentless only in the demands of caste. By caste men are placed in watertight compartments. Beyond the caste circle there is no real social life, no inter-dining and certainly no inter-marriage. There is no worse force in the whole world that operates for separating man from man, and creating jealousy, suspicion and strife between communities, than this hydra-headed monster—caste. In such a land there is being planted, by the grace of God, a divine Society which is meant to be one, which was created by God to be one, and whose one characteristic worship is, by the ordinance of its divine Master, participation in one common sacred Food. Division in this Society means exclusive communions and severed fellowship, and produces all the worst effects of the Hindu caste system. When, added to this, different sects aim at establishing churches, each among people of a different caste, the evil is complete. Separate castes merge into separate denominations and once more continue their unholy warfare of generations. This is actually taking place in some parts of the country.

On the other hand, movements for union are being set on foot in different parts of India. The most striking is the movement in South India between the Anglican, the Presbyterian and Congregational Churches. Here among the Dravidian peoples of South India is a community, one in race, one in language, one in social life, one in political aspirations. For a generation they have shared a common spiritual experience. A common ambition to bring the whole country to the feet of Christ possesses them. The Church is the only thing that divides. They say : We want one Church for India, a Church that will be really one, that will express outwardly our inward unity.

We are working together to discover some way of getting one united Church. We do not desire any one Church to absorb the others. We do not ask any one to deny its past spiritual heritage, we cannot demand the severance of fellowship of any of these

Churches with the Churches in Europe or America that have planted them. But *we must have one Church.* We want a Church of India, a Church which can be our spiritual home, a Church where the Indian religious genius can find natural expression, a living branch of the Holy, Catholic and Apostolic Church, a Church which, being a visible symbol of unity in that divided land, will draw all men to our blessed Lord.

Fathers and brothers! Be patient with us if we cannot very whole-heartedly enter into the controversies of either the sixth or the sixteenth centuries. Recollection of these embitters church life ; they may alienate the young Churches from all ecclesiastical connections.

Unity may be theoretically a desirable ideal in Europe and America, but it is vital to the life of the Church in the mission field. The divisions of Christendom may be a source of weakness in Christian countries, but in non-Christian lands they are a sin and a scandal.

Great things, then, are at stake. The world is ready to hear the message of Christ. The young Churches in the mission field are waiting for a lead. They turn with wistful eyes to Lausanne. God wills unity. Christ prays for unity. The Holy Spirit works for unity. Let us also with penitence and sorrow and love confess our divisions and together will, pray, and work, " that we all may be one."

THE REV. PROFESSOR TIMOTHY TINGFANG LEW, D.D.
Yenching University, Peking (Congregationalist)

The subject assigned by the Conference for this evening is the necessity of Christian unity for the missionary enterprise of the Church. I shall first present to you the message of the Chinese Church concerning the necessity of unity. In 1922 there was held in Shanghai the National Christian Conference of China, the greatest Conference of its kind ever held in China. One thousand delegates, 500 Chinese and 500 missionaries, representing every Protestant communion, were assembled. That Conference issued a message to the Christian Church. The very first passage of the message is entitled, " The United Church." It reads as follows :

" We Chinese Christians who represent the various leading denominations express our regret that we are divided by the denominationalism which comes from the West. We are not unaware of the diverse gifts through the denominations that have been used by God for the enrichment of the Church. Yet we recognise fully that denominationalism is based upon differences the historical significance of which, however real and vital to the missionaries from the West, are not shared by us Chinese. Therefore, denominationalism, instead of being a source of inspiration, has been and is a source of confusion, bewilderment, and inefficiency. We recognise also most vividly the crying need of the Christian salvation for China to-day, and we firmly believe that it is only the united Church that can save China, for our task is great and enough strength can only be obtained through solid unity. Therefore, in the name of the Lord, who prayed that all may be one, we appeal to all those who love the same Lord to follow His command and be united into one Church, catholic and indivisible, for the salvation of China. We believe that there is an essential unity among all Chinese Christians, and that we are voicing the sentiment of the whole Chinese Christian body in claiming that we have the desire and the possibility to effect a speedy realisation of corporate unity, and in calling upon missionaries and representatives of the Churches in the West, through self-sacrificial devotion to our Lord, to remove all the obstacles in order that Christ's prayer for unity may be fulfilled in China."

Since 1922, the necessity for Christian unity has become even greater than before, particularly in the following aspects :

First of all, the magnitude of the work of evangelisation continually demands a united Church. There are in China over 400 million souls, and only 400 thousand are members of Protestant Communions ; that is, only one in a thousand. There are about one million and a half in the Roman Communion, which is only one in 260. There are over 2,000 walled cities in China ; the Gospel has only been carried to two-thirds of these. Among the hundreds of thousands of villages and small towns a large number have not heard the message of the Gospel. There are provinces as large as the whole of France or Switzerland which have no permanent churches.

Secondly, not only the magnitude, but also the nature of the work is urging us with increasing force for unity. It is the glory of the Christian Gospel that it has been presented to China not as a mere system of philosophical thought or a mere set of theological doctrines or a mere system of ecclesiasticism, but as a life of service. Christianity is known in China through its magnificent service rendered by schools and colleges, hospitals, dispensaries and other institutions of social service. Only unity can make it possible for such institutions to maintain decent standards, guarantee their growing life and assure their continual progress.

Thirdly, there is rising in China the all-powerful nationalism which challenges Christianity. Underneath all the civil strife and disturbed conditions in China there is a fundamental unity of the Chinese people, a unity which has never been impaired. Anything that either interferes with such unity, or may threaten its permanency is looked upon as the very enemy of the nation. Christianity is being looked upon with grave suspicion at this moment in China because, while it professes to teach love and unity, it is divided against itself. Some national leaders have pointedly asked " Can Christianity, which has caused and supported so many wars in Western history, which is at present minutely divided in its own household, be a factor of help to China at all in her present life and death struggle for national unity ? " Only a united Church can meet such a challenge.

Facing such great necessity for unity, Chinese Christians are praying for a common confession of faith. In this matter three points are of special importance for us.

Our common confession of faith should not be a mere intellectual statement. Thousands of Christians gave up wealth, health, livelihood, social standing, life-careers, and everything that human beings crave for and hold dear, in order to accept Christianity and to confess their faith in Jesus Christ. Some of them did so at the cost of their lives and died martyrs' deaths. But the confession of these Chinese Christians usually consisted of John iii, 16, together with the great Commandment and the Ten Commandments, the Sermon on the Mount and the Lord's Prayer. Their confession was the Gospel itself, learnt from the Word of God and made real by the lives Christians lived.

Next, our common confession of faith should not fail to give explicit interpretation of human relationships in terms of the divine. Our philosophy of life is built upon ethical human relationships. Our religions emphasise these relationships. Chinese Christians believe that in confessing faith in Jesus Christ they confess their faith in the Saviour who came to fulfil and not to destroy. We wish to know how our faith in Him fulfils the need of all human relationships, especially those between men and women, employers and employed, nation and nation.

Further, we need a definite and courageous statement of the attitude of our faith to scientific discovery. It is perilous to leave materialism unchallenged. This is the peril, not only of the West, but also of the East. It cannot be overcome by mere contemptuous indifference, or unintelligent dogmatism. It can only be overcome by a united confession of faith on the part of all Christians, a confession which understands science and spiritualises it.

Concerning order, there are two outstanding thoughts in the minds of Chinese Christians. They have seen in the last hundred years men from different nations who came to China with the sanction of different Communions, under different orders, and some from Communions that give no formal ordination. They have watched their work and their lives ; they have found in every Communion both saintly servants and also others who are unworthy of the order they claim. The same is true of the Chinese ministers who receive ordination from them. Chinese Christians, with all their appreciation and traditional respect for institutional form and symbolic authority, fully realise the problem of apostolic succession ; yet they can only set little value on the *mere* formal sanction of the ministry by external authority. The great majority of Chinese Christians will not ask how a man is ordained, but how he lives, how he preaches and how he serves.

Again, in the development of the Chinese Church, we find that women have played a very important part. To an increasing number of Chinese Christians of this generation there is a definite hope that in the completely united Church of God there should be nothing that can be interpreted as " prejudice against women." They shall serve the Church in every capacity so long as they are qualified for it.

The vision of the united Church is very real to Chinese Christians. May I share with you a few glimpses of it ?

First of all the united Church should be a Church richer in spiritual grace. We are standing now at the threshold of a new era of the Christian Church. Looking forward, we see a vision of the united Church. We cannot help but glance back at the roads by which we have severally come. There we see that the path of division was stained with the tears of the saints and sanctified by the blood of the martyrs. We must preserve those witnesses heroically made. We must treasure the richness which they have bequeathed to us. I believe that I am voicing the sentiments of the Chinese Christians that the united Church must be a Church richer in God's grace and fuller in the understanding of His will than any single Communion heretofore has ever attained alone.

Secondly, the united Church should be a growing Church. The centre of our Gospel is Jesus Christ. He is not only the Way and the Truth, but also the Life. Life is never static : it either grows or declines. The united Church must have a divine vitality for continuous growth. She must continually " grow in grace and in the knowledge of our Lord and Saviour, Jesus Christ." I believe I am again voicing the sentiments of Chinese Christians that it is only with such capacities of all-round, complete, and never-ceasing growth that the united Church can for ever be united and never again suffer divisions as she has in the past.

And, finally, the united Church should be a Church not for a section of the world, but for the entire world. The peoples in the Far East have their own spiritual and religious inheritance, which is in some aspects different from that of the Western nations. Their inheritance helps them to understand the purpose of God in Jesus Christ in their own way. It may give them a certain insight and understanding which the West has not yet seen. There is among the Chinese Christians now a felt command of God to interpret Christianity in terms of the spiritual inheritance of the Chinese race. They believe that such interpretation, when made together with their own spiritual experience, should find a wider expression. It does not belong to them alone, but should become the possession of the whole Church Universal. The movement for an indigenous Church is growing more audible and more persistent in China. It is the hope of the Chinese Christians that the united Church will be enriched by the contribution of the indigenous Churches not only of China but also of Japan, India and other lands.

Fellow Christians, to achieve our unity we must follow our Master into the Garden of Gethsemane once more, facing the cup of complete self-denial, and pray with one accord, " Father, thy will, not mine, be done." To achieve unity we must follow the Saviour all the way to Golgotha, and there nail on the Cross all our personal preferences, individual habits, group prejudices, petty jealousies and deeply entrenched interests. To achieve unity we must die with Him and rise again. We must follow the risen Lord to Mount Olivet, there to acquire a new vision, a vision that takes in the entire world.

IV. THE NECESSITY OF CHRISTIAN UNITY FOR THE SOCIAL FUNCTION OF THE CHURCH

WEDNESDAY, AUGUST 17TH, 8.30 P.M.

Chairman: Dr. ERICH STANGE

THE REV. A. E. GARVIE, D.D.
Principal of Hackney and New College, London (Congregationalist)

From the biological standpoint man may be described as a gregarious animal. Psychology and sociology converge in the proof that man realises himself individually as he relates himself socially. It is as son, brother, husband, father, worker, citizen that he becomes most fully man. Religion, too, is social in its earliest phases, tribal and national; and if it passes into an individual stage (as in the teaching of Jeremiah and Ezekiel) on the way from its national to its universal form it does not thereby cast off its social relations, as the individual in this as in all his other activities is affected by and affects the society of which he is a member. Christianity does assert the value of the individual soul (the single sheep and the single coin) but as the value is that of the child of God, the universal Father, the relation to God places each man in relation to all who share that relation to God; and just as in the relation to God love is the law, so in the relation to other men. Love cannot be fulfilled, however, in this relation to the same degree in all individuals: the more intimate the relation to God of individuals, the more intimate is it possible for their mutual relations to be. The New Testament distinguishes *philadelphia* from *philanthropia*, love of the brethren from love of men. The one is not an exclusion of the other, but a concentration of it. The *philadelphia* cannot fully develop unless as it freely expands into the *philanthropia*. The missionary obligation of the Church is to bring all men into the relation of children to God as Father; and thus as each convert passes into the communion of the Church, the *philanthropia* becomes *philadelphia*. But evangelisation is not the only expression of *philanthropia*: it must express itself in all the service for the whole good of others for which the individual has the capacity, his situation gives him the opportunity, and the conditions around him impose the necessity.

For this demand the following among other reasons may be suggested : (1) Man is so affected by his environment that its conditions may hinder or further his development mentally, morally and spiritually. The slum does not promote, but prevents saintliness. Conditions must often be altered to secure the necessary receptivity and responsiveness for the Christian message. Care for the whole life of man must often be the herald of solicitude for the soul, the relation to God. (2) The Christian community does not and cannot realise its moral ideal fully within a society which is indifferent or hostile to it. As Christians are related to other members of society, they cannot be fully Christian unless the relationship on both sides is being Christianised. In the industrial as in the international sphere a man cannot give full expression to his Christian manhood in conditions and relations which fall far below the Christian level. (3) The Christian character is to be manifested in all the relations of life ; a man cannot fulfil even his individual duty as a Christian unless he is using every channel of influence, not only to develop his own personality, but in so doing to conform the world around him to the ideal which he recognises for himself. God is the Creator, Preserver and Father of all the world, Jesus Christ is the Saviour and Lord of all men, the Spirit of God is given for the cleansing and hallowing of the whole of life. The Christian religion is not a private privilege, it is a public responsibility. The Church in promoting saintliness in its members must promote a Christian citizenship. (4) It was for a long time assumed that social miseries and wrongs could be, if not removed, at least relieved by individual philanthropy. It is now acknowledged that the extent of the evil is so great and its causes are so deeply rooted in the social system that the resources of individual philanthropy are not adequate, nor can it so alter the system as to uproot the causes of evil. What is necessary is *social politics*, the collective and corporate effort of the whole community, whether local, national, or world-wide. Thus Christian citizenship in the widest possible range of interest and activity is a primary obligation.

Once more, (5) the individual member of the Church will not in his activity as citizen be adequately effective unless he has the sympathy and support of the Church in its testimony and influence as the Christian community amid the other communities of which human society is composed. While the Church is not committed to and must allow itself to be entangled in sectional solutions of the problems, economic or political, it has an ideal to present of what human society should be, and it is the guardian of principles of conduct which are applicable to all conditions and relations. It must assert that ideal. It must show the application of those principles. It must assert the authority and efficacy of Jesus Christ as Saviour and Lord in all the manhood of all mankind.

Lastly, (6) what is ever needed in human society for the solution of its problems is goodwill, the new heart, the love of the neighbour as well as, and as much as, self. Not only must the Church in its evangelisation produce in individual men the adequate motive of such love to men, the constraining love of Christ, but it must surely in its own life show the realisation of the ideal. The *philadelphia* must be the pattern of the *philanthropia* as well as an encouragement and support of it ; the fellowship of believers in the Lord must show the way to that community in human society which will harmonise differences and so prevent division and conflict in human relations. Again, it should be possible for the world amid all its suspicions, rivalries and hates to point to Christians and say, " See how these Christians love one another." How can this challenge of the world, and must we not add, this summons of Jesus Christ Himself be met ?

A characteristic feature of our own age is the manifold differences of sex, class, interest, nation, and race, which are asserting themselves as divisions leading to conflict.

Paul lived in a world as divided, and to all these divisions he applied his Christian *universalism ;* the differences, if not abolished, are transcended in the unity of the life of believers in Christ, in whom there is neither male nor female, learned nor unlearned, bond nor free, barbarian nor Greek, Jew nor Gentile, but only a new man. There is no truth which the Christian Church needs so much to assert as this Christian universalism, and no duty it must urge more than the application of this universalism in all human relations. This application will, however, have a two-fold result. There are differences so opposed to the recognition of a common humanity that only their abolition can be an adequate application : the institution of slavery is acknowledged to be such ; the practice of war is being increasingly recognised as inconsistent with the realisation of the Christian ideal. There are other differences, which may by the Spirit of Christ be so harmonised that there is no need for their abolition : sex cannot be abolished, but any antagonism to which it may give rise can be removed by a cleansing and hallowing of the relation of man and woman as in Christian marriage. This harmonisation may need time ; it must be a gradual process, and cannot be accomplished safely if rushed too speedily. This is what reformers in a hurry do not adequately recognise, and so blame men of deeper insight and wider vision for compromising, as they call it, principle to expediency. Paul is not to be depreciated because he did not at once advocate the emancipation of the slave, or the release of Christian women from the rules of propriety recognised at that time. The reformer should always take into account the total conditions as affecting the principle to which he is seeking to give practical application. Evolution is the mode of God's creative activity; it must also be the mode of man's social progress. Applying this lesson of history to our own time, we must recognise that the existing industrial system cannot be broken up in the hope of making a better out of its fragments. It is within the system that human relations must be so Christianised that gradually and inevitably the system itself will be so modified as to conform much more closely to the Christian ideal. So, also, perilous as are the divisions among the nations, a cosmopolitanism which ignores or is indifferent to nationality cannot afford a remedy. The differences of nations must be recognised, but harmonised into an internationalism which transforms these differences into contributions to human unity.

The Church must be the exponent and the agent of this Christian universalism; it must show the pattern of, and provide the power for, human unity. But may not the taunt be brought against it, "Physician, heal thyself?" How can a Church which has not reconciled its divisions exercise this ministry of reconciliation in the world? How can it show the world what differences must be abolished to secure unity, and how some differences must be transformed to become consistent with it? It is to be feared that the majority of Christians do not realise how much the witness of the Church is blurred, its work hindered, its influence weakened by the divisions of Christendom. If it be said that the spiritual unity is deeper and wider than these ecclesiastical differences indicate, it must be answered, that the world to be influenced can only apprehend and appreciate a unity which is manifest and effective. If it was necessary that the Word should become flesh in order that men might behold the glory of the only-begotten of the Father in Him, is it not necessary that the vision of the one Church of Jesus Christ which the Epistle to the Ephesians presents to us should be seen in the world? The Church cannot deliver its message of "peace on earth to men of goodwill" to a divided world as long as it itself appears divided in the world; it cannot fulfil its mission of the unification of mankind in the one Kingdom of God until its own unity is seen of all men.

It is not ecclesiastical interests which bring us together, but vital practical interests for human good. The differences which still divide are so deeply rooted in human history ; they have so strong a hold on human memories, associations, affections and convictions, they have so contributed to the fuller expression of the contents of the Christian religion, that they cannot be treated lightly as of no consequence ; only as we fully recognise the reality of them can we with reality deal with them. It is not with mere words or names that we are engaged, but with what have become most sacred concerns. The way to the goal of unity is difficult and long and demands wisdom, patience and courage ; but in following that way under the leadership of Christ Himself the Churches may give the world a good example of how differences should be recognised so that divisions may be removed in human life. Lausanne may become a guide to Geneva, and all other centres where men are seeking to reconcile differences and remove divisions.

In this task let us recognise the principle already alluded to, of diversity-in-unity. All differences need not be abolished, but only transformed, in the removal of divisions. Uniformity is not necessary for unity, for it has again and again when enforced provoked conflict and discord. Within the limits which the truth and the grace of Christ set, variety of creed, code, ritual and polity, must be allowed, in recognition of the variety of human thought and life. There is one difference which we must harmonise or transcend, the difference of Catholic and Protestant in regard to the sacraments and the ministry, so that the division at the Table of the Lord and in the proclamation of the Word of the Lord may be abolished. One theory there need not be, but one practice, which would allow all Christian believers to hear without doubt or scruple the same Gospel and to partake together the same Sacrament. Do we need more, and can we be content with less, in order that the spiritual unity of the Church may be made manifest and effective among men? Does not our heartfelt yearning for full and free fellowship with all Christians demand this at the very least, whatever more may follow ? And is not this the least expression of unity which will enable one Church, reconciled within itself, to exercise effectively the ministry of reconciliation in the world so divided by sex, class, interest, nation and race ? The world is calling " Come over and help," and Christ is commanding " Answer the call! "

PROFESSOR DR. DEMETRIOS BALANOS
University of Athens (Orthodox)

It has been manifest for some time that Christian minds are everywhere turning towards unity as a necessity for the effective realisation of Christian purposes. This is a turning-point in Christian history; it is a movement which has been specially noticeable since the War—so clearly have the War and the post-war period shown that the dissipation of Christian energies made them wholly unable to meet the needs of these terrible times and the aspirations of mankind.

The Church, it seemed, was called by its very essence to be the one spiritual harbour in which the heart could find peace in the midst of this turmoil. We have to confess that it has not been so, and that while this and that national Church threw itself, now and again, with more or less energy into the changing fortunes of the conflict, the Church as a whole was powerless to prevent it or to bring it to a speedy end. Nor could it mitigate, for all its good intentions, the cruelties of the war—it was not prepared beforehand for the task, nor were its energies adequate. And yet, at the heart of the severed Confessions, was there not enshrined that spirit of unity and peace which might have been the world's example?

Our divisions, recriminations, misunderstandings, rivalries, and the habit of throwing the cloak of religion over political motives and national self-seeking—all this was hardly calculated to diffuse in the world an atmosphere of unity and peace.

There must be an end to this! The world is athirst for real peace; yet the words of Isidore of Pelusium are as true now as when they were first uttered: " When men speak of peace, there we see them making ready for battle." The world needs peace; and if the Church —the salt of the earth—is to keep its savour, it must not allow its message of peace to be unheard.

Let the Churches unite with sincerity on the basis of their common faith in their Lord and Saviour, proclaiming their certitude that the kingdom of God alone can save the world. Fired by this faith, inspired by love, let us weld ourselves into a Christendom one and indivisible, remembering that nothing but co-operation can ensure the triumph of the Christian ideal. We are severed from each other by differences of rite, of order, of dogma, I know; yet Christ said, " hereby shall all men know that ye are my disciples, if ye love one another "; that is the great commandment of love, and we have too often turned away from it to fix our minds on secondary or valueless problems.

The sacred bond of love ought not to be broken by differences of thought or of usage. Christ is for us all the one beginning and the one end. Can we then suffer differences of opinion about the intermediate steps to keep us separate ? God forbid ! This bond is strong enough to create a unity in which the Christian ideal could be realised ; one in which the particular Churches would run no more risk of compromise than do the peoples who form the League of Nations. Let me remind you of the wise words of the Bishop of Manchester : " I could wish that in the sphere of moral and social questions all Christians would acquire the habit of acting together as though they were one body. Such common action is possible without betraying any theological convictions."

Nothing would do more to promote such a co-ordination of effort than the holding of annual meetings of churchmen and theologians like this Conference which we are happy to hold in Lausanne. The purpose of such meetings would be to bring our agreements into the foreground, to dissipate misunderstanding, to provide against possible differences, not by artificial compromises, but by facing the facts in the spirit of free and generous interchange of thought. The results should then be brought home to the whole Christian people, for, it must be remembered, we shall never reach real unity till we have taught even the humblest of the faithful to desire it.

We shall thus learn, moreover, to see how we have cause to differ, and we shall have more respect for usages and teachings which are not our own. Theologians, priests and believers of different Churches will come to know each other as members of one communion in Christ ; the places where others worship, the priests who minister there, will be sacred in our eyes.

Such a brotherhood of Christians, if we can picture it, would be a new epoch for Christianity, a renaissance of the faith, in which Christians, ceasing to spend their strength against each other, would fight the good fight side by side, working for the triumph of truth and righteousness and for good of all mankind. Then the Saviour's saying, that there shall be one flock and one shepherd, would be fulfilled.

Thus the Church could devote itself fruitfully to the moral and social problems of the day, could wage successful war against the forces of anarchy, could succour the oppressed and heavy-laden. So alone could she find the road to peace and salvation ; so alone could we become fellow-workers for the kingdom ; so alone could the Church stand firm against the gates of hell, the earthly hell of anarchy and wickedness.

Be sure that the Greek Catholic Church is ready to labour for the realisation of this high ideal. Even in her darkest hour she has never abandoned this dream. Inspired by her Saviour's teaching, and conscious of the tasks laid on her, it will be her desire to labour side by side with other Churches towards the Christian goal, for the establishment of God's kingdom on earth. God help her to achieve it !

LIST OF MEMBERS

OFFICERS OF THE CONFERENCE

President :   The Rt. Rev. CHARLES H. BRENT, D.D.

Deputy Chairman :   Rev. ALFRED E. GARVIE, D.D.

Vice-Presidents :   The Most Rev. NATHAN SÖDERBLOM, D.D.
The Most Rev. ARCHBISHOP GERMANOS.
Pastor CHARLES MERLE D'AUBIGNÉ, D.D.
Prof. Dr. ADOLF DEISSMANN.

Treasurer :   GEORGE ZABRISKIE, D.C.L.

General Secretary :   Mr. RALPH W. BROWN, P.O. Box 226, Boston, Mass., U.S.A.

STAFF OF INTERPRETERS

Mr. H. CYRIL KERR.   Pastor ANDRÉ MONOD.
Pastor JULES RAMBAUD.   Pastor Lic. HERMANN SASSE.
                                 Col. H. H. WADE.

MEMBERS

The following list has been revised and, of necessity, abbreviated from the "Who's Who," printed for the Conference at Lausanne.

Numbers in brackets refer to the pages on which the address or remarks of the member are printed.

*Deceased.

AALDERS, W. J., Dr.Theol.—Professor of Theology, University of Groningen. Editor, *N. Theol. Tydschrift*. Reformed Church of the Netherlands. [222]

ABBOTT, Rev. B. A.—Editor, *The Christian Evangelist*, St. Louis, Mo., U.S.A. Disciples of Christ.

ABBOTT-SMITH, GEORGE, D.D., D.C.L.—Canon of Christ Church Cathedral, Montreal. Professor of N.T. Literature, Montreal Theological College. Church of England in Canada.

ADELAIDE, Bishop of—see Thomas, A. N.

AINSLIE, PETER, D.D., LL.D.—Minister of Christian Temple, Baltimore, Md., U.S.A. Editor, *The Christian Union Quarterly*. Disciples of Christ. [222, 342, 407]

ALIVISATOS, HAMILCAR S., D.D.—Professor of Canon Law and Practical Theology, University of Athens. Orthodox Church of Greece. [106, 386]

ALIVISATOS, IRENE H.—27 Voulis St., Athens. Orthodox Church of Greece.

AMBROSIOS (A. NICOLAIDES)—Metropolitan of Naupactos, Greece. Orthodox Church of Greece ; also delegate from the Archbishopric of Cyprus. [386]

ANDERSEN, J. OSKAR, D.D.—Professor of Theology, University of Copenhagen. Editor, *Theological Review*. Church of Denmark.

ANKAR, GUSTAF ALFRED, Lic.Theol.—Komminister, Gustav Vasa Church, Stockholm. Church of Sweden.

ANTAL, G. VON, Dr. Phil.—Bishop, Hungarian Reformed Church. Member of Upper House of Parliament. Papa, Hungary.

APPIA, LOUIS—Inspecteur ecclésiastique, Consistoire de Paris. Pastor Church of St. Marcel, Paris. Evangelical Lutheran Church of France. [373, 381]

ARMAGH, Archbishop of—see D'Arcy.

ARMITAGE, W. J., Ph.D., D.D.—Canon and Archdeacon of Halifax, N.S. Rector of St. Paul's Church, Halifax. Church of England in Canada.

ARSENIEW, NICOLAS, Dr. Phil.—Professor of Theology at Warsaw; Privat-docent at University of Königsberg, Prussia. Orthodox Church of Russia. [104, 386, 402]

ASHWORTH, ROBERT A., D.D.—Pastor, Baptist Church of the Redeemer, Yonkers, N.Y. Northern Baptist Convention of the U.S.A. [313]

ATKINSON, HENRY A., D.D.—Secretary of Church Peace Union, 70, Fifth Ave., New York. National Council of Congregational Churches in the U.S. [222, 393]

AULÉN, GUSTAF, D.D.—Professor at the University of Lund, Sweden. Editor, *Svensk Teologisk Kvartalskrift.* Church of Sweden.

AZARIAH, VEDENAYAKAM SAMUEL, LL.D. (Cantab.)—Bishop of Dornakal, Deccan. Church of England in India. [103, 422, 491]

BAER, SAMUEL HAROLD, Ph.D..—31 Dartford Ave., Hillcrest, St. Louis, Mo., U.S.A. National Council of Congregational Churches in the U.S.

BAGNALL, MRS. MARY AURORA—17 Maxwell Rd., Rathgar, Dublin. Methodist Church in Ireland.

BAGNAIL, THOMAS ST. JOHN—Secretary of Church Committee, Methodist Church in Ireland. Address, 17 Maxwell Rd., Rathgar, Dublin.

BAGNELI, ROBERT, Ph.D., D.D.—Pastor, Grace Church, Harrisburg, Pa., U.S.A. Methodist Episcopal Church.

BAKER, HAROLD NAPIER, M.A.—Rector of St. Thomas' Church, North Sydney. Church of England in Australia.

BALAKIAN, KRIKORIS—Bishop, Armenian Apostolic Church. Apostolic Delegate for the Armenians of Europe. Address, 8c Ave. Pereire, Asnières sur Seine, Paris. [395]

BALANOS, DEMETRIOS S., Dr. Theol.—Professor at University of Athens. Orthodox Church of Greece. [386, 505]

BALASSA, FRANÇOIS RAGÀLYI—Member, Upper House of Parliament. Address, Ragàly, Hungary. Reformed Church of Hungary.

BANNINGA, JOHN J., D.D.—Principal, Union Theological Seminary, Pasumalai, S. India. South India United Church. [263]

BARBER, WILLIAM T. A., D.D.—Principal, Richmond Theological College, Surrey. Wesleyan Methodist Church.

BARBOUR, G. F., D.Phil.—Finscatle, Pitlochry, Perthshire. Elder, United Free Church of Scotland. [357]

BARNES, CLIFFORD W., LL.D.—10 La Salle St., Chicago, Ill., U.S.A. Presbyterian Church in the U.S.A.

BARSAUM, SÉVÉRIUS APHRAM—Archbishop of Syria and of Lebanon. Syrian Orthodox Church. Address, Homs, Syria. [382]

BARTLET, J. VERNON, D.D.—Professor of Church History, Mansfield College, Oxford. Congregational Union of England and Wales. [206, 290, 422, 429]

BARTON, WILLIAM E., D.D., LL.D., Litt.D.—Member, Executive Com., National Council of Congregational Churches in U.S. Corresponding Editor, *The Congregationalist.* Address, Oak Park, Ill., U.S.A. [228, 380, 381]

BATE, HERBERT NEWELL, M.A.—Canon of Carlisle Cathedral. Church of England. [36]

BATES, MINOR LEE, LL.D.—President, Hiram College, Hiram, Ohio, U.S.A. Disciples of Christ in N. America.

BELL, W. COSBY, D.D.—Professor of the Philosophy of the Christian Religion, Virginia Theological Seminary, Alexandria, Va. Protestant Episcopal Church in U.S.A.

BÉNÉDICTOS—see Papadopoulos, B.

BENSOW, OSCAR, D.Theol.—Hauptpastor. Akersberge, Sweden. Church of Sweden.

BERRY, SIDNEY M., D.D.—Secretary, Congregational Union of England and Wales. Address, Memorial Hall, Farringdon St., London.

BERTRAND, A. N.—President, General Com. of the National Union of the Reformed Churches of France. Pastor, Oratory of the Louvre, Paris. [106, 205]

BIELER, CHARLES, D.D.—Professor of Theology, United Theological College, Montreal. United Church of Canada. [429]

DE BILDT, HARALD—Swedish Minister to Egypt. Address, Swedish Legation, Cairo, Egypt. Church of Sweden. [483]

BIRD, PHILIP SMEAD, D.D.—Pastor, First Presbyterian Church, Utica, N.Y. Presbyterian Church in U.S.A.

BLAIR, JOHN C., M.A.—Missionary, United Church of Northern India. Address, Deese Camp, Bombay Presidency, India. [285, 381, 415]

BLAKE, HOWARD—449 East 55 St., Kansas City, Mo. Presbyterian Church in U.S.A.

BLEAKNEY, EDWARD MILTON ADDISON, B.D.—Pastor, Tabernacle Baptist Church, Utica, N.Y. Northern Baptist Convention, U.S.A.

BLEAKNEY, GUY GARFIELD, B.D.—Pastor, First Baptist Church, Corning, N.Y. Northern Baptist Convention, U.S.A.

DE BOËR, ALEXIS, LL.D.—Professor of University, Chief Curator of Transylvanian Reformed Church, Judge of the Supreme Court for Administration of Hungary. Address, 1 Kiralyhàgo ut 5 à, Budapest. Reformed Church of Hungary.

BONCZAK, FRANCIS—Bishop, Polish National Catholic Church. Professor of Dogmatic Theology, etc., at Cracow Seminary. Editor, *Polska Odrodzona*. Address, Ul. Madalinskiego 10, Cracow.

BOND, AHVA J. C., D.D.—Pastor, Seventh Day Baptist Church. Address, Plainfield, N.J., U.S.A.

BOYD, Mrs. WESLEY—106 South Jardin St., Shenandoah, Pa. Primitive Methodist Church in U.S.A.

BRENT, CHARLES HENRY, D.D., LL.D.—Bishop of Western New York. Address, 250 Summer St., Buffalo, N.Y. Protestant Episcopal Church in U.S.A. [3, 33, 404]

BREWIS, JOHN THOMAS, B.D.—Principal, United Methodist Theological College, Manchester, England. United Methodist Church.

BRILIOTH, INGVE TORGNY, D.Phil., D. Theol.—Professor of Church History in the Academy of Abo, Finland. Co-editor, *Svensk Teologisk Kvartalskrift*. Church of Sweden.

BRISTOW, JOHN—Greenview, Dunmurry, Co. Antrim, Ireland. Member of the General Synod and of the Representative Church Body, Church of Ireland.

BRODERSEN, PAUL—Pastor, Kvislemark bei Sandved. Church of Denmark.

BROWN, ARTHUR J., D.D., LL.D.—General Secretary, Board of Foreign Missions, Presbyterian Church in U.S.A. Address, 156 Fifth Ave., New York.

BROWN, WILLIAM ADAMS, Ph.D., D.D.—Professor in Union Theological Seminary, New York. Presbyterian Church in U.S.A. [78, 223, 393, 422]

BUDD, REV. W. R.—General Secretary of the Home Missions Fund, Methodist Church in Ireland. Address, 34 Dartmouth Rd., Dublin.

BUDD, DR. ELIZABETH, L.R.C.P. and S.I.—34 Dartmouth Rd., Dublin. Methodist Church in Ireland.

BUKOVINA, Metropolitan of—see Nectarie.

BULGAKOW, SERGIUS, DR.—Archpriest. Professor of Dogmatic Theology at the Russian Orthodox Theological Institute in Paris. Orthodox Church of Russia. [208, 258, 386]

BURN, ANDREW E., D.D.—Dean of Salisbury. Church of England.

BURNTVEDT, T. O., C.T.—Pastor, Trinity Lutheran Church, Minneapolis, Minn., U.S.A. Lecturer, Augsburg Theological Seminary, Minneapolis. Lutheran Free Church of America.

CADMAN, S. PARKES, D.D., S.T.D., L.H.D., LL.D.—Pastor, Central Congregational Church, Brooklyn, N.Y. President, Federal Council of Churches of Christ in America. National Council of Congregational Churches in U.S. [115]

CANNON, JAMES, jun., D.D.—Bishop, Methodist Episcopal Church South. Address, 52 Bliss Building, Washington, D.C., U.S.A. [105, 389, 394, 428, 430]

CERNAUTI, ARCHBISHOP OF—see Nectarie.

CHOISY, J. EUGÈNE, D.Theol.—Professor of Ecclesiastical History at the University of Geneva. Reformed Church of Geneva. [28, 409]

CHRIST CHURCH, DEAN OF—see Kennedy.

CHRISTOPHOROS—Archbishop of Leontopolis. Greek Orthodox Patriarchate of Alexandria. [386]

CLARK, LUCIUS C., D.D.—Chancellor, American University, Washington, D.C. Methodist Episcopal Church., U.S.A.

CLAUDIUS PASHA, SALIB—Senator, Egypt. Address, Ramleh, near Alexandria. Coptic Church.

COCHRAN, JOSEPH WILSON, D.D., LL.D.—Pastor, American Church of Paris (Interdenominational). Presbyterian Church in U.S.A.

COLE, ELMER WARD, D.D.—Pastor, First Christian Church, South Bend, Ind., U.S.A. Registrar, International Convention, Disciples of Christ.

COMBA, ERNESTO—Professor of Theology at the Faculty of Theology of Rome. Editor, La Luce. Waldensian Evangelical Church.

CONSTANTINIDIS, MICHAEL, D.Theol.—Great Archimandrite. Vicar of the Greek Church of St. Sophia, London. Ecumenical Patriarchate of Constantinople. [386]

COOPER, A. ORLTON, L.Th.—Chaplain at Buenos-Aires. Church of England.

COWDEN, REV. JOHN B.—Christian Unity Evangelist. Address, West Nashville, Tenn., U.S.A. Disciples of Christ.

D'ARCY, CHARLES FREDERICK, D.D.—Archbishop of Armagh and Primate of Ireland. Church of Ireland. [23, 222, 396, 403, 435]

DAVEY, JAMES ERNEST, B.D.—Professor of Biblical Literature and Vice-Principal. Presbyterian College, Belfast. Presbyterian Church in Ireland.

DAVIES, EDWARD OWEN, M.A., B.Sc.—Moderator Elect of General Assembly, Presbyterian Church in Wales. Address, Bodnant, Bangor.

DAVIS, DARIUS ALTON, L.H.D.—Associate General Secretary, World's Committee. Y.M.C.A. Address, 347 Madison Avenue, New York. Presbyterian Church in U.S.A.

DAY, WILLIAM HORACE, D.D.—Pastor, United Church, Bridgeport, Conn., U.S.A. President, Home Board, National Council of Congregational Churches in the U.S.

DEISSMANN, ADOLF, D.Theol., D.D.—Professor at University of Berlin. Geheimer Konsistorialrat. Evangelical Church of the Old Prussian Union. [43, 95, 217]

DENYS, METROPOLITAN—see Dionisy.

DIBELIUS, MARTIN, D.Theol., D.Phil.—Professor at Heidelberg University, and Rector 1927-28. German Evangelical Church. [280, 414]

DIBELIUS, OTTO, D.Dr.—General Superintendent of the Kurmark, Evangelical Church of the Old Prussian Union. Address : Kaiser Wilhelmstr. 11a, Berlin-Steglitz. [232, 397]

DICKEY, Rev. SAMUEL, M.A.—Former Professor of N.T. in McCormick Theological Seminary, Chicago. Address, Oxford, Penna., U.S.A. Presbyterian Church in U.S.A.

DIOBOUNIOTIS, CONSTANTINE, Dr.Theol.—Professor of Theology, University of Athens Orthodox Church of Greece. [386]

DIONISY (WALEDINSKY), D.D.—Metropolitan of Warsaw and all Poland. Rector and Professor of the Orthodox Theological Faculty, Warsaw University. Editor, Woskresnoie Cztenie. Orthodox Church of Poland. [386]

DIXON, WILLIAM GRAY, M.A.—Minister Emeritus and ex-Moderator, Presbyterian Church of New Zealand. Address, St. Leonard's, Dunedin, N.Z.

DONALD, GEORGE H., D.D.—Minister, Church of St. Andrew and St. Paul, Montreal. Secretary of Committee on Correspondence with Other Reformed Churches. Presbyterian Church in Canada.

DORNAKAL, BISHOP OF—see Azariah.

DOUGLAS, J. A., B.D., Ph.D.—Canon. Vicar of St. Luke's, Camberwell, London. Editor, The Christian East. Church of England. [221, 415]

DUBLIN, ARCHBISHOP OF—see Gregg.

DUNN, EDWARD ARTHUR, D.D.—Bishop of British Honduras. Church of England, Province of West Indies.

DUPPUY, CHARLES RIDLEY, D.D.—Bishop of Victoria, Hong Kong. Chung Hwa Sheng Kung Hui (Chinese Holy Catholic Church, Anglican Communion).

DYCE, ARTHUR W., S.T.B.—Pastor, First Congregational Church, Franklin, Mass., U.S.A. National Council of Congregational Churches in the U.S.

DYSINGER, HOLMES, D.D., LL.D.—Dean and Professor of Systematic Theology. Western Theological Seminary of United Lutheran Church, Fremont, Neb., U.S.A. United Lutheran Church in America.

EGYPT AND THE SUDAN, BISHOP OF—see Gwynne.

ELDERDICE, HUGH LATIMER, D.D., LL.D.—President, Westminster Theological Seminary, Westminster, Md., U.S.A. Methodist Protestant Church.

ELERT, WERNER, D.Theol., D.Phil.—Professor at University of Erlangen and Rector, 1927-8. Lutheran Church of Bavaria. [13]

EMERSON, CHESTER B., D.D.—Pastor, Congregational Church, Detroit, Mich. U.S.A. President, Board of Trustees, Conference of Michigan ; Executive Committee of Commission on Missions, National Council of Congregational Churches in U.S.

ENDERS, GEORGE CHRISTIAN, D.D.—Dean, Christian Divinity School, Defiance, Ohio, U.S.A. Christian Church.

ENNIS, REG.—Melbourne, Australia. Church of Christ.

EULOGIOS, METROPOLITAN—Archbishop of the Russian Orthodox Churches in Western Europe. Address, 12 rue Daru, Paris. Russian Orthodox Church. [386]

FABRICIUS, CAJUS, D. Theol.—Professor, University of Berlin. Evangelical Church of the Old Prussian Union.

FALCONER, JAMES WILLIAM, D.D.—Professor of New Testament, Halifax, Nova Scotia, Canada. United Church of Canada.

FARGAS, VICTOR—Pastor. Secretary of Bishop Raffay. Editor of *Ev. Lep* (Press). Address, Debrecen. Evangelical Lutheran Church in Hungary.

FEHL, ANDREAS—Konsistorialrat. Address, Magdeburg. Evangelical Church of the Old Prussian Union.

FIERO, RAYMOND H.—Deacon, Central Congregational Church, Brooklyn, N.Y. U.S.A. National Council of Congregational Churches in the U.S.

FISHER, B. H. B.—Canon of Lucknow. Head of S. P. G. Brotherhood, Cawnpore. Church of England in India.

FISHER, FREDERICK B., D.D., LL.D.—Bishop, Methodist Episcopal Church, U.S.A. Address, Calcutta, India. [381, 402]

FLEURY, GUSTAVE—Vice-President of the Synodal Commission of the National Church of the Canton of Vaud. Address, Morges, Switzerland.

FORGAN, ROBERT, D.D.—Convener of Foreign Missions, United Free Church of Scotland. Address, 5 Hermitage Terrace, Edinburgh. [438]

FORNEROD, ALOÏS AUGUSTE—Professor of Systematic Theology, University of Lausanne. Reformed Church of Canton of Vaud. [382, 395]

FOTHERINGHAM, JOHN TAYLOR, C.M.G., M.D., C.M.—Professor of History of Medicine, University of Toronto. Elder, St. Andrew's Church, Toronto. Presbyterian Church in Canada.

FRANK, GRAHAM, D.D.—Pastor, Central Christian Church, Dallas, Texas, U.S.A. General Secretary, International Convention, Disciples of Christ.

FURNAJIEFF, D. N.—Pastor, Sofia, Bulgaria. Editor, *Zornitza.* Evangelical Church of Bulgaria. [104]

FYFFE, DAVID, D.C.L.—Pastor, Jesmond Church, Newcastle-on-Tyne. Moderator. Presbyterian Church of England. [274]

GARDINER, Rev. J. BRUCE—Minister, St. George's Church, Johannesburg, S. Africa. Presbyterian Church of South Africa.

GARDNER, MISS LUCY—General Secretary of Copec. Editor, *Copec News,* 92 St. George's Sq., London. Society of Friends. [372]

GARRETT, ALFRED E., Ph.D.—Logan, Philadelphia, Pa., U.S.A. Society of Friends.

GARVIE, ALFRED ERNEST, D.D.—Principal of Hackney and New College, London. Congregational Union of England and Wales. [35, 500]

GAUGLER, ERNST, D.Theol.—Professor of Theology, Berne. Old Catholic Church of Switzerland. [156]

GELLER, SAMUEL, Dr.—Pastor in Sagan, Silesia. Evangelical Church of the Old Prussian Union.

GERMANOS (STRENOPOULOS), D.D., D.Ph.—Archbishop and Metropolitan of Thyateira. Representative of the Ecumenical Patriarchate in Western Europe, with seat in London. Address, 20 Newton Rd., London. Ecumenical Patriarchate of Constantinople. [18, 43, 95, 217, 382, 408, 443]

GEORGE, BISHOP OF—see Sidwell.

GERRARD, THOMAS LEE—Treasurer of Hartley College, Manchester. Local preacher. Primitive Methodist Church.

GIBSON, THERON—303 Kendal Ave., Toronto. Elder, United Church of Canada.

GIESECKE, FRIEDRICH, Dr.Phil.—Oberkirchenrat. Pastor, Leitmaritz, Bohemia. German Evangelical Church in Bohemia, Moravia and Silesia.

GILMORE, CHARLES, D.D.—Pastor, First United Presbyterian Church, Cadiz, Ohio. U.S.A. United Presbyterian Church of North America. [402]

GLOUCESTER, BISHOP OF—see Headlam.

GLUBOKOWSKY, NIKOLAJ, D.D.—Professor Emeritus. Professor in University of Sofia, Bulgaria. Orthodox Church of Russia. [67, 386, 402]

GOGARTEN, FRIEDRICH, D.Theol.—Pastor, Dorndorf. Evangelical Church of Thuringia. [102]

GOODALL, CHARLES, B.D.—Minister, St. Oswald's Church, Edinburgh. Church of Scotland.

GORE, CHARLES, D.D., LL.D., D.C.L.—Bishop. Address, 27 Eaton Terrace, London. Church of England. [42, 156, 160, 221, 222, 394, 402, 403, 422]

GOUNELLE, ELIE, Chevalier of the Légion d'honneur—Pastor, Reformed Church of St. Etienne (Loire). Editor, *La Revue du Christianisme social.* Vice-President, National Union of the Reformed Churches of France. [415, 451]

GRAFTON, WARREN, B.D.—Minister of First Christian Church, Los Angeles, Cal., U.S.A. Disciples of Christ.

GREEVER, W. H., D.D.—Professor of Ethics, Apologetics and Symbolics, Lutheran Theological Seminary, Columbia, S.C. Editor, *American Lutheran Survey.* United Lutheran Church in America.

GREGG, JOHN ALLEN FITZGERALD, D.D.—Archbishop of Dublin. Church of Ireland. [222, 394, 428]

GWYNNE, LLEWELLYN H.—Bishop of Egypt and the Sudan. Church of England. [283]

HADORN, WILHELM, Dr.Theol.—Professor of Theology, Berne. Reformed Church of Berne. [95]

HAENISCH, G.—Geheimer Konsistorialrat. Senior der Ev. Unität in Poland. Pastor. Address, Ul. Sw. Jozefa 2, Posen. United Evangelical Church in Poland.

HAGEMEYER, FRANZ, D.Phil.—Pastor at the Stephanuskirche, Halle, a.S. Evangelical Church of the Old Prussian Union.

HALL, FRANCIS J., D.D.—Professor of Dogmatic Theology, General Theological Seminary, New York. Protestant Episcopal Church in U.S.A. [101, 222, 403]

HAMILTON, L. A., C.E.—14 King St. E., Toronto. Treasurer, General Synod. Church of England in Canada.

HANDMANN, RUDOLF, Dr.Theol.—Pastor and Professor of Theology, Basle. President of the Kirchenrat, Reformed Church of Basle.

HARVEY, FREDERICK G., L.Th.—Minister, Congregational Church, Knoxville, S. Australia. Congregational Union of Australia and New Zealand.

HAVILAND, WALTER W.—Friends' Select School, Philadelphia, Pa., U.S.A. Society of Friends.

HAUGE, SVEND—Prediger. Secretary of Inner Mission in Copenhagen. Editor *Sing Lys.* Church of Denmark.

HAUSSLEITER, GOTTLOB, D.Theol.—Geheimer Konsistorialrat. Professor at the University of Halle. Address, Burgbergstr. 38, Erlangen. Evangelical Lutheran Church. [155, 415]

HEADLAM, ARTHUR CAYLEY, D.D.—Bishop of Gloucester. Church of England. [202, 283, 331, 376, 424]

HEARD, WILLIAM H., D.D., LL.D.—Bishop, African Methodist Episcopal Church. Address, 438 North 53rd St., Philadelphia, Pa., U.S.A.

HEATH, CARL—Secretary of the Friends' International Service, Friends' House, Euston Rd., London. Society of Friends in Great Britain and Ireland. [410]

HEILER, FRIEDRICH, D.Theol., Dr. Phil.—Professor of Theology in Marburg. Evangelical Lutheran Church. [393]

HELD, GEORG, Dr. Theol.—Kirchenrat. Pastor, Asch, Bohemia. German Evangelical Church in Bohemia, Moravia and Silesia.

HENRY, Rev. JERRY M., Ph.D.—Chairman of General Welfare Board, Church of the Brethren. Address, New Windsor, Maryland, U.S.A.

HERMELINK, HEINRICH, Dr. Theol., Dr. Phil.—Professor of Theology, University of Marburg. Evangelical-Lutheran Church in Germany.

HEROLD, OTTO, Dr. Theol.—President of the Federation of the Protestant Churches of Switzerland. President of the Kirchenrat, Reformed Church of Zurich. Address, Römerstrasse 14, Winterthur, Switzerland. [11]

HERRON, CHARLES, D.D.—Professor of Church History, Omaha Theological Seminary, Omaha, Neb., U.S.A. Presbyterian Church in U.S.A.

*HERTZBERG, MIKAEL—Pastor in Oslo. Editor, *Kirkens Budshap til Tiden*. Church of Norway. Died at Lausanne, August 11th, 1927. [232]

HINDERER, AUGUST, Dr. Theol.—Professor. Director of the Evangelical Press Association of Germany. Editor, *Das Evangelische Deitschland, Der Evangelische Pressedienst*. Address, Beymestr. 8, Berlin-Steglitz. Evangelical Church of the Old Prussian Union.

HINDES, Rev. WILLIAM—Wesleyan Methodist Church of S. Africa. Address, Jagersfontein, S. Africa.

HOGNESTAD, PETER—Bishop of Bergen. Church of Norway. [362, 375]

HOLDEN, ALBERT THOMAS, C.B.E. General Superintendent, Home Missions, Victoria, Australia. Principal, Missionaries' Training College, Melbourne. Chaplain-General, Australian Military Forces. Methodist Church of Australasia. [160]

HOLLAND, Rev. WILLIAM EDWARD SLADEN, M.A.—Lecturer, Union Christian College, Alwaye, Travancore, India. Church of England. Address, C.M.S., Salisbury Sq., London, E.C.4.

HONDURAS, BISHOP OF—see Dunn.

HORNE, FRANK A.—409 Grand Ave., Brooklyn, N.Y. Methodist Episcopal Church, U.S.A.

HORNYANSZKY, ALADAR, Dr.—Professor of Theology in the Theological Seminary in Pressburg-Bratislava. Evangelical Church in Slovakia.

HORSTMANN, PETER FREDERIK—Chaplain of the Cathedral Church, Viborg, Denmark. Church of Denmark.

HOUGHTON, ROY M., D.D.—Pastor, Church of the Redeemer, New Haven, Conn., U.S.A. National Council of Congregational Churches in the U.S.

HOWIE, Rev. R. H., B.D.—Address, 7 Tudor Ave., Gidea Park, Essex. Delegate from Methodist Church of Australasia.

HOYOIS, EMILE—Pastor and Secretary-General of Belgian Christian Missionary Church. Editor, *Chrétien Belge*. Address, 25 Avenue Jean Linden, Brussells.

HUGHES, HENRY MALDWYN, D.D.—Principal of Wesley College, Cambridge. Wesleyan Methodist Church. [317]

HUME, ROBERT A., D.D.—First Moderator, United Church of Northern India. Address, 165 Grove St., Auburndale, Mass. [399]

HUMPHRIES, A. LEWIS, M.A.—Professor of New Testament Greek and Systematic Theology, Hartley College, Manchester. Primitive Methodist Church.

HUNTER, Rev. GRAHAM C., D.D.—Presbyterian Church in the U.S.A. Address, Fullerton, California.

HURST, JOHN, D.D.—Bishop of Florida, African Methodist Episcopal Church. Address, Baltimore, Md., U.S.A. [283, 491]

IHLEN, CHRISTIAN, Dr. Theol.—Professor of Systematic Theology, University of Oslo. Editor, *Missionsblatt für Israel*. Church of Norway.

INAGAKI, YOICHIRO, D.D.—Professor at Central Theological College, Tokyo. Nippon Sei Kokwai (Japanese Holy Catholic Church—Anglican Communion). [154, 232]

IRELAND, PRIMATE OF—see D'Arcy.

IRBE, KARL—Bishop, Evangelical Lutheran Church in Latvia. Address, Riga, Latvia. [375]

IRINEY (GEORGEVITCH), D.Ph., Lic.Theol.—Bishop of Novi Sad, Serbia. Orthodox Church of Serbia. [386]

JAMES, JAMES ALTON, Ph.D., LL.D.—Dean of the Graduate School and Professor of History, Northwestern University, Evanston, Chicago. Methodist Episcopal Church, U.S.A.

JENKINS, Rev. THOMAS—Education Officer, Welsh League of Nations Union. Address, 8 The Grove, Barry ¡S. Wales. Presbyterian Church in Wales.

JENSEN, PAUL TH.—Bishop of the Moravian Church. Chairman of Board of the Moravian Church in Germany. Address, Herrnhut, i.Sa. [409, 422, 444]

JESCH, ADOLF—Pastor, Atäse, Ostrau. Editor, *Berichte für kirchliche Blätter in der Czechoslovakischen Republik*. Evangelical Church in Slovakia.

JÉZÉQUEL, JULES—Chevalier of the Légion d'honneur. Pastor. International Secretary of Life and Work and of the World Alliance. National Union of the Reformed Churches of France. Address, 11 Villa Brune, Paris, XIV.

JONES, THOMAS J.—Pastor, First Congregational Church, Scranton, Pa., U.S.A. National Council of Congregational Churches in the U.S.

JOYCE, G. C., D.D.—Archdeacon of St. Davids. Church of Wales. [430]

KAAS, BARON ALBERT VON, LL.D.—Lecturer at the University of Budapest. Evangelical Lutheran Church in Hungary.

KALIINICOS—see Scoumperdis.

KATZ, PETER—Pastor in Fahrenbach, Baden. Evangelical Church of Baden.

KAY, Rev. DAVID MILLAR, D.S.O., D.D.—Professor of Hebrew, University of St. Andrews. Church of Scotland. [439]

KELLER, Rev. ADOLF, D.D.—Secretary, Federation of the Protestant Churches of Switzerland. General Secretary of the International Social Institute. Editor, *Bulletin of the Institute*. Address, Sonneggstrasse 16, Zurich. Reformed Church of Zurich. [99]

KELLEY, Rev. WILLIAM MUSSON—General Secretary of the Primitive Methodist Church. Address, St. Osyth, Lowther Hill, London, S.E.23.

KENDRICK, ELIZA H., Ph.D.—Professor of Biblical History, Wellesley College, Wellesley, Mass. National Council of Congregational Churches in the U.S.

KENNEDY, HERBERT B., B.D.—Dean of Christ Church, Dublin. Church of Ireland.

KENNINCK, F.—Archbishop of Utrecht. Old Catholic Church.

KLEIN, WILLIAM E., D.D.—Director, Division of Evangelism, Board of National Missions of the Presbyterian Church in the U.S.A. Address, Montclair, N.J., U.S.A.

KLINGMAN, GEORGE A., Ph.D.—Dean of Bible Department, Thorp Spring Christian College, Texas, U.S.A. Editor, *Christian Leader*. Churches of Christ in N. America.

KOREN, Rev. LAURENTIUS—General Secretary, Norwegian Bible Society. Address, Minechsjt 2, Oslo. Church of Norway.

KORTHEUER, BISHOP, D.Theol.—Bishop of Nassau. Address, Wiesbaden. Evangelical Church in Germany.

KRAFFT, FERDINAND CHARLES FRANCIS, Lic.Theol.—Pastor of the Walloon Church of Haarlem, Holland. Editor, *L'Eglise Wallonne*. Reformed Evangelical Church of the Netherlands.

KULP, EDMUND JAMES—Pastor, First Church, Des Moines, Iowa. Methodist Episcopal Church, U.S.A.

KÜRY, ADOLF, Dr. Theol.—Bishop. Professor at University of Berne. Old Catholic Church of Switzerland. [353]

LANG, AUGUST, Dr. Theol. *hon. causa*—Superintendent and first Cathedral preacher at Halle a.S. Professor of Theology, University of Halle. Moderator des Reformierten Bundes für Deutschland. Evangelical Church of the Old Prussian Union. [301]

LANG, THEODOR, Dr. Theol.—Oberkonsistorialrat. Member, Evang. Oberkirchenrat Pastor in Berlin-Wilmersdorf (120 Wilhelmsauer) Evangelical Church of the Old Prussian Union.

LAUN, JUSTUS FERDINAND, Lic Theol.—Lecturer, University of Giessen. Editor, *Für die Einheit der Kirche*. Evangelical Church in Hesse. [403]

LEHTONEN, Rev. ALEKSI, D.D.—Lecturer on Pastoral Theology in Helsingfors University, Finland. Member of editorial staff, *Kirko ja Kansa*, and of *Teologisk Tiddskrift*. Lutheran Church of Finland.

LENCZ, GEZA, D.Lic., D. Theol.—Professor, Hungarian University, Debrecen. Reformed Church of Hungary.

LEO, PAUL, Lic.Theol.—Pastor, Neuhaus, Solling. Evangelical Lutheran Church of Hanover.

LEONTOPOLIS, ARCHBISHOP OF—see Christophoros.

LEW, TIMOTHY TINGFANG, Ph.D., D.D.—Professor, Yengching University, Peking. Honorary Pastor, Chinese Independent Church, Peking. Editor, *Life and Truth Journal*. North China Kung-Li-Hui (Congregational Church of China). [103, 402, 438, 495]

LEWINS, WILLIAM ALFRED—1 Redclyffe Rd., Withington, Manchester. Church Secretary, Member of General Connexional Committee and College Committee. A Guardian Representative of the Church. United Methodist Church.

LIMERICK, BISHOP OF—see White.

LINDSKOG, HANS JONAS, D.D.—Rector of Braennkyrka, Stockholm. Church of Sweden. [181]

LIVINGSTONE, W. P., F.R.S.G.S.—121 George St., Edinburgh. Editor, *Record of United Free Church*, and *Other Lands*. United Free Church of Scotland.

LOFTHOUSE, WILLIAM FREDERICK, D.D.—Principal, Handsworth Wesleyan College, Birmingham. Wesleyan Methodist Church. [105, 413]

LUNN, SIR HENRY, M.A., M.D., B.Ch.—5 Endsleigh Gardens, London. Elected Lay Representative of Conference 1910-31. Local Preacher. Trustee. Editor, *Review of the Churches*. Wesleyan Methodist Church. [286]

LYMAN, Mrs. ALBERT J.—255 President St., Brooklyn, N.Y. National Council of Congregational Churches in the U.S.

MACARTHUR, KENNETH C., B.D.—Rural Secretary, Massachusetts Federation of Churches. Address, Sterling, Mass. Northern Baptist Convention, U.S.A.

MACAULAY, J. J.—Minister, Christ Church, Rathgar, Dublin. Presbyterian Church in Ireland.

*M'CLYMONT, JAMES A., D.D., C.B.E.—Principal Clerk of the General Assembly, Church of Scotland. Died, September 20th, 1927. [228, 415]

McCONNELL, FRANCIS J., D.D., LL.D.—Bishop, Methodist Episcopal Church, U.S.A. Address, Pittsburg, Pa. [54]

MacCRACKEN, JOHN HENRY, Litt.D., LL.D.—15 East 83rd St., New York. Former President, Lafayette College. Presbyterian Church in the U.S.A.

McDOWELL, WILLIAM FRASER, D.D., LL.D., L.H.D.—Bishop, Methodist Episcopal Church, U.S A. President Board of Temperance, Prohibition and Public Morals, Methodist Episcopal Church. Address, Washington, D.C. [28]

MACHICHAN, DUGALD, D.D., LL.D., F.R.S.E., R.A.S. (Bombay Branch).—Hon. Principal, Wilson College, Bombay. United Free Church of Scotland. Address, 18, Douglas Cres., Edinburgh. [402]

MACLAGAN, REV. PATRICK JOHNSTON, M.A., D.Phil.—Foreign Missions Secretary, Presbyterian Church of England. Address, 78 Airedale Ave., London.

MACLEAN, Right Rev. NORMAN, D.D.—Moderator of the Church of Scotland and Chaplain in Ordinary to His Majesty the King. 6 Grosvenor Gardens, Edinburgh.

MACNUTT, FREDERICK BRODIE, M.A., F.R.Hist. S.—Provost of Leicester Cathedral, Archdeacon of Leicester. Church of England.

MALAN, AONIO—Pastor. Chiesa Evangelica Italiana. Address, 40 Via San Stefano, Bologna.

MANCHESTER, BISHOP OF—see Temple.

MANN, THEOPHIL—Lecturer at the Theological College of the Methodist Church, Frankfurt-a-M. Methodist Episcopal Church.

MANNING, WILLIAM T., D.D., D.C.L., LL.D.—Bishop of New York. Protestant Episcopal Church in the U.S.A. [204, 402, 424]

MARGETSON, W. J., M.A.—Provost, St. Mary's Cathedral, Edinburgh. Episcopal Church in Scotland.

MARQUIS, JOHN A., D.D., LL.D.—General Secretary, Board of National Missions, Presbyterian Church in the U.S.A. Address, 156 Fifth Ave., New York.

MARSH, DANIEL L., S.T.B., LL.D., Litt.D.—President of Boston University. Methodist Episcopal Church, U.S.A.

MARTIN, ALFRED VON, Dr. Jur., Dr. Phil.—Professor at University of Munich. Editor, *Una Sancta*. Evangelical Lutheran Church. [228]

MASTER, HENRY B., D.D., LL.D.—General Secretary, Board of Pensions, Presbyterian Church in U.S.A. Secretary, Western Section, Alliance of Reformed Churches. Address, 91 Witherspoon Bldg., Philadelphia, Pa.

MAUCK, JOSEPH W., LL.D.—President Emeritus, Hillsdale College, Hillsdale, Mich., U.S.A. Northern Baptist Convention, U.S.A.

MÉJAN, FRANÇOIS—Pastor. Secretary General, National Union of the Reformed Evangelical Churches of France. Address, 47 rue de Clichy, Paris. [209]

MÉNÉGOZ, FERNAND, Dr. Theol.—Professor of Dogmatic Theology at the Protestant Faculty of Theology, University of Strasburg. Church of the Confession of Augsburg of Alsace and of Lorraine. [139]

MERLE D'AUBIGNÉ, CHARLES, Dr. Theol.—Pastor at Neuilly sur Seine. National Union of the Reformed Evangelical Churches of France. [95, 412, 418, 439, 476]

MERRILL, WILLIAM P., D.D.—Pastor of the Brick Church, New York. Presbyterian Church in the U.S.A. [106]

MILL, W. H.—21 Drummond Place, Edinburgh. Solicitor in Supreme Courts (Scotland). Elder. Church of Scotland.

MILNE, JAMES, M.A.—Minister, St. James' Presbyterian Church, Thames, New Zealand. Presbyterian Church of New Zealand. [285]

MOE, OLAF, Dr. Theol.—Professor, Gemeindefakultät, Oslo. Church of Norway. [199]

MONAHAN, ALFRED EDWIN, M.A.—Vicar of Monmouth, Church in Wales. [403]

MONNIER, HENRI, Dr. Theol., Chevalier of the Légion d'honneur.—Pastor. Professor, Protestant Faculty of Theology, Paris. National Union of the Reformed Evangelical Churches of France. [321]

MONOD, WILFRED, Lic. Phil., Dr.Theol.—Hon. President of National Union of the Reformed Churches of France. Professor, Protestant Faculty of Theology, Paris. Pastor of the Oratory of the Louvre. Editor, *Bulletin des Veilleurs*. President, French Section of the World Alliance for International Friendship through the Churches. [88, 391, 431]

MOORE, JOHN M., Ph.D., D.D.—Bishop, Methodist Episcopal Church, South. Address, Dallas, Texas, U.S.A. [479].

MOORE, REV. T. ALBERT, D.D.—Secretary of the General Council of the United Church of Canada. Address, 421 Wesley Building, Toronto, Canada. [479]

MOREHOUSE, FREDERIC COOK, L.H.D.—1801, Fond du Lac Ave., Milwaukee, Wis. Editor, *The Living Church.* Deputy to General Convention since 1910, Protestant Episcopal Church in the U.S.A. [437, 439].

MOSEL, HEINRICH G. W.—Pastor in Rohrberg, Altmark, Germany. President, 1924-27, Hochkirchliche Vereinigung. Evangelical Church of the Old Prussian Union.

MOTT, JOHN R., Ph.D., LL.D.—President, World's Committee of the Y.M.C.A.; Chairman, International Missionary Council; Chairman, World Student Christian Federation; Chairman, Institute of Social and Religious Research. Address, 347 Madison Ave., New York. Methodist Episcopal Church, U.S.A. [215]

MUDGE, LEWIS SEYMOUR, D.D., LL.D.—Stated Clerk of the General Assembly, and Secretary of the General Council, Presbyterian Church in the U.S.A. Address, Witherspoon Bldg., Philadelphia, Pa. [381].

NASH, J. O., D.D.—Co-adjutor Bishop of Capetown. Church of the Province of South Africa (Anglican).

NAUPACTOS, METROPOLITAN OF—see Ambrosios.

NEANDER, HERMAN, Dr. Theol.—Pastor in Estuna, Sweden. Church of Sweden.

NEIIENDAM, MICHAEL NICOLAJ, D.D.—Church of Denmark. Address, Espergärde, Denmark.

NECTARIE (COTLARCIUC), D.D.—Archbishop of Cernauti and Metropolitan of Bukovina. Orthodox Church of Roumania. [215, 386]

NEUSCHÄFER, CARL—Studiendirektor, German Baptist Theological Seminary. Address, Wandsbeck, Germany.

NIKOLAOS (EVANGELIDIS), Dr. Theol.—Archbishop of Nubia. Professor of the College at Janina. Chancellor, Greek Orthodox Patriarchate of Alexandria. [207, 386].

NOLLEN, JOHN S., Ph.D., LL.D.—Dean of Grinnell College, Grinnell, Iowa, U.S.A. National Council of Congregational Churches in the U.S.

NOOE, ROGER T., D.D.—Professor of Pastoral Theology, Vanderbilt University. Pastor of Vine Street Christian Church, Nashville, Tenn., U.S.A. Disciples of Christ.

NORREGAARD, J., D.D.—Professor. Address, Gl. Kongevej 72, IV, Copenhagen. Church of Denmark.

NORBERG, OTTO, D.D.—Dean of Strängnäs, Church of Sweden.

NOVI SAD, BISHOP OF—see Iriney.

NOYES, EDWARD M., D.D.—Pastor, Congregational Church, Newton Centre, Mass. President, American Congregational Association. National Union of Congregational Churches in U.S.

NUBIA, ARCHBISHOP OF—see Nikolaos.

NUELSEN, JOHN LOUIS, D.D., LL.D.—Bishop, Methodist Episcopal Church, U.S.A. Address, 69 Badenstr., Zurich. [404].

NYGREN, ANDERS, D. Theol.—Professor of Systematic Theology, University of Lund. Church of Sweden.

OCHIAI, J. K., D.D.—Principal, Central Theological College, Tokio. Nippon Sei Kokwai (Japanese Holy Catholic Church—Anglican Communion).

OHLEMÜLLER, Dr. GERHARD—General Secretary of the Evangelical Prussian Church. General Secretary, Evangelical League, and International Association for the Defence of Protestantism. Editor, *Protestantische Rundschau* and *Täglische Rundschau* (supplement, *Dienst am Volk*). Address, Friedrich-Wilhelmstr., 2 a, Berlin. Evangelical Church of the Old Prussian Union.

OSTENFELD, HARALD, D.D.—Bishop of Seeland. Church of Denmark. [84].

OTTAWA, BISHOP OF—see Roper.

PALMER, EDWIN JAMES, D.D.—Bishop of Bombay. Church of England in India. [233, 403, 412, 431].

PAPADOPOULOS, BENEDICTOS K.—Deacon. Address, 14 Odos Erectheos, Athens. Greek Orthodox Patriarchate of Jerusalem. [386]

PARASKEVAIDIS, THEOLOGOS, Dr. Theol.—Archimandrite. Priest of the Greek Orthodox Church in Leipzig. Ecumenical Patriarchate of Constantinople. [154, 386]

PARKER, GEORGE, M.A., B.D.—Principal, London Missionary Society College, Nagercoil, Travancore, India. Address, L.M.S., 48 Broadway, London, S.W. South India United Church.

PARKER, LEWIS DAVID—Pastor, Montreuil, France. Secretary of the Synod and of the Bureau of the Evangelical Methodist Church of France.

PARSONS, EDWARD L., D.D.—Bishop of California. Address, San Francisco, Cal. Protestant Episcopal Church in U.S.A. [447].

PEAKE, ARTHUR S., D.D.—President-elect of the National Free Church Council. Professor of Exegesis in the University of Manchester. Tutor in Hartley Primitive Methodist College, Manchester. Editor, *Holborn Review*. Primitive Methodist Church.

PEEL, ALBERT, Litt.D.—Minister, Clapton Park Congregational Church, London. Editor, *Congregational Quarterly*. Congregational Union of England and Wales.

PEET, WILLIAM W., LL.D.—Representative for Near East, Federal Council of Churches, U.S.A. Address, 105 East 22nd St., New York City. National Council of Congregational Churches in the U.S.

PERADSE, GREGOR, Dr. Phil., Cand. Theol.—Reader in Armenian-Georgian philology at the University of Bonn. About to return to Georgia. Orthodox Church of Georgia. [366, 386]

PERRY, JAMES DE WOLF, D.D.—Bishop of Rhode Island. Address, Providence, R.I. Protestant Episcopal Church in U.S.A.

PFANNENSTILL, MAGNUS—Professor and Dean of Lund. Editor, *Kristendomen des Värtid*. Church of Sweden.

PHILIP, ADAM, D.D.—Minister of Longforgan, Scotland. United Free Church of Scotland.

PHILIPPS, WILHELM, Dr. Theol.—Pastor, Head of the Berlin City Mission, Stubbenstr. 8, 1, Berlin Schöneberg. Evangelical Church of the Old Prussian Union. [94, 415].

PHILPUTT, Rev. JAMES M., D.D.—Special Worker in Dept. of Missions, Disciples of Christ. Address, c.o. Brown Bros. & Co., 59 Wall St., New York.

PIPER, OTTO, Lic. Theol.—Privatdozent at the University of Göttingen. Lutheran Church of Hanover.

PONGRÁCZ, JOSEPH—Professor of N.T. Exegesis in Theological Seminary at Papa. Editor, *Dunantuli Protestans Lap*. Reformed Church of Hungary.

PRÖHLE, KARL, Dr. Theol., Dr. Phil.—Dean of the Evangelical Theological Faculty, Sopron, Hungary. Professor of Systematic Theology. Evangelical Lutheran Church of Hungary. [204].

PROCHAZKA, GUSTAV A.—Bishop of the Czechoslovak Church. Address, Hradec, Königrätz-Bohemia.

PRYS, OWEN, D.D.—Principal of Theological College, Aberystwyth. Presbyterian Church in Wales.

PUSTOWKA, OTTO—Pastor in Mähren-Schönberg, Czechoslovakia. German Evangelical Church in Bohemia, Moravia and Silesia.

PYKE, RICHARD—President, United Methodist Church. Pastor of United Methodist Church, Bristol, England. Editor, *United Methodist Newspaper*. [228].

QUICK, OLIVER CHASE, M.A.—Canon of Carlisle Cathedral. Church of England. [305].

RAFFAY, ALEXANDER, D.D.—Bishop, Evangelical Lutheran Church in Hungary. Address, Deakter 4, Budapest IV. [128].

RAGG, LONSDALE, D.D.—Canon of Lincoln Cathedral. British Embassy Chaplain in Rome. Church of England.

RAVASZ, LADISLAS, D.Ph.—Bishop of the Danubian Diocese, Reformed Church of Hungary. Member of the Hungarian Upper House. Address, Radayntea, 28 Budapest IX.

REED, LEWIS T., D.D.—Pastor of Flatbush Congregational Church, Brooklyn, N.Y. Chairman of Commission on Evangelism and Devotional Life, National Council of Congregational Churches in the U.S.

REICHEL, Sir HARRY R., M.A., LL.D.—Principal of the University in N. Wales, Vice-Chancellor of the University of Wales. The Church in Wales.

RICHARDS, GEORGE W., D.D., LL.D., D. Th. (Heidelberg)—President and Professor of Church History, Theological Seminary, Lancaster, Pa. Secretary of Conference of Theological Seminaries and Colleges of the U.S. and Canada. Reformed Church in the U.S.

RICHARDS, T. T., D.D.—Pastor, First Baptist Church, Scranton, Pa. Northern Baptist Convention, U.S.A.

RICHMOND, Rev. MAURICE, M.A.—Secretary, Y.M.C.A., Cairo. Acting Secretary, Egyptian Fellowship of Unity. Church of England.

RILEY, ATHELSTAN, M.A., F.S.A.—Seigneur de la Trinité, Jersey, Channel Islands. Vice President, English Church Union. Chairman, Anglican and Eastern Churches Association. Chairman, Alcuin Club. Church of England. [412].

RITCHIE, DAVID LATRIE, D.D.—Principal of Congregational College of Canada. Dean, United Theological College, Montreal. United Church of Canada.

ROBERTS, Rev. J. E., D.D.—Ex-President of the Baptist Union of Great Britain. Address, 8 Queen's Gate, Glasgow. [43].

ROBINSON, WILLIAM, M.A., B.Sc.—Principal, Overdale College, Birmingham. Churches of Christ in Great Britain.

ROGERS, B. TALBOT, D.D.—Rector, St. Matthew's Church, Sunbury, Pa. Protestant Episcopal Church in U.S.A.

ROPER, JOHN CHARLES, D.D.—Bishop of Ottawa, Canada. Church of England in Canada. [434].

ROSE, IVAN MURRAY, M.A.—Pastor, First Baptist Church, Philadelphia, Pa. Northern Baptist Convention, U.S.A. [394]

ROSENKJAR, JENS, Mag. Sc.—Principal of High School, Roskilde, Denmark. Church of Denmark.

ROY, Rev. THOMAS J.—Northern Baptist Convention, U.S.A. Address, 38 Oakdale St., Brockton, Mass.

RUST, Dr. J. A.—Preacher. Evangelical Lutheran Church of the Netherlands. Address, Lane Nieuwstraat, 3, Utrecht. [393].

DE SAINT-ANDRÉ, LOUIS, D.S.O., M.C.—Pastor at Tours. National Union of the Reformed Evangelical Churches of France.

SALISBURY, DEAN OF—see Burn.

S

SANDEGREN, Rev. PAUL, Cand. Phil., Cand. Theol.—Associate Secretary, Church of Sweden Mission. Address, Kungstengaten, 5 Stockholm. Church of Sweden. [284].

SANDS, The Hon. Lord (CHRISTOPHER N. JOHNSTON), LL.D.—Judge of Supreme Court of Scotland. Elder, Church of Scotland. Lay Reader. Joint Chairman, Church of Scotland Union Committee. Address, 4 Heriot Row, Edinburgh. [185, 229, 388].

SANFORD, Mrs. WILLIAM E.—Hamilton, Ontario, Canada. United Church of Canada. [373, 443].

SASSE, HERMANN, Lic. Theol., S.T.M.—Pastor in Oranienburg. Address, Bernauerstr. 60, Oranienburg bei Berlin. Evangelical Church of the Old Prussian Union.

SCHEER, CHARLES—Pastor at Mulhouse, Alsace. Deputy from Haut-Rhin to the French Chamber of Deputies. Reformed Church of Alsace and of Lorraine.

SCHEMPP, JOHANNES—Director of the Theological Seminary, Reutlingen, Wurtt. Evangelische Gemeinschaft.

SCHENCK, HAROLD W., A.M.—Pastor of Franklin Reformed Church, Nutley, N.J. Reformed Church in America. [400].

SCHERER, Rev. M. G. G., D.D.—Secretary of the United Lutheran Church in America. Address, 39 East 35th St., New York. [221, 248, 375, 430, 435]

SCHIAN, MARTIN, D. Theol., Dr. Phil.—General Superintendent of the Church in province of Silesia. Address, Schlossplatz 8, Breslau, 4. Evangelical Church of the Old Prussian Union. [286].

SCHMIDT, KARL LUDWIG, Dr. Theol.—Professor at Jena University. Editor, *Theologische Blätter.* Evangelical Church of Thuringia. [483].

SCHMITZ, OTTO, Dr. Theol.—Professor of New Testament Theology and Exegesis, University of Münster. Editor, *Neutestamentliche Forschungen und Furche.* Evangelical Church of the Old Prussian Union. [158].

SCHNEIDER, FRANCIS, Ph.D.—Professor. Member of the Central Board, Czechoslovak Church. Address, Akademicka 42, Bruo, Czechoslovakia.

SCHOELL, D., Dr.—Prälat, Evangelical Church in Wurtemberg. Address, Alter Postplatz 4, Stuttgart. Member of the Oberkirchenrat. Editor, *Monatsschrift für Pastoraltheologie.* [309, 375]

SCHOU, AAGE—Advocate. Address, Rosenborggabe 5, Oslo. Church of Norway.

SCOUMPERDIS, KALLINICOS J.—Archimandrite, Greek Orthodox Patriarchate of Jerusalem. Address, Odos Erectheos 14, Athens. [386]

SELECMAN, CHARLES C., D.D., LL.D.—President, Southern Methodist University, Dallas, Texas. Methodist Episcopal Church South, U.S.A.

SHATFORD, ALLAN P., D.C.L., O.B.E.—Canon of Cathedral, Montreal. Church of England in Canada.

SHAW, JOHN MACKINTOSH, D.D.—Professor of Systematic Theology, Halifax, N.S. United Church of Canada. [347].

SIDWELL, H. B., D.D.—Bishop of George, Cape Province. Church of the Province of South Africa (Anglican).

SIEBEL, JACOB GUSTAV—Freudenberg bei Siegen, Westphalia. Manufacturer. Evangelical Church of the Old Prussian Union. [222].

SIEGMUND-SCHULTZE, FRIEDRICH, D.D.—Professor in the University of Berlin. Social worker. Editor, *Die Eiche.* Evangelical Church of the Old Prussian Union. [146, 476].

SIGMOND, S. O., M.A.—Pastor of Trinity Lutheran Church, Brooklyn, N.Y. Norwegian Lutheran Church of America.

SILLS, KENNETH C. M., LL.D.—President of Bowdoin College, Brunswick, Maine. Protestant Episcopal Church in U.S.A.

DA SILVA, ALFREDO—Professor. Superintendent of Portuguese Methodist Church. Director of Industrial and Commercial Institute of Oporto. Editor, *Portugal Evangelico*. Address, Rua Quental 125, Porto. Delegate from Protestant Churches of Portugal.

SIMONS, WALTER, D.Dr.—President of the Supreme Court at Leipzig. Evangelical Lutheran Church of Saxony. [415, 417].

SJÖSTEDT, Major ANDERS—Address, Stockholm. Church of Sweden.

SJÖSTRAND, BERTIL, Cand. Phil.—Missionary in Madura, South India, Swedish Church Mission. Tamil Evangelical Lutheran Church.

SLOSSER, GAIUS JACKSON, S.T.M.—Pastor. Author. Address, 7 Oakfield Rd., Clapton, London. Methodist Episcopal Church, U.S.A.

SMILEY, WILLIAM B., D.D.—Ex-Moderator, General Assembly, United Presbyterian Church of North America. Address, Rochester, Pa., U.S.A. [422].

SMITH, Rev. FRANCIS E.—Secretary, Ministerial Relief and Pensions, Disciples of Christ. Address, Indianapolis, Ind., U.S.A.

SMITH, J. CROMARTY, B.D.—Minister. Address, Coatdyke Manse, Coatbridge, England. Church of Scotland. [228].

SLATTERY, Miss MARGARET.—Associate Editor, Pilgrim Press. Address, 14 Beacon St., Boston, Mass. National Council of Congregational Churches in the U.S.

SÖDERBLOM, NATHAN, D.D., Ph.D., D.C.L., LL.D., M.D.—Archbishop of Upsala. Prochancellor of the University of Upsala. Church of Sweden. [75, 95, 159, 160, 321, 375, 396]

SOFIA, ARCHBISHOP OF—see Stefan.

SOMMER, T. W. ERNST, M.A.—Superintendent of the Frankfort District, Methodist Episcopal Church. Preacher. Lecturer in the Methodist Theological Seminary, Frankfort-a-M.

SOPER, EDMUND S., D.D., LL.D.—Dean and Professor of the History of Religion, School of Religion, Duke University, Durham, N.C. Methodist Episcopal Church, U.S.A.

SOUČEK, JOSEF, D.D.—Senior and President of the Church, Evangelical Church of Bohemian Brethren in Czecho-Slovakia. Address, Jungmannova, Prague, II. [268].

STANGE, ERICH, Dr. Theol.—President of the Federation of Y.M.C.A. in Germany. Editor, *Pastoralblätter, Führerdienst*. Address, Wilhelmshöhe, Kassel. [500]

STEFAN, Dr. Phil., Mag. Theol.—Archbishop and Metropolitan of Sofia. Professor of Homiletics at the University of Sofia. Editor, *Naroden Strage*. Orthodox Church of Bulgaria. [148].

STEIMLE, AUGUSTUS, D.D.—Pastor, Church of the Advent, New York. President, Board of Education of the United Lutheran Church. President, Inner Mission Society of the Lutheran Church in New York. United Lutheran Church in America. [373].

STEJSKAL, R. T., Dr. Theol.—Bishop, Czechoslovak Church. Address, Olomouc, Czechoslovakia.

STEVENSON, J. ROSS, D.D., LL.D.—President of the Theological Seminary of the Presbyterian Church at Princetown, N.J. Chairman, Department of Church Co-operation and Union. Presbyterian Church in the U.S.A. [12].

STEVENSON, Rev. J. SINCLAIR, M.A., B.D.—Presbyterian Church in Ireland. Address, Shottery, Killiney, Co. Dublin. [438]

STEWART, GEORGE CRAIG, D.D., L.H.D.—Rector of St. Luke's Church, Evanston, Chicago. Member of the National Council of the Episcopal Church. Associate Editor, *Anglican Theological Review*. Protestant Episcopal Church in U.S.A. [394]

STEWART, R. W., B.D., B.Sc.—Minister at Cambusland, near Glasgow. United Free Church of Scotland.

STÖREN, J. N.—Bishop of Haalogaland, Church of Norway. Address, Tromsö, Norway.

STURGIS, WILLIAM C., Ph.D.—Address, 325 E. 72nd St., New York. Formerly Educational Secretary, Department of Missions, Protestant Episcopal Church in U.S.A.

SUMITRA, Rev. H.—Missionary in area of South India United Church. Address, London Mission, Ballary, S. India. [196, 421].

SWARTZ, HERMAN FRANK, D.D., M.Sc.—President, Pacific School of Religion, Berkeley, Cal. National Council of Congregational Churches in U.S.

SYDNEY, ARCHBISHOP OF—see Wright, John C.

SYRIA, ARCHBISHOP OF—see Barsaum, S. A.

TAEKEMA, P., Cand. Theol.—Minister, Seventh Day Baptist Church. Address, Nieuwe Pekela, Holland.

TARAFDAR, S. K.—Canon of St. Paul's Cathedral, Calcutta. Principal, C.M.S. High School, Bhagalpur, Bekar, India. Church of England in India. [403].

TARANGER, ABSALON, Dr. Jur.—Professor of Jurisprudence, University of Oslo. Address, Slemdal, Aker, Norway. Church of Norway.

TATLOW, TISSINGTON, D.D.—Hon. Canon of Canterbury Cathedral. Rector of All Hallows, Lombard St., London. General Secretary of the Student Christian Movement of Great Britain and Ireland. Church of England. [299, 423]

TEMPLE, WILLIAM, D.D., D.Litt.—Bishop of Manchester. Chairman of Copec. Church of England. [132, 416, 443, 488].

THOMAS, ARTHUR NUTTER, D.D.—Bishop of Adelaide. Church of England in Australia. [422].

THOMAS, J. S. LADD, D.D.—Pastor, First Methodist Episcopal Church, German-town, Philadelphia. Methodist Episcopal Church, U.S.A.

THOMPSON, ERNEST TRICE, D.D.—Professor of Ecclesiastical History and Polity, Union Theological Seminary, Richmond, Va. Presbyterian Church in the U.S.A.

THOMPSON, Rev. LESLIE M., M.A.—Secretary for Methodist Mission, Fiji. Address, Dilkusha, Nausori, Fiji. Methodist Church of Australasia.

THOMPSON, WILLIAM OXLEY, D.D., LL.D.—President Emeritus, Ohio State University, Columbus, Ohio. Presbyterian Church in the U.S.A. [372].

THVEDT, NIELS B., M.A., B.D.—Rector of Trinity Church, Oslo. Chairman, Norwegian Missionary Council of International Missionary Council. Church of Norway. [431].

THYATEIRA, ARCHBISHOP OF—see Germanos.

TINNEVELLY, BISHOP OF—see Tubbs.

TITIUS, ARTHUR, Dr. Theol.—Geheimer Konsitorialrat. Professor in the University of Berlin. Address, Friedrich-Wilhelmstr. 23, Berlin, W.10. Evangelical Church of the Old Prussian Union. [231].

TOURIAN, LEON—Bishop of Manchester, Armenian Apostolic Church. Address, 229 Upper Brook St., Manchester. [197].

TUBBS, NORMAN, D.D.—Bishop of Tinnevelly and Madura. Church of England in India. [207].

TURK, MORRIS H., Ph.D., D.D.—Pastor, Williston Church, Portland, Maine. Member of Commission on Interchurch Relations, National Council of Congregational Churches in the U.S.

TURKEVICH, BENEDICT J.—Rector of the Parish Church, Ostrog-u-H., Wolhynia. Orthodox Church of Poland. [386]

UNRUH, BENJAMIN, Professor Lic.—Conference of the South German Mennonites. Address, Auerstr., 24 Rüppurr, Karlsruhe. [157, 443].

UPSALA, ARCHBISHOP OF—see Söderblom.

UTRECHT, ARCHBISHOP OF—see Kenninck.

VALIADIS, CONSTANTINE—Archimandrite. Pastor of the Greek Orthodox Church at Lausanne. Ecumenical Patriarchate of Constantinople. [386]

VANCE, JOSEPH A., D.D., LL.D.—Pastor, First Presbyterian Church, Detroit, Mich. President of the Board of National Missions, Presbyterian Church in the U.S.A.

VERNER, ANTOINE, Th.B., Ph.C.—Pastor, Litomysl, Czechoslovakia. Evangelical Church of Bohemian Brethren in Czechoslovakia.

VICKREY, CHARLES V., A.M., B.D.—General Secretary, Near East Relief, 151 Fifth Ave., New York. Methodist Episcopal Church, U.S.A.

VICTOR, JOHN, B.D., Ph.D.—Professor of Philosophy and Comparative Religions, Theological Academy, Budapest. Reformed Church of Hungary.

VICTORIA, BISHOP OF—see Duppuy.

VAN VLIJMEN, T. J.—Bishop of Haarlem. Old Catholic Church.

VURPILLOT, EMILE—Inspecteur Ecclésiastique, Consistoire de Montbéliard. Pastor, Audincourt, Doubs, France. Evangelical Lutheran Church of France. [154].

WADSWORTH, JULIAN S., Dr. Theol.—Director of the Methodist Memorial at Chateau-Thierry, France. Methodist Episcopal Church, U.S.A.

WALKER, GEORGE, D.D.—Minister of the East Parish of St. Nicholas, Aberdeen. Church of Scotland.

WALLAU, RENÉ H., Lic. Theol.—Pastor, St. Peterskirche, Frankfort-a.-M. Assoc. Editor, Una Sancta and Liturgischen Blatter. Evang. Church of Frankfort.

WARSAW, METROPOLITAN OF—see Dionysy.

WASHBURN, HENRY BRADFORD, D.D., LL.D.—Dean of Episcopal Theological School, Cambridge, Mass. Protestant Episcopal Church in U.S.A.

WATT, THOMAS M., M.A.—Chaplain, Scottish Church in Geneva. Church of Scotland.

WESTERN, FREDERICK JAMES, M.A.—Canon of Lahore Cathedral. Head of Cambridge Mission to Delhi. Church of England in India. [155].

WHITE, HARRY VERE, D.D.—Bishop of Limerick. Church of Ireland.

WIGHAM, JOSEPH T., M.D., F.R.C.P. (Ir.)—Professor of Pathology, University of Dublin. Society of Friends in Great Britain and Ireland.

WILLIAMS, J. W., D.D.—Bishop. Address, Claremont, Cape of Good Hope. Church of the Province of South Africa (Anglican).

WILSON, DAVID MOFFAT—Churches of Christ in Australia.

WISEMAN, C. LUKE, M.A.—Headmaster, Queen's College, Taunton, England. Wesleyan Methodist Church.

WISEMAN, FREDERICK LUKE, D.D.—Secretary of Home Mission Department, Wesleyan Methodist Church. Address, 1 Central Buildings, Westminster, London.

WOBBERMIN, GEORG, D. Theol., Dr. Phil.—Author. Professor of Systematic Theology, University of Göttingen. Evangelical Lutheran Church of Hanover. [176].

Woods, Edward S., M.A.—Hon. Canon of Canterbury. Vicar of Croydon, England. Church of England. [382, 438].

Workman, Herbert Brook, D.Litt., D.D.—Principal, Westminster College, London. Wesleyan Methodist Church. [121, 142].

Wotherspoon, H. J., D.D.—Church of Scotland. Address, 14 Grange Terrace, Edinburgh. [157, 222, 431].

Wright, Horace C., B.D.—Pastor, Dunnville Baptist Church, Dunville, Ont., Canada. Baptist Union of Ontario and Quebec.

Wright, John Charles, D.D.—Archbishop of Sydney and Primate of Australia. Church of England in Australia.

Zabriskie, George, D.C.L.—49, Wall St., New York, Lawyer. Chancellor of the Diocese of New York. Protestant Episcopal Church in U.S.A. [34, 406].

Zankow, Stefan, Dr. Theol., Dr. Jur.—Protopresbyter. Professor of Canon Law, University of Sofia. Orthodox Church of Bulgaria. [190, 386]

Zarnovicky, Milan—Pastor, Pepinok, Czechoslovakia. Evangelical Church in Slovakia.

Zoch, Samuel—Bishop of the West District, Evangelical Church in Slovakia. President of the Federation of Evangelical Churches in the Czechoslovakian Republic. Member of Parliament. Address, Modra, Czechoslovakia.

Zoellner, Wilhelm, Dr. Theol.—General Superintendent, Westphalia, Evangelical Church of the Old Prussian Union. Address, Münster, Westphalia. Appointed to the Conference as Friendly Visitor from the German Evangelical Kirchenausschuss. [166, 186, 373.]

Zwemer, Samuel M., D.D., LL.D.—Missionary and Travelling Secretary A.C.L.S.M. Address, American Mission, Cairo, Egypt. Editor, *The Moslem World*, New York. Reformed Church in America. [104, 215, 229].

STAFF

Ames, Allan P.—1133 Broadway, New York. Head of the Press Bureau of the Conference.

Benedict, Mrs. Helena Marja—Address, Seabrook, N.H., U.S.A.

Bredenberg, Miss Stina—Church of Sweden. Teacher at the Commercial School, Pahlmans Handelsinstitut, Stockholm. Address, Riddaregatan, 19, Stockholm.

Brent, Miss Helen C. C.—Protestant Episcopal Church in U.S.A. Address, 250 Summer St., Buffalo, N.Y.

Brown, Ralph W., A.B.—General Secretary, World Conference on Faith and Order. P.O. Box 226, Boston, Mass., U.S.A. Protestant Episcopal Church in U.S.A. [34, 405, 406].

Dumm, Rev. B. Alfred, Ph.D.—Associate Secretary, World Conference on Faith and Order. Congregational Church. Address, Newton, N.H., U.S.A.

Gordon, Rev. Linley V.—70 Fifth Avenue, New York. Press Bureau, Correspondent for American Religious Press.

Jessup, Charles A., D.D.—Rector of St. Paul's Cathedral, Buffalo, N.Y. Protestant Episcopal Church in U.S.A.

Lytle, Rev. R. Ridgely, Jr., M.A. (Oxon.)—Superintendent, City Mission of Rochester, N.Y. Protestant Episcopal Church in U.S.A.

Porritt, Arthur, 7 Arundel Street, Strand, London, W.C.2

Ringrose, T. H.—Protestant Episcopal Church in U.S.A. Address, Cotmaton Cottage, Sidmouth, Devon, England. [441].

Tomkins, Rev. Floyd W., Jr.—Associate Secretary, World Conference on Faith and Order. Protestant Episcopal Church in U.S.A. Address, 12 South Water St., Providence, R.I. [441].

LIST OF CHURCHES REPRESENTED AT LAUSANNE

Most of the Churches listed below were represented by delegates officially appointed. In some cases the representatives were credentialled as friendly visitors, and in the case of the German Churches they were selected by a committee formed for that purpose. A few Churches, members of which were present *ex officio* or by co-option, are not listed.

ANGLICAN

Church of England.
Church of Ireland.
Episcopal Church in Scotland.
The Church in Wales.
Protestant Episcopal Church in the U.S.A.
Church of England in Canada.
Province of the West Indies.
Diocese in Argentina and Eastern South America.
Church of England in India.
Chung Hua Sheng Kung Hui (China).
Nippon Sei Kokwai (Japan).
Church of the Province of South Africa.
Church of England in Australia and Tasmania.

BAPTIST

Northern Baptist Convention, U.S.A.
Seventh Day Baptist General Conference, U.S.A.
Baptist Union of Ontario and Quebec.
Seventh Day Baptist Churches of Holland.
Baptist Churches in Germany.

BRETHREN

Church of the Brethren, U.S.A.

CHRISTIAN

General Convention of the Christian Church, U.S.A.
Churches of Christ in North America.

CONGREGATIONAL

Congregational Union of England and Wales.
National Council of Congregational Churches in the United States.
North China Kung Li Hui.
Congregational Union of South Africa.
Congregational Union of Australia and New Zealand.

DISCIPLES

Disciples of Christ in North America.
Churches of Christ in Great Britain.
Churches of Christ in Australia.

EASTERN CHURCHES

Ecumenical Patriarchate of Constantinople
Patriarchate of Alexandria.
Patriarchate of Jerusalem.
Church of Greece.
Church of Cyprus.
Church of Rumania.
Church of Serbia.
Church of Bulgaria.
Church of Russia.
Orthodox Church of Poland.
Church of Georgia.
Armenian Church.
Syrian Patriarchate of Antioch.

EVANGELICAL CHURCHES OF GERMANY

Evangelical Church of the Old Prussian Union.
Evangelical Church of Baden.
Evangelical Church of Frankfort.
Evangelical Church of Hanover.
Evangelical Church of Hesse.
Evangelical Church of Thuringia.
Evangelical Church of Wurtemberg.

FRIENDS

Society of Friends in Great Britain and Ireland.
Society of Friends in America.

LUTHERAN

United Lutheran Church in America.
Lutheran Free Church of America.
Norwegian Lutheran Church of America.
Evangelical Lutheran Church of Bavaria.
Evangelical Lutheran Church of Hanover.
Evangelical Lutheran Church of France.
Church of the Confession of Augsbourg (Alsace and Lorraine).
Church of Denmark.
Church of Norway.
Church of Sweden.
Evangelical Lutheran Church in Hungary.
Evangelical Lutheran Church in Latvia.
Evangelical Church in Slovakia.
Tamil Evangelical Lutheran Church (India).

MENNONITES

Conference of South German Mennonites.

METHODIST.

Wesleyan Methodist Conference.
United Methodist Church.
Primitive Methodist Church.
Methodist Church in Ireland.
Methodist Episcopal Church, U.S.A.
Methodist Episcopal Church, South, U.S.A.,
Methodist Protestant Church in the United States.
African Methodist Episcopal Church, U.S.A.
Primitive Methodist Church, U.S.A.
Evangelical Methodist Church of France.
Wesleyan Methodist Church of South Africa.
Methodist Church of Australasia.

MORAVIAN

Moravian Church in Germany.

OLD CATHOLIC CHURCHES

Old Catholic Church in the Netherlands.
Old Catholic Church in Switzerland.

PRESBYTERIAN AND REFORMED

Church of Scotland.
United Free Church of Scotland.
Presbyterian Church of England.
Presbyterian Church in Ireland.
Presbyterian Church in Wales.
Presbyterian Church in the U.S.A.
Presbyterian Church in the U.S.
United Presbyterian Church of North America.
Reformed Church in the United States.
Reformed Church in America.
Presbyterian Church in Canada.
Reformed Churches of Switzerland.
National Union of the Reformed Evangelical Churches of France
National Union of the Reformed Churches of France.
Reformed Church of Alsace and of Lorraine.
Reformed Church of Hungary.
Evangelical Church of Bohemian Brethren in Czecho-Slovakia.
German Evangelical Church in Bohemia, Moravia and Silesia.
Italian Evangelical Church.
Waldensian Evangelical Church.
Belgian Christian Missionary Church.
Presbyterian Church of New Zealand.

OTHER CHURCHES

Czechoslovak Church.
Protestant Churches of Portugal.
United Church of Canada.
South India United Church.
United Church of Northern India.

APPENDIX

The Continuation Committee appointed at Lausanne

Rt. Rev. Charles H. Brent, D.D., *Chairman*
Rev. Alfred E. Garvie, D.D., *Vice-Chairman*
George Zabriskie, D.C.L., *Treasurer*
Ralph W. Brown, *General Secretary*,
    P.O. Box 226, Boston, Mass., U.S.A.
Rev. Peter Ainslie, D.D.
Dr. Hamilcar Alivisatos
Rev. Prof. Nicholas Arseniew
Rev. Robert A. Ashworth, D.D.
Rev. Henry A. Atkinson, D.D.
Rev. Robert Bagnell, D.D.
*Rev. Harold N. Baker, M.A.,
    alternate for Bishop White
Rt. Rev. Mgr. K. Balakian, D.D.
Most Rev. Metropolitan Balan
*Rev. John J. Banninga, D.D.
Rev. Clarence A. Barbour, D.D.
G. F. Barbour, D.Phil.
Rev. Canon H. N. Bate, M.A.
President Miner Lee Bates, LL.D.
Rt. Rev. the Bishop of Bombay
*Rev. Ahva J. C. Bond, D.D.
Very Rev. Dr. Sergius Bulgakow
*Rev. Erasmo Braga, D.D.
Rev. G. A. Brandelle, D.D.
Prof. Yngve Torgny Brilioth, D.Phil.
Rev. William Adams Brown, D.D.
Rev. Bishop James Cannon, Jr., D.D.
Very Rev. the Dean of Canterbury
Rev. Samuel H. Chester, D.D.
Prof. Eugène Choisy, D.D.
*His Holiness the Metropolitan Chrysostom
Judge Alexis deBoér, LL.D.
Prof. Dr. Adolf Deissmann

Gen. Sup. D.Dr. Otto Dibelius
*Most Rev. the Metropolitan of Warsaw and
  all Poland, Dionisy
*Rt. Rev. the Bishop of Dornakal
Most Rev. the Archbishop of Dublin
Prof. Dr. Werner Elert
Miss Lucy Gardner
Most Rev. Metropolitan Germanos
Rt. Rev. the Bishop of Gloucester
President William Allen Harper, LL.D.
Rev. Bishop William H. Heard, D.D.
Prof. Friedrich Heiler, D.theol.
Prof. D.Dr. Hermelink
Rt. Rev. Peter Hognestad, D.D.
*Rev. Albert T. Holden, C.B.E., B.A.
Rt. Rev. the Bishop of Honduras
Rt. Rev. Iriney, Bishop of Novi Sad
Prof. James A. James, Ph.D., LL.D.
Rt. Rev. Bishop Paul Th. Jensen, D.D.
Freiherr Albert v.Kaas, Dr.,
  alternate for Bishop v.Raffay
Rev. Adolf Keller, D.D.
Prof. Eliza H. Kendrick
Bischof D. Kortheuer
Bishop Dr. Adolf Küry
Dr. theol. August Lang
Rev. Aleksi Lehtonen, D.D.
Prof. Geza Lencz,
  alternate for Judge deBoér
*Rev. Timothy Tingfang Lew, Ph.D.
Rev. Jonas Lindskog, D.D.
Rev. William F. Lofthouse, D.D.
Sir Henry Lunn, M.D.
President John H. MacCracken, LL.D.
Rt. Rev. William T. Manning, D.D.
Rev. Bishop Francis J. McConnell, D.D.
Rev. Charles Merle d'Aubigné, D.D.
Rev. A. E. Monahan, M.A.
Rev. Wilfred Monod, D.D.

Rt. Rev. the Bishop of Montreal
Rev. Bishop John M. Moore, D.D.
Rev. T. Albert Moore, D.D.
*Rt. Rev. James Okey Nash, D.D.
Rev. Bishop John Nuelsen, D.D.
Rt. Rev. Harald Ostenfeld, D.D.
Rev. Albert W. Palmer, D.D.
Rt. Rev. Edward L. Parsons, D.D.
*K. T. Paul, B.A.
Rt. Rev. James DeWolf Perry, D.D.
Bishop Alexander v.Raffay, D.D.
Rev. George W. Richards, D.D.
Rev. J. E. Roberts, D.D.
Mrs. Kingman Mott Robins
Hon. Lord Sands, LL.D.
Rev. M. G. G. Scherer, D.D.
D. Dr. Prälat Schoell
Prof. Friedrich Siegmund-Schultze, D.D.
Rev. P. Carnegie Simpson, D.D.
*Rev. William B. Smiley, D.D.
Rev. Edmund D. Soper, D.D.
Rt. Rev. Rotislav Stejskal, Th.D.
Rev. J. Ross Stevenson, D.D.
Rev. J. Sinclair Stevenson, M.A.
Rev. Canon Tissington Tatlow, D.D.
Pastor Niels B. Thvedt, B.D.,
    alternate for Bishop Hognestad
Rev. Floyd W. Tomkins, Jr.,
    alternate for Bishop Brent
Rt. Rev. Leon Tourian, D.D.
*Rt. Rev. Gilbert White, D.D.
Rev. F. Luke Wiseman, M.A.
Rev. Canon Edward S. Woods, M.A.
*Rev. David Z. T. Yui, Litt.D.
Prof. Dr. Stefan Zankow
Prof. Dr. Francis Žilka
Rt. Rev. Samuel Zoch, D.D.
*Rev. Samuel M. Zwemer, D.D.

*Corresponding member.

BUSINESS COMMITTEE

constituted by the Continuation Committee,
Lausanne, Switzerland, August 20, 1927.

Rt. Rev. Charles H. Brent, D.D., *Chairman*
George Zabriskie, D.C.L., *Treasurer*
Ralph W. Brown, *General Secretary*
Rev. Peter Ainslie, D.D.
Most Rev. Archbishop Alexander
Rev. Robert A. Ashworth, D.D.
Rev. Henry A. Atkinson, D.D.
Rev. Robert Bagnell, D D ,
  alternate for Bishop McConnell
Rev. Clarence A. Barbour, D.D.
Judge Alexis deBoér, LL.D.
Rev. William Adams Brown, D.D.
Rev. Bishop James Cannon, Jr., D.D.
Prof. James A. James, LL.D.
Rev. Bishop Francis J. McConnell, D.D.
Rev. T. Albert Moore, D.D.
Rt. Rev. James DeWolf Perry, D.D.
Rev. M. G. G. Scherer, D.D.
Prof. Edmund D. Soper, D.D.
Rev. J. Ross Stevenson, D.D.

THE SECRETARIAT:

P.O. Box 226, Boston, Mass., U.S.A.